MARK

THE NEW TESTAMENT LIBRARY
Current and Forthcoming Titles

COMMENTARY SERIES

MATTHEW. BY R. ALAN CULPEPPER, MCAFEE SCHOOL OF THEOLOGY, MERCER UNIVERSITY

MARK. BY M. EUGENE BORING, BRITE DIVINITY SCHOOL, TEXAS CHRISTIAN UNIVERSITY

LUKE. BY JOHN T. CARROLL, UNION PRESBYTERIAN SEMINARY

JOHN. BY MARIANNE MEYE THOMPSON, FULLER THEOLOGICAL SEMINARY

ACTS. BY CARL R. HOLLADAY, CANDLER SCHOOL OF THEOLOGY, EMORY UNIVERSITY

ROMANS. BY BEVERLY ROBERTS GAVENTA, PRINCETON THEOLOGICAL SEMINARY

I CORINTHIANS. BY ALEXANDRA R. BROWN, WASHINGTON & LEE UNIVERSITY

II CORINTHIANS. BY FRANK J. MATERA, THE CATHOLIC UNIVERSITY OF AMERICA

GALATIANS. BY MARTINUS C. DE BOER, VU UNIVERSITY AMSTERDAM

EPHESIANS. BY STEPHEN E. FOWL, LOYOLA COLLEGE

PHILIPPIANS AND PHILEMON. BY CHARLES B. COUSAR, COLUMBIA THEOLOGICAL SEMINARY

COLOSSIANS. BY JERRY L. SUMNEY, LEXINGTON THEOLOGICAL SEMINARY

I & II THESSALONIANS. BY SUSAN EASTMAN, DUKE DIVINITY SCHOOL

I & II TIMOTHY AND TITUS. BY RAYMOND F. COLLINS, THE CATHOLIC UNIVERSITY OF AMERICA

HEBREWS. BY LUKE TIMOTHY JOHNSON, CANDLER SCHOOL OF THEOLOGY, EMORY UNIVERSITY

JAMES. BY REINHARD FELDMEIER, UNIVERSITY OF GÖTTINGEN

I & II PETER AND JUDE. BY LEWIS R. DONELSON, AUSTIN PRESBYTERIAN THEOLOGICAL SEMINARY

I, II, & III JOHN. BY JUDITH M. LIEU, UNIVERSITY OF CAMBRIDGE

REVELATION. BY BRIAN K. BLOUNT, UNION PRESBYTERIAN SEMINARY

CLASSICS

HISTORY AND THEOLOGY IN THE FOURTH GOSPEL. BY J. LOUIS MARTYN,
UNION THEOLOGICAL SEMINARY, NEW YORK

IMAGES OF THE CHURCH IN THE NEW TESTAMENT. BY PAUL S. MINEAR,
YALE DIVINITY SCHOOL

PAUL AND THE ANATOMY OF APOSTOLIC AUTHORITY. BY JOHN HOWARD SCHÜTZ,
UNIVERSITY OF NORTH CAROLINA, CHAPEL HILL

THEOLOGY AND ETHICS IN PAUL. BY VICTOR PAUL FURNISH, PERKINS SCHOOL
OF THEOLOGY, SOUTHERN METHODIST UNIVERSITY

THE WORD IN THIS WORLD: ESSAYS IN NEW TESTAMENT EXEGESIS AND THEOLOGY.
BY PAUL W. MEYER, PRINCETON THEOLOGICAL SEMINARY

GENERAL STUDIES

THE LAW AND THE PROPHETS BEAR WITNESS: THE OLD TESTAMENT IN THE NEW.
BY J. ROSS WAGNER, PRINCETON THEOLOGICAL SEMINARY

METHODS FOR NEW TESTAMENT STUDY. BY A. K. M. ADAM, UNIVERSITY OF GLASGOW

NEW TESTAMENT BACKGROUNDS. BY CARL R. HOLLADAY, CANDLER SCHOOL OF
THEOLOGY, EMORY UNIVERSITY

M. Eugene Boring

Mark

A Commentary

WJK WESTMINSTER
JOHN KNOX PRESS
LOUISVILLE · KENTUCKY

2012 paperback edition
Originally published in hardback in the United States
by Westminster John Knox Press in 2006
Louisville, Kentucky

12 13 14 15 16 17 18 19 20 21—10 9 8 7 6 5 4 3 2 1

Book design by Jennifer K. Cox

Library of Congress Cataloging-in-Publication Data is on file at the Library of Congress, Washington, D.C.

ISBN: 978-0-664-22107-2 (hardback)

ISBN: 978-0-664-23899-5 (paperback)

CONTENTS

PREFACE

In this commentary I have attempted to present the information readers of Mark need in order to engage the text, without merely assembling a collection of miscellaneous comments—a commentary in the worst sense of the word. Combining historical, literary, and theological approaches, I have attempted to offer an interpretation of Mark as a whole, without simply imposing my reading on readers of either Mark or this volume. I have not striven for novelty, to go where no commentator has gone before; I have not restricted what I say by the principle "if somebody else has said it, you won't find it here." Such striving is sometimes the result of trying to justify yet another commentary on a thoroughly-studied text, addressed to colleagues in the academic community attempting to ward off the dreaded critique in scholarly reviews, "There is little that is new here." Such commentaraies are written for those who have already read numerous other commentaries on Mark and are looking for new methods, data, and conclusions. There is a place for such studies in pushing the envelope of the discipline, but they can be unhelpful or misleading to the students who choose a particular commentary as one of their few resources in understanding the text. Such students do not evaluate it in terms of the dozen other commentaries they have read on the same text, but in terms of the text of the Bible itself, i.e., whether or not it provides information and insight to facilitate their own understanding of the Bible. I have attempted to provide such a commentary on the Gospel of Mark.

Many students and colleagues have helped along the way. I am particularly grateful to C. Clifton Black and Joel Marcus, who shared copies of their own forthcoming commentaries on Mark with me, and to Jerry L. Coyle and J. T. Williams for their careful work in proofreading; J. T. Williams also worked through my translation of the Greek text of Mark, providing several helpful suggestions. It has been a pleasure to work with Jon L. Berquist and Daniel Braden and their staff at Westminster John Knox Press, and to them also I express my heartfelt thanks.

ABBREVIATIONS

AB	Anchor Bible
ABD	*The Anchor Bible Dictionary*
ABRL	Anchor Bible Reference Library
ACCS	Ancient Christian Commentary on Scripture
AnBib	Analecta Biblica
ANRW	*Aufsteig und Niedergang Der Römischen Welt*
ANTC	Abingdon New Testament Commentaries
ATANT	Abhandlungen zur Theologie des Alten und Neuen Testaments
AUSDDS	Andrews University Seminary Doctoral Dissertation Series
BDAG	*A Greek-English Lexicon of the New Testament and Other Early Christian Literature*
BETL	Bibliotheca Ephemeridum theologicarum Lovaniensium
BEvT	Beiträge zur evangelischen Theologie
BGBE	Beiträge zur Geschichte der biblischen Exegese
Bib	*Biblica*
BibInt	Biblical Interpretation
BJRL	*Bulletin of the John Rylands Library*
BNTC	Black's New Testament Commentary
BRS	Biblical Resource Series
BTS	Biblisch-Theologische Studien
CB/NT	Commentaire biblique: nouveau testament
CBQ	*Catholic Biblical Quarterly*
CBQMS	Catholic Biblical Quarterly Monograph Series
DSB	Daily Study Bible
EBib	Etudes bibliques
EHPR	Etudes d'histoire et de philosophie religieuses
EKK	Evangelisch-Katholischer Kommentar zum Neuen Testament
ETL	*Ephemerides theologicae lovanienses*
ExpTim	*Expository Times*
FB	Forschung zur Bibel
FBBS	Facet Books, Biblical Series

FRLANT	Forschungen zur Religion und Literatur des Alten und Neuen Testaments
GNS	Good News Studies
Hermeneia	Hermeneia—A Critical and Historical Commentary on the Bible
HNT	Handbuch zum Neuen Testament
HNTC	Harper's New Testament Commentary
HTKNT	Herders Theologischer Kommentar zum Neuen Testament
HTS	Harvard Theological Studies
IB	The Interpreter's Bible
IBC	Interpretation: A Bible Commentary for Teaching and Preaching
IDBSup	*The Interpreter's Dictionary of the Bible, Supplementary Volume*
Int	*Interpretation*
IRT	Issues in Religion and Theology
ITS	International Theological Studies
JBL	*Journal of Biblical Literature*
JSNT	*Journal for the Study of the New Testament*
JSNTSup	Journal for the Study of the New Testament: Supplement Series
JSOTSup	Journal for the Study of the Old Testament: Supplement Series
JTC	*Journal for Theology and the Church*
JTS	*Journal of Theological Studies*
KBANT	Kommentare und Beiträge zum Alten und Neuen Testament
KEK	Kritisch-Exegetischer Kommentar über das Neue Testament
LBS	Library of Biblical Studies
LD	Lectio Divina
LEC	Library of Early Christianity
LHD	Library of History and Doctrine
LTQ	*Lexington Theological Quarterly*
MdB	Le Monde de la Bible
Neot	*Neotestamentica*
NIB	The New Interpreter's Bible
NICNT	New International Commentary on the New Testament
NIGTC	New International Greek Testament Commentary
NovT	*Novum Testamentum*
NovTSup	Supplements to Novum Testamentum
NPNF[1]	A Select Library of the Nicene and Post-Nicene Fathers of The Christian Church, First Series

NTL	New Testament Library
NTR	New Testament Readings
NTS	*New Testament Studies*
NTTh	New Testament Theology
OBO	Orbis Biblicus et Orientalis
ÖTK	Ökumenischer Taschenbuchkommentar zum Neuen Testament
SANT	Studien zum Alten und Neuen Testament
SBB	Stuttgarter Biblische Beiträge
SBF	Studium Biblicum Franciscanum
SBLDS	Society of Biblical Literature Dissertation Series
SBLSP	Society of Biblical Literature Seminar Papers
SBM	Stuttgarter biblische Monographien
SBS	Stuttgarter Bibelstudien
SBT	Studies in Biblical Theology
SJT	*Scottish Journal of Theology*
SNTI	Studies in New Testament Interpretation
SNTSMS	Society of New Testament Studies Monograph Series
SNTU	Studien Zum Neuen Testament und Seiner Umwelt
SNTW	Studies of the New Testament and Its World
SP	Sacra Pagina
Str-B	Strack, Hermann, and Paul Billerbeck, eds. *Kommentar zum Neuen Testament aus Talmud und Midrasch*
SUNT	Studien zur Umwelt des Neuen Testaments
TDNT	*Theological Dictionary of the New Testament*
THKNT	Theologischer Handkommentar zum Neuen Testament
ThSt	Theologische Studien
WBC	Word Biblical Commentary
WC	Westminster Commentaries
WdF	Wege der Forschung
WMANT	Wissenschaftliche Monographien zum Alten und Neuen Testament
WD	*Wort und Dienst*
WUNT	Wissenschaftliche Untersuchungen zum Neuen Testament
WUANT	Wissenschaftliche Untersuchungen zum Alten und Neuen Testament
ZNW	Zeitschrift für die neutestamentliche Wissenschaft und die Kunde der älteren Kirche

BIBLIOGRAPHY

Texts and Reference Works

Bauer, Walter, and Frederick W. Danker, eds. *A Greek-English Lexicon of the New Testament and Other Early Christian Literature*. Translated by Frederick W. Danker and William Arndt. Edited by Frederick W. Danker, 3d ed. Chicago: University of Chicago Press, 2000.

Boismard, Marie-Émile, ed. *Synopse des quatre évangiles en français, Tome 2: Commentaire*. 2 vols. Paris: Cerf, 1972.

Boring, M. Eugene, et al., eds. *Hellenistic Commentary to the New Testament*. Nashville: Abingdon, 1995.

Bratcher, Robert G. *Old Testament Quotations in the New Testament*. London: United Bible Societies, 1961.

Bratcher, Robert G., and Eugene A. Nida. *A Translator's Handbook on the Gospel of Mark*. Leiden: Brill, 1961.

Freedman, David Noel, ed. *The Anchor Bible Dictionary*. 6 vols. New York: Doubleday, 1992.

The Interpreter's Dictionary of the Bible, Supplementary Volume. 5 vols. Nashville: Abingdon, 1976.

Kittel, Gerhard, and Gerhard Friedrich, eds. *Theological Dictionary of the New Testament*. Translated by Geoffrey W. Bromiley. 10 vols. Grand Rapids: Eerdmans, 1964–1976.

Kloppenborg, John S. *Q Parallels: Synopsis, Critical Notes, and Concordance*. Sonoma, Calif.: Polebridge, 1988.

Metzger, Bruce M. *A Textual Commentary on the Greek New Testament*. 2d ed. Stuttgart: United Bible Societies, 1994.

Oden, Thomas C., and Christopher A. Hall, eds. *Mark*. Ancient Christian Commentary on Scripture, NT/2. Downers Grove, Ill.: InterVarsity, 1998.

Robinson, James M., et al. *The Critical Edition of Q: Synopsis including the Gospels of Matthew and Luke, Mark and Thomas with English, German, and French Translations of Q and Thomas*. Hermeneia—A Critical and Historical Commentary on the Bible. Minneapolis: Fortress, 2000.

Ross, Allen P. *Introducing Biblical Hebrew*. Grand Rapids: Baker, 2001.

Strack, Hermann, and Paul Billerbeck, eds. *Kommentar zum Neuen Testament aus Talmud und Midrasch.* 6 vols. Munich: Beck, 1924.

Commentaries on Mark

Achtemeier, Paul J. *Invitation to Mark.* Garden City, N.Y.: Image, 1978.

———. *Mark.* 2d ed. Proclamation Commentaries. Philadelphia: Fortress, 1986.

Barclay, William. *The Gospel of Mark.* 2d ed. Philadelphia: Westminster, 1956.

Black, C. Clifton. *Mark.* Abingdon New Testament Commentaries. Nashville: Abingdon, forthcoming.

Cranfield, C. E. B. *The Gospel According to Saint Mark.* Cambridge: Cambridge University Press, 1966.

Donahue, John R., and Daniel J. Harrington. *The Gospel of Mark.* Sacra Pagina. Collegeville, Minn.: Liturgical Press, 2002.

Dowd, Sharyn. *Reading Mark: A Literary and Theological Commentary on the Second Gospel.* Macon, Ga.: Smyth & Helwys, 2000.

Evans, Craig. *Mark 8:27–16:20.* WBC 34B. New York: Nelson, 2001.

Focant, Camille. *L'évangile selon Marc.* Commentaire biblique: nouveau testament 2. Paris: Cerf, 2004.

France, R. T. *The Gospel of Mark: A Commentary on the Greek Text.* New International Greek Testament Commentary. Grand Rapids: Eerdmans, 2002.

Gnilka, Joachim. *Das Evangelium nach Markus.* Evangelisch-Katholischer Kommentar zum Neuen Testament. 2 vols. Zurich: Benziger, 1978, 1979.

Grant, Frederick C. "Introduction and Exegesis of Mark." Pages 629–917 in *The Interpreter's Bible* 7. Edited by George Arthur Buttrick. Nashville: Abingdon, 1951.

Grundmann, Walter. *Das Evangelium nach Markus.* THKNT 2. Berlin: Evangelische Verlagsanstalt, 1973.

Guelich, Robert A. *Mark 1–8:26.* WBC 34A. Dallas: Word, 1989.

Gundry, Robert H. *Mark: A Commentary on His Apology for the Cross.* Grand Rapids: Eerdmans, 1993.

Haenchen, Ernst. *Der Weg Jesu.* Berlin: Töpelmann, 1966.

Hooker, Morna D. *The Gospel according to Saint Mark.* Black's New Testament Commentaries. Peabody, Mass.: Hendrickson, 1991.

Iersel, Bas M. F. van. *Mark: A Reader-Response Commentary.* Translated by W. H. Bisscheroux. Journal for the Study of the New Testament: Supplement Series 164. Sheffield: Sheffield Academic, 1998.

Johnson, Sherman E. *A Commentary on the Gospel According to St. Mark.* Black's New Testament Commentaries. London: Adam & Charles Black, 1960.

Juel, Donald H. *The Gospel of Mark.* IBT. Nashville: Abingdon, 1999.

Lane, William L. *The Gospel According to Mark.* New International Commentary on the New Testament. Grand Rapids: Eerdmans, 1974.

LaVerdiere, Eugene. *The Beginning of the Gospel: Introducing the Gospel according to Mark.* 2 vols. Collegeville, Minn.: Liturgical Press, 1999.

Lohmeyer, Ernst. *Das Evangelium des Markus.* 16th ed. KEK. Göttingen: Vandenhoeck & Ruprecht, 1937.

Lührmann, Dieter. *Das Markusevangelium.* Handbuch zum Neuen Testament 3. Tübingen: Mohr, 1987.

Mann, C. S. *Mark: A New Translation with Introduction and Commentary.* AB 27. New York: Doubleday, 1986.

Marcus, Joel. *Mark 1–8: A New Translation with Introduction and Commentary.* AB 27. New York: Doubleday, 2000.

———. *Mark 8–16: A New Translation with Introduction and Commentary.* AB 27a. New York: Doubleday, forthcoming.

Moloney, Francis J. *The Gospel of Mark: A Commentary.* Peabody, Mass.: Hendrickson, 2002.

Painter, John. *Mark's Gospel: Worlds in Conflict.* New Testament Readings. London: Routledge, 1997.

Perkins, Pheme. "Introduction, Commentary, and Reflections on Mark." Pages 507–734 in *The New Interpreter's Bible* 8. Edited by Leander Keck. Nashville: Abingdon, 1995.

Pesch, Rudolf. *Das Markusevangelium: I. Teil. Kommentar zu Kap. 1:1–8:26; II. Teil. Kommentar zu Kap. 8:27–16:20.* 4th ed. Herders Theologischer Kommentar zum Neuen Testament. 2 vols. Freiburg i. B: Herder, 1984.

Rawlinson, A. E. J. *St. Mark.* Westminster Commentaries. London: Methuen, 1960.

Schmithals, Walter. *Das Evangelium nach Markus: Kapitel 1–9.* ÖTK 2/1. 2 vols. Würzburg: Gütersloher Verlagshaus, 1979.

———. *Das Evangelium nach Markus. Kapitel 9,2–16,18.* ÖTK 2/2. Würzburg: Gütersloher Verlagshaus, 1979.

Schweizer, Eduard. *The Good News According to Mark.* Translated by Donald H. Madvig. Richmond: John Knox, 1970.

Taylor, Vincent. *The Gospel According to St. Mark.* New York: Macmillan, 1959.

Wellhausen, Julius. *Das Evangelium Marci.* Berlin: G. Reimer, 1903.

Witherington, Ben. *The Gospel of Mark: A Socio-Rhetorical Commentary.* Grand Rapids: Eerdmans, 2001.

Monographs, Books, Articles

Achtemeier, Paul J. "'He Taught Them Many Things': Reflections on Marcan Christology." *CBQ* 42 (1980): 465–81.

———. "The Origin and Function of the Pre-Markan Miracle Catenae." *JBL* 91, no. 2 (1972): 198–221.

————. "Toward the Isolation of Pre-Markan Miracle Catenae." *JBL* 89, no. 3 (1970): 265–91.

Allison, Dale C., Jr. *The End of the Ages Has Come: An Early Interpretation of the Passion and Resurrection of Jesus.* Philadelphia: Fortress, 1985.

Ambrozic, Aloysius M. *The Hidden Kingdom: A Redaction-Critical Study of the References to the Kingdom of God in Mark's Gospel.* CBQMS 2. Washington: Catholic Biblical Association of America, 1972.

Anderson, Hugh, ed. *Jesus.* Great Lives Observed. Englewood Cliffs, N.J.: Prentice-Hall, 1967.

Arens, Eduardo. *The HΛΘON Sayings in the Synoptic Tradition: A Historico-critical Investigation.* OBO 10. Freiburg: Universitätsverlag, 1976.

Aune, David E. *The New Testament in Its Literary Environment.* LEC. Philadelphia: Westminster, 1987.

Baarlink, Heinrich. *Anfängliches Evangelium.* Kampen: Kok, 1977.

Bacon, Benjamin W. *Is Mark a Roman Gospel?* HTS 7. Cambridge, Mass.: Harvard University Press, 1919.

Bagatti, Bellarmino. *The Church from the Circumcision: History and Archaeology of the Judaeo-Christians.* Translated by Eugene Hoade. Studium Biblicum Franciscanum Smaller Series 2. Jerusalem: Franciscan Press, 1971.

Bailey, Kenneth E. *Poet and Peasant and Through Peasant Eyes: A Literary-Cultural Approach to the Parable in Luke.* Grand Rapids: Eerdmans, 1980.

Balabanski, Vicky. *Eschatology in the Making: Mark, Matthew, and the Didache.* SNTSMS 97. Cambridge: Cambridge University Press, 1997.

Balch, David L., and Carolyn Osiek. *Families in the New Testament World: Households and House Churches.* Louisville, Ky.: Westminster John Knox, 1997.

Barr, James. "'Abba' Isn't 'Daddy.'" *JTS* 39 (1988): 28–47.

Barrett, C. K. "The Background of Mark 10:45." Pages 1–18 in *New Testament Essays: Studies in the Memory of T. W. Manson, 1893–1958.* Edited by A. J. B. Higgins. Manchester: Manchester University Press, 1959.

Barth, Karl. *Church Dogmatics, Volume I: The Doctrine of the Word of God.* Translated by G. T. Thomson. Edinburgh: T. & T. Clark, 1936.

————. *Church Dogmatics, Volume II: The Doctrine of God, Second Half-Volume.* Translated by Geoffrey Bromiley, et al. Edinburgh: T. & T. Clark, 1957.

————. *Church Dogmatics, Volume IV: The Doctrine of Reconciliation, Part Four (Fragment), The Christian Life (Fragment), Baptism as the Foundation of the Christian Life.* Translated by Geoffrey Bromiley. Edinburgh: T. & T. Clark, 1969.

————. *Church Dogmatics, Volume IV: The Doctrine of Reconciliation, Part One.* Translated by Geoffrey Bromiley. Edinburgh: T. & T. Clark, 1956.

———. *The Teaching of the Church Regarding Baptism.* Translated by Ernest A. Payne. London: SCM Press, 1948.

Bauckham, Richard. "The Brothers and Sisters of Jesus: An Epiphanian Response to John P. Meier." *CBQ* 56, no. 4 (1994): 686–700.

———. "For Whom Were Gospels Written?" Pages 9–48 in *The Gospels for All Christians: Rethinking the Gospel Audiences.* Edited by Richard Bauckham. Grand Rapids: Eerdmans, 1998.

Baumbach, G. "Das Sadduzäerverständnis bei Josephus Flavius und im NT." *Kairos* 23 (1971): 17–37.

Beare, Francis Wright. *The Earliest Records of Jesus: A Companion to the Synopsis of the First Three Gospels by Albert Huck.* Nashville: Abingdon, 1962.

Beasley-Murray, George R. *Jesus and the Last Days: The Interpretation of the Olivet Discourse.* Peabody, Mass.: Hendrickson, 1993.

Beavis, Mary Ann. *Mark's Audience: The Literary and Social Setting of Mark 4:11–12.* JSNTSup 33. Sheffield: JSOT Press, 1989.

Ben-David, Arye. *Talmudische Ökonomie.* Hildesheim: Olms, 1974.

Berger, Klaus. "Die königlichen Messiastraditionen des Neuen Testaments." *NTS* 20, no. 1 (1973): 1–44.

Bertram, Georg. *Die Leidensgeschichte Jesu und der Christuskult: Eine formgeschichtliche Untersuchung.* FRLANT N.F. 15. Göttingen: Vandenhoeck & Ruprecht, 1922.

Best, Ernest. *Following Jesus: Discipleship in the Gospel of Mark.* JSNTSup 4. Sheffield: University of Sheffield, 1981.

———. *Mark: The Gospel as Story.* SNTW. Edinburgh: T. & T. Clark, 1983.

———. "The Role of the Disciples in Mark." *NTS* 23 (1976): 377–401.

Black, C. Clifton. *The Disciples according to Mark: Markan Redaction in Current Debate.* JSNTSup 27. Sheffield: JSOT Press, 1989.

———. "The Face Is Familiar—I Just Can't Place It." Pages 33–50 in *The End of Mark and the Ends of God: Essays in Memory of Donald Harrisville Juel.* Edited by Beverly R. Gaventa and Patrick D. Miller. Louisville, Ky.: Westminster John Knox, 2005.

———. *Mark: Images of an Apostolic Interpreter.* Columbia: University of South Carolina Press, 1994.

———. "Was Mark a Roman Gospel?" *ET* 105, no. 2 (1993): 36–40.

Bligh, P. H. "A Note on *Huios Theou* in Mark 15:39." *ExpTim* 80 (1968): 51–53.

Blount, Brian K. "Is the Joke on Us? Mark's Irony, Mark's God, and Mark's Ending." Pages 15–32 in *The End of Mark and the Ends of God: Essays in Memory of Donald Harrisville Juel.* Edited by Beverly R. Gaventa and Patrick D. Miller. Louisville, Ky.: Westminster John Knox, 2005.

Bock, Darrell L. *Blasphemy and Exaltation in Judaism and the Final Examination of Jesus: A Philological-historical Study of the Key Jewish Themes Impacting Mark 14:61–64.* WUNT 2/106. Tübingen: Mohr, 1998.

————. "The Son of Man Seated at God's Right Hand and the Debate over Jesus' 'Blasphemy.'" Pages 181–91 in *Jesus of Nazareth: Lord and Christ.* Edited by Joel B. Green and Max Turner. Grand Rapids: Eerdmans, 1994.

Boismard, Marie-Émile. *L'Évangile de Marc: Sa préhistoire.* Etudes bibliques nouv. sér. 26. Paris: Librarie Lecoffre, 1994.

Bolt, Peter. *Jesus' Defeat of Death: Persuading Mark's Early Readers.* SNTSMS 125. Cambridge: Cambridge University Press, 2003.

Bonneau, Guy. *Stratégies rédactionnelles et fonctions communautaires de l'évangile de Marc.* EBib nouv. sér. 44. Paris: J. Gabalda, 2001.

Borgen, Peder. *Bread from Heaven: An Exegetical Study of the Concept of Manna in the Gospel of John and the Writings of Philo.* NovTSup 10. Leiden: Brill, 1965.

Boring, M. Eugene. "The Christology of Mark: Hermeneutical Issues for Systematic Theology." *Semeia* 30 (1985): 125–54.

————. *The Continuing Voice of Jesus: Christian Prophecy and the Gospel Tradition.* Louisville, Ky.: Westminster John Knox, 1991.

————. "How May We Identify Oracles of Christian Prophets in the Synoptic Tradition? Mark 3:28–29 as a Test Case." *JBL* 91, no. 4 (1972): 501–21.

————. "The Kingdom of God in Mark." Pages 131–46 in *The Kingdom of God in 20th-Century Interpretation.* Edited by Wendell Willis. Peabody, Mass.: Hendrickson, 1987.

————. "Mark 1:1–15 and the Beginning of the Gospel." *Semeia* 52 (1990): 43–82.

————. "Markan Christology: God-Language for Jesus?" *NTS* 45 (1999): 451–71.

————. "Matthew: Introduction, Commentary, and Reflections." Pages 87–505 in *The New Interpreter's Bible*, 8. Edited by Leander Keck. Nashville: Abingdon, 1995.

————. *1 Peter.* ANTC. Nashville: Abingdon, 1999.

————. *Revelation.* Interpretation. Louisville, Ky.: Westminster John Knox, 1989.

————. *Sayings of the Risen Jesus: Christian Prophecy in the Synoptic Tradition.* SNTSMS 46. Cambridge: Cambridge University Press, 1982.

————. "The Synoptic Problem, 'Minor' Agreements and the Beelzebul Pericope." Pages 587–619 in *The Four Gospels 1992—Festschrift Frans Neirynck.* Edited by Frans van Segbroeck, et al. 3 vols.; 1. Leuven: Leuven University Press, 1992.

————. *Truly Human / Truly Divine: Christological Language and the Gospel Form.* St. Louis: CBP Press, 1984.

————. "The Unforgivable Sin Logion Mark 3:28–29 / Matt 12:31–32 / Luke 12:10: Formal Analysis and History of the Tradition." *NovT* 17 (1976): 258–79.

Bornkamm, Günther. *The New Testament: A Guide to Its Writings.* Translated by Reginald Fuller and Ilse Fuller. Philadelphia: Fortress, 1973.

―――. "The Stilling of the Storm in Matthew." Pages 52–58 in *Tradition and Interpretation in Matthew.* Edited by Günther Bornkamm, et al. Translated by Percy Scott. NTL. Philadelphia: Westminster John Knox, 1963.

Boucher, Madeleine. *The Mysterious Parable: A Literary Study.* CBQMS 6. Washington: Catholic Biblical Association of America, 1977.

Brandenburger, Egon. *Markus 13 und die Apokalyptik.* FRLANT Heft 134. Göttingen: Vandenhoeck & Ruprecht, 1984.

Brandon, S. G. F. *Jesus and the Zealots: A Study of the Political Factor in Primitive Christianity.* New York: Scribner, 1967.

Breytenbach, Cilliers. "Das Markusevangelium als episodische Erzählung: Mit Überlegungen zum 'Aufbau' des zweiten Evangeliums." Pages 137–70. In *Der Erzähler des Evangeliums: Methodische Neuansätze in der Markusforschung.* Edited by Ferdinand Hahn. SBS 118 / 119. Stuttgart: Verlag Katholisches Bibelwerk, 1985.

Broadhead, Edwin K. *Mark.* Readings, A New Biblical Commentary. Sheffield: Sheffield Academic, 2001.

―――. *Naming Jesus: Titular Christology in the Gospel of Mark.* JSNTSup 175. Sheffield: Sheffield Academic, 1999.

―――. *Teaching with Authority: Miracles and Christology in the Gospel of Mark.* JSNTSup 74. Sheffield: JSOT Press, 1992.

Brown, Raymond E. *The Death of the Messiah: From Gethsemane to the Grave: A Commentary on the Passion Narratives in the Four Gospels.* ABRL. 2 vols. New York: Doubleday, 1994.

―――. *The Semitic Background of the Term 'Mystery' in the New Testament.* FBBS 21. Philadelphia: Fortress, 1968.

Bryan, Christopher. *A Preface to Mark: Notes on the Gospel in Its Literary and Cultural Settings.* New York: Oxford University Press, 1993.

Bultmann, Rudolf. *The Gospel of John: A Commentary.* Translated by G. R. Beasley-Murray, et al. Philadelphia: Westminster, 1971.

―――. *The History of the Synoptic Tradition.* Translated by John Marsh. New York: Harper & Row, 1963.

―――. *Theology of the New Testament.* Translated by Kendrick Grobel. 2 vols. New York: Scribner, 1951.

Burger, Christoph. *Jesus als Davidssohn: Eine traditionsgeschichtliche Untersuchung.* FRLANT 98. Göttingen: Vandenhoeck & Ruprecht, 1970.

Burkett, Delbert. *Rethinking the Gospel Sources: From Proto-Mark to Mark.* New York: T. & T. Clark, 2004.

Burridge, Richard A. *What Are the Gospels? A Comparison with Graeco-Roman Biography.* SNTSMS 70. Cambridge: Cambridge University Press, 1992.

Cadoux, Arthur Temple. *The Sources of the Second Gospel.* London: J. Clarke, 1935.

Carlson, Stephen C. *The Gospel Hoax: Morton Smith's Invention of Secret Mark.* Waco, Tex.: Baylor University Press, 2005.

Casey, Maurice. *Aramaic Sources of Mark's Gospel.* SNTSMS 102. Cambridge: Cambridge University Press, 1998.

Catchpole, David R. "The Answer of Jesus to Caiaphas." *NTS* 17, no. 2 (1971): 213–26.

Charlesworth, James H., ed. *The Messiah: Developments in Earliest Judaism and Christianity.* Minneapolis: Fortress, 1992.

Chilton, Bruce. *A Galilean Rabbi and His Bible: Jesus' Use of the Interpreted Scripture of His Time.* Wilmington, Del.: Glazier, 1984.

———. *God in Strength: Jesus' Announcement of the Kingdom.* SNTSU B/1. Freistadt: Plèochl, 1979.

Christ, Felix. *Jesus Sophia: Die Sophia-Christologie bei den Synoptikern.* ATANT 57. Zürich: Zwingli-Verlag, 1970.

Collins, Adela Yarbro. *The Beginning of the Gospel: Probings of Mark in Context.* Minneapolis: Fortress, 1992.

———. *Is Mark's Gospel a Life of Jesus? The Question of Genre.* Milwaukee: Marquette University Press, 1990.

Colwell, Ernest Cadman. "A Definite Rule for the Use of the Article in the Greek New Testament." *JBL* 52 (1933): 12–21.

Combet-Galland, Corina. "L' Évangile selon Marc." Pages 35–61 in *Introduction au Nouveau Testament: Son histoire, son écriture, sa théologie.* Edited by Daniel Marguerat. *MdB* 41. Geneva: Labor et Fides, 2004.

Conzelmann, Hans. "Present and Future in the Synoptic Tradition." *JTC* 5 (1968): 26–44.

———. *The Theology of St. Luke.* Translated by Geoffrey Buswell. New York: Harper & Row, 1961.

Cook, John G. *The Structure and Persuasive Power of Mark: A Linguistic Approach.* Semeia Studies. Atlanta: Scholars Press, 1995.

Cook, Michael L. *Christology as Narrative Quest.* Collegeville, Minn.: Liturgical Press, 1997.

Cotter, Wendy, CSJ. "Mark's Hero of the Twelfth-Year Miracles: The Healing of the Woman with the Hemorrhage and the Raising of Jairus' Daughter (Mark 5:21–43)." Pages 54–78 in *A Feminist Companion to Mark.* Edited by Amy-Jill Levine and Marianne Blickenstaff. Cleveland: Pilgrim Press, 2004.

Cranfield, C. E. B. "St. Mark 13." *Scottish Journal of Theology* 6–7 = 6 (1953) 189–96; 287–303; 7 (1954) 284–303.

Crossan, John Dominic. *The Cross That Spoke: The Origins of the Passion Narrative.* San Francisco: Harper & Row, 1988.

————. *The Dark Interval: Towards a Theology of Story.* Niles, Ill.: Argus Communications, 1975.

————. "Empty Tomb and Absent Lord." Pages 135–52 in *The Passion in Mark: Studies on Mark 14–16.* Edited by Werner H. Kelber. Philadelphia: Fortress, 1976.

————. *In Parables: The Challenge of the Historical Jesus.* New York: Harper & Row, 1973.

————. *Jesus: A Revolutionary Biography.* San Francisco: HarperSanFrancisco, 1994.

Croy, N. Clayton. *The Mutilation of Mark's Gospel.* Nashville: Abingdon, 2003.

Cullmann, Oscar. *Baptism in the New Testament.* SBT 1. Translated by J. K. S. Reid. Naperville, Ill.: Alec R. Allenson, 1958.

————. *The Christology of the New Testament.* Rev. ed. NTL. Translated by Shirley C. Guthrie and Charles A. M. Hall. Philadelphia: Westminster, 1963.

————. *Peter: Disciple, Apostle, Martyr.* Rev. ed. Cleveland: World, 1958.

Cuvillier, Elian. *Le concept de ΠΑΡΑΒΟΛΗ dans le second évangile: Son arrière-plan littéraire, sa signification dans le cadre de la rédaction marcienne, son utilisation dans la tradition de Jésus.* EBib nouv. sér. 19. Paris: J. Gabalda, 1993.

Dahl, Nils Alstrup. *Jesus in the Memory of the Early Church.* Minneapolis: Augsburg, 1976.

D'Angelo, Mary Rose. "'Abba' and 'Father' Imperial Theology and the Jesus Traditions." *JBL* 111, no. 4 (1992): 611–30.

Danove, Paul L. *The End of Mark's Story: A Methodological Study.* BibInter 3. Leiden: Brill, 1993.

————. "The Stone That the Builders Rejected." Pages 64–65 in *Studies in the New Testament* 2. Edited by J. Duncan M. Derrett. 5 vols. Leiden: Brill, 1977.

Davis, Phillip G. "Mark's Christological Paradox." *JSNT* 35 (1989): 3–18.

Derrett, J. Duncan M. *Law in the New Testament.* London: Darton, Longman & Todd, 1970.

————. "The Stone That the Builders Rejected." Pages 2:64–65 in *Studies in the New Testament.* Edited by J. Duncan M. Derrett, M. Leiden: Brill, 1977.

Devisch, M. "La relation entre l'évangile de Marc et le document Q." Pages 59–91 in *L'Évangile selon Marc: Tradition et rédaction.* Edited by M. Sabbe. BETL 34. Leuven: Leuven University Press, 1974.

Dewey, Joanna. "'Let Them Renounce Themselves and Take Up Their Cross': A Feminist Reading of Mark 8:34 in Mark's Social and Narrative World." Pages 23–36 in *A Feminist Companion to Mark.* Edited by Amy-Jill Levine and Marianne Blickenstaff. Cleveland: Pilgrim Press, 2004.

————. *Markan Public Debate: Literary Technique, Concentric Structure and Theology in Mark 2:1–3:6.* SBLDS 48. Chico, Calif.: Scholars Press, 1980.

Dewey, Kim. "Peter's Curse and Cursed Peter." Pages 96–114 in *The Passion in Mark: Studies on Mark 14–16*. Edited by Werner H. Kelber. Philadelphia: Fortress, 1976.

Dibelius, Martin. *From Tradition to Gospel*. New York: Scribner, 1935.

Dinkler, Erich. "Comments on the History of the Symbol of the Cross." *JTC* 1 (1965): 124–46.

Dodd, C. H. *The Parables of the Kingdom*. New York: Scribner, 1961.

Donahue, John R. *Are You the Christ? The Trial Narrative in the Gospel of Mark*. SBLDS 10. Missoula, Mont.: Society of Biblical Literature, 1973.

———. *The Gospel in Parable*. Philadelphia: Fortress, 1988.

———. "Jesus as the Parable of God in the Gospel of Mark." *Inter* 32, no. 4 (1978): 369–86.

Doudna, John Charles. *The Greek of the Gospel of Mark*. Journal of Biblical Literature Monograph Series 12. Philadelphia: Society of Biblical Literature and Exegesis, 1961.

Dowd, Sharyn. *Prayer, Power, and the Problem of Suffering*. SBLDS 105. Atlanta: Scholars Press, 1988.

———. "Reading Mark Reading Isaiah." *LTQ* 30, no. 3 (1995): 133–44.

Duling, Dennis C., and Norman Perrin. *The New Testament: Proclamation and Parenesis, Myth and History*. 3d ed. Fort Worth, Tex.: Harcourt, Brace, & World, 1994.

Dunn, James D. G. *Christology in the Making. A New Testament Inquiry into the Origins of the Doctrine of the Incarnation*. Philadelphia: Westminster, 1980.

———. *The Evidence for Jesus*. Philadelphia: Westminster, 1985.

Dupont, Jacques. *Études sur les évangiles synoptiques*. BETL 70. 2 vols. Leuven: Leuven University Press, 1985.

Dyer, Keith D. *The Prophecy on the Mount: Mark 13 and the Gathering of the New Community*. International Theological Studies 2. Bern: Lang, 1998.

Elliott, J. K. "An Eclectic Textual Commentary on the Greek Text of Mark's Gospel." Pages 189–211 in *The Language and Style of the Gospel of Mark: An Edition of C. H. Turner's "Notes on Marcan Usage" Together with Other Comparable Studies*. Edited by J. K. Elliott. NovTSup 71. Leiden: Brill, 1993.

Evans, C. F. "'I will go before you into Galilee.'" *JTS* 5 (1954): 3–18.

Evans, Craig A. *To See and Not Perceive: Isaiah 6.9–10 in Early Jewish and Christian Interpretation*. JSOTSup 64. Sheffield: JSOT Press, 1989.

Farmer, William R. *The Last Twelve Verses of Mark*. SNTSMS 25. London: Cambridge University Press, 1974.

Feldmeier, Reinhard. "Die Syrophönizierin (Mk 7, 24–30)—Jesus 'verlorenes' Streitgespräch?" Pages 211–27 in *Die Heiden: Juden, Christen und das Problem des Fremden*. Edited by Reinhard Feldmeier and Ulrich Heckel. WUNT 70. Tübingen: Mohr, 1994.

Fendler, Folkert. *Studien zum Markusevangelium.* Göttingen: Vandenhoeck & Ruprecht, 1991.

Filson, Floyd V. *A Commentary on The Gospel According to St. Matthew.* HNTC. New York: Harper & Brothers, 1960.

Fitzmyer, Joseph A., S.J. "*Abba* and Jesus' Relation to God." Pages 15–38 in *A cause de l'Evangile: Études sur les Synoptiques et les Actes: Offertes au P. Jacques Dupont, O.S.B. à l'occasion de son 70e anniversaire.* Edited by Jacques Dupont. LD 123. Paris: Cerf, 1985.

Fleddermann, Harry T. *Mark and Q: A Study of the Overlap Texts.* BETL 122. Leuven: Leuven University Press, 1995.

Fowler, Robert M. *Let the Reader Understand: Reader-response Criticism and the Gospel of Mark.* Minneapolis: Fortress, 1991.

———. *Loaves and Fishes: The Function of the Feeding Stories in the Gospel of Mark.* SBLDS 54. Chico, Calif.: Scholars Press, 1981.

———. "The Rhetoric of Direction and Indirection in the Gospel of Mark (1989)." Pages 207–28 in *The Interpretation of Mark.* Edited by William R. Telford. Studies in New Testament Interpretation. Edinburgh: T. & T. Clark, 1995.

Fuller, Reginald H. *The Foundations of New Testament Christology.* New York: Scribner, 1965.

———. *The New Testament in Current Study.* New York: Scribner, 1962.

Funk, Robert W. *Language, Hermeneutic, and Word of God.* New York: Harper, 1966.

———. "The Looking-Glass Tree Is for the Birds." *Int* 26, no. 1 (1973): 3–9.

Gaston, Lloyd. *No Stone on Another: Studies in the Significance of the Fall of Jerusalem in the Synoptic Gospels.* NovTSup 23. Leiden: Brill, 1970.

Gaventa, Beverly R., and Patrick D. Miller, eds. *The End of Mark and the Ends of God: Essays in Memory of Donald Harrisville Juel.* Louisville, Ky.: Westminster John Knox, 2005.

Geddert, Timothy J. *Watchwords: Mark 13 in Markan Eschatology.* JSNTSup 26. Sheffield: JSOT Press, 1989.

Gerhardsson, Birger. "The Parable of the Sower and Its Interpretation." *NTS* 14 (1968): 165–93.

Giesen, Heinz. "Christliche Existenz in der Welt und der Menschensohn: Versuch einer Neuinterpretation des Terminwortes Mk 13,30." SNTSU 8 (1983): 18–69.

Goodacre, Mark. *The Synoptic Problem: A Way through the Maze.* London: Sheffield Academic, 2001.

Goodspeed, Edgar J. *An Introduction to the New Testament.* Chicago: University of Chicago Press, 1937.

Hahn, Ferdinand. "Einige Überlegungen zu gegenwärtigen Aufgaben der Markusinterpretation." Pages 173–97 in *Der Erzähler des Evangeliums:*

Methodische Neuansätze in der Markusforschung. Edited by Ferdinand Hahn. SBS 118/119. Stuttgart: Verlag Katholisches Bibelwerk, 1985.

————. *The Titles of Jesus in Christology: Their History in Early Christianity.* Translated by Harold Knight and George Ogg. New York: World, 1969.

Harner, Philip B. "Qualitative Anarthrous Predicate Nouns: Mark 15:39 and John 1:1." *JBL* 92 (1973): 75–87.

Hassler, I. "The Incident of the Syrophoenician Woman (Matt XV, 21–28; Mark VII, 24–30)." *ExpTim* 45 (1934): 459–61.

Hedrick, Charles W. *Many Things in Parables: Jesus and His Modern Critics.* Louisville, Ky.: Westminster John Knox, 2004.

Hengel, Martin. *Christ and Power.* Translated by Everett R. Kalin. Philadelphia: Fortress, 1977.

————. "The Gospel of Mark: Time of Origin and Situation." Pages 1–30 in *Studies in the Gospel of Mark.* Edited by Martin Hengel. Philadelphia: Fortress, 1985.

————. "The Titles of the Gospels and the Gospel of Mark." Pages 64–84 in *Studies in the Gospel of Mark.* Edited by Martin Hengel. Philadelphia: Fortress, 1985.

Herzog, Rudolf. *Die Wunderheilungen von Epidauros: Ein Beitrag zur Geschichte der Medizin und der Religion.* Leipzig: Dieterich, 1931.

Holtzmann, Heinrich Julius. *Die Synoptische Evangelien: Ihr Ursprung und Geschichtlicher Charakter.* Leipzig: Wilhelm Engelmann, 1843.

Hooker, Morna D. *Jesus and the Servant: The Influence of the Servant Concept of Deutero-Isaiah in the New Testament.* London: SPCK, 1959.

————. *The Son of Man in Mark: a study of the background of the term "Son of Man" and its use in St. Mark's Gospel.* Montreal: McGill University Press, 1967.

————. "Trial and Tribulation in Mark XIII." *BJRL* 65, no. 1 (1982): 78–99.

Horsley, Richard A. *Hearing the Whole Story: The Politics of Plot in Mark's Gospel.* Louisville, Ky.: Westminster John Knox, 2001.

————. *Jesus and the Spiral of Violence: Popular Jewish Resistance in Roman Palestine.* San Francisco: Harper & Row, 1987.

Horsley, Richard A., and John S. Hanson. *Bandits, Prophets, and Messiahs: Popular Movements in the Time of Jesus.* Minneapolis: Winston, 1985.

Incigneri, Brian J. *The Gospel to the Romans: The Setting and Rhetoric of Mark's Gospel.* BibInt 65. Leiden: Brill, 2003.

Jackson, Howard M. "The Death of Jesus in Mark and the Miracle from the Cross." *NTS* 33 (1987): 16–37.

————. "Why the Youth Shed His Cloak and Fled Naked: The Meaning and Purpose of Mark 14:51–52." *JBL* 116, no. 2 (1997): 273–89.

Jeremias, Joachim. *Abba: Studien zur neutestamentlichen Theologie und Zeitgeschichte.* Göttingen: Vandenhoeck & Ruprecht, 1966.

————. *The Eucharistic Words of Jesus*. Translated by Norman Perrin. New York: Scribner, 1966.

————. *Infant Baptism in the First Four Centuries*. Library of History and Doctrine. Translated by David Cairns. Philadelphia: Westminster, 1960.

————. *Jesus' Promise to the Nations*. SBT 24. Naperville, Ill.: Alec R. Allenson, 1958.

————. "Die Salbungsgeschichte Mc 14,3–9." *ZNW* 35 (1936): 75–82.

————. *New Testament Theology: The Proclamation of Jesus*. New York: Scribner, 1971.

————. *The Parables of Jesus*. 2d rev. ed. New York: Scribner, 1972.

————. *The Prayers of Jesus*. SBT 2/6. Naperville, Ill.: Alec R. Allenson, 1967.

————. "Zum nicht-responsorischen Amen." *ZNW* 64 (1973): 122–23.

Johnson, Earl S. "Is Mark 15.39 the Key to Mark's Christology?" *JSNT* 31 (1987): 3–22.

Juel, Donald. "A Disquieting Silence: The Matter of the Ending." Pages 1–14 in *The End of Mark and the Ends of God: Essays in Memory of Donald Harrisville Juel*. Edited by Beverly R. Gaventa and Patrick D. Miller. Louisville, Ky.: Westminster John Knox, 2005.

————. *A Master of Surprise: Mark Interpreted*. Minneapolis: Fortress, 1994.

————. *Messiah and Temple: The Trial of Jesus in the Gospel of Mark*. SBLDS 13. Missoula, Mont.: Scholars Press, 1977.

————. "The Origin of Mark's Christology." Pages 449–60 in *The Messiah: Developments in Earliest Judaism and Christianity*. Edited by James H. Charlesworth. Minneapolis: Fortress, 1992.

Jülicher, Adolf. *Die Gleichnisreden Jesu*. Freiburg i. B. Mohr, 1888.

Kafka, Franz. *Parables and Paradoxes*. New York: Schocken Books, 1958.

Käsemann, Ernst. "Sentences of Holy Law in the New Testament." Pages 66–81 in *New Testament Questions of Today*. London: SCM Press, 1969.

Keck, Leander. "Mark 3:7–12 and Mark's Christology." *JBL* 84, no. 4 (1965): 341–58.

Kee, Howard Clark. *Community of the New Age: Studies in Mark's Gospel*. Philadelphia: Westminster, 1977.

————. *Miracle in the Early Christian World: A Study in Sociohistorical Method*. New Haven, Conn.: Yale University Press, 1983.

————. "Scriptural Quotations and Allusions in Mark 11–16." Pages 475–502 in *SBLSP* 2. Atlanta: Society of Biblical Literature, 1971. 475–502.

————. "The Terminology of Mark's Exorcism Stories." *NTS* 14 (1968): 231–46.

Kelber, Werner H. "Conclusion: From Passion Narrative to Gospel." Pages 153–80 in *The Passion in Mark: Studies on Mark 14–16*. Edited by Werner H. Kelber. Philadelphia: Fortress, 1976.

————. *The Kingdom in Mark: A New Place and a New Time.* Philadelphia: Fortress, 1974.

————. *Mark's Story of Jesus.* Philadelphia: Fortress, 1979.

————. *The Oral and the Written Gospel: The Hermeneutics of Speaking and Writing in the Synoptic Tradition, Mark, Paul, and Q.* Philadelphia: Fortress, 1983; 2d ed. with new introduction by the author, 1997.

————, ed. *The Passion in Mark: Studies on Mark 14–16.* Philadelphia: Fortress, 1976.

Kermode, Frank. *The Genesis of Secrecy: On the Interpretation of Narrative.* Cambridge, Mass.: Harvard University Press, 1979.

Kertelge, Karl. *Die Wunder Jesu im Markusevangelium.* SANT 23. Munich: Kösel, 1970.

Kingsbury, Jack Dean. *The Christology of Mark's Gospel.* Philadelphia: Fortress, 1983.

Klauck, Hans-Josef. *Vorspiel im Himmel? Erzältechnik und Theologie im Markusprolog.* BTS 32. Neukirchen: Neukirchener Verlag, 1997.

Koester, Helmut. *Ancient Christian Gospels: Their History and Development.* Philadelphia: Trinity Press International, 1990.

Kuhn, Heinz-Wolfgang. *Ältere Sammlungen in Markusevangelium.* SUNT 8. Göttingen: Vandenhoeck & Ruprecht, 1971.

Künzi, Martin. *Das Naherwartungslogion Markus 9, 1 par [und Parallelstellen]: Geschichte seiner Auslegung: Mit einem Nachwort zur Auslegungsgeschichte von Markus 13, 30 par.* BGBE 21. Tübingen: Mohr, 1977.

Lambrecht, Jan. *Die Redaktion der Markus-Apokalypse: Literarische Analyse und Strukturuntersuchung.* AnBib 28. Rome: Päpstliches Bibelinstitut, 1967.

Lampe, Peter. *From Paul to Valentinus: Christians at Rome in the First Two Centuries.* Translated by Michael Steinhauser. Edited by Marshall D. Johnson. Minneapolis: Fortress, 2003.

————. "The Roman Christians of Romans 16." Pages 216–30 in *The Romans Debate.* Rev. and expanded ed. Edited by Karl P. Donfried. Peabody, Mass.: Hendrickson, 1991.

Lee-Pollard, Dorothy A. "Powerlessness as Power: A Key Emphasis in the Gospel of Mark." *SJT* 40 (1987): 173–88.

Lightfoot, R. H. *The Gospel Message of St. Mark.* Oxford: Oxford University Press, 1962.

————. *Locality and Doctrine in the Gospels.* London: Hodder & Stoughton, 1938.

Lindemann, Andreas. "Die Kinder und die Gottesherschaft." *WD* 17 (1983): 77–104.

Linnemann, Eta. *Studien zur Passionsgeschichte.* FRLANT 102. Göttingen: Vandenhoeck & Ruprecht, 1970.

Lohmeyer, Ernst. *Die Briefe an die Philipper, an die Kolosser und an Phile-mon*. 14th ed. KEK IX/1. Göttingen: Vandenhoeck & Ruprecht, 1974.

———. *Galiläa und Jerusalem*. FRLANT n.F. 34. Göttingen: Vandenhoeck & Ruprecht, 1936.

Lohse, Eduard. *Märtyer und Gottesknecht: Untersuchungen zur urchristlichen Verkündigung vom Sühntod Jesu Christi*. FRLANT 46. Göttingen: Vandenhoeck & Ruprecht, 1955.

Love, Stuart A. "Jesus Heals the Hemorrhaging Woman." Pages 85–101 in *The Social Setting of Jesus and the Gospels*. Edited by Wolfgang Stegemann, Bruce J. Malina, Gerd Theissen. Minneapolis: Fortress, 2002.

Luz, Ulrich. "The Secrecy Motif and the Marcan Christology (1965)." Pages 75–96 in *The Messianic Secret*. Edited by C. M. Tuckett. IRT 1. London: SPCK, 1983.

MacDonald, Dennis Ronald. *The Homeric Epics and the Gospel of Mark*. New Haven, Conn.: Yale University Press, 2000.

Mack, Burton L. *A Myth of Innocence: Mark and Christian Origins*. Philadelphia: Fortress, 1988.

Malbon, Elizabeth Struthers. "The Christology of Mark's Gospel: Narrative Christology and the Markan Jesus." Pages 33–48 in *Who Do You Say That I Am? Essays on Christology*. Edited by Mark Allen Powell and David R. Bauer. Louisville, Ky.: Westminster John Knox, 1999.

———. "Fallible Followers: Women in the Gospel of Mark." *Semeia* 28 (1983): 29–48.

———. "Galilee and Jerusalem: History and Literature in Marcan Interpretation (1982)." Pages 253–67 in *The Interpretation of Mark*. Edited by William R. Telford. Studies in New Testament Interpretation. Edinburgh: T. & T. Clark, 1995.

———. "The Jesus of Mark and the Sea of Galilee." *JBL* 103, no. 3 (1984): 363–77.

———. *Narrative Space and Mythic Meaning in Mark*. San Francisco: Harper & Row, 1986.

Maloney, Elliott C. *Semitic Interference in Marcan Syntax*. SBLDS 51. Chico, Calif.: Scholars Press, 1981.

Mansfield, M. Robert. *Spirit and Gospel in Mark*. Peabody, Mass.: Hendrickson, 1987.

Manson, T. W. "The Cleansing of the Temple." *BJRL* 33 (1951): 271–82.

———. *Only to the House of Israel? Jesus and the Non-Jews*. FBBS 9. Philadelphia: Fortress, 1964.

———. *The Teaching of Jesus*. Cambridge: Cambridge University Press, 1963.

Marcus, Joel. "The Jewish War and the Sitz im Leben of Mark." *JBL* 111 (1992): 441–62.

———. *The Mystery of the Kingdom of God*. SBLDS 90. Atlanta: Scholars Press, 1986.

————. "Mark 4.10–12 and Markan Epistemology." *JBL* 103 (1984): 557–74.

————. *The Way of the Lord: Christological Exegesis of the Old Testament in the Gospel of Mark.* Louisville, Ky.: Westminster John Knox, 1992.

Marguerat, Daniel. "Le Problème Synoptique." Pages 11–33 in *Introduction au Nouveau Testament: Son histoire, son écriture, sa théologie.* Edited by Daniel Marguerat. MdB 41. Geneva: Labor & Fides, 2004.

Marshall, Christopher D. *Faith as a Theme in Mark's Narrative.* SNTSMS 64. Cambridge: Cambridge University Press, 1989.

Martin, Ralph P. *Mark: Evangelist and Theologian.* Contemporary Evangelical Perspectives. Grand Rapids: Eerdmans, 1973.

Marxsen, Willi. *Mark the Evangelist.* Translated by Roy A. Harrisville. Nashville: Abingdon, 1969.

————. *Mark the Evangelist: Studies on the Redaction History of the Gospel.* Translated by James Boyce et al. Nashville: Abingdon, 1969.

Masson, Charles. *L'Évangile de Marc et l'Église de Rome.* Bibliothèque théologique. Neuchâtel: Delachaux & Niestlé, 1968.

Matera, Frank J. *New Testament Christology.* Louisville, Ky.: Westminster John Knox, 1999.

Mauser, Ulrich. *Christ in the Wilderness.* SBT 39. Naperville, Ill.: Alec R. Allenson, 1963.

McArthur, Harvey K. "Son of Mary." *NovT* 15 (1973): 38–58.

McNeill, John T., ed. *Calvin: Institutes of the Christian Religion.* Translated by Ford Lewis Battles. 2 vols. LCC 20–21. Philadelphia: Westminster, 1960.

Meier, John P. "The Brothers and Sisters of Jesus in Ecumenical Perspective." *CBQ* 54, no. 1 (1992): 1–28.

————. "The Debate on the Resurrection of the Dead: An Incident from the Ministry of the Historical Jesus?" *Journal for the Study of the New Testament* 77 (2000): 3–24.

Merkel, Helmut. "Peter's Curse." Pages 66–71 in *The Trial of Jesus: Cambridge Studies in Honour of C. F. D. Moule.* SBT 2/13. Naperville, Ill.: A. R. Allenson, 1970.

Meye, Robert P. *Jesus and the Twelve: Discipleship and Revelation in Mark's Gospel.* Grand Rapids: Eerdmans, 1968.

Miller, Susan. *Women in Mark's Gospel.* JSNTSup 259. London: T. & T. Clark, 2004.

Moloney, Francis J. *The Gospel of John.* SP 4. Collegeville, Minn.: Liturgical Press, 1998.

Moltmann-Wendel, Elizabeth. "Mit der Schwiegermutter fing alles an: Petrus und die Frauen." Pages 12–20 in *Petrus, der Fels des Anstoßes.* Edited by Raul Niemann. Stuttgart: Kreuz, 1994.

Montefiore, C. G., and Israel Abrahams. *The Synoptic Gospels.* 2d ed. Library of Biblical Studies. New York: Ktav, 1968.

Montefiore, C. G., and H. Loewe, eds. *A Rabbinic Anthology*. Meridian Books. New York: World, 1963.

Moore, Stephen D. "Deconstructive Criticism: The Gospel of the Mark." Pages 84–102 in *Mark and Method: New Approaches in Biblical Studies*. Edited by Janice Capel Anderson and Stephen D. Moore. Minneapolis: Fortress, 1992.

Moule, C. F. D. "Mark 4:1–20 Yet Once More." Pages 95–113 in *Neotestamentica et Semitica: Studies in Honour of Matthew Black*. Edited by E. Earle Ellis and Max E. Wilcox. Edinburgh: T. & T. Clark, 1969.

Mowinckel, Sigmund. *He That Cometh: The Messiah Concept in the Old Testament and Later Judaism*. Biblical Resource Series. Translated by G. W. Anderson. Grand Rapids: Eerdmans, 2005.

Munro, Winsome. "Women Disciples in Mark?" *CBQ* 44, no. 2 (1982): 225–41.

Myers, Ched. *Binding the Strong Man: A Political Reading of Mark's Story of Jesus*. Maryknoll, N.Y.: Orbis, 1988.

Neirynck, Frans. *Duality in Mark: Contributions to the Study of the Markan Redaction*. Peeters: Leuven University Press, 1988.

———. "Le discours anti-apocalyptique de Mc. XIII." *ETL* 45 (1969): 154–64.

Neyrey, Jerome H. "The Idea of Purity in Mark's Gospel." *Semeia* 36 (1986): 91–128.

Nickelsburg, George W. E. *Resurrection, Immortality, and Eternal Life in Intertestamental Judaism*. HTS 26. Cambridge, Mass.: Harvard University Press, 1972.

Ogden, Schubert M. *The Point of Christology*. San Francisco: Harper & Row, 1982.

Parker, D. C. *The Living Text of the Gospels*. Cambridge: Cambridge University Press, 1997.

Perkins, Pheme. *Resurrection: New Testament Witness and Contemporary Reflection*. Garden City, N.Y.: Doubleday, 1984.

Perrin, Norman. "The Christology of Mark: A Study in Methodology (1971, 1974)." Pages 125–40 in *The Interpretation of Mark*. Edited by William R. Telford. Studies in New Testament Interpretation. Edinburgh: T. & T. Clark, 1995.

———. "The High Priest's Question and Jesus' Answer." Pages 80–95 in *The Passion in Mark: Studies on Mark 14–16*. Edited by Werner H. Kelber. Philadelphia: Fortress, 1976.

———. *The New Testament, an Introduction: Proclamation and Parenesis, Myth and History*. New York: Harcourt Brace Jovanovich, 1974.

———. "The Use of (*Para-*)didonai in Connection with the Passion of Jesus in the New Testament." Pages 94–103 in *A Modern Pilgrimage in New Testament Christology*. Edited by Norman Perrin. Philadelphia: Fortress, 1974.

Pesch, Rudolf. *Naherwartungen: Tradition und Redaktion in Mark 13.* KBANT. Düsseldorf: Patmos-Verlag, 1968.

Petersen, Norman R. "When Is the End Not the End? Literary Reflections on the End of Mark's Narrative." *Int* 34 (1980): 151–66.

Pokorný, Petr. "Die Bedeutung des Markusevangeliums für die Entstehung der christlichen Bibel." Pages 409–27 in *Text and Contexts: Biblical Texts in Their Textual and Situational Contexts: Essays in Honor of Lars Hartman.* Edited by Tord Fornberg et al. Oslo: Scandinavian University Press, 1995.

———. "From a Puppy to a Child: Some Problems of Contemporary Biblical Exegesis Demonstrated from Mark 7.24–30 / Matt 15.21–28." *NTS* 41 (1995): 321–37.

———. *Der Gottessohn: Literarische Übersicht und Fragestellung.* ThSt 109. Zürich: Theologischer Verlag, 1971.

———. "Das Markusevangelium: Literarische und theologische Einleitung mit Forschungsbericht." Pages 1970–2035 in *ANRW* II.25.3. Berlin: De Gruyter, 1984.

Preuss, H. R. "Galiläa im Markus-Evangelium." Dissertation, Göttingen, 1966.

Price, Reynolds. *The Three Gospels.* New York: Scribner, 1996.

Pryke, E. J. *Redactional Style in the Marcan Gospel: A Study of Syntax and Vocabulary as Guides to Redaction in Mark.* SNTSMS 33. Cambridge: Cambridge University Press, 1978.

Quesnell, Quentin. *The Mind of Mark: Interpretation and Method through the Exegesis of Mark 6, 52.* AnBib 38. Rome: Pontifical Biblical Institute, 1969.

Räisänen, Heikki. *The 'Messianic Secret' in Mark.* Edinburgh: T. & T. Clark, 1990.

Rau, Gottfried. "Das Markusevangelium: Komposition und Intention der ersten Darstellung christlicher Mission." Pages 2037–257 in *Aufstieg und Niedergang Der Römischen Welt*; II.25.3. Berlin: De Gruyter, 1984.

Reploh, Karl-Georg. *Markus, Lehrer der Gemeinde: Eine redaktionsgeschichtliche Studie zu den Jüngerperikopen des Markus-Evangeliums.* SBM 9. Stuttgart: Verlag Katholisches Bibelwerk, 1969.

Rhoads, David. *Reading Mark, Engaging the Gospel.* Minneapolis: Fortress, 2004.

Rhoads, David, Joanna Dewey, and Donald Michie. *Mark as Story: An Introduction to the Narrative of a Gospel.* 2d ed. Minneapolis: Fortress, 1999.

Riches, John Kenneth. *Conflicting Mythologies: Identity Formation in the Gospels of Mark and Matthew.* Studies of the New Testament and Its World. Edinburgh: T. & T. Clark, 2000.

Ringe, Sharon H. "A Gentile Woman's Story." Pages 65–72 in *Feminist Interpretation of the Bible.* Edited by Letty M. Russell. Philadelphia: Westminster, 1985.

————. "A Gentile Woman's Story, Revisited: Rereading Mark 7:24–31a." Pages 79–100 in *A Feminist Companion to Mark*. Edited by Amy-Jill Levine and Marianne Blickenstaff. Cleveland: Pilgrim Press, 2004.

Robbins, Vernon K. *Jesus the Teacher: A Socio-Rhetorical Interpretation of Mark*. Philadelphia: Fortress, 1984.

Robinson, James M. "Jesus: From Easter to Valentinus (or to the Apostles Creed)." *JBL* 101 (1982): 5–37.

————. *The Problem of History in Mark and Other Marcan Studies*. Philadelphia: Fortress, 1982.

Rogers, P. "The Desolation of Jesus in the Gospel of Mark." Pages 53–74 in *The Language of the Cross*. Edited by P. Rogers. Chicago: Franciscan Herald Press, 1977.

Root, Michael. "Dying He Lives: Biblical Image, Biblical Narrative, and the Redemptive Jesus." *Semeia* 30 (1985): 155–70.

Roskam, Hendrika Nicoline. *The Purpose of the Gospel of Mark in Its Historical and Social Context*. NovTSup 114. Leiden: Brill, 2004.

Sabin, Marie Noonan. *Reopening the Word: Reading Mark as Theology in the Context of Early Judaism*. Oxford: Oxford University Press, 2002.

Saldarini, Anthony J. *Pharisees, Scribes and Sadducees in Palestinian Society: A Sociological Approach*. Biblical Resource Series. Grand Rapids: Eerdmans, 2001.

Sanders, E. P. *Jesus and Judaism*. Philadelphia: Fortress, 1985.

————. *The Historical Figure of Jesus*. New York: Penguin, 1993.

Schaff, Philip, ed. *Chrysostom: Homilies on the Gospel of Saint Matthew*. NPNFI 10. Peabody, Mass.: Hendrickson, 1888, 1994.

Schenke, Ludger. *Das Markus-Evangelium*. Stuttgart: Kohlhammer, 1988.

————. *Studien zur Passionsgeschichte des Markus: Tradition und Redaktion in Markus 14, 1–42*. FB 4. Würzburg: Echter Verlag, 1971.

————. *Die Wundererzählungen des Markusevangeliums*. SBB 5. Stuttgart: Verlag Katholisches Bibelwerk, 1974.

Schille, Gottfried. *Anfänge der Kirche: Erwägungen zur apostolischen Frühgeschichte*. BEvT 43. Munich: Kaiser Verlag, 1966.

Schmithals, Walter. *Einleitung in die drei ersten Evangelien*. Berlin: De Gruyter, 1985.

————. *Der Rahmen Der Geschichte Jesu: Literarkritische Untersuchungen zur ältesten Jesusüberlieferung*. Darmstadt: Wissenschaftliche Buchgesellschaft, 1969.

Schnelle, Udo. *The History and Theology of the New Testament Writings*. Translated by M. Eugue Boring. Minneapolis: Fortress, 1998.

Schulz, Siegfried. *Die Stunde der Botschaft: Einführung in die Theologie der vier Evangelisten*. Hamburg: Furche-Verlag, 1970.

Schüssler Fiorenza, Elisabeth. *In Memory of Her: A Feminist Theological Reconstruction of Christian Origins*. New York: Crossroad, 1983.

Schweizer, Eduard. "Anmerkungen zur Theologie des Markus." Pages 93–104 in *Neotestamentica: Deutsche und Englische Aufsätze 1951–1963*. Zürich: Zwingli Verlag, 1963.

Scott, Bernard Brandon. *Hear Then the Parable*. Minneapolis: Fortress, 1990.

Sellew, Philip. "Oral and Written Sources in Mark 4:1–34." *NTS* 36, no. 2 (1990): 234–67.

Selvidge, Marla J. "Mark 5:25–34 and Leviticus 15:19–20." *JBL* 103, no. 4 (1984): 619–23.

Senior, Donald P. "The Struggle to Be Universal: Mission as Vantage Point for New Testament Interpretation." *CBQ* 46, no. 1 (1984): 63–81.

Shepherd, Tom. *Markan Sandwich Stories: Narration, Definition, and Function*. Andrews University Seminary Doctoral Dissertation Series 18. Berrien Springs, Mich.: Andrews University, 1993.

———. "The Narrative Function of Markan Intercalation." *NTS* 41 (1995): 522–40.

Sherwin-White, A. N. *Roman Society and Roman Law in the New Testament*. Sarum Lectures, 1960–1961. Grand Rapids: Baker, 1978.

Shiner, Whitney Taylor. *Follow Me! Disciples in Markan Rhetoric*. SBLDS 145. Atlanta: Scholars Press, 1995.

———. *Proclaiming the Gospel: First-century Performance of Mark*. Harrisburg, Pa.: Trinity Press International, 2003.

Shires, Henry. *Finding the Old Testament in the New*. Philadelphia: Westminster, 1974.

Smith, Morton. *Clement of Alexandria and a Secret Gospel of Mark*. Cambridge, Mass.: Harvard University Press, 1973.

———. *Jesus the Magician*. San Francisco: Harper & Row, 1978.

———. *The Secret Gospel: The Discovery and Interpretation of the Secret Gospel according to Mark*. 1st ed. New York: Harper & Row, 1973.

Snodgrass, Klyne R. "The Parable of the Wicked Husbandmen: Is the Gospel of Thomas Version Original?" *NTS* 21 (1974): 142–44.

Stanton, Graham. *Gospel Truth? New Light on Jesus and the Gospels*. Valley Forge, Pa.: Trinity Press International, 1995.

Steck, Odil Hannes. *Israel und das gewaltsame Geschick der Propheten: Untersuchungen zur Überlieferung des deuteronomistischen Geschichtsbildes im Alten Testament, Spätjudentum und Urchristentum*. WMANT 23. Neukirchen-Vluyn: Neukirchener Verlag, 1967.

Stendahl, Krister. *The School of St. Matthew and Its Use of the Old Testament*. Philadelphia: Fortress, 1968.

Stock, Augustine. *Call to Discipleship: A Literary Study of Mark's Gospel*. GNS 1. Wilmington, Del.: Glazier, 1982.

Strange, James F. "Crucifixion, Method of." Pages 199–200 in *The Interpreter's Dictionary of the Bible, Supplementary Volume*. Edited by Keith Crim et al. Nashville: Abingdon, 1976.

Strange, James F., and H. Shanks. "Has the House Where Jesus Stayed in Capernaum Been Found?" *BAR* 8 (1982): 26–37.

Strecker, Georg. *The Sermon on the Mount: An Exegetical Commentary*. Translated by O. C. Dean. Nashville: Abingdon, 1988.

———. *Theology of the New Testament*. Translated by M. Eugene Boring. New York: De Gruyter, 2000.

Streeter, Burnett Hillman. *The Four Gospels: A Study of Origins*. London: Macmillan, 1964.

Sugirtharajah, R. S. "The Widow's Mites Revalued." *ExpTim* 103 (1991–1992): 42–43.

Suhl, Alfred. *Die Wunder Jesu*. Gütersloh: Güterloher Verlagshaus, 1968.

———, ed. *Der Wunderbegriff im Neuen Testament*. Wege der Forschung 295. Darmstadt: Wissenschaftliche Buchgesellschaft, 1980.

Sundberg, A. C. "On Testimonies." *NovT* 3 (1959): 268–81.

Tagawa, K. *Miracles et Évangile, la pensée personnelle de l'évangéliste Marc*. Etudes d'histoire et de philosophie religieuses 62. Paris: Presses universitaires de France, 1966.

Talbert, Charles H. *What Is a Gospel? The Genre of the Canonical Gospels*. Philadelphia: Fortress, 1977.

Tannehill, Robert C. "The Disciples in Mark: The Function of a Narrative Role (1977)." Pages 169–96 in *The Interpretation of Mark*. Edited by William R. Telford. Studies in New Testament Interpretation. Edinburgh: T. & T. Clark, 1995.

———. "The Gospel of Mark as Narrative Christology." *Semeia* 16 (1980): 57–96.

———. "The Gospels and Narrative Literature." Pages 56–70 in *NIB* 8. Edited by Leander Keck. Nashville: Abingdon, 1995.

———. *The Sword of His Mouth*. Philadelphia: Fortress, 1975.

Telford, William. *The Barren Temple and the Withered Tree: A Redaction-critical Analysis of the Cursing of the Fig-tree Pericope in Mark's Gospel and Its Relation to the Cleansing of the Temple Tradition*. JSNTSup 1. Sheffield: JSOT Press, 1980.

———. "The Pre-Markan Tradition in Recent Research (1980–1990)." Pages 693–723 in *The Four Gospels 1992—Festschrift Frans Neirynck*. Edited by Frans van Segbroeck et al. Leuven: Leuven University Press, 1992.

———. *The Theology of the Gospel of Mark*. New Testament Theology. Cambridge: Cambridge University Press, 1999.

Theissen, Gerd. *The Gospels in Context: Social and Political History in the Synoptic Tradition*. Translated by Linda M. Maloney. Minneapolis: Fortress, 1991.

———. *The Miracle Stories of the Early Christian Tradition.* Translated by Francis McDonagh. Philadelphia: Fortress, 1983.

———. *The Religion of the Earliest Churches: Creating a Symbolic World.* Translated by John Bowden. Minneapolis: Fortress, 1999.

Tödt, H. E. *The Son of Man in the Synoptic Tradition.* NTL. Translated by Dorothea M. Barton. Philadelphia: Westminster, 1965.

Tolbert, Mary Ann. *Sowing the Gospel: Mark's World in Literary-Historical Perspective.* Minneapolis: Fortress, 1989.

Tuckett, Christopher M. "Mark's Concerns in the Parables Chapter (Mark 4,1–34)." *Biblica* 69, no. 1 (1988): 1–26.

———. "Synoptic Problem." *ABD* 6:263–70.

Turner, C. H. "*Ferein* in St Mark." Pages 13–15 in *The Language and Style of the Gospel of Mark: An Edition of C. H. Turner's "Notes on Marcan Usage" Together with Other Comparable Studies.* Edited by J. K. Elliott. NovTSup 71. Leiden: Brill, 1993.

Turner, C. H., and J. K. Elliott, eds. *The Language and Style of the Gospel of Mark: An Edition of C. H. Turner's "Notes on Marcan Usage" Together with Other Comparable Studies.* NovTSup 71. Leiden: Brill, 1993.

Vanhoye, Albert. "La fuite du jeune homme nu (Mc 14,51–52)." *Biblica* 52 (1971): 401–6.

Via, Dan O., Jr. *The Ethics of Mark's Gospel: In the Middle of Time.* Philadelphia: Fortress, 1985.

Vorster, Willem S. "Literary Reflections on Mark 13:5–37: A Narrated Speech of Jesus." *Neot* (1987): 203–22.

Watts, Rikki E. *Isaiah's New Exodus in Mark.* WUNT 88. Tübingen: Mohr Siebeck, 1997.

Weeden, Theodore J. *Mark—Traditions in Conflict.* Philadelphia: Fortress, 1971.

Wills, Lawrence M. *The Quest of the Historical Gospel: Mark, John, and the Origins of the Gospel Genre.* London: Routledge, 1997.

Wrede, William. *The Messianic Secret.* Library of Theological Translations. Translated by James C. G. Greig. London: James Clarke, 1971.

Wright, Addison G. "The Widow's Mites: Praise or Lament?—A Matter of Context." *CBQ* 44 (1982): 256–65.

Wright, N. T. *Jesus and the Victory of God.* Christian Origins and the Question of God 2. Minneapolis: Fortress, 1996.

———. *The Resurrection of the Son of God.* Christian Origins and the Question of God 3. Minneapolis: Fortress, 2003.

Wuellner, Wilhelm H. *The Meaning of "Fishers of Men."* Philadelphia: Westminster, 1967.

Zahn, Theodor. *Introduction to the New Testament.* Translated by John Moore Trout et al. 3 vols. Edinburgh: T. & T. Clark, 1909.

Zeller, Dieter. "Bedeutung und religionsgeschichtlicher Hintergrund der Verwandlung Jesu." Pages 303–21 in *Authenticating the Activities of Jesus.* Edited by Bruce Chilton and Craig A. Evans. Leiden: Brill, 1999.

Zerwick, Maximillian, and Joseph Smith. *Biblical Greek.* Rome: Scripta Pontificii Instituti Biblici, 1963.

Zimmermann, Alfred. *Die urchristlichen Lehrer: Studien zum Tradentenkreis der Didaskaloi im frühen Urchristentum.* WUANT 2.12. Tübingen: Mohr, 1984.

INTRODUCTION

The Gospel of Mark is a written text composed to be read aloud, all at once, in the context of a worshiping congregation.[1] Mark's potent story cannot be summarized; it must be experienced. Before proceeding, the reader is advised to cease and desist from reading all secondary literature (including this commentary) and to read the Markan narrative itself as a whole—or better yet, to listen as the story is read aloud by someone else. This requires about an hour and a quarter, the length of a good movie. The following sketch is provided as an aid to analysis and appreciation.

1. Story

The opening words inform the reader that the following narrative is the beginning and norm of the good news of Jesus Christ the Son of God. Somewhere offstage, the voice of God addresses the Christ in the words of Scripture, declaring that the way of the Lord will be prepared by God's messenger (1:2–3). When the narrative curtain opens, the reader sees the strange figure of John the Baptizer, preaching repentance and baptism for the forgiveness of sins, and announcing the future advent of a powerful figure who will baptize with the Holy Spirit (1:4–8). Jesus appears and is baptized without another word from John, but the heavenly voice speaks to Jesus declaring him to be God's Son. The Holy Spirit descends on him and drives him into the wilderness, where he is tested by Satan. John is arrested, and Jesus begins to preach the good news of the kingdom of God (1:14–15).

The first words the reader hears Jesus speak are "Follow me," addressed to the fishermen whom he calls to be his disciples. With his few disciples, Jesus begins a vigorous ministry of preaching, teaching with authority, casting out demons, healing the sick, cleansing lepers, raising the dead, feeding the hungry, and giving sight to the blind (1:21–8:26). In the midst of his activity, Jesus

---

1. This well-based hypothesis is now widely accepted. Cf., e.g., Christopher Bryan, *A Preface to Mark: Notes on the Gospel in Its Literary and Cultural Settings* (New York: Oxford University Press, 1993), 67–162; Whitney Taylor Shiner, *Proclaiming the Gospel: First-century Performance of Mark* (Harrisburg, Pa.: Trinity Press International, 2003), and the literature they list.

delivers a long parabolic discourse to the crowds, but it is intended to be understood only by his disciples—though they too fail to understand. His mighty works include power over nature: he calms the storm (4:35–41) and walks on the water (6:45–51). While God and the demons (and the reader) know Jesus' identity, despite his mighty works the characters in the narrative do not recognize him.

The story takes a dramatic turn in the episode described in 8:27–9:1. Jesus asks his disciples, "Who do people say that I am?" and receives a variety of impressive answers. Jesus then directs his question to the disciples themselves, and Peter answers for the group: "You are the Christ." Jesus' response is not to congratulate Peter (contrast Matt 16:17–19), but to command silence. For the first time, Jesus states that the Son of Man is to go to Jerusalem where he will be killed, but will rise from the dead (8:31). This pattern is repeated three times, so that there are two further "passion predictions" (9:31; 10:33–34). Through it all, the disciples remain uncomprehending, despite their witnessing the dramatic transformation of Jesus when Moses and Elijah appear to him on the mountain. The voice that spoke to Jesus at the beginning ("You are my beloved son," 1:11) now addresses the disciples directly ("This is my beloved son," 9:7). But their hearts are hardened.

In Mark, Jesus makes one trip to Jerusalem (10:1–52). His arrival is hailed by the crowds as the "one who comes in the name of the Lord" who will inaugurate "the coming kingdom of our ancestor David" (11:1–10). Jesus' response is to drive those buying and selling animals from the temple, which sharpens his conflicts with the Jewish leaders (11:15–33). Jesus' debates with Jewish scribes in Galilee (2:1–3:6) intensify in Jerusalem (12:1–40). Jesus leaves the temple, takes four of his disciples to the Mount of Olives, and delivers the longest discourse in Mark, announcing the destruction of the temple, future persecution of his disciples, and the coming of the Son of Man in clouds with great power and glory (13:1–37).

On his fourth day in Jerusalem, at a dinner party in Bethany at the house of Simon the Leper, a woman pours a large amount of expensive perfumed oil on Jesus' head; Jesus explains that this anticipates his coming death (14:3–9). The next evening Jesus celebrates the Passover with his disciples, declares the bread and wine to be his body and blood, and departs with them to pray in Gethsemane (14:12–42). With the help of Judas, one of the special group of twelve Jesus himself had chosen, a crowd sent by the Jewish leaders apprehends Jesus in Gethsemane. They take him to the house of the high priest, where he is interrogated and confesses himself to be the Christ, the Son of God, and promises that they will see him as the Son of Man seated at God's right hand and coming with the clouds of heaven (14:43–62). The Jewish leaders turn Jesus over to Pilate, who has him crucified as one who claims to be "King of the Jews"

(15:1–41). His disciples had already disappeared, so Jesus is buried by a friendly member of the Jewish governing council in a tomb cut from the solid rock (15:42–46).

Even in the early Galilean part of the story, while Jesus appears to be having great success, people begin to reject and abandon him. Early on, the Pharisees and Herodians conspire to put him to death (3:6). Jesus' mother, brothers, and sisters fail to understand him, consider him deranged, and attempt to bring him back home (3:21, 31–35). When Jesus returns to preach in his hometown, the people of Nazareth are scandalized by him (6:1–6). In the latter part of the story, the misunderstanding and rejection of Jesus gains momentum: the crowds that welcome him to Jerusalem turn on him and call for his life (11:1–10; 12:37; 14:43; 15:11–15). One of the Twelve betrays him to the authorities (14:1–2, 10–11, 43–45). Another denies with a curse that he knows him (14:66–72). In Gethsemane at the arrest, they all forsake him and flee (14:50). The story that had begun with men leaving all to become Jesus' disciples (1:16–20; cf. 10:28) concludes with a young man literally leaving everything to avoid being a disciple (14:51–52). The next day, Jesus' only utterance from the cross is a loud cry, "My God, my God, why have you forsaken me?" (15:34).

Late in the narrative, Mark mentions that there were women who had followed him in Galilee, had supported his mission, had come to Jerusalem with him, and had observed the crucifixion and burial from a distance when the other disciples had fled (15:40–41, 47). They are the only exception to the almost unmitigated misunderstanding and rejection of Jesus, and only they come to the tomb on Sunday morning (16:1–4). There they find the empty tomb and are told by a young man in a white robe to go and tell the others that Christ is risen and goes before them to Galilee. All others have misunderstood, rejected, betrayed, denied, and failed. These women are the only hope that the message from and about Jesus will endure. Mark concludes his narrative with a sentence that breaks off in the middle, "But they said nothing to anyone, for they were afraid . . ."

This is a strange story, fraught with reversal and paradox.

What is this story *about*? The obvious answer: it is about Jesus, who appears in almost every scene and is the subject of most of the verbs in Mark. One could also say: it is about the disciples, who are called in the first chapter and accompany Jesus and are taught by him throughout until they abandon him in chapters 14 and 15; they are the goal of the final revelation pointed to in 16:7. The real answer, however: the story is about God, who only rarely becomes an explicit character, but who is the hidden actor in the whole drama, whose reality spans its whole narrative world from creation to eschaton, and who is not an alternative or competitor to the view that regards Jesus as the principal subject. To tell the story of Jesus is to tell the self-defining story of God.

2. Structure

The author's rhetoric, his strategy of communication, is built into the text itself by the way he has arranged the narrative. Numerous outlines have been proposed.[2] Since an outline must necessarily be diachronic and static, no one outline can do justice to all the dimensions of Mark's rhetorical structure. The interpreter should not think of divisions, the crisp lines of an outline, but of overlapping pivotal or transitional sections.[3] The original hearers were more aware of *links* that hold the story together than of *divisions*.

Mark seems to be structured in two major parts corresponding to the author's christological emphases. The narrator declares Jesus to be the Christ in the opening line and recounts many mighty works of Jesus, but no human being recognizes his true identity until about halfway through the narrative when Peter confesses Jesus to be the Christ—clearly a turning point in the story (8:27–29). From 8:30 to the end, Jesus reveals his own identity as the Son of Man who will suffer, die, be raised by God, and return in glory at the end of history. Thus the narrative can be thought of as bipartite, 1:1–8:29 / 8:30–16:8. Yet the carefully structured 8:22–10:52 is clearly a unit that would be divided by such a bipartite structure (see analysis at 8:22). Topographical and other considerations point to part one as comprising 1:1–8:21 and part two as 11:1–16:8, joined by the transitional section 8:22–10:52, which overlaps and unites the bipartite structure 1:1–8:29 / 8:30–16:8.

The following characteristics distinguish the two parts:

Part One 1:1–8:21	Part Two 11:1–16:8
Galilee	*Jerusalem*
Calling, sending disciples	*No calling or sending disciples*
Miraculous ministry	*Nonmiraculous ministry*
Exorcisms	*No exorcisms*
Success	*Rejection*
Major central discourse: parables	*Major central discourse: apocalyptic*
Kingdom parables	*No kingdom parables*
Mystery of the kingdom	*Jesus the king*

2. Heinrich Baarlink gives an analysis of twenty-seven outlines of Mark, dividing them into seven categories based on the number of major sections in each, from two to more than ten (*Anfängliches Evangelium* [Kampen: Kok, 1977], 75–78).

3. Rather than the sharply defined national boundaries that map the continents, the reader might better think of the rhetorical "narrative flow" as represented by the way rivers and oceans are mapped: while different bodies of water can be distinguished, where does the Missouri River become the Mississippi, the South China Sea become the Pacific Ocean?

> *Purity, Sabbath, synagogue*   *Temple*
> *Secrecy commands*   *No secrecy commands*
> *Unhealed blindness*   *Blindness healed*
> *No valid confession*   *Valid confession: Jesus,*
>   *centurion*
> *Key symbols: bread,*   *Key symbols: cup, way,*
>   *sea, boat*   *cross*

The two major parts correspond to the emphases of Mark's Christology. Neither "Galilee" nor "Jerusalem" is merely a topographical indication; both have symbolic overtones. Part one begins with Jesus' call of the disciples to become "fishermen who fish for people" (1:16–20) and concludes with Jesus' challenge to them, "Do you not yet understand?" (8:21). Part two begins with Jesus' welcome by the crowds in Jerusalem, who finally join those who crucify Jesus, and concludes with the postresurrection command to return to Galilee to follow Jesus, who "goes before" them. The two parts are joined by the important transitional section 8:22–10:52, which both separates and joins part one and part two by representing the "way" of Jesus from Galilee to Jerusalem (and back, 16:7!) and the transition from blindness to sight.

Mark has two, and only two, extended discourses of Jesus. The parables discourse is inserted in the middle of part one, the apocalyptic discourse in the middle of part two, each providing interpretation of its major narrative unit. Other subdivisions are indicated by Mark's summary and transitional statements (1:32–34[–39]; 3:7–12; 6:6; 6:53–56) and are discussed in the commentary. The complete outline can be seen in the table of contents.[4] The major structural elements can be represented as follows:

> 1:1–15   Title and Prologue: Judea and Galilee
> PART 1 GALILEE   1:16–8:21
> 1:16–3:35   Authority, Rejection, and the New Community
> *4:1–34   Central Discourse: Parables and the Mystery of the Kingdom of God*
> 4:35–8:21   Crossing Borders
> "THE WAY"   GALILEE TO JERUSALEM 8:22–10:52

---

4. The division of the unified narrative into units and giving titles to individual sections and pericopes is not a neutral act, but already an interpretation. I have attempted to make divisions and provide titles appropriate to Mark's meaning as I have discerned it, but often have been constrained to use conventional divisions and labels for convenience. Several different Markan motifs and patterns may be interwoven into a single episode. To reduce these to a single title can distort the reader's perception of what the pericope is "about." See examples at 4:1–9 and 7:24–30.

3. Genre

The most important issue for interpreting any Gospel text is the decision about Gospel genre. Texts in the Gospel of Mark will be understood differently depending on whether they are taken as, for example, Peter's memoirs, accurate historical reports, theological interpretations of historical events, historical novel, drama, legend, fiction, allegory, or "gospel" in the sense of a distinctive new genre created in early Christianity for the propagation of its faith. These and several more options[5] have been advocated for the generic identification of Mark and other early Christian Gospels.

For some time the dominant scholarly view prevailed that the Gospels are not biographies, but examples of a new kerygmatic genre devised by Mark.[6] It is still universally accepted that the Gospels are not biographies in the modern sense, but there is currently a growing movement to regard the Gospels as *bioi*, biographies in the ancient Hellenistic sense.[7] While there are significant points of contact between Mark and Hellenistic biographies, it is important to see Mark as

---

5. Among the more provocative is Dennis Ronald MacDonald, *The Homeric Epics and the Gospel of Mark* (New Haven, Conn.: Yale University Press, 2000), who argues, "the earliest gospel indeed used the *Odyssey* as his primary literary inspiration but also imitated Books 22 and 24 of the *Iliad* for narrating Jesus' death and burial . . . Mark wrote a prose epic modeled largely after the *Odyssey* and the ending of the *Iliad*" (p. 3).

6. Cf., e.g., Rudolf Bultmann, *The History of the Synoptic Tradition* (trans. John Marsh; New York: Harper & Row, 1963), 346–50; Reginald H. Fuller, *The New Testament in Current Study* (New York: Scribner, 1962), 78; Udo Schnelle, *The History and Theology of the New Testament Writings* (trans. M. Eugene Boring; Minneapolis: Fortress, 1998), 153–61; Petr Pokorný, "Das Markusevangelium: Literarische und theologische Einleitung mit Forschungsbericht," in *ANRW* II.25.3 (Berlin: De Gruyter, 1984), 2003, 2022.

7. Cf. Richard A. Burridge, *What Are the Gospels? A Comparison with Graeco-Roman Biography* (SNTSMS 70; Cambridge: Cambridge University Press, 1992); Charles H. Talbert, *What Is a Gospel? The Genre of the Canonical Gospels* (Philadelphia: Fortress, 1977); David E. Aune, *The New Testament in Its Literary Environment* (LEC; Philadelphia: Westminster, 1987), 17–76; Vernon K. Robbins, *Jesus the Teacher: A Socio-Rhetorical Interpretation of Mark* (Philadelphia: Fortress, 1984), who considers Mark a distinctive (not "unique") combination of Old Testament prophetic biographical form and Greco-Roman biography of the disciple-gathering teacher, all of which fits into the Hellenistic genre of biography.

having written a distinctive narrative that fits only awkwardly (if at all) into the literary categories already available to him. Mark does not simply adopt an available pattern and compose a "life of Jesus" on this basis. Though Mark does not invent an absolutely new genre, the narrative he composes is so distinctive from existing genres as to be considered a quantum leap, a mutation rather than merely a Christian example of an existing genre or an evolution from preceding models.[8]

Five elements are especially distinctive in setting Mark apart from Hellenistic biographies:

(1) The narrative presents a tensive juxtaposition of pictures of Jesus as truly human and truly divine, facilitated by the narrative-rhetorical device of the messianic secret.

(2) The story of Jesus is presented as the definitive segment of universal history that extends from creation to eschaton; Jesus the Christ and Son of Man who has already appeared in history will appear at the end of history as its goal and judge. For the importance of the apocalyptic perspective in assessing the genre of Mark, see notes 44 and 46, pp. 356–57, and the diagram on p. 247.

(3) The main character is presented as both a figure of past history who once spoke and the present Lord of the community who still speaks. The Jesus of the narrative speaks not only to the characters in the story, but as the bearer of the present word of the risen Christ to post-Easter believers.[9] The narrative throughout is implicitly a two-level drama, which becomes evident in numerous specific scenes (see comments on, e.g., 4:35–41; 5:35–43; 6:2, 31–44, 45–52; 7:24–30; 8:3; 9:2–8; 10:2–12; 12:18–27; 16:5–7), and sometimes becomes explicit (e.g., 13:37).[10]

8. So also Guy Bonneau, *Stratégies rédactionnelles et fonctions communautaires de l'évangile de Marc* (EBiB nouv. sér. 44; Paris: J. Gabalda, 2001), 65–111, who argues Mark neither invented an absolutely new literary genre nor merely adopted the Hellenistic *bios* for Christian purposes, but is influenced by a number of literary models. His final product, in Bonneau's view, is most like a "life of a prophet."

9. So, e.g., Willi Marxsen, *Mark the Evangelist: Studies on the Redaction History of the Gospel* (trans. James Boyce et al.; Nashville: Abingdon, 1969), ch. 3 and passim; Walter Grundmann, *Das Evangelium nach Markus* (THKNT 2; Berlin: Evangelische Verlagsanstalt, 1973), 2–3, 36 and passim.

10. See, e.g., Gottfried Rau, "Das Markusevangelium: Komposition und Intention der ersten Darstellung christlicher Mission," in *Aufstieg und Niedergang Der Römischen Welt* (ANRW II.25.3; Berlin: De Gruyter, 1984), 2067. Walter Schmithals is correct that Mark's basic intention is to tell the story of the risen Lord within the framework of the pre-Easter life of Jesus, even arguing that specific scenes were originally stories about the risen Jesus first inserted by Mark within the pre-Easter setting (e.g., 9:2–8; 3:13–19; *Das Evangelium nach Markus. Kapitel 9,2–16,18* [ÖTK 2/2; Würzburg: Gütersloher Verlagshaus, 1979], 715–52).

(4) The narrative is episodic but not anecdotal, composed on the basis of individual units of tradition that had themselves been utilized in preaching and teaching the gospel. These aspects of the Gospel are not incidental but fundamental, and they set Mark apart from other Hellenistic authors and place his narrative in a distinct category.

(5) As Jesus had communicated the inexpressible reality of the kingdom of God in parables that point to it in ambiguous, deceptively history-like, open-ended stories that called for participation and decision by the hearer, so Mark wrote his Gospel that points beyond itself to the meaning of God's act in the Christ-event as an ambiguous, deceptively history-like open-ended narrative that calls for participation and decision by the reader. As Jesus spoke of the kingdom in parables, so Mark speaks of Jesus in the new narrative form that is an extended parable.[11]

These distinctive features are all christological. The Gospel of Mark is narrative Christology; Mark devised a new literary form to express a new content (see *Excursus: Markan Christology* at 9:1 and *Excursus: The Messianic Secret* at 9:13). Mark writes to show who God is, not to reveal the character or greatness of the protagonist. The Gospel is a kerygmatic genre, expressed in narrative, not a wisdom genre, expressed in sayings. It is the genre appropriate to the Christian message as good news, not good advice or good principles and insights. What Mark has to say cannot be translated into other genres or media. Medium and message are not identical, but the message is inseparably bound to the medium.[12]

Though in continuity with more than one stream of previous Christian theology, Mark is not simply the natural, evolutionary next step in the development of early Christian literature. The author does much more than merely edit received tradition. With the Gospel of Mark something radically new came into

11. This point is elaborated in, e.g., John R. Donahue, "Jesus as the Parable of God in the Gospel of Mark," *Int* 32, no. 4 (1978); John R. Donahue, S.J., *The Gospel in Parable* (Philadelphia: Fortress, 1988), 194–216; Timothy J. Geddert, *Watchwords: Mark 13 in Markan Eschatology* (JSNTSup 26; Sheffield: JSOT Press, 1989).

12. See Marie Noonan Sabin, *Reopening the Word: Reading Mark as Theology in the Context of Early Judaism* (Oxford: Oxford University Press, 2002), especially the autobiographical statement on p. ix, reflecting the author's discovery of Mark's Jewish heritage: "But in the thought-processes of religious Jews, I discovered, the Bible cannot be subsumed into some other category. In itself it represents a point of engagement between human beings and the divine being, and to be 'theological' is to enter its world of reality." So also the conclusion of C. Clifton Black, *The Disciples according to Mark: Markan Redaction in Current Debate* (JSNTSup 27; Sheffield: JSOT Press, 1989), 252: ". . . when Mark the evangelist presents us with certain claims about discipleship, viewed in the light of God's activity in the world through the ministry, death, and resurrection of Jesus, as exegetes we cannot forever shunt such *sachkritisch* considerations to systematic theologians without ultimately becoming irresponsible in our exegesis."

being. Paul and other early missionaries had pointed to the cosmic story of the preexistent Christ who became a human being, suffered, died, and was raised, with a bare minimum of reference to the life and teaching of Jesus of Nazareth. Mark is the first New Testament author to express Christian faith through the narrative medium of a comprehensive story of the earthly Jesus. Many of the incidents and sayings that make up the content of Mark had been proclaimed and taught previously. Mark writes for those who already know the basic story. They will not be surprised when at the end Jesus is crucified rather than being hailed as God's Messiah by the religious and political leaders. They believe in the resurrection. But *"Whatever the first readers knew of the life-story of Jesus of Nazareth was subverted by the Markan story. They were not familiar with this plot: Jesus' presence in Galilee, his single journey to Jerusalem to be rejected, tried and crucified, the resurrection, and the surprising silence of the women.* It saw the light of day for the first time when Mark invented it. It is this radical newness of the Markan story which must be kept in mind."[13]

4. Sources

The Gospel of Mark is a composition by an author, not an anthology assembled by an editor.[14] But neither is it a fictional story composed from whole cloth. The narrative is rooted in historical tradition. Where did the author get his information?

1. *The author was not an eyewitness; he did not know the historical Jesus.* The Gospel itself makes no claim to be or include eyewitness tradition (contrast, e.g., the consistent use of the first person in the *Gospel of Peter*, and the secondary claim in John 21:24). Although a few modern scholars have argued that the author was the young man who fled away naked on the night of Jesus' arrest (see on 14:51–52), the ancient tradition agreed with the earliest discussion of the Gospel that the author "had neither heard the Lord, nor had he followed him" (Papias [ca. 60–130], bishop of Hierapolis, as cited in Eusebius *HE* 3.39.15).

---

13. Francis J. Moloney, *The Gospel of Mark: A Commentary* (Peabody, Mass.: Hendrickson, 2002), 16. So also Petr Pokorný, "Die Bedeutung des Markusevangeliums für die Entstehung der christlichen Bibel," in *Text and Contexts: Biblical Texts in Their Textual and Situational Contexts: Essays in Honor of Lars Hartman*, ed. Tord Fornberg et al. (Oslo: Scandinavian University Press, 1995), 409: "this writing marked a decisive turn in the life of the Christian church, and set the switches for the development of later orthodoxy with its canonized collection of writings (the New Testament)."

14. Classical form criticism, represented, e.g., by Rudolf Bultmann, *History of the Synoptic Tradition*, and Martin Dibelius, *From Tradition to Gospel* (New York: Scribner, 1935), argued that "The composers [of the Synoptic Gospels] are only to the smallest extent authors. They are principally collectors, vehicles of tradition, editors" (Dibelius, *Tradition to Gospel*, 3). See, more recently, Helmut Koester, *Ancient Christian Gospels: Their History and Development* (Philadelphia: Trinity Press International, 1990), 286, ". . . Mark was more of a collector than an author."

2. *The author did not receive his information directly from eyewitnesses.* From the second century onward, the tradition developed that the author was the Mark of Philemon 24, the companion of Paul who later became Peter's associate in Rome.[15]

> Mark became Peter's interpreter and wrote accurately all that he remembered, not, indeed, in order, of the things said or done by the Lord. For he had not heard the Lord, nor had he followed him, but later on, as I said, followed Peter, who used to give teaching as necessity demanded but not making, as it were, an arrangement of the Lord's oracles, so that Mark did nothing wrong in thus writing down single points as he remembered them. For to one thing he gave attention, to leave nothing out of what he had heard and to make no false statements in them. (Papias, as cited in Eusebius *HE* 3.39.15)

This tradition was repeated and elaborated with numerous variations and inconsistencies in later patristic writings:

> From the second century: Irenaeus, *Against Heresies* 3.1.1;
> *Anti-Marcionite Prologues; Muratorian Canon;* Clement
> of Alexandria [as cited in Eusebius *HE* 2.15.2; 6.14.6–7]
> From the third century: Tertullian, *Against Marcion* 4.5.3;
> Origen [as cited in Eusebius *HE* 6.25.5]
> From the fourth century: Eusebius *HE* 2.16.24 reports fur-
> ther traditions current in his time; Jerome, *Lives of Illus-
> trious Men,* on Simon Peter 1.1; *Commentary on Matthew*
> "Preface" 6

A survey of New Testament and patristic references indicates that:

a. There was a historical figure "Mark" who was a missionary coworker of Paul. There is no primary evidence that this Mark was a Jerusalem or Judean Christian. He may have accompanied Paul to Rome and continued there after his death.

b. By the end of the first century, the developing traditions about Paul and Peter had also associated Mark with Peter. *If* this Mark was ever in Rome and *if* he remained there after Paul's death, he *may* have become acquainted with Peter prior to Peter's own death.

---

15. For a full and engaging treatment of this tradition, see especially C. Clifton Black, *Mark: Images of an Apostolic Interpreter* (Columbia: University of South Carolina Press, 1994). For the trajectory that led to the combination of Petrine and Pauline traditions in Rome at the end of the first century, cf. M. Eugene Boring, *1 Peter* (ANTC; Nashville: Abingdon, 1999), 20–28.

   c. In Rome at the end of the century, we see a clear tendency to associate Peter and Paul as two martyr apostles who had died in Rome, whose joint legacy is entrusted to the Roman church (cf. 1 Peter, *1 Clement*). Historical differences between Peter and Paul are smoothed out (cf. Acts). Pauline ideas and persons are now associated with Peter. In 1 Peter, for example, the Pauline letter form and the Pauline Christology are advocated by "Peter," who now claims the Pauline assistants Mark and Silvanus as his own associates.

   d. Still later, in the second century, as numerous Gospels were circulated throughout the church, points of contact with eyewitness tradition were sought for the anonymous Gospels by the emerging stream of Christian tradition that would become early catholic mainstream orthodoxy, partly as a defense against developing Gnosticism and other Christian movements later deemed heretical. We observe this interest in legitimization by eyewitnesses in other Christian documents at the turn of the century and later (cf., e.g., 1 John 1:1–3; Luke 1:1–4; Acts 1:1–2, 21–22).

   e. The developing tradition about Mark documented in the above canonical and patristic references was applied to the Gospel, and henceforth it was assumed that its author was Mark the companion of Peter.

   f. At first it was assumed that Mark wrote only after Peter's death, but later the claims were made that Mark wrote during Peter's lifetime, either at his request or without Peter being aware of it—though a revelation from the Holy Spirit to Peter validated the composition as written at God's will. The Gospel was then inspected and approved by him. The final stage in this legendary development is that Peter had taken the initiative and instructed Mark to write the Gospel, or even dictated it to him.

   g. In all this it is clear that the church's interest was in theological legitimization of Mark as representing the apostolic faith, not the historical accuracy of the claim that John Mark, resident of Jerusalem and disciple of Simon Peter, was the actual author, though the first generations of the church did not distinguish these two aspects of the claim to Markan authorship. The ancient tradition makes clear that Mark's Gospel was accepted and valued in the church not because of its historical accuracy, but because it represented Peter's apostolic authority.

   h. Though the Gospel of Mark may have been written by a person named Mark—it was the most common name in the Roman world—the evidence is that this attribution was only made late and for theological reasons. Though the Gospel contains materials that go back to eyewitnesses of Jesus' ministry, these materials bear the marks of having been mediated to the author not by an individual, but by a generation of community teaching, preaching, and worship.

3. *Mark did not know other Gospels, canonical or noncanonical.* In the fifth century C.E., Augustine apparently initiated the tradition, at odds with the Mark-as-Peter's-interpreter tradition, that Mark abbreviated the Gospel of Matthew (*Harmony of the Gospels* 1.2). This view was regnant during the Middle Ages; a small minority of contemporary scholars still advocates it, mostly in the form of the Griesbach hypothesis (Mark conflated Matthew and Luke).[16] Likewise, a few scholars have argued that narrative Gospel-like writings existed prior to Mark and influenced Mark directly or indirectly: (1) the *Gospel of Peter*,[17] (2) an earlier version of canonical Mark, that is, an Urmarkus or Secret Gospel,[18] (3) other noncanonical or lost Gospels.[19] The line between the second and third

16. The Synoptic problem has been thoroughly restudied in the last generation, with the majority of scholars continuing to affirm the priority of Mark. For succinct summaries of the present state of research and arguments for Markan priority, see C. M. Tuckett, "Synoptic Problem," in *ABD*, 6:263–70; Mark Goodacre, *The Synoptic Problem: A Way through the Maze* (London: Sheffield Academic, 2001), 13–105.

17. John Dominic Crossan, *The Cross That Spoke: The Origins of the Passion Narrative* (San Francisco: Harper & Row, 1988). For thorough arguments opposing this hypothesis, see Raymond E. Brown, *The Death of the Messiah: From Gethsemane to the Grave: A Commentary on the Passion Narratives in the Four Gospels* (ABRL; 2 vols.; New York: Doubleday, 1994), 2:1317–49.

18. Prior generations of scholars have frequently sought help in resolving the intricacies of the synoptic problem or the present form of Mark by postulating an Urmarkus, an earlier form of Mark revised into canonical Mark. This theory was developed in the early nineteenth century, popularized by Heinrich Julius Holtzmann, *Die Synoptische Evangelien: Ihr Ursprung und Geschichtlicher Charakter* (Leipzig: Wilhelm Engelmann, 1843), and assumed by, e.g., Bultmann, *Theology of the New Testament*, 1:3. The postulate of an Urmarkus still forms a constituent element in the complex theory of Markan origins proposed by Koester, *Ancient Christian Gospels*, who argues for a five-stage trajectory beginning with Urmarkus, including the Secret Gospel of Mark, and concluding with the expansion of canonical Mark made by second-century scribes who added the Long Ending (pp. 285–86).

For description of the alleged discovery and detailed analysis of the text by the one who claimed to have made the original discovery and photographed the manuscript, see Morton Smith, *Clement of Alexandria and a Secret Gospel of Mark* (Cambridge, Mass.: Harvard University Press, 1973). For a more popular account by the same author, see Morton Smith, *The Secret Gospel: The Discovery and Interpretation of the Secret Gospel according to Mark* (1st ed.; New York: Harper & Row, 1973). Stephen C. Carlson has presented what appears to be a convincing case that the Secret Gospel was a hoax, although his arguments are yet to be evaluated by the scholarly community; see *The Gospel Hoax: Morton Smith's Invention of Secret Mark* (Waco, Tex.: Baylor University Press, 2005).

19. Some sample theories: Arthur Temple Cadoux, *The Sources of the Second Gospel* (London: J. Clarke, 1935), posited three different Gospel-like sources used by Mark, designated "A" (40 C.E., Petrine and Palestinian), "B" (66–70, Diaspora Jewish Christianity), and "C" (50 C.E., Pauline

categories is not distinct; how different from canonical Mark does a postulated predecessor have to be in order to be regarded as a different composition? None of these theories has proved convincing to the majority of scholars. This commentary is written from the perspective that Mark is the first Gospel, not dependent on prior Gospels or Gospel-like narratives.

4. *Mark was written on the basis of living Christian tradition from and about Jesus that circulated in his church as the substance of preaching and teaching, including pre-Markan collections of material.* Two generations of form-critical study of this tradition have shown that it circulated mostly as individual units that can be categorized in terms of form and function.[20] Much of the material is traditional, but the framework is redactional. While there was no pre-Markan Gospel, some of this material was likely already arranged in small topical collections, such as the traditional nuclei of the collection of conflict stories in 2:1–3:6, the parable discourse of 4:1–35, the apocalyptic discourse of 13:1–37, and shorter collections such as 9:41–49. It is probable that Mark knew collections of Jesus' sayings, to which he responded both positively and negatively. It is unlikely that the collection of sayings known as the *Gospel of Thomas* had been compiled early enough to have influenced Mark. Even those who argue

---

Gentile Christianity). In 1968 Charles Masson argued canonical Mark is the result of abbreviating and extensively revising the primitive gospel used in Rome (*L'Évangile de Marc et l'Église de Rome* [Bibliothèque théologique; Neuchâtel: Delachaux & Niestlé, 1968], 13–23). In 1972 Marie-Émile Boismard gave detailed arguments for a complex series of Gospel-like documents prior to Mark on which Mark was dependent; Boismard subsequently revised and simplified his theory in 1984 and 1994 (M.-E. Boismard, ed., *Synopse des quatre évangiles en français, Tome 2: Commentaire* [2 vols.; Paris: Cerf, 1972]; M. E. Boismard, *L'Évangile de Marc: Sa préhistoire* [Etudes bibliques nouv. sér. 26; Paris: Librarie Lecoffre, 1994]). Walter Schmithals, *Einleitung in die drei ersten Evangelien* (Berlin: De Gruyter, 1985), 406–31, argues a Hellenistic Christian composed a Gospel-like document now lost ("Grundschrift") that Mark redacted into the canonical Gospel. Cf. also Walter Schmithals, *Das Evangelium nach Markus: Kapitel 1–9* (ÖTK 2/1; 2 vols.; Würzburg: Gütersloher Verlagshaus, 1979), 1:34–36, with other examples and bibliography. Lawrence M. Wills, *The Quest of the Historical Gospel: Mark, John, and the Origins of the Gospel Genre* (London: Routledge, 1997), assumes that the Fourth Gospel was independent of Mark, and on this basis argues that the parallels between them point to an earlier Gospel-like document on which they were both dependent. The most recent effort along these lines is that of Delbert Burkett, who argues canonical Mark is dependent on two lost recensions of a lost Proto-Mark (Delbert Burkett, *Rethinking the Gospel Sources: From Proto-Mark to Mark* [New York: T. & T. Clark, 2004]). For a convenient chart of parallels between the Gospel of Mark and extant noncanonical Gospels, with an argument that all such parallels are later than Mark, see Craig A. Evans, *Mark 8:27–16:20* (WBC 34B; New York: Nelson, 2001), xxxii–xliii.

20. In addition to the classical studies of Bultmann, *History of the Synoptic Tradition*; Dibelius, *Tradition to Gospel*; and Karl Ludwig Schmidt, *Der Rahmen Der Geschichte Jesu: Literarkritische Untersuchungen zur ältesten Jesusüberlieferung* (Darmstadt: Wissenschaftliche Buchgesellschaft, 1969), see especially William Telford, "The Pre-Markan Tradition in Recent Research (1980–1990)," in *The Four Gospels 1992—Festschrift Frans Neirynck* (ed. Frans van Segbroeck et al.; Leuven: Leuven University Press, 1992), 2:693–724, and the literature he gives.

for an early date do not posit a literary connection between the *Gospel of Thomas* and Mark (see, e.g., Koester, *Ancient Christian Gospels*, 107–13). The case with Q is more debated: while the majority of Gospel scholars affirm the existence of Q, only a minority of these suppose that Mark knew this collection of Jesus' sayings.[21] The central argument against this has been the difficulty of explaining Mark's minimal use of Q had he known it. The present study is written from the perspective that Mark was aware of Q or Q-like collections of Jesus' sayings but is suspicious of the genre of sayings collections not rooted in the narrative of the crucified Jesus, which were dangerously open to contamination by sayings of Christian prophets.[22]

5. Date

On the one hand, the Gospel must have been written late enough to allow for the development of the oral tradition on which it is based, that is, about a generation, and, on the other hand, early enough to have been used by Matthew and Luke near the end of the first century C.E. These general considerations would locate Mark roughly between 60 and 80 C.E. This period is narrowed somewhat by the apocalyptic discourse of chapter 13, with its prediction of the temple's destruction, which seems to reflect the tumultuous times of the war in Judea 66–73, but it is not clear whether Mark was written just before, during, or just after the war. The reference to the death of James and John in 10:39 is also relevant. In the story line all these events are still in the future and predicted by Jesus; the question is whether the narrative itself reflects that they have already happened. Thus virtually all scholars date Mark in the period 65–75, with the major issue being whether or not Mark 13 is understood to reflect the destruction of Jerusalem as something that has already occurred.

By any reckoning, this was a tumultuous time for the empire, for Judaism, and for the new Christian community. Serious earthquakes occurred in 60 and 63 (Tacitus, *Annals* 15.44). The Roman army suffered defeat at the hands of the Parthians on the eastern border of the empire in 62 (Tacitus, *Annals* 15.13–17). In 64, Roman Christians became scapegoats for the disastrous fire that destroyed much of the inner city of Rome: they were rounded up and put to death in the

---

21. The question of whether Mark *knew* Q must be kept separate from the question of whether he *used it as a source*. For a careful analysis of the issue, see M. Devisch, "La relation entre l'évangile de Marc et le document Q," in *L'Évangile selon Marc: Tradition et rédaction* (ed. M. Sabbe; BETL 34; Leuven: Leuven University Press, 1974), 59–91. Among scholars who argue for Mark's knowledge of Q, see especially Harry T. Fleddermann, *Mark and Q: A Study of the Overlap Texts* (Leuven: University Press, 1995), and Burton L. Mack, *A Myth of Innocence: Mark and Christian Origins* (Philadelphia: Fortress, 1988), 315–24.

22. For an elaboration of this argument see M. Eugene Boring, *The Continuing Voice of Jesus: Christian Prophecy and the Gospel Tradition* (Louisville, Ky.: Westminster John Knox, 1991), 191–246.

most cruel ways. Both Peter and Paul probably died in this purge. Other Christian leaders had been martyred by the time Mark was written. Nero committed suicide in 68, and struggles for the emperor's throne ensued, with three emperors within one year. Meanwhile, the Roman army put down a revolt in Palestine in a bloody war that devastated the region and destroyed Jerusalem and its temple. During the siege, the commanding general became emperor, and his son completed the war, burned the temple, and carried its sacred objects through the streets of Rome in a triumphal procession. At some point in this chaotic time Mark was written. The readers live in the time when the Holy City and temple had just been destroyed or when its destruction was imminent and certain. More precise than this we cannot be.

6. Provenance

Interpreters have traditionally assumed that each Gospel originated in a particular Christian community, reflecting its concerns and directed to its needs, and that this information is helpful for contemporary understanding of the text of each Gospel. Thus exegetes regularly speak of the "Markan community," "Johannine community," and the like. This assumption has recently been challenged by arguments that each Gospel was addressed not to the evangelist's particular community but to the early Christian movement at large. Richard Bauckham rightly points out that since Matthew and Luke used Mark as a source, this must mean that by the time of the later Synoptics (twenty to thirty years after the composition of Mark), the Gospel of Mark was widely circulated, not limited to the Markan community. "Whatever Mark had meant his Gospel to be, his work, when Matthew and Luke knew it, had already in fact come to be useful and valued in many Christian churches."[23] Bauckham's second argument assumes that the Gospels are Hellenistic *bioi*, and that such documents were not written for a limited community, but for the reading public at large. His third argument is that early Christianity was not composed of discrete isolated communities but a network of congregations extending around the Mediterranean in active communication with each other; anyone writing something like the Gospel of Mark would have not merely his own community, but the broader church in view as the target audience. The argument from genre is questionable, but there is some strength in his other observations. When they are taken into consideration, the best approach to the Gospel of Mark seems to be that it was in fact written for a particular Christian community reflecting its problems, needs, and interests, but that such communities recognized that they were part of a worldwide network of churches. Furthermore, these communities were not sectarian conventicles

---

23. Richard Bauckham, "For Whom Were Gospels Written?" in *The Gospels for All Christians: Rethinking the Gospel Audiences* (ed. Richard Bauckham; Grand Rapids: Eerdmans, 1998), 12.

turned in upon themselves, but were directed outward to the world. As Mark writes, he is aware of this broader context (cf., e.g., 13:10, 37; 14:9),[24] but nonetheless does not write for Christians in general but for the church in a particular situation. Despite Bauckham's protests, there is a certain appropriateness in the analogy to Pauline letters, addressed to particular Christian communities (not merely congregations), but with the awareness that they have a wider relevance (cf., e.g., 1 Cor 1:1–2; Gal 1:2, and the ambiguities associated with the endings of Romans suggesting the particularities of the letter also address a wider readership). When Paul's letters were collected and circulated throughout broad streams of early Christianity shortly after his death, and the deuteropauline letters recognized that the specificity of the letter form was appropriate for the wider church, this was not a violation of their original particularity (cf. Col 4:16; Eph 1:1 [with or without the varia lectio *en Epheso* found in most late MSS]). When Matthew and Luke adopted Mark as a basic source for their own Gospels, this was indeed a recognition that it was adaptable for a different readership than originally addressed—but that it must be adapted, not simply repeated. Like Matthew and Luke, readers of the Gospel of Mark in the twenty-first century recognize that it has a message that transcends its original situation. Contemporary readers, however, will hear the Markan message better if they are aware of the particularity of its original context. What was this original situation?

While there is nothing direct in the book about the readers (in contrast to the Pauline Letters), a good bit about them can be inferred.

(1) The author writes in Greek and translates lingering Aramaic elements in his tradition (5:41; 7:34; 14:36; 15:22, 34). He explains Jewish practices, not always accurately (2:19; 7:3–4; 10:2; 14:1; 14:12; 14:64; 15:42) and does not seem to have a clear picture of Jewish leadership groups (3:6; 6:17; 8:15; 12:13). The readers, or most of them, thus seem to be a Greek-speaking community that reads its Bible in Greek translation (the LXX), with a limited knowledge of Judaism, apparently a predominantly Gentile community on the edge of Judaism. But since Sabbath keeping, fasting, and purity laws are issues (e.g., 2:1–3:6; 7:19), the Markan church is a mixed community for whom the integration of Jews and Gentiles in one church was a major issue. The Jewish Scripture is recognized as authority by all, but not the authority claimed by Jewish elders and scribes.

(2) The lack of reference to large cities (except Jerusalem), the primarily agrarian imagery, the lack of urban metaphors, the preponderance of situations in which poor people play leading roles, and the limitation of reference to monetary units to small-denomination coins suggest that the community from which Mark came belonged to the lower socioeconomic stratum.

---

24. Cf. Mary Ann Beavis, *Mark's Audience: The Literary and Social Setting of Mark 4:11–12* (JSNTSup 33; Sheffield: JSOT Press, 1989), 171.

(3) Chapter 13 points to a community directly affected by the Jewish revolt in Palestine.[25] The readers are themselves in the situation of crisis brought about by the war (13:14, 37). The community is not undergoing direct persecution in the sense that it is criminal to confess Christian faith, yet it stands in tension with its environment and may be harassed and suffer violence from both Jewish and Gentile authorities (13:9). In chapter 13 Jesus speaks past the disciples to the readers. The chaos brought about by the war is their problem.

(4) As in the earlier Pauline churches (e.g., 1 Cor 14) and those later pictured in Acts (e.g., Acts 11:27–29), the Markan community knows the phenomena of charismatic gifts of the Spirit in its midst (13:11; cf. 1:8, 3:28–29), including prophets who speak in the name of the risen Lord (13:6). The harassed community of believers needs a message from the risen Lord to interpret its own situation and to know how to be authentic disciples. Mark affirms the power of the Spirit, but is suspicious of prophets who deliver new oracles in the name of the risen Lord (13:22).

(5) In the distress of this situation the community experienced some tensions in how to understand their faith in Jesus Christ. These were not theoretical christological abstractions but burning existential issues: Did the political tumult and ravages of war mean the Son of Man was to appear immediately? Did the stories of Jesus' amazing deeds of power mean that those who followed him could overcome present troubles by having faith in Jesus' miraculous help? What did it mean that the miracle-working Jesus had not overcome the Romans but had been crucified by them? What did discipleship to such a Jesus mean? Mark is narrative Christology, but it addresses real issues of life and death, not merely conceptual ones.

Where was this community located? An early tradition, still often advocated in the present, places the composition of the earliest Gospel in Rome. The question affects the understanding of numerous Markan passages. For instance, should the modern reader interpret 12:13–17 as though both evangelist and his first readers had regularly heard Rom 13:1–7? Are they affected by the suspicion in Rome that they do not pay taxes, and/or that they support the revolt in Palestine? Another example: Should Mark's suspicious stance toward "Son of David" Christology be read in the context of a church that affirms a creedal statement confessing Jesus to be Son of David (Rom 1:3–4)? Another example: It is sometimes argued that 10:12 presupposes Roman divorce law (and therefore Rome), but Hermas (*Mand.* 1.5.1.6), presumably from Rome, does not have this clause. Such examples show how tricky arguments from and about

25. See especially Ludger Schenke, *Das Markus-Evangelium* (Stuttgart: Kohlhammer, 1988), 11–27; Joel Marcus, "The Jewish War and the Sitz im Leben of Mark," *JBL* 111 (1992): 441–62; Joel Marcus, *Mark 1–8: A New Translation with Introduction and Commentary* (AB 27; New York: Doubleday, 2000).

provenance can be. A final and very important example: When reading the few Markan texts that interpret Jesus' death as salvific (10:45; 14:24), should the modern reader presuppose that this Gospel comes from a church familiar with the atonement theology of Romans (e.g., 3:21–31; 5:1–21)? If so, does the author presuppose it and thus does not repeat it, or oppose it—and thus does not repeat it? These issues do not arise if Mark was written in a non-Roman context.

The tradition that Mark was written in Rome is not based on data from the Gospel itself, but on the traditions cited above regarding authorship, all of which basically go back to the Papias testimony. The traditions concerning the Gospel's provenance are not uniform (see citations above). In the earliest extant tradition, Papias relates Mark to Peter but not to Rome. Later tradition sometimes associated both author and Gospel with Egypt.[26] It was even later that the tradition tended to consolidate around a Roman origin for the Gospel, a view still prevalent today.[27] Some data in Mark is compatible with a Roman origin if this could be demonstrated or made probable on other grounds, but cannot be used as evidence for a Roman origin. The allusions to suffering and persecution (e.g., 8:34–38; 13:9–13) may well reflect Nero's persecution of Roman Christians in 64 C.E., but this would have affected Christian self-understanding throughout the Roman world. Likewise, the number of Latinisms is sometimes taken as evidence of a Roman origin, but the influence of the language of the Romans was not restricted to the city of Rome or to Italy, but pervaded the empire.

There are serious objections to the theory of a Roman provenance. Paul had written his longest extant letter to the Roman church about fifteen years before the composition of Mark. Peter and Paul had both worked and died in Rome a few years before Mark wrote. Yet, in contrast to other literature emanating from Rome, the Gospel of Mark does not reflect Paul's letter to the Romans. Not only are key words of Pauline theology in general and Romans in particular missing from Mark (e.g., "law," "the righteousness of God"), but the general christological perspective of the Gospel is different from that of Paul, who never communicated his Christology by telling stories of the earthly Jesus, but concentrated everything on the death and resurrection. Nor is there any internal evidence that links the contents of Mark to the preaching of Peter. The Markan negative picture of Peter and all the disciples argues against this connection. So also, the Gospel of Mark is not reflected in the earliest Christian writings emanating from

---

26. Chrysostom stated that the Gospel was composed in Egypt: "Homilies on Matthew" 1:7, in Philip Schaff, ed., *Chrysostom: Homilies on the Gospel of Saint Matthew* (NPNF1 10; Peabody, Mass.: Hendrickson, 1888, 1994), 3–4, and the tradition reported in Eusebius *HE* 2.16 can be understood in the same way.

27. Cf. C. Clifton Black, "Was Mark a Roman Gospel?" *ET* 105, no. 2 (1993): 36–40. A recent full-length monograph has attempted to strengthen this possibility by imaginative rhetorical arguments that Mark is a thinly disguised attack on Roman leaders, written in the city of Rome in 71 C.E. (Brian J. Incigneri, *The Gospel to the Romans: The Setting and Rhetoric of Mark's Gospel* (BibInt 65; Leiden: Brill, 2003).

Rome. First Peter and *1 Clement* both come from Rome near the end of the first century; neither indicates directly or indirectly any awareness of the Gospel of Mark, and neither incorporates or reflects the gospel type of narrative Christology, but only the Pauline cosmic Christology. So also the Old Roman Creed, ancestor of the Apostles' Creed, represents the confession of the Roman church at the end of the second century C.E. and has the Pauline Christology that goes directly from the birth of Jesus to "crucified under Pontius Pilate," with no place for the kind of Markan narrative Christology portraying the ministry of Jesus. Though the Gospel of Mark was certainly accepted and current in Rome at the end of the *second* century, the creed was apparently formulated in Rome before narrative Christology became the accepted norm. This creed is compatible with 1 Peter and *1 Clement*, but not with Mark, which suggests that the Gospel of Mark came to Rome from someplace else, sometime after the death of Peter.[28]

While Mark was probably not written in Rome, the actual geographical setting for the composition of Mark remains unknown. The positive orientation toward Galilee has led several scholars to postulate a Galilean provenance,[29] but the author's imprecise knowledge of Palestinian geography seems to point to a setting outside Palestine (compare, e.g., 7:31 with the map, and cf. 5:1; 6:45; 7:31; 8:22; 10:1; 11:1).[30] Thus other scholars have located the Gospel in neighboring Syria.[31] The Gospel's existence is first documented by its use in Matthew in the 90s, very probably in Antioch of Syria or its environs. Antioch and the Christian community there had contacts with Cyrene (Acts 11:20), which could mean that Simon of Cyrene's sons were known there (Mark 15:21).[32] Interpretation of several texts treated in the commentary seems to

28. The strongest defense of the traditional view of the Roman origin of Mark is still probably Benjamin W. Bacon, *Is Mark a Roman Gospel?* (HTS 7; Cambridge, Mass.: Harvard University Press, 1919).

29. E.g., Ched Myers, *Binding the Strong Man: A Political Reading of Mark's Story of Jesus* (Maryknoll, N.Y.: Orbis, 1988), 43; Edwin K. Broadhead, *Mark* (Readings; Sheffield: Sheffield Academic, 2001), 16. Most recently, a full-length monograph argues for a Galilean provenance: Hendrika Nicoline Roskam, *The Purpose of the Gospel of Mark in Its Historical and Social Context* (NovTSup 114; Leiden: Brill, 2004). All are in the wake of Ernst Lohmeyer, *Galiläa und Jerusalem* (FRLANT n.F. 34; Göttingen: Vandenhoeck & Ruprecht, 1936), and R. H. Lightfoot, *Locality and Doctrine in the Gospels* (London: Hodder & Stoughton, 1938).

30. H. R. Preuss, "Galiläa im Markus-Evangelium" (Dissertation, Göttingen 1966) has made a convincing case that most of the Gospel's geographical detail belongs to the tradition, and that lack of geographical knowledge belongs in the redactional level.

31. Among several scholars who argue for a Syrian provenance, cf. Howard Clark Kee, *Community of the New Age: Studies in Mark's Gospel* (Philadelphia: Westminster, 1977), 100–105; Gerd Theissen, *The Gospels in Context: Social and Political History in the Synoptic Tradition* (trans. Linda M. Maloney; Minneapolis: Fortress, 1991); Schenke, *Markus-Evangelium*, 45–48, lists nine reasons for a Syrian or Phoenician setting for the Gospel.

32. On the alleged connection between the Rufus of 15:21 and Rome, see commentary there. It makes at least as much sense to appeal to Acts 11:20 as evidence for an Antiochene origin. In neither case, however, do we have "evidence."

make more sense if the Gospel was written in Syria or Galilee, but it is not possible to be more precise than this.

7. Author

Who composed such a narrative? The Gospel of Mark, like the other canonical Gospels, is anonymous; even the authorial "I" or "we" does not appear (contrast Luke 1:1–4; John 21:25). Yet the second-century Christian community considered it important to designate the Gospel as from "Mark." Who was this Mark, why did the church attribute the Gospel to him, and was the church historically correct in doing so? If one begins with the ancient tradition and challenges others to prove that it could not be true, one will always win the argument. We have seen, however, that the tradition itself is inconsistent and is oriented not to historical accuracy but to theological validity. The later Christian community rightly accepted the Gospel of Mark as an authentic representative of the apostolic faith. The historical decision as to actual authorship should be made by examining the Gospel itself. The preceding discussion has already made clear that, while it contains materials that go back to the time of Jesus, the Gospel of Mark is not composed on the basis of either personal or second-hand reminiscences, and not composed by someone who is directly familiar with Palestine or Palestinian Judaism. The materials available to Mark come through the experienced faith of the Christian community in its teaching, preaching, worship, and debates, not via a chain of individual eyewitnesses.

Defenders of Markan authorship sometimes argue that since Mark was not an apostle and not a heroic figure in early Christianity, the Gospel would not have been attributed to him unless he was the actual author.[33] This argument is not made with reference to noncanonical Gospels, however (*Thomas, Judas, Matthias, Bartholomew, Mary, Nicodemus, Gamaliel*). So also, the "graphic details" of Mark are sometimes presented as evidence of eyewitness testimony despite the fact that apocryphal Gospels are often replete with such details.

We should probably best think of the author as a Christian teacher who writes not as a charismatic individual but as a member of the community.[34] The "pre-

---

33. E.g., Robert A. Guelich, *Mark 1–8:26* (WBC 34A; Dallas: Word, 1989), xxviii.

34. The lack of research on the role and function of teachers in the early church has now been remedied by the thorough study of Alfred Zimmermann, *Die urchristlichen Lehrer: Studien zum Tradentenkreis der Didaskaloi im frühen Urchristentum* (WUANT 2.12; Tübingen: Mohr, 1984). See also Beavis, *Mark's Audience*, 50–67. Cf. Christopher D. Marshall, *Faith as a Theme in Mark's Narrative* (SNTSMS 64; Cambridge: Cambridge University Press, 1989), 11 n. 3: "What was Mark doing before he wrote his gospel? What qualified him to write down a definitive record of the stories about Jesus? Surely the evangelist had a thorough familiarity with, and participated in, the oral life and traditions of the community." Clifton Black has pointed out that redaction criticism overreacted to the "community" emphasis of form criticism, insisting that the evangelists were individualistic "authors in their own right" rather than merely editors of community tradition (Black, *Disciples*, 223–24). We can now see that the two perspectives need not be mutually exclusive.

Markan" tradition was known not only to Mark but to his readers; he does not first mediate it to them in the Gospel, but places it in a new framework. Redaction criticism of the miracle stories indicates that Mark writes for readers who already know the *tradition*, but do not know it in the Markan *framework* and with Markan *redactional changes*. This is what would be striking to them.[35] Thus Jesus-the-teacher in the narrative represents the teaching function in Mark's church, probably including Mark himself as an "inspired teacher" who is in tension with church prophets who claim a direct vertical relation to the risen Christ but not the horizontal relation to the tradition handed on historically. Mark himself is an inspired teacher who curbs the "irresponsible excesses" of the Christian prophets.[36] As a teacher, Mark has likely already been occupied with the transmission and interpretation of the tradition before writing the Gospel. The pre-Markan elements did not come to Mark from some other planet; he doesn't start cold with pre-Markan tradition and ask what to do with it. There is every reason to think of continuity, even personal and "official" continuity, between the stages of pre-Markan church tradition and Markan redaction, just as there are elements of continuity between the pre-Easter Jesus and post-Easter teaching of the church. But it is the Christian community, not Peter or Mark, that forms the bridge between the historical Jesus and the Gospel of Mark. As a Christian teacher, Mark is the heir and interpreter of this tradition.

8. Purpose

The author gives no explicit statement of his purpose(s) in writing (vs. Luke 1:1–4; John 20:30–31). His purpose must be inferred from the document itself. As a teaching document, the references to teaching and Jesus as teacher provide reliable clues (see *Excursus: Jesus the Teacher versus the Scribes* at 7:23). In the dualistic framework of Mark's apocalyptic perspective, Jesus' teaching is primarily to "insiders." The Gospel presupposes readers aware of the essential elements of the Christian message; it is thus not basically an evangelistic or apologetic tract. Yet the lines between insiders and outsiders are not rigid or crisp, and outsiders overhear the didactic message directed primarily to the Christian (see *Excursus: Crowds, Followers, Disciples, and the Twelve* at 6:6). This community includes prophetic claims and understandings of Jesus and discipleship that Mark

35. Karl Kertelge, *Die Wunder Jesu im Markusevangelium* (SANT 23; Munich: Kösel, 1970), 182–84: the Markan redaction of the miracle stories indicates a didactic, even catechetical interest. So also Ludger Schenke, *Die Wundererzählungen des Markusevangeliums* (SBB 5; Stuttgart: Verlag Katholisches Bibelwerk, 1974), 90–91, who illustrates this in a detailed exegesis of 4:35–41.

36. M. Robert Mansfield, *Spirit and Gospel in Mark* (Peabody, Mass.: Hendrickson, 1987), 50, 83. This thesis has recently been argued by Guy Bonneau, who regards Mark as himself a Christian prophetic figure who is suspicious of the growing institutional authority within the church and current manifestations of Christian prophecy. In response, he associates himself with the classical prophetic line—Isaiah, John the Baptist, Jesus—and conveys his prophetic message in narrative form (*Stratégies rédactionnelles*, 323–27).

considers inadequate and dangerous. As narrative Christology, Mark's teaching document is aimed at helping the church clarify its understanding of the meaning of the Christ event and discipleship to Jesus in a threatening, confused, and conflicted situation. The devastating war was raging, or was just concluded. The temple had just been destroyed or was about to be. The meaning of who Jesus was and what it meant to be his follower in this situation was interpreted in conflicting ways.[37] Yet Mark is not a polemical document targeting a specific heresy within the community, but a constructive statement intended as a help and norm for articulating and living out the Christian faith in a particular situation. "Mark's purpose was pastoral. He wrote primarily to build up his readers in faith."[38] The Markan author, as representative of the Markan Jesus, looked upon the harassed people of God and "had compassion for them, because they were like sheep without a shepherd; and he began to teach them many things" (6:34). Modern hearers, like ancient ones, can be "spellbound by his teaching" (11:18).

9. Text and Transmission

Though composed for oral presentation, the Gospel of Mark was from the first a written document, participating in both orality and textuality. As is the case with all other biblical documents, the original manuscript has perished and we have only copies of copies. The dozens of Markan manuscripts that have survived are all different from each other, each having a large number of minor variants, as well as some major variations (cf. the endings of Mark after 16:8). Mark was not the favorite Gospel in early Christianity; it was copied less than the others, and is thus only minimally represented in the papyri. Of 118 extant New Testament papyri, Mark is represented in only three, and that fragmentarily: $\mathfrak{P}^{45}$ (III cent.; fragments from 4:36–12:28), $\mathfrak{P}^{84}$ (VI cent., fragments from chs. 2 and 6), and $\mathfrak{P}^{88}$ (IV cent., 2:1–26). Thus our earliest text of Mark is a papyrus fragment from the third century C.E.[39] The earliest extant complete manuscripts of Mark come from the fourth and fifth centuries C.E.: Sinaiticus ($\aleph$), Vaticanus (B), Alexandrinus (A), and codex Bezae Cantabrigensis (D, 05).

---

37. Paul J. Achtemeier, *Invitation to Mark* (Garden City, N.Y.: Image, 1978), 18–22, helpfully sums up Mark's purpose as his creative response to three problems threatening the community: destruction of the temple, threatening persecution, varied interpretations of Jesus.

38. Ernest Best, *Mark: The Gospel as Story* (SNTW; Edinburgh: T. & T. Clark, 1983), 51. Guy Bonneau, who rightly regards Mark as a prophetic figure, unnecessarily regards "pastoral" and "prophetic" as mutually exclusive alternatives, and so concludes that Mark has no pastoral purpose and cannot identify him as a teacher or his narrative as teaching (*Stratégies rédactionnelles*, 353–55). Mark's use of pastoral imagery and the designation "teacher" for the Markan Jesus should warn us against such rigid distinctions.

39. The sensationalizing claim that fragments of Mark have been found at Qumran has been soundly refuted. Cf., e.g., Graham Stanton, *Gospel Truth? New Light on Jesus and the Gospels* (Valley Forge, Pa.: Trinity Press International, 1995), 20–32, and the bibliography he provides.

The text of Mark is almost complete in the Freer Codex (W) and Codex Ephraemi Rescriptus (C) from the fifth century. Several other majuscules contain fragments of Mark, but all told, from the first eight centuries C.E. we have only eight complete MSS of Mark and four more that are almost complete. From the ninth century and later we have a host of minuscules, nearly all of which represent the late Byzantine form of the text, but a few (e.g., 1342 from the 13th/14th century and 2427 from the 14th century) illustrate that an early form of the text can be found in a late manuscript.

The textual phenomena raise the question whether the document underwent only the more-or-less random changes that occur in the process of repeatedly copying any document over the centuries, or whether in the times prior to the earliest extant manuscripts Mark circulated in more than one edition. Allowing for accidental scribal miscues, Matthew and Luke appear to have used nearly, but not exactly, the same text of Mark now found in our critical texts. Many of their "minor agreements" against the dominant text tradition of Mark now extant are probably best explained by their having used a slightly revised edition ("Deutero-Markus") no longer extant as a complete manuscript.[40]

10. Language, Translation, and Interpretation

Mark is a carefully composed literary composition expressing a profound theology. This does not mean that the author was striving for literary elegance, or that he was capable of doing so.[41] The author's straightforward rough-and-ready Greek does not measure up to classical literary standards and is less elegant than that of any of the other Gospels.[42] He occasionally uses Greek words

---

40. Cf., e.g., Folkert Fendler, *Studien zum Markusevangelium* (Göttingen: Vandenhoeck & Ruprecht, 1991), 147–83; Daniel Marguerat, "Le Problème Synoptique," in *Introduction au Nouveau Testament: Son histoire, son écriture, sa théologie* (ed. Daniel Marguerat; MdB 41; Geneva: Labor & Fides, 2004), 26–27; Schnelle, *New Testament Writings*, 170–75, and the bibliography he provides.

41. Since Mark is obviously among the minority of the population that was literate, he had probably attended a primary school until age twelve, but not the secondary school in which the composition and analysis of texts was rigorously pursued. See Beavis, *Mark's Audience*, 20–31, and the literature she cites. Burton L. Mack's picture of a document "composed at a desk in a scholar's study lined with texts and open to discourse with other intellectuals" is a gross exaggeration (*Myth of Innocence*, 322–23).

42. For Mark's vocabulary, syntax, and literary style, see Vincent Taylor, *The Gospel According to St. Mark* (New York: Macmillan, 1959), 44–54; C. H. Turner and J. K. Elliott, eds., *The Language and Style of the Gospel of Mark: An Edition of C. H. Turner's "Notes on Marcan Usage" Together with Other Comparable Studies* (NovTSup 71; Leiden: Brill, 1993); John Charles Doudna, *The Greek of the Gospel of Mark* (SBLMS 12; Philadelphia: Society of Biblical Literature and Exegesis, 12); Frans Neirynck, *Duality in Mark: Contributions to the Study of the Markan Redaction* (Peeters: Leuven University Press, 1988); E. J. Pryke, *Redactional Style in the Marcan Gospel: A Study of Syntax and Vocabulary as Guides to Redaction in Mark* (SNTSMS 33; Cambridge: Cambridge University Press, 1978), has received mixed reviews, from very positive to despairing; see summaries in Black, *Disciples*, 205–12; Neirynck, *Duality in Mark*.

incorrectly or writes awkward or ungrammatical sentences.[43] He strings together clauses with a monotonous use of *kai* ("and," 1,078 times) or participles (e.g., 5:25–27), and makes a somewhat tedious use of a limited number of adverbial connectives such as *euthys* ("immediately," forty-two times) and *palin* ("again," twenty-eight times). His use of verb tenses is colloquial, employing the historical present more than 150 times, sometimes alternating between the historical present and other tenses in the same sentence. He often uses dual expressions for the same reality. Matthew and Luke improve Mark's style on all these and other points. Some of the features previously considered indications of a semitizing style have been shown by more recent study to belong to the ordinary Koine.[44] Combined with the fact that Mark's tradition is of ultimately Semitic origin, and that both tradition and redaction reflect a Hellenistic context, it becomes very difficult to use Mark's language as evidence that the author himself had Aramaic as his mother tongue, though it is likely that both tradition and author are located in a context where Aramaic is spoken.

Because of the differing structures of Greek and English, and the overlapping but not identical semantic fields of virtually all the vocabulary involved, it is neither desirable nor possible to produce a truly literal, word-for-word translation. Nonetheless, the translation provided with this commentary is quite literal, not attempting to be more refined than Mark himself, and thus preserving, for example, his monotonous use of *kai*, use of the imperfect tense, and shifts from aorist tense to the historical present and back within the same sentence.

The Gospel of Mark is located at the intersection of historical, literary, and theological trajectories. Understanding Mark calls for methods appropriate to all three dimensions; all three approaches are interwoven in the following commentary. Mark is *historical* in a double sense: it deals with a particular historical figure (30 c.e. historical Jesus) and addresses a particular historical situation (ca. 70 c.e. Markan context). Historical methods are necessary to get within hearing distance of Mark's narrative. *Literary* approaches concerned with plot, characterization, narrator, and "reader response" are not alternatives to historical considerations, but are their necessary complement. Literary methods and perspectives facilitate a *reading* (= hearing) of the text as opposed to merely *investigating* it.[45] The substantive content of Mark's narrative is *theological.*

43. See, e.g., notes on 10:20 and 14:68. The number of such notes could be multiplied.

44. See Ferdinand Hahn, "Einige Überlegungen zu gegenwärtigen Aufgaben der Markusinterpretation," in *Der Erzähler des Evangeliums: Methodische Neuansätze in der Markusforschung* (ed. Ferdinand Hahn; SBS 118 / 119; Stuttgart: Verlag Katholisches Bibelwerk, 1985), 177–80.

45. Cf. Bastiaan M. F. van Iersel, *Mark: A Reader-Response Commentary* (trans. W. H. Bisscheroux; JSNTSup 164; Sheffield: Sheffield Academic, 1998), 16. See especially the thorough commentary of Camille Focant, *L'évangile selon Marc* (CB/NT 2; Paris: Cerf, 2004), who unobtrusively utilizes the full range of narratological methods without imposing its technical vocabulary on the reader, and without considering this an alternative to historical criticism or theological exegesis (47–48).

While the text can be studied profitably by limiting one's questions to matters of language, sociology, literary structure, and the like, these are all secondary to what Mark is *about*. The driving force of this commentary is to use the full spectrum of methods to facilitate a hearing of this theological message in all its strangeness and terror, in the conviction that Mark rightly designated his narrative as ultimate good news (1:1).

COMMENTARY

1:1–15 Title and Prologue

1:1 The Author's Title[1]

To perceive how Mark has chosen to begin his narrative, one must first make a judgment on the syntax of the first four verses. This is not easy; remember that ancient MSS had neither punctuation nor spaces between words or sentences, so that all such divisions in modern Bibles are to be credited to editors of the Greek text and translators into modern languages. The number of textual variations in the manuscript tradition of verses 1–4 indicates that the syntactical arrangement was already obscure in the early centuries, as scribes attempted to clarify the meaning of the text by "correcting" its syntax.

Taking 1:1 to be the author's original opening line, one can construe this verse as the title for the whole Gospel, as a section head for the prologue, as the first sentence of the Gospel, or as part of a longer introductory sentence, for example: "The beginning of the gospel of Jesus Christ is just as it is written in Isaiah the prophet. . . ." The option chosen here argues that Mark 1:1 is best understood as the author's title to the whole Gospel, rather than as an element in the first sentence of the narrative.[2]

---

1. The biblical form of the document has two titles, one of which is the author's (1:1) and one of which (in varying forms) was added to the document as part of the tradition and canonizing process. Most MSS entitle the document "The Gospel according to Mark" or "The Markan Holy Gospel," but the oldest MSS available to us, ℵ and B from the fourth century (cf. Introduction 10.1) entitle the document *Kata Markon*, "according to Mark." Since the other canonical Gospels are analogously entitled *Kata Maththaion, Kata Loukan,* and *Kata Iōannēn* ("according to Matthew," "according to Luke," "according to John"), it is apparent that the titles are not original, but were added late in the second century in the process of forming the fourfold Gospel. The title "The Gospel" headed the fourfold collection, testifying to the early Christian faith that there is one gospel in four different narrative versions. This is the majority scholarly view; the minority is represented by Martin Hengel, "The Titles of the Gospels and the Gospel of Mark," in *Studies in the Gospel of Mark* (ed. Martin Hengel; Philadelphia: Fortress, 1985), 64–84, who argues, "the Gospels took on their titles before they were combined in the canon of the four Gospels" (81) and derive from the first century.

2. For evidence for and against the various possibilities, and a detailed argument for the option here chosen, see M. Eugene Boring, "Mark 1:1–15 and the Beginning of the Gospel," *Semeia* 52 (1990): 43–82. John G. Cook, *The Structure and Persuasive Power of Mark: A Linguistic Approach* (Atlanta: Scholars Press, 1995), 138–40, 173, argues on technical linguistic grounds that it is important to see 1:1 as the author's title for the whole work.

Beginning / Norm[a] of the gospel of Jesus Christ,[b] the Son of God[c]

a. Mark's first word *archē* means both "beginning" and "norm." English unfortunately has no single word that combines both meanings, but either alone misses Mark's point. The definite article is lacking in the Greek text, corresponding to ancient titular style, and is thus not added in the English translation.

b. The genitive *Iēsou Christou* can be either subjective, the gospel proclaimed by Christ, or objective, the gospel about [God's act in] Jesus Christ. Mark's understanding combines both meanings,[3] so the nonspecific "of" is retained here.

c. *Huiou theou* (Son of God) is present in most ancient MSS, but missing from a few key early ones (ℵ*, Q 28c. *al*). It is probably better to regard the phrase as original, since the two words could easily have been omitted by *homoioteleuton* (similarity of endings; thirteen words end in *-ou* in vv. 1–3), since it is well attested (B, D, W, and most later MSS), since it fits Mark's technique of disclosing to the reader what is withheld from the characters in the narrative, and since it forms a bracket with 15:39.

The typical title for a biography began with *Peri* ("about, concerning") plus the name of the subject. If Mark had followed the ancient biographical convention, he would have entitled his document *Peri Iēsou* (About Jesus). His title is distinctive, already setting his composition apart from Hellenistic biography (see Introduction 3.).

"Gospel" (*euangelion*) means "good news." It is the noun form related to the verb *euangelizō* (evangelize, proclaim the gospel, tell good news). The precise form *euangelion* is not found in the LXX, but the plural is found in 2 Sam 4:10, and the feminine *euangelia* five times (2 Sam 18:20, 22, 25, 27; 2 Kgs 7:9). The verb occurs twenty-three times, including the Isaiah texts 40:9; 52:7; 60:6; 61:1, especially important for shaping Mark's understanding of the gospel. One meaning of *euangelion* in Hellenistic culture was "good news of victory from the battlefield," which was then extended to mean something like "the good news of peace and prosperity, the good life resulting from military victory." Such victory and the resulting good life were associated with the Pax Romana and the emperor. That *euangelion* played a role in the emperor cult is documented by the famous Priene inscription of 9 B.C.E., which declares Augustus to be "savior" (*sōtēr*) and concludes with the line "the birthday of the god Augustus was the beginning for the world of the good tidings [*euangeliōn*] that came by reason of him." Mark's use of the term for the Christian message places it in parallel and opposition to the Roman ideology, and places Jesus as true Son of God in opposition to the imperial claims.[4] The issue of

3. Corresponding to "gospel of God" in 1:14, as argued by numerous scholars since at least Ernst Lohmeyer, *Das Evangelium des Markus* (16th ed.; KEK; Göttingen: Vandenhoeck & Ruprecht, 1937), 7.
4. See the documented list of divine titles given the various emperors in Evans, *Mark 8:27–16:20*, lxxxii–lxxxiii.

using God-language for the man Jesus is already adumbrated in the opening line of the document.

Euangelion did not become the designation for a book until the second century, a development to which Mark 1:1 no doubt contributed (Justin, *Apol* 1.66.3; Irenaeus, *Against Heresies* 1.7.4; 1.8.4, etc.; *2 Clem* 8.5; perhaps *Did.* 15.4). Here, however, "the gospel of Jesus Christ" refers not to a book but to the good news of God's saving act in Jesus Christ, the message proclaimed by the church of Mark's day (8:35; 10:29; 13:10; 14:9).

This gospel had a beginning (*archē*); it derives from and is in continuity with the gospel Jesus himself preached (1:14–15). Prior to Mark, *euaggelion* had been used for the good news of God's saving act in the death and resurrection of Jesus (1 Cor 15:3–5). By extending the term "gospel" to embrace not only the church's kerygma about Jesus but to include Jesus' own words and deeds, Mark takes a radically new step. The Jesus who proclaims the gospel in the narrative continues to address the post-Easter reader precisely through this narrative that is both "about" and "from" him (see on 13:37). The Gospel of Mark is not merely a report of what Jesus once said and did. Jesus stands at the beginning of the church's story as the one who preached the word (1:45; 2:2; 8:32, 38; 13:31; cf. also 4:1–20), and who identifies himself with the later church's message, in which he continues to live and speak (8:35; 10:29). Continuity is important for Mark, but not replication. Mark does not believe that the gospel Jesus preached in 1:14 is identical with that the church preaches, but that there is continuity, that the one was the *archē* of the other.

Mark only uses the term *archē* three times elsewhere in the Gospel, in each case in the sense of "beginning" (10:6, 13:8, 19). This is not merely a matter of chronology; it connotes "source, origin" (as translated in Rev 3:14). The word is resonant with the opening line of the Bible, "In the beginning . . ." (Gen 1:1), and suggests that the story that begins with John the Baptist and Jesus and extends through death and resurrection into the readers' present is a new, creative act of God (cf. on 7:37). The point is not that the story of Jesus begins with his baptism by John, but that the gospel proclaimed by the church of Mark's day had its beginning and origin in the events narrated in Mark as a whole. Cross and resurrection are not the end of something that begins in Mark 1:1; the Gospel of Mark as a whole narrates the beginning of a story that continues in the readers' own day and of which they are a part. The open "ending" of the story at 16:8 suggests that the whole of Mark's story is only a beginning, that "the *beginning* of the gospel story is over on Easter morning,"[5] and that every reader is challenged to continue the story in his or her own time.

---

5. Joel Marcus, *The Mystery of the Kingdom of God* (SBLDS 90; Atlanta: Scholars Press, 1986), 231. Cf. Luke's analogous understanding in Acts 1:1. The Gospel of Luke had narrated what Jesus *began*, a story that continues into the book of Acts. Mark's "Book of Acts" is the present life of the Christian community reading his text. Cf. Phil 4:15, the only New Testament linguistic parallel to *archē tou euaggeliou.*

Archē not only means "beginning"; it also means "authority" (as translated in Luke 12:11; 20:20), "norm, rule, ruler" (as in Rom 8:38; 1 Cor 15:54; Eph 1:21; 3:10; Col 1:16; 2:10; Titus 3:1). "Ruler" can refer not only to a person, but to a norm; just as the word for "canon" is the same word as "yardstick, measuring norm," so we also speak of a twelve-inch measuring device as a "ruler." *Archē tou euangeliou Iēsou Christou* can thus legitimately be translated "the norm for the proclamation of the gospel of Jesus Christ." Many versions of the Christian message were being propagated in Mark's day. Mark clearly did not believe that only one version of this message could be authentic (cf. on 9:38–40). But he regarded some expressions of the Christian message as dangerously seductive; in particular he was concerned about the problems presented by those Christian prophets who claimed to speak in behalf of Jesus by promulgating new revelations from the risen Lord (see commentary on 13:5, 20–21, 32; 16:1–8).[6] By committing his story to writing and presenting the Christian community with a document to be read in the church's worship, Mark composed a narrative that both portrayed the there-and-then event of salvation as it unfolded in the life, death, and resurrection of Jesus—the *beginning* of the story that continues into the readers' present—and a *norm* by which later claims to present the gospel could be measured. "Beginning" thus does not mean "preliminary," as though the later church would outgrow this beginning, which is also source and norm.[7] Mark does not see himself writing a canonical document in the later ecclesiastical sense. Like his predecessor Paul who believed that the risen Christ continues to speak, but who also wrote letters that could serve as a norm by which claims to later revelation could be tested (cf. 1 Cor 14:37–38), so Mark composes a narrative that both communicates the message from and about Jesus and provides the norm for the continuation of this proclamation in the mission of the church (cf. 13:10). He points to this multifaceted function by the title with which he prefaces the narrative as a whole.

That Jesus is the Christ, the Son of God (*Iēsou Christou huiou theou*), is revealed to the reader in the first line of the document, though Jesus' identity will be concealed from the characters in the story until the conclusion (see *Excursus: The Messianic Secret* at 9:13).

---

6. See Boring, *Continuing Voice of Jesus,* 242–46; Werner H. Kelber, *The Oral and the Written Gospel: The Hermeneutics of Speaking and Writing in the Synoptic Tradition, Mark, Paul, and Q* (Philadelphia: Fortress, 1983; 2d ed. with new introduction by the author, 1997), 44–139, 199–210; Michael L. Cook, *Christology as Narrative Quest* (Collegeville, Minn.: Liturgical, 1997), 67–108.

7. On the literary correlation between beginning and end in Mark's narrative, see especially Focant, *L'évangile selon Marc,* 56–57; 594–99. *Archē* as "beginning" has a double sense that can be perceived only in retrospect, by the reader who sees the narrative from the perspective of the epilogue, in which the story comes to an end, but without closure (see note 14 at 16:7).

1:2–15 The Markan Prologue

The function of the prologue is to set the stage for the (post-Easter) audience, so that they may see and hear the body of the narrative in the perspective intended by the author, a frame of reference the (pre-Easter) characters in the narrative itself do not and cannot yet have. Somewhat like the prologue of the Gospel of John (1:1–18), or Job 1–2, Mark's prologue moves on a different level than the narrative as a whole. The body of the narrative takes place in the everyday world, in the villages of Galilee and Jerusalem, with ordinary people: crowds and disciples, priests, scribes, and Pharisees. The prologue, however, begins in a transcendent, offstage setting, then narrates what transpires in the "wilderness"—never mentioned in the body of the Gospel—with an extraordinary cast: God, Isaiah, "the Lord," John the Baptizer, Holy Spirit, Satan, wild animals, and angels. The figure of the Lord Jesus himself is the point of intersection and line of continuity between these two worlds: he is addressed by God in the metahistorical world (1:2–3), and he is the this-worldly figure addressed by the heavenly voice and into whom the divine Spirit descends (1:10–11).[8] The reader, but not the participants in the body of the narrative, is party to these extraordinary scenes, events, and voices, and is prepared to understand the story in a way that they cannot—until after the cross and resurrection.

For Mark, John and Jesus are not parallel figures—John is clearly subordinate to Jesus, and Jesus' identity is not derived from John. Mark indicates Jesus' superior role by means of the offstage transcendent voice identifying Jesus as Lord and John as the messenger who prepares the way, so that when John appears in verse 4, the reader already places him in his proper role. This is represented by the two subsections 1:4–8 (John) and 1:9–15 (Jesus), each of which begins with *egeneto* (NRSV "appeared," "came"), the whole prefaced by a transcendent voice that makes it clear that Jesus is the Lord and John the messenger who prepares the way. The structure is thus best visualized as:

Transcendent Prelude: (1:2–3)

John (1:4–8)	**Jesus (1:9–15)**
Baptizing	Baptized
———	Tested
Preaching	Preaching

The parallelism is disrupted by the middle element in the second section (1:12–13) in which Jesus is tested by Satan—the cosmic power of evil is absent from the story of John; it only appears to challenge the Son of God.

---

8. Cf. Hans-Josef Klauck, *Vorspiel im Himmel? Erzähltechnik und Theologie im Markusprolog* (BTS 32; Neukirchen: Neukirchener Verlag, 1997), 113.

1:2–3 Transcendent Prelude: The Messenger, the Lord, and the Way

Like 1:1, so 1:2–3 is a discrete unit, the narrative proper beginning with the *egeneto* of 1:4 that introduces a new scene. The unit 1:2–3 should thus be followed by a period, as in the NIV, REB, NAB, NJB, and others (contrast NRSV). The unit stands by itself, hovering in a realm unspecified by spatial or temporal markers. The audience hears the offstage voice of God speaking in words of Scripture, before the onstage action begins in verse 4. There is nothing comparable elsewhere in the Markan narrative or the New Testament, but Mark's compositional strategy corresponds somewhat to the manner in which Deutero-Isaiah opens with voices from a heavenly scene, the text of which Mark takes as his key introductory quotation (Isa 40:1–11).

1:2 The following narrative corresponds to Scripture as written[a] in Isaiah the prophet[b]: Attention![c] I am sending my messenger[d] ahead of you, who will prepare your way. 3 A voice of one calling out in the wilderness,[e] "Prepare the way of the Lord, make his paths straight."

a. The familiar *kathōs gegraptai* (six times LXX; twenty-five times NT), "as it is written [in Scripture]," is normally related syntactically to what precedes. The extraordinary function of the unit has interfered with normal syntax, so that here *kathōs* indicates that the whole of the following narrative corresponds to Scripture.

b. Some relatively early textual witnesses (A, W, *f*¹³), and part of the Syriac, Old Latin, and Coptic tradition, as well as the bulk of later Greek MSS, read *en tois prophētais* (in the prophets), an obvious attempt at correction. The KJV followed this text, but the older MSS not yet discovered in 1611 (e.g., א, B) undoubtedly represent the original.

c. *Idou* (1,092 times, LXX; 200 times, NT; 7 times, Mark) represents the Hebrew demonstrative particle *hinneh,* a mild exclamatory call for attention, traditionally represented by the biblical-sounding "lo," "behold," or more colloquially, "look!" Often best left untranslated, as frequently in NRSV, NIV, and other modern translations, here it is an initial call for attention.

d. *Angelos* may be translated generically as "messenger" or specifically as "angel." In Exod 23:20 the reference is to the "angel of the Lord" who will go before Israel in the exodus from Egypt; in Mal 3:1, the messenger is a human figure who will purify the people in preparation for the advent of God.

e. *Erēmos* is an adjective, "deserted, uninhabited," as in 6:31, 32, 35. When it refers to the desert expanse that Israel had to traverse between Egypt and the promised land, or en route from the Babylonian captivity back to the Judean homeland, it has been traditionally translated "wilderness." This translation is preserved here in order to maintain its biblical connotations.

Mark begins with a transcendent offstage voice speaking in words of Scripture, declaring that the story about to be heard accords with Scripture. The audience is not directly addressed, but overhears words that are spoken to another offstage figure, addressed as "you" (sing.) in verse 2, then identified as "the Lord" in verse 3, a different figure from God the speaker (see on 12:35–37). The voice of God announces a third figure, the messenger, further identified as the voice in the wilderness. When the this-worldly voice of John is heard in the opening paragraph of the narrative that immediately follows, it comes with the authority and commission of the transcendent voice of God.

The Scripture with which Mark begins is programmatic for the narrative as a whole. The first citation in 1:2 is basically the LXX of Exod 23:20, combined with elements of the Mal 3:1. This combination of texts is not an amalgamation concocted by Mark; he joins a long trajectory of reinterpretation and fusion of different texts already present in the Old Testament and Judaism. The trajectory begins with the promise of Exod 23:20, which Malachi reflected in his oracle of Mal 3:1. These two texts were then associated and conflated in rabbinic exegesis, identifying the angel of the Lord promised to lead Israel through the wilderness and the Elijah *redivivus* promised in Mal 3:1 (cf. Mal 4:5–6), and together representing "the Law and the prophets" (cf. *Exod. Rab.* 32.9; *Deut. Rab.* 11.9). Mark thus takes over a mélange that was already traditional.[9] It is Mark himself, however, who adds the citation from Isa 40:3, and who attributes the whole to "the prophet Isaiah." The *archē* of the gospel, Mark 1–16, corresponds to what is written in Isaiah. Since Mark's citation of the Isaiah text has virtual verbatim agreement with Matt 11:10 / Luke 7:27 (Q), which differs from both the MT and the LXX, Mark draws this text from Q or from the same Greek source or tradition used by Q. Numerous other points of contact in 1:2–13 with the tradition common to Matthew and Luke point to this section as representing a Mark / Q overlap.

[1:2] Even though 1:1 is a title, there is no crisp separation between the first and second verses. Not only were there no verse numbers, there was no punctuation in the earliest manuscripts. Thus 1:1 flows into 1:2 and can be read with it. Yet *kathōs* connects directly neither to 1:1 ("The beginning is just as it is written . . .") nor with 1:4 (Just as it is written . . . John appeared . . .). Either is awkward. There are no non-awkward ways of construing the syntax of these verses. It seems best to understand "Just as it is written in Isaiah the prophet . . ." to introduce the offstage prelude, which is indeed suspended in midair. *Kathōs* links with the preceding; the connection, however, is not just to 1:1, but to the biblical story represented by "Isaiah." The sense seems to be something like "The gospel of Jesus Christ, and the following narrative, are in accord with what God spoke through the prophet Isaiah . . . ," without any particular scheme of

---

9. Cf. documentation and further examples in Krister Stendahl, *The School of St. Matthew and Its Use of the Old Testament* (Philadelphia: Fortress, 1968), 50. The procedure was not arbitrary, but followed recognized rules. The Qumran scrolls offer many examples of the fusion of texts. Mark elsewhere combines Old Testament texts without calling attention to it (1:11; 12:36; 14:24).

prediction / fulfillment, promise / fulfillment, or typology being presupposed. The hearer-readers of the narrative that is about to begin simply hear an off-stage, divine voice speaking in the words of Scripture, announcing that what is about to transpire on the narrative stage is in accord with (*kathōs*) Scripture.

Mark cites this combination of texts as "Isaiah." It is remotely possible that this is simply a mistake. Both Matthew and Luke apparently thought so, silently "correcting" it, as did some early scribes, who "corrected" the text to refer to "the prophets." It seems that Mark intentionally moved the Isaiah reference to the beginning of the combined quote in order to designate the whole story that is about to unfold as corresponding to [*kathōs*] Isaiah. Mark writes "an Isaian story"; not only the prologue, but the Gospel as a whole, can be called "The Gospel according to Isaiah" (see further in *Excursus: Mark and the Scriptures* at 14:52).

Of the ca. thirty-three instances where Mark directly quotes or clearly paraphrases or alludes to Scripture, only here is Scripture cited in the voice of the narrator, which is transparent to the voice of Isaiah, which is in turn transparent to the voice of God (cf. also 14:27). Christ is addressed by God in an off-stage scene not located in space and time, but the reader hears the voice of God speaking to Jesus before the appearance of either John or Jesus on the narrative stage. This does not mean Mark has a doctrine of preexistence such as Paul's, or of incarnation such as John's. Mark is not so conceptually crisp. Mark refers to the creation of the world by God (13:19), but it is the act of God alone, with no suggestion that a preexistent Christ participated in it or existed before it. But this prenarrative offstage voice also excludes understanding the baptismal scene of 1:9–11 in adoptionist terms (see on 1:10). As in 1:11 Jesus hears (and the audience overhears) the voice of God speaking to Jesus, so already the audience (over-)hears the voice of God speaking to "the Lord" in 1:2–3.

The reader gets no picture of when, where, or how this declaration from God to Jesus as "Lord" occurred. Before the action ever begins on the this-worldly narrative stage, before the readers have ever seen the earthly Jesus in the story line of the Gospel, they have (over-) heard God declare that Jesus is transcendent Lord who has a "way" in this world, and is conditioned to hear the whole story within this framework.

[1:3] Mark's appropriation and interpretation of Isa 40:3 is dependent on the LXX. The MT of Isaiah portrays a voice in the heavenly court crying out "Prepare the way of the Lord [Yahweh] in the wilderness." The way, not the messenger, is in the wilderness. In the original context, heavenly beings are commanded (plural imperative) to prepare the way for God to lead the captives from Babylon back to Judah for the grand eschatological restoration. This eschatological hope was not realized in Deutero-Isaiah's time, but the text continued to be understood eschatologically. Thus the Qumran community understood its withdrawal to the wilderness in terms of this text, with "way" now understood as "way of life" (1QS 8.12–16). As the eschatological community, they would live the "way of the Lord" in the wilderness in preparation for the advent of God. In the LXX translation, however, it is the voice of someone in the wilderness who calls out "Prepare the way of the Lord." Mark's interpretation is dependent on the LXX. If Mark had the same LXX text now extant, he changed "my way" of Mal 3:1 to "your way," which facilitates his identification of "the way of the Lord" as meaning the way of Jesus. Those who respond to the messenger's proclamation are to prepare the way of the Lord. How they are to do this is explicated in 1:4–6.

This transcendent prelude to the action of the narrative itself reveals to the audience that the story about to begin is in line with the Scriptures of Israel, with Isaiah in particular, that the one God of Israel addresses another transcendent being as "the Lord" (cf. Phil 2:5–11) and that this Lord has a way which not only the messenger in the wilderness is to prepare. Jesus' way is already announced, affirmed to be part of God's plan revealed in Scripture, in some way related to the Scriptures of Israel. He is commissioned to go that way. He will not merely teach a way of life, but will live it out. The following account of *Jesus* is the "way of the *Lord*": it begins in baptism and reception of the Spirit, which leads to mission, opposition, and persecution that costs him his life, but is vindicated by God in the end. The story of Jesus is the pattern for the disciples' own life. Others will be called to follow.

Excursus: The Way

From the opening Isaian epigraph onward, the word *hodos,* translated variously in the NRSV as "way," "path," "road," "journey," is a key theological term in Mark. Of the sixteen occurrences in Mark (1:2, 3; 2:23; 4:4, 15; 6:8; 8:3, 27; 9:33, 34; 10:17, 32, 46, 52; 11:8; 12:14), only 2:23 and 8:3 have the ordinary literal sense; all the others carry the overtones of Mark's distinctive theology. Mark uses it only in the singular. The initial citation from Isa 40:3 sets the tone for Mark's usage: "the way of the Lord" means God's own way through the wilderness, leading the captive Israelites triumphantly back to Zion. The way of the Lord is not the ethical pattern the Lord wants people to follow, but the Lord's own way, which he himself walks at the head of his redeemed people. For Mark, "the Lord" whose way is to be prepared is the Lord Jesus. The way of the Lord leads from Galilee to the cross. When Jesus calls people to follow him, it is on this way of self-denial that leads to the cross—the way of the Lord modulates into the way of the readers. This does not become clear, however, until the crucial scene of 8:27–38. Seven of Mark's fourteen theological uses of the term are then concentrated in the section 8:22–10:52, and the section is bracketed by the formulalike *en tē hodō* ("in the way," "on the road"). In the transcendent, offstage scene that begins the Gospel, Jesus is already commissioned to walk this way that leads to rejection, suffering, and death. This is not a rejection of or alternative to the triumphal march of the Lord to Zion proclaimed by Isaiah, but its reinterpretation in the light of Jesus' actual destiny. The triumph of God joyfully promised by Isaiah will be realized in Jesus' way to the cross: this is Mark's theme. Thus "the way of the Lord" Jesus is not the ethical life to which he calls, but the way of suffering and death he himself follows to its bitter—and ultimately triumphal—end. This way of Jesus continues into the reader's own time, and Jesus' call to discipleship is not a call to adopt his "way of life" in the sense of adopting his ideals and principles, but to follow behind him in the path he himself walked.

Since these opening words clearly use "way" primarily in a metaphorical, symbolic manner, the reader is sensitized, from the first page, to be alert to other symbolic overtones (e.g., "boat," "loaf"), but without reading profound theological meaning into their every occurrence. The narrative is not a mystical allegory, but takes place in the everyday world: a road is a road and a boat is a boat. Yet, like the parables that begin in the everyday world and then point beyond themselves without being obvious about it, the narrative as a whole is charged with transcendent potential. "Let the reader understand" (13:14).

1:4–8 John the Baptizer:
Preaching and Baptizing in the Wilderness

The narrative moves from the transcendent world to the stage of history. When the narrative curtain rises, the first scene portrays the ministry and message of John the Baptist. John was a significant historical figure in his own right (Josephus, *Ant.* 18.5.2 §116–19), with his own prophetic message, his own disciples, and a considerable following among the people (Matt 3:7–12; Luke 3:1–9, 16–17; Luke 11:1; John 3:25; 4:1; Acts 19:1–7). Mark has no interest in John as an independent figure, but pictures him entirely in relation to Jesus (see commentary on 6:21–29; 8:28; 9:11–13; 11:27–33).

> 1:4 John the Baptizer[a] appeared in the wilderness, proclaiming a baptism of repentance for the forgiveness of sins. 5 And all the Judean country and all the inhabitants of Jerusalem were going out to him and were being baptized[b] by him in the Jordan river, confessing their sins. 6 And John was clothed with camel's hair and a leather belt around his waist, and ate locusts and wild honey. 7 And he kept proclaiming, "After me[c] there comes the one mightier than I, whose sandal strap I am not worthy to stoop down and untie. 8 I baptize you in[d] water, but he will baptize you in[d] the Holy Spirit."

a. Reading *egeneto Iōannēs ho baptizōn en tē erēmō* with B 33 892 cop[bo(MSS)]. The usual title for John is *ho Baptistēs* ("the Baptist"), as in 6:25 and 8:28, but Mark also uses the participial form, as 6:14, 24. Other MSS do not recognize "the Baptizer" as a title, take the participle adverbially in parallel with "proclaiming," and thus omit the article and add the conjunction: "John appeared in the wilderness, baptizing and proclaiming. . . ."[10]

10. For the reading adopted here, see J. K. Elliott, "An Eclectic Textual Commentary on the Greek Text of Mark's Gospel," in *The Language and Style of the Gospel of Mark: An Edition of C. H. Turner's "Notes on Marcan Usage" Together with Other Comparable Studies* (ed. J. K. Elliott; NovTSup 71; Leiden: Brill, 1993), 191–94.

b. *Ebaptizonto* can be construed grammatically as either middle ("were baptizing themselves") or passive, as above. In Jewish proselyte baptism, the candidates immersed themselves. While the following *hyp' autou* ("by him") could conceivably mean "under his authority," the more likely meaning is that John immersed the penitents in the Jordan—which is confirmed by the active *ebaptisa* in v. 8 and the passive *ebaptisthē* in v. 9.

c. *Opisō mou* can also mean "after me" in the sense of "following me as my disciple" (the identical phrase is used in 1:17 and 8:34; cf. John 1:30).

d. "Water" is preceded by the preposition *en* ("in," "with") in some early and the great majority of later MSS, apparently an addition to correspond to its presence before *pneumati hagiō* ("Holy Spirit") and to the parallels in Matt 3:11, John 1:26. The dative case, with or without the preposition, can mean either "with" or "in." The point is the contrast between the different elements, not the manner of baptism—which in any case was most likely immersion.

[1:4] If Mark's Bible, like our Old Testament, ended with Malachi, its closing words promised the coming of "Elijah" to prepare the way for the coming of God (see below). Mark, however, subsumes the biblical collage of verses 2–3 under the heading "Isaiah," and declares that John appears in the "wilderness" as the one announced by the transcendent voice, the word of God that comes through the words of Isaiah. The wilderness then becomes the setting for John's preaching and for Jesus' baptism and testing. The wilderness is to identify John and to set the stage for the events to come. John has no call for others to abandon civilization and retreat to the wilderness; it is not an idealized setting for living the godly life where his disciples should gather as a special congregation.

The wilderness is an ambivalent image in the Hebrew Bible and Jewish tradition (see note "e" on 1:3). The wilderness is the deserted, inhospitable area where there is no food or water, the haunt of wild animals, demons, and death, but this means it is also the place where Israel was utterly dependent on God, the place where Israel was faithful to God before entering into the land.[11] The wilderness was thus the place of new beginnings, the place where Israel stood before crucial decisions (Deut 30:19), where they entered into the covenant and became God's people (Deut 29:12), where Israel is called to make a fresh start (Jer 2:2; Hos 2:14; 9:10), the route to a new Exodus (Isa 40–55). Thus the Qumran community, likewise hearing Isa 40:3 as a key text, proceeds to the "wilderness" to prepare for the climactic act of God in history. When some of the eschatological prophets and charismatic leaders who appeared in the first century, promising deliverance from the yoke of Rome, led their followers into the wilderness (cf. Acts 5:36; 21:38; Josephus, *Ant.* 29.97–98, 169–72; *War* 2.261–63), this was not mere strategy, but a symbolic act laden with the overtones of God's promised eschatological deliverance. Mark's emphasis on the

---

11. Ulrich Mauser, *Christ in the Wilderness* (SBT 39; Naperville, Ill.: Alec R. Allenson, 1963), 77–138.

wilderness as the setting for his opening scenes signifies the new beginning, the inauguration of the new age by the act of God the Creator.

Mark's story begins in the wilderness, not in the Jerusalem temple where water rites of purification were practiced and priests daily offered sacrifice for sins (contrast Luke 1:5–25). Since John is forerunner and model for Jesus, this opening scene already manifests to the discerning reader a tension between the temple and the John/Jesus story (cf. 1:14; 6:21–29; 11:11–17; 13:1–2; 14:58; 15:29). John proclaimed a baptism, a gracious gift of God that offered forgiveness of sins and called for repentance. The Markan order should not be reversed, as though his message was a moralizing "you should repent," of which baptism then became a symbol.[12] John did not proclaim repentance, but baptism (cf. Acts 10:37; 13:24, analogous to the proclaiming of a fast in 2 Chron 20:3; Jonah 3:5). In Mark, John is not a fire-and-brimstone preacher; he does not proclaim the imminent judgment of God or explicitly call for bringing forth the "fruit" of good works (contrast Matt 3:8–10; Luke 3:8–9), but announces the forgiveness of sins available in the baptism he proclaims and points to the coming powerful one who will baptize with the Holy Spirit. The proclamation of grace precedes the call to change one's life. Baptism mediated the forgiveness of sins, yet it is inseparably bound to repentance, a new mind-set that reverses conventional values and calls for a complete reorientation of one's life in view of the decisive act of God to occur immediately. This repentance is not an individualistic being-sorry for one's personal wrongdoings—though it does not exclude that—but a joining in the corporate renewal of the people of God preparing for God's eschatological act, concretely expressed in going out to the wilderness and receiving the gift of forgiveness offered in John's baptism.

Later Jewish sources document the practice of proselyte baptism. If this practice existed in John's day, it would be the closest analogy to John's baptism: just as Judaism required baptism (along with temple sacrifice and circumcision) of new converts, so John calls Jews to make the same new beginning they require of Gentiles. Since John also called people to go out into the wilderness, where the original covenant was made, and then to reenter the "promised land," baptism as entry into the eschatological people of God awaiting the coming deliverance would fit Mark's understanding of his baptism, however John himself may have understood it.

[1:5] Galilee is conspicuously absent (see on 1:14). When Mark says that *all* Judea and *all* Jerusalem went out to him and were being baptized by him in the

---

12. As already in Josephus's report, tailored to the understanding of his Hellenistic readers: "In his view this [sc., the practice of justice toward their fellows and piety toward God] was a necessary preliminary if baptism was to be acceptable to God. They must not employ it to gain pardon for whatever sins they committed, but as a consecration of the body implying that the soul was already thoroughly cleansed by right behavior."

Jordan, this is not to be seen in historical terms and labeled an excusable exaggeration (11:31 shows the statement is not a historical description). Mark is thinking in terms of the continuation and fulfillment of biblical history. As Israel had once come out of the wilderness, passed through the waters of the Jordan, and settled in Judea and Jerusalem, now the whole people are pictured as returning to the wilderness, passing through the waters of the Jordan, confessing their former sinfulness, and reemerging as the nucleus of the renewed people of God. The fundamental human problem is here conceived to be not ignorance or inherent human imperfection, but sin, understood as corporate active rebellion against the creator (see on 2:5–10).

[1:6] This brief description of John is withheld until the summary of his message and the response of the people had been given, and even then Mark relates nothing of John's "background" (as in Luke 1), but restricts his characterization to John's strange clothing and diet. Camel's hair clothing is the rough attire of the desert Bedouin, and locusts and wild honey form part of their diet, as also in the desert community of Qumran (cf. Lev 11:21–22; CD 12.14). The depiction of John in such terms is not a romantic back-to-nature portrayal of John as anticulture, anticivilization as such, but it has the overtones of Eden, in accord with the other creation motifs in this introductory section (cf. on 1:13). Mark later makes it clear, however, that his primary intent is to portray John as Elijah. In Mark, one's clothing, like one's name, involves one's personal identity (see on 10:50). Of all that Mark could have told us about this outlandish character, why mention the "leather belt"? The discerning reader will pick up the unmistakable signal pointing to Elijah (cf. 2 Kgs 1:8), even before Mark makes the identification explicit in 9:11–13. Malachi was always copied with the "Book of the Twelve," consistently as the last. Mark used the LXX, in which the Twelve were often, but not always, thought of and copied as the last books of Scripture. If Mark thought of Mal 3–4 as the concluding words of Scripture, John's appearance as the promised Elijah is all the more significant: his book begins where Scripture left off, and as its continuation and fulfillment.

[1:7] John's message is summarized in the first direct speech in the plotted narrative (the citation from "Isaiah" in 1:2–3 does not belong to the this-worldly plotted action). It alludes to Jewish hope of "the coming one" who will be the agent of God's eschatological salvation. For the historical John, this was probably God himself (cf. Mal 3:1; Zech 14:5; Luke 1:15–17), or perhaps a similar agent from heaven, the Son of Man or Elijah (Mal 4:5; note that John does not identify *himself* as "Elijah" in Mark). Even at the narrative level, the crowds that flocked to hear John do not expect another human figure to come after John— even if this figure is the Messiah—but the "mighty one," God himself or a heavenly figure like the Son of Man. But the reader already knows that Jesus is the fulfillment of this hope. Historically, Jesus had been baptized by John and had become an adherent of his movement, that is, his disciple (*opisō mou*, "after me," is the same phrase as 1:17). Early on, the young Christian movement co-opted John into their understanding of salvation history as the one who prepares the way for the Messiah, namely Jesus. John's reference to his unworthiness to untie the "coming one's" sandal strap points to a divinely empowered human figure rather than to God. In Mark's view, John had no other role than to prepare the way for Jesus, and he certainly referred to Jesus as the coming one. The significant point here is that *the first reference to Jesus identifies him as the "mighty one,"* indeed the *mightier* (comparative) one, the one who will represent the God of Deutero-Isaiah whose eschatological "coming" is marked by power and "strength" (Isa 40:10, 26, 29, 31; 45:24; 50:2; 52:1; 63:1, 15).[13] Jesus' ministry in the first half of Mark will indeed be a manifestation of this divine strength.

[1:8] This difference in John's status and power and that of Jesus is expressed in their respective baptisms, which represent the mission of each in its entirety: John's mission is to prepare a people for the coming of the Messiah, represented by his water baptism; Jesus' mission is to manifest the eschatological power of God effective through the Spirit (1:10, 12; 3:29). In Mark, *pneuma* (Spirit) is never used in reference to John (contrast Luke 1:15–17). John uses the aorist *ebaptisa*, suggesting that his baptismal ministry comes to an end with the advent of Jesus. Mark draws a clear line between the time of John and the time of Jesus (cf. 1:14): John is the precursor, Jesus is the fulfillment. Jesus represents the eschatological age of the Spirit and operates in its power; John does not. Jesus is not only the one given and empowered by the Spirit, but the one who dispenses the Spirit, sharing its power with his disciples (cf. 6:7; 13:11), the one who operates as the functional equivalent of God who gives the Spirit (see on 1:10).

"Baptize in the Holy Spirit" is an odd phrase—"baptize" is naturally related to water but not to Spirit (though cf. 1 Cor 12:13). Mark seems to have connected baptism and Spirit to contrast the ministries of John and Jesus; since John's ministry was summed up in his baptism, he characterizes Jesus' ministry in the same terms (cf. 10:38–39). Mark never specifically narrates the fulfillment of John's promise that Jesus will baptize in the Spirit. We should not fill in the content of this promise too quickly. By the promise of "baptism in the Holy Spirit" does Mark have in mind an event that happens after Easter, in the narrative world of the Gospel that he does not plot?[14] Or does Mark mean that the baptism with the Holy Spirit given by Jesus does not refer to a specific event in the life of the disciples, but to the life of discipleship as such, characterized by the Spirit given by Jesus?[15] As in 10:38–39 where death-baptism is not a

---

13. Cf. Bruce Chilton, *God in Strength: Jesus' Announcement of the Kingdom* (SNTSU B/1; Freistadt: Plèochl, 1979).

14. So Donald H. Juel, *The Gospel of Mark* (IBT; Nashville: Abingdon, 1999), 55.

15. Cf. Klauck, *Vorspiel im Himmel*, 88–89; Mansfield, *Spirit and Gospel*, 24–25.

one-time event but the nature of discipleship, so Spirit-baptism may be a powerful metaphor for the gift of the Spirit that empowers Jesus' disciples. In any case, it should not be assumed that Mark has the scenario of the later Acts 1–2 in mind.

1:9–15 Jesus of Nazareth: Baptized, Tested in the Wilderness, and Preaching

1:9–11 Baptism: God Reveals Jesus as His Son and Empowers Him with the Spirit

1:9 And it came to pass in those days[a] that Jesus came from Nazareth of Galilee and was baptized in the Jordan by John. 10 And just as[b] he was coming up from the water, he saw the heavens being torn open and the Spirit descending into[c] him like[d] a dove. 11 And a voice came from heaven, "You are my beloved Son; in you I have taken[e] great delight."

a. This biblicism, archaic and quaint to modern English ears, translates *kai egeneto*, found 559 times in the LXX, mostly as the translation of the MT's redundant *wyhy*, which was rendered "it came to pass" in the KJV. *Kai egeneto* is not found in nonbiblical Greek. Mark's use of it (seven times) gives his narrative a biblical ring; the translation above attempts to preserve this for the English reader. Likewise, *en ekeinais tais hēmerais* ("in those days"; ninety-eight times, LXX) is a "biblical" phrase. The combination *kai egeneto en ekeinais tais hēmerais* is found five times in the LXX.

b. Here translating *euthys,* a word Mark uses more than any other New Testament writer, forty-two of the fifty-nine New Testament occurrences. The adjective means "straight," "direct" [hence the KJV's "straightway"], the derived adverb thus "directly," "immediately." The meaning is often weakened to simply "next," or to a function word with little content (as when "well," "then," "so," and the like are used to introduce an English sentence). Both Matthew and Luke considered Mark to have overused the word, either eliminating it altogether (Luke eliminates all Markan instances) or changing it to the more common *eutheōs.* I have rendered *euthys* in a variety of ways, depending on the context. The word is probably a remnant of oral style and gives a certain vividness to the narrative, but by no means does it always mean "immediately" (this cannot be the meaning in, e.g., 1:21; 4:5), and it should not be taken to indicate that the Markan Jesus always acted quickly and directly as a "man of action."

c. In such a context *eis* can mean "into" or be a synonym of *epi* ("on," "upon").

d. *Hōs* is here taken as an adverb modifying *katabainon* (descending), rather than in an adjectival sense modifying dove (also theoretically possible). The point is not that the Spirit is compared to a dove, but that it descended dovelike upon Jesus (fluttering, hovering, brooding; cf. Gen 1:2).

e. The aorist *eudokēsa* can be gnomic, but more likely has its usual temporal sense in Koine Greek, i.e., it refers to a specific event in past time. The meaning here is thus not that God is in general pleased with Jesus, but God takes delight in Jesus' coming to be baptized by John.

[1:9] The man Jesus appears for the first time in the narrative. In contrast to the crowds who stream from Jerusalem and Judea, a lone individual comes from Nazareth of Galilee: the Galilee / Jerusalem tension that structures the narrative as a whole is implicit in the terse depiction (see Introduction 2.), and Jesus' initial journey from Galilee to Judea to be baptized foreshadows his final journey to Jerusalem and death (cf. 10:38).[16] There is no Bethlehem or City of David in Mark, no reference to Davidic descent (see commentary on 10:47; 11:10; 12:35). The Markan Jesus has no prior connections with Judea or Jerusalem. Nazareth is mentioned only here in Mark (though presupposed as Jesus' *patris* [home town] in 6:1–6). There is no reference to Nazareth in the Old Testament, Josephus, or the Talmud, but Mark's point is not Nazareth's obscurity (contrast John 1:46) but its location: Galilee. When Jesus appears on the Markan stage of history, he is obviously the one addressed in the transcendent scene of 1:2–3, but he comes "from Nazareth," not from heaven. Mark narrates no miraculous birth and has no doctrine of preexistence; the Markan Jesus has nothing to say about his prior life either in this world or beyond. *How* it is that Jesus is both from God and from Nazareth Mark leaves as an unnarrated, unconceptualized mystery.

Virtually all interpreters regard Jesus' baptism by John as one of the most certain historical events of the New Testament narrative. It was difficult for early Christianity to assimilate this historical reality into their developing theology. Their master and Lord had in fact been baptized by, and had for a while been the disciple of, the leader of a parallel and somewhat competing movement. The difficulties of integrating this event into Christian consciousness are seen in the ripple effect of reinterpretations represented in early Christian narratives, including the New Testament Gospels. Mark is the earliest of these. He has already dealt with the issue of the relation of John and Jesus in the preceding verses, and the narration of Jesus' baptism by John is given without further comment, either from John or the narrator (contrast Matt 3:14–15; John 1:19–34). It is nonetheless surprising that the one announced in 1:8 as the baptizer in the Holy Spirit is baptized, and receives the Holy Spirit rather than dispenses it. Mark does not make it explicit, but Mark's Christian readers recognize Jesus' act as the initiating paradigm of their own new life. Without a word of explanation, Jesus takes his place in the line of repentant humanity preparing for the eschatological act of God. Jesus' initial appearance in Mark is in solidarity with sinful humanity. The one we readers have heard addressed in 1:2 as belonging to the transcendent world appears in this world as one *of* us. The one whose blood will mediate the ultimate renewal of God's covenant with humanity (14:24) joins with those who confess their sins and throng to the

---

16. Cf. Elizabeth Struthers Malbon, "Galilee and Jerusalem: History and Literature in Marcan Interpretation (1982)," in *The Interpretation of Mark* (ed. William R. Telford; 2d ed.; SNTI; Edinburgh: T. & T. Clark, 1995), 258.

wilderness locus of the covenant. On the interwoven strands of baptism, cup, sonship, discipleship, cf. 10:38–39; 12:1–11; 15:39.

[**10**] The Spirit descends into Jesus (see note *c* above). He is a "Spirit-possessed" person, but both his opponents and his family could question what had "gotten into Jesus," what kind of spirit had control of him (cf. 3:20–35). Jesus' reception of the Spirit is not portrayed as the direct effect of John's baptism, but the Spirit descends into him immediately afterward, as he comes out of the water. After 1:9, John disappears from the Markan stage (cf. 1:14; 6:14, 21–29). Only Jesus (and the reader) see the heavens split and the Spirit descending; only he (and the reader) hear the voice. This is an aspect of Mark's messianic secret (see *Excursus: The Messianic Secret* at 9:13). The coming of the Spirit is not a soft, warm-fuzzy image (despite the analogy of the dove). "Spirit" connotes power, eschatological power, as in Isa 11:1–5—another Isaiah connection in this context.

The "open heaven" is an apocalyptic motif, the language of theophany, epiphany, vision. The splitting of the heavens is portrayed violently, toned down by both Matt 3:16 and Luke 3:21 (but corresponding to 15:38). As elsewhere, Mark gives no explanation, but leaves the reader to grasp the allusion. The imagery may point backward to Isa 64:1 (LXX 63:19), where the author longs for God to break open the heaven and appear in this world, causing the mountains to shake and the nations to tremble at God's presence, and forward to Mark 15:38, where the temple curtain is ripped from top to bottom (*schizō* in each instance, only these two times in Mark). Each text may have the overtones of both threat (God is no longer safely in heaven or in the temple but is loose in the world) and promise (the time of waiting and longing is over, the ultimate act of God's revelation is already beginning).

As in 1:2–3, the heavenly voice is a fusion of Scripture texts, Ps 2:7 and Isa 42:1, with probable allusions to the "beloved son" of Gen 22:2, 12, 16. The citation of Ps 2:7 evokes the royal imagery and inauguration ceremony of the Judean king, who was declared to be God's son (see *Excursus: Markan Christology* at 9:1). The citation of Isa 42:1 is from the first of the Servant Songs, with the immediate context referring to the Servant's divine endowment with the Spirit to bring God's justice to the Gentiles (42:2–4), and the wider context of the Servant Songs including the climactic act of vicarious suffering and death (52:13–53:12). While Mark is not always aware of or interested in the context of the Scripture he cites, here he again seems to connect with the comprehensive network of Isaiah's Servant theology. The "beloved Son" terminology may be intended to evoke the imagery of Abraham's binding of Isaac as well—this phrase is not found in either Ps 2 or Isa 42. In the LXX, "beloved" (*agapētos*) often translates the Hebrew *yahid*, "only" (as in Gen 22:2, 12, 16), and points to the uniqueness of Jesus as Son of God. The Spirit of Yahweh would rest on the coming king (Isa 11:2), on the chosen Servant (Isa 42:1), and on the anointed herald of good news (Isa 61:1). Mark cites none of these texts explicitly, but his predilection for Isaiah suggests their influence on his Christology. The tension between royal power as God's anointed Son and human weakness as the Suffering Servant is built into the initial identification of Jesus and maintained throughout the narrative.

The declaration from heaven should not be misunderstood in an adoptionist sense.[17] Mark does not speculate on "when" Jesus "became" the Son of God, but the affirmation in 9:7 must be the declaration of a reality that already exists, and it cannot be regarded as performative language (unless Jesus was "adopted" twice!). So also the addition of the Greek article to "my Son," absent in Ps 2:7, and the omission of "Today I have begotten you," which is found there, indicate Mark is not thinking of Jesus' adoption as Son of God at his baptism. Likewise the earliest interpretations in Matt and Luke, who regard Jesus as Son of God from his birth, show that they wanted to prevent Mark's being misunderstood in terms of adoptionist Christology.

The identity of Jesus is a matter of revelation, not deduction. Mark is concerned to communicate the reality of Jesus as he truly is, that is, as seen in the eyes of God. The narrator has already revealed to the reader that Jesus is Son of God. The heavenly voice confirms the narrator's point of view as aligned with God's own perspective; the narrator is reliable, and can be trusted to guide the reader through the unfolding story.[18] The ripping open of the heavens, the descent of the Spirit, and the heavenly voice have no effect on John or the crowds. Here as elsewhere, the reader is privileged to see, hear, and know that which is hidden from the characters in the story. This is something readers do not have the liberty of choosing; it is not something they achieve or may feel smug about, but something given to them or even imposed upon them. They are privileged, elected, to share a terrible secret (cf. 4:10–12), the elect who have their status by grace (cf. 13:20, 22, 27).

1:12–13 Jesus Is Tested in the Wilderness

> 1:12 And at once the Spirit thrusts him out[a] into the wilderness. 13 And he was in the wilderness forty days, being tested by Satan,[b] and he was with the wild animals, and the angels were serving him.

a. *Ekballei*, the same term used repeatedly for casting out evil spirits, and often in the LXX for "drive out" (e.g., Gen 3:24; Exod 10:11; 34:24).

17. Contra the view classically expressed by Julius Wellhausen, *Das Evangelium Marci* (Berlin: G. Reimer, 1903), 7: "In any case, the essential meaning of the baptism of Jesus is found in the fact that it transforms him into the Messiah, that he went into the water as a mere human being and came out as the Son of God." More recently, e.g., Georg Strecker, *Theology of the New Testament* (trans. M. Eugene Boring; New York: De Gruyter, 2000), 353.

18. Jack Dean Kingsbury, *The Christology of Mark's Gospel* (Philadelphia: Fortress, 1983), 60 and passim. M. Cook, *Narrative Quest*, 70.

b. *Satanas* is not a native Greek word, but a loan word from the Hebrew Bible. It is found only occasionally in the LXX and Jewish Greek (Sir 21:27), where it preserves its generic sense as a common noun meaning "adversary," "accuser." In the New Testament it is used only as a title or name for the devil, *the* transcendent accuser and adversary of God's people. Mark does not use "devil," but Satan is equated with "Beelzeboul" and "Prince of Demons" in 3:22.

It is difficult for modern readers who know Matthew and Luke not to read their stories between the lines of Mark's spare narrative. The reader should note what is not there: No initiative from Jesus, who is not the subject of any active verb; no movement from the wilderness to temple or mountain; no fasting; no dialogue, saying of Jesus, or citation of Scripture; no "temptation" in the moral sense at all; no example for believers in their "temptations."

[1:12] The episode begins "at once" (cf. note *b* on *euthys* at 1:10); Mark allows neither Jesus nor reader to bask in the reassurance of the heavenly voice.[19] This scene is connected with the previous one by the common elements of Spirit and wilderness (not, as in Matthew and Luke, by the Son of God motif). Again, the Spirit is not a "soft" image, but operates with an almost violent power (cf., e.g., 1 Kgs 18:12; Acts 8:39–40). As in the baptismal scene, Jesus is "passive" throughout; the only verb of which he is the subject is the repeated "was." Jesus is tested in the context of a cosmic conflict between the power of God represented by the Spirit that he has received, and Satan, the ruler of evil spirits (3:22). Jesus' own initial act will be narrated in 1:14–15, 16–20.

The wilderness location is emphasized by being mentioned twice within six words, and despite the fact that Jesus is already in the wilderness where John is baptizing. Here, however, the Spirit drives him away from the other people into a setting that, while still the this-worldly scene of John's ministry and repentant sinners, is also a transcendent context peopled by Satan and angels. The forty days could be simply the common biblical round number (second in frequency only to "seven" in biblical narrative), but in connection with "wilderness" it evokes again the experience of Israel (Deut 8:2), Moses (Exod 34:28), and especially Elijah, who was also fed by angels (1 Kgs 19:1–8).

Peirazō can mean either "tempt" in the moral sense ("entice to do evil") or "test" in the sense of a test of strength. The elaborate Q account followed by Matthew and Luke understands the experience in the former sense: Jesus has been declared to be Son of God; now the devil tempts him to be disobedient. The Markan account makes no reference to the Son of God motif, and *peirazō* here points to a test of strength, a contest of opposing forces. It lasts forty days (not, as in Q / Matt / Luke, only at the end of a forty-day period of fasting). John has announced the coming of the "mighty one." The powerful Spirit of God has descended into Jesus. The power at work in him now immediately confronts the

---

19. Cf. C. Clifton Black, *Mark* (ANTC; Nashville: Abingdon, forthcoming), ad loc.

transcendent power of evil. Who will prevail? Satan's power has previously overcome all. Even after this wilderness encounter, Satan continues to be active in opposing the preaching of the gospel (4:15; 8:11) and can even speak through leading disciples (8:33).

Did Jesus too fail to meet the test? The outcome is not explicitly announced; the reader must await further developments (see on 1:21–28; 3:22–27). But this brief narrative already presents evocative hints: during this wilderness testing, Jesus was served by angels and was with the wild animals. The angels do not arrive only at the end of a successful resistance to Satan (contrast Matt 4:11b), but sustain him throughout. This is not merely an answer to the prosaic question of how Jesus was provided with food during the forty days—though overtones of 1 Kgs 19:1–8 may be present. There is a close connection between Spirit and angels; both represent the power and presence of God (Acts 23:8; 1 Tim 3:16; Heb 1:14; Rev 22:6; cf. Rev 1:4; 3:5). Psalm 91:11 may also hover in the background, specifically so in the Q version of the temptation (Matt 4:6; Luke 4:10). While the presence of angels is clearly a positive, victorious image (8:38; 13:27), the animals are somewhat ambiguous. Do they stand on the side of Satan, representing the dangers of the wilderness testing? If Ps 91 is in the background, defeat of wild animals is the counterpart of the ministry of angels. During Nero's action against Christians in Rome a few years before Mark was written, followers of Jesus had been arrested and thrown to wild animals. Some readers may have been reminded by this scene that in his encounter with demonic power, Jesus too had faced wild animals. In concert with the other eschatological imagery in this section, Jesus' presence with the animals may represent the Messiah as restoring the original creation's paradisiacal peace with nature, which was to be restored at the eschaton (cf. Isa 11:6–8; 65:25; Hos 2:18; Ps 91:11–13; Job 5:22; *2 Bar.* 73.6; *T. Naph.* 8.4).[20] The phrase "with the wild animals" (*meta tōn thēriōn*) suggests harmonious coexistence. Since both wilderness and peace with the animals are Isaian motifs, Mark's interest in Isaiah as interpretative key to the Jesus story gives some credence to this view.[21] Mark has no explicit Adam Christology but does present Jesus as more than merely the survivor of Satan's onslaught; he is the victor over Satanic power. The conflict has taken place in the wilderness, observed only by God and the angels—and the reader, who can only perceive it as a victory hidden from the world at large (cf. 4:10–12). Yet the scene does not end on an idyllic note, but is open-ended: we have not seen the last of Satan (3:23–26; 4:15; 8:33).

20. So, e.g., Siegfried Schulz, *Die Stunde der Botschaft: Einführung in die Theologie der vier Evangelisten* (Hamburg: Furche-Verlag, 1970), 56; Kingsbury, *Christology of Mark's Gospel*, 68. Cf. Dan O. Via Jr., *The Ethics of Mark's Gospel: In the Middle of Time* (Philadelphia: Fortress, 1985), 47–49, on Mark's eschatology as anticipation of the new creation.

21. Klauck, *Vorspiel im Himmel*, 58–59. Paradisiacal conditions as God's people are led by an angel in the way through the wilderness are also features of Isa 35; 40, which may also be in the background here.

1:14–15 Ministry in Galilee

This compact transitional summary both concludes the prologue and sets up the next scene. There is both continuity with the preceding (John, Jesus, Galilee, gospel, repent) as well as discontinuity: "after" demarcates the time of John from that of Jesus; John is removed from the scene before Jesus takes center stage; Jesus is now active rather than passive; a new time begins as the fulfillment of the old; John's message was exclusively about the "coming one," while Jesus' message is the good news of the kingdom of God; "all Judea" responded to John, but Jesus was the sole Galilean to respond. Jesus does not continue John's baptizing work in Judea, but proceeds to Galilee, which will come to symbolize the Gentile mission.

1:14 Now after John had been delivered up,[a] Jesus came into Galilee proclaiming the gospel[b] of God,[c] 15 saying "The time is fulfilled, and here comes the kingdom of God;[d] repent, and believe in the gospel."

a. While *paradidōmi* can mean simply "arrested," the word has overtones of Jesus' and the disciples' being "delivered up" or "handed over," both by human agents and as God's act (see on 9:31).

b. As in 1:1, "gospel" is better than "good news," in order to preserve the continuity between Jesus' preaching and the later Christian message.

c. The genitive *tou theou* can here be either a subjective genitive of source, "the gospel from God," or an objective genitive of description, "the gospel about God," but these need not be alternatives (cf. 1:1).

d. The case made by C. H. Dodd that *ēngiken* means simply "has come," "has arrived," has not convinced most scholars. One could translate it "has come near," which would express the perfect tense of *engizō* and Mark's view that the kingdom is still future but so near that it already affects the present (see on 14:42). This is the intent of the colloquial translation above.

[1:14] John has fulfilled his mission and is arrested and removed from the stage before Jesus begins his ministry. John's death is narrated as a flashback in 6:17–29, but he is never to be heard from again (contrast Matt 11:2–6 / Luke 7:18–23). In Mark, John and Jesus do not have overlapping ministries (contrast John 3:22–4:3). John's being "delivered" up is a model and premonition of what is in store for both Jesus and his disciples (see on 9:31); he had "prepared the way" not just by his preaching. In Mark, John's announcement of the coming of the mighty one was the whole burden of his ministry and content of his message. In the Markan story line he is arrested, imprisoned, and killed, without the reader hearing another word from him—a faithful minister who never knew that the word he proclaimed had found its divinely given fulfillment, a model for ministers of all time, who are called simply to be faithful to the word they are given, without claiming to see its "success."

Galilee was conspicuously absent in 1:5. Jerusalem and Judea responded to John, but Jesus is the sole Galilean to do so—representatively, as it turns out. The people had to go out into the wilderness to John; Jesus goes to the people, bringing the ultimate good news to Galilee. Jerusalem and Judea will end up rejecting Jesus, but Jesus will have Galilean followers, and Galilee will be the scene of the new beginning (14:28). Thus Jesus' ministry, which opens with his return from Judea to Galilee as the preacher of the gospel, foreshadows Jesus' return to Galilee as the crucified and risen one whose word will continue to be heard in the preaching of his disciples (16:7). Galilee is not specifically "Gentile" in Mark (contrast Matt 4:15 citing Isa 9:1); the Galilean west bank of the Sea of Galilee will represent Judaism (cf., e.g., commentary on 1:21–28, 39; 5:21–24; 7:24), but it is a Judaism that borders Gentile territory and will be the transitional scene to the church of Jews and Gentiles of Mark's time. Yet Mark's interest in the Gentile mission (11:17; 13:10; 14:9) and his orientation toward Isaiah may give Galilee a Gentile overtone. Mark's conclusion sends the reader "back to Galilee" (16:7), thus forming a bracket with this text, and allowing the Galilean ministry of Jesus to be read in the light of his cross and resurrection.

Jesus came *proclaiming* (*kēryssōn;* note the prominence of this verb in the opening section). In this summary, all Jesus does is speak. His ministry is epitomized as ministry of the word (cf. 1:38, 39; 2:2; 4:14; 8:32; 13:31). Healing and exorcisms are not alternatives to his ministry of the word but integral to it. Like being "delivered up," preaching binds together John, Jesus, and his disciples (1:4, 7; 3:14; 6:12; 13:10; 14:9).

[15] The content of Jesus message is indicative / imperative. Neither can stand alone. The announcement of God's act calls for response; the command to repent and believe rests on the preceding gracious act of God. The indicative is stated in two perfect-tense forms, each of which characteristically points to a past act with results and implications that continue into the present: (1) In God's act in the advent of Jesus, the time is fulfilled (*peplērōtai*); something has happened that means the time of waiting is over, and (2) in God's act in the advent of Jesus, the promised kingdom of God has come near (*ēngiken,* as also in Q, Matt 10:7 / Luke 10:9). It has not completely arrived and is not simply present (see *Excursus: Kingdom of God* below), but neither is it merely future. The perfect tense conveys the sense that something has already happened that has brought the kingdom effectively near.[22] Compare Luke 21:20, where *ēngiken* refers to the encirclement of the city during a siege: the city has not yet fallen, but its fate is sealed and life is already different. Likewise in Rom 13:12, *ēngiken* expresses

---

22. The Greek perfect tense here signals a past act that endures in the present and makes it radically different (cf. on 2:5; 9:1; 16:4, 6). Contemporary English has no true equivalent to the Greek perfect, but cf. old English "Joy to the world, the Lord *is* come"—different from the simple past "has come," which only reports a past event.

the arrival of the dawn: the new day is not yet here, but neither is it simply some-time during the night; "first light" calls for living in terms of the dawning day rather than the past darkness (cf. also *ēngiken* in Jas 5:8; 1 Pet 4:7).

The dawn of the kingdom calls for response. Like John the Baptist and the prophets of Israel, the Markan Jesus calls for repentance, a message that will be continued by his disciples (6:12). In this context, repentance means a reorientation of one's whole life, a turn to the new reality that is dawning, not a return to the past. Likewise, "believe" means not merely to accept something as true; it involves a response with one's total self, an uncalculating obedience-in-personal-trust that involves one's whole life (cf. 2:5; 4:40; 5:34, 36; 9:23–24, 42; 10:52; 11:22–24).

Mark has no picture of Jesus conducting an extensive solo ministry. Mark here is likely summarizing in advance the whole Galilean ministry to be plot-ted immediately, not describing a period of Jesus' activity when he toured Galilee alone, without disciples. The Markan summary begins in the mode of diegetic narrative and modulates in midsentence to become direct address (second-person imperatives rather than third-person report). What begins as there-and-then report modulates into here-and-now address to the reader. This illustrates the character of the Gospel as a whole, ostensibly reporting past events that stealthily and seamlessly become contemporary.

At the end of this compressed introductory section that functions as the key to the whole narrative, we can see that Mark has woven many of the major themes of his Gospel into it. The hoped-for events that were to happen at the eschaton, when God brings history to a worthy conclusion, are already hap-pening in the advent of Jesus Christ: Scripture is fulfilled, Elijah returns, the heaven is opened, God's voice speaks again, the Spirit and angels descend, the ultimate testing, binding and victory over Satan, eschatological peace with the animal world in the new creation—in short, the advent of the Messiah, the coming of God's kingdom.

Excursus: Kingdom of God[23]

Basileia can be understood and translated either in the dynamic sense of "reign," "rule," "exercising kingly power," or in the territorial sense of "kingdom," "realm." The En-glish word "dominion" has something of the same twofold aspect. "The reigning pres-ence of God"[24] captures both the dynamism and personal dimension of the phrase, which is about Someone, not an abstraction or principle. The exact phrase "kingdom of God"

---

23. For a more detailed discussion, see M. Eugene Boring, "The Kingdom of God in Mark," in *The Kingdom of God in 20th-Century Interpretation* (ed. Wendell Willis; Peabody, Mass.: Hen-drickson, 1987), 131–46.

24. Moloney, *Mark: Commentary*, 49 and passim, so translates *hē basileia tou theou*.

is not found in the Old Testament (though cf. Wis 10:10), but declarations that God is king or that God will rule are fairly common (e.g., 1 Sam 12:12; Pss 5:2; 10:16; 44:4; 47:7–8; 68:24; 93:1; 96:10; 99:1; 146:10; Isa 6:5; 33:22; 44:6; 52:7; Zeph 3:15; Zech 14:9, 16; Mal 1:14).

In first-century Judaism "kingdom of God" was understood in a threefold perspective. (1) The eternal rule of God, independent of all human action. God is always the creator and ruler of the universe, and there is no other power that can ultimately resist God's rule; as in Ps 103:19, "The LORD has established his throne in the heavens, and his kingdom rules over all." God is already king de jure, but not de facto, since rebellious humanity has rejected God's kingship. (2) The present rule of God in the individual lives of those who are obedient to God. Rabbis spoke of "taking upon oneself the yoke of the kingdom," i.e., submitting oneself to God's rule, especially as symbolized in the daily recitation of the Shema (Deut 6:4). God's kingdom is present in the midst of a rebellious world as faithful members of God's covenant people obey God's will revealed in the Torah. (3) The future rule of God. The present rebellious state of the world is not the last word. God will reestablish his kingdom over the whole creation, bringing the world and history as we know it to an end, and restoring the creation to its unity under God's sovereignty. Mark's understanding of the kingdom of God is rooted in this Jewish apocalyptic hope.[25] One such apocalyptic vision of the coming kingdom is found in *Assumption of Moses*, contemporary with Mark:

> Then his kingdom will appear throughout his whole creation.
> Then the devil will have an end.
> Yea, sorrow will be led away with him.
> Then will be filled the hands of the messenger,
> who is in the highest place appointed.
> Yea, he will at once avenge them of their enemies.
> For the Heavenly One will arise from his kingly throne.
>
> (10.1–3a)

Sometimes the future coming of the kingdom involved a messiah that God would anoint from this world; sometimes it involved the coming of a heavenly figure such as the Son of Man (cf. *Excursus: Markan Christology* at 9:1); sometimes God is pictured as coming directly to establish his kingdom.

The future coming of the kingdom of God was an object of daily prayer. The Kaddish, which probably was already part of the synagogue liturgy in the first century, expresses this hope:

> Magnified and sanctified be his great name in the world which he hath created according to his will. May he establish his kingdom during your life and during your days, and during the life of all the house of Israel, even speedily and at a near time.

God is at present king over the whole creation, but God's kingship has been usurped by hostile powers. The coming kingdom of God will thus mean God's mighty reestab-

---

25. See notes 44 and 46, pp. 356–57, and the diagram on p. 247.

lishment in fact of a kingship that is presently real but not actualized. The kingdom is not a hidden reality of the heart, or a hidden dimension of the world. It is not the church, or an improved social reality that Jesus' disciples are urged to "build" or "work for." There is no text in Mark that clearly declares that the kingdom is present, even in some hidden way.

Mark's language of the kingdom is not abstract but related to God's act in Jesus. The kingdom dawns and becomes real in the ministry of Jesus, is presently hidden in this-worldly reality, and will be revealed in power when Jesus reappears as the apocalyptic Son of Man (9:1). Mark expected this to happen soon, so that it already affected Mark's present, as it had affected Jesus'. The kingdom is future, but the time of waiting is over, and the present is already transformed.

Part 1

Galilee
Mark 1:16–8:21

1:16–3:35 Authority, Rejection, and the New Community

1:16–3:6 Acting with Authority

1:16–20 The Call of the Disciples

The Prologue is complete, and the body of the narrative itself begins. The stage has been set: the long-awaited eschatological act of God is already beginning. The "Powerful One" has been announced and empowered by the Spirit, has encountered the demonic power of evil, and is ready to begin his work. What will be his first "mighty act" initiating the kingdom of God that he has announced as already dawning?

He calls four rather ordinary people to follow him. They will be with him throughout, present in almost every scene, until Gethsemane (14:50). At the end of the narrative, Jesus will leave behind no monuments or institutions—only a group of very fallible disciples. The last words of the narrative will point the reader to their renewal, with the risen Jesus going before them, and their continuation of his mission in the world. Jesus is not thought of as a solitary individual, a "great man" who affects history, but throughout as Jesus-in-relation-to-his-disciples. From the very beginning the story of Jesus is the story of a community, and there is no Christology apart from ecclesiology and discipleship. For readers whose perception has not been deadened by familiarity, the calling of disciples must appear to be a great reversal of expectations. If *this* Jesus is the Christ, the Son of God (1:1), both the Christ and the nature of God's kingdom must be rethought.

> **1:16** And passing along beside the Sea of Galilee he saw Simon and Andrew the brother of Simon[a] casting their nets[b] into the sea, for they were fishermen by trade.[c] **17** And Jesus said to them, "Come,[d] follow me, and I will make you into fishermen who fish for people." **18** And they immediately left their nets and followed him. **19** And he went a little farther and saw James the son of Zebedee and John his brother, who were likewise in a boat, preparing their nets, **20** and he immediately called them. And they left their father Zebedee in the boat with their hired men, and went away, following behind him.

a. The somewhat awkward rendering is to preserve the point that Andrew's identity is in relation to Simon, who will be renamed Peter in 3:16. This Simon is called first, and will be the primary disciple, the spokesperson for the group, and the leading figure in the early church.

b. "Nets" is supplied as the object of the participle *amphiballontas,* which refers to the act of casting the large round nets with weights along the edges, which pulled the net down around the fish, trapping them.

c. "By trade" is added to make Mark's point that they are not amateurs fishing for pleasure or to gain additional food for their families; instead they are engaged in the thriving fishing business for which the towns along the shore of the Sea of Galilee were widely known beyond Palestine, mentioned not only by Josephus (*War* 3.506–508) but by Strabo (*Geog.* 16.2.45) and Pliny (*Nat.* 5.15.71).

d. *Deute* is an adverb used as a hortatory and imperative particle (sing. *deuro*), combining both invitation and command (elsewhere in Mark 6:31; 10:21; 12:7; cf. Matt 11:28; 22:4; John 4:29; 11:43; Acts 7:3; Rev 19:17). *Opisō mou* is lit. "behind me." "Follow me" is thus not only metaphorical, "take my life and teachings as your model," but literal: "walk behind me on the same way I am going" (cf. *Excursus: The Way* at 1:3). *Deute opisō mou* is clearly the equivalent of *akolouthei moi,* "follow me" (1:18; 2:14).

[1:16] The Sea of Galilee is about seven miles wide and twelve miles long, and would normally be called a *limnē* ("lake") by Hellenistic authors (so consistently by Luke). Referring to it as a *thalassa* ("sea") is not mere provincialism—the Mediterranean was not far away, and every Galilean knew what a real ocean was like—but Semitic usage, as Aristotle (*Mete.* 1, 13 p. 351a, 8) had already recognized. Jewish sources referred to it as the Sea of Chinnereth, Gennesaret, or Tiberias. "Sea of Galilee" is peculiar to Mark and sources dependent on him, reflecting Mark's focus on Galilee as the "Holy Land," the place of Jesus' proclamation and mighty deeds (cf. 1:14). Using "sea" rather than "lake" allows the Markan narrative to evoke the chaos and anticreation motif associated with "sea" in ancient Near Eastern imagery and the Hebrew Scriptures.

Jesus "passes along beside" (the phrase is somewhat awkward), in divine sovereignty (cf. Exod 33:18–23; 1 Kgs 19:19; cf. Mark's similar usage in 2:14 and 6:48). He "sees" two fishermen working at their trade. He sees them; they do not see him. They are not looking for anything except fish. Their becoming disciples is not the fulfillment of their religious quest. The initiative is entirely with Jesus, his call is intrusive and disruptive; their new status as disciples is conferred, not attained. The narrator has introduced Jesus to the readers, but Jesus does not introduce himself to the fishermen, nor cultivate them for his call. His powerful word is effective. While there were some Hellenistic stories in which philosophers took the initiative to call promising students to study with them,[1] it was unheard of for a rabbi to call students, who were expected to apply on their own initiative. The paradigm is the biblical God who calls prophets (cf.,

---

1. M. Eugene Boring et al., eds., *Hellenistic Commentary to the New Testament* (Nashville: Abingdon, 1995), §§ 27–28, and cf. Plato, *Sophist* 218d–222d.

e.g., Exod 3; Isa 6; Jer 1). That Jesus calls his first disciples in pairs already anticipates their being sent out two-by-two (6:7).

[1:17] Jesus' first, paradigmatic words in the Gospel are "Come, follow me."[2] The invitation / command is not to join Jesus in the study of philosophy or the common pursuit of truth, but to join with Jesus himself on the way he is going. Jesus has a "way" (1:3), they are called to walk behind him on this road, but they will not learn the destination until later (see on 8:27–38). Jesus' word is both command and promise. With the words "I will make you into . . ." he takes responsibility for their future transformation. *Poiēsō* ("will make, create") is the first verb in Mark's Bible, occurring frequently in the creation story and in Deutero-Isaiah (e.g., 43:1; 44:2). They must decide whether or not to follow, but when they later become "fishermen for people," it will not be their own achievement.

The fishing metaphor for the act of the gods or of God has a long history in pagan and biblical religion and Jewish tradition, and must not be filled in by modern understandings of fishing.[3] In the Old Testament, such imagery has primarily an ominous, threatening tone and content (cf. Jer 16:16; Ezek 29:4–5; Amos 4:2; Hab 1:14–17; cf. Matt 13:47). At the end of history there will be a great judgment, and the fish will be caught and sorted out. In the Hellenistic world, fishing was a metaphor for teaching, as a skilled teacher fished out good students from the masses. Pagan and Jewish tradition had used the image in a variety of ways, often of the deity's work in history in calling people to a new life, to participate in the god's own saving work. The imagery and connotations are multilayered. Here the meaning may be that God's own judging / saving mission to the world is represented by Jesus, who calls disciples to participate in the divine mission to humanity. This first scene in which the disciples appear is thus utterly theological, not only picturing Jesus' pre-Easter call to certain Galileans, but transparent to the post-Easter situation in which the risen Christ calls disciples and sends them forth. This is not a special call to the exclusive group of the Twelve, which will be narrated in 3:13–19. The "call" vocabulary was often used in early Christianity for the risen Christ's call to discipleship through the preaching of the

---

2. These are Jesus' first words in the mimetic mode of "showing," in which the narrator presents the action directly. Throughout the Gospel, the narrator projects the story directly before the reader's imagination in the mode of mimesis, allowing the audience to see and hear what occurs on the narrative "stage," rather than in the diegetic mode of "telling" in which the action and speech are summarized in the narrator's own words. This distinction, common in modern literary study of narrative, goes back to Plato (*Republic* 392–95).

3. Wilhelm H. Wuellner, *The Meaning of "Fishers of Men"* (Philadelphia: Westminster, 1967). In particular, the fishing portrayed here is labor-intensive, strenuous, and persistent work, involving long hours, often without success (cf. the elaboration of this scene in Luke 5:4–11). The modern image of using bait and a line, passively waiting for fish to be attracted and caught, is completely out of the picture here.

church, so that Christians can be designated simply as "the called" (e.g., Rom 1:6–7; 8:28, 30; 9:24; 1 Cor 1:2, 9, 24; 7:17; 2 Thess 2:14; Heb 9:15; 1 Pet 1:15; 2:21; 3:9; Jude 1; Rev 17:14; 19:9). So also, people can "follow" [*akoloutheō*] Christ "wherever he goes" even after the resurrection (Rev 14:4). The followers of Jesus are not a voluntaristic society for promoting good, but those whose business-as-usual lives have been disrupted by a draft notice.

[1:18] Jesus' first miracle, the first "mighty act," occurs before the startled eyes of readers not anesthetized by familiarity: Jesus calls, and without a word, the fishermen respond and begin to follow. Mark gives no explanation. Common sense longs to fill in this gap. Ancient scholars spoke of Jesus' "divinely compelling face"; a modern scholar speaks of the force of Jesus' "personality."[4] Those who harmonize the Gospels can look to Luke or John, where those called have had an opportunity to observe Jesus' miracles or listen to his teachings.[5] Mark intends to portray the event of the fishermen becoming disciples as wholly the work of Jesus, who works entirely by his powerful word (cf. 1:14). There is no parallel to such an unmotivated call story in ancient literature.

[1:19] The preceding scene is virtually repeated, this time in the diegetic mode. The two brothers are preparing their nets between catches for the next haul. "James" is the anglicized form of the biblical name "Jacob," as "John" represents the biblical name "Johanan." "Son of Zebedee" is not only to distinguish James from the brother of Jesus of the same name, but calls attention to his family that he will leave in order to become a disciple.

[1:20] Jesus *sees* and *calls*, this time using the verb common for the call to Christian discipleship (see above). Jesus chooses, elects; Zebedee and the hired men are not called. It is specifically not the case that Jesus called all and only James and John responded; this would give the credit and responsibility to those who responded, and ignore the divine initiative and grace involved. It is a mistake to try to fit the scene into a psychologically plausible or theologically voluntaristic biographical mode of reporting. Though something like this may have happened during the ministry of Jesus, what we have in Mark's narrative is the paradigmatic representation of the gathering of the Christian community by the call of God in Christ.

James and John likewise drop what they are doing and fall in line behind Jesus, Peter, and Andrew. They leave their father and employees in the boat,

4. Cf. Jerome, *Hom* 83, cited in Thomas C. Oden and Christopher A. Hall, eds., *Mark* (ACCS NT/2; Downers Grove, Ill.: InterVarsity, 1998), 20; Morna D. Hooker, *The Gospel according to Saint Mark* (BNTC; Peabody, Mass.: Hendrickson, 1991), 39.

5. E.g., Theodor Zahn, *Introduction to the New Testament* (trans. John Moore Trout, et al.; 3 vols.; Edinburgh: T. & T. Clark, 1909), 3:306–7; James D. G. Dunn, *The Evidence for Jesus* (Philadelphia: Westminster, 1985), 37. Haenchen's interpretation is to be preferred: "[The Markan story] deals 'only' with the miracle of Jesus' compelling word" (Ernst Haenchen, *Der Weg Jesu* [Berlin: Töpelmann, 1966], 80).

heightening even Elisha's response to the prophetic call of Elijah (cf. 1 Kgs 19:19–21) that had served as something of a model for this narrative. That the fishermen have a boat and employees indicates they are not penniless peasants; they have something to leave, and they leave it. They will later rightly claim to have "left all" (10:28; cf. Luke 5:11). The absoluteness of the claim made upon them and the completeness of their response should not be mitigated by pointing out that elsewhere in the New Testament and later in Mark's own story they seem to still have a house, boat, and family (cf. 1 Cor 9:5; John 21:3; Mark 1:29–31; 3:9; 4:1, etc.). The paradigmatic scene in 1:16–20 is not intended to portray the domestic practicalities of discipleship, but to present the absolute claim of God mediated through Jesus' word, and its effective result.

1:21–34 The Day of the Lord

A new day begins at 1:21—the call of the fishermen could not have been on a Sabbath—and extends through 1:34, with another new day beginning at 1:35. All that Jesus does on this day is salvific and redemptive: he teaches, casts out demons, heals. Mark seems to have created this model day as an example of Jesus' work as such.[6] Mark does not present the reader with a random collection of stories, but illustrates the "day of the Lord," what happens on the human scene when the Lord is present.

> 1:21 And they are entering into Capernaum, and as soon[a] as the Sabbath came, he entered the synagogue and was teaching. 22 And they were amazed at his teaching, for he was teaching them as one who has authority, not like the scribes. 23 Just then, there was in their synagogue a man possessed by an unclean spirit,[b] and he cried out, 24 "What do you have to do with us,[c] Jesus of Nazareth? Have you come to destroy us?[d] I know who you are, the Holy One of God." 25 And Jesus rebuked it,[e] saying "Silence!" and "Come out of him!" 26 And the unclean spirit threw him into convulsions, let out a loud scream, and came out of him. 27 And all were amazed, so that an intense discussion ensued, as they kept asking each other, "What is this? A new teaching, and with authority! He even commands the unclean spirits, and they obey him." 28 And immediately the report about him went out everywhere, into all the surrounding region of Galilee.

6. Schenke, *Wundererzählungen*, 109–18, argues 1:29–39 is built on pre-Markan traditions that had already been combined into a unit, introduced by 1:21a, to which Mark only adds the introductory exorcism 1:21b–28. It has often been argued that the material derives from eyewitness testimony (e.g., Haenchen, *Der Weg Jesu*, 89), or even directly from Peter (e.g., Taylor, *Mark*, 178). If so, the transmission is not direct; layers of church tradition lie between the events themselves and Markan redaction (see Introduction 4.).

1:29 And they came out of the synagogue and went directly into the house of Simon and Andrew, with James and John. 30 And Simon's mother-in-law was lying sick with a fever, and they immediately tell Jesus about her. 31 And he came up and grasped her hand and raised her up,^f and the fever left her, and she served^g them.

1:32 Now when evening came, after the sun had set, people were bringing to Jesus all who were sick and those possessed by demons. 33 And the whole town formed a congregation^h at the door. 34 And he healed many of those sick with various diseases, and cast out many demons, and he would not permit the demons to speak, because they knew him.^i

a. This periphrastic phrase here renders the ubiquitous and flexible term *euthys* (see on 1:10), rendered "just then" in v. 23.

b. Literally "in" an unclean spirit. While the Greek *en* ("in") may be a Semitism, a remnant of the story's origin in Aramaic, to Mark's Hellenistic audience it would suggest that the man is actually engulfed in the demonic power of evil, an apt portrayal of the human situation apart from the kingdom of God. Cf. 12:36 *en tō pneumati tō hagiō*, "in the Holy Spirit." "Unclean spirit" (six times in Mark) is Mark's distinctive term, found in each of his exorcism stories.

c. *Ti hēmin kai soi*, lit. "what [is there that is both] to us and to you," i.e., "what do we have in common" (cf. Judg 11:12; 1 Kgs 17:18; Mark 5:7; John 2:4).

d. Since there was no punctuation in the ancient manuscripts, the words can be punctuated as a statement, "You have come to destroy us," or as in most English translations, as continuing the preceding question.

e. The Greek *autō* can be either masculine or neuter, here translated "it" to refer to the spirit as the object of Jesus' command.

f. *Ēgeiren* is the same word used for Jesus' resurrection, not his "rising," but his being-raised by God. The translation should preserve this image of Jesus lifting her up (as in, e.g., NRSV) rather than her "rising" of her own accord or being assisted by Jesus (vs. "helped her up" as in NAB, NJB, NIV, TEV, CEV).

g. *Diēkonei*, like *diēkonoun* of 1:13, is from *diakoneō*, and can be translated "serve" or "minister."

h. *Episynēgmenē* is related to the word for synagogue. Mark uses it elsewhere only at 13:27. Cf. the related noun at 2 Thess 2:1; Heb 10:25.

i. Some MSS, including B L W θ *f*¹, append some form of "to be the Christ," but this is an obvious secondary reading probably derived from the parallel Luke 4:41. The shorter reading above is attested by ℵ* A and most later MSS, and as the more difficult reading, it is clearly original.

[1:21–28] The Jewish fishing town of Capernaum will become the center of Jesus' ministry in Galilee—not his hometown Nazareth (1:9; 6:1–6), and not the Hellenistic cities of Sepphoris (only four miles from Nazareth) or Tiberias on the southwest shore of the Sea of Galilee, neither of which Jesus is ever reported as entering. The description of the synagogue as "their" synagogue, here as in 1:39, may serve only to designate it to Mark's primarily Gentile readership as a Jewish synagogue in a region somewhat removed from the readers' own, but may also convey a certain aloofness, a distancing overtone—compare the narrator's rather dissociating reference to "the Jews" in 7:3. Nonetheless, as a faithful Jew Jesus attends the synagogue as a matter of course on his first Sabbath in town, and avails himself of the opportunity to teach, a right belonging to all adult Jewish males. In practice, however, "teaching" had become the function of rabbis and scribes (see *Excursus: Jesus the Teacher vs. the Scribes* at 7:23), and visitors preached only at the invitation of the leader of the synagogue (cf. Acts 13:14–16). As in the case of the exorcism to follow, Jesus does not wait for invitation or challenge, but takes the initiative.

Verses 21–28 should be considered one paragraph. This opening scene is composed by Mark as the first of the Markan intercalations (see on 5:21). Jesus' authoritative new teaching forms the framework and main theme (cf. 22, 27) within which an exorcism story is inserted, with the result that the response to the *exorcism* is the acclamation of a new *teaching*.[7] It is not the content of Jesus' teaching that is important for Mark, nor is it his manner of teaching, as though he taught vigorously and forcefully, while the scribes taught timidly. Rather, the focus is on the authority of Jesus as such, an authority to which the demonic world is already subject. Exorcism is not a separate, parallel aspect of Jesus' ministry alongside "teaching" and "healing," but is inseparably incorporated into Jesus message. "Authority" (*exousia*) is found nine times in Mark, always with reference to Jesus (not attributed even to John the Baptist, despite 11:28–33), and conferred on the disciples (3:15; 6:7). The same powerful word that calls people to discipleship (1:16–20) is present in Jesus' teaching with authority and conquest of the demonic element in human life (1:21–28), all of which is an aspect of the word of the dawning kingdom of God (1:14–15). Of course, for Judaism and early Christianity, God was the ultimate authority; the issue was how God's authority is mediated. In Judaism, the divine authority is mediated by the Torah, which then must be interpreted through debate and voting by qualified scholars. For Mark, God's authority is mediated by the word of Jesus, who simply pronounces.[8]

It is not incidental that among the Gospels only Mark chooses an encounter with the demonic power of evil as the opening scene of Jesus' ministry.[9] The

7. It is historically unlikely that a demoniac would be present in the synagogue service (cf. 5:1–5). It is Mark who has brought the exorcism story into the framework of Jesus' teaching in order to clamp together teaching and exorcism as dual manifestations of Jesus' authority.

8. Modern sensitivities, especially American, are often bothered by such claims to authority. Popular affirmations of Jesus as Lord are sometimes hardly aware that Jesus does not speak in the mode of "May I suggest . . . ," "It seems to me that . . . ," or "Perhaps you might want to consider. . . ."

9. Cf. James M. Robinson, *The Problem of History in Mark and Other Marcan Studies* (Philadelphia: Fortress, 1982), 81–90. Mark not only portrays Jesus' ministry as exorcising a few demoniacs in Galilee, but as the Christ-event in which a cosmic battle is fought and won; cf. Marcus, *Mark 1–8*, 72–73.

unclean spirit[10] (in contrast to Jesus as the *Holy One of God* who has been filled with the Holy Spirit, 1:10, 24) represents every manifestation of evil—sickness, sin, death—and the whole kingdom of evil. The scene thus concentrates into one incident God's act in Christ that overcomes the enslaving demonic power, and it is understandable that in Markan terms to willfully misunderstand this work of God is related to the one unpardonable sin (3:28–30). In addition to the four individual accounts of exorcisms (1:21–28; 5:1–20; 7:24–30; 9:14–29), Mark makes them a prominent part of his summaries of Jesus' ministry (1:32–34, 39; 3:11–12; cf. 3:22–30; [absent 6:53–56]), and includes power over demons in Jesus' commission to his disciples (3:15; 6:7, 13; cf. 9:38–39).

Though addressed by Jesus in the singular (v. 25) and referred to by the narrator as one demon (v. 26), the unclean spirit refers repeatedly to "us" (v. 24), and the crowd also speaks of "the unclean spirits" in the plural (v. 27). This is not because a horde of demons inhabits the poor man; it indicates that in this initial paradigmatic event Jesus encounters the whole demonic world. The possessed man does not seek Jesus out, does not ask for aid. He is helpless. Jesus takes the initiative and is not reactive but on the attack as the leading edge of the coming kingdom of God. The demons are on the defensive, knowing in fact that they are already beaten. Their immediate challenge, "What do you have to do with us?" is not an informational question, nor a confession of the ontological difference separating them from Jesus; the issue is a matter of jurisdiction, of realms of authority. They recognize Jesus as the representative of God's dawning kingdom. The "Holy One of God" points to Jesus as the one filled with the Holy Spirit (rather than the unholy spirit of the demons), and to the divine title used for God thirty times in Isaiah, the key Old Testament book to which Mark orients his narrative (see on 1:2). Jesus will challenge the conventional purity system, but not as an unholy violator of God's sacred realm. He is God's agent of holiness, himself authorized both to violate traditional boundaries and draw new, clear lines.[11] Over against the scribes stands the one who teaches with authority; over against the unholy spirits that plague humanity stands the Holy One of God. In the pre-Markan form of the story, that the demons know Jesus' name and identity is part of their self-defense mechanism in the presence of the exorcist: knowing the adversary's identity and pronouncing his name gives power. Jesus commands the demon to be silent, preventing it from using its knowledge as an apotropaic force. In the larger Markan story, this is one of the elements of Mark's messianic secret important to his theological framework (see *Excursus: The Messianic Secret* at 9:13). At the level of the Markan nar-

---

10. Mark uses "unclean spirit" (eleven times) interchangeably with "demon" (seven times). "Unclean" is not, of course, a matter of hygiene, but of ritual purity. The unholy spirit stands over against the Holy Spirit.

11. Cf. Jerome H. Neyrey, "The Idea of Purity in Mark's Gospel," *Semeia* 36 (1986): 91–128.

rative, the demon's "disclosure" of Jesus' identity has no effect; it is as though the participants in the story had not heard it. They are impressed but do not perceive Jesus' true identity (1:27).

Jesus operates entirely by his powerful word. There is only his *rebuke* and his *command*. The "rebuke" (*epetimēsen*), though common in New Testament exorcisms, is not found in Hellenistic exorcism stories. Its background is related to the divine rebuke of evil powers in the Old Testament (cf. Pss 9:5; 68:30; 106:9; 119:21; Zech 3:2).[12] There are no incantations, no magic words, no props, no ceremonies or rituals. It is also important to see that there is no struggle. From the very first, Jesus stands before a defeated enemy, an enemy that *knows* it is defeated. The reader begins to perceive that, though the demonic powers continue to have influence, Jesus is already the victor, already anticipating 3:23–27. In military terms, this is not the "opening battle" but the "mopping up exercise." Though the forces of evil still occupy much territory, Satan is present only as a vanquished opponent. It is not merely that the eschatological battle is here joined, but from Mark's post-Easter perspective the decisive battle has already been fought and the victory can already be celebrated. When "all" speak of a "new teaching" thus manifested, the Markan point is not novelty but the eschatological renewal of creation (see on 2:21–22). As elsewhere, the characters in the story do not and cannot (yet) see what the readers see. They are amazed, but amazement is not faith.[13]

[1:29–34] Visitors to Capernaum today are struck by the fact that when exiting the excavated ruins of a fourth- or fifth-century synagogue built on the site of a first-century synagogue, they "immediately" see the excavated ruins of a first-century house. This dwelling apparently had served as a meeting place for Christians in the late first century and was incorporated into a church building of the fourth or fifth century. A plausible case has been made that this was the house of Simon Peter.[14] While the story from pre-Markan tradition may well reflect such historical data, Mark's own point more likely echoes the theological history of the church for which he writes: from synagogue beginnings to the house churches

12. Though it goes too far to say with Joachim Gnilka, *Das Evangelium nach Markus* (EKK NT; 2 vols.; Zürich: Benziger, 1978, 1979), 1:81, that here "Jesus steps in Yahweh's place," it is correct to see Mark's language as evoking the image of God acting in Jesus. Cf. Howard Clark Kee, "The Terminology of Mark's Exorcism Stories," *NTS* 14 (1968).

13. Even so, Mark does not deprecate this response. The synagogue congregation cannot perceive Jesus identity, but their response to his authority is authentic. K. Tagawa argues that the amazement (v. 22 *ekplēssomai*, v. 27 *thambeō*) typical of Hellenistic miracle stories as response to the miracle of a divine being is reinterpreted by Mark as a response to the life and work of Jesus as a whole, his existence as such. See *Miracles et Évangile, la pensée personnelle de l'évangéliste Marc* (EHPR 62; Paris: Presses universitaires de France, 1966), 92, 121.

14. See, e.g., Bellarmino Bagatti, *The Church from the Circumcision: History and Archaeology of the Judaeo-Christians* (trans. Eugene Hoade; SBF Smaller Series 2; Jerusalem: Franciscan Press, 1971); J. F. Strange and H. Shanks, "Has the House Where Jesus Stayed in Capernaum Been Found?" *BAR* 8 (1982): 26–37.

of the readers' own time. Jesus meets with his disciples in a house in 2:1; 3:20; 7:17, 24; 9:28, 33; 10:10 (cf. also 3:31–35; 4:10–12). Eventually, after the destruction of the temple, this "house" will become the "house of prayer for all nations," the place of healing, table fellowship, and instruction of disciples.

"Lying sick with a fever" does not sound critical to modern ears, but in the ancient world fever was not regarded as a symptom, but as itself a deadly power. The situation here portrayed is life-threatening. In addition, the woman is robbed of status and dignity, unable to offer hospitality in her own home. They tell Jesus of her malady, more likely to excuse her conduct than as a request for healing—Jesus has as yet performed no healings in Mark. Jesus again takes the (divine) initiative, approaches her, grasps her hand (cf. 5:41; *touching* is all that is needed for healing, 5:23, 27–28), and raises her (*ēgeirein*, the same word used in the accounts of Jesus' resurrection; cf. also 2:9, 11; 3:3; 9:27; 10:49). As in the preceding exorcism, but in contrast to the stereotyped practices of ancient healers, there are no techniques, rituals, or magic words. The fever "leaves" her, like the unclean spirit of 1:25 and the leprosy of 1:42.[15] Mark says nothing about her faith or that of the disciples. Jesus does not pray, but acts with sovereign authority. As the fever had represented the leading edge of death, the story represents the leading edge of the divine power at work in Jesus' resurrection. Mark's comment that the woman rises up and immediately serves them can be understood at two levels. On the one hand, she serves them a meal. While for contemporary sensitivities this may smack of first-century patriarchy and the servility of women, in Mark's own context this means that she is now restored to fullness of life, that she can serve guests in her own home, which she had been prevented from doing by the devastating fever. On the other hand, the word for "serve" (*diakoneō*) is resonant throughout Mark with the overtones of Christian ministry. Jesus was served by angels (1:13), he himself has come to serve (10:45), and the Gospel will conclude with a remembrance of the women followers of Jesus in Galilee who had served him (15:41; the same phrase is used in Acts 19:22 for Paul's coministers Timothy and Erastus, and in Rom 15:25 of Paul's own ministry). The cognate noun *diakonos* ("servant," "minister") in 9:35 and 10:43 designates the ministry of Jesus' male disciples. In ministering to Jesus and the disciples, this woman who has been healed and raised by Jesus performs a ministry to the nascent church, analogous to later pastoral ministry.[16] In all this, Mark narrates with a knowing look to the post-Easter reader, but the full meaning of the event is lost on the characters in the story.

15. The point is not lost on Luke, who adds that Jesus "rebuked" the fever (Luke 4:39) as though it were a demonic power (cf. notes on Mark 1:25).

16. So, e.g., Elizabeth Moltmann-Wendel, "Mit der Schwiegermutter fing alles an: Petrus und die Frauen," in *Petrus, der Fels des Anstoßes* (ed. Raul Niemann; Stuttgart: Kreuz, 1994), 12–20, and Susan Miller, *Women in Mark's Gospel* (JSNTSup 259; London: T. & T. Clark, 2004), 164–66.

Mark's characteristic double expression in verse 32[17] is his clarification that the setting of the sun officially signaled the conclusion of the Sabbath, so that the townspeople could bring all the sick and afflicted to the house where Jesus healed in the presence of his disciples. All the preceding activities, including exorcism and healing, had occurred on the Sabbath, but for the moment Mark withholds making any point of this; the salvific picture of the "day of the Lord" is his focus on this paradigmatic day. He reserves its problematic character for contemporary religion for the next section (cf. 2:23–3:6). Although Mark presents all sickness as having a demonic aspect, he here distinguishes "sick" and "demon possessed" —showing that he does not superstitiously regard all sickness as caused by demons. He brackets them together as symbolizing all the threats to a full life, and can elsewhere embrace all Jesus' healing ministry as "casting out demons" (1:39). Mark's alternation of "all" and "many" does not mean that they brought all the sick and Jesus healed a lot of them, but not all. The semitizing use of "many" is here not exclusive (many-not-all) but inclusive (many-not-few), as in 10:45—all were brought, he healed them, and there were many of them.[18] As in 1:24–25 which is here echoed, Jesus' prohibiting the demons from speaking "because they knew him" represents both his sovereign power in overcoming their defensive tactics and, at the comprehensive Markan narrative level, as expression of the messianic secret (see *Excursus: The Messianic Secret* at 9:13).

1:35–39 Ministry in All Galilee

This brief section weaves together important Markan concerns: presence and absence of Jesus, the purpose of Jesus' "coming," the disciples' commitment to and misunderstanding of Jesus, the lure of resting on past success and the call of future mission, Jesus' ministry of word and deed, and the divine / human character of the person of Jesus himself. The whole pericope is vaguely reminiscent of the Easter story of 16:1–8: here too it is a Sunday, very early (*prōi*, *lian* are common to both accounts), Jesus "rises," leaving the disciples behind. They are distressed at his absence, but are directed to the mission that lies before them. He goes before them into Galilee (14:28; 16:7). This is not to suggest that the story is an allegory of the resurrection, but that all the events of Jesus' ministry are seen in the light of Easter and that the narrative as a whole is shaped by the resurrection faith. The high point of the pericope is Jesus' declaration of the purpose of his "coming" in verse 38.

1:35 And very early the next morning, while it was still dark, Jesus arose, left the house, and went away to a deserted, wilderness place, where he

---

17. Cf. Neirynck, *Duality in Mark*.
18. Cf. Joachim Jeremias, *"polloi,"* in *TDNT*, 6:540–42.

was praying. **36** And Simon and those with him pursued him[a] **37** and found him, and say to him, "Everybody is looking for you!" **38** And he says to them, "Let us go elsewhere, into the neighboring market towns, so that I may preach there too. For it was for this reason that I have come." **39** And he went, preaching in their synagogues in the whole of Galilee, and casting out demons.

a. *Katedioxen* may have a slightly hostile overtone, "tracked him down," but need not. I have translated it with "pursue," which has roughly the same ambiguity in English.

[1:35] Jesus rises early, leaves house and town, and goes to a lonely "wilderness" spot to pray. This is the first reference to prayer in the Gospel. Jesus will also depart to pray alone in 6:46, again after a day of miracles, and at the end of the narrative in the paradigmatic Gethsemane scene of 14:32–39. He instructs the disciples to pray in 11:24–25 and 13:18, and criticizes the scribes for praying hypocritically (12:40). The content of Jesus' prayer is not given, nor his reasons. There is no indication that he is praying for power to do more miracles, as though his spiritual batteries, drained by the intensity of the preceding day, needed recharging. Nor is it merely as an example to the disciples, a reminder of the need for "quiet time." Mark's point seems rather to be christological: Jesus has been acting with sovereign divine power, healing and casting out demons on his own authority. In the preceding scenes, he does not pray *to* God but acts *as* God. He will be criticized for appearing to set himself in the place of God (2:7). But divine beings do not pray. Mark here juxtaposes the picture of the weak human being and the preceding picture of the powerful Son of God, so that already in these opening scenes there is a mini-summary of the Gospel as a whole: the "day in Capernaum" anticipates the powerful Jesus of chapters 1–8; the lonely prayer already portrays the weak human Jesus of 9–15, culminating in Gethsemane and cross.

[1:36–38] The men of the small group, not yet designated "disciples," are identified as "Simon (not yet 'Peter') and those with him." He was called first, is the leader and spokesperson for the group throughout, and will be singled out in the postresurrection assignment of 16:7.

Just as Mark does not explicate the reason(s) for Jesus' prayer, so the motives behind the disciples' pursuit of Jesus are left for the reader to fill in, a miniature of the stance of the narrative as a whole, which is open, unfinished, left for involved readers to complete. In the light of the Gospel as a whole, it is likely that here we have the first instance of the disciples' misunderstanding, which will deepen and intensify as the story develops: they want Jesus to *stay*, he is determined to *go elsewhere*. They want more miracles, he wants to preach. They want to go back to Capernaum, where he and they have enjoyed success. He wants to go ahead to the mission that awaits him, "elsewhere" (*allachou*, only here in the

New Testament).[19] As portrayed by Mark, the healings and exorcisms of the previous day are not local, individual episodes, but each points beyond itself to a universal need and mission. The single demon refers to "us," the demonic realm. "All" congregate at the door. Now, "all" are looking for him. There is no suggestion here that to respond to Jesus in the light of the miracles of the preceding day is an inadequate response of "miracle mongers" who only perceive Jesus as a "magician" or "divine man." Here, the contrast is not between miracles and the cross, or miracles and ministry of the word, but between the localized and a universal mission. That "everyone is looking for you" means for Peter and those with him a return to the success of the preceding day. But Jesus is not a "great *man*," who will bask in the favor of those who have marveled at his achievements. He is the proclaimer and agent of the kingdom of *God*, and he knows that the miracles point beyond themselves to the universal reign of God that is dawning. He knows that preaching has priority over miracles; the Markan church is commissioned to continue *preaching*, whether or not it experiences miracles. He must thus preach "*elsewhere*," because "It was for this reason that I have come." Like much else in Mark, this can be heard at the pedestrian level: "This is why I left the house early and came out here." Like much else in Mark, this can be heard with the deeper overtones of the meaning and purpose of Jesus' advent as a whole, resonant in Mark's other "I have come" saying in 2:17 (cf. also 1:24; 4:3; 10:45; connections with the resurrection story of 16:1–8), and explicitly developed in the Fourth Gospel.[20] The disciples have been called to follow, but they are still in Capernaum, still at home. Now they want Jesus to follow them back to Capernaum, but Jesus is propelled forward and outward, "elsewhere." They follow.

[1:39] The saving power of God that is present in Jesus' ministry and illustrated by the "day of the Lord" in Capernaum is extended to all Galilee, and summarized as preaching and casting out demons. As the following story makes clear, this does not exclude healings and other saving acts. All Jesus' proclamation can be summarized as the announcement of the dawning of God's kingdom and the response this calls for (1:14–15). All Jesus' acts can be summarized as the expulsion of demonic powers from people's lives. The hidden victory of 1:12–13 is becoming manifest.

1:40–45 The Cleansing of the Leper

This pericope is a further transition from pictures of Jesus' saving acts that have received an entirely positive response in 1:21–39 to the controversy section

19. This "elsewhere" becomes a thematic image of the boundary-crossing mission of Jesus. Cf. Broadhead, *Mark*, 26, 50, 61.

20. John 8:14; 9:39; 10:10; 12:27; 15:22; cf. Eduardo Arens, *The* HΛΘON *Sayings in the Synoptic Tradition: A Historico-critical Investigation* (OBO 10; Freiburg: Universitätsverlag, 1976), 272.

2:1–3:6. On the one hand, it is a retrospective illustration that the preceding "everyone" is meant seriously, including even those excluded from society by leprosy. On the other hand, the story has a prospective view, showing in advance Jesus' respect for law, temple, and priesthood.

The story is paradigmatic, with no reference to a particular time, place, or person. The leper is not named; the disciples are not mentioned. The story typifies the saving act of God in Jesus.

1:40 And a leper[a] comes to him, begging him and bowing before him, saying, "If you are willing, you are able to cleanse me." 41 Jesus[b] became angry,[c] stretched out his hand, touched him, and says, "I am willing. Be cleansed." 42 And immediately the leprosy left him, and he was cleansed. 43 And Jesus[b] stormed at him[d] and thrust him out[e] 44 and says to him, "See that you say nothing to anyone, but go, show yourself to the priest, and offer the sacrifices prescribed by Moses appropriate for your cleansing, as a testimony to them." 45 But he went out and began to proclaim openly and everywhere,[f] and to spread the word, so that Jesus[b] was no longer able to enter publicly into a town, but stayed out in the deserted places. And people were coming to him from all over the place.

a. Instead of a more accurate and sensitive translation such as "a person with a scabby skin disease," the traditional translation of *lepros* as "leper" is here retained. Despite its medical inaccuracy and contemporary sensitivity regarding referring to afflicted persons only in terms of their maladies, "leper" preserves the revulsion, hopelessness, and social ostracization inherent in Mark's term taken from the LXX.[21]

b. Here and in vv. 43 and 45, the name "Jesus," which does not occur in this pericope, has been added for clarity. From 1:40b through 1:45, both Jesus and the leper are referred to by pronouns, with subject and direct object distinguished only by context.

c. Most MSS read *splagchnistheis*, "having compassion," and the reading is followed by most English translations (REB is an exception). Most commentators, however, regard *orgistheis*, "having become angry," as original, though found only in D a ff² r¹ Ephraem, since it is the more difficult reading. A change from "being angry" to "having compassion" is readily explained, but not vice versa. Both Matthew and Luke simply omit the troublesome word.

d. *Embrimēsamenos* can mean "snorting" (in indignation) as in 14:5; John 11:33, 38; "sternly order" as Matt 9:30.

e. *Exebalen*, the same word used of the Spirit's powerful thrusting of Jesus into the wilderness in 1:12 and Jesus' own casting out of evil spirits (e.g., 1:34, 39).

f. *Polla*, adverbial use of the common word for "much, many," often used simply to intensify the action of the verb (e.g., 3:12, "sternly warned"; 5:10, 23, "earnestly"; 5:38, "loudly"; 5:43, "strictly"; 6:23, "in all seriousness"; 9:26, "terribly"; 15:3, "solemnly").

21. While there are no real modern analogies to such understandings of ritual defilement, one thinks of the way HIV patients are often regarded in contemporary society.

[1:40] During Jesus' wider ministry in Galilee, a person afflicted with leprosy takes the initiative to come to him. The biblical term is not identical with leprosy in the modern sense (Hansen's disease), but covers a variety of skin diseases, several of them curable and noncritical, as well as scaly fungal growths that can infect plants, houses, and clothing. It is clear, however, that Mark thinks of the plight of the afflicted man in terms of Lev 13–14, where "leprosy" is physically and socially a living death that renders the person ritually unclean (Lev 13:45–46: "He shall live alone. . . . He shall wear torn clothes . . . he shall cover his upper lip and cry out 'Unclean, unclean.'"). The Mishnah tractate *Negaim* provides extensive discussion and regulations, comparing its healing to resurrection from the dead. In accord with biblical and Jewish usage, the man asks for "cleansing" (not "healing"), which will not only restore him physically but give him his life back by reinstating him in society. While the word "faith" is not used (2:5 is its first occurrence in Mark), the man is convinced that Jesus is able to cleanse him. He makes no confession or claims, uses no christological titles, but makes his fate dependent on Jesus' willingness. Jesus is willing.

[1:41–43] Jesus is not only willing and able, but also angry (reading *orgistheis,* see note *c* above). Mark's lack of explanation of the reason for Jesus' anger has been filled in by the speculations of interpreters, which have included Jesus' irritation at having his preaching ministry interrupted or his anticipation of the man's disobedience to his command to silence. Such explanatory attempts based on reconstructing Jesus' psychological response to a literal 30 C.E. scene are off-target. More cogently, others have argued on the basis of the history of the tradition Mark incorporates that the story retains traces of an earlier portrayal of Jesus as a Hellenistic miracle worker who snorts and growls as a result of the divine spirit at work within him (see on 7:31–37). At the level of the Markan narrative, the reader should more likely ponder Jesus' divine anger at the power of evil that dominates the human scene and resists the kingdom of God he embodies and proclaims, a response analogous to the "storming at him" of verse 43 and the "sighing" of 7:34 (cf. also John 11:33, 38 and Jesus "weeping" in John 11:35). While leprosy was rarely associated with demon possession in Jesus' or Mark's context, Mark tends to categorize everything that threatens the fullness of life intended by God, whether sickness or "natural" evil such as storms, as part of the demonic kingdom, so that the cleansing of the leper has overtones of Jesus' confrontation with demonic evil—Jesus "casts out" the man (v. 43),[22] and the leprosy "leaves" him (v. 42), as though leprosy is an evil, objective power from which Jesus liberates. Jesus touches the man (in contrast to 2 Kgs 5:10), but does not thereby become ritually unclean: his cleansing power overcomes the man's uncleanness, and purity replaces ritual

---

22. Here the "casting out" is positive, as when the Spirit thrusts Jesus out into the wilderness in 1:12, but the exorcistic and violent overtone is still present.

defilement (cf. 1 Cor 7:12–14). Jesus words "Be cleansed" (not "I cleanse you") are a divine passive, with God as the hidden actor.

[**1:44**] In accord with biblical and Jewish law (Lev 13:49; 14:2–4), Jesus commands the healed man to go immediately to the priest and be certified that he has been cleansed of ritual defilement and can reenter society. This is to be done "as a testimony to them," which probably means not only official evidence to the priests and the public at large that he has been cleansed, but testimony to Jesus' and his followers' respect for the law. The stance of the Markan Jesus toward the law is nuanced and dialectical (see on 7:1–23). Even though John the Baptist has conferred God's forgiveness without the temple apparatus of priesthood and sacrifice (1:4), and Jesus has both taught on his own authority without citing the law and healed on the Sabbath in violation of the law (1:21–31), nothing has been made of it. In the next section, Jesus will be accused of violating both the written law and the Jewish tradition (2:1–3:6, esp. 2:23–3:2). By placing this story here, Mark makes a preemptive strike at the accusations to come. Moses, priests, and sacrifice are here affirmed. The law itself, including its regulations about the exclusion of lepers from society, is not merely narrow-minded exclusiveness or bigotry but a testimony to God's will and safeguard for community life, and it is to be respected. Jesus respects it, his challengers need to know this in advance, and his followers need to respect it too. Just what this means for Mark's readers is not clear, and requires further development in the following stories (2:1–3:6; 7:1–23).

Jesus also commands the man to "say nothing to anyone." On the surface, the command is as strange as that of 5:43 and as difficult to imagine being kept: restoration to society is the point and purpose of the man's cleansing; if he keeps quiet about it, the healing has been in vain. But in the comprehensive Markan narrative where the dialect of secrecy and openness plays a crucial role, this command functions at a deeper level. The tension between proclamation and silence runs throughout Mark (see *Excursus: The Messianic Secret* at 9:13).

[**1:45**] Despite Jesus' command, the healed man begins to proclaim the good news of what has happened to him (cf. 5:20; 7:36). The vocabulary reflects the early Christian mission: *kēryssō* (preach, announce, proclaim) is the standard term for proclamation of the gospel (e.g., 13:10; 14:9), and *logos* (word, message) is its content (e.g., seven times in 4:14–20). Though it violates the chronological and narrative framework of the messianic secret, the man is portrayed in post-Easter terms as a missionary of the Christian faith: those liberated and restored by God's power at work in Jesus cannot keep silence, they have been liberated for service in the Christian mission and must offer their own testimony; the "them" of verse 44 embraces the readers as well. The logic is rhetorical rather than that of linear narrative. The command to silence accentuates the explosive nature of the gospel itself, which must come to expression. Mark shares the view that the gospel-embodied-in-miracle-stories *generates* authentic Christian proclamation, though this can be done only within the framework of the narrative that climaxes in cross and resurrection.

2:1–3:6 Authority and Conflict

The preceding section has presented Jesus in triumphal terms, in conflict with the cosmic powers of evil, but without opposition on the human level—except for a mere hint of the disciples' misunderstanding. Now, resistance and conflict emerge in each of five stories, which are not randomly assembled but arranged to form a major literary unit of the narrative. This arrangement is topical, and does not reflect different periods in Jesus' ministry, as though he proceeded idyllically through Galilee for a while (1:39–45), and then had a series of conflicts all at once (2:1–3:6). There are clear markers that set the section off from what precedes and follows: (1) Conflict surfaces in the first story, continues throughout, reaches its climax in 3:6 with the resolution to destroy Jesus, but then all but disappears until Jesus arrives in Jerusalem. (2) "Son of Man" as a self-designation of Jesus emerges (2:10, 28), and then disappears until the first passion prediction in 8:31. These two sayings are the only sayings in Mark that present Jesus as acting with the authority of the Son of Man during his earthly life. (3) There is no overt expression of the messianic secret in this section. (4) The whole section seems to take place in Capernaum, beginning abruptly with Jesus' entrance into the town itself, an awkward transition from the statement in 1:45. (5) The next section begins with a summary of Jesus' activity that could join seamlessly to 1:45. (6) Each of the stories has the same general form of a pronouncement story in which the powerful word of Jesus settles the issue. (7) The five stories of the section not only manifest a common theme but fit together into a tightly woven structure:

> A. *The Healing of the Paralytic / Forgiveness of Sin*   (2:1–12)
> B. *The Call of Levi / Eating with Sinners*   (2:13–17)
> C. *The Question about Fasting / Old and New*   (2:18–22)
> B¹. *Plucking Grain on the Sabbath*   (2:23–28)
> A¹. *Healing on the Sabbath / Doing Good or Evil*   (3:1–6)

The section as a whole is structured on the A B C B¹ A¹ pattern, with A corresponding to A¹, B to B¹, and the central C element providing the hermeneutical key for the section as a whole:[23] A and B are connected by the theme of sin /

---

23. Persuasively argued by Joanna Dewey, *Markan Public Debate: Literary Technique, Concentric Structure and Theology in Mark 2:1–3:6* (SBLDS 48; Chico, Calif.: Scholars Press, 1980), esp. 109–30. The arrangement has some problematic aspects, but Mark was not composing freely; his arranging and adapting traditional elements leave some rough edges in the basic chiastic arrangement he has created.

sinners, while A¹ and B¹ are related by the issue of Sabbath observance. C is not related to either, and thus can be seen as standing at the center as the central focus of the whole structure. The contents of this central story lend plausibility to this arrangement: there is the contrast between old and new, with the time of Jesus' presence as the pivotal period; that Jesus himself makes the declaration of the time of the bridegroom's presence is exceptional, as is Jesus' predicting his being taken away.

2:1–12 Healing and Forgiveness

2:1 And several days later, after he had again entered Capernaum, people heard that he was in the house.ᵃ **2** And so many were gathered together that there was no longer room for them, not even at the door. And he was speaking the word to them. **3** And people come, bringing to him a paralyzed man carried by four people. **4** And since they were not able to bring him in because of the crowd, they dug through the roof over the place where Jesus was, and when they had made an opening they lower the mat on which the paralytic was lying. **5** And when Jesus saw their faith, he says to the paralytic, "Child,ᵇ your sins are forgiven."ᶜ **6** And some of the scribes were sitting there, questioning in their hearts, **7** "How can this fellow say such a thing? He is blaspheming! Who can forgive sins except the one God?" **8** And Jesus knew immediately in his spirit what they were thinking and says to them, "Why are you thinking this in your hearts? **9** Which is easier, to say to the paralytic, 'Your sins are forgiven,' or to say 'Rise up, and take your mat and walk?' **10** But that you may know that the Son of Man has authority on earth to forgive sins"ᵈ—he says to the paralyzed man—**11** "I say to you, Rise up, take your mat and go home." **12** And he arose,ᵉ and immediately took up his mat and went out while everyone was watching, so that all were amazed and glorified God, saying, "We have never seen anything like this."

a. *En oikō*, lit. "in a house," is the standard Greek phrase for "at home" (cf. German *zu Hause*) and is often so translated. Yet the more literal rendering enables the modern reader to hear the overtone present for the original Markan readers, who gathered in house churches to hear the word.

b. *Teknon*, the generic word for a child without regard to age or gender, can be used in specific contexts to mean "son" or "my son" or "my dear son," as often in English translations (cf., e.g., Luke 15:31). In 10:24 Jesus addresses his disciples with this term of endearment, which also connotes membership in the "children of Israel," the people of God.

c. Present tense *aphientai* "are [being] forgiven" is read in B, 28, 33, 565, 1241, 2427, and a few other MSS, plus the Latin tradition and later translations. The perfect *apheōntai* "have been forgiven" is read in ℵ A C D K L W and most of the later tradition, probably representing a harmonization with Luke 5:20. Mark's Greek usage does not typically distinguish between these two forms. In either case, for Mark, Jesus is represented as acting in God's place, forgiving sins, rather than in the role of a priest, who declares that God has forgiven sins—as is made clear by the scribes' response.

d. Some scholars have argued that the first clause of v. 10 is an editorial aside to the reader (like 13:14),[24] which would call for a different punctuation (the ancient MSS, of course, were without punctuation). The majority construal adopted here assumes that the second clause, "he says to the paralyzed man," is editorial, and that in v. 10a Jesus addresses the scribes, while in 10b the author addresses the reader.

e. Though sounding a bit quaint in English, "arose" translates *ēgerthē*, corresponding to *egeire* ("rise") of Jesus' command, in both cases reflecting the language of death / resurrection, as in 3:3–4, 5:41–42, and elsewhere in the miracle stories. The passive verb is lit. "was raised," but the form is often used intransitively as a synonym of *anistēmi*. (Cf. notes on 1:31, 35–39, 40; 2:11–12, 14, and commentary on 8:33.)

An original miracle story in typical form has been expanded by adding elements of a controversy dialogue concerning Jesus' announcement of forgiveness of sins and divine authority as Son of Man, thereby shifting the focus of the whole.[25] There can be no doubt that the historical Jesus performed acts of healing and announced God's forgiveness. However, several observations indicate that this story is not merely a report of a particular incident. (1) The form of the story is that of a typical Markan intercalation (see on 5:21), with the insertion of the secondary element marked by the repeated *legei tō paralytikō* (vv. 5, 10, "he says to the paralytic"). (2) The details of the scene are difficult to imagine historically. Hostile scribes are present among the small group in the house, while crowds of sincere inquirers stand outside. Jesus seems to continue his teaching undistracted by the clamor and noise as the men dig a hole through the mud and straw thatch roof, and his hearers seem not to notice either. (3) No one in the narrative has raised a protest against John the Baptist, who also mediated the forgiveness of sins (1:4); only now does the announcement of forgiveness become problematical. There is no reference in the rest of the narrative to Jesus' forgiving the sins of a particular individual or group. Even in this scene, the pronouncement of forgiveness is spoken only to the paralyzed man, the others presumably remaining unforgiven, including the four men who carried the paralyzed man to Jesus, and *they* are the ones to whom "faith" is attributed. (4) The

24. Cf. Robert M. Fowler, "The Rhetoric of Direction and Indirection in the Gospel of Mark (1989)," in *The Interpretation of Mark* (ed. William R. Telford; 2d ed.; SNTI; Edinburgh: T. & T. Clark, 1995), 207–28, esp. 213. Fowler argues that not only 2:10 but the Son of Man saying in 2:28 and much else is communicated at the discourse rather than the story level.

25. This view of the tradition history of the unit is widely, but not universally, held. Among dissenters who regard the story as an original unity are William L. Lane, *The Gospel According to Mark* (NICNT; Grand Rapids: Eerdmans, 1974), 97, and Robert H. Gundry, *Mark: A Commentary on His Apology for the Cross* (Grand Rapids: Eerdmans, 1993), 121–23, who gives a detailed argument.

omniscient narrator knows, and lets the reader know, the thoughts of the scribes before Jesus reveals them in the story itself. Such observations are not intended as negative pickiness, but as pointers to the nature of the story; it operates on a level other than mere report. Mark has combined and retold traditional material in such a way that it communicates something of the meaning of the Christ-event as such, seen from the post-Easter perspective of Mark's own situation: both Jesus' healings and his announcement of forgiveness point to his *authority*, central in this whole section.

[2:1–2] At one narrative level, the reference is probably to the house of Peter and Andrew, which becomes the adopted "headquarters" of Jesus' mission in Galilee (see on 1:29–34). But the private home has become a public place, reminiscent of the house churches of Mark's own time. Not only is the house filled with listeners, there was no room "even at the door," in contrast to 1:33, where the whole town was gathered "at the door." Mark pictures the increasing attractiveness and drawing power of Jesus and his message. By Mark's time "the word" had practically become a technical expression for the Christian kerygma (cf. 4:33; 8:32; Acts 4:29, 31; 8:25; 11:19, and elsewhere). This does not anachronistically portray Jesus as having preached the later Christian message, but carries the overtones of what happens in the proclamation of the gospel in Mark's time: Jesus continues to be the preacher, because in the proclamation of Christian preachers the risen Christ makes his own voice heard (cf. on 1:16–20).

[2:5] Though Jesus has issued a general call to "believe in the gospel" (1:15), this is Mark's first reference to "faith" (elsewhere only 4:40; 5:34; 10:52; 11:22). No content is given, but the apparent meaning is that they have heard of Jesus' ability to heal and are confident that it is true. Faith is attributed to the bearers, not to the paralyzed man, whose faith or lack of it is not a factor in his being healed or forgiven (contrast 5:34, 36; 9:23; 11:22–24).

By inserting the dialogue about forgiveness within the healing story, Mark has made it the central emphasis. The man had not come seeking forgiveness, but had been brought in hopes of being physically healed. There is no speculation here on the theological relation of sin and sickness or the connection between healing and forgiveness (contrast John 9:1–38 and cf. Jas 5:15–16). Nor is there any suggestion of psychosomatic paralysis—neither Mark nor any other New Testament author thinks in such modern categories. The man does not begin to walk by receiving forgiveness; the healing is a separate act. The whole focus is on the unilateral authority of Jesus, who pronounces forgiveness unsought and unexpected. Jesus does not wait until the man realizes his guilt and asks for forgiveness; there is nothing here about subjective guilt *feelings*. As in 2:17, it is assumed that to be human is to be enmeshed in objective guilt, that every human being as such is in need of God's forgiveness. While Jesus does not specifically say "I forgive you of your sins," the passive *aphientai* points to God as the actor and portrays Jesus as acting in God's stead. The scribes rightly understand that Jesus is going beyond the priestly or prophetic claim to announce God's forgiveness (cf. 2 Sam 12:13), and in the concluding line of the story Jesus identifies himself as the Son of Man who has authority to forgive. The scene portrays God's reconciling act in the Christ-event.

[2:6–7] The scribes have been contrasted with Jesus in 1:22, but here appear for the first time in the narrative (see *Excursus: Jesus the Teacher versus the Scribes* at 7:23). The scene is paradigmatic: those who will be involved in putting Jesus to death already raise the charge on which he will be condemned (14:64; see on 3:6), and resist him on the grounds that he improperly casts himself in the role that only God can fill. The scribes are not advocates of "works righteousness" who view the law as a means of salvation, and their objection to Jesus is not on the grounds that he announces salvation and forgiveness apart from the works of law. This Pauline issue does not emerge in the Markan account (see on 2:17). Instead they see themselves as defenders of the fundamental confession of Israel's faith: the holiness of the one God. The modern "enlightened" reader cannot understand this story if blasphemy is regarded as only a quaint element of religious paraphernalia of the narrow-minded. It was the most serious of sins, the blurring of the line between Creator and creature, the denial of God's holiness or arrogation of it as one's own. Their objection was not a matter of false messianic claims, for there is no suggestion in Jewish tradition that the Messiah will forgive sins. The scribes understand themselves as striving on God's behalf and defending the divine prerogative. The uniquely Markan formulation "the one God" echoes the Shema (Deut 6:4–5) and the monotheistic claim of deutero-Isaiah that God alone forgives sins (Isa 43:25). It reflects the live issue in Mark's own situation of whether devotion to Jesus as Son of God constitutes blasphemy in that it compromises monotheism. While implicit here, the same issue is explicitly developed in John 10:31–39. Leviticus 24:10–23 had made "blaspheming the name" a capital offense. The later Mishnah had defined this narrowly as "fully pronouncing the divine name" (*m. Sanh* 7:5). The charge here and in 14:64 does not correspond to either definition, but seems to mean any conduct in which one violates God's honor by assuming divine prerogatives. Taken with 3:6 and 14:64, the silent charge of the scribes shows that Mark has framed the controversy section 2:1–3:6 with allusions to the death penalty that will ultimately be carried out.

[2:9] Which is in fact easier, to forgive sins or to heal the paralyzed man? For Mark, forgiveness of sins is clearly the more difficult, for in fact only God can forgive. But in the situation portrayed in the narrative, it is easier to *say* "Your sins are forgiven"—which cannot be objectively proved or disproved—than to *do* the act of healing, which can be immediately demonstrated. At the narrative level, the argument thus functions as a kind of *qal vahomer* argument: if Jesus can heal the man, which is subject to empirical verification, then his pronouncement of forgiveness is also valid, though it cannot be empirically verified. Jesus does heal the man, with words that reverse his previous condition. He had been carried (*airomenon*) to Jesus but now is commanded to carry (*aron,* the imperative form of the same word) his own bed. At the word of Jesus, the passive victim has become an active participant in life.

[2:10] This is the first of fourteen Son of Man sayings in Mark (see *Excursus: Markan Christology* at 9:1). Only here and in 2:28 does the Son of Man *exercise authority on earth.* The declaration reflects Mark's situation, in which God's forgiveness was pronounced in Jesus' name. Jesus, though absent from the world until the Parousia, already exercises the eschatological authority of the Son of Man in the church's pronouncement of forgiveness. Matthew 9:8's change of Son of Man to "men" (= human beings) changes Mark's conceptuality and terminology, but preserves his point. In the pre-Markan story, the miracle is supposed to demonstrate the divine authority of Jesus. By placing the story in a context that concludes with the decision to kill Jesus, the evangelist shows that miracles did not in fact serve to convince people, but must be seen in the context of cross and resurrection.

[2:11–12] "Rise" . . . "he arose" echoes the language of resurrection. As in the Psalms, sickness is already the leading edge of death, and to be delivered from sickness is to be saved from death (Pss 6; 22:14–15; 31:9–10; 41:1–10; 55:4–5; 56:13 [cf. v. 8]). The paralyzed man was carried by others, lowered through the roof as into a grave, powerless to help himself or even know his own real need. The man is not just given the use of his legs—he is given his life back. The story as a whole points beyond the once-upon-a-time healing of a paralyzed person in Galilee to God's act of forgiveness represented in the Christ-event as a whole. It represents not merely Jesus' healing act of raising a Galilean individual but God's redemptive act for humanity in raising up Jesus.

The conventional "choral conclusion" to the miracle story presents the crowd as glorifying *God* for what *Jesus* had done; that is, they do not make the false scribal distinction between "Jesus" and "God." But neither do they identify Jesus as Messiah, and his self-identification as Son of Man has no effect on them; the messianic secret remains intact despite the epiphany of divine power. The "all" who are amazed and glorify God does not include the scribes, who are not represented as converted by the miracle—they immediately reappear as critics and enemies in 2:16 and 3:22. Though Mark knows of a "good" scribe, who sees no conflict between Jesus' claims and authentic monotheism and can join Jesus in recitation of the Shema (12:28–34), the scribes in the conflict scenes are typically "flat," mono-dimensional characters who represent the opposition to Jesus throughout the narrative and extending into Mark's own time.

2:13–17 Calling Sinners and Eating with Them

> **2:13** And he went out beside the sea again, and the whole crowd kept coming to him, and he was teaching them. **14** And as he was passing by, he saw Levi[a] the son of Alphaeus sitting at the tax collector's booth, and says to

him, "Follow me." And he arose[b] and followed him. 15 And he was reclining at dinner in his house,[c] and many tax collectors and sinners were reclining with Jesus and his disciples—for there were many who were following him. 16 And the scribes who belonged to the Pharisees,[d] when they saw that he was eating with sinners and tax collectors, were saying to his disciples, "He eats[e] with tax collectors and sinners."[f] 17 And when Jesus heard, he says to them, "It is not those who are well who need a physician, but those who are sick. I have not come to call righteous people, but sinners."

a. The reading *Iakōbon* (James) in D θ *f*[13] 565 and a few other MSS is an obvious effort to harmonize this text with 3:18, where James the son of Alphaeus is listed as one of the Twelve. Levi, called here, is missing there.

b. *Anastas* is here translated as having the overtones of resurrection language, as in 2:11–12. While the word can mean simply "get up" (as, e.g., 14:57, 60), it is used repeatedly of Jesus' resurrection in 8:31; 9:9–10, 27, 31; 10:34, is specifically identified with resurrection in 12:23–25, and has resurrection connotations in 1:35 and 5:42.

c. The translation preserves the ambiguity of the Greek pronouns. See on 1:40–45.

d. Literally "scribes of the Pharisees," replaced in A C θ *f*[1] *f*[13] and the mass of latter MSS by the expression "scribes and Pharisees" that became common in early Christianity due to the influence of Matthew. The more unusual expression documented in ℵ B W 28 and a few other MSS is to be preferred as the more difficult reading.

e. Many later MSS add *kai pinei* (and drinking), perhaps to make clear the eucharistic overtone already present in Mark's text. Luke 5:30 had already made this explicit, and this cross-fertilization of the MSS tradition influenced Mark's text as well.

f. *Hoti* is not here interrogative, a very rare usage in any case. Some editions of the Greek text, including UBS[4] and Nestle-Aland[27], nevertheless punctuate the utterance as a question, a construal often followed by English translators. There is no interrogative *ti*, however, so that if the expression is understood as a question, it does not belong formally in the same series as 2:7, 18, 24. If a question, it is not asking for information, but is a challenge. The punctuation above represents the scribes' words as a statement, a charge warning that the disciples should dissociate themselves with Jesus.

Three scenes, originally perhaps independent, have been fused by Mark into one unit, framed by Jesus' call of Levi the tax collector / sinner (v. 14) and Jesus' declaration that he has come to call sinners (v. 17). As in the preceding pericope, the middle element of the unit portrays a dispute between Jesus and the scribes, this time over table fellowship. The later church would face the disputed issue of table fellowship between Jewish Christians and Gentile Christians, regarded by Jews as "sinners," that is, ritually unclean (cf. 7:24–30; 14:41; Acts 11:1–3; Gal 2:11–15; cf. Luke 6:32–34). The relation of Jewish and Gentile Christians within one church was not an issue during Jesus' ministry. Mark's predominately Gentile church would find such stories addressing their own situation, and could hear in Jesus' earlier pronouncements the authority for their own inclusive practice.

[2:13–14] Again, Mark provides no content of his teaching; *that* Jesus teaches with divine authority is Mark's emphasis, not *what* he teaches (see on 1:21–22). Levi, however, does not hear Jesus' teaching, and his call takes place not because he has evaluated and been convinced by Jesus' message, but as the direct result of Jesus' powerful word. The crowds come to Jesus, but Jesus calls Levi, who had not taken any initiative and was not seeking Jesus. There is no reference to repentance or faith; Levi is not a volunteer, but a draftee. In form, content, and function, Levi's call is modeled on that of the first four disciples called in 1:16–20.

Jesus calls Levi away from his everyday work. As with the fishermen in 1:16–20, for Levi responding to Jesus' call meant leaving his livelihood. He was sitting *epi to telōnion*, which probably refers to one of the toll booths located along main highways and at bridges and waterways where customs were collected for the regime of Herod Antipas, puppet "king" at the pleasure of Rome.[26] In Galilee, which was not under direct Roman rule, Levi would not have been involved in collecting the poll taxes that went directly to the Roman government (see on 12:13–17), but he would still have been regarded as being involved in shady and unpatriotic business. He was not a government official or bureaucrat, but more like a private businessman who leased the privilege of collecting taxes from the government, or an employee who worked for those who did so. Tax collectors were considered both ritually unclean and morally corrupt.

This Levi is not mentioned elsewhere in Mark and is noticeably absent from the list of the Twelve in 3:16–19 (see Commentary there). The tradition has made various efforts to remedy Mark's supposed lack: (1) Matt 9:9 simply replaces "Levi" with the name "Matthew" found in Mark 3:18, but Mark provides no indication that Levi and Matthew are the same person. (2) A few scribes substituted "James" for "Levi" (see note *a* above). (3) The *Gospel of the Hebrews* understands the "Matthias" chosen to be Judas's successor in Acts 1:23 to be the same as Mark's "Levi." The common denominator of these efforts is to identify Levi as one of the Twelve. Mark's point in this pericope, however, is to present Jesus' call as inclusive, not limited to the Twelve, but extending to all "sinners." The "many" who "follow him" (v. 15) does not refer only to tax collectors, but to disciples, whom Mark does not limit to the Twelve (see *Excursus: Crowds, Followers, Disciples, the Twelve* at 6:6). Jesus' call generates discipleship; Levi "rises" (see note *b* above) and follows.

[2:15] Jesus' call and Levi's response eventuates in a festive meal (*katakeisthai*, "recline," suggests an upscale banquet at which guests reclined Roman-

---

26. The story presupposes a border crossing in the vicinity, a political situation that did not exist after 39 C.E. when Galilee was united with the territory of Philip to the east. This is one indication that Mark has early traditions formulated within a decade of Jesus' death. Cf. Theissen, *Gospels in Context*, 235–89.

style in a U-shaped pattern around a central table). As in 1:16–20, 29–31, Jesus calls people to discipleship, then joins them in their house and eats with them—reflecting the house churches of Mark's situation. To become a follower of Jesus is to be incorporated into an inclusive group that eats and drinks together in an atmosphere of celebration. The Greek pronouns can relate the house to either Levi or Jesus (cf. 1:40–45). Mark is not concerned to identify the house historically, though Jesus does seem to act as host. As in, for example, 7:17; 10:10, "the" house is simply the place where Jesus meets with his followers. The whole scene has overtones of the inclusive eucharistic celebrations of early Christianity, the proleptic celebration of the messianic banquet in the dawning kingdom of God. "The" house points beyond a particular house in Capernaum, whether Levi's or Jesus', to the early Christian house churches, as do the themes of call, banquet, healing, and reception of "sinners." "Eating with" is taken seriously in the ancient Mediterranean world as a sign of acceptance. Jesus eats with sinners.

[2:16] Small houses, or the dining rooms of larger houses, were adjacent to courtyards that made it easy for passersby to look in and overhear the conversations inside.[27] The scribes, already introduced as Jesus' challengers in 2:6, are now related to the Pharisees. They reflect actual opponents of Mark's and the readers' own time (see *Excursus: Jesus the Teacher versus the Scribes* at 7:23). In Mark's narrative they play a literary role, so the reader should not ask the historicizing question of how it came about that such scribes were present at the dinner party of which they are so critical. As was the case with the scribes of 2:6, and like the Pharisees of 2:24, they are present to raise the objection to which Jesus may then respond with authority. They do not ask Jesus directly, but ask the disciples. This corresponds to Mark's church situation in which predominately Gentile congregations and integrated Christian congregations of Jewish and Gentile Christians are challenged by Jews and strict Jewish Christians regarding their inclusive fellowship. The Gentile and integrated Jewish/Gentile congregations respond not by arguments based on Scripture or tradition but by appealing to Jesus' authority.

What is the nature of the scribes' protest? The modern reader must avoid either stereotyping the Pharisees or romanticizing the "sinners." "Tax collectors and sinners" does not refer to two groups, as though tax collectors were not sinners; it has the sense of "tax collectors and other sinners." The latter designation has been understood in two ways, either as ritually unclean or morally lax. Tax collectors were in fact regarded as engaged in a business that made them ritually impure—they came in contact with all sorts of Gentile impurity, and so their occupation meant that they had essentially abandoned their own

---

27. Cf. David L. Balch and Carolyn Osiek, *Families in the New Testament World: Households and House Churches* (Louisville, Ky.: Westminster John Knox, 1997), 10–11, 17, passim.

religious community and its provisions for purity. They were not welcome in the synagogue, and those who associated with them were assumed to have contracted their cultic uncleanness. On this understanding, the scribes' objection is that of strict Pharisees concerned with ritual purity, which Jesus violates by entering Levi's house and eating with Jews whose essential defect is that they do not abide by the strict cultic rules of the Pharisees, that is, they are not bad people but simply "nonobservant Jews." In the other view, "sinner" refers to flagrant violators of the moral law, including thieves, liars, prostitutes, and other unsavory types avoided by those concerned not only with ritual purity but with common human decency.[28]

[2:17] Jesus' response is twofold. (1) He cites a proverb popular in both Gentile and Jewish tradition, that the physician goes where he is needed, namely among sick people, not to those who are healthy. Especially in the Jewish form of the aphorism, God is the physician who heals, so that here too Jesus casts himself in the role of God (see on 2:6–10). In a Jewish context, the proverb would also suggest that just as the physician communicates healing to the sick rather than the sick infecting him with their sickness, so Jesus communicates his own holiness to others, making them clean, rather than becoming unclean by his contact with them (cf. on 1:40–45).

(2) The parallel saying, and punch line of the unit, is Jesus' christological pronouncement on the purpose of his "coming" (cf. n. 20 at 1:38 on Jesus' *ēlthon*, "I have come," sayings). He does not call the "righteous." Who are these? Should the term be enclosed in quotes, as though the Markan Jesus refers ironically to the "so-called righteous," or the "self-righteous" who are not aware of their need for forgiveness? Then "sinners" would refer to all human beings in the Pauline sense (cf. Rom 3:19–23), and the "righteous" would be those who arrogantly deny that they are sinners. While there may be some influence of Pauline theology in Mark, this text is not an explication or reflection of Paul's view of universal human sinfulness. And while Mark would hardly claim that there are righteous people who need no forgiveness, that is not the point here. Instead, Jesus' declaration utilizes the Semitic form of "dialectic negation,"[29] and means "more than" instead of "rather than." Jesus' mission is to the outcast and rejected, those with no claim to be accepted and who in fact were not. The kingdom of God that is dawning in his ministry will be a banquet in which all are accepted: if these are accepted and celebrate with Jesus at God's table, then all are accepted. Jesus' call excludes no one—including the righteous. The call

---

28. C. S. Mann, *Mark: A New Translation with Introduction and Commentary* (AB 27; New York: Doubleday, 1986), 228–30, represents the first option, and simply translates *hamartōloi* as "nonobservant Jews." The second option is championed by, e.g., E. P. Sanders, *The Historical Figure of Jesus* (New York: Penguin, 1993), 225–33.

29. Cf., e.g., Rudolf Pesch, *Das Markusevangelium: I. Teil. Kommentar zu Kap. 1:1–8:26; II. Teil. Kommentar zu Kap. 8:27–16:20* (4th ed.; HTKNT; 2 vols.; 1984), 1:166, and Hos 6:6.

of Levi and the party at his house are not an individual case, but a paradigm of God's reconciling act.

2:18–22 Now and Later; Old and New

This pericope is the central unit in the chiastic structure of 2:1–3:6, illuminating the whole section and defining its central issue: the relation of the eschatological newness represented by Jesus to both the "old" world of the Scripture and Judaism and the later world of Mark and his post-Easter Christian readers. This pericope makes clear that, while there is continuity from the Old Testament through the ministry of Jesus within its Jewish context to the time of the Markan church, there is also a double disjunction. Jesus and his disciples, including the Markan Christians, stand in the new time, while the Old Testament and Judaism (including John the Baptist) represent the old. Yet there is not a simple continuity, but also disjunction, between the time of Jesus' ministry and Mark's own time. The threefold periodization of salvation history explicitly found in Luke-Acts[30] is already implicit in Mark, but less neatly and more dialectically.

2:18 And John's disciples and the Pharisees observed regular fasts.[a] And people[b] are coming and saying to him, "Why do the disciples of John and the disciples of the Pharisees fast, but your disciples do not fast?" **19** And Jesus said to them, "The wedding guests[c] are not able to fast while the bridegroom is with them, are they?[d] As long as they have the bridegroom with them, they are not able to fast. **20** But days will come when the bridegroom will be taken from them, and then they will fast on that day. **21** No one sews a patch of unshrunk cloth on an old garment. Otherwise, the fullness[e] pulls away from it, the new from the old, and a worse split[f] happens. **22** And no one puts new wine in old wineskins. Otherwise, the wine breaks through the skins, and the wine is destroyed, as are the skins. On the contrary: 'New wine into new skins.'"

a. The periphrastic construction imperfect *ēsan* + participle *nēsteuontes* is taken to represent the customary imperfect, i.e., that John's disciples and the Pharisees included fasting as part of their regular religious observance, not that they happened to be fasting

---

30. See Hans Conzelmann, *The Theology of St. Luke* (trans. Geoffrey Buswell; New York: Harper & Row, 1961), and the many later appropriations and adjustments of Conzelmann's scheme found in later literature on Luke-Acts. Donald Senior and Eugene LaVerdiere have rightly argued that the salvation history perspective is already important in Mark's theology (Donald P. Senior, "The Struggle to Be Universal: Mission as Vantage Point for New Testament Interpretation," *CBQ* 46, no. 1 (1984): 78–81; Eugene LaVerdiere, *The Beginning of the Gospel: Introducing the Gospel according to Mark* (2 vols.; Collegeville, Minn.: Liturgical Press, 1999), 62–63 and passim.

at the time the dialogue takes place. While this pericope, like the preceding one, deals with religious observance of eating practices, it is not part of the same scene: the fasting question does not arise during the dinner party at Levi's house, as though John's disciples and Pharisees were present but abstaining.

b. The third-person-plural verb *erchontai* could have "John's disciples and the Pharisees" as subject, but the context requires that it be taken impersonally, referring to "they," i.e., people in general.

c. Literally, "sons of the wedding hall," reflecting the Semitic use of "son" to mean those who belong to a particular category.

d. Greek sentences beginning with the particle *mē* are not informational questions, but rhetorical questions expecting a negative answer.

e. *Plērōma* is lit. "that which fulfills, fills up," and so can be used for a "patch," but is never so used elsewhere in the New Testament, in the LXX, or in any pagan Greek literature. Since the word has overtones of the messianic fulfillment (6:43; 8:20, its only other occurrences in Mark; cf. John 1:16; Rom 11:12, 25; 13:10; 15:29; Gal 4:4; Eph 1:10; 4:13), it is here rendered "fullness" despite its awkwardness.

f. *Schisma* can mean simply "tear," "hole," when applied to a garment, but, except for this text and its Matt 9:16 parallel, elsewhere it is always used for the undesirable division in a religious community (John 7:43; 9:16; 10:19; 1 Cor 1:10; 11:18; 12:25). The translation "split," while awkward for a garment, preserves the overtone of the growing rift between Judaism and developing Christianity, which had originally been one community.

[2:18] In the Old Testament and Judaism, fasting was not a matter of asceticism and world rejection, but a sign of repentance and humility before God. The Scripture prescribed only one fast, in connection with the annual Day of Atonement (Lev 16), but already in the history of Israel and Judaism, occasional voluntary fasts were called for and practiced, and additional fasts became customary in some circles. Zechariah 8:19 indicates that by the sixth century B.C.E. four annual fasts were observed, and the people are exhorted to make them occasions of celebration and rejoicing (cf. Est 9:31; Luke 2:37). In first-century Judaism, many pious Jews observed voluntary times of fasting, a practice that continued into the early church (cf. Matt 6:16–18; Luke 2:37; Acts 10:30; 13:2; 14:23; 27:9; 2 Cor 6:5; 11:27). The Pharisees fasted twice every week (Luke 18:12; according to *Did.* 8:1 this was on Tuesdays and Thursdays). The disciples of John the Baptist also fasted regularly, presumably continuing and expressing John's call to national repentance.[31] In the case of both John's disciples and the Pharisees,

31. For the first time the reader learns that John the Baptist not only proclaimed the "mighty one" to come (1:4–8), but had disciples of his own, parallel to the group of Jesus' disciples. While the Christian community interpreted John as only the forerunner of Christ, the historical reality was that a Baptist community existed alongside the Christian community, and partly in competition with it (cf. Luke 7:18; 11:1; Acts 19:1–7). Mark here incorporates a pre-Markan element and perspective without integrating it into his own understanding of John's role in salvation history.

two "renewal movements" within Israel, the call to a rigorous religious practice was in preparation for the eschaton, and was believed to help implement its arrival. The coming of the kingdom could be facilitated by signs of repentance such as fasting. In this context, Jesus and his disciples seemed to be out of step with, or actually impeding, the arrival of the promised kingdom. Though Mark regards John as a true prophet of God, here his disciples stand with the Pharisees in the old order, over against Jesus and the eschatological newness he brings. In Mark, the question is raised not by John's own disciples (as in Matt 9:14), but by anonymous interested observers of the three "renewal movements," who see Jesus and his followers as out of step with serious efforts to inaugurate the time of redemption. The dispute is not merely about how somber religious people should be, but what time it is on God's redemptive schedule. Jesus and his disciples do not fast in order to encourage God to bring the kingdom, but celebrate in the light of the kingdom that is already dawning (cf. comment on 7:24–30 and *Excursus: Kingdom of God* at 1:15).

[2:19–20] Jesus' response is his most extensive statement in this series of controversy stories. He replies not by citing Scripture or making an authoritative pronouncement, but with three parables,[32] all of which deal with impossibilities: fasting at a wedding celebration, patching an old garment with a new piece of cloth, and putting new wine in old wineskins. All three sayings point to the time of Jesus as a special time that cannot be combined either with the old world of Scripture and Judaism or the later time of the church, though it is definitive for how readers should understand both. This is the surprising point: the reader expects Jesus to defend his disciples' failure to fast, not to get an explanation of the difference between periods of time. The "time of Jesus" stands in contrast to both the old world of Judaism and the later time of the church. Jesus and his disciples had proleptically celebrated the messianic banquet, the time of the kingdom when all would eat and drink together. This dawning eschatological reality is focused in the person and presence of Jesus. Thus Mark does not base the neglect of fasting and the permission to feast on Jesus' command or teaching, but on the person of Jesus himself. The Christ-event, not doctrine or ideology, is the basis of the new reality, and Christology, not mealtime practice or the value of fasting as such, becomes the point at issue.

Jesus clearly, though indirectly, identifies himself as the bridegroom (see *Excursus: Markan Christology* at 9:1) and his presence as the sign and authorization of the time of messianic celebration. In Mark, it is Jesus' personal presence

---

32. Though the word "parable" does not appear until 3:23, its use there indicates that Mark includes even such brief metaphorical expressions in the category of parable. Mark does not use *parabolē* for a specific literary genre, but for a variety of different literary forms that communicate indirectly. See on 4:10, and the recent analysis of Elian Cuvillier, *Le concept de ΠΑΡΑΒΟΛΗ dans le second évangile: Son arrière-plan littéraire, sa signification dans le cadre de la rédaction marcienne, son utilisation dans la tradition de Jésus* (EBib nouv. sér. 19; Paris: J. Gabalda, 1993), 195–205.

that authorizes feasting instead of fasting. An ominous note, the first hint of a "passion prediction," intrudes into the festive scene: this presence is only temporary; the bridegroom will be "taken away." This imagery does not fit the wedding metaphor, but is a retrojection of the Jesus story into the image. The characters in the narrative could not have understood the allusion, but the post-Easter reader knows that Jesus will be violently taken away. The prediction is not only shaped by the actual course of events, but its language again reflects that of Isaiah (53:8; cf. on 1:2–3). As in all expressions of the messianic secret, the story works at two levels.

"The days will come" points to the readers' own time. Although the story looks back on the ministry of Jesus, when the bridegroom was present and fasting was inappropriate, the church of the author's own time practices fasting. Mark himself is aware of the difference between the time of Jesus and the time of the church, and he tells the story in such a way that it impinges on and authorizes present practice. Mark assumes, but does not prescribe, fasting as an element of Christian discipline. His perspective is entirely christological, but in the controversy dialogues of this section Christology functions in a variety of ways to justify the faith and practice of Mark's church. This pericope is different from the others in that church practice is not legitimized by Jesus' practice, but is contrasted to it.

[21–22] Each of the two sayings points to the impossibility of mixing old and new. To sew a patch of new (unshrunk) cloth on an old garment means that at the next washing the patch will shrink and tear away from the old garment. New (still fermenting) wine placed in old wineskins that have lost their elasticity will break the skins. Here, two wisdom sayings become eschatological parables of the relation of old and new. They function as parables, so that their application must avoid the pedestrian "moral of the story" that can dispense with the provocative multilayered dimensions of meaning in the image itself. While Mark's parabolic imagery is clearly an affirmation of the new reality that has come into the world in Jesus, it can legitimately be interpreted in more than one way, as illustrated by the respective ways Matthew and Luke understood it.[33] The following reflections are evoked by this catalytic imagery; though not neatly harmonizable, they are all in line with Mark's presentation of Jesus' words:

- "New" in such biblical contexts is an absolute term, not a relative one. It points to God's eschatological renewal, and does not mean "up to date" or "new and improved" in the cultural sense. Compare Paul's use of "new creation" (2 Cor 5:17; Gal 6:15), John's

---

33. Matt 9:14–17 characteristically takes it as affirming both old and new (cf. also Matt 13:52), while Luke 5:39 affirms that "the old is better" (unless this appended concluding interpretation is to be taken ironically).

use of "new Jerusalem" (Rev 22:1, 2, 5), the Fourth Gospel's use of "new commandment" (John 13:34), all of which connote ultimacy, not "more recent and therefore better." In such usage, there is a dialectical relation between "old" and "new," for the new is not the replacement of the old, but its eschatological fulfillment. Thus the Markan affirmation of the new does not merely present Jesus as an innovative figure whose efforts to introduce new perspectives were opposed by stodgy, hidebound defenders of tradition, committed to doing things as they had always been done.

- There is no magic in the particular terminology for newness used by Mark. *Neos* and *kainos* are each used twice, and as synonyms.[34]
- The parables should not be allegorized, as though the "old garment" and "old wineskins" refer disparagingly to worn-out and inflexible Judaism. This line of thought would call for the old to be cast aside and the new to be used in place of it, but such imagery works neither for the patch nor the wine. Both sayings in fact not only affirm the power of the new, but show a concern lest the old be lost. While the new is stronger than the old, it neither replaces it nor merely supplements it. While there is concern lest the two be mixed, it is assumed they can continue to exist alongside each other.[35] Mark's narrative as a whole, from the first lines onward, is concerned to express continuity between Judaism and its Scripture and the eschatological newness manifest in Christ.
- Perhaps the main thrust of the imagery is best grasped as a protest against seeing the eschatological newness that came into the world with Jesus as merely a supplement to Judaism, a repairing of the deficiencies of the old. As in the case of the rich man in 10:17–22, what Jesus offers is not merely a supplement to what one already has.

2:23–28 Keeping the Sabbath Holy: Jesus Challenged and Warned

This pericope is joined to the preceding one by the theme of eating / not eating and to the following one by the issue of what constitutes authentic Sabbath observance. In Mark's situation his predominately Gentile church did not adhere strictly to the Sabbath, and was beginning to or had already replaced the Jewish seventh day with the Christian first day of the week, the "Lord's Day." This was an issue not only between Christians and their Jewish neighbors, but

34. Contra, e.g., Johannes Behm, "*kainos*," in *TDNT*, 3:447–54, who argues that *neos* means "new" in the chronological sense, while *kainos* denotes that which is new in nature . . . better than the old, superior in value or attraction. This view is often reflected in the commentaries, but has little or no basis in New Testament usage, and none at all in Mark.

35. Cf. Hooker, *Mark*, 100; van Iersel, *Mark*, 157.

an inner-church issue, and not only between Gentile and Jewish Christians. The affirmation of the Hebrew Bible as Christian Scripture necessarily raised the question of how to interpret the Sabbath command. Only here and in the following story does the Sabbath become a topic of controversy in the Markan narrative. In 2:23–28, as required by law, Jesus is challenged and warned about the conduct of his disciples, and when he continues to "violate" the Sabbath, in 3:1–6 he is condemned in accordance with the law. On the structure of 2:1–3:6 as a whole, see above at 2:1.

> 2:23 And it came to pass[a] that on a Sabbath he was going through the grainfields, and as his disciples made their way[b] they were picking ears of grain. 24 And the Pharisees were saying to him, "Look! Why are they doing what is not lawful[c] on the Sabbath?" 25 And he says to them, "Have you never read what David did when he had need and got hungry, he and those with him, 26 how he entered into the house of God when[d] Abiathar was high priest and ate the bread of the Presence, which no one may lawfully eat except the priests, and also gave to those who were with him?" 27 And he was saying to them,[e] "The Sabbath was made[f] for the man,[g] and not the man for the Sabbath. 28 So, then, the Son of Man is Lord even of the Sabbath."

a. On *kai egeneto* as "it came to pass," see note *a* on 1:9.

b. The expression *hodon poiein* does not refer to making a path or building a road, but as in the comparable Latin and English expressions, simply to "go along."

c. [*Ouk*] *exestin*, "[not] permitted," is used six times in Mark (2:24, 26; 3:4; 6:18, 10:2; 12:14), always in the semi-technical sense of "[not] according to the revelation of God's will in the Torah." The phrase does not merely express the pickiness of those sensitive to the niceties of tradition, but belongs to the juristic terminology of scribal discussion and is used, e.g., by John the Baptist in his charge against Herod (6:18). It is thus not only a matter of what is "permitted" but what is positively commanded in the law in order to do God's will.

d. *Epi* is an extremely flexible preposition, but here clearly designates "the time within which an event or condition takes place" (BDAG 367), as in Luke 3:2; 4:27; Acts 11:28. More general translations such as "in the days of" or "in the time of," or construing the phrase to mean "in the section of Scripture dealing with Abiathar" (on the analogy of 12:26) are efforts to save Mark or Jesus from confusing Ahimelech, who was priest in the Old Testament story (1 Sam 21:1), with Abiathar (cf. 1 Sam 22:20). A few Greek MSS including D and W, the Latin translations, and the Sinaitic Syriac solve the problem by omitting the troublesome phrase, as do Matthew and Luke.

e. The two additional sayings are introduced by *kai elegen autois*, a distinctively Markan phrase. Twelve of fifteen New Testament occurrences are found in Mark (2:27; 4:2, 11, 21, 24; 6:4, 10; 7:9; 8:21; 9:1, 31; 11:17 + Luke 6:5 = Mark 2:8; John 5:19; 8:23). The phrase is usually redactional, and at least four times represents Markan introduction of new sayings into a pericope.

f. *Egeneto*, lit. "came into being," here has the overtones of creation and evokes the creation story of Gen 1, where *egeneto* is used repeatedly as the counterpart for *epoiēsen*.

g. The Greek *ho anthrōpos* is generic, "human being," and the Markan Jesus clearly refers not just to men but to human beings as such. "Man" is here retained, along with the definite article, despite its lack of gender-inclusiveness and the awkwardness of "*the* man," in order to make the wordplay between "the man" and "the Son of Man" clear in the English translation. The expression was also awkward in Greek. Cf. on 8:34.

[2:23–24] In the Jewish Scriptures that became the only Bible of the early church, Sabbath keeping was no trivial matter. The Sabbath had been instituted by God at creation, and God himself had observed it (Gen 2:2), as had the angels in heaven and the patriarchs even before the law was given (*Jub.* 2:18–23; *Gen. Rab.* 11 [8c]). The Sabbath is thus on earth a foretaste of the eschatological joy, pictured as a perpetual Sabbath celebration (2 Esd 7:31; *2 En.* 33.1–2), and even now the Sabbath is observed in heaven, while the unrighteous tormented in gehenna are granted a reprieve from their sufferings every Sabbath.[36] Keeping the Sabbath holy was one of the Ten Commandments, where it was elaborated more extensively than any of the others, and it was based on both God's creative act at the beginning and God's liberating act at the exodus (Exod 20:8–11; Deut 5:12–15). The Sabbath is God's gift to Israel for their refreshment and enjoyment, a day when slaves and animals may rest from their labor (Exod 23:12). No exceptions are to be made, even in plowing time and harvest time (Exod 34:21). The strict Sabbath rules were not regarded as a burden; keeping them was a sign of joyous obedience to God and of God's acceptance. Sabbath keeping was not merely a matter of individual piety; the Sabbath was a testimony and sign to Israel and to the world of God's covenant with Israel; from the oldest biblical laws through the Judaism of Jesus' and Mark's time into the later period when the Mishnah was codified, those who violate it are to be put to death (Exod 31:12–17; Num 15:32–36; *Jub.* 2:25; *m. Sanh* 7.4). Israel's failure to sanctify the Sabbath brought the disaster of war and exile as God's punishment (Jer 17:21–27; Neh 13:15–22). Especially after the exile, when Israel's national identity was gone and the existence of Israel as the covenant people depended on observance of the law that distinguished them from Gentiles, Sabbath observance became increasingly important (Isa 56:2–6; 58:13; 66:23). Far more than a sign of petty religiosity, the Sabbath was a mark of Israel's very identity, the sign of God's work in history. Like fasting in the previous pericope, Sabbath observance could hasten the day of God's redemption, and violation of the Sabbath could postpone the day of salvation or cause God to turn away

36. Hermann Strack and Paul Billerbeck, eds., *Kommentar zum Neuen Testament aus Talmud und Midrasch* (Str-B; 6 vols.; Munich: Beck, 1924), 4:839–40; Eduard Lohse, "*sabbaton*," in *TDNT*, 7:8.

from Israel once again, and perhaps finally. Unlike fasting, Sabbath observance was a matter of obligation for every Jew, and was not only a matter of tradition but a direct command of Scripture. Jews were willing to die rather than violate the Sabbath, and did so (1 Macc 2:29–38).

In this perspective, violation of the Sabbath was a serious charge. The commandment read "the seventh day is a Sabbath to the Lord your God; *you shall not do any work*," but the Bible itself did not define what constituted "work." In order to keep the Sabbath at all, one needed to know when one was doing work and when not. This meant that the definition of "work" was literally a matter of life and death, not to speak of the integrity of the community of Israel and the fulfillment of God's eschatological promises, and therefore could not be left to individual whims or each person's sense of freedom. Lists of what is to be considered "work," and the issue of who has the authority to make such lists, were thus matters of supreme importance. Numerous representative lists of prohibited activities were developed by Israel's teachers (e.g., *Jub.* 50.6–13; CD 10.14–11.18; *m. Besach* 5.2; *m. Shabbath* 7). When the Pharisees challenge Jesus' disciples for plucking grain on the Sabbath, they represent this tradition. The disciples' offense was not plucking the grain itself, which was permitted in biblical and Jewish law as a help to those in need, and could have been done on other days (Deut 23:25). They are charged with profaning the Sabbath. They are not accused directly, however; the charge is made to Jesus, who is considered responsible for their behavior. Thus here as elsewhere in 2:1–3:6, the authority of Jesus is the root issue, and the agenda modulates from Halakah to Christology.

[2:25–28] As in the preceding pericope, Jesus pronounces a threefold response to the charge, consisting of an interpretation of Scripture (which has priority over human tradition, here as in 7:1–13), a general humanitarian statement appealing to God's intention in creation (as in 10:2–12), and a pronouncement on the authority of the Son of Man. The warrant of the first is derived from Scripture and functions in a Jewish context; the second has a wider perspective embracing Gentiles and common human wisdom. Mark affirms and includes both types of argument, but regards neither as final. All such issues are settled not by Scripture or human wisdom, but by the universal authority of the Son of Man expressed in verse 28. The differing genres and logical bases of the three sayings, as well as the fresh beginning at verse 27, indicate that the three sayings did not all originate in the same setting. Whatever the pre-Markan history of the sayings, for Mark they form a unit, climaxing in the Son of Man saying of verse 28 (cf. the similar structure in 2:8–11, with the Son of Man saying of v. 10 as its linchpin).

[25–26] The general point of the appeal to the David story is clear: just as the Scripture reports that David did "what was not lawful" when he ate the sacred bread and shared it with those with him (1 Sam 21:1–9), so Jesus authorizes his disciples to transgress the biblical and traditional norms. Mark (in contrast to Matt 12:1) does not make it a matter of human need: in Mark the disciples are not hungry, and they do not eat, so the Markan argument is not that "human need is more important than Sabbath rules." Nor is there a rabbinic *qal vahomer* argument, along the lines of "if you Pharisees acknowledge that King David exercised authority over sacred objects, how much more does the true king exercise over the Sabbath." Mark's Christology has no Davidic typology and is extremely cautious about interpreting Jesus in Davidic terms (see on 12:35–37), so Mark does not base his argument on the pattern "something greater than David is here" (contrast Matt 12:42 / Luke 1:32). Even in this first saying, the focus is entirely on Jesus' authority.

[2:27] The two additional sayings are related by their use of "man" / "Son of Man" (cf. note *g* above). Although Mark has not based his argument on the priority of human need to religious rules, the first saying does fit into the Jewish tradition in which Sabbath laws could be set aside if emergency human need called for it.[37] There is no emergency in Mark, however; Mark's appropriation of this line of argument corresponds more to the appeal to the law of God implicit in creation than to general humanitarian concerns, and then quickly modulates from "man" to "Son of Man." His point is not individualistic autonomy freed from traditional rituals, but the authority of Jesus.

[2:28] The Markan Jesus has already identified himself as the Son of Man who exercises eschatological authority (see on 2:10). Here, the authority by which he authorizes his disciples to violate the norms of tradition and Scripture is the climactic self-declaration that the Son of Man is Lord even of the Sabbath. Since "man" and "son of man" are interchangeable expressions in the Hebrew Bible, some interpreters have seen them as variant expressions for "human being" and understand both verse 27 and verse 28 to refer to authority over the Sabbath granted to human beings as such. This connection between the "man" of verse 27 and "Son of Man" of verse 28 has sometimes been understood to mean that "man," that is, human beings as such, are Lord of the Sabbath, as though the dominion over the world given by God at creation *also* includes freedom to dispose of Sabbath rules as each human being sees fit. This is a too post-Enlightenment, humanist reading of Mark. In the one instance where "son of man" terminology refers to human beings in general, 3:28, Mark uses the plural. In every instance, including the present one, where Mark uses the phrase "Son of

---

37. Cf. 1 Macc 2:38–41; 2 Esdras 6:54; *2 Bar.* 14.18; Mekilta 109b on Exod 31:14, "The Sabbath is handed over to you, not you to it," is the closest parallel to the Markan declaration, though this is stated not as a general maxim but as applying specifically to life-threatening situations. Philo, *On the Life of Moses* 2.22 and *Special Laws* 2.60–64 provide extensive examples of the way Hellenistic Judaism appealed to the general humanitarianism of the Law's intent in interpreting it to Gentiles.

Man," he refers to the unique authority of Jesus. Mark applies the title "Lord" to Jesus only ambiguously; while the reader perceives Jesus' identity as both Son of Man and Lord, Jesus' self-identification is lost on the characters in the narrative (see *Excursus: Markan Christology* at 9:1, *Excursus: The Messianic Secret* at 9:13, and comments on 1:3; 2:10; 5:19; 7:28; 11:3; 12:36–37).

In all of this, the Markan Jesus never sets aside the law or abrogates the Sabbath as such—the reader must remember 1:40–45—but affirms it as the gift of God to humanity (v. 27), yet subject to the authority of the Son of Man (v. 28).

3:1–6 Keeping the Sabbath Holy: Jesus Persists and Is Condemned

Like 2:1–12, the opening unit in this section, this pericope is formally a combination of miracle story and controversy story, and as in the initial story, attention is focused on the controversy and Jesus' pronouncement rather than the miracle itself. The chapter division is unfortunate, for the Sabbath issue of the preceding pericope continues. The opposition to Jesus is not merely personal pique but a matter of gathering evidence for a legal proceeding against someone who has been properly warned (see on 2:24). There is a tradition of capital punishment for profaning the Sabbath that extends from Exodus through *Jubilees* and Qumran into the Mishnah. In Jesus' situation, Jewish religious leaders could administer discipline in the synagogue for breach of Jewish law (cf. 2 Cor 11:24–25), but in order to execute radical offenders, they would have to obtain the cooperation of the political authorities. In Galilee, this would mean the Herodian dynasty that ruled at Rome's behest; in Judea, a Roman province directly under Roman rule, the Roman governor would have to see Jesus as a criminal or threat.

In this scene that concludes the controversy section 2:1–3:6, the narrative thus reaches a crucial point. The dawning of the kingdom of God in Jesus' ministry brings the fullness of life that means forgiveness and freedom from sin, reconciliation of those who could not eat together, deliverance from demonic power, the overcoming of death and the negative effects of law. Many respond in joy, but some have hard hearts, and on the basis of Scripture, tradition, and sincere religious conviction, consider Jesus a threat to the community of faith and God's purpose for the world. They begin plans to put him to death.

3:1 And again he entered the synagogue, and a man was there with a withered hand. 2 And they were observing Jesus carefully, to see if he would heal him on the Sabbath, so that they could bring charges against[a] him. 3 Then he says to the man with the withered hand, "Rise,[b] stand in the midst of the congregation." 4 And he says to them, "Is it lawful on the Sabbath to do good, or to do evil, to save someone's life,[c] or to destroy it?" But they remained silent. 5 Then he looked around on them, with wrath,[d] grieved at the hardness of their hearts, and says to the man, "Stretch out your hand." And he stretched it out, and his hand was restored. 6 And the Pharisees immediately went out with the Herodians and held a consultation^e against him, how to put him to death.

a. *Kategoresosin* has the legal sense of bringing charges in a court, and is related to the preceding *pareteroun* ("observing him carefully," with the connotation of looking for legal evidence) and the following *symboulion edidoun* (see the following notes).

b. Again, *egeire* can be taken in its pedestrian sense, "stand up," but the word has the connotation of resurrection (cf. comments on 1:31, 35–39, 40; 2:11–12, 14).

c. *Psychen* is not an abstraction, but refers to a particular life, that of the man with the withered hand whom Jesus will restore, and that of Jesus, whom the Pharisees and Herodians are plotting to kill. On *sozo*," save," see on 5:23.

d. Since *orge* is the standard term for the wrath of God in the LXX (e.g., Exod 4:14; 32:11; Num 11:10; Amos 4:10; Isa 5:25; 9:19; 59:19; Zeph 1:18), this term is used here rather than "anger," the usual translation for *orge* in this passage.

e. The awkward combination *symboulion edidoun* is found no place else in Greek literature. *Symboulion* can refer to the act of consulting, to a consultation or council session or its results, i.e., a plan or purpose ("counsel"), or to a deliberative body itself, a council. The more usual verb with "counsel," *poieo* (lit. "make"), is found in a ℵ A C Δ θ and most later MSS. *Edidoun* (lit. "give") translated here and preferred as the more difficult reading is found in B L *f*^13 and a few other MSS. While it may simply represent Mark's inelegant Greek, confusing "counsel" and "council," Mark may have used the awkward phrase in anticipation of 15:1, and the translation above attempts to preserve this connection.

[3:1] The man is designated not by the general *tis* ("someone," "a certain person") but by *anthropos* just referred to in 2:27, the "living being" of Gen 1 for whom the Sabbath was made. But the description of the man's present condition connotes death. In a dry land where moisture means life, *exerammenen* ("withered") often implies "death" (cf. LXX Job 8:12; 12:15; 18:16; Pss 90:6; 101:5, 12; 128:6; Isa 37:27; 40:7, 24; 51:12; Ezek 19:12; Dan 7:8). The man's affliction prevented him from making a living. Correspondingly, the man's healing is narrated in resurrection language (v. 4 and note above).

[2] Whether miracles happen at all, and if so, whether Jesus can perform them, is not an issue in the Markan miracle stories (see *Excursus: Miracle Stories in Mark* at 6:56). The answer to *this* question, crucial in modern Western consciousness, is assumed in Mark's world. In 1:40, the question is Jesus' willingness, not his power, and in 3:22, the issue is the source of his power, not the fact of it. Here, too, the Pharisees assume Jesus can perform the miracle, and the question is entirely a matter of religious law: will he do it on the Sabbath?

[3–4] The man does not ask for healing (cf. 2:5), nor do the opponents respond to Jesus' challenging question. Jesus is the only speaker in the entire scene. He takes the initiative, forces the issue, calls the man to stand up before all, and addresses not the man but the Pharisees. He operates entirely by his powerful word (cf. 1:16–20). Thus the scene should not be understood as political theater staged by Jesus[38]—we do not have here an exact transcript of a particular event—but as Markan theology. God's act in Christ precedes human seeking. Mark's own church should not keep a low profile in order to avoid harassment and persecution, concealing its freedom in Christ, but should boldly live out its faith.

At the level of everyday life, the Pharisees have a reasonable point: unless there is a life-threatening situation, Sabbath laws should be observed, and the man's healing should be postponed a few hours until after the Sabbath.[39] Jesus' posing the issue in life-or-death terms should not be understood merely as exaggeration; from Mark's perspective it has a triple theological point. (1) Concretely, Jesus is restoring life to a particular individual, while his challengers are working out a strategy to put Jesus to death. Jesus' response is oriented not to the abstract issue of the law, but to the concrete issue of what he is doing and what his opponents are doing. (2) The incident focuses the issue on the purpose of the Torah, namely to bring life and to do God's will, ultimately expressed in the love command by which all commandments are to be judged (cf. 12:28–34; Deut 30:15). (3) As a symbolic portrayal of the deliverance effected by God in the Christ-event as such, the man is in the realm of death, and his restoration sets him in the realm of life and salvation.

[5] The Pharisees respond wrongly because of the hardness of their hearts. In biblical theology, Greek *kardia* as the primary translation of Heb. *lēb* and *lēbāb*, refers not only, or mainly, to the center of the emotions, but to the locus of the will and understanding.[40] For the Markan narrative throughout, the principal problem is lack of understanding. For early Christianity in general it was a profoundly troubling problem that the Jews as God's own people, with their Scripture and tradition, for the most part failed to recognize Jesus as Messiah and did not respond in faith to the church's proclamation. Early Christian theologians found some help in the biblical concept of "hardening," which was dialectically both human responsibility and expression of the sovereignty of

---

38. So Myers, *Binding the Strong Man*, 161–62, who interprets this section in terms of political ideology under the heading "Civil Disobedience as Theater: Jesus' Deuteronomic Ultimatum."

39. Cf. 1:29–34; 2:23–28; Luke 13:10–17. Scribal law in Jesus' day allowed work on the Sabbath in exceptional cases, e.g., the service of a midwife at childbirth and the work of a physician where life was threatened. Later Rabbinic teaching had a very moderate interpretation of such rules—even a sore throat could be treated on the Sabbath, since it could develop into something serious (*Yoma* 8:6). There was a spectrum of understandings in first-century Judaism concerning how rigidly the rules should be applied, with the Qumran teachers being more rigid than others. The Pharisees' point in the Markan story is not that the man should not be healed, but that the healing should be delayed a few hours in order to preserve the sanctity of the Sabbath.

40. Friedrich Baumgärtel and Johannes Behm, "*kardia*," in *TDNT*, 3:605–13.

God. Here and 10:5, the Pharisees' hearts are "hard," as though it was their own choice; in 6:52 and 8:17 the disciples' hearts are "hardened," a passive participle pointing to God as the one responsible. The classic example was the pharoah of the exodus, who both willfully refused to hear God's word through Moses and was the unwilling object of God's sovereign power. Pharaoh hardens his own heart (Exod 8:15), but God hardens his heart (Exod 4:21). Both affirmations are made simultaneously in 9:34–10:1. So also the mystery of why Israel did not respond to the message of the prophets was classically expressed by Isa 6:9–13, a text that became central not only to Mark (cf. 4:12), but to broad streams of New Testament theology (cf. Matt 13:14–15; Mark 4:12; Luke 8:10; John 12:40; Acts 28:26; Rom 11:8). In Mark, it is not only Jesus' opponents whose hearts are hardened, but the crowds that follow him (4:12), Israel in general (10:5), and even his disciples (6:52; 8:17). The modern reader should therefore not view this scene superficially as merely portraying some particularly obtuse, evil, or obstinate individuals who rejected Jesus' liberal attitude toward the Sabbath because they were bound by their own narrow orthodoxy—as though, if we had been there, we would have responded differently—but as exemplifying the miracle of God's initiative and election. Jesus thus responds with a combination of wrath and sorrow, expressing not only the emotion of a truly human being, but the dialectic of the divine wrath and compassion. He can unilaterally heal a withered hand, but not a hard heart.

The actual healing is something of an anticlimax. Jesus only speaks, which by any standard could hardly be considered "work," but the point is lost in this context, which is oriented to larger issues. To ask whether Jesus "actually violated the Sabbath" is to pose the question in un-Markan categories, as though the conduct of the Lord of the Sabbath could be judged by other norms. As throughout 2:1–3:6, the issue is primarily christological, to which questions of practice are then subordinated. Likewise, the effect on the healed man, and even his name, are not mentioned. The story points beyond itself.

[6] In order to have Jesus executed, the Pharisees, who are lay religious leaders without political authority, need the support of those with political influence, and collaborate with the Herodians.[41] Their plan, however, is never realized. While John the Baptist does fall victim to Herod Antipas—an ominous foreshadowing of Jesus' fate, since Herod was also interested in Jesus (see on 6:14–29)—the

---

41. The Herodians were not an identifiable religious party comparable to Pharisees and Sadducees. They are referred to elsewhere in the New Testament only in 12:13 and the Matthean parallel at 22:16, though the "leaven of the Pharisees and the leaven of Herod" appear together in the warning of 8:15. Josephus, *War* 1:326, refers to "those of Herod's party" (*tous ta Hērōdou phronounta*, lit. "those who think along Herodian lines"; Polyaenus 8.14.3 refers to those who belong to the Roman party as *ta Rōmaiōn phronein*, "those who think along Roman lines"; cf. Mark 8:33). The phrase apparently refers to supporters of Herod Antipas, puppet king of Galilee during Jesus' ministry, and likely to those who backed the reigns of his son Agrippa I and grandson Agrippa II.

events that do happen in Jerusalem that bring about Jesus' death are remarkably similar. The story probably reflects Mark's own stylization, retrojecting the pattern of the passion story into the controversies of the Galilean period. The pericope 3:1–6 does have several traits of the passion story: (a) The religious leaders want to execute Jesus on religious charges, but need the political authorities to carry out their plan; (b) "blasphemy" is the primary religious charge, and in each case Jesus responds by identifying himself as Son of Man (2:7–10, 28; 14:62–64);[42] (c) Jesus manifests divine wrath in the temple cleansing and cursing of the fig tree and manifests grief in Gethsemane; (d) there is the identical vocabulary of *apolesōsin* (11:18) *symboulion* (15:1); (e) the central motif of Jesus' response in 3:4, "do good or do harm, save life or destroy life," proleptically portrays what is at stake as the Jerusalem religious and political leaders make their decision in response to Jesus. Thus all of 3:1–6 is a dramatic foreshadowing of what will transpire in Jerusalem. Mark did not want the death of Jesus in Jerusalem to appear only as the conclusion of the story, but also was unwilling to unrealistically bring the Jerusalem chief priests and Roman governor to Galilee early in the story. In 3:1–6, though based on older tradition, Mark arranges the narrative so that the pattern (but not the personnel) of the passion permeates the story throughout. Major turning points of part 1 end in rejection (see Introduction 2.): as in 3:6 Jesus is rejected by the religious leaders, so in 6:6 he is rejected by his family and hometown, and in 8:21 even his disciples do not understand.

3:7–12 International Multitudes, the Sick, and the Demonized—and Jesus' Response

Part 1 of Mark's narrative portrays the Jesus who, filled with divine power, effects salvation by his mighty acts of healing and exorcism, but who conceals his identity by the messianic secret. This pattern has briefly receded to accommodate other Markan interests in the preceding controversy section 2:1–3:6. With this transitional paragraph, Mark now reestablishes the pattern that had dominated the opening section, 1:21–45, in which mighty acts attract throngs of followers who nonetheless fail to discern Jesus' true identity. This most extensive summary in the Gospel could in fact attach seamlessly to 1:45, but Mark's insertion of the controversy section now gives a different tenor to all that follows.

---

42. Blasphemy is not explicitly found in 3:1–6, but the common elements and pattern this pericope shares with 2:1–12 suggests that the charge of 2:7 is carried over into this pericope, since in both stories Jesus acts with divine authority. "Son of Man" of 2:10 connects with 2:28, which in turn connects with the Sabbath theme binding together 2:23–3:6.

3:7 And Jesus, with his disciples, withdrew to the sea, and a great multitude from Galilee followed,[a] and from Judea 8 and from Jerusalem and from Idumea and Transjordan and the area around Tyre and Sidon, a great multitude, when they heard all that he was doing, came to him. 9 And he told his disciples to keep a boat ready for him because of the crowd, to keep them from crushing him. 10 For he healed many, so that all who were afflicted were falling upon him in order to touch him,[b] 11 and the unclean spirits, whenever they saw him, were falling prostrate[c] before him, crying out, "You are the Son of God." 12 And he sternly[d] warned them not to reveal his identity.

a. *Akoloutheō*, if original (it is missing from some MSS), can here mean either "accompany" in the ordinary sense or "follow" in the sense of discipleship. It seems to be parallel to the neutral "came to him" that concludes the sentence, but may nonetheless have the overtones of discipleship.

b. From *epipiptō*, lit. "fall upon," which can be understood in a favorable (as Luke 15:20) or hostile sense (e.g., LXX Gen 14:15). The latter would correspond to the translation of *thlibōsin* in v. 9 as "crush," a word that often has the negative sense of "oppress, persecute," as in, e.g., 2 Cor 1:6; 4:8; 1 Thess 3:4.

c. From *prospiptō*, lit. "fall before," which can be understood in the positive sense of worship, but here means subjection, servility (as 5:33; 7:25; so Gundry, *Mark*, 163). The afflicted "fall on" him imploringly or threateningly, the demonized "fall before" him in subjection or worship. Cf. also the double meaning of *krazō*, "cry out," which can be either the anguished cry of the defeated demon or the worshipful response to Jesus' authority. Both uses are found in Mark 9:24–26.

d. *Polla*, neuter plural of *polys*, "much, many," could be translated "repeatedly." *Polla* can also be used adverbially to intensify the verb (as 5:10, 38, 43; 6:20, 23; 9:26).

[3:7–8] Jesus does not launch a counterattack against the plot to have him killed, nor does he take flight; he simply "withdraws." The location beside the sea is reminiscent of the previous scenes of calling his disciples (1:16–20; 2:13–14), who now accompany him. "Disciples" need not refer to the five explicitly called; Mark's narrative is not so linear. Now, again beside the sea, great multitudes (*plēthos*) "follow" him (see note *a* above). The indistinct use of "disciples" and "follow" raises the question of what constitutes discipleship, and whether only those specially called are disciples (cf. 2:15, 16, 18, 23), to which Mark will respond in the next pericope (see also *Excursus: Crowds, Followers, Disciples, and the Twelve* at 6:6).

In response to reports of what Jesus was doing, that is, his miraculous healings and exorcisms rather than his teaching, people come from long distances and form an international gathering. The list of cities and countries is presented from the perspective of Galilee as the center, then Judea and Jerusalem to the south, Idumea (mentioned only here in the New Testament) even farther to the south, then the area across the Jordan to the east, then the area around Tyre and

Sidon to the north. Since the Mediterranean borders Galilee on the west, no crowds could be pictured as coming from that direction. Otherwise, the four points of the compass are represented, and this is clearly Mark's intent: a very large crowd, from diverse and distant locations, gathers around Jesus in Galilee. Mark is likely suggesting the international, far-flung response to Jesus in the reader's own time (and place?), since various aspects of the scene make it difficult to imagine as a historical event during Jesus' ministry: the great distances and long travel times involved, the absence of reference to provisions (contrast 6:34–36; 8:2–3), and the lack of any concern on the part of Herod Antipas regarding the political implications of such a large and excited gathering at the beginning of Jesus' ministry (contrast his response to John the Baptist, who attracted only people from Judea, 1:5; 6:17–29).

[9–12] To this overwhelming response, which also has undertones of threat (see note *b* above), Jesus makes two precautionary responses:

(1) *To avoid being crushed by the enthusiastic crowd, Jesus orders a boat to stand ready as a means of escape.* The boat is not used, and, after an intervening journey to the mountains and other events, another (?) boat appears as a speaking platform (4:1). The mysterious boat of 3:9 is thus not a lakeside pulpit but insurance against being mobbed and physically hurt. The puzzling presence of the boat here has supported source theories, and also raised theological questions: the reader wonders about Jesus' preoccupation with his own safety— should he not rather be concerned with the sick? The issue is analogous to the quandary posed by 4:10–12, and is perhaps already preparing the reader for such thinking. Furthermore, if Jesus has the power to heal and evoke the submission and acclamation of demons, does he not have power to avoid being harmed by the press of the crowd? Jesus seems at once to be all-powerful and vulnerable. Is there already a dim premonition that those who seek to save their life will lose it, and those who lose their life in the service of others will save it? In any case, the thoughtful reader already perceives that the story cannot be appropriated at the level of mere descriptive report, wonders if the boat has more than an incidental meaning (see on 4:1), and reflects on how to think of Jesus as both filled with divine power yet humanly weak and vulnerable.

(2) *Jesus is acclaimed as Son of God by the demons, who prostrate themselves before him, but orders them to be silent precisely because they—in contrast to the admiring crowds—know his true identity.* In this scene, Jesus does not cast out the unclean spirits, and there are no pictures of people rejoicing in their deliverance from demons. The reader sees another indication that the account is not merely informational, as the narrative camera focuses on only one aspect of the scene: the demons (i.e., the people they possess and through whom they speak) prostrate themselves before Jesus and cry out that he is the Son of God. This may represent mere deferential submission or worshipful homage (cf. Phil 2:10–11; Col 1:20; 2:15). In contrast to the defensive identi-

fication of Jesus made by the demons of 1:24, the acclamation is the same as the authentic confession made by Christian believers, confirmed by God's own confession of Jesus as his Son (1:1, 11; 9:7; 15:39). As always, the characters in the narrative do not perceive, and remain unaffected by this privileged information shared by the reader.

3:13–19 The Choosing of the Twelve

The preceding pericope, verses 7–12, had served as a transition, reestablishing Mark's basic story perspective. This scene thus functions somewhat as a second introduction to the next main section, as 1:16–20 did for the first section. Here the call that was initiated there advances to a new level. There, they were called to be disciples, and their call could be a model for the reader. Here, they are constituted as a special group that is important for the Christian community to which the reader belongs, but it is not transparent to the believer's own experience in the same way as the previous call story—Mark's readers can see themselves as disciples, but not as apostles called to "be with" Jesus during his earthly life. The international community just described in 3:7–12, an anticipatory picture of the church of Jews and Gentiles of Mark's own time, evokes the question of how the authority of Jesus will be mediated to this community. The creation of the Twelve is Jesus' response.

3:13 And he goes up the mountain[a] and summons those he himself chose,[b] and they came away to him. 14 And he appointed twelve[c] so that they might be with him and he might send them out to preach 15 and to have authority to cast out demons.[d] 16 So he appointed them as the Twelve[e]: Simon (to whom he gave the name Peter[f]); 17 James son of Zebedee and John the brother of James (to whom he gave the name Boanerges, that is, Sons of Thunder); 18 and Andrew, and Philip, and Bartholomew, and Matthew, and Thomas, and James son of Alphaeus, and Thaddaeus, and Simon the Cananaean,[g] 19 and Judas Iscariot, who nevertheless[h] betrayed him.

a. *Eis to oros* could be translated "into the hill country," but Mark probably intends the mountain as the locus of Jesus' authoritative pronouncement, with overtones of Sinai. Attempting to identify the particular mountain intended is too biographical and historicizing, confusing theology with geography, and thus misses Mark's point.

b. The verb *ēthelen* would be lit. "was wanting." The phrase *hous ēthelen autos*, with the emphatic pronoun, could also be translated "those whom he wanted / chose personally."

c. The phrase *hous kai apostolous ōnomasen* ("whom he also named apostles") has very strong attestation in the MSS, including both ℵ and B, and is thus included in the text of NA²⁷, albeit in brackets, and in the NRSV, NIV, TEV, CEV, [NAB]. The NA²⁶ had relegated the phrase to the apparatus, and it is not included in the RSV, REB, NJB. Since Mark elsewhere uses "apostle" only in 6:30, in the nontechnical sense, and since it is difficult to find a reason for its omission in A C² D K Π, *f* ¹ and numerous minuscules, the phrase here is considered a scribal insertion from Luke 6:13.

d. The parallelism of the Greek syntax is difficult to preserve in English. There are two purpose clauses, each introduced with *hina*, the second having two subheadings. The Twelve are the subject of the first clause and "he" [Jesus] the subject of the second:

> He appointed Twelve
>> A. that they might be with him
>> B. and that he might send them out
>>> 1. to preach
>>> 2. and to have authority to cast out demons

e. The second reference to the Twelve is missing from A C² D L Θ 0133, 0134, *f* ¹³ and most later MSS, but its absence is probably due to scribal tightening of the syntax, omitting the repetition from v. 14. It is here retained on the basis of its presence in several good MSS including both ℵ and B, and because it is part of the structure of the passage (missed by the scribal "correction"). The addition of the definite article (missing in v. 14) gives the phrase a quasi-official sense, expressed in the English translation above by capitalization. They were twelve individuals; now, by Jesus' creative act, they are "the Twelve."

f. *Petros* is the Greek word "rock," but it is here transliterated, instead of translated, because for Mark's readership as in modern English it had already become the name by which the disciple was known.

g. *Kananaion* was also a foreign word in Mark's Greek, and so is left here untranslated. Unrelated to the geographical names Cana or Canaan, it is a transliteration of Aramaic *qan'an* ("enthusiast, zealot"), related to the Hebrew *qin'ah* ("zeal, jealousy").

h. Translating the common conjunction *kai*, which normally means "and, also, even," but can also be used to emphasize a fact as surprising, unexpected, or noteworthy (cf. Bauer, BDAG, 495).

[13] *Anabainei eis to oros* ("he goes up the mountain") is a stock phrase occurring twenty-four times in the LXX, eighteen times in the Pentateuch, mostly of Moses, and for the reader familiar with the Bible it conjures up images of Sinai and God's establishment of Israel as the twelve-unit covenant people (Exod 18–20). There, too, the one God acts through his authorized mediator, who appoints further authorized representatives. As in 1:16–20, the initiative is entirely with Jesus, who summons those he personally chooses. The verb *proskaleitai* here has the connotation of "summons" or "order" in the legal or military sense (cf. 15:44). "Invite" is too soft a translation; the Twelve receive a draft notice, not merely an invitation.

[14] The verb *epoiēsen* ("appointed") is used in a manner that contrasts with classical Greek but corresponds to LXX usage for appointment (1 Sam 12:6; 1 Kgs 13:33). Since it is used repeatedly for God's act of creation in Gen 1–2 and elsewhere, it may also have the overtones of a new creative act. Likewise, the number twelve is not arbitrary, but resonant with biblical associations of the twelve-tribe covenant people. Mark does not make explicit precisely what these associations are: does Jesus constitute the Twelve as the nucleus of the eschatologically renewed people of God, or does he appoint them as missionaries *to* Israel? The Twelve and the "apostles" were different, overlapping groups in early Christianity (cf. 1 Cor 15:5–7). Mark does not use "apostle" in the official sense, but only in its functional sense as "missionary" (6:30). Unlike later tradition, he never speaks of "twelve apostles" or "twelve disciples" (Matt 10:1; 11:1; Luke 6:13; Acts 6:2; Rev 21:14), but simply of "the Twelve," a phrase he uses more than any of the other Gospels, despite their greater length (ten times; Matt three times; Luke six times; John four times). The Twelve are not "promoted" out of the rank of the disciples. Though for Mark they are a distinct group with a unique function, they do not represent a higher level in a hierarchy; Mark is suspicious of hierarchical imagery among the disciples (cf. 9:33–37; 10:35–45; see *Excursus: Crowds, Followers, Disciples, and the Twelve* at 6:6).

The Twelve do, however, have a unique role and function not fulfilled by all disciples (see further on 6:7–11, 30). Jesus appoints the Twelve[43] for two seemingly contrasting purposes, each introduced by a *hina* ("in order that") clause: "that they might be with him" and "that he might send them out." (1) "Being with him" distinguishes the Twelve from other followers and disciples. The Twelve leave their homes and jobs and follow him on his itinerant ministry. The phrase thus carries more freight than its pietistic sense of personal, individualistic "being with Jesus." Jesus and the Twelve will function as a unit throughout the remainder of the narrative until 14:50–52. They will form the connecting link between the time of Jesus narrated in the Gospel and the time of the church, the readers' present.[44] They will have the same message and ministry of exorcism as Jesus himself, and will also represent the missionaries of Mark's own church. Just as God sends Jesus, so Jesus sends his missionaries (9:37; 6:7). (2) Jesus' ultimate purpose in selecting them is not the spiritual self-indulgence of "being with Jesus," but "that he might send them out." The Twelve are subjects

---

43. The Twelve do not apply or volunteer. Here, too, Jesus takes the initiative. Thus Judas cannot be said to have "infiltrated" Jesus' group (contra Myers, *Binding the Strong Man*, 407).

44. Gnilka, *Markus*, 1:171, rightly points out that Mark has a dialectical view of the disciples / Twelve. On the one hand, they are the bearers of the tradition, the sign and means of continuity between Jesus and the church, between his preaching and church proclamation and instruction. Shiner's study of teachers in the Hellenistic world, comparing the Gospels and, e.g., Iamblichus's *Life of Pythagoras,* notes that "The listing of the twelve in Mark . . . would have been understood as succession lists legitimating the twelve as the authorized repositories of the traditions concerning Jesus." Shiner, *Follow Me!* 91. On the other hand, the appointing of the Twelve also functions within the framework of the messianic secret, illustrating that Jesus' message was not and could not be understood until after Easter. As Shiner points out, the two portrayals of the disciples are not linear; they overlap. "Jesus continues with his progressive commissioning of the disciples in spite of their incomprehension" (200).

of the first *hina* clause, but Jesus himself is the active subject of the second (not, as in the NRSV, where the Twelve are passive subjects). "Send" translates *apostellō*, the verb from which the noun "apostle" is derived. God is the original Sender, whose sending is manifest in John the Baptist (1:2) and Jesus (9:37; cf. John 17:18). The sending, like the calling / electing, is Jesus' own sovereign act. This sending is summarized in two components, expressed in parallel infinitives: (a) *kēryssein*, "proclaim the message," the activity of John (1:4, 7), of Jesus (1:14, 38–39), and of the later Christian community throughout the world (13:10; 14:9). (b) *Echein exousian ekballein ta daimonia* ("to have authority to cast out demons") completes the summary purpose of the Twelve's selection. The Twelve's mission is the extension of Jesus' own, and represents his authority. It is striking that "healing" is here omitted (though present in 6:13). Jesus' and the Twelve's mission is summarized as a ministry of word and deed, and Mark is here content to summarize their deeds under the one heading of expulsion of the demonic from this world, the meaning of the Christ-event as such (cf. 1:27, 39; 3:22; cf. John 12:31).[45]

[16–19] The second reference to "*the* Twelve," now constituted as a distinct group (see note *e* above), gives their names, including the new names Jesus gives to its first three members. These three constitute something of an inner group within the Twelve (cf. 5:37; 9:2, 14:33; *Excursus: Crowds, Followers, Disciples, and the Twelve* at 6:6). In several streams of biblical theology, naming is more than labeling; the name represents the person as such, so that to bestow a new name represents a change of being and status.

Simon is given the name "Peter," a Greek word meaning "rock." It is not simply a nickname, "Rocky," but suggests foundation (Matt 16:18) and pillar (Gal 2:9). "Rock" also evokes the renaming of Abram as Abraham, who stands at the beginning of God's covenant with Israel as the channel of blessing to all peoples (Gen 12:1–3; 17:5), and who in this role is called "rock" (Isa 51:1–2).[46] Both Jesus and the narrator will always use this new name for Simon throughout the narrative until 14:37. Just as Peter was called first (1:16–20), and functions throughout as leader and spokesperson for the Twelve (1:36; 5:37; 8:29–33; 9:5; 10:28; 11:21; 13:3; 14:37), so he will be acknowledged as their leader after Easter (16:7).

Peter's brother Andrew is not named until fourth in the list, in order to name John and James, who with Peter constitute an inner circle within the Twelve. They, too, and only they, are given new names by Jesus, further distinguishing

---

45. Cf. note 9, p. 63.

46. Mary Ann Tolbert, *Sowing the Gospel: Mark's World in Literary-Historical Perspective* (Minneapolis: Fortress, 1989), explains Simon's new name from within the text of Mark, by relating it to the "rocky soil" of Mark 4:16 that fails under persecution. This explanation has not been persuasive to many interpreters. Although Peter does fail within the plotted narrative, he is restored as the primary disciple after Easter (13:9–13; 16:7). Mark's readers would have been aware that Peter had died as a martyr, and would not associate his name with failure but steadfast endurance. After 64 C.E. Peter was recognized as the rock he proved to be.

them from the other disciples. They are also distinguished from Peter in this regard, for they do not receive new individual names, but together are called "Boanerges," and, unlike Peter, they are never referred to later in the narrative by this name, either by the narrator or by anyone in the narrative. Though it has occasioned many attempts at explanation, the meaning of "Boanerges" and Mark's translation "Sons of Thunder" remain as mysterious to us as to Matthew and Luke, who omit both the original name and its translation. Probably it designated their status in early Christianity rather than a personality trait.

The designation of Judas as "Iscariot" could be understood in Mark's time as related to the *sicarri*, the "dagger men" who assassinated sympathizers with the Romans. *If* these connotations are valid—and the evidence is not strong in the case of Judas—then the fact that Judas is already identified as the one who betrayed Jesus may reflect the situation of Mark's own times, when members of the Christian community who resisted the war were betrayed and put to death by their closest friends and family who were fighting the Romans. Even though "Iscariot" more likely designates Judas's place of origin, meaning "man from Kerioth," Mark and his readers may have taken it in the sense related to their own situation—just as Judas the "Zealot" had betrayed Jesus and contributed to his death, so it was happening in their own time (cf. 13:12, where the same verb is used of those who "hand over" Jesus' followers to be killed). This first reference to Judas that already, and without explanation, identifies him as the betrayer shows that Mark writes for initiated readers who already know the basic outline of the Jesus-story, and that only the naive, first-time "outsider" reader will be surprised or perplexed by this reference.[47] None of the other names in the list play any further role in the story.

3:20–35 God's Kingdom and Family

This segment represents the Markan adaptation of a very complex set of traditions (note the various locations of parallel passages in Matt 9:32–34; 12:22–37; 46–50; Luke 8:19–21; 11:14–15, 17–23; 12:10). As found in Mark, these verses are a unit that he composed from traditional elements, constructed according to the interlocking pattern typical of Markan composition (see on "Intercalations" at 5:21). Elements of the tradition history prior to Mark are disputed,[48] but the Markan structure is clear: he begins with a scene in which Jesus'

47. Contra Robert M. Fowler, *Let the Reader Understand: Reader-response Criticism and the Gospel of Mark* (Minneapolis: Fortress, 1991), 105–6. On the fallacy of the "virginal reader" among some narrative critics, see Francis J. Moloney, *The Gospel of John* (SP 4; Collegeville, Minn.: Liturgical Press, 1998), 13–20.

48. On the details of the tradition history here assumed, see the arguments, alternative views, and bibliographies in M. Eugene Boring, "The Unforgivable Sin Logion Mark 3:28–29 / Matt 12:31–32 / Luke 12:10: Formal Analysis and History of the Tradition," *NovT* 17 (1976): 258–79, and M. Eugene Boring, "The Synoptic Problem, 'Minor' Agreements and the Beelzebul Pericope," in *The Four Gospels 1992—Festschrift Frans Neirynck* (ed. Frans van Segbroeck et al.; 3 vols.; Leuven: Leuven University Press, 1992), 1:587–619.

"people" go looking for him because they believe he is out of his mind, inserts a scene in which scribes from Jerusalem charge Jesus with operating by the power of Beelzebul, then concludes with Jesus' family finding him without either apprehending him or joining his group. While verses 22–27 and 31–35 are Markan adaptations from tradition, Mark himself has combined them into this format, added the independent saying 28–30 into this context, and created verses 20–21 as the opening scene that sets the tone for the whole.

3:20 And he enters a house,[a] and again a crowd gathers, so that they were not even able to eat. 21 And when his people[b] heard, they came out to get[c] him, for they were saying[d] "He's not in his right mind."

22 And the scribes who had come down[e] from Jerusalem were saying, "He is possessed by Beelzebul,"[f] and "It is by the ruler of demons that he casts out demons." 23 And he summoned them and was speaking to them in parables: "How can Satan cast out Satan? 24 And if a kingdom is divided against itself, that kingdom cannot endure; 25 and if a house is divided against itself, that house cannot endure. 26 And if Satan has rebelled against himself and is divided, he cannot endure but is coming to an end. 27 But no one can enter the strong man's house and plunder his property, unless he first binds the strong man, and then he can plunder his house. 28 Amen[g] I say to you, people will be forgiven all their sins, and however many[h] blasphemies they have uttered. 29 But whoever blasphemes against the Holy Spirit will never receive forgiveness, but is guilty of an eternal sin—30 for they had been saying, "He is possessed by an unclean spirit."

31 And his mother and his brothers and sisters[i] arrive, and standing outside they sent to him, calling him. 32 And a crowd was sitting around him, and they tell him, "Look, your mother and your brothers and sisters are outside, looking for you." 33 And he replies, "Who is my mother, and who are my brothers and sisters?" 34 And looking around at those seated around him in a circle, he says, "You look[j]—these are my mother and brothers and sisters. 35 For whoever does the will of God is my brother and sister and mother."

a. See on 2:1.

b. *Hoi par' autou* (lit. "those beside him") was used idiomatically for close associates (as in 1 Macc, six times, for Jonathan and his men / troops / companions) or family (as in LXX Prov 31:21, "her family and friends"; cf. Sus 33 NRSV "those with her"; NAB "her relatives"). The phrase is here translated "people," which in colloquial English can mean family, friends, associates, one's own group. It is in fact Jesus' family that shows up in v. 30, but the initial ambiguity dramatizes the scene for the reader, who does not learn their specific identity until the scene is concluded.

c. *Kratēsai* is a strong word that can often be translated "seize," "apprehend," "arrest," as in 6:17; 12:12; 14:46, but can also mean "firmly grasp" in a benevolent sense (as 1:31). I thus translate it here with the colloquial "get," which could mean that they want to bring Jesus back home for his own good, but as the story turns out, is to be understood with a hostile, almost violent overtone.

d. The imperfect third plural *elegon* could be understood impersonally, "people were saying," but the parallel to the *elegon* of the next sentence, where the scribes are clearly the subject, indicates that here it is Jesus' family who say this.

e. "Coming down" is meant literally, not in the sense of "from the north." Jerusalem is on a mountain; people "go up" to and "come down" from the Holy City, from whatever direction.

f. Practically all Greek manuscripts read *beelzeboul*, though B reads *beezeboul*. Both are different from the traditional "Beelzebub" of the NIV, following the KJV, which had followed the Vulgate. No Greek MS reads "Beelzebub." This name was related to the Hebrew epithet given to the god of the Philistines in 2 Kgs 1:2, Baal-zebub, "god of flies." The etymology and meaning of both Beelzebub and Beelzebul are disputed (cf. *IDB* 1:332, 374), though "Beelzebul" may well have been used as the name of a pagan god, "Lord of the House" (= Heavenly Temple). Even if by New Testament times the etymology had been forgotten, the name was then adapted in Judaism as a pejorative name for the chief demon, equivalent to Satan and Belial.

g. The adverbial form of the Hebrew root *'mn*, which basically means "to be firm, to confirm, to support," was used as a strong response to something that had been said, i.e., "may it be so," "that is certainly true." The historical Jesus apparently used it in a distinctive way at the *beginning* of certain utterances, a usage adopted by the early church when transmitting his sayings.[49] Since the word was transliterated into Greek rather than translated, and thus would appear as a strange element to Greek readers and hearers, that practice is here preserved (as in NAB).

h. The translation obscures a grammatical irregularity in the sentence, which is awkward in any case. The indefinite relative pronoun *hosa* is neuter plural in agreement with "sins," when proper grammar requires it to be feminine in concord with "blasphemies"—a problem remedied in A C K L Γ and other MSS—but the original text is preserved in ℵ B D Δ Θ and other MSS.

i. *Adelphoi*, the plural of *adelphos*, "brother," is found in vv. 31, 32, 33, 35, supplemented in some MSS by "sisters" in v. 32. Then the singular "brother" and "sister" are found in Jesus' concluding statement in v. 35. Mark 6:3 refers to Jesus' sisters. The masculine plural *adelphoi* was sometimes used generically to mean "brothers and sisters," both in general usage (e.g., Luke 21:16)[50] and as a quasi-technical term for the Christian community (e.g., 1 Cor 1:1 and in Paul's letters generally). "*Hoi adelphoi*," "the brothers," thus had the ring of "the brethren," a term for the inclusive Christian community.

---

49. See Joachim Jeremias, *New Testament Theology: The Proclamation of Jesus* (New York: Scribner, 1971), 35–36, and the bibliography he gives. This view has been repeatedly challenged, but remains essentially intact. See Jeremias's response to his critics in Joachim Jeremias, "Zum nicht-responsorischen Amen," *ZNW* 64 (1973): 122–23. For initial "amen" as a mark of Christian prophetic speech, see Boring, *Continuing Voice of Jesus*, 163–65.

50. See numerous examples in Walter Bauer and Frederick W. Danker, eds., *A Greek-English Lexicon of the New Testament and Other Early Christian Literature* (3d ed.; trans. Frederick W. Danker and William Arndt; Chicago: University of Chicago Press, 2000), 18.

On the issue of whether Mark intends natural brothers of Jesus (rather than stepbrothers or cousins), see on 6:3.

j. *Ide* corresponds to the *idou* of the crowd in v. 32. Both are stereotyped particles with equivalent meaning, not really an imperative but an attention-getting particle used to begin a sentence.

[20–21] The house and crowd are stock elements in Mark's narrative and carry theological freight.[51] Jesus is pictured once again as in a house, surrounded by those who turn out to be his true brothers and sisters in the family of God (vv. 32, 34–35), a scene that evokes in Mark's readers the image of their own house churches. Jesus is so involved with the crowd that he and those with him could not so much as eat. Such frenzied behavior is taken by his family as an indication that Jesus has lost his mind. Numerous efforts by interpreters and scribes who transmitted the MSS have attempted to soften this obvious meaning,[52] but that *exestē* must here refer to berserk behavior is clear from its usage elsewhere (e.g., 2 Cor 5:13), by the parallel between what the scribes are saying and what his family is saying (*elegon gar hoti exestē* is paralleled by *elegon hoti Beelzeboul echei*), and by the strong word *kratēsai* expressing the family's intent. More is going on here than Mary's motherly instincts making her wonder if Jesus is eating well. Jesus' mother and brothers are not merely concerned about his welfare and about getting him discreetly out of the public eye. They are not malicious in their misunderstanding, like the scribes who attribute his works to Satan; they merely think he is crazy. And they not only abstain from becoming his followers, but join the scribes in actively opposing his ministry. The Markan Mary is unaware of a virginal conception, and she plays out her role in terms of the messianic secret (see *Excursus: The Messianic Secret* at 9:13).

[22] With the arrival of scribes from Jerusalem, the opposition becomes more sinister. Scribes have heretofore been at the forefront of those who challenged Jesus (2:6, 16), but they have been local religious authorities. Now, just as the family comes from elsewhere (presumably Nazareth) to restrain Jesus, so scribes arrive from Jerusalem. The two previous references to Jerusalem have been positive, as people from Jerusalem flock to both John and Jesus (1:5; 3:8); Mark is not suspicious of Jerusalem as such. But the religious leadership

51. On the "house," see on 1:29; 2:1, 15. To ask from a historicizing perspective whether the house is the same as that of 1:29; 2:1, 15 and the crowd is the same as 3:7–12 are questions likely to miss Mark's point, just as are speculations on whether the "crowd" could fit inside the "house" or only gather at the door (2:2).

52. If it were not the obvious meaning, scribes would not have attempted to "correct" it (cf. the variations for *exestē* in the MSS), and Matthew and Luke would not have omitted it. Among those who have offered alternate explanations is John Painter, *Mark's Gospel: Worlds in Conflict* (NTR; London: Routledge, 1997), 69–71, who argues it is the crowd that considers Jesus "beside himself," and the disciples who attempt to restrain him.

of Jerusalem has now taken note of Jesus, the initiated reader knows that their scribes will be involved in the machinations that lead to his death (8:31; 10:33; 11:18; 14:1, 43, 53; 15:1, 31), and the reference to Jerusalem thus sounds an ominous note. The local religious leaders and their political collaborators have already resolved to put Jesus to death (3:6), but their charges have been that he is a blasphemer and lawbreaker who has been properly warned (2:7, 24; 3:1). This charge is now escalated: Jesus operates with satanic power. Prior to the passion story, Jesus' power to work miracles is not the issue (cf. notes on 1:40; 9:22–23 and *Excursus: Miracle Stories in Mark* at 6:56). Previously, the problem has been that he performs his miraculous deeds on the Sabbath; now, that he performs them by satanic power.

In the Q version of this scene, the scribes' charge is in response to a particular incident of exorcism (Matt 12:22–23; 9:32–33 / Luke 11:14). If Mark knew this introduction, he has omitted it, so that in Mark the charge is evoked not by an individual occasion, but by the ministry of Jesus as a whole, which Mark can sum up as "casting out demons" (see on 1:39; 1:12, 21–28). Mark poses the issue dualistically, with no middle ground (cf. 3:4): does the power all acknowledge to be at work in Jesus represent the kingdom of God or the forces of transcendent evil? By speaking of Beelzebul as the "ruler of demons," the scribes acknowledge that the question concerns more than an individual instance of evil, that there is a whole demonic system, the negative counterpart to the kingdom of God. That the scribes "were saying" this (*elegon*, iterative imperfect) suggests that this was their typical and repeated charge against Jesus and his group, not that it was directly said to Jesus on a particular occasion. Once again, the reader has privileged information unavailable to the characters in the story, and already knows this charge is false, having observed the descent of the Holy Spirit on Jesus (1:10) and Jesus' first encounter with the demons in which the demonic world itself acknowledges that the power they fear is that of the Holy One of God (1:24).

[23–29] Jesus first summons the scribes (see on *proskaleō* at 3:13), who have been bandying this charge about, and confronts them directly with a threefold response (3:23–27; cf. 2:25–28) followed by a solemn pronouncement concerning blasphemy against the Holy Spirit (3:28–29).

[23–26] This is the first occurrence of the term "parables" in Mark, though Jesus has previously responded to his critics in figurative, allusive speech (2:20–22; see on 4:2). The first two responses utilize the imagery of Satan's kingdom and Satan's household. Each image conceives of the demonic realm as a unified entity that is more than the aggregate of individual demons. Just as Jesus is not a "great man" in the individualistic sense of an outstanding personality, a religious celebrity, or a genius, but represents the kingdom of God, so the opposition comprises not merely individual evil forces but united "systemic evil." The Markan Jesus argues that even if one assumes the false scribal interpretation of Jesus' ministry to be true, this would still mean that Satan's kingdom or household is self-destructing from within (vv. 24–25 deal with metaphors and are constructed with subjunctives, unreal conditions). Verse 26 then shifts to the indicative to pose the issue in real terms: if Jesus represents Satanic power, then Satan is divided against himself and his rule is coming to an end in Jesus' ministry—even on the scribes' own understanding, Jesus' ministry represents the beginning of the end of Satan's domain. The whole discussion conceives the dawning kingdom of God within the dualistic apocalyptic framework (see *Excursus: Kingdom of God* at 1:15). If God is to rule, Satan the "strong man" must be bound. Jesus is not only the herald of this dawning kingdom, but in some sense its agent, the "stronger one" announced by John (1:7).

[27] In the preceding verses Jesus has been arguing on the scribes' own terms. Each of the statements of verses 24, 25, 26 is introduced with the common coordinating conjunction *kai*. But with verse 27, introduced with the adversative conjunction *alla* indicating a strong contrast, Jesus presents the real situation: the dynamism of his ministry does not reflect internal troubles within the realm of evil, but an invasion from without. Jesus' parabolic speech does not hesitate to utilize bold, disconcerting imagery—a burglar cannot break into a strong man's house and plunder it without first tying up the strong man. Jesus pictures what is happening in his ministry as the eschatological binding of Satan; as he and his disciples preach, heal, and cast out demons, they are plundering Satan's kingdom and setting the captives free. One image of the eschatological victory of God found in biblical texts and Jewish tradition is that at the end, God, either directly or through his agents, would overcome or bind the power of evil, sometimes represented as a strong or mighty man. This liberating act allows God's people and the creation itself to celebrate the liberty of the abundant life God intends, a celebration sometimes portrayed as dividing the booty taken from the enemy. The prominence of Isaian imagery in this tradition, and the key role of Isaiah in the formation of Mark's theology, should be noted (cf. Isa 24:21–22; 49:24–26; 53:12; *T. Dan* 5.11; *T. Levi* 18.12; *T. Zeb.* 9.8; *1 En.* 10.4–5; 11QMelch; Rom 8:18–25; Rev 20:1–2). Now the reader can see what had transpired when Jesus was tested by Satan in the wilderness (1:12–13) and what is in progress in the ministry of Jesus (1:23–28, 39). Jesus and the reader already look back on the decisive defeat of Satan; his present ministry is not a battle in which the outcome is in doubt, but the mopping-up exercise in the territory of a defeated enemy. The power of evil has not disappeared—Jesus still casts out demons and Mark's church is still confronted by demonic situations—but the decisive event has already taken place. Mark and his community look back on God's saving act in the Christ-event as a whole, and thus do not regard this decisive event only as Jesus' victory over Satan in the wilderness encounter or in the exorcisms of his ministry; the stories of each of these points beyond the event it narrates to God's act in Christ as such, narrated in the Markan Gospel as a whole.

[28–29] Jesus, who is already regarded as a blasphemer (2:7) and will finally be condemned to death on the charge of blasphemy (14:64), here reveals the true nature of blasphemy and declares it forgivable—except for the ultimate blasphemy. From Mark's point of view, to refuse to believe in this good news is bad enough, but to pervert it into its opposite, and consider it the work of Satan rather than the work of God, is the ultimate human evil, the rejection of God's definitive last word. It is in this perspective that the saying about the "unpardonable sin" should be understood. Mark brings an independent saying into this context and is the first to do so. The core of the original saying, which goes back to the historical Jesus, had been an unconditional pronouncement of universal amnesty: all sins will be forgiven to all people. The saying circulating in Mark's setting had been elaborated in the course of tradition, probably by a Christian prophet pronouncing God's judgment on those who rejected the Holy Spirit that inspired prophecy.[53] The Markan form thus juxtaposes two different statements. The first declares that all sins will be forgiven; the second specifies one sin that will not be forgiven. This is not the same as "All sins will be forgiven except one . . ." (found in none of the Gospels), nor is it the same form as the Matthean and Lukan saying, "This sin (speaking against the Son of Man) will be forgiven, but a different sin (speaking against the Holy Spirit) will not be forgiven." These forms are more readily amenable to ordinary human logic than the Markan form, which is the paradoxical juxtaposition of two different statements, each coherent and complete in itself, but logically problematical when placed together. The Markan form belongs to the same category as the pair of clashing statements in 9:24. The Markan form is dialectic: without compromising the original pronouncement of unconditional and universal forgiveness, it solemnly declares that those who reject the message given by the Holy Spirit can only anticipate God's eschatological judgment.

[30] Christian tradition has combined this text with its Matthean and Lukan forms and attempted to interpret it in conjunction with other New Testament references to an "unpardonable sin" (Luke 12:10; Matt 12:31–32; Heb 6:4–8; 10:26–29; 1 John 5:16–17). However, verse 30 shows that Mark does not present this text as material for a general discussion of which sins may be forgiven and which not, but regards it as addressing one particular situation. While later readers may not dismiss or trivialize the terror of this warning, it is to be interpreted in the context of the dualistic apocalypticism of Mark's theology as a whole (see on 4:10–12; 9:40). This dualistic theology of "insiders" and "outsiders" is already being prepared for in the next scene.

[3:31–35] Jesus' family that set out in verse 21 now arrives. In the meantime the reader has come to see what is at stake in one's response to Jesus. Jesus is

53. For evidence for this view and alternatives to it, see M. Eugene Boring, "How May We Identify Oracles of Christian Prophets in the Synoptic Tradition? Mark 3:28–29 as a Test Case," *JBL* 91, no. 4 (1972): 501–21, and Boring, "Unforgivable Sin Logion," 258–79.

inside the house, surrounded by his circle. His mother, brothers, and sisters stand outside, send (*apesteilan*; cf. 3:14; 6:7) for him, and call (*kalountes;* cf. 1:20, 2:17) him. Mark heightens the irony of the situation by using the same terminology that expresses Jesus' own calling and sending disciples. Jesus does not go out to them, but sends his reply indirectly. Mark offers no explanation for Jesus' rude behavior to his own mother and siblings, for he is narrating on another level than reporting personal relationships and familial behavior during the earthly ministry of Jesus. The scene is theological throughout. The appearance of Jesus as the representative of God's kingdom calls for a radical decision, and nothing can have a higher priority, not even family (cf. 1:20; 10:17–31). Mark's own church was facing existential decisions that sometimes forced them to choose between Christian faith and family, and they were sometimes betrayed to the authorities by members of their own families (cf. 13:9–12, which, as here, includes speaking by the Holy Spirit). But this extraordinary scene not only indicates that it may be necessary to forsake one's biological family, the closest ties in this world, in order to be a disciple of Jesus, it declares that this circle of disciples has been constituted as a new family. Remarkably, the one who is the Son of God here declares that those about him are not only followers and disciples, and not only brothers and sisters to each other, but that as their brother they belong *with* him as brothers and sisters to the family of God (cf. 10:28–30; Matt 25:40; 28:10; Rom 8:29; John 20:17; Heb 2:11). That "father" is missing from this metaphor is not merely a matter of the absence of Joseph from the Markan narrative but part of the theological imagery: the family of God to which both Jesus and the disciples belong can have many mothers, brothers, and sisters, but only one father (cf. 8:38; 11:25; 13:32; 14:36).

Mark here leaves the content of "doing the will of God" undefined. Undoubtedly the scribes understood "doing the will of God" to be the reason they had made the arduous trip from Jerusalem to Galilee in the first place. While Mark does not prescribe or legally define what "doing the will of God" means, the macro-narrative makes it clear that it must be related to repentance in response to Jesus' proclamation of the kingdom (1:14–15) and the command to love God and neighbor that sums up the law (12:28–34), as articulated by a Jerusalem scribe. Mark thus does not give a clear yes / no response to the issue of whether one must be a believer in Jesus in order to "do the will of God" and be included in God's family. Most of Mark's readers will have made the decision to become Christians as adults, and some will have broken family ties in order to be Christian disciples and will hear these words as embracing them in the larger family of God.

All the Gospels portray Jesus' family as not believing in him as the Messiah until after the resurrection. This is the only scene in Mark in which Mary appears. Humanity is divided into two groups, insiders and outsiders, and Jesus' mother and siblings belong to the outsiders, along with the scribes, whose opposition is also radicalized in this scene. But Mark's theology is not monodimensional. This same scene contains the declaration of universal forgiveness, and over against the closed circle that separates insider and outsider is the open-ended "whoever" of verse 35. Jerusalem scribes are roundly condemned, but Mark also knows of the good scribe of 12:28–34. Mary here stands among the outsiders, but Easter brings the renewed possibility of [the same?] Mary in 15:40–41, 47; 16:1, and the "whoever" can expand the circle of those around Jesus to include readers of Mark's own time and later, including those who have denied him or failed to recognize him.

4:1–34 Central Discourse of Part 1: Parables and Mystery of the Kingdom of God

The fast-paced narrative now pauses, and for the first time Jesus makes an extended speech. The two major parts of Mark's composition each have a lengthy discourse situated approximately at the midpoint of the section: 4:1–34 in the midst of 1:1–8:21; 13:1–37 bisecting 11:1–16:8 (see Introduction 2.). Like the apocalyptic discourse, the parable discourse serves to interpret the meaning of the narrative as a whole.

The parable discourse is not intended to give a "summary of Jesus' teaching." This passage can be read in a few minutes, but it is only an excerpt from a teaching session that lasted until evening and included "many things" (vv. 2, 33, 35). Rather than a summary, it is more like "teaching about teaching" (Hooker, *Mark*, 120), the how and why of Jesus' message, and the reader still looks in vain for an extended presentation of the substance of Jesus' message. Mark's understanding of "Jesus the teacher" is not primarily related to the content of his teaching, which in any case could not be understood until after the resurrection, in the light of the cross (see *Excursus: Jesus the Teacher versus the Scribes* at 7:23 and *Excursus: The Messianic Secret* at 9:13).

Mark's purpose in including the discourse here seems to be related to questions plaguing the Markan community.

(1) Jesus had announced that the kingdom of God was dawning in his own ministry, which was devoted to announcing this good news and calling people to repentance (1:14–15). In conflict with the scribes from Jerusalem, Jesus had indicated that the "strong man" had been bound and that his "house" was being ransacked: Satan had been overpowered and the kingdom that was dawning in Jesus' ministry meant freedom for those held captive (3:27). But the world

continued as usual, and Mark's community was experiencing distress and persecution. The community of Christian believers was hearing that Jesus and his followers were not the advance wave of God's kingdom, but an obstacle to it (see on 2:18–3:6), that Jesus' ministry, now carried on by his followers, even represented the demonic kingdom rather than God's (3:22). The challengers of Jesus in the narrative and the church's opponents of Mark's own time believed in the coming kingdom of God; their daily prayer included "thy kingdom come." The issue was not whether one believed in the promised kingdom of God, but whether the unorthodox, out-of-step ministry of Jesus and his followers represents and initiates God's kingdom or is a barrier to its coming.

(2) In Mark's setting the community of Christian believers was primarily Gentile, and most Jewish people encountering the new faith had rejected it. The experience of Mark's church in history had been recapitulated in the preceding two chapters: Jesus' proclamation had received a broad positive response, but the Jewish leadership had rejected it. From the perspective of the Markan church, the Messiah was being generally rejected by Israel, the biblical people of God, and the Messiah was forming a new family of God (3:31–35). This new situation in which former insiders are now outsiders, and vice versa, called for an explanation. One function of 4:1–34 is to explain in biblical terms how this could be. This is then followed in 4:35–5:17 by Jesus' first venture into Gentile territory. Thus the section 4:1–20 (the seed parable, the reason for speaking in parables including the "hardening theory," and the interpretation of the parable) is not merely an isolated episode in the Markan narrative, but "provides the audience with the fundamental typology of hearing-response that organizes the entire plot of the Gospel . . . a theological vision of the world and Jesus' mission in it" (Tolbert, *Sowing the Gospel*, 164–65). The first parable of 4:3–9, the key to them all (v. 13), comes after the Jerusalem leadership rejects Jesus (3:22–30), as does the parable of 12:1–11 in its context. These are the only two parables that are extended narratives, and each has an explanatory Scripture citation to clinch the point. Mark understands both parables allegorically, portraying Israel's mostly negative response to Jesus.

(3) A third, and related, question is internal to Mark's own theological thought and that of his community: what does it mean that Jesus was not recognized and understood more fully by his own disciples until after Jesus' death and resurrection? The issues dealt with in 4:1–34 are not only apologetic, but internal to Markan Christology and interwoven with the messianic secret.

In the present text of Mark, 4:1–34 is a discrete unit, bracketed by a redactional introduction (1–2) and conclusion (33–34) and designed by Mark to be grasped as a whole. Yet the individual subunits of which it is composed did not all originate at the same time, but represent the growth of an extensive tradition. The details of the development of the tradition are not obvious; efforts to reconstruct its stages vary.[54] The present structure, even if it reflects elements of a pre-Markan collection from a variety of stages in tradition history, is from Mark; since he could have arranged it otherwise, it should be carefully noted:

1–2	Setting		
3–9	Seed Parable 1		
	10–12 . . .	"Parable theory" 1	
		13–20 . . .	Interpretation of Parable 1
	21–25 . . .	"Parable theory" 2	
26–29	Seed Parable 2		
30–32	Seed Parable 3		
		33–34 . . .	"Parable theory" 3

It is immediately clear that the arrangement is not systematic, not designed to present a logical case. A more logically satisfying structure might have been to present the three seed parables, with the explanation of the first as a key, either preceded or followed by an integrated discussion of why Jesus taught in parables. Nor is the structure concentric, which would have provided a more aesthetic sense of satisfaction and closure.[55] Mark's own rhetorical strategy is to intersperse the explanatory material into the narrative flow of the presentation of the parables themselves, using traditional materials from a variety of sources. This tactic inhibits a satisfying explanation in terms of a logical system exterior to the text, and makes Mark's own presentation parabolic rather than systematic and discursive, corresponding to the narrative mode he has chosen for the Gospel form as a whole. The reader is not given a ready-made essaylike explanation of either the parables or Jesus' motives in employing them, but must work through the narrative engaging each issue as it arises. The term "Markan parable theory" has become common as a designation for Mark's distinctive presentation of why Jesus taught in parables, but "theory"

---

54. E.g., Pesch, *Markusevangelium*, 1:226–27; Gnilka, *Markus*, 1:156–92; Dieter Lührmann, *Das Markusevangelium* (HNT 3; Tübingen: Mohr, 1987), 80–81; Philip Sellew, "Oral and Written Sources in Mark 4:1–34," *NTS* 36, no. 2 (1990): 234–67; Schenke, *Wundererzählungen*, 9–10, and the literature they list.

55. Contra, e.g., Beavis, *Mark's Audience*, 133–55; van Iersel, *Mark*, 176–77; John R. Donahue and Daniel J. Harrington, *The Gospel of Mark* (Sacra Pagina; Collegeville, Minn.: Liturgical Press, 2002), 143 (reflecting Jacques Dupont, *Études sur les évangiles synoptiques* [BETL 70; 2 vols.; Leuven: Leuven University Press, 1985], 264); Black, *Mark*, ad loc. Though Mark can use concentric structures effectively (cf. on 2:1–3:6), here his structure is linear and progressive. Thus this unit starts out with straightforward instruction that presupposes the goal of teaching in parables is that the crowd understand Jesus' message. Only en route and at the end does the reader perceive that most did not, could not, and were not intended to understand.

should not be taken to mean a coherent logical explanation, which Mark does not intend.

4:1–2 The Markan Setting

4:1 And again he began to teach beside the sea. And a very large crowd gathers about him, so that he got into a boat and was sitting[a] there in the sea, and the whole crowd was beside the sea on the land.[b] 2 He was teaching them many things in parables, and in his teaching was saying to them:

a. *Kathēmai* is the normal word for sitting, found eleven times in Mark, but only here and 13:3 of Jesus, further emphasizing that the parable discourse of ch. 4 and the apocalyptic discourse of chap. 13 are the two blocks of teaching material in the midst of their respective major sections (see Introduction 2 on structure.).

b. *Gē* is the same word translated "earth," "ground," "soil," or "dirt" in 4:5, 8, 20, 26, 31. The traditional "land" is preserved here, but it seems that Mark's description of the setting is already influenced by the pattern of what follows, in which Jesus the teacher is the sower and the crowd is the land / earth / ground / soil. Matthew changes to the expected word *aigialon*, "beach," and both Matthew and Luke omit the awkward reference to sitting "in the sea."

[1–2] If there was an introduction to a pre-Markan parable collection, it has been lost or completely rewritten by Mark. These two verses are replete with Markan vocabulary and themes: linking with the simple *kai*, "and"; *palin*, "again"; an *ochlos pleistos*, "large crowd," that *synagetai*, "gathers"; pleonistic *ērxato*, "began"; the setting *para tēn thalassan*, "beside the sea"; result clause with *hōste*, "so that"; Jesus' activity as *didaskein*, "teaching"; the content as *didachē*, "teaching"; *en parabolais*, "in parables" as the mode; sayings introduced with *kai elegen autois*, "he was saying to them"; Jesus and his disciples in the *ploion*, "boat"; Jesus *sits* to teach, only here and for the speech beginning at 13:3 corresponding to this speech in Mark's macrostructure—all of these are typical of Markan composition.

The boat requisitioned in 3:9 is finally used. The scene is vaguely symbolic: Jesus and his disciples in the boat (see on v. 36), the crowd of potential disciples on the land / soil. Will Jesus' teaching fall in good soil? There is no suggestion that the hearers do not understand. The scene continues the reality presupposed in Jesus' successful and popular teaching ministry previously described (1:21–27; 2:2, 13, 19–22; 3:23): Jesus communicates clearly, including his use of parables, and is understood by friend and foe alike. However, Mark has built in a premonition of what is to come. Jesus *sits* in the posture of an authoritative teacher—as we think of kings seated on their throne and judges sitting behind the bench. In describing Jesus as sitting in the boat, he somewhat redundantly describes the crowd as "on the land," instead of the normal word "beach," using the same word that will be used for the four kinds of soil in the following parable (see note *a* above).

4:3–9 Seed Parable 1: "The Sower"[56]

3 "Listen! Look! A sower went out to sow. 4 And it came to pass[a] that as he was sowing, some[b] seed fell along[c] the path, and birds came and ate it up. 5 And other seed fell on rocky ground, where it did not have much dirt, and it sprang up immediately because it had no depth of soil. 6 And when the sun rose, it was scorched, and because it had no root, it was dried up. 7 Other seed fell into the thorns, and the thorns came up and choked it, and it produced no grain.[d] 8 And other seed fell into good soil and was growing up and increasing and bearing fruit,[d] some[e] thirty, some sixty, and some a hundredfold." 9 And he was saying, "The one who has ears to hear with had better listen."[f]

a. On *kai egeneto* as "it came to pass," see note *a* on 1:9.

b. *Ho* is neuter singular, referring to seed in the collective sense, not "a seed," and so throughout.[57]

c. *Para tēn hodon* can mean either "on" or "alongside" the path; see commentary below.

d. *Karpos* is the generic word for "product," and can be rendered "fruit," "grain," "harvest," etc. as the context requires. It is thus used metaphorically of the products of a life obedient to God, the "fruits of the Spirit," and the like (cf., e.g., Matt 3:8, 10; 7:16, 17; Gal 5:22). Mark uses it in 4:7, 8, 29; 11:14; 12:2. While "grain" is required by the imagery of the present context, the metaphor of "bearing fruit" in the spiritual sense was so widespread in early Judaism and Christianity that this overtone is present even before the interpretation of vv. 13–20. I have thus translated "grain" in v. 7 but "fruit" in v. 8 to preserve this nuance, although *karpos* is found in both cases (so also NAB).

e. The MSS have a confusing plethora of readings for the series of prepositions preceding the numbers (not required by the English translation in any case), generated in part by the ambiguity of both *eis* and *en* in the oldest MSS, written without accents. Thus both *eis* and *en* can be construed as either the numeral "one" or the preposition "in / into." Mark's original was probably *hen . . . hen . . . hen,* the neuter of the numeral "one," understood distributively.

---

56. Matthew was the first to designate the parable as "The Sower" (13:18). For convenience, I use the terminology to designate a parable that has become traditional, though the reader is reminded that every title for a parable is not a neutral label, but already expresses an interpretation. E.g., Gnilka, *Markus,* 1:155, "The Parable of the Confident Sower"; R. T. France, *The Gospel of Mark: A Commentary on the Greek Text* (NIGTC; Grand Rapids: Eerdmans, 2002), 188, "The Parable of the Seeds"; Painter, *Mark's Gospel,* 76, "The Parable of the Soils." See note 4 in Introduction 2.

57. Contra, e.g., Gundry, *Mark,* 192, and France, *Gospel of Mark,* 150, who understand the whole parable to refer to six individual seeds. Gundry explicitly rejects the idea that the word is here used in the collective sense; France says each seed is typical of a whole group. But a group of birds does not eat the same individual seed (4:4).

f. The Greek third-person imperative *akouetō*, often translated with the "let . . ." construction, does not mean permission, but command. English has no corresponding imperative form.

[3–9] Two barriers inhibit modern readers from hearing this parable. (1) The modern Western reader thinks in terms of contemporary agriculture, its methods and expectations. These are different from those of the ancient eastern Mediterranean countries, where sowing preceded plowing and the expected yield was dramatically less. Most importantly, modern Western consciousness is generally unaware of the fragility of the natural cycle and does not think in terms of the food necessary for life as threatened by every bad harvest and called into question at every sowing. In the ancient world, harvest was not taken for granted at the time of sowing—so many things can happen before the harvest, and if there is no harvest there is famine and death. Bread is a basic human need, but modern urbanized Western people do not reflect on the threat to our life involved in every sowing and do not look at the bare fields with life-and-death hope.

(2) The modern reader is already aware of the parable's allegorizing interpretation and has never thought of the parable without it. This would also have been the case for Mark and his readers, for in its Markan context (literary and historical), the parable is not heard apart from the interpretation given along with it. Nonetheless, Mark has preserved the original parable, and the reader can still be struck by its provocative original impact that projects itself through the layers of later meaning. In biblical interpretation, this "original" meaning may not be substituted for the later Markan meaning, for in understanding the text before us, the point is not to peel away layers of tradition and redaction in an effort to get back to Jesus' original meaning, but to understand the text of Mark.

[3] The double introduction "Listen! Look!" is unusual, not being found elsewhere in the New Testament or the LXX, the nearest approximation being the prophetic "hear . . . behold" (*akoue . . . idou*) of Jer 6:19. The parable is bracketed with another call to hear (v. 9); the keyword "hear" permeates this section, occurring ten times (vv. 3, 9, 12, 15, 16, 18, 20, 23, 24, 33). The call is for hearers to listen in more than a superficial way, a warning that what is being said does not lie on the surface. For Jewish Christian readers and those Gentiles influenced by their biblical heritage, "Hear!" may have evoked the fundamental confession of Israel, the Shema (*Shema* means "hear!" and is the first word of Deut 6:4–5).[58]

The identity of the sower is not given; he does not appear in the story after the opening line, and is not interpreted in the allegory of 13–20, but the reflec-

---

58. So Birger Gerhardsson, "The Parable of the Sower and Its Interpretation," *NTS* 14 (1968): 165–93. The Shema is important to Mark (see on 12:28–34), even in his primarily Gentile context.

tive hearer may think of Jesus himself. Jesus' teaching the word to those "on the land" corresponds to the sower's casting seed on the ground; the sower "goes out" (*exēlthen*), parallel to Jesus' own "I have come" (*exēlthon*: see on 1:38). Furthermore, in Old Testament imagery the transcendent sower who sows in the earth is God (Isa 61:11; Jer 31:27; Hos 2:23; cf. 2 Esd 9:30), and the parable is another instance of imagery that hints that it is Jesus who functions in the divine role. In Mark's view, Jesus preached the word during his earthly ministry, and the risen Jesus continues to speak in the church's proclamation. Though in the proclamation of the historical Jesus, the sower will have been only a figure in the story, Mark already understands him in a veiled theological sense, even prior to the appended interpretation.

The parable has a binary structure (Marcus, *Mystery*, 31, 59), its dualism corresponding to Jewish apocalyptic thought. On the one hand, there is a sowing that produces no fruit, with three categories: soil on / alongside the path, on rocky ground, among the thorns. On the other hand, there is sowing that produces abundant fruit, in three categories, from surprisingly good to practically incredible. The typical storytelling "law of three," in which the *third* element is the decisive one, here undergoes a parabolic deformation—the third sowing, among the thorns, is just as unfruitful as the preceding two. It is not the third phase that provides the resolution, the story's dénouement, but the binary opposition bad soil / good soil.

In Mark's understanding of the parable, it is clear that the seed of the first does not fall *on* but *alongside* the path (see note *c* above). For him, to be on the path is good, for it means to be following the same road / path / way that Jesus is going and on which he calls disciples to follow (see, e.g., 10:46, 52; *Excursus: The Way* at 1:3). In first-century Palestine, seed was sometimes first broadcast and then plowed under. In the original parable, the hearer is thus probably to think of the path as the temporary beaten path that went through the field, used between harvest and sowing as a shortcut, to be plowed up in the planting of the new season. It would not be unusual for seed to be broadcast in this manner, since it was expected that seed that fell on the path would also produce fruit. But in this case, the birds eat it before it can be plowed under. Likewise the "rocky ground" does not refer to ground with many rocks lying about the surface—much of Palestinian soil is like this, and farmers gather the rocks and place them at the edge of the field. The "rocky ground" is the thin layer of soil covering a large rock beneath the surface. Since this rock cannot be seen, it is expected that this soil too will produce fruit, but the grain that sprouts up quickly cannot develop roots and thus withers and dies without producing any fruit. The apparent carelessness of a sower who sows seed among the thorns and thistles may raise eyebrows among knowledgeable farmers, but here, too, the idea is that the seed is sown in hope of producing fruit, frustrated only by the pernicious growth of thorns that choke the good seed. However the agricultural practice is understood, the work of the sower, while not bizarre, can hardly be called standard practice. Already in the first three sowings, prudence and caution seem low on the priority list, and there is a certain lavishness, an indiscriminate sowing bordering on carelessness. The Markan reader (but not the crowds on the shore!) may think of the scenes of 2:15–17, 18–22.

While the sower's practice is realistic, but marginally so, the harvest of the final scene is indeed a surprise. There is some evidence that a normal harvest was four to ten times what had been sown, and that a yield of fifteen times the seed sown was considered exceptionally good.[59] On this understanding, the lowest producer of the good soil was twice as fruitful as anyone's highest expectations, and a harvest one hundred times what one had sown would be off the charts. This understanding has recently been challenged, with some evidence indicating that a hundredfold yield was considered within the realm of possibility, so that the imagery of the parable remains in the everyday world throughout; in this view the kingdom of God is pictured in relation to the ordinary rather than as eschatological extravagance.[60] The data cited for this view is from Greece, Italy, Africa, and Babylon, and the evidence that such a harvest could have been considered normal in a Palestinian setting is ambiguous at best. That the point can be debated at all implies the borderline character of the imagery—it is not the normal picture of everyday life, but also not the out-of-this-world phantasmagoria of eschatological plenty prevalent in apocalyptic literature.[61] The hundredfold yield brings the parable to a conclusion with a harvest that exceeds all expectation. There is one place, however, where a Galilean farmer had heard of a hundredfold harvest that he could take seriously. In the biblical story read in the synagogue (and, in Mark's time, in the church), he heard, "Isaac sowed seed in that land, and in the same year reaped a hundredfold. The Lord blessed him . . ." (Gen 26:12), words that are echoed in the parable ("sowed," "seed," "land," "hundredfold"). "Maybe in the Bible," a local farmer might have mused, "but not in the real world where I work." Jesus' story begins in the ordinary world and ends in the world of the Bible where "the Lord" blesses beyond anything one can imagine, and the hearer is left asking which is the "real" world. This "hundredfold," repeated in 10:29–30, recasts the story in eschatological terms already impinging on this world. Readers may wonder where they stand on God's time line. The seed has been planted, but the end is not yet. Is the kingdom here, in some hidden way, like seed invisibly germinating? Or is

---

59. Arye Ben-David, *Talmudische Ökonomie* (Hildesheim: Olms, 1974), 1:104–5.

60. E.g., Bernard Brandon Scott, *Hear Then the Parable* (Minneapolis: Fortress, 1990), 358; Charles W. Hedrick, *Many Things in Parables: Jesus and His Modern Critics* (Louisville, Ky.: Westminster John Knox, 2004), 172–73.

61. Cf., e.g., *2 Bar.* 29.5: "The earth also shall yield its fruit ten thousandfold and on each vine there shall be a thousand branches, and each branch shall produce a thousand clusters, and each cluster produce a thousand grapes, and each grape produce a cor of wine."

it only the word that is here, promise and guarantor of the kingdom yet to come? Readers too may find themselves in that group about the Twelve, asking about the parables.

4:10–12 The Markan "Parable Theory"—First Statement

The interpreter must be wary of speaking of a Markan "parable theory," which (like "messianic secret") is only a convenient modern scholarly label for a Markan narrative strategy. Mark presents no comprehensive, systematic, discursive "explanation," but a narrative embracing a number of related insights. Just as the "point" of a parable cannot be summarized in nonparabolic language, so one cannot summarize Mark's understanding of how parables functioned in Jesus' ministry and his own Gospel in a series of theoretical "points" that can replace Mark's narrative. Nonetheless, the following reflections are derived from Mark's narrative and may illuminate the modern reader's effort to grasp Mark's portrayal of the parabolic teaching of Jesus:

(1) *Jesus* taught in a provocative, parabolic manner that subverted people's mythologies, the framework of thought that prohibited their hearing the message of the kingdom. People had to respond to Jesus' teaching before there could be meaning at all. The parables contained no built-in meaning to be excavated. Meaning comes into being in the interaction between hearers and Jesus' parables.

(2) The *church* responded to and saw meaning in Jesus' parabolic teaching, in the light of its postresurrection situation, often developing allegorizing interpretations to express its new insights.

(3) *Mark's* Christology did not allow characters in the narrative to come to an authentic understanding of Jesus Christ prior to the cross / resurrection. Insight was a matter of sovereign grace, finding oneself an "insider," a matter of election.

10 And when he was alone, those around him with the Twelve were asking him about the parables.[a] 11 And he was saying to them, "To you has been given the mystery of the kingdom of God, but to those outside everything comes in parables,

12 in order that, 'even though they see, they may see and not perceive, and that, although they hear, they may hear and not understand, so that they may not repent[b] and be forgiven.'"

a. The singular *parabolē* is read by D W Θ *f*[13] and a few other MSS, an obvious scribal correction to correspond to the fact that only one parable has been told. Mark, however, signals by the plural that he intends Jesus' response to apply to the parables generally (cf. v. 13).

b. *Epistrepsōsin* represents the standard LXX translation of the Hebrew *shuv,* "repent, return" (to God). Elsewhere, Mark always uses *epistrephō* in the sense of physical turning

(5:30; 8:33; 13:16), but here he is not using his own idiom but quoting the Scripture. Hence the translation is "repent," as 1:4, 15; 6:12.

In the present structure arranged by Mark, these three verses are another intercalation (see on 5:21), inserted into the unity comprising the parable and its interpretation 3–9 / 13–20). Since in the pre-Markan tradition verse 10 served to connect 3–9 and 13–20, the insertion is actually 11–12,[62] with the effect that verse 10 now introduces 11–12 rather than 13–20. Mark has probably changed the singular "parable" he found in his tradition to "parables," in order to make the disciples' question apply to parables in general rather than the one parable that has just been told.[63] Their question concerns parabolic teaching as such. Jesus teaches the crowds *only* in parables (v. 34); the disciples ask about this way of teaching, not about a particular parable or group of parables.

The modern reader too asks, What is a parable, and what does it mean that Jesus' teaching as such is called "in parables"?[64] The Greek word *parabolē* means simply "something cast beside" something else to explain or clarify it, that is, "comparison," "analogy." Markan usage, however, reflects the LXX, which employs the word for the wide range of meanings of the Hebrew *mashal*, which it translates: figure, proverb, aphorism, riddle, lesson, allegory, or almost any kind of indirect or metaphorical speech. Mark has his own distinctive understanding, however—hence this paragraph he inserts at this point. Since Mark includes verses 13–20, his understanding embraces allegory, but the ref-

62. That 11–12 is a discrete unit that circulated separately is indicated by (1) the *kai elegen autois* introduction, as in 4:21, 24 (the phrase is not in the LXX; elsewhere in the New Testament only Luke 6:5 = Mark 2:27, but twelve times in Mark; John 5:19, 8:23, but twelve times in Mark; (2) the character of the insertion itself, which has traits of old Aramaic tradition: antithetical parallelism, threefold divine passive (*dedotai, ginetai, aphethē*) superfluous *ekeinois* ("to those"); (3) the fact that the Isaiah quotation is different from both the MT and the LXX, but has similarities to the Palestinian Targum (see Joachim Jeremias, *The Parables of Jesus* [2d rev. ed.; New York: Scribner, 1972], 15, and T. W. Manson, *The Teaching of Jesus* [Cambridge: Cambridge University Press, 1963], 75–78. While Mark seems to have taken the basic form of the saying from tradition, he has modified it to fit precisely his own understanding of the parables. Whatever its prior meaning(s), Mark seems to have been attracted to it because of its usefulness in explicating his understanding of the parables, and by its use of a text from Isaiah, Mark's key biblical book (see on 1:2, and *Excursus: Mark and the Scriptures*, at 14:52). As Beavis's study has shown, these verses are not an "alien element" in the Gospel, but integral to its narrative and theology as a whole (Beavis, *Mark's Audience*, 175 and passim).

63. This is a more likely explanation than regarding the plural as including the parables of 3:23–27 (Pesch, *Markusevangelium*, 1:237) or considering each of the four sowings of 4:3–8 as a separate parable (Marcus, *Mystery*, 44). Cf. also 12:1 that promises "parables" but then relates only one parable. "In parables" seems a semi-technical phrase to designate Jesus' teaching as such, not a quantitative reference to how many parables were spoken on a certain occasion.

64. The following material summarizes and partly reproduces M. Eugene Boring, "Matthew: Introduction, Commentary, and Reflections," in *NIB* 8 (ed. Leander Keck; Nashville: Abingdon, 1995), 298–300.

erence to "mystery" in verse 11 and the intention expressed in verse 12 associated with the messianic secret shows that Mark's "parable theory" is far different from the understanding of allegory traditional in the later church.

For centuries, the Gospel parables were understood to be primarily allegories, that is, encoded doctrine that could be decoded into edifying lessons for Christian life. The first major turning point in modern parable study was made by Adolf Jülicher's 1888 work, which made a sharp distinction between parable and allegory.[65] In Jülicher's view, an allegory has many points, a parable but one, which he understood to be a general point of moral or religious instruction. C. H. Dodd and Joachim Jeremias followed in this train, emphasizing that "the point" of each parable is eschatological, not a general moralism.[66] For Dodd, each parable in its original setting in the message of Jesus communicated something about Jesus' realized eschatology, that is, the kingdom of God as already present in Jesus' ministry; Jeremias modified this to "eschatology in the process of realization," understanding the kingdom in Jesus' message to be both "already" and "not yet." Dodd's classic definition has served as the point of departure for much contemporary study of the parables: "At its simplest the parable is a metaphor or simile drawn from nature or common life, arresting the hearer by its vividness or strangeness, and leaving the mind in sufficient doubt about its precise application to tease it into active thought" (Dodd, *Parables*, 5). Recent study would give widespread, but not unanimous, support for the following points:

(1) Jülicher's distinction between parable and allegory was valuable, but too rigid, not allowing for the broad spectrum of usages in biblical thought, just as the lines he drew between parable, similitude, and example story were too neat.

(2) A parable is not an illustration of a prosaic "point," but is itself an inseparable unity of form and meaning. Parables are a means of disclosing new truth that cannot be reduced to nonparabolic, discursive language. Not only was allegorical interpretation offtrack in looking for a number of points in each parable, but Jülicher, Dodd, and Jeremias were wrong in looking for the single "point" of each parable—a parable has no "point" at all that can be stated in nonparabolic language.[67] Parables are thus not mere comparisons or analogies, supplementary illustrations of truth already known but in need of illustration. Parables bring the truth itself to expression, which cannot be expressed abstractly (cf.

---

65. Adolf Jülicher, *Die Gleichnisreden Jesu* (Freiburg i. B.: Mohr, 1888).

66. C. H. Dodd, *The Parables of the Kingdom* (New York: Scribner, 1961); Jeremias, *Parables*.

67. This approach to interpreting parables has been recently advocated by, e.g., Robert W. Funk, *Language, Hermeneutic, and Word of God* (New York: Harper, 1966), 124–222; John Dominic Crossan, *In Parables: The Challenge of the Historical Jesus* (New York: Harper & Row, 1973); John Dominic Crossan, *The Dark Interval: Towards a Theology of Story* (Niles, Ill.: Argus Communications, 1975); and Scott, *Hear Then the Parable*.

Lührmann, *Markusevangelium*, 82–83). To reduce a parable to a "point" is to domesticate its message to more comfortable and manageable categories.

(3) Parables are polysemic; that is, they generate new meaning in new situations. While a parable cannot "mean" simply anything (it is not a Rorschach blot), it has no one meaning that can be ferreted out by objective methods. It takes on meaning as it gently forces the hearer / reader to participate in the construction of meaning. This process can subvert the life-world of the hearer, opening up a new vision of reality. Parables thus often function by beginning in the familiar world of the hearer, but then they present a different vision of the world that challenges the everyday expectations of the hearer. In the preaching of Jesus, parables were not pleasant stories to decorate a moralistic point, but were disturbing stories that threatened the hearer's secure mythological world. This mythological world is the world of assumptions by which we habitually live, the unnoticed framework of our thinking within which we interpret other data. Parables surreptitiously attack this framework of our thought-world itself. "'You have built a lovely home,' myth assures us; 'but,' whispers parable, 'you are right above an earthquake fault'" (Crossan, *Dark Interval*, 57).

These reflections apply more to the original function of parables in Jesus' ministry than to their allegorical interpretations in the early church and in later centuries. Though Mark's "parable theory" was tailored to respond to the theological needs of his own time, its disconcerting aspects for modern readers can be seen as preserving something of the original function of the parables in the proclamation of Jesus.

[10] The situation corresponds to the typical Markan pattern of public teaching followed by private explanation to his disciples (7:17; 9:28; 10:10; 13:3). Elsewhere, the typical house setting evokes the "insiders" of the Markan house churches (cf. comments on 1:29–34; 2:1, 15, 20–21; 3:31–35). Here, the boat replaces the house as the setting for Jesus, and "those around him with the Twelve" are identified as "his own disciples" in 4:34. On the possible symbolism of the boat, see on 4:1, 36. The scene and action of 4:1–34 is difficult to follow, if one attempts to imagine it historically. Jesus is never depicted as leaving and reentering the boat, which he and the Twelve are still in for the departure at 4:36. Yet it is difficult to picture Jesus, the Twelve, and his (large?) group of disciples gathered in one end of the boat for private instruction while the crowd waits patiently on the shore. Jesus begins to speak exclusively to the disciples in verse 11, and the *autois* ("to them") of verse 13 continues the address to the disciples, as does the repeated *autois* of verses 21 and 24. Yet, without any overt transition, the parables of verses 26–29 and 30–32 seem to be addressed to the crowds, and the concluding summary of 33–34 contrasts what was said to the crowds in parables and what was explained privately to the disciples. The scene is thus composed to present the reader, an "insider," the theological dimensions of Jesus' strategy of teaching in parables, rather than describing what happened on a particular day.

[11] The contrast between "you" and "those outside," more appropriate to the house church image than the boat setting and thus merging the imagery of the church as "boat" and "house," allows the reader to hear both the explanation for the preceding parable and the reason for Jesus' teaching in parables as such. The explanation is conceived in terms of the apocalyptic dualism that permeates Mark's theology: there are two groups, and only two. Mark is not distinctive in this. Not only had sectarian groups such as the Qumran covenanters used such dualistic conceptuality, "those outside" is an expression used in rabbinic school discussion for Gentiles and unbelieving Jews. The imagery was adopted by early Christianity (e.g., 1 Thess 4:12; 1 Cor 5:12–13; Col 4:5), and then by Mark and the later Gospels. "Insider" and "outsider" terminology is not institutional, but existential. The line between insider and outsider is not the line that separates Christianity and Judaism or church members from others, but is determined by one's response to Jesus.[68] The Markan narrative as a whole will illustrate that insiders behave as outsiders, outsiders as insiders, and that no one may smugly assume he or she is "in." The address is to the reader, not to the crowds on the lakeshore.

Likewise, the language of "mystery," which occurs only here in Mark, is found frequently in the Pauline tradition and Revelation, and the use of Isa 6:9–10 is appealed to not only in Mark and the parallels in Matthew and Luke, but in Acts 28:26–27; Rom 11:8; John 12:40. "Mystery" was used in the mystery cults of Mark's day to refer to the secret information explained only to initiates; doubtless many of his readers would have thought in these terms when hearing this text, and Mark's text certainly includes this meaning. "Mystery" is thus like "secret," in that it is not necessarily something that is inherently difficult to understand ("the mystery of existence," "the mysteries of the theory of relativity"), but something that is not understood until it is revealed—a matter of hiddenness, not complexity. It is thus "not a mystery of dogma, but a mystery of application . . . not an intellectual, but an existential mystery."[69] Again, this corresponds to its meaning in the Old Testament and apocalyptic Judaism, where "mystery" represents Aramaic *raz*, God's plan for the ages that will be fully disclosed only at the eschaton (eight times in Dan 2:18–47; 4:9).[70] This in

68. Donahue, *Gospel in Parable*, 44; cf. Donald Juel, *A Master of Surprise: Mark Interpreted* (Minneapolis: Fortress, 1994), 51–52.

69. Madeleine Boucher, *The Mysterious Parable: A Literary Study* (CBQMS 6; Washington: Catholic Biblical Association of America, 1977), 84, elaborates: "The term 'mystery of application' is employed . . . for the purpose of distinguishing the Markan mystery of the parables, which has to do with hardness of heart, from a mystery which has to do with secret knowledge. . . . It would be best, perhaps, to say that the parables are the means by which God judges the hearers, and by which the hearers bring judgment upon themselves."

70. Cf. Raymond E. Brown, *The Semitic Background of the Term 'Mystery' in the New Testament* (FBBS 21; Philadelphia: Fortress, 1968).

turn corresponds to Mark's view of the kingdom of God (see *Excursus: Kingdom of God* at 1:15). The mystery of the kingdom is *given* to the disciples. They have been granted the insight that the kingdom of God that is to appear at the eschaton in power (9:1) is already dawning in the ministry of Jesus. This is not an attainment on their part, but a gift.[71] While Mark is here thinking within the conceptuality of apocalyptic predestination, he stops short of saying God refuses to grant this insight of faith to those outside, of whom it is said more impersonally that "everything comes in parables."

The mystery of the kingdom *has been given* to the disciples. The reader must ask not only what this is, but when it has been given. The reader has not been previously informed of this, and becomes aware that he or she has been excluded from something that some people within the narrative know.[72] Thus, although the readers are generally addressed by the narrator as "insiders," here they are excluded from the circle of insiders, and become aware that some people in the narrative have received revelation from Jesus of which the reader remains ignorant. This is not to be explained as a quantitative or temporal inclusion, as though they know some things but not everything, or as though their lack of knowledge is remedied at some later point, but in terms of Markan dialectic—readers both know and don't know (see notes in *Excursus: The Messianic Secret* at 9:13).

[12] Jesus' response to the disciples' question about parables concludes with words taken from Isa 6:9–10, not explicitly designated as such. At an initial, surface reading, Jesus seems to say that he teaches in parables in order to prevent his hearers from understanding, for if they did understand, they might turn to God and be forgiven. Jesus' teaching in parables seems intentionally designed to prevent that from happening. Can this have been the intention of the historical Jesus? Can this be the meaning of the Markan text? Before attempting to formulate a response to these unavoidable questions, it will be helpful to consider the trajectory of the text itself:

- In the MT of Isa 6, the prophet is called and sent to "this people," with the command, formulated in the second-person imperative, *"Keep listening, but do not comprehend; keep looking, but do not understand."* The prophet is then commanded in the second-person imperative, *"Make the mind of this people dull, and stop their ears, and shut their eyes, so that they may not look with their eyes, and listen with their ears, and comprehend with their minds,*

---

71. The view that the ability to hear and understand is God's gift is not peculiar to Mark. The Qumran community, too, saw itself as God's elect community of the last days, and the author of the Hodayoth praises God "for having uncovered my ears to marvelous mysteries" (1QH 1.21; cf. 1QM 10.11).

72. See elaboration of this point in Fowler, "Rhetoric," 217–26.

and turn and be healed." How these words should be understood in their Old Testament setting is a disputed point among exegetes, with some seeing them as fusing the actual result with the statement of intent, in accord with Semitic thought, and others seeing them as irony or sarcasm.

- The LXX already attempts to ameliorate the perceived difficulty: *"You shall hear indeed, but you shall not understand; and you shall see indeed, but you shall not perceive. For the heart of this people has become thick, and they can hardly hear with their ears, and they have closed their eyes; lest they should see with their eyes, and hear with their ears, and understand with their heart, and be converted, and I should heal them."* The imperatives have become indicatives, no longer commanding the people to become deaf and blind, but describing what they in fact will be. The people themselves have closed their eyes, and this is what keeps them from the hearing and seeing that would allow them to return to God and be healed.

- The Targum, the Aramaic paraphrase of the Hebrew text read in the synagogue, reads as follows: *And he said: Go and speak to this people who hear indeed and do not understand, and see indeed but do not know . . . lest / unless they repent and it be forgiven them.* (The final phrase can be understood in a conditional sense, "unless," giving hope to those who repent.) The Targum differs from both MT and LXX in the following points: (1) the verbs are placed in the third person rather than the second; (2) the command is to go and speak to the people *who* hear but do not understand, and (3) the final phrase deals with forgiveness rather than healing. In points (1) and (3), Mark agrees with the Targum, and the sticky point remains point (2): Mark still seems to say that Jesus teaches in parables *in order that* (Greek *hina*) people may not understand, rather than *to those who* (already are determined to) misunderstand.

- The Markan Jesus takes up the words in a form that agrees neither with the MT, LXX, or Targum. In their present context, they express Mark's theology of divine sovereignty and the messianic secret.

- Matthew perceived the difficulty of Mark's view, and alleviated it somewhat by a number of strategic hermeneutical moves: (1) He changes the offending *hina* to *hoti* ("in order that" to "because"). (2) He recasts the whole discourse in wisdom terms so that Jesus teaches in parables in order to evoke responses from good students, moving Mark 4:25 ahead to this point. (3) He makes clear that Mark's use of biblical language is actually a quotation of Scripture, by citing the whole text of Isa 6:9–10, showing that however difficult Jesus' pedagogical strategy may appear, here as elsewhere Jesus is simply fulfilling Scripture. (4) He augments the discourse with other material showing that the disciples do indeed understand as Jesus intended.

• So also Luke moderates the apparent harshness of Mark, but with less rigor (since he portrays the ministry of Jesus as a special time, and has Acts in which to set forth his own theology of how the message of Jesus was perceived before and after Easter). By omitting the final clause of 4:12 and adding an analogous clause at Luke 8:12, it becomes the devil, not God, who is to blame for the lack of perception! (Cf. the roles of God / Satan in 2 Sam 24:1; 1 Chr 21:1.)

• Such efforts on the part of Mark's earliest interpreters point up the difficulty of the Markan text, which has continued to plague later exegetes, many of whom have sought to incorporate Mark's or Jesus' statement into a more congenial theology.[73] The approach followed most often is to understand Mark's troublesome *hina* to mean "because"—as Matthew had already done in the first century—and the concluding *mēpote* to mean "unless," thus both making the Markan Jesus' statement a declaration about the way people already are rather than his own intention, and leaving the way open for forgiveness to those who repent.[74] This rationalization can fit more comfortably into later understandings of evangelization and mission: God's offer is made to all; those who refuse to hear are responsible for their own damnation, and those who accept can take some credit for having made the right decision— "self selected" in R. T. France's phrase.[75]

73. These have been catalogued and discussed by Craig A. Evans, *To See and Not Perceive: Isaiah 6.9–10 in Early Jewish and Christian Interpretation* (JSOTSup 64; Sheffield: JSOT Press, 1989). Cf. Fowler, "Rhetoric," 221–22, who argues the Markan Jesus does not intend the statement seriously ("tongue in cheek," . . . "a little bit humorous"). Fowler's argument is that since Jesus in 1:14–15 calls people to repent, he cannot be serious when he explains that his teaching is to keep people from repenting. Fowler's explanation simply illustrates the problem of trying to make Mark consistent, all on one level. Verses 10–12 make sense only within the framework of the messianic secret, which Mark does not attempt to make consistent with the rest of the story at the narrative level. See *Excursus: The Messianic Secret*, at 9:13.

74. The "causal" use of *hina* is rare and disputed, and the translation of *mēpote* as "unless" is problematical (see Bauer and Danker, eds., BDAG, 477, 648). The combination is thus extremely problematical.

75. France, *Gospel of Mark*, 195, and cf. 199: Jesus' "challenge to think through the significance of the image, and to respond appropriately to its demand, will inevitably show up the division which already exists between those who are open to new insight and those who are resistant to change." The mystery of divine sovereignty and human responsibility expressed in the Markan text here verges on the moralism of "we should all be open to new insights." Similarly, Ben Witherington, *The*

In my own view, the harsh Markan statement should stand; the initial impression is correct: in this text Jesus is portrayed as having taught in parables to keep people from understanding, and Mark found a saying of Jesus in his tradition, bolstered by a Targumic citation from Isaiah, that supported this view. Just as Isaiah 6:9–10 is not a verbatim report of what happened on a particular day in Isaiah's life, but includes retrospective theological reflection on how it all turned out, so Mark 4 does not present a picture of what happened in a boat on a particular day in the life of Jesus, but a retrospective theological reflection on what had happened in the Christ-event. In Markan Christology, it had not been possible for people to understand the truth about Jesus and his message during Jesus' ministry; this had to await the cross and resurrection. Yet Jesus had taught, in public and private. What was the meaning of *this*? Jesus had taught in a secretive manner, not intending to be understood (by the characters in the narrative), as the ministry of Jesus as such was a mystery to be disclosed only later.

In Mark's time, the people of Israel had by and large rejected the Christian message. What was the meaning of *this?* Could Jesus the teacher not make his message clear? Had people to whom it was clear rejected it nonetheless? Mark rejects each of these options. This is somewhat analogous to Paul's struggle with the same issue in Rom 9–11, which also cites Isa 6 (Rom 11:8), and also speaks of "mystery" (11:25) and "hardening" as God's sovereign act (Rom 9:18; 11:7, 25; cf. 2 Cor 3:14 and commentary above on Mark 3:5). As in Paul's argument, despite Israel's rejection, there was in fact a continuing group of "insiders," the elect people of God, and "outsiders." In Mark's day, the invitation is indeed universal, just as it was in Jesus' day. But people in Jesus' day could not make an authentic response of Christian faith, prior to the cross and resurrection. Yet Mark had a firm tradition that Jesus had taught—was he not a good teacher, could he not get people to understand? That the teaching had been in parables was a helpful feature for Mark's theological approach: "parables" can be understood as "secrets," and thus Jesus' teaching could be understood as teaching in a secretive manner that could not be understood until after the resurrection. His teaching was purposely veiled from the outsiders. For Mark, Jesus' teaching had to be understood in terms of the messianic secret (see *Excursus: The Messianic Secret* at 9:13). In Mark's time, too, all are invited, but most do not respond. Yet some, the "insiders" in which the reader is included, have responded. How should insiders explain this to themselves—that "we" are

---

Gospel of Mark: A Socio-Rhetorical Commentary (Grand Rapids: Eerdmans, 2001), 167: "The parables give insight to the open-minded but come as a judgment on the obdurate." Hooker, *Mark,* 126, "To those who respond, the meaning of the parables is explained." This is difficult to imagine either historically or in the Markan story line: Does Jesus tell a parable, then ask for those who want to know more to step forward (as "inquirers" come forward as the hymn is sung at the conclusion of an evangelistic sermon), and to such inquiring minds he then gives the additional teaching?

smarter or better than "they"? Mark makes this a matter of grace, of God's choice, not ours, for which "insiders" can only be grateful. Further: in painting the pre-Easter picture, Markan dialectic comes into play: the "insiders" too do not really understand, until later (cf., e.g., 8:17–18), and "outsiders" can be addressed as people who are intended to understand, and do (e.g., 7:14–15; 12:1–12).[76] For the characters in the story, this promised later understanding meant "after the revelation of the resurrection." But the insiders of Mark's own time, after Easter, still waver and misunderstand, and still await the ultimate revelation, at the Parousia, which will be a revelation to all. So understood, as confessional Markan theology rather than objectifying report, Mark's harshness can be allowed to stand without mitigation, for in Mark's time and perspective it is not the last word, either for the characters in the story or for both insiders and outsiders of his own time and ours.

4:13–20 Interpretation of "The Sower"

4:13 And he says to them, "You don't understand this parable?[a] Then how will you understand all the parables? 14 It is the word[b] that the sower is sowing. 15 These are the ones[c] alongside[d] the path where the word is being sown, and when they hear, Satan comes immediately and takes away the word that has been sown in[e] them. 16 And these are those being sown in rocky ground, who, when they hear the word, immediately receive it with joy, 17 and they have no root in themselves, but last only a short time. Then, when 'tribulation'[f] or persecution arises on account of the word, immediately they fall away.[g] 18 And others are the ones being sown in / among the thorns; these are those who hear the word 19 and the cares of the world, and the deceitful lure of wealth, and the desire for other things come in and choke the word, and it produces no fruit. 20 And those are those who have been sown on the good soil, who hear the word and accept it and bear fruit, thirtyfold and sixtyfold and a hundredfold."

a. The second clause is clearly a question, since it is introduced by the interrogative particle *pōs*. It is not clear whether the first clause should be punctuated as a separate sentence, and if so, whether it is a question or a statement. If a question, it is introduced with the negative particle *ouk*, expecting a positive answer: "You understand this parable, don't you." The translation above attempts to communicate that the disciples should have been able to answer yes, but could not, as evidenced by their question.

b. The word order of the Greek places the emphasis on *logon*, "word." The initial statement of the interpretation emphasizes that the parable is being understood as an allegory: "we are not talking about sowing seeds, but 'sowing' the *word*."

76. Cf. Beavis's conclusion to her study of 4:1–34: "The distinction between 'insiders' and 'outsiders' is not fixed, but depends on individual response" (*Mark's Audience*, 154–55). Mark's use of the apocalyptic dualistic perspective here is analogous to 13:20: there is an apocalyptic perspective, but God is not captive to any system. God has set a boundary between "insiders" and "outsiders," but the boundary can be crossed in both directions.

c. The Greek word for "seed" is neuter, and pronouns referring to it in vv. 3–9 are all neuter. In the interpretation, Mark uses the generic masculine plural throughout, which corresponds to *logos*, which is masculine, which also makes the transition from seed to person. The contrast, of course, is not female / male, but impersonal / personal.

d. Here the word translated ambiguously in v. 4 must be clearly translated in its natural sense, at the side of the path / road rather than on it (see note *c* and comments on 4:3).

e. Reading *eis autois* with N^{27}, which follows B W $f^{1, 13}$ 28, which may mean either "in them" individually or "among them" collectively. Other MSS read *en tais kardiais autōn*, "in their hearts," apparently a later scribal "clarification."

f. On the semi-technical tone of 'tribulation,' see note *d* on 13:19.

g. On *skandalizō*, see notes *a* and *c* on 6:3.

As the parables were handed on and around in the church's teaching and preaching, they were interpreted and modified to address new situations. These post-Easter additions and modifications can often be identified with a great degree of probability, but they are not merely to be stripped away in order to get back to the original parable. They illuminate the ways Jesus' potent message was heard and interpreted as the early Christians struggled to apply it to their own situations, and show how Jesus' parables continued to illuminate Christian existence after Easter. The interpretation has its own validity as part of the Gospel of Mark and as part of Scripture. It is neither a second-rate alternative to the parable nor "the" meaning of the parable; it lets the modern reader hear a canonical response to and interpretation of the original parable.

That these verses are not part of Jesus' original parabolic teaching, but represent later Christian interpretation,[77] is indicated by the following considerations: (1) The interpretation (mis-)construes the parable as an allegory. While the distinction is not absolute, verses 3–9 function as a parable, and the interpretation represents it as a different literary genre. A parable is open-ended, polysemic, challenging the hearer to decide, and has no self-contained meaning until someone responds to it. The meanings of an allegory have already been decided by the teacher (as here), who delivers them in a point-by-point explanation or makes them transparent in the allegory itself (as in *Pilgrim's Progress*). (2) The parable has a dualistic, binary structure, while the interpretation is structured in four parts.[78] (3) The parable is eschatological in tone; the interpretation is oriented to the vicissitudes of the present Christian mission.

---

77. So most critical scholars. For arguments to the contrary, see, e.g., Gerhardsson, "Sower," 165–93; C. F. D. Moule, "Mark 4:1–20 Yet Once More," in *Neotestamentica et Semitica: Studies in Honour of Matthew Black* (ed. E. Earle Ellis and Max E. Wilcox; Edinburgh: T. & T. Clark, 1969), 95–113.

78. Marcus has pointed out, however, that while the interpretation as it circulated in pre-Markan tradition had a four-part structure, Mark himself understands 4:13–20 in binary terms ("bad soil / outsiders" = 4:15–19; "good soil / insiders" = 4:20), just as he will understand 4:24–25a as "insiders" and 4:25b as "outsiders." Marcus, *Mystery*, 156–57.

Thus in the parable the amazingly good yield points to the eschatological harvest, while in the interpretation it is understood more prosaically as discipleship. (4) The interpretation is not self-consistent (in Mark 4:14, seed = word, but in 4:16, 18, 20 seed = hearers). Matthew has noticed this and slightly adjusted it; compare Matt 13:19b–20. (5) In the interpretation, much more attention is given to the losses than is the case in the parable itself, where the focus is on the surprising harvest. The interpretation explains and elaborates the three unsuccessful sowings, giving the reasons; the "good soil," however, is not really interpreted, but simply repeated from the parable itself. The post-Jesus, pre-Markan composer of the interpretation could have taken the interpretation in another, more positive direction, explaining what constitutes "good soil" and portraying the "fruits" it produces (one thinks, e.g., of Gal 5:22). (6) The interpretation reflects the situation of the post-Easter church, not that of the pre-Easter historical Jesus or the Jesus of the Markan story line. The attempt to represent the interpretation as "the varying response to this proclamation which has been the focus of interest in chapters 2 and 3, and of which this discourse offers an explanation" (France, *Gospel of Mark,* 204) must remain unconvincing—in the preceding narrative, where have persecutions and the lure of riches and the like kept the word from bearing fruit in those who heard Jesus? Thus, if the historical Jesus *had* explained the parable in this way to the 30 C.E. crowds, they would not have understood the interpretation any better than the parable itself, for it presupposes the Christian mission and church life. It is post-Easter believers who can look back on widespread failure and still have confidence that the word does after all find a response in some people in whom it produces the fruit of the Christian life. (7) The vocabulary is that of the church, not of Jesus. Examples: absolute use of *ho logos* ("the word"); several words that occur nowhere else in the teaching of Jesus are found regularly in early Christian parenesis (e.g., *speirō*, "sow," for "preach"; *apatē*, "deception"; *ploutos*, "wealth"; *akarpos*, "unfruitful"; *karpophoreō*, "bear fruit" in a metaphorical sense; the combination *thlipsis kai diōgmos*, "tribulation and persecution"; *skandalizō*, "fall away"). (8) The parable can be readily translated into Aramaic; the interpretation cannot, but seems to have been *composed* in Greek. (9) In the parable, the seed terminology is in the neuter singular; in the interpretation, the "seeds" are generic masculine plural, except for the final unelaborated listing of three categories of good seed, reproducing the vocabulary of the parable. (10) There are indications that the parable circulated in some streams of early Christianity without the interpretation. Some church fathers interpreted it without the allegorical interpretation (Justin, Pseudo-Clementine homilies). *Gospel of Thomas* 41 has the parable in essentially the same form as Mark but has no allegorical interpretation.

[13] The reproachful tone indicates the disciples should know the meaning of the parables, that is, that the parables themselves are transparent, that Jesus

expects them to be understood. Yet he immediately gives the explanation, without which they cannot be understood. This dialectic of revelation and concealment is interwoven into the parable discourse throughout, and cannot be reduced to a logically satisfying resolution on one side or the other. The relation between "this parable" and "all the parables" presents the Sower as the key to Jesus' parabolic teaching as such: it is the parable about parables—and therefore must itself be understood parabolically. Mark regards the initial parable as the key to them all, in a fivefold perspective: (1) The parable is about preaching and responding to the word / gospel, which in Mark's view is what Jesus and his own Gospel are about. (2) Jesus himself must give the interpretation; parables are not discrete conundrums that may be figured out independently but are integrally related to the person of Jesus without being directly christological. Thus verse 13 restates the same claim as verse 11. (3) The parable and its interpretation connect the pre-Easter ministry of Jesus and the post-Easter proclamation of the church and its mission experience; the parables of Jesus must be illuminated by the resurrection event. (4) Mark affirms the allegorical interpretation of the church, regarding allegory as the proper approach to all the parables.[79] (5) Mark himself probably regarded the interpretation, like the parable, as coming from the historical Jesus, yet he did not make the distinction between "historical" and "post-Easter" Jesus nearly so neatly as modern historians. The risen Christ who speaks in the tradition of the church and Mark's own Gospel is not a different Jesus from the Jesus who spoke at the Galilean lakeside. The interrelation of these two is part of the dynamic of the Gospel form Mark devised for this purpose.

[14] The sower himself is not given an allegorical interpretation (contrast Matt 13:24, 37), which both illustrates the generic difference between parable and allegory and allows the figure of the sower to modulate between the sowing of the word in the ministry of Jesus, the *archē* of the gospel proclaimed in Mark's own time (see on 1:1), and the sowing of the word by Christian missionaries of Mark's day.[80] All emphasis is placed on the *logos,* "the word," used seven times in this paragraph (+v. 33), which had become a quasi-technical term for the Christian message (cf. 1 Thess 1:6; Gal 6:6; Col 4:3; Acts 4:4; Jas 1:21). The role of the initial parable as the key to them all is enhanced, so that, however the original parables may have functioned in their original settings, at the level of the Markan narrative one can see a comprehensive picture projected by

79. Boucher, *Mysterious Parable,* 17–25, 45–53, 83–84. Donald Juel recounts the revelatory impact of his decision to read the parables in their narrative setting: "Jesus' parable must be read as an allegory for which Mark provides an authorized interpretation" (*Master of Surprise,* 48).

80. Marcus, *Mystery,* 69, argues it is Jesus who continues to sow the word through Christian missionaries, and that this is signaled by the fact that "the parable is narrated in the past because it deals with the past, while the interpretation is narrated in the present because it deals with the present."

the three seed parables: the seed broadcast by Christian preaching falls on unresponsive soil, but there is an amazing harvest nevertheless (3–20); the seed germinates and produces without human effort (26–29); the seed proceeds from impossibly small beginnings to eschatological fulfillment (30–32).

[15–20] When the Markan Jesus speaks of a time when "'tribulation' or persecution [that] arises on account of the word," he addresses an experienced reality of the church for which he writes. Modern, more comfortable readers may "not trivialize the pain and danger of persecution. It costs people their faith. . . . If God does not shorten the time of persecutions, no one would survive" (13:20).[81]

As pointed out above, in these verses the imagery fluctuates between "seed" equals "word" to "seed" equals various kinds of believers. The imagery does not particularly lend itself to parenesis; each type of soil cannot decide to change its character. The imagery seems to fit the givenness of the predestinarian conceptuality that forms part of the framework within which the discourse is conceived. The seed / word is good throughout. The soil is passive and cannot change. Understanding is a gift; lack of it is divine hardening (see on 3:5; 4:11–12). Nonetheless, as illustrated by the preaching experience of the church through the centuries, the broad parenetic thrust of the interpretation has not been deterred by either the modulation of the imagery or its fixity, and the general message has always been perceived: the word falls on various kinds of soils in different circumstances; sometimes the seed produces no fruit, but when it falls in good soil, it is amazingly productive. Although homiletical points are not explicitly made, the audience can be implicitly warned—"what kind of soil are *you?*"—or missionaries can be encouraged—"despite the lack of response, be faithful in your sowing, and a bountiful harvest will result." Thus despite, or perhaps because of, the inconsistent application of the parable's metaphors, even the allegorical interpretation retains some of the dynamic of the original, and even readers of the explanation do not have a ready-made interpretation, but must interact with it and formulate their own response. Nor has Mark exerted himself to fit the imagery here into a systematic structure consistent with the rest of the Gospel. Satan, apparently overcome in 1:12–13 and bound in 3:27, is still active during the ministry of Jesus (8:33) and still opposing the Christian mission in Mark's own time (4:15; cf. 1 Thess 3:5; 2 Cor 11:3).

4:21–25 Markan "Parable Theory"—Second Statement: "Parables about Parables"

In this section, composed by Mark from prior traditions and placed in this setting to further illuminate Jesus' parabolic pedagogy, the argument goes a step beyond

---

81. Pheme Perkins, "Introduction, Commentary, and Reflections on Mark," in *NIB* 8 (ed. Leander Keck; 12 vols.; Nashville: Abingdon, 1995), 651.

10–12, building on the interpretation in 13–20: the word is *meant* to be heard, and finally *will* be. The "hiding" and "hardening" are only temporary, and correspond to God's wisdom, not human "common sense." Yet it is not just a matter of chronology; the Markan dialectic of secrecy and revelation is also at work here.

4:21 And he was saying to them, "The[a] lamp does not come[b] in order that[c] it may be placed under the measuring bowl or under the bed, does it? Is it not rather the case[d] that it comes in order that it may be placed on the lampstand? 22 For nothing is hidden, except in order that it may be revealed, neither is anything concealed, except in order that it may be brought out into the open. 23 Whoever has ears to hear with had better listen."[e] 24 And he was saying to them, "Be careful how[f] you hear. With the measure you measure out to others with, it will be measured[g] out to you, and it will be added to you. 25 For to the one who has, more will be given, and whoever does not have, even what he or she has will be taken away."

a. The articles with lamp, measuring bowl, bed, and lampstand are generic and could be translated with the English indefinite article (cf. "I must find the drugstore," which can be said in a strange town where no particular drugstore is intended, and is the equivalent of "I must find a drugstore"). The English definite article is retained here, however, in order to preserve the particular personal reference of "the lamp" to Jesus and his message (see below).

b. That a lamp "comes" is as awkward in Greek as it is in English, and may reflect the underlying Aramaic idiom. It is preserved here, since Mark appears to understand the imagery not impersonally but christologically. Some scribes were bothered by the strange usage and changed *erchetai* "comes" to *haptetai* "is lit" (the Greek MSS D [W f^{13}], the Latin translations, some MSS in the Coptic translations). The versions of the saying in Matt 5:15 and Luke 8:16, 11:33, reflecting the Q wording, likewise set the Markan usage in sharp profile by speaking of people "lighting" a lamp rather than Mark's unique image of the lamp's "coming."

c. The conjunction *hina* occurs four times in this brief text. I have rendered it each time with the purposive "in order that" to correspond to the purpose-*hina* of 4:12.

d. This fulsome rendering is chosen to bring out the contrast in the two Greek questions. The first begins with *mēti*, which expects a negative answer, the second with *ouch*, expecting a positive response.

e. On the rendering of the third-person imperative, see on v. 9.

f. *Blepete ti akouein* can also be translated "watch what you hear," or "pay attention to what you hear." If *ti* is translated "what," the latter translation is preferable. But since the *ti* can be adverbial, the translation above preserves Mark's emphasis. In any case, the point is not that hearers should be discriminating regarding the content of what they hear, but that they should take care to hear in more than a superficial way. Luke 8:18 rightly takes it in this way, changing Mark's ambiguous *ti* to the explicit *pōs*, "how."

g. Better English style would call for something like "what you have meted out to others will be meted out to you," but I have chosen the inelegant English to correspond to Mark's threefold use of the words for "measure."

These four sayings, some or all of which may go back to Jesus, circulated in early Christianity as four independent sayings in a variety of forms, each with its own meaning, both meaning and form changing as they were adapted to various historical and literary contexts. Each was derived from the wisdom tradition, affirming sage perspectives. For instance, 4:25 originally expressed the commonplace that the rich get richer and the poor get poorer. When adopted and adapted to express Jesus' message, whether by Jesus himself or his post-Easter disciples, the sayings received an eschatological tone. Most reconstructions of Q include all four sayings; in Q they were not in the same context.[82]

The present form of the collection is elegantly arranged: two pairs of two sayings each, with the Markan trademark *kai elegen autois* introducing each subunit, in each case the second element being introduced by an explanatory *gar* clause. The first unit begins with a question, corresponding to the opening question of verse 13. There are four *hina* purpose clauses, linking the whole section to the crucial *hina* of verse 12. The first unit concludes with an exhortation to hear; the second unit begins with an analogous admonition, giving the whole a quasi-chiastic AABBCCB^{1}B^1 structure: two questions, two statements, two imperatives, two statements.

The sayings were originally aphoristic wisdom tradition. Mark places them in this parabolic context, where they function as a further step in explicating Mark's "parable theory" (cf. the structure of 4:1–34 outlined above). However, the sayings are not mere comments on Jesus' parabolic speech but are themselves parables. The repeated call for more than superficial hearing in 23–24 corresponds to the repeated call that brackets 4:3–9. The evocative metaphors call for interpretation rather than themselves providing a discursive explanation, and the way in which they lend themselves precisely to an allegorizing interpretation in Mark's literary framework suggests that Mark regarded the sayings as parables. "Explanations" of Jesus' parabolic pedagogy are not straightforward, but are themselves parables (cf. comments on v. 13).[83]

[21–22] The saying begins with two rhetorical questions about what is self-evidently *not* done: placing a lamp under a *modion*, a two-gallon measuring ves-

---

82. For details, bibliography, arguments, and counter-arguments, see John S. Kloppenborg, *Q Parallels: Synopsis, Critical Notes, and Concordance* (Sonoma, Calif.: Polebridge, 1988) ad loc.; James M. Robinson et al., *The Critical Edition of Q: Synopsis including the Gospels of Matthew and Luke, Mark and Thomas with English, German, and French Translations of Q and Thomas* (Hermeneia; Minneapolis: Fortress, 2000), ad loc.

83. Cf. Kafka's well-known "Von den Gleichnissen / On Parables," Franz Kafka, *Parables and Paradoxes* (New York: Schocken Books, 1958), 10–11.

sel, or under a bed or dining couch (*klinē* may have either meaning, 7:4). While it has been suggested that extinguishing a lamp by placing a bowl over it rather than using a snuffer or blowing it out was not extraordinary, there seems to be no reason to place a lamp under a bed. The point is that lamps are placed where they can give light; this is their purpose. The strange combination in which "lamp" is subject (not object) and "come" is the verb, suggests that he understands the "lamp" in personal, christological terms. Though Mark never makes the explicit equation that Jesus or his teaching is the light, to represent a prophet or teacher or his teaching as "light" was a common enough metaphor in both Judaism and the Gentile Hellenistic world (cf., e.g., Ps 119:105, where "light" is "word," key term for Mark's Christology). The Christ has "come" (cf. the *ēlthon* "I have come sayings," and note 20 on 1:38 above); the Christ and his teaching are indeed presently "hidden," like the seed in the parables. But this cannot be the last word—the light does not come *in order to* be hidden, and the presently hidden Christ has come *in order to* bring light to all. Though the blindness and hardening of 4:11–12 are mysteriously real, the reality is penultimate. Likewise, that things are hidden only *in order to* be revealed later is not commonsense wisdom, but corresponds to Mark's narrative Christology and its essential means of expression, the messianic secret (see *Excursus: The Messianic Secret* at 9:13). In its Markan framework, this saying no longer explains Christology, but must be explained from it.

The saying in verse 22 as proverbial wisdom probably meant something like "you can't keep things secret; the truth comes out sooner or later," and then was taken over to express the eschatological conviction of Jesus or early Christianity that all things will be revealed at the last judgment. Mark understands it primarily in the sense that the hidden Messiahship will finally be revealed. In the narrative framework of Jesus' ministry, this pointed to the Easter revelation; in Mark's own time, while interpreting the past hiddenness of Jesus' ministry, it also pointed to the Parousia, when Jesus' messiahship will be revealed to all. Thus the blindness and hardening of 4:11–12 that seemed so absolute there is now, without retracting the previous statement, seen to be short term one step in the divine plan for history (see on 13:20 and diagram in *Excursus: Markan Christology*, p. 247). Both sayings show that the insider / outsider language of verses 10–12 does not mean the Markan church understood itself as a sect into which people were invited to learn its secrets; the "mystery" is finally for all.

[23] The command to attend to how one hears is important for the hearer / readers of Mark's Gospel, not just for the characters in the story who hear the words of Jesus. Mark's Gospel as a whole functions as the continuing voice of Jesus. From 1:2 onward, where the "way of the Lord" points beyond the surface meaning to a way that involves the readers, Mark has communicated that what is to be heard in these words calls for more than a superficial hearing.

The interpretation of the key parable in 13–20 shows that Mark sees the meaning of Jesus' words as pointing beyond the literal. This is not a call to allegorize every item and feature of Mark, but a call to listen reflectively, not assuming the meaning is on the surface (where Satan can take it away, 4:15), but asking where the text points beyond the obvious.

[24–25] Here, too, Mark's readers overhear the private instruction to disciples in the story. And here, too, a saying that previously had been commonsense wisdom—"don't be so critical of others, unless you want them to be just as critical of you"—had been reinterpreted in an eschatological sense as fostering a nonjudgmental attitude among Jesus' followers—"don't judge others too harshly, for God will judge us as we have judged others." The folk wisdom of "the rich get richer and the poor get poorer" becomes in this context an exhortation to really look and listen, for the divine gift of perceiving God's kingdom is not arbitrary, but is given to those who strive to understand and have developed their own insight. Once again, Mark applies proverbial wisdom to how his readers must *hear*. Those who hear with insight receive more insight; those who hear only superficially have even that taken away from them. The divine passives throughout indicate that the one who both gives and takes away is God. As those who initially received the mystery of the kingdom of God as a gift cannot celebrate their own ingenuity but can only give thanks, so those who continue to hear with perception must regard this as God's continuing grace.

While this section does project the image of a progression from concealment to revelation in the way God deals with the world, this should not be understood in a purely diachronic way. It is not the case that Jesus' ministry was simply the time of concealment, followed by the time of revelation after Easter—already in Jesus' ministry, the hidden light broke through in a prolepsis of the ultimate revelation, and after Easter the revelation remains mysterious.[84] Both Jesus' time and the time of Mark and his readers have a dialectic, paradoxical juxtaposition (not just a quantitative "mixture" or perspectival "balance") of hiddenness and revelation, of darkness and light, of divine presence and christological absence. While Mark affirms the dualistic view of 4:11–12 that seems so ultimate, he does not cancel it out with the more hopeful view of 4:21–25. He allows a tension to remain, just as within 4:21–25 itself there is a tension between the hope of 21–22 and the threat of 24–25.

4:26–29 Seed Parable 2: "The Seed Growing Secretly"

4:26 And he was saying, "The kingdom of God is like this:[a] a man scatters seed on the ground 27 and sleeps at night and gets up in the morning, and

---

84. Cf. the provocative description of Mark's narrative as a whole as a paradoxical "secret epiphany," Dibelius, *Tradition to Gospel*, 297.

the seed sprouts and grows—he does not know how. 28 The earth brings forth fruit without any visible cause,[b] first the stalk, then the head, then the full head of grain. 29 But when the grain is ripe, at once he puts the sickle to it, because the harvest has come."

a. Mark's *houtōs . . . hōs* corresponds to the Aramaic l[e], "it is the case with . . ." that probably served as the typical introduction to Jesus' parables. The introductory phrase suggests that it is the parable as a whole that in some way corresponds to the kingdom of God, not that the kingdom is compared with any one element. The kingdom is not like the man, the sowing, the seed, or the harvest, but like the whole situation narrated in the parable.

b. *Automatē*, only here and Acts 12:10 in the New Testament, can be translated "by itself."

This parable is one of the few texts peculiar to Mark (though Matt 13:24–30 has several verbal points of contact and may represent Matthew's reworking of this parable). The differing introductory formula (*kai elegen* "and he was saying"), and the concluding allusion to Scripture sets it off from the Sower, though both features bind it to the following parable of the Mustard Seed, as does its brevity, general structure, and analogous "point." Yet this parable is different from both the Sower and the Mustard Seed in its predominant use of the narrative present tense. This suggests that the three seed parables did not all originate at one time and had been brought together in the pre-Markan tradition. It is Mark who placed them into this context (cf. on the structure of 4:1–34 above).

This is the first parable explicitly designated a parable of the kingdom of God, though 4:11 indicates that Mark understands all the parables of this section to be kingdom parables. The perspective has shifted from the sower of verses 3–9; the reader sees things from the perspective of the "man," who is never called a "sower," and who only sows the seed and then, after some time, reaps the harvest. There is no reference to the man's work—no plowing or cultivating. There is no surprise ending in the sense of the Sower parable. The marvelous aspect is not that there is an amazing harvest despite losses, as in verses 3–9, but that there is a harvest at all—the earth produces its yield without any visible cause. First-century farmers did not think of this as "natural," but as the mysterious power of God. Nor could the harvest be assumed; every planting was a life-or-death matter. Yet the man only sleeps and rises, and does not know how it is that the seed sprouts and produces fruit. Nonetheless, when the time is ripe, the harvest comes, and he puts the sickle to the ripe grain.

The parable almost certainly goes back to the historical Jesus, but we cannot recover the original meaning(s) of the parable in the context of his ministry. While the harvest vocabulary of verse 29, which reflects the MT and Targum of Joel 3:13, is a stock symbol that points to the eschatological harvest, including the separation of wheat and chaff, this does not mean that Jesus intended the whole parable allegorically. The man in the parable did not represent God, Jesus, or his disciples, but was simply the man in the story, the equivalent of the usual *tis*, "someone," "a certain man." Yet Mark has indicated that the parable of the Sower of verses 3–8 is the key to all the parables (v. 13), and the allegorical interpretation of 13–20 indicates Mark expected all the parables to be interpreted allegorically. Thus it is likely that he understood the "man" in the same terms as the sower of verse 3, representing Jesus who sowed the word in his own ministry and continued to sow the word through his disciples in Mark's own time. The harvest would be the Parousia. The general message of the parable would be that Christian preachers could sow in confidence that the word would produce fruit, though how this happens is a mystery not understood by the preacher. The details of this allegorical approach should not be pressed. The interpreter need not wonder whether the "man" is Jesus (who in Mark sometimes sleeps and does not know, cf., e.g., 4:38; 5:30; 13:32), God (who will be the Harvester; God as Sleeper and Not-Knower is somewhat problematical), or the disciples (who indeed sleep and do not know, e.g., 4:13, 38; 14:37–40). Mark probably did understand the time after the sowing of the seed but prior to the harvest as the time of preaching the gospel prior to the eschaton, but did not have a precise periodization of history corresponding to the three phases of stalk, head, full head of grain. In a way corresponding to his own time and theology, he reaffirmed the original thrust of the parable: those who sow the gospel need not suppose that their own exertions bring or hasten the kingdom. Nor does their having received the mystery of the kingdom mean that they understand how or when the kingdom will come. The seed has been sown in the Christ-event (see on *archē* of 1:1), and they may continue to sow in confidence, for the present hiddenness of the kingdom will be made manifest in God's own time.

4:30–32 Seed Parable 3: "The Mustard Seed"

This is the only parable found in both Q and Mark, as well as in the *Gospel of Thomas*. It had a complicated tradition history prior to Mark's locating it in this context. The Q-form (Matt 13:31–32 / Luke 13:18–19) was paired with the parable of the Leaven. In the *Gospel of Thomas*, it is logion 20, unrelated contextually either to other seed parables (the Sower, *Gos. Thom.* 9) or the Leaven (*Gos. Thom.* 96).

> 4:30 And he was saying, "How may we picture the kingdom of God, or with what parable may we present[a] it? 31 It is like this:[b] as is the case with a grain of mustard seed, which, when it is sown in the earth, is the smallest of all the seeds on earth, 32 and when it is sown, it comes up and becomes larger than all the garden plants, and grows large branches, so that 'the birds of heaven can live'[c] under its shade."

a. A C² D Θ *f*¹ 33 and the mass of later MSS have *parabalōmen,* "set beside, apply," as the verb. While this is the cognate to the noun *parabolē,* it is never used in the LXX or elsewhere in the New Testament in this sense. The above translation represents the reading of ℵ B and a few other MSS, *thō,* from *tithēmi,* "set, place, put."

b. Translating *hōs* in the sense of "it is the case with." See note *a* on 4:26; here also the kingdom is not compared to any particular item within the simile, but to the picture as a whole. The structure of the Greek sentence, which is one long subordinate clause with no main verb, is here retained.

c. The usual translation "build nests" or "roost" is appropriate for birds, but the Greek text *kataskēnoun* is the typical word for "live," "dwell," and is here so translated in order to preserve the connotation of living in the land promised by God, in the presence of God, which became an image of the future kingdom (cf. the use of *kataskēnoō* in, e.g., the LXX of Num 14:30; 35:34; Deut 33:28; Josh 22:19; 2 Sam 7:10; 1 Chron 23:25; Pss 5:11; 14(15):1; 15(16):9 [cited Acts 2:26]; 36(37):3; Zech 2:10–11 [echoed in this Markan text]; 8:3, 8; Jer 23:6).

Since at the Markan level each unit of the parable section 4:1–34 can only be understood as part of the whole complex, I will here discuss only the distinctive features of this parable. It is helpful to begin at the end of the parable, which is also the end of the whole unit. The tiny mustard seed has become a large plant. This is realistic in botanical terms, for in Galilee mustard plants could attain a height of nine or ten feet, and birds could be attracted to them both for shade and to eat their seed. Yet the final description is not merely taken from observing mustard plants but reflects biblical terminology in which the final kingdom of God is portrayed as a great world-tree, under which the nations of the world find shelter and nourishment (Dan 4:12, 21; Ezek 17:23; 31:6). The image is conceived within the apocalyptic framework in which at the eschaton God's own rule replaces the tyrannical succession of worldly empires (Dan 2; 4; 7).[85] The parable portrays neither the worldwide success of the church, as in medieval theology, nor the gradual development of the kingdom within history until the political and economic structures of society are permeated by the ethic of Jesus, as in the older liberal theology. Thus the parable is not simply a straightforward promise that, despite appearances, the tiny seed will finally become a great tree.[86] Though the power of the symbolism is often lost on modern Westerners who do not live in a dry, almost treeless steppe where a large tree is virtually a miracle, the Old Testament had portrayed the final kingdom as a great, life-giving tree. A mustard

85. Yet in Dan 4:12, where Nebuchadnezzar's kingdom is a great tree whose top reaches to heaven, it is *cut down,* with only its stump remaining. God's kingdom, by contrast, is everlasting.

86. While the mustard seed itself was not literally the smallest of all seeds, its smallness was proverbial. However, in the Jewish context, the contrast of small beginnings and impressive endings was not illustrated by the mustard seed; thus the parable should not be interpreted as conventional reassuring wisdom, as in "mighty oaks from little acorns grow." On the connection between the understanding of the kingdom here expressed and Mark's apocalypticism, see on 13:5–37.

plant, however, is not a tree and not necessarily desirable—Palestinian farmers did not welcome it, for it tended to take over. Yet the "birds"—representing the Gentile nations in the Old Testament imagery—welcomed it. The image is thus somewhat double-edged. The Q version of the parable that influenced both Matthew and Luke had already changed "plant" to "tree," which, though botanically incorrect, seemed to be more theologically valid.[87] Mark's is the more original form on this point, and preserves the somewhat jarring image: the expected grandeur of the world-tree turns out to look like a big weed (as the expected Messiah turns out to look like a blasphemer, and his crown is a crown of thorns).[88] It is true that the parable is a parable of contrast: the tiny beginnings of Jesus and Mark's own day will grow to fill the world and become the ultimate, all-embracing kingdom. But the reader must ponder whether the unconventional Jesus and his unconventional band of followers represented this kingdom.

This concluding parable is distinctive in that it begins with a double question posed in the first-person plural. Instead of a straightforward declaration, it presents itself as a certain pondering of what sort of language and imagery is appropriate in speaking of the kingdom of God. If God's kingdom can be spoken of at all, the kingdom must come into speech parabolically. The "we" is not an "editorial we" or "plural of majesty," but an "ecclesial we."[89] The Markan Jesus includes his disciples in the address; they are not only the addressees, but participate with him in the pondering and speaking. As in 9:39–40, Jesus associates himself with the disciples by using the first-person plural, and throughout the Gospel the Jesus who speaks is not only the Jesus "back there" in history, but the Jesus who becomes contemporary and continues to speak through the Markan narrative. This "we" blurs the line between the word of Jesus and the word of his disciples in Mark's day who speak in his behalf.

4:33–34 The Markan "Parable Theory"—Third Statement

4:33 With many such parables he was speaking[a] the word to them, in accordance with their ability to hear. 34 Without parables he was not speaking[a] to them, but privately to his own disciples he was explaining[a] everything.

---

87. Technically, the mustard plant was in fact considered something of a borderline case by ancient botanists. See Theophrastus, *Hist. Pl.* 1.3.1–4, who discusses the fact that some flora are in a category between plants and trees, and gives them a specific designation, *dendrolachana,* "tree-plants."

88. This interpretation is developed especially, and somewhat exaggeratedly, by Robert W. Funk, "The Looking-Glass Tree Is for the Birds," *Int* 26, no. 1 (1973): 3–9; with more restraint, Scott, *Hear Then the Parable,* 373–87. In any case, the contrast made by the parable is not between conventional expectation (mighty tree) and parabolic image (lowly shrub), but between the shrub's own seed and its result.

89. This narrative mode in which the post-Easter community of faith speaks with the voice of the risen Christ located in the pre-Easter narrative was extensively developed in the Johannine literature. Cf. John 3:1–21, the Farewell Discourses John 14–17, and the "we" of the Johannine epistles.

a. The three verbs are all imperfects, denoting continuous and repeated action, Jesus' customary practice, not just the way he did it this one afternoon.

This is the third installment of Mark's "parable theory," which in the nature of the case could not be presented all at once, essaylike, in one coherent set of principles, but had to be presented parabolically. It interweaves and juxtaposes the two views of parabolic teaching we have seen throughout the section: the parables represent a didactic strategy intended to communicate Jesus' message by adapting it to the hearers, and the parables are a means of concealing Jesus' message from all except the elect. There is throughout a dialectic of secrecy and revelation, divine sovereignty and human choice, universalism and election. This is already seen in the commands to hear that surround the opening, paradigmatic parable, the key to them all (v. 13). The command *akouete* of verse 3 seems universal, and the concluding *hos echei ōta akouein akouetō* in verse 9 can be understood as addressed to everyone—but the addition of *akouein* can already be understood as gift of authentic hearing, not just physical hearing or common-sense understanding. That Mark has no single consistent "parable theory" is also seen in his treatment of the parable in 12:1–12.

The distinction between tradition (v. 33) and redaction (v. 34) is helpful:[90] in the pre-Markan tradition, Jesus adapted his teaching to the capacity of his hearers; he taught in order to be understood, and he was understood. Mark's "parable theory" requires that Jesus not be understood until after the resurrection, and that he intended it to be so; "ability to hear" in the pre-Markan verse 33 had indicated the crowds had a certain capacity, and Jesus adapted his message to it so they could understand.[91] In Mark's own view, they *could* not hear, since the parables themselves had made them deaf and blind (see on 4:10–12). Although later in the narrative Jesus will continue to teach publicly, comprehensively, and in an understandable manner (e.g., 6:34; 12:13–40), using parables only on selected occasions (12:1–22; 13:28–37), Mark here subsumes all Jesus' teaching under the heading of "parable" that intentionally conceals his meaning from those who do not have the revelatory key provided only to his

90. Scholars disagree on how precisely to sort out pre-Markan tradition and Markan redaction in these two short verses. Christopher M. Tuckett, "Mark's Concerns in the Parables Chapter (Mark 4,1–34)," *Bib* 69, no. 1 (1988): 6–8, catalogues six reconstructions of the apportionment of tradition and redaction. Yet the assignment of v. 33 to tradition and v. 34 to Mark is widely supported.

91. Gundry, *Mark*, 234, resolves the difficulty by referring v. 33 to the "attention span" of the crowd, to which Jesus adapted his teaching. Witherington, *Mark*, 173, makes it a matter of the audience's own choice; Jesus intended to reveal his message to all, but all were not willing to hear it. Cf. France, *Gospel of Mark*, 218, who interprets the tension between these two verses as Mark's intending to remind us of the "variety of response" to parables. Some would be left cold by them, others would seek out more insight. Jesus taught in order to evoke such response (v. 33) and provided it to those who "responded" (v. 34). This is not what Mark says.

disciples (v. 34). Yet Mark's christological perspective includes more than overlaying the overtly revelatory teaching of Jesus with his own messianic secret. For him, the parables are not stand-alone vehicles of religious insight, but are understood only in relation to the one who tells them, and as his gift. The gift without the giver, however, is bare; the tale requires the teller. In Mark's view, one must first accept Jesus as the parable of God, the Messiah who upsets our expectations, before the parables are opened to his disciples: Jesus' person before Jesus' teaching, the Revealer before the revelation. *This* insight is not an attainment based on sound reasoning from valid evidence that meets our criteria; it must be given by God. Those who see it must not congratulate themselves, but give thanks to God. What we hear is the message, the story itself, but Jesus stands on the margin of his own discourse.[92] In Mark's view, this could not be seen, and was not seen, until illumined by the light of cross and resurrection.

The long section ends without reaction either from the crowd or the disciples, either positive or negative (contrast, e.g., 1:22). The reader must await further developments.

4:35–8:21 Crossing Borders

4:35–41 Stilling the Storm

While this story has connections with the preceding—4:35–36 has a clear relation to 4:1—with 4:35 the narrative takes a new turn, both geographically and in regard to its focus. Here begins a series of dramatic miracle stories in which Jesus is increasingly portrayed as an epiphany of divine power. While the miracles become more spectacular, the focus remains on Jesus himself, not on the miracles as such. The calming of the storm (4:35–41) is followed by a vivid and lengthy description of a spectacular exorcism in Gentile territory (5:1–20). Then a story in which a woman is healed in the presence of pressing crowds is intercalated into the account of Jesus' raising a little girl from the dead (5:21–43). The series of miracle stories continues intermittently through 6:52, with the stories of feeding the five thousand (6:32–44) and walking on the water (6:45–52), and concludes with a summary in which Jesus' saving / healing power attracts multitudes from "the whole region" (6:53–56). The similarity of this summary to 3:7–12 has encouraged some scholars to posit a pre-Markan miracle source here used by Mark. This possibility has sometimes been supported by pointing

---

92. Funk, *Language*, 179–80, 93, 215–16, Funk sees the parables as pointing obliquely to a Christology. The hearers of Jesus' parables "also perceive who it is that gives it. . . . the parable is an oblique invitation on the part of Jesus to follow him" (197); ". . . Jesus 'appears' in the penumbral field of the parable as one who has embarked on this way" (216).

to an analogous pattern of similar miracles later in Mark; that is, in this view Mark would have had available to him two versions of a traditional document or cycle of oral traditions portraying Jesus as filled with divine power.[93] It does seem likely that Mark's context included cycles of traditions and even structured documents that presented Jesus as a powerful divine figure, even though our present state of knowledge does not allow us to reconstruct their contents with any precision or to analyze their theology; pointing out variations in scholars' attempts at reconstructions and their differing assessments of the theological perspective of such putative sources does not disprove the hypothesis as such. Mark does not take up such traditions merely to neutralize them, but as vehicles of his own dialectical theology (see *Excursus: Miracle Stories in Mark* at 6:56). Mark also recounts each story in terms of the messianic secret; the picture of Jesus as divine epiphany is set in the framework of inadequate understanding or secrecy (cf. 4:41; 5:6, 21–24, 31, 43; cf. *Excursus: The Messianic Secret* at 9:13).

The story has some of the typical formal characteristics of a Hellenistic miracle story: the description of the dire threat, the call for help, the miracle itself, and the response.[94] Yet Mark reflects not only the Hellenistic miracle story but the influence of the Old Testament. In the Jonah story (Jonah 1), a divinely commissioned prophet boards a boat en route to Gentile territory, there is a violent windstorm at sea, Jonah sleeps but the seasoned sailors panic, God calms the storm in relation to what happens to Jonah, and the sailors are converted. Not only themes, but overlapping vocabulary connect the two stories: for example, the words for *boat, waves, sea, sleeping, waking up, being about to die,* the wind *ceasing, awesome fear.* This story has also been shaped by texts in which God is the creator who rebuked and drove back the watery chaos at creation and continues to be Lord of wind and wave (Gen 1:1–10; Pss 65:7; 74:13–14; 89:9–13; 104:5–9; 107:23–32; Job 38:8–11; Jer 5:22; 31:35, and see on 1:16), as well as by psalms in which the troubles of God's people are represented by stormy waters (cf. Pss 69:1–2; 124:4–5). So also, Mark has already placed his own

---

93. Cf., e.g., Leander Keck, "Mark 3:7–12 and Mark's Christology," *JBL* 84, no. 4 (1965): 341–58; Heinz-Wolfgang Kuhn, *Ältere Sammlungen in Markusevangelium* (SUNT 8; Göttingen: Vandenhoeck und Ruprecht, 1971), 30–32, 191–214; Pesch, *Markusevangelium,* 1:277–81; Paul J. Achtemeier, "Toward the Isolation of Pre-Markan Miracle Catenae," *JBL* 89, no. 3 (1970): 265–91; Paul J. Achtemeier, "The Origin and Function of the Pre-Markan Miracle Catenae," *JBL* 91, no. 2 (1972): 198–221. All these (and other such proposals based on the supposed history of the pre-Markan tradition) are weighed and found wanting by, among others, Robert M. Fowler, *Loaves and Fishes: The Function of the Feeding Stories in the Gospel of Mark* (SBLDS 54; Chico, Calif.: Scholars Press, 1981), 5–42, and Lührmann, *Markusevangelium,* 95.

94. Cf. Bultmann, *History of the Synoptic Tradition,* 216; for more recent analyses and qualifications, cf. Schenke, *Wundererzählungen,* 49–59. In particular, pagan rulers were pictured as able to command wind and sea (2 Macc 9:8 [Antiochus Epiphanes]; Dio Cassius 41.4.13; 59.28.6 [Caesar, Caligula]).

stamp on the typical miracle story form, reformulating this story as a disciple-ship story. A dialogue, internal to the group, becomes central in a way not typical of miracle stories.

4:35 On that day, when evening had come, he says to them, "Let us go[a] across to the other side." **36** And they left the crowd and take him with them in the boat, just as he was, and there were other boats with him. **37** And a great windstorm came up, and the waves were breaking over the boat, so that the boat was already being swamped. **38** And he was in the stern, sleeping on the cushion. And they wake him and say to him, "Teacher, don't you care that we're about to die?" **39** And he woke up and rebuked the wind, and spoke to the sea, "Silence! Be still!" And the wind ceased, and there was a great calm. **40** And he said to them, "Why are you so miserably afraid?[b] Do you not yet have faith?" **41** And they were filled with awesome fear, and kept saying to each other, "Who then is this, that even the wind and the sea obey him?"

a. Jesus' "Let us go . . ." is not a suggestion, but a command. Greek, like English, has no first-person imperative, but uses the hortatory subjunctive that functions as an imperative, which comes into English with the "let . . ." form. Cf. note on 3:9 regarding the third-person imperative.

b. From Homer onward, *deilos,* which means "fearful," "cowardly," could be used in the negative sense of "vile," "worthless," or in a compassionate sense, "miserable, poor, wretched, in need of help." The manuscript tradition of the last five words of this verse is very confused, with several groups of MSS including *houtōs* ("thus," "such") in various locations, and many MSS, including most later ones, introducing the second question with *pōs,* "how is it that . . . ?" The translation above follows most modern critical texts, which are based on ℵ B, and several early uncials. Although the word *houtōs* was probably not in the original text, I have included "so" to express the intended sense. Important for the Markan understanding is *oupō* ("not yet"), which is well attested.

[35] The verse is transitional, binding this pericope both to the teaching scene just completed and to the "other [Gentile] side." The "birds" in the conclusion of the final parable, representing the Gentiles, had already pointed to this next move in Jesus' ministry, constituting a further link between the two pericopes.

[36] The disciples obey. They are the active agents, and Jesus is passive. They leave the crowd, with which they have been contrasted in verses 33–34, and take Jesus with them "in the boat, just as he was." The meaning of this somewhat awkward phrase is not entirely clear. It may simply signal that Jesus had been teaching from the boat (4:1), and they took him with them without disembarking. Since the boat is a necessary part of the story in any case, the phrase seems to call attention to it. At Jesus' command, a boat has been standing ready since 3:9, where it was to serve to separate Jesus (and his disciples) from the crowd. Then the Twelve are appointed, to "be with" Jesus, so that he could send them out to preach, and to have authority over demons (3:14). All these elements recur in this pericope, which is linked to the image of Jesus and his disciples forming a group in contrast to "the crowd." The boat is thus the encompassing image that includes Jesus-who-teaches and the Twelve as the core of a larger group of disciples who are called to proclaim, crossing through stormy waters to Gentile territory, encountering threatening demonic power en route that terrifies them, but delivered and rebuked by Jesus who acts and speaks with the power of God. All these elements cohere in the symbol of boat-as-church. Christian interpreters after Mark, beginning with Matthew, certainly developed this symbolism, placing it in a context of discipleship and rewriting it so that Jesus calls people to follow him, gets into the boat, and others follow (Matt 8:18–27).[95] In the second century, the ark became the symbol of the church in which the redeemed are delivered from divine judgment, and the mast of sailboats was seen as symbolizing the cross (Minucius Felix, *Octavius* 29; Justin, *I Apology* 55). In the next century Origen could declare, "as many as are in the bark of the holy church will voyage with the Lord across this wave-tossed life" (*On Matthew*, Homily 6). The central section of the church building is still called the "nave" (Latin for "ship"). This is not to suggest an allegorical interpretation of every occurrence of a boat in Mark, for sometimes the boat as a means of transportation is simply a natural part of the story. For instance, the initial appearance of a boat in the narrative disrupts any attempt to impute a consistent "boat symbolism" to Mark, for there disciples *leave* the boat in order to follow Jesus (1:19). Nor should the details of this story be allegorized, as though for Mark the boat conveying Jesus and the disciples represents the church, the storm stands for persecution, Jesus' sleep means the delay of the Parousia, and the calming of the storm is the peace Jesus brings at his return. Nonetheless, without employing a rigid allegorical method, Mark rewrites his tradition in such a way that the meaning is rarely on the surface, and the boat here seems to point beyond its literal signification.[96] The "other boats," however, are probably only a fragment of pre-Markan tradition; they were part of the traditional story, but play no role in the narrative at the Markan level—unless they are a minor protest

95. Classically developed by Günther Bornkamm, "The Stilling of the Storm in Matthew," in *Tradition and Interpretation in Matthew* (ed. Günther Bornkamm et al.; trans. Percy Scott; NTL; Philadelphia: Westminster John Knox, 1963), 52–58.

96. Cf. Ernest Best, *Following Jesus: Discipleship in the Gospel of Mark* (JSNTSup 4; Sheffield: University of Sheffield, 1981), chap. 29: "The Church as Ship," 230–34. Kertelge, *Wunder*, 97–98, argues the boat symbolism was already in the pre-Markan tradition, and Mark develops it without making it explicit. The ship had already become a symbol for Israel, the people of God (cf. T. Naph. 6; 1QH 6.22–23). The church fathers would interpret the boat specifically as the church (Tertullian *On Baptism* 12; Clement of Alexandria, *Salvation of the Rich Man* 34.3).

against exclusivism of the Markan church: they are not the only boat on the sea (cf. 9:38–49).

[38] The picture of Jesus asleep in the raised stern of the boat on the cushion normally occupied by the helmsman should not be interpreted psychologically, as though he was worn out after a long day of teaching. That Jesus sleeps points to his humanity, for while pagan gods may sleep, the true God of Israel does not (Ps 121:4; pleas such as Pss 35:23; 44:23; 59:4 reveal Israel's conviction that it is contrary to God's nature to sleep; cf. 1 Kgs 18:27). Human beings may lie down and sleep in peace as a sign of their trust in God (Pss 3:5; 4:8); Jesus is here fully human in both senses. By their lack of faith, the disciples betray their lack of authentic humanity, that is, they fall short of the true humanity manifest in Jesus' calm sleep, which is that of those who trust in God. The first words the disciples speak to Jesus in the Gospel—except for 1:37, which also indicate their failure to understand him and his mission—reveal the paradoxical combination of faith and unfaith, understanding and obtuseness, that will characterize them throughout the Gospel. They address him as "Teacher"—odd for a storm-and-exorcism story, where "master" or "Lord" would be more fitting—a clue that Mark recasts the miracle story in terms of discipleship. Their prayer-protest, reminiscent of Israel's reproachful prayers in the Psalter, implies they believed Jesus *could* do something to save them from the storm. The disciples' cry—"Don't you care that we're about to die?"—extends the story into the Markan readers' present, reflecting the anguished prayers of Christians in the time of Nero's rampage against Christians in Rome in 64 C.E. and the terrors faced by Christians in Palestine and Syria during the Jewish revolt. The kind of faith the story calls for, however, is not only that Jesus could save them from the storm, but that if he is with them—literally in the same boat—he can save them even if he and they go under, a faith in the Lord of the storm who can save beyond death. Mark's readers know that God did not deliver Jesus from death, but raised him from the dead, and already look back on the martyrdoms of Peter, Paul, and other Christians. This story calls them to a faith in the God who saves through and beyond death, not necessarily from death. At the narrative level, the disciples do not and cannot know that *the* epiphany of the Son of God will be on the cross (15:39); to insist that God manifest his saving power to keep them from dying is here pictured as profound *lack* of faith (Schenke, *Wundererzählungen*, 84–92).

[39] Jesus rebukes the wind and sea, using the same vocabulary as in the initial exorcism of 1:25 (*epetimēsen*, "rebuke"; *pephimōso*, "silence!"). In Jonah 1:4, the term for "wind" is *pneuma*, the same word used for [unclean] *spirit* in Mark (e.g., in the story that follows immediately, 5:2, 8). While Mark never uses *pneuma* in the sense of "wind" (but always *anemos*, as here; cf. 6:48, 51; 13:27), the underlying imagery is transparent: in the windstorm Jesus faces another expression of the demonic threat and overcomes it by his sovereign authority. Here Jesus is implicitly contrasted with Jonah, the guilty party who

caused the storm sent by God, a storm that only God can calm. While the sleeping Jesus evokes the image of Jonah, one "greater than Jonah is here," and Jesus' calming of the storm casts him in the role of God.[97]

[40–41] Even though the disciples had believed Jesus could do something about the storm, Jesus addresses them with severity and compassion as "miserably afraid" (see note *b* above). Believing Jesus could work a miracle is not identical with authentic faith (see on 15:29–32). While Mark is not carrying on a corrective Christology that is only concerned with criticizing faith in miracles—he in fact uses the miracle stories as a vehicle of his Christology—belief that Jesus can work miracles is inadequate, is *not yet* faith, which will come only in the light of crucifixion and resurrection. Thus their "awesome fear" has the same ambiguity as their "faith." It is expressed in different vocabulary than that of their terror of the storm and Jesus' description of their lack of faith ("we're about to die"; "miserably afraid"). It represents their state after the storm has been calmed and is the same word used of the women's state after hearing the message of the resurrection (16:8). While Mark can use it negatively as the fear that is the opposite of faith (5:36), it can also represent numinous awe in the presence of the holy, the "fear of the Lord" in the reverential sense. Mark does not tell the readers how to understand it here. In the slot reserved for the concluding acclamation of a typical miracle story, the disciples fail to grasp Jesus' identity, and acclamation is replaced with wonderment (cf. 1:27 and 5:30–34, where the woman "knows" and has "faith," but the disciples do not know). The final question shows the story is not focused on the "nature miracle" itself, but christologically on Jesus. In Markan perspective, "Who then is this?" *can* only be answered from the perspective of 16:6; the readers already stand there, but not the disciples in the narrative. Not *yet* (v. 40!).[98]

5:1–20 The Gerasene Demoniac

5:1 And they came to the other side of the sea, to the territory[a] of the Gerasenes.[b] 2 And just as he had gotten out of the boat, a man who had an unclean spirit came to meet him out of the tombs, 3 a man who lived in the tombs, and no one was able bind him any more, not even with a

---

97. While Jonah is an antihero in the biblical story, in postbiblical tradition Jonah had become a heroic figure who threatens the chaos monster with eschatological destruction (see Marcus, *Mark 1–8*, 1:337, who cites *Pirqe R. El.* 10; *Tanhuma* on Leviticus, 8). The Q tradition had already declared that what Jesus brings is "something greater than Jonah" (Matt 12:39–41; Luke 11:29–32), referring to the kingdom of God. Mark taps into this tradition, identifying king and kingdom: some-*one* greater than Jonah is here! God as master of the stormy sea is a biblical motif, e.g., Job 38:8–11.

98. Schenke, *Wundererzählungen*, 40–43, gives detailed redactional arguments that v. 40 is a Markan insertion and the point of the story at the Markan level.

chain, 4 for he had often been bound with leg irons and chains, but he had broken the chains and smashed the leg irons, and no one was mighty enough to control him. 5 And throughout the night and day, in the tombs and on the mountains, he kept yelling and cutting himself up with stones. 6 And when he saw Jesus from a distance, he ran and knelt before him, 7 and yelled in a loud voice, "What do you have to do with me,[c] Jesus, Son of the Most High God? I adjure you by God that you not torment me." 8 For Jesus was already saying to him,[d] "Come out of the man, you unclean spirit!" 9 And he asked him, "What is your name?" And he says to him, "My name is Legion; for there are many of us." 10 And they[e] pleaded with him earnestly not to send them out of the territory.[f] 11 Now there was a large herd of pigs feeding there on the hillside; 12 and they pleaded with him, "Send us into the pigs; let us go into them." 13 And he permitted them. And the unclean spirits came out and went into the pigs. And the herd rushed down the steep bank into the sea—there were about two thousand of them—and were drowned in the sea.

14 And the herdsmen fled and told it in the city and the countryside, and people came to see what had happened. 15 They come to Jesus, and are looking at the demoniac sitting quietly, [g] clothed, and in his right mind, the same man who had had the legion; and they were afraid. 16 And those who had seen it told them what had happened to the demoniac—and about the pigs. 17 And they began to plead with Jesus to leave their region.

18 And as he was getting back into the boat, the man who had been demon-possessed was pleading with him that he might be with him. 19 And he did not permit him, but says to him, "Go to your house and your own people, and tell them how much the Lord has done for you, how he has had mercy on you." 20 And he went away and began to proclaim in the Decapolis how much Jesus had done for him, and everyone was amazed.

a. Gerasa is a city, so *chōra* does not mean "country" in the political sense, but "the territory around the city," its "environs."

b. Two actual cities are named in the text tradition: (1) *Gerasa* (ℵ* B D latt sa) is a Hellenistic city belonging to the Decapolis in Transjordan, near the Jabbok River, more than 30 miles SE from the Sea of Galilee (two days hard walking up and down steep hills), identified with the nearby modern city of Jerash, 22 miles N of Amman. (2) *Gadara* (A C *f*[13] 𝔐 sy[p, h]), another city of the Decapolis, is about 6 miles from the Sea of Galilee (three hours of hard walking), on the southeast side of the Yarmuk River. Each of these sites presents difficulties for the setting of the story, which takes place on the bank of the sea. In the third century, Origen postulated that there had been a town "Gergasa," whose ruins are supposedly identified with *Kursa* on the eastern shore of the sea. All three names occur in MSS of each of the Synoptics. On the basis of attestation in the best MSS and the principle of *lectio difficilior,* Mark apparently wrote *Gerasēnōn,* changed by Matthew to *Gadarēnōn*. Under the influence of Origen, *"Gergasēnōn"* penetrated the MSS traditions of all three Synoptics.

c. See note *c* at 1:24 on the same phrase (there in plural, here in singular).

d. The imperfect tense here is used as the equivalent of the pluperfect and expresses continuous action, thus making the demons' shout a response to Jesus' prior command (as 5:28, 6:18; Luke 8:29).

e. There is no pronoun subject in the Greek text; the subject indicator is included in the third-person singular verb *parekalei*. A peculiarity of Greek grammar, however, is that neuter plural subjects regularly take singular verbs; thus the subject can be either the demonized man (so most English translations) or the neuter plural unclean spirits. The story throughout oscillates between singular and plural, depicting the man's deranged state.

f. *Chōra*, same word as v. 1. The demons are at home in Gentile territory and do not want to be displaced.

g. The Greek text has only *kathēmenon*, "sitting"; "quietly" is implicit, in contrast to his previous uncontrollable raging about. "Same" is likewise implied but not explicit.

As Jesus inaugurated his ministry in his Jewish context by attending a synagogue where he encountered and vanquished a demon (1:21–28), so his first act after setting foot on Gentile soil is to exorcise a demon. The sacred setting of Jewish synagogue worship is clearly contrasted with the unclean tombs in Gentile territory (which also served as places of pagan worship; cf. Isa 65:4), but Jesus is sovereign over the demonic power that pervades each sphere.

This longest, most detailed, and most vivid of the Synoptic miracle stories lacks smoothness and consistency. The disciples arrive in the boat with Jesus (v. 1) but play no role in the story. The location is confused in the tradition (on Gerasa, Gadara, and Gergasa, see note *b* above). There are repetitions (Jesus seems to meet the demoniac twice, vv. 2, 6; two proofs of the demoniac's cure, vv. 11–13, 15). The exorcism itself is not narrated, and Jesus' command to come out seems awkwardly inserted (v. 8). The demon knows Jesus' name (v. 7), but Jesus, though in charge throughout, must ask the name of the demon (v. 9). Verbs and pronouns referring to the demon(s) and the victim alternate between singular (vv. 2, 6, 7, 8, 9a, 10a) and plural (9b, 10b, 12, 13). The gender of the words referring to the spirits also varies between neuter, corresponding to *pneuma* ("spirit"), and masculine, corresponding to *anthrōpos* ("man"). The demons seem both deferential (v. 6) and aggressive (v. 7). There is no explicit messianic secret, and contrary to his usual practice, Jesus commands the healed man to tell others (v. 19), but it is not clear whether the man obeys or disobeys (v. 20).

While a detailed history of the tradition can no longer be reconstructed, it is likely that the story gained accretions as it was repeatedly retold in the pre-Markan tradition. A story of an exorcism by the sea, in which the healed man became a "missionary" to his compatriots in the Gentile territory on the east bank, was associated with Gerasa, the large and influential Hellenistic city of the Decapolis, and became the "foundation story" for churches in the area. At its origin or along the way, the story picked up the folk motifs of the defrauded demon and the destruction of the swine—in which Jewish and Jewish-Christian hearers would delight—and the reference to "legion" and its anti-Roman, anti-war overtones, and reflections on Isa 65:1–7.[99] At the Markan level, it is located as a parallel to 1:21–28, and its vocabulary is recast to make the parallel obvious. Since Isaiah plays a key role in Mark's formation of the Gospel (see on 1:1–3), the echoes of Isaiah may have been introduced or augmented at the redactional level. The length and placement of the story indicate the central importance of God's triumph over the demonic world in the Christ-event for Mark's theology.

[1–5] The group arrives on the eastern bank, and Jesus disembarks. Mark does not specify the chronology he has in mind (is it very late evening or, presumably, the morning after the events of 4:1–41?), or whether the disciples join Jesus on the shore. All attention focuses on Jesus. A man immediately comes to meet him who is triply unclean (on "unclean," see on 1:21–28): possessed by unclean spirits, living in unclean tombs, in a land populated by hordes of pigs and demons. Like the leprous man in 1:40–45—associated with the demons of 1:39—the man here is a picture of death, of one already banished from the land of the living, from human community that makes human life possible. Like the other exorcisms and healing stories, this story has overtones of the resurrection story, a prolepsis of what God did for humanity in the resurrection of Jesus. This is not a story about the response of faith and its transforming power, but about an invasion of alien territory and reclaiming it for the kingdom of God. The man had often been bound, but not successfully; the army of demons within him was too strong. No one was "mighty enough" (*ischyen,* cf. 1:7) to subdue him. Without explicitly calling attention to it, the story evokes the previous images of Jesus as the mightier one who will receive and dispense the Holy Spirit (see on 1:7–10), the one who will bind the strong man (3:27; Rev 20:1–2).

[7–8] The demonized man falls before Jesus, not worshiping him but acknowledging his authority and power, but also with a challenge. "What do you have to do with me?" here means something like "we belong to two different realms." In this encounter the kingdom of God confronts the kingdom of evil (cf. 3:22–27). As elsewhere, the demons recognize Jesus' true identity (cf. 1:24; 3:11). The answer to the disciples' question in 4:41 is given, but only the readers hear it, and it has no effect on the characters in the narrative. At some pre-Markan level, the peculiarity of knowing names and their power has played

99. Since Simon bar Giora, one of the leaders of the Jewish revolt, came from Gerasa (Josephus, *War* 4.503), this may be another link between this story and the Jewish war that would have been known to (some of) Mark's readers.

a role in the story; to know the demon's or exorcist's name gives one power. Here, the demons know Jesus' name and even adjure Jesus by God, attempting a kind of reverse exorcism, as unclean spirit opposes Holy Spirit, but they have no power. Strangely, Jesus, who must ask the demon's name, acts with sovereign authority. Only after the demon's outburst does the narrator, with a peculiar use of the imperfect tense (see note *d*), let the reader know that this is a response to what Jesus had already been saying. Jesus takes the initiative, is on the attack. He is not reacting to the request or aggression of the demons. The reader never hears the word of command, which has already evoked the submission and bargaining of the demons. There are no rituals, no struggle. Terrible as the situation is for the demonized man, in this scene Jesus encounters a defeated enemy.

[9–10] The demons' self-designation as "legion" has sometimes been taken as a direct allusion to the Roman occupation of Palestine, perceived as demonic by the inhabitants and by Mark, as though the story of the exorcism and resulting drowning of the pigs represents expelling the Romans and driving them into the sea.[100] The Tenth Legion, stationed in Palestine, had the insignia of a wild boar on its banners. In the latter part of the Jewish revolt against Rome, Vespasian sent troops under the command of Lucius Annius on a punitive raid to Gerasa, burned the city, and devastated the surrounding villages. If Mark was written shortly after 70 C.E., this would have been a recent event. It has often been noted that *agelē*, the word for "herd," is not really appropriate for pigs, but was used for military units, and "he permitted them" of verse 13 could be translated as "he dismissed them," with a military overtone, just as "rushed" could be translated "charged," with a military connotation. The demons' plea not to be sent out of the country can be seen as transparent to the unwillingness of the Roman occupation force to leave Palestine. Yet Horace, devoted supporter of Rome, two generations before had spoken of a "cohort of fever-demons" (*Odes* 1.3.30), and Mark's explicit interpretation of "legion" is not directly anti-Roman but refers only to the vast number of demons inhabiting the poor man (a standard legion comprised six thousand men, even though they were often not at full complement). Thus for Mark, the meaning of the story cannot be reduced to an allegory of liberation from the Romans—its horizon is broader than that, within a cosmic and eschatological framework—but it could hardly have been read in Mark's time without political overtones. It is also important to note that the demons do not ask to remain in the *man*, but that they not be forced to leave the *territory*. Jesus' first foray into Gentile territory not only frees individuals from demonic power but purges the country itself

100. This interpretation has been especially popular among advocates of liberation theology, e.g., Myers, *Binding the Strong Man*, 190–93, and Richard A. Horsley, *Hearing the Whole Story: The Politics of Plot in Mark's Gospel* (Louisville, Ky.: Westminster John Knox, 2001), 141–48.

(cf. LaVerdiere, *Beginning*, 1:130). Israel is no longer exclusively the Holy Land—the Christ-event exorcizes Gentile territory; analogous to 7:19, Jesus proleptically makes all lands clean.

[11–13] The Jew-Gentile contrast could hardly be more forcefully expressed than by the presence of swine. For Jews, pigs were prohibited as food not because they were unclean in themselves, but because the Torah declared them to be ritually "unclean for you"—ritually impure, not dirty (Lev 11:7–8; Deut 14:8). Abstinence from pork, like Sabbath observance, was a matter of God's law that set Israel apart as a distinctive, holy people. Refusal to eat pork was a boundary marker between faith and unfaith, and Jewish martyrs had given their lives on this account (1 Macc 1:47; 2 Macc 6–7). For Romans and other Gentiles, the pig was a sacred animal, to be sacrificed to the gods and consumed in sacred meals, including at ancestral tombs on ritual occasions. The destruction of the pigs was thus not only, or not primarily, an economic issue but a religious confrontation, with pigs constituting an appropriate refuge for demons, and their destruction representing not only the folk motif of tricking the demons but the victory of Israel's God over paganism.[101]

Both ancient and modern interpreters have been bothered by the destruction of the large number of swine. Ancient sources indicate that even a herd of three hundred pigs was considered extraordinary; two thousand is a an extravagantly large number, and would have been worth a fortune. Jerome explained that the destruction of the large number of pigs was necessary to convince the bystanders that in fact such a horde of demons had been expelled, and that in any case one soul saved is priceless.[102] Modern readers might also think in terms of cruelty to animals and the ethics of destroying so much food in a hungry world. But pointing to the evidential power on bystanders turns out to be wide of the mark, for they end up rejecting Jesus anyway, and appealing to the "greater good" seems to presuppose that Jesus was faced with the choice of destroying pigs or saving a human life.[103] In terms of such logic, however, surely the one who calmed the storm and walked on the water could have delivered the man *and* spared the pigs. It is better not to pose the question within this framework, to grant that neither the Jesus in the story nor Mark the storyteller ever raised such questions, and that the language of the story is to be under-

101. According to Rikki E. Watts, *Isaiah's New Exodus in Mark* (WUNT 88; Tübingen: Mohr Siebeck, 1997), 160, the story portrays Jesus as Isaiah's Yahweh-Warrior of the second exodus "who defeats the hostile powers, now in their New Testament demonic manifestation as 'Legion,' by drowning them in the sea, just as in the first exodus. Whereas in Isaiah it was the downfall of the nations' idols which would signal the coming of deliverance, in Mark it is the demise of the demons." Cf. Isa 65:1–7 as the background for this imagery, and the LXX's interpretation of "nations" as "demons."

102. *The Life of St. Hilarion* 32; *Homily* 54, cited in Oden and Hall, *Mark*, 70.

103. So, e.g., Witherington, *Mark*, 183, "a matter of priorities."

stood as oriented to the one confessional point of God's saving act in Christ, not as a kind of objectifying language from which inferences must be made.[104] In any case, the story itself makes nothing of the financial loss, which is more the concern of a modern capitalist society. The villagers do not argue that Jesus should have found a more cost-effective means of exorcism; they do not bemoan their financial loss, demand financial restitution, or try to have Jesus arrested for destruction of property. They merely ask the intruder to leave. For the demoniac, Jesus' appearance had meant salvation. His neighbors had become accustomed to the status quo and considered Jesus' presence uncomfortable or dangerous.

[14–16] The conclusion of the story is different from other exorcism and miracle stories, and much longer. The story's repercussions and the conclusions drawn from it seem to be as important as the exorcism itself. The narrative lens shifts away from the healed man to the herdsmen. There is no positive reaction, but flight. Curious crowds come from the city and surrounding villages to see what has happened. They see the healed man, restored to a normal human life, and they respond with fear. Mark uses exactly the same word as in 4:40–41, where fear is the opposite of faith (see commentary there). They had not been afraid of the raging of the madman; they had become accustomed to his ravings as an aspect of their given, normal world. Now they realize they are in the presence of someone for whom such a world is not the unchangeable, unnoticed givenness of everyday life, and this is scary indeed.

[17–20] Two responses follow, both of which accept the reality of the miracle. The crowds implore Jesus to leave their region. The healed man asks to be "with Jesus" (*met' autou*, as 3:14). The reader may be surprised that Jesus complies with the crowd's request but refuses the man's—he had granted the demon's plea expressed with the same verb (*parakaleō*, v. 12). No reason for the refusal is given. One can think of possible reasons: the man may be a Gentile, and it is "not time yet" for Gentiles to be included (see on 7:24–30), or the man wants to be a member of the Twelve, which is now a closed circle (see on 3:13–19), or Jesus, in contrast to the rabbis, does not accept applicants, but always takes the initiative to call (see on 1:16–20). Or this element may have

104. This does not mean that such language is "merely subjective." It refers to something beyond itself, but the referent is not an object within the world of propositional language, constituting a premise in a logical chain from which necessary inferences can and must be made. Confessional, referential language says what it says, but does not take responsibility for further statements that may be inferred from it, for it is not that kind of language. Here, the "point" is christological, and that point stands: the God of Israel represented in Jesus meets and vanquishes the powers of the demonic world. Such a confessional affirmation does not raise the objectifying issue of alternative fates for the pigs, their economic value, the hungry people who could have been fed by them, and the morality of destruction of property in a good cause. On referential, nonobjectifying language, cf. M. Eugene Boring, *Revelation* (Int; Louisville, Ky.: Westminster John Knox, 1989), 51–58.

already been in the traditional story, and Mark exploits it because he wants to use the man as a proleptic symbol of the later Gentile mission. In any case, only here in Mark does Jesus command someone he has healed to go and spread the news, something he elsewhere explicitly forbids (cf. 1:44, a story with some similarities to this one; 5:43; 7:31–37). There are other ambiguities and reversals of expectations: The man is told to go *home* and *tell* (*apangelō*, as v. 14) his *own people* what *"the Lord"* had done for him. However, the man goes to the whole *Decapolis*,[105] where he *preaches* (*kēryssō*, as 1:14; 3:14; 6:12; 13:10; 14:9) what *Jesus* has done for him. Does this represent obedience and understanding, or misunderstanding and unintended disobedience? While the reader knows that Jesus is indeed "the Lord," with regard to the characters in the story this title is used only ambiguously (see *Excursus: Markan Christology* at 9:1). At the narrative level, the man is told to declare what the Lord *God* has done for him, and he mis-takes this in terms of *Jesus*, as though Jesus were a separate character, while in Mark's own view the figures of God and Jesus modulate into each other under the designation "Lord." We thus see here another aspect of the messianic secret. In this perspective, the command to go home and tell his own people, a typical feature of miracle stories Mark preserves elsewhere (2:11; 8:26; cf. 7:30; 8:3), is probably also an expression of the Markan secrecy theory. Mark apparently takes a traditional story that reported the founding of the Decapolis churches—not by Jesus himself, to be sure, but by someone he had healed and sent[106]—and retells it in such a way that the later Christian mission is indeed reflected in it, but also maintaining his view that Jesus was not truly understood until after Easter. Here as elsewhere, Mark is wrestling with the problem of narrating the pre-Easter story in such a way that it is translucent (not entirely transparent) to the later Gentile mission and faith in Jesus as Lord. This is not a historicizing account, but a collapsing of horizons in which elements of the post-Easter revelation shine through the pre-Easter narrative. The healed demoniac-turned-missionary in Decapolis is an example, somewhat like the man of 9:38, whose work is affirmed by Mark, though it does not fit within his theological and chronological categories. When Jesus leaves the east bank, he has not proclaimed the kingdom or called people to repentance (cf. 1:14–15), but he has exhibited his conquest of Satan. The lib-

---

105. The Decapolis ("Ten Cities") was a league of several cities in southern Syria and northern Jordan (except Scythopolis, located south of the Sea of Galilee, just west of the Jordan). Decapolis came to be a traditional name, though membership in the group was sometimes as high as eighteen or nineteen. The cities were quasi-independent, proud of their Hellenistic tradition, some claiming to have been founded by Alexander the Great, though the league itself originated in the second century B.C.E. They represented Gentile culture and tradition parallel to the surrounding Jewish culture.

106. Gottfried Schille, *Anfänge der Kirche. Erwägungen zur apostolischen Frühgeschichte* (BEvT 43; Munich: Kaiser Verlag, 1966), 64.

erated ex-demoniac can represent Jesus' ministry as a whole; Jesus has left behind a missionary in Gentile territory whose obedience and understanding are incomplete but who is nonetheless effective ("all," v. 20).

5:21–43 Jairus's Daughter and the Woman with a Hemorrhage

5:21 And when Jesus had crossed back to the other side in the boat, a large crowd gathered around him, and he was beside the sea. **22** And the leader of one of the synagogues[a] comes, named Jairus, and when he saw him he falls at his feet, **23** and earnestly pleads with him, "My daughter is at the point of death. Come and place your hands on her, so that she may be saved from death, and live." **24** And he went away with him. And a large crowd was following him, and was pressing in on him.

25 And a woman had been suffering from hemorrhages for twelve years **26** and had suffered much under many physicians, and had spent everything she had and not gotten any better but in fact had gotten worse, **27** and she heard about Jesus and came up in the crowd behind him and touched his clothes.[b] **28** For she had been saying,[c] "If I touch even his clothes, I will be saved."[d] **29** And at once the source of her bleeding dried up, and she sensed in her body that she had been healed of her affliction. **30** And Jesus instantly noticed that power had gone out of him, turned about in the crowd, and was saying, "Who touched my clothes?" **31** And the disciples were saying to him, "You see the crowd pressing in on you, and you are saying, 'Who touched me?'" **32** And he was looking around to see the one who had done this. **33** But the woman, fearful and trembling, knowing what had happened to her, came and fell before him, and told him the whole truth. **34** And he said to her, "Daughter, your faith has saved you.[d] Go in peace, and remain[e] healed from your affliction."

35 While he was still speaking, people come from the synagogue leader's house, saying, "Your daughter has died. Why bother the teacher any further?" **36** But Jesus overheard[f] what they were saying and says to the leader of the synagogue, "Stop being afraid; just keep on believing."[g] **37** And he did not permit anyone to follow him except Peter, James, and John, James's brother. **38** And they come to the house of the leader of the synagogue, and he sees a commotion and people crying and wailing loudly, **39** and he entered and says to them, "Why are you making such a commotion and crying? The child is not dead but sleeping." **40** And they laughed at him. But he forced[h] them all outside and takes along the child's father and mother and those with him and goes in to where the child was. **41** And he grasped the hand of the child and says to her, "Talitha koum,"[i] which means, "Young woman,[j] I say to you, arise." **42** And immediately the young woman arose[k] and started walking around, for she was twelve

years old. They were utterly astounded. 43 And he strictly[1] ordered them
that no one should know this, and told them to give her something to eat.

  a. Each synagogue had a single leader; "synagogues," not "leaders," is plural. *Heis
tōn archisynagōgōn* refers to the leader of one of the synagogues, not one of several leaders of a single synagogue.

  b. The long series of aorist participles ending with a finite verb could be mechani-
cally translated: "And a woman having a flow of blood for twelve years and having suffered much from many physicians and having spent everything she had but not having
gotten better but rather having gotten worse, having heard about Jesus and having come
up behind him, *touched* his clothes."

  c. On the use of the imperfect *elegen* for the pluperfect, see note *d* on 5:8.

  d. Three of Mark's fourteen usages of the verb *sōzō* are found in this story (3:4; 5:23,
28, 34; 6:56; 8:35; 10:26, 52; 13:13, 20; 15:30, 31). The NRSV translates it with "save,"
"be made well," "be healed." It is a rich word, which connotes deliverance from the enemies of life that threaten authentic existence (cf. 10:17, 25, 26, where *sōzō* is paralleled
and equated with "have eternal life," "enter the kingdom of God," and "be saved"). Thus,
even when it refers "only" to physical healing, the connotation of restoration to fullness
of life, this-worldly and eschatologically, is not far away.

  e. The present imperative *isthi* implies a continuing state. It is not the case that the
woman is only now healed by Jesus' word. She has already been healed, but is now told
that the healing is not a temporary episode, but entering into the peace of God. Cf. REB
"Go in peace, free from your affliction."

  f. Since *parakousas* can mean "overhear" (so, e.g., NRSV, REB, NJB) or "ignore, dis-
obey" (as in Matt 18:17; so, e.g., NIV, NAB, RSV), some MSS (including ℵ² A C D K Θ
Π) replace it with *akousas*, which clearly means "hear." *Parakousas* has good MSS attestation (including ℵ*·ᶜ B L W Δ), and as the more difficult reading is to be regarded as
original—Mark likes ambiguity, and scribes did not typically replace a clear reading
with an ambiguous one.

  g. Both imperatives are in the present tense. While the distinction between aorist and
present cannot often be pressed, here it seems appropriate to indicate it in the translation.

  h. While *ekballō* can mean simply "send away," "dismiss," with no connotation of force
(e.g., Matt 9:38; Luke 10:2), all the other fifteen Markan instances have the sense of
"expel," "cast out," often with the overtone of exorcising demons. See on 1:12; 11:15, 23.

  i. The Aramaic phrase, unfamiliar to scribes, has generated a number of variations in
the MSS tradition, including "Tabitha" (without *koum*) in W and much of the Latin tradition under the influence of Acts 9:40, and *koumi* (feminine) in the majority of later
MSS for the grammatically incorrect masculine imperative *koum*. But the masculine was
sometimes used generically, and the reading above supported by ℵ B C L *f*¹ and others
is undoubtedly correct.

  j. The word used here, *korasion*, is different from *paidion*, "child." *Korasion* is the
diminutive of the common classical Greek *korē*, "young woman," not found in the New
Testament, and used in the LXX only in the metaphorical sense for the pupil ("apple") of
the eye. Mark has *korasion* elsewhere only at 6:22, 28 of the daughter of Herodias.

  k. See note *e* on 2:12.

l. *Polla*, adverbial use of the common word for "much, many," often used simply to intensify the action of the verb (see on 1:45; 3:12; 5:10).

This dramatic combination of two stories represents a distinctive Markan literary technique, variously called intercalation, insertion, interpolation, dovetailing, sandwich, interweaving, interlocking, framing of one story by another, interlude of one story within another, or, in the jargon of narratology, "heterodiegetic analepsis." As many as twenty-six Markan passages have been so identified.[107] While some of these are borderline or questionable, six are all but universally acknowledged (3:22–30; 5:21–43; 6:6b–29; 11:12–25; 14:1–11; 14:53–72), and six others are widely so identified (1:4–8; 1:21–28; 4:3–20; 6:7–30; 13:5–27; 14:18–25). Mark did not invent this pattern, nor is it unique to him in the New Testament, but it is a distinctive literary technique he utilizes far more than the other Gospel writers.

The function of such intercalations is seldom merely to fill time lapses, but to combine two stories that interact with and illuminate each other, often with an element of irony. The parade example is the framing of Jesus' hearing before the chief priests with the story of Peter's denial—as Jesus confesses himself to be the Christ, the Son of God, Peter denies that he knows him (14:53–72). While stories may have occasionally been combined in the pre-Markan tradition—including possibly by Mark himself as a teacher of the tradition before composing the Gospel—the two stories in 5:21–43 are evidently combined by Mark himself. The combination of sickness / healing pointing to death / resurrection was more apparent to ancient readers than to modern ones. In the biblical world, sickness was the leading edge of death. To be sick was already to be in the grasp of death, and to be healed was to be restored to life. Both stories spoke to the human condition as such, the condition of mortality, not only to those who happened to be sick or have a death in the family.

The figure of Jesus himself (with his disciples) binds the stories together. The other two main characters, the woman with the flow of blood and Jairus, the leader of the synagogue, represent striking contrasts:[108] Jairus is named and is male, wealthy, the leader of a synagogue, a parent concerned about his sick daughter, who approaches Jesus publicly to ask for healing for his daughter but receives a far greater miracle privately and is commanded not to tell anyone. The woman is nameless, poor, and excluded from the synagogue; she has no children and can have none; and she is concerned about the living death she bears in her own body, approaches Jesus surreptitiously, receives the miracle in

107. Cf. Tom Shepherd, *Markan Sandwich Stories: Narration, Definition, and Function* (AUSDDS 18; Berrien Springs, Mich.: Andrews University, 1993); Tom Shepherd, "The Narrative Function of Markan Intercalation," *NTS* 41 (1995): 522–40.

108. Ibid., 529–30. For details and rationale for these characterizations, see commentary below.

the most intimate secrecy, but is compelled by Jesus to make it public. Jairus and the woman also share features in common: each comes to Jesus with faith derived from hearing about him from others; their faith leads both to overcome the impurity barrier; they both respond to Jesus' powerful deed on their behalf not with gratitude but with fear and amazement. Jesus' salvific power is extended to both; the story does not play off women against men, poor against rich, unclean against pure. As in 5:1–20 the Jew / Gentile gap is bridged, in 5:21–43 the male / female barrier is overcome. Both cases reflect the newness of the Christian community generated by the Christ event.

The woman and the girl are closely linked by contrasts and parallels: both are female; both are unclean and cannot touch or be touched; both are restored to community, family, and sexuality; both are given life, but also become life-givers: the healed woman can now bear children; the young woman now stands on the threshold of puberty, marriage, and family; both are called "daughter"; both can now be mothers. They are both affected by a time span of twelve years: the one entered her living death the year the other was physically born. On the same day, when everything seemed hopeless, each is delivered into a new life. The verb *sō-zō* is used of both, and both are saved from more than physical sickness and death. One has the bold faith that dares to touch; the other is absolutely passive and unable to do anything for herself but receives Jesus' life-giving touch.

[21–24] That Jesus is now back in Jewish territory is made clear by the virtual repetition of the setting of 4:1, by the assumed concern with purity rules, by the approach of the leader of a synagogue, by the use of Aramaic, and by the repeated "twelve." As pigs and tombs had signaled Gentile territory, so synagogue and purity rules signal the Jewish setting. *Archisynagōgos*, all four Markan instances in this context, does not refer to a rabbi or scribe, but to the lay officer of a synagogue presumably responsible for the building, for leading in worship, and general administration—though the exact nature of the office is no longer clear (cf. Acts 13:15; 18:8, 17). As the leader of a synagogue, Jairus is a person of some social standing; he is identified first by his office, not by his name (not "Jairus, the leader of a synagogue," but "the leader of a synagogue, named Jairus"). He also is relatively wealthy, for his daughter has a separate room (v. 40; houses of ordinary people consisted of only one room). If, as is likely, the setting is Capernaum, Jesus' last appearance in the synagogue had resulted in a plot to kill him (3:1–6), but this seems to have been forgotten. This narrative is to be interpreted primarily for itself, not in a historicizing manner that makes inferences from other scenes.

As in 12:28–34 and 15:42–57, Mark here presents a Jewish leader in a favorable light. Falling at Jesus' feet indicates respect, but not worship. Jairus is the first Jewish religious official to show interest in Jesus and respond in faith. He asks Jesus to deliver his daughter from death that will certainly ensue if Jesus does not come to her, and to do so not by praying for her, but by his own touch.

"Be saved and live" already anticipates the later resurrection imagery. Jesus sets out with him, surrounded by a large crowd, and he is jostled as they move along—not threatened with being crushed, as in 3:9. The stage is set for the intervening scene.

[25–29] Among the data indicating that this story was originally separate is the change in grammatical style from predominantly present-tense Greek verbs to predominantly past-tense (aorist and imperfect), and the extraordinarily long chain of participles with which the scene begins (see note *b* above). The rhetorical effect is to focus attention on the final finite verb. A story that had begun with a plea for Jesus to come and touch the utterly passive daughter who can take no initiative on her own is interrupted by, and turns out to enclose, a story of a woman who takes all the initiative as "toucher" rather than "touchee."

Mark does not specify that the woman's hemorrhage was continual vaginal bleeding, nor that it made her ritually unclean, but the use of language from Leviticus (5:25 reflects Lev 12:7; 15:25) made this clear enough to the ancient reader. The Old Testament and Jewish tradition was deeply concerned about contamination by contact with blood, the potent source of life. As in the case of leprosy (see on 1:40), "unclean" in such cases is a matter of ritual purity.[109] It does not connote dirtiness or disgust associated with bodily liquids and functions, but is a matter of the power associated with blood and with reproductive functions and organs, a power that must be safeguarded—somewhat as we speak of "contamination" and "decontamination" from radiation. A whole tractate of the Mishnah deals with the precautions that must be taken in regard both to menstruation and irregular bleeding—the community must be insulated from such potency as a matter of life and death (see *Niddah* and parts of *Zabim*). The reference to having spent all her money on physicians to no avail emphasizes her hopelessness.[110] The woman is thus physically sick and weak, ritually unclean and unable to participate in synagogue and community life, and impoverished (though once a person of means). Mark does not mention husband or children. Since vaginal bleeding prohibited marriage and was grounds for divorce, in the understanding of her culture which she shared, the woman

109. See Marla J. Selvidge, "Mark 5:25–34 and Leviticus 15:19–20," *JBL* 103, no. 4 (1984): 619–23; Stuart A. Love, "Jesus Heals the Hemorrhaging Woman," in *The Social Setting of Jesus and the Gospels* (ed. Wolfgang Stegemann et al.; Minneapolis: Fortress, 2002), 85–101; Wendy Cotter, CSJ, "Mark's Hero of the Twelfth-Year Miracles: The Healing of the Woman with the Hemorrhage and the Raising of Jairus' Daughter (Mark 5:21–43)," in *A Feminist Companion to Mark* (ed. Amy-Jill Levine and Marianne Blickenstaff; Cleveland: Pilgrim Press, 2004), 54–78, and the bibliography they provide.

110. The contrast between charismatic healers and professional physicians was a common one in the Hellenistic world, with each side disdaining the other. Cf. data in Gnilka, *Markus*, 1:215, who points out that physicians were for the wealthy. The inscriptions at, e.g., Epidauros indicate that many poor came there for miraculous healing. While Mark reflects this traditional cultural feature, also present in other Hellenistic miracle stories, this is not his main point.

cannot fulfill her function as a woman, to bring new life into being as a mother (cf. Gen 16:1–6; 30:1–8; 1 Sam 1:3–10). Like the leper of 1:40, her life is actually a living death, and her healing would be a restoration to life. Like the child who waits in Jairus's house, she is beyond all human hope.

[28–34] The woman had heard about Jesus and had derived her faith from the testimony of others (v. 27). This hearing had generated faith (v. 34; cf. Rom 10:17). Here as elsewhere the narrative functions at two levels, and the there-and-then account modulates into the here-and-now experience of the readers. The woman knows she is unclean and believes that touching Jesus will heal her—but will this touch also render the Teacher unclean? This, and not shyness or modesty about her condition, is the reason for her secretive approach. The belief that touching a person charged with holy power can heal was widespread in antiquity (cf. 3:10; 6:56; Acts 19:12) and smacks of the magical views prevalent in the Hellenistic world. So also, that Jesus was charged with divine power, which could be transmitted by touch without his knowing or willing it, can be understood in terms of magic and superstition. Mark does not disguise or explain this, but reinterprets it in terms of faith—others were jostling Jesus, but only the woman with faith was healed. Mark adds the element of faith to a story originally told with Hellenistic "divine man" overtones. The woman's faith was real, but was expressed in an inadequate theology; Mark considers practical faith more important than conceptually correct theology (see also 9:38–41). Her faith was not a matter of believing the right things about Jesus, but believing in his power to help despite all appearances to the contrary—a prolepsis of resurrection faith. Her faith had caused her to violate conventional social constraints by appearing in public and especially by touching the revered holy man (to touch someone's garments is to touch the person; see on 10:50). Jesus too transgresses the customary norms by stopping, touching, and talking with a woman (cf. John 4:27).

The focus is christological. Mark is untroubled by human traits such as having Jesus ask informational questions. Mark's dialectic of humanity and divinity are woven into this story too. Divine power comes *ex autou* ("out of him," v. 30), not *di' autou* ("through him"). He himself is the source of the power, not merely its vehicle—he does not pray to someone else but acts on his own. It is not the "power of faith" but the divine "power of Jesus" that heals. She does not say to herself, "If *I* believe strongly enough . . . ," but believes in *Jesus'* power to heal. Yet Jesus does not say "My power has healed you," but "Your faith has saved you." Neither Jesus' power nor saving faith exist in isolation from each other, as the next story will show (6:5–6). Jesus himself awakens faith—it is not an independent religious attitude or conviction that can be brought *to* him.

The woman knows within her own body that she has been healed, and Jesus knows power has gone forth from him. The readers know, for here the omniscient narrator makes them aware of the most intimate internal feelings of the woman and of Jesus' supernatural power and perception. The jostling crowds do not know, and the disciples not only stand with the imperceptive crowds but their protestations sound very much like the mocking crowds at the house of Jairus (v. 40). In contrast, Jesus addresses the woman as "daughter," which is not condescending, but includes her in the people of God and family of believers (see on 3:31–35).

The typical conclusion of a miracle story involves some demonstration that the miracle had truly happened. In this case, the miracle can be confirmed only by the woman herself, and she does so. There is no expression of joy or gratitude—interpreters should be wary of describing how the woman "must have felt." Called by the word of Jesus, she becomes a witness and declares the "whole truth," albeit in "fear and trembling," corresponding to 4:41, 16:8, and the *ekstasei megalē* ("profound astonishment") of verse 42. Once again, Markan readers can see the story as transparent to their own situation. They too have heard, believed, and are called to be witnesses in a fearful situation.

[35–36] When the story is read aloud, the audience becomes impatient with the pause to heal the woman, knowing that "amidst the hubbub, the searching, and the pedestrian conversation, the sands of the little girl's hourglass have been running out" (Black, *Mark*, ad loc.). The woman has been sick a long time anyway and can be healed later. The detailed description of her plight and fruitless efforts to be healed causes the hearer to experience the delay. "What about the little girl? Get there before it is too late!" When the original story begun at 5:21 resumes, it *is* too late—the issue is no longer sickness but death, and the messengers conclude that the daughter is now beyond all hope. But two words signal continuity with the preceding story: Jesus has just addressed the healed woman as "daughter" and has commended her "faith." One daughter has just been restored to authentic life by her faith. Jesus responds to the message not addressed to him (see note *f* above on "overheard"). He does not wait to be asked, and the reader never knows what Jairus would have done if the decision had been left to him. He has been one who believes and hopes. But is literal, physical death the death of hope (cf. Luke 24:21; John 11:37; Rom 4:16–25)? The present imperatives of verse 36 are important. Jairus had already manifested faith in coming to Jesus; now he has become fearful. He is challenged by the new report: he can no longer ask for healing. Jesus challenges him to overcome his fear, as had the woman, and to continue his faith in imitation of the woman's.

[37] Despite the lack of understanding, Jesus takes the three disciples who will constitute the inner circle along with him. Only these three will be present at the transfiguration (9:2) and in Gethsemane (14:33), joined by Andrew at the private revelatory discourse (13:3; cf. 1:16–20). Obtuse as they are, they will be witnesses in the later church of the key revelatory moments of the Christ event (cf. *tous met' autou*, "those with him" of v. 40, correlated with *met' autou* of 3:14).

[**38–40**] In the ancient Mediterranean world, without embalming or refrigeration facilities, the dead were often buried on the day they died. Mark does not note or feel constrained to explain that the funeral had already begun (in the father's absence) when Jesus and the entourage arrive—his focus is on christological meaning, not psychological realism or family feelings. The commotion of loud crying and wailing belongs to the customary ritual, in which flute players and professional mourners were hired (cf. Jer 9:17–20; Matt 9:23; 11:16–17; Luke 23:27).[111] When Jesus declares the girl is not dead but sleeping, the professional experts on death laugh him to scorn, but he was expressing resurrection faith in the later Christian language (cf. 1 Thess 4:13–14; 1 Cor 15:51; John 11:11–14). Death is called "sleep," not to pretend it is not real, but to deny that it is ultimate. Jesus does not say "The girl only seems to be dead," but in the presence of death speaks the word of eschatological victory over death. At the story level, the professional mourners and attending crowd laugh, not at Jesus' claim to raise the dead, which he has not made, but at his foolish misdiagnosis without ever seeing the patient. But the reader knows, and hears it as misplaced scorn at Christian resurrection faith (cf. Acts 17:32).

[**41–43**] As elsewhere, the Synoptic miracle stories have some affinities with the Elijah and Elishah stories (cf., e.g., 1 Kgs 17:19–22; 2 Kgs 4:33–37). Here, there is an obvious contrast: Jesus does not pray, engages in no rituals, has no "technique"—he only touches and speaks, and the dead girl is raised. As Jesus was not defiled by the touch of the unclean woman, so he is not defiled by touching the corpse. Their touch does not communicate defilement; his touch communicates holiness and restoration to life. Even the Aramaic phrase, foreign to Mark's Greek-speaking readers, is no magic word,[112] but when translated is seen to be the simple speech that anyone could employ in waking someone from sleep. By translating the phrase, Mark removes the story from the world of magic and focuses on the authority of Jesus that cannot be resisted even by the power of death. In combination with the other features mentioned above, the reference to the girl's age seems deliberate. The reader has not been able to picture the daughter until this disclosure by the narrator (contrast Luke 8:42, which places this information in the opening lines of the story). Now, at the end of the combined stories, a revelatory insight is disclosed: the child is a young woman, ready to launch on a meaningful and fulfilled life, just as the woman sick for twelve years is restored to such a life. That she "walks around" is incidental to this. In typical Hellenistic miracle stories, this note would have served as con-

---

111. Cf. Josephus, *War* 3.437; Strack and Billerbeck, *Kommentar*, 1:521–23; Gustav Stählin, "*kopetos*," in *TDNT*, 841–46; Ketub 4.4, "Even the poorest in Israel do not hire less than two flute players and one wailing woman."

112. Philostratus, somewhat skeptical himself, reports of Apollonius of Tyana, a contemporary of Jesus, that when he raised a dead girl to life he "whispered in secret some spell over her"; *Life of Apollonius* 4.45.

firmation of the miracle. Here, in addition, it reveals that we have not been talking about a baby. The command to give her something to eat may indeed serve as the traditional confirmation of the reality of the miracle, and also serves to bring the story back to earth with a directive about her practical needs, to reintegrate her into the social world of the living, and to link her story to the post-Easter experience of the readers' faith in the reality of Jesus' own resurrection (cf. Luke 24:30, 42–43; Acts 10:41; John 12:2). The story points beyond itself to the Christ-event as a whole, to Jesus' own resurrection.[113] Readers are not asked whether they believe that once-upon-a-time Jesus raised a little girl from the dead, but are challenged to believe that once-for-all-time God raised Jesus from the dead. This, too, is indicated by the concluding Markan overlay of the messianic secret, extremely difficult to imagine historically, but making sense in terms of Mark's Christology: the ministry of Jesus was indeed an epiphany of God's power, but this must remain secret for the present, for it could only be perceived after and in terms of his own death and resurrection.

6:1–6a Jesus Is Rejected at Nazareth

6:1 And he left that place and comes to his hometown, and his disciples follow him. 2 And when the Sabbath came he began to teach in the synagogue, and the large congregation who heard him were terribly shocked.[a] And they kept asking, "Where does this guy[b] get this from? What is the wisdom that has been given to him, and such deeds of power that happen through his hands? 3 Isn't this the construction worker,[c] the son of Mary, and brother of James and Joses and Judas and Simon, and aren't his sisters here with us?" And their encounter with him led to their downfall.[d] 4 And Jesus was saying to them, "Prophets[e] are not without honor, except in their hometown, and within their own family, and in their own house." 5 And he was not able to do there any deed of power, except that he did lay his hands on a few sick people and healed them. 6 And he was amazed because of their unbelief.

---

113. See, e.g., Alfred Suhl, *Die Wunder Jesu* (Gütersloh: Güterloher Verlagshaus, 1968), 7–18, 52–53, who illustrates the Markan understanding of miracle, Christology, and faith on the basis of this story. He points out the story does not presuppose faith on the part of the reader, but functions as a call to faith. Here, too, the reader is not asked to believe something about "what really happened" on a particular day in Galilee, but to believe in what God did in the Christ-event as such (see commentary on 2:11–12 and *Excursus: Miracle Stories in Mark* at 6:56 and *Excursus: Markan Christology* at 9:1). This story has proleptic echoes of Mark 15–16: one is on the way to death, there is mocking and derision, death as the abandonment of hope, God's saving act in a way that transcends what those involved could imagine. Matthew recognizes this, and has Jairus confess such faith from the beginning (Matt 9:18–26), as though the Matthean Jairus had already responded to the call to faith in Mark 5!

a. *Ekplēssō,* lit. "knocked out" of one's senses, "bowled over," can be understood in a positive sense (as 7:37; Luke 9:43; Acts 13:12), or in a neutral or negative sense (as 10:26; Eccl 7:16). It is not clear at first how Mark intends it. Likewise, the questions of v. 2 can be understood as initial admiration. In v. 3 it becomes clear that their response and questions are disdainful, and the final verb *skandalizō* (see note *d* below) reveals that [all along] their response has been negative. The translator must choose whether to translate the initial ambiguous words positively, so that there is progression from initial positive to final negative response, or to render it as negative from the beginning. The latter option is chosen here.

b. The thrice-repeated *houtos,* lit. "this" [one] has a contemptuous tone.

c. *Tektōn* is a generic term for anyone who builds, especially for those who work in metal, wood, or stone, being used in the LXX for blacksmiths, masons, and carpenters. "Construction worker" is chosen to preserve something of the implied disdainful tone of those who look down on manual labor. "The son of the *tektōn* and Mary" is the apparent reading of $\mathfrak{P}^{45}$ (our oldest MS of Mark), and of f^{13} and the old Latin translations. It seems to be supported by Origen's comment that none of the authentic Gospels call Jesus a *tektōn* (*Against Celsus* 6.34, 36), but this is probably due to his using MSS of Mark assimilated to Matthew. The reading above has the best MSS attestation and is very likely original.

d. *Skandalizō* is difficult to render into English with any one word. The cognate noun *skandalon* is an object over which one might trip, and is used both for the thing itself and for the action of being tripped up. Its meaning is then extended metaphorically to refer to "an action or circumstance that leads one to act contrary to a proper course of action or set of beliefs, temptation to sin, enticement to apostasy, false belief, etc.," and then to "that which causes offense or revulsion and results in opposition, disapproval, or hostility, fault, stain, etc." Mark uses only the verbal form (4:17; 6:3; 9:42, 43, 45, 47; 14:27, 29), in the common New Testament sense of "to cause to be brought to a downfall, cause to sin" and "to shock through word or action, give offense to, anger, shock" (Bauer and Danker, BDAG, 926). In the context of Markan theology, the word here means far more than that the people in the synagogue were upset by what Jesus said, but that their encounter with Jesus hardened them in their unbelief.

e. The Greek text has the singular "prophet" and corresponding verb and pronoun. The translation here renders it as a plural in order to use gender-inclusive language (cf. NRSV), which is appropriate since the saying does not refer to a specific prophet but is proverbial, and since there were both male and female prophets.

The narrative moves directly from the scene at Jairus's house to Jesus' return to his hometown, where he is rejected by those who should be most familiar with him—the hometown folk, his relatives, his own family (note the Markan elaboration of the familiar proverb in 6:4). Thus far, the only negative responses to Jesus have come from Jewish leaders, the scribes and Pharisees. The only exception has been that his own family considers him deranged, and Jesus begins to constitute a new community as the family of God (3:30–35). That incident is now writ large, reflecting the experience of the missionary church of Mark's own time.

[6:1] Nazareth is not mentioned in this pericope but is clearly presupposed as Jesus' hometown (cf. 1:9). Jesus' disciples (here clearly the Twelve) play no role in the story, but are mentioned as present because in the next scene they themselves will be sent out with a missionary task. As they have been witnesses to Jesus' mighty works and the positive response, so they are here witnesses of Jesus' rejection, preparing them for their own experience. This, too, is transparent to the experience of the post-Easter church.

[6:2] It is presupposed that Jesus, as an observant Jew, attends the synagogue (cf. 1:21). While it is true that every Jewish male had the right to speak in the synagogue assembly (cf. Luke 4:16; Acts 13:15), that is not the point here; Jesus teaches on his own authority, not as authorized by custom or tradition (1:22). Nor does Mark raise the historicizing question of whether his family, who had already rejected him (3:30–35) is present to "hear him preach." To ask such questions is to miss the two-level drama Mark presents. At the narrative level the scene from the life of Jesus is seen by the reader in the light of Jesus' ministry as a whole, in which his own people refused to believe in him despite his teaching with authority and his deeds of power.

Everyone in the synagogue responds negatively, and does so immediately (cf. note *a* above). There is no progression from an initial positive response to a subsequent rejection. As elsewhere, Mark combines Jesus' message ("wisdom," only here in Mark) and his miracles ("deeds of power"). It is not the content of his teaching or particular miracles to which they respond, but the authority implicit in both. They accept the fact that Jesus works miracles, that is, that they happen "through his hands," but this only raises the question of the source of his power, and does not lead to faith (see on 3:20–30). Mark does not oppose the tradition of the miracle-working Jesus, but is intent on showing that belief in miracles does not necessarily lead to or represent Christian faith.

[3] Sophisticated Greeks disdained manual laborers and could not grasp the idea of a laborer who could teach with authority. Jews tended to affirm working with one's hands, and many Pharisees were craftsmen—Paul was by no means an isolated example (1 Cor 4:12; Acts 18:3). Yet Sir 38:24–34, while valuing the labor of farmers, artisans, and manual workers (the *tektōn* is specifically mentioned), is clear that no such person can speak in the assembly or expound the Torah, for "wisdom . . . depends on the opportunity of leisure." In Mark, the disdainful "this guy" and the presence of the article with *tektōn* suggests that it is *this* construction worker who is disparaged, not the class as such. Familiarity, not elitist prejudice against the "working class," is a key factor in their rejection. Likewise, referring to Jesus as "son of Mary" simply designates him as one well known, "Mary's boy from down the street," as does the reference to Jesus' brothers and sisters. The designation does not suggest that the local residents imply Jesus is illegitimate, nor is it Mark's veiled reference to virginal conception and birth, of which he manifests no knowledge or

interest.[114] Mary (= Miriam) is named only here in Mark. Like James (= Jacob), Joses (= Joseph), Judas (= Judah, Jude), and Simon (= Simeon), she bears a biblical name reflecting leaders in Israel's early history, suggesting a pious family. Jesus' family did not believe in him during his earthly life (John 7:5). James was converted by a resurrection appearance (1 Cor 15:7) and became a leader in the Jerusalem church (Gal 1:19; Acts 15:13; 21:18); the canonical Letter of James was attributed to him, along with considerable noncanonical literature. The canonical Letter of Jude is attributed to Jesus' brother "Judas." Nothing historical is known about the other brothers or his sisters. They have appeared in the history of Christian thought in regard to the later doctrine of the perpetual virginity of Mary. The question of their identity became important in the later history of dogma, but is unimportant for the exegesis of Mark—though there is no exegetical reason to suggest that Mark understands Jesus' brothers and sisters in any other way than his biological siblings. The issue is no longer resolved along confessional lines, with, for example, some Roman Catholic scholars opting for biological siblings and some Protestant scholars arguing for the Epiphanian view that Jesus' "brothers and sisters" were children of Joseph by a former marriage.[115]

[4] Jesus' only word in this scene is to quote a traditional proverb, current in both the Hellenistic world to show that wandering philosophers were often not appreciated by those who knew them, and in Jewish circles with the additional connotation current in first-century Judaism that true prophets were often rejected. Mark considers Jesus to be more than a prophet (cf. 6:15–16; 8:28–29), yet is not hesitant to have Jesus apply the proverb to his own situation.

[5–6] The narrator concludes this scene with two extraordinary statements. (1) He does not hesitate to say that Jesus *could* do no deed of power in Nazareth, and gives no explanation. Luke omits the statement, while Matthew changes *could* to *did*, and presents the unbelief of the Nazarenes as the explanation. It is puzzling that even in Mark the absolute statement is qualified with the exception clause—Jesus did heal a few sick people after all. This seems to be a correction of a too-radical statement of Jesus' inability, but whether in the pre-Markan tradition or by Mark himself is not clear.

(2) Jesus *was amazed* at their unbelief, a statement omitted by both Matthew and Luke. Mark presumably sees a connection between Jesus' inability (or min-

114. Since both Matthew and Luke, who have stories of Jesus' virginal conception, rephrase Mark's words to avoid the possible defamatory implication of "son of Mary" (Matt 13:55; Luke 4:22), the phrase may have fueled later Jewish polemic questioning Jesus' legitimacy. The detailed study of Harvey K. McArthur, "Son of Mary," *NovT* 15 (1973): 38–58, examines all the possible backgrounds for a Jewish male being identified by his mother's name and concludes it is simply an informal, ad hoc description.

115. See, e.g., on the Roman Catholic side, John P. Meier, "The Brothers and Sisters of Jesus in Ecumenical Perspective," *CBQ* 54, no. 1 (1992): 1–28, and on the Protestant side, Richard Bauckham, "The Brothers and Sisters of Jesus: An Epiphanian Response to John P. Meier," *CBQ* 56, no. 4 (1994): 686–700, and the literature they give.

imal competence) to work miracles and the absence of faith, but does not make this explicit. Faith and miracles are related in Markan perspective, but Mark does not seem to have a coherent, systematic explanation of their relation (see *Excursus: Miracle Stories in Mark* at 6:56). Modern interpreters might well respect this wariness, especially if it results in affirming that Jesus always has the power, but miracles do not happen where there is no faith. This is a difficult thesis to sustain in the Markan texts, serving to save Jesus' power at the price of generating guilt among those who must attribute absence of miracles in their experience to their own lack of faith (see 1:40; 2:5; 4:40; 5:34–36; 9:23–24; 10:52; 11:22–24; 15:32).

6:6b–30 Mission of the Twelve and the Death of John the Baptist

Major turning points of part 1 end in rejection (see Introduction 2.). As in 3:6 Jesus is rejected by the religious leaders, so in 6:6 he is rejected by his family and hometown (each time in a synagogue), and in 8:21 even his disciples do not understand (in the boat, representing the church; see on 4:36).

However the structure of the narrative as a whole is understood, the episode of the rejection at Nazareth in the preceding scene constitutes a turning point in the story, so that the present scene is the beginning of a new section. The segment that begins here portrays Jesus and his disciples as en route (the "way" motif), with dramatic episodes involving great crowds in the "wilderness," concerned with feeding, eating, and encounters with Gentiles. Thus after being rejected in his hometown, there are progressive steps in the direction of the Gentile Christianity of Mark's own time. Each section of part 1 begins with a discipleship story including the *kaleō* (call) vocabulary, which progresses from initial call (1:16–20) to constitution of the group of the Twelve (3:13–19) to sending them forth in mission (6:6b–13). The section 6:6b–30 is another Markan intercalation (see on 5:21). Jesus sends out the Twelve, and while they are gone, the narrator inserts the story of the death of John the Baptist before reporting their return.

Excursus: Crowds, Followers, Disciples, and the Twelve

It is possible to chart an overly schematic view of the Markan understanding of God's relation to the world of humanity.

All such charts are excessively schematic. Mark did not write an essay or present a diagram, but told a story. Stories can communicate the truth of things in a manner impossible for a diagram (or commentary). Yet diagrams and comments may help Mark's readers grasp and be grasped by his story.[116]

---

116. That two-dimensional diagrams do not necessarily violate the dynamism of narrative, but may facilitate its understanding, is illustrated by Elizabeth Struthers Malbon *Narrative Space and Mythic Meaning in Mark* (San Francisco: Harper & Row, 1986) with its many charts and diagrams oriented to explicating the *narrative* communication of Mark.

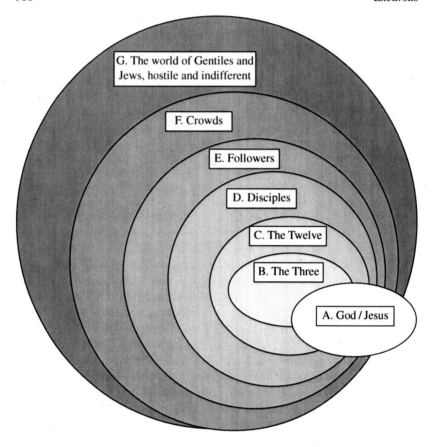

Mark's own use of insider / outsider terminology, as well as his speaking of "circles" around Jesus and the Twelve, also suggest that an effort to schematize Mark's perspective is not necessarily misdirected (3:21; 4:10).

The two-dimensional chart is necessarily conceived in terms of space, but this does not mean that "G." is further from God / Jesus than the other groups. This is why the circle overlaps all the other circles and is immediately related to them, not only indirectly through the other circles. Mark emphasizes that God is the Creator (10:6; 13:19), and that all who do God's will belong to the family of God (3:34–35). This affirmation is not surrendered by Mark's understanding that God separates out an elect people; the two affirmations stand in a dialectical relationship.

God, and Jesus as God's representative (9:37), stand at the initiating center. God has taken the initiative in sending the Christ, and Christ takes the initiative in calling disciples (1:16–20), constituting the Twelve (3:13–19), and sending them forth in mission (6:7–30). The gospel is "from God" (1:14) and is centrifugal, from God through Jesus and the disciples to the world, so one could begin at the innermost circle and follow the divine initiative outward to the whole creation. Since it is also helpful to understand Mark's groupings of humanity as a progressive narrowing—Mark's word is election (13:20, 22, 27)—we will begin with the totality and attend to Mark's progressively more selective grouping. In each case, the smaller group remains part of the larger unit from which it is selected.

The following categories may be distinguished:

G. The whole world and all its people belong to God the Creator

While Mark thinks in the categories of apocalyptic dualism, his dualism, like that of Jewish apocalyptic generally, is penultimate. All things and all people are in the hand of the one God, the Creator.

F. Crowds (*Ochlos*, thirty-eight times, and *plēthos*, two times)

In general, the crowds are positively disposed toward Jesus: they are attracted to him and leave their ordinary occupations to come and be taught and healed by him. The crowd(s) belong to the world, and are not yet disciples; crowd and disciples are often clearly distinguished (3:9; 5:31; 6:45; 7:17; 8:1; 8:6; 9:14). Yet the crowds have made a first step toward following Jesus in that they have come apart from the world in general to hear Jesus and make up their mind whether they will take further steps.

E. Followers (*akoloutheō*, nineteen times)

Of the several concentric circles, only one ultimately counts—the line that divides "insiders" from "outsiders" (cf. 4:10–12). The line that separates these two groups is identical to the line that separates those who follow Jesus and those who do not. "Follow" (*akoloutheō*) is for Mark a theologically laden word. While *akoloutheō* can occasionally be used in the pedestrian sense of "walk behind" (11:9; 14:13), it most often involves a life-changing religious commitment. In this sense, there is a clear line between crowds and followers (8:34). Thus "followers" seems sometimes to be used as a synonym for "disciples" (cf. 1:18; 2:14; 10:28, and the ambiguous 2:15). Yet the counterpart of "follower" is "leader" (10:32; 16:7), while the correlative for "disciple" is "teacher" (13:1; 14:14).[117]

D. Disciples (*mathētēs,* forty-six times, all but three times in 2:18 of Jesus' disciples)

This is the most frequently used word for those associated with Jesus. Though the line dividing followers and disciples is not crisp and absolute, for the most part "disciples" refers to a narrower group, distinguished not only from the crowd (3:9; 4:34; 5:31; 6:41, 45; 7:17; 8:1, 6, 34) but from those who follow (3:7), a group that can fit into one boat

117. This point is elaborated by LaVerdiere, *Beginning,* 63–64.

(6:45; 8:10; though cf. the peculiar 4:36b), a house (7:17; 9:28; 10:10), or one guest room (14:14); those whom Jesus has called and who have left everything to follow him (1:16–20; 2:15; 10:28—though "disciple" is not found in these texts). It appears that *mathētēs* can be used in a narrower or a broader sense, sometimes including not only the Twelve but all those who follow Jesus, but not vice versa: all the disciples follow, but not all followers are disciples; all the Twelve are disciples, but not all disciples belong to the Twelve.

C. The Twelve (*dōdeka,* eleven times of Jesus' disciples)

Mark speaks of disciples and the Twelve, but never of "the twelve disciples" (contrast Matt 10:1; 11:1; 20:17). He speaks once, perhaps twice, of apostles ([3:14]; 6:30), but never of "the twelve apostles" (contrast Matt 10:2; Luke 6:13; 9:10–12; Rev 21:14). References to the Twelve occur mostly in redactional passages, indicating that Mark had a special interest in the original Twelve chosen from among Jesus' followers.[118]

The key issue here is Mark's understanding of the relation of the Twelve to disciples. Several Markan texts may be read as though the two groups are identical (e.g., 2:15, 23; 6:1, 35; 7:2; 8:4, 27, 33–34; 9:14, 18, 28; 10:13; 12:43; 14:32; 16:7). In some contexts they are interchangeable in the narrative (e.g., 11:11, 14 and 14:16–17). And some texts presuppose the disciples are a small group (cf. 8:10; 7:17; 9:28; 10:10; 14:14). There are no instances where the disciples are clearly distinguished as a larger group of Jesus' followers from which the Twelve are chosen. Thus Bultmann, for example, supposed that Mark had not reflected on the issue, and naively and imprecisely identified disciples with the Twelve.[119] Robert P. Meye's dissertation-length study attempts to show that this assumption is the consistent and considered view of Mark, who understood Jesus to have had only twelve disciples.[120] There are, however, several key texts in which a group larger than the Twelve seem to be included in the disciples of Jesus. In 2:14 Levi is called and follows, but is not listed among the Twelve in 3:13–19. The descriptions of "those about him with the Twelve" seem to be identified as disciples (3:32–34; 4:10 with 4:34). Some descriptions of disciples seem to apply to a larger group than the Twelve. In 2:18, is it only the Twelve who do not fast? In 7:2, is it only the Twelve who do not observe ritual handwashing? In 2:15 are the "many" who follow him distinguished from the disciples, or identified with them—in which case there are more than twelve. In 10:28–30, the family of God, Jesus' "mother, brothers and sisters" constitute a much larger group than the Twelve. The group often pictured as alone with Jesus in the house (reflecting

---

118. William Telford, *The Theology of the Gospel of Mark* (New Testament Theology; Cambridge: Cambridge University Press, 1999), 127–28, contra Ernest Best, "The Role of the Disciples in Mark," *NTS* 23 (1976): 377–401.

119. Bultmann, *History of the Synoptic Tradition,* 344–45: "Indeed when Mark speaks of the *mathētai* as a group he obviously has the Twelve in mind (in all probability naively and without any reflection, even in the passages before their appointment 2:15–16; 3:7–9)."

120. Robert P. Meye, *Jesus and the Twelve: Discipleship and Revelation in Mark's Gospel* (Grand Rapids: Eerdmans, 1968); see esp. 97–191. So also Schenke, *Markus-Evangelium,* 90–95 and elsewhere, argues repeatedly and explicitly that by "disciples" Mark always means "the Twelve," who play a key role in mediating Jesus' teaching to the present. So also Painter, *Mark's Gospel,* 57–58.

the house churches of the Markan community) is never designated as "the twelve," but always as "the disciples." Disciple terminology is not used, but this group of Jesus' true family that does the will of God (3:30–35) is much larger than the Twelve.

Mark thus seems to use "disciple" both for the Twelve and for a larger group. More importantly, there are key functions exercised by the Twelve that do not involve disciples in general: "being with" Jesus, authority to cast out demons, teach, preach, and heal (3:14; 6:12–13, 30; though 9:40 relativizes this). Mark has no firm doctrine of apostles or apostleship, but does understand the Twelve to have been called to maintain continuity between the time of Jesus and the time of the church (so, e.g., Gnilka, *Markus*, 1:136–43). While Mark's readers cannot explicitly identify with the Twelve as a closed group with a unique function for the later church, they can identify with them and the wider group as disciples, and this may well have been intentional on Mark's part. It is clear that the reader cannot become a member of the group of the Twelve, yet the call of Jesus for some Christians to be missionaries, and the instructions for their mission in 3:14–15 and 6:7–11, has something to say to the missionaries of Mark's own church, just as the church's missionary experience has influenced the way the story is told.

B. The Three (or Four)

Although the Twelve have a special role, there is also an inner circle within the Twelve[121] who are called first (1:16–20), listed first and given new names (3:16–17), and witness the extraordinary events of the resurrection of Jairus's daughter (5:37), the Transfiguration (9:2), the apocalyptic discourse (13:3), and Jesus' agony in Gethsemane (14:33). Although Andrew is included in 13:3 as in 1:16–20, the distinctive listing of "Peter, James, and John" first should be noted, as also in 3:16–17, rearranging the pairing of brothers to correspond to the three "pillars" of the early church (Gal 2:9, corresponding to Abraham, Isaac, and Jacob).

A. Jesus/God

The Markan Jesus himself does not belong to the group of the Twelve or the Three. In appointing the Twelve as the core of the new Israel and the Three as the new "patriarchal" pillars, Jesus does not include himself, but in a certain sense stands over against the people of God, old and renewed, standing, as it were, on God's side.

*****

Issues, tensions, and problems remain in this and all such analyses. Except for the Twelve, an exclusive group identified with the apostles, there is some fluidity in Mark's terminology and categories. The "crowd" can be in the house with Jesus, not distinguished

---

121. When Mark refers to the "inner circle" of Peter, James, and John, he always distinguishes them from "the disciples," not from "the Twelve." That Andrew twice appears with them, making "the Four" rather than "the Three," shows that Mark's categories do not have rigid boundaries and are not strictly hierarchical.

from "*hoi peri autou*" (those around him, 3:20, 32). The "Twelve" are also "disciples" and "followers," though Satan can speak through their leader, and they can still be challenged to follow (8:33–34). In 10:32 three groups are mentioned in quick succession: the "disciples," "those who followed him," and the "Twelve." Mark has not taken pains to indicate whether the reader should imagine one, two, or three groups. Throughout Mark the "disciple" category is the most numerous and most significant, but also the most vague. While clearly demarcated from the world and the crowds, "disciples" fade into the category of "follower" on the one side and "Twelve" on the other.

Nor is such an analysis as presented without remainder. All that Mark has to say about the nature of the community called into being by God through Jesus does not fit into the schema sketched above. Thus the "family of God" language of 3:31–35 and 10:30 represent a vital aspect of Markan ecclesiology, but on another plane than that portrayed in the somewhat hierarchical chart presented above. So also, the metaphors of flock, temple, people of God, and ship are not embraced in this approach (cf. Best, *Following Jesus*, 208–45).

There are "minor characters," the "little people," who resist classification. Joseph of Arimathea lived in expectation of the kingdom of God announced by Jesus and boldly associated himself with the crucified Jesus when his disciples had abandoned him, but he is not called a disciple (15:42–46). Bar-Timaeus, healed of his blindness and following Jesus on the way, is not said to be a disciple, yet obviously he portrays discipleship (10:46–52). So also, those who are said to have faith and / or experience Jesus' salvific power are not included as disciples, yet the post-Easter readers of Mark's Gospel are clearly to learn something about discipleship from them. The "many" women of 15:40–41, 47, 16:1, who also have a core group of three, are said to "follow" Jesus, but none are called disciples or apostles, or numbered among the Twelve. The three women at the tomb are distinguished from "his disciples and Peter," yet are given a commission to carry the message to this primary group—which they fail to carry out.

In all this, the basic perspective is apocalyptic dualism. Election is an apocalyptic category. The specific terminology of election occurs only in 13:20–27, but since Mark as a whole is conceived within the framework of apocalyptic categories, the conceptuality of election is present throughout. Dualism is implicit in the doctrine of election. One is either chosen or not; there is no third or fourth category, no "almost" or "sort of" chosen. There are only insiders and outsiders (3:31–32; 4:11–12) (see Malbon, *Narrative Space*, 129–31), those for and those against (9:40), those who save life and those who destroy it, those who do good and those who do evil (3:4), only those who enter into life (i.e., enter into the kingdom of God) and those cast into hell (9:48). However, the line between "insiders" and "outsiders," elect and nonelect, is blurred by at least two considerations: the disciples themselves seem to migrate back and forth across the line, and outsiders are affirmed even though they do not "follow with us" (9:40).

6:6b And he was going around among the villages teaching. 7 And he calls the Twelve to him, and began to send them out two by two, and he was giving them authority over unclean spirits, 8 and he ordered them to take nothing for the way[a] except a staff—no bread, no bag, no money in their belts—9 but to wear sandals, "and do not wear two tunics."[b] 10 And he was saying to them, "Wherever you enter a house, stay there until you leave that place. 11 And whatever place will not receive you or listen to you, as you leave shake off the dust that is on your feet as a testimony against[c] them." 12 And they went out and proclaimed that people should repent, 13 and were casting out many demons, and were anointing many sick people with oil, and were healing them.

14 And king Herod heard of it, for Jesus' name had become publicly known, and people were saying[d] "John the Baptizer has been raised from the dead, and this is why miraculous powers are at work in him." 15 But others were saying, "He is Elijah," and still others were saying, "A prophet, like one of the prophets." 16 But when Herod heard, he was saying, "The one I beheaded, John, has been raised."

17 For Herod himself had sent men and had John arrested, bound, and put in prison on account of Herodias,[e] his brother Philip's wife, because he had married her. 18 For John had been saying to Herod, "It is not lawful for you to have your brother's wife." 19 Now Herodias had it in for him[f] and was wanting to kill him, but she could not. 20 For Herod feared John, since he knew he was a righteous and holy man, and kept him in protective custody, and when he heard him he was deeply disturbed, and yet he liked to listen to him.

21 But an opportune day came when Herod for his birthday had a banquet for his ranking officials and military officers and the prominent people of Galilee. 22 And when his[g] daughter Herodias came in and danced, she pleased Herod and his guests. The king said to the young woman,[h] "Ask of me whatever you want, and I will give it to you." 23 And he swore to her in all seriousness, "Whatever you ask of me, I will give to you, as much as half of my kingdom." 24 And she went out and said to her mother, "What should I ask?" And she said, "The head of John the Baptizer." 25 And she immediately rushed back to the king and asked, "I want you to give me, right now, on a platter—the head of John the Baptizer." 26 And even though the king was deeply grieved, because of the oaths and his guests, he was unwilling to refuse her; 27 And immediately the king sent one of his bodyguards, with orders to bring John's head. And he went out and beheaded him in the prison 28 and brought his head on a platter and gave it to the young woman, and the young woman gave it to her mother. 29 And when his disciples heard they came and took away his body and placed it in a tomb.

30 And the apostles gather together with Jesus and told him all they had done and taught.

a. On the translation of *hodos* see *Excursus: The Way* at 1:3.
b. The sentence begins in the indirect third-person report of the narrator, then modulates into second-person direct address. Verse 10 then begins afresh with a new

quotation formula *kai elegen autois* (cf. 2:27; 4:11, 21; 6:10; 7:9; 9:1). Such phenomena point to the formation of the speech from disparate elements in the history of the tradition, but this history can no longer be reconstructed. The traditional "tunic" is retained as the translation for *chitōn*, since there is no English equivalent for this long loose undergarment worn next to the skin by both sexes.

c. Many translations render "against them," as here, in which case the meaning would be that this symbolic act will be damning testimony against them in the last judgment— to reject Jesus' emissaries is ultimately serious business. But *eis martyrion autois* is the same phrase as 1:44 and 13:9, in each case in a neutral or positive sense, and the meaning may be that this symbolic prophetic act is testimony that might yet move the inhabitants to repentance. It is impossible to preserve this ambiguity in English, but the REB's "as a solemn warning" comes close; it is a warning that may still be heeded, but if not, will be testimony against them in the last judgment.

d. Reading *elegon* (3rd pl.) with B (D) W and others, rather than *elegen* (3rd sg.) with א A C L Θ f¹ f¹³ and the majority of later MSS. The latter reading makes it easier to imagine Jesus identified as the resurrected John (see commentary on v. 18 below).

e. The prepositional phrase *dia Hērōdiada* does not make clear whether Herod arrests John because John condemned his marriage to Herodias or to protect him from Herodias's displeasure.

f. The Greek *eneichen autō* corresponds exactly to this colloquialism.

g. The reading *autou* ("his"), which makes the daughter Herod's and her name Herodias, has very strong MS support (א B D L Δ 565), is the *lectio difficilior*, and is thus placed in the text by WH, GNT³, NA²⁶⁻²⁷ and is so translated in, e.g., the NRSV. The familiar reading *autēs* ("her"), which makes the unnamed girl the daughter of Herodias, is supported by A C Θ f¹³ 33, 2427 and the vast majority of later MSS, and placed in the text by N²⁵ and other editions of the Greek text, and is so translated in most English versions (e.g., NIV). This reading seems to be influenced by an awareness of the historical facts as reported in Josephus, *Ant.* 18.111.

h. *Korasion,* as in 5:41–42 (see note *j*, p. 156).

[6b–7] The Twelve have already been constituted as a special group. They have been with Jesus and have witnessed both his deeds of power and his rejection. Now they are commissioned for a special task. Jesus' calling them to him (*proskaleō*) is thus more than a matter of location. As in Acts 13:2, 16:10, where the same word is used, the reference is to being set apart for mission. The word "apostles" is not used here, though it is found in some MSS of 3:14 (see note *c*, p. 99) and is used in the nontechnical sense of "missionaries" in the report of their return at 6:30. However, the cognate verb *apostellō* is used, and it presents the Twelve as sent forth as authorized representatives of Jesus, with his own authority. If Jesus himself sent out disciples "two by two," this probably indicated that his representatives were not solitary individualists but represented a community, and it was in accord with the biblical precept that the testimony of one witness is inadequate (e.g., Deut 17:6). The practice was continued in the early church, or the description here is derived from early Christian practice (e.g., Peter and John, Acts 3:1–11; 8:14–25; Paul and Barnabas, Acts

13:42–15:12; Paul and Silas, 15:40–17:15; Titus and "the brother," 2 Cor 12:18). As in 1:39, Jesus' ministry as a whole can be encapsulated in his victory over the demonic; the Twelve are now authorized and empowered to extend Jesus' victory through their own mission. As the extension of Jesus' ministry, their mission includes preaching and teaching (vv. 11, 12, 30). Jesus does not call a reclusive Qumran-like group *to* him, but sends them *from* him to all Israel. This is the symbolism of the Twelve (see on 3:13–19). The church of Mark's own time sees this same mission as now continued to embrace the whole world (13:10; 14:9). While much of the Markan Jesus' instruction on discipleship applies to every Christian, the present passage is directed to the Twelve, and so here we have special instructions for Christian missionaries.[122]

[8–9] The instructions for the journey (*hodos*, see *Excursus: The Way* at 1:3) reflect the exodus motifs of food, sandals, tunic, and staff (cf. Exod 12:11; Deut 8:4; 29:5). Perceptive readers in Mark's church will remember that the whole narrative is conceived in terms of the new exodus, the way (*hodos*) through the wilderness promised in Isaiah. The instructions also reflect, in comparison and contrast, the practice of traveling philosophers and preachers as represented by Cynics and Pythagoreans among the Gentiles, and Essenes among the Jews.[123] Cynics were instructed to take a staff for self-defense, and a begging bag for their provisions, but to go barefoot, beg their living from supportive hearers, and dwell alone. Essene emissaries carried a staff and wore sandals, but needed to carry no provisions because they lodged en route with fellow members of their sect who provided for them. Mark or his tradition seems to have received an early set of instructions expressing eschatological severity, which he readjusts in the direction of more practical reality. Q had forbidden both staff and sandals, both of which Mark permits (Luke 10:1–12 / Matt 10:1–14). The variations in the rules for mission praxis show they were adapted to circumstances, adjusted to fit the mission and the people the mission is designed to serve.[124] Nonetheless, the missionary instructions of Markan Jesus call for radical trust in God and confidence in the hospitality of fellow believers to take care of their needs. This is indicated by the instructions about what they are to wear and what they are not to wear; in Mark, clothing, like one's name, is an aspect of one's being (see on 10:50).

[10–11] With a fresh introduction *kai elegen autois* (and he was saying to them; see note *e* on 2:27), two sayings are included reflecting two responses to their mission. Some will receive and provide for them. In Mark's time, these

122. So Best, *Following Jesus*, 194, who argues there is a general mission for the church as a whole, but a special mission for some, represented by the Twelve. Contra, e.g., Kee, *Community of the New Age*, 89, who applies 6:8–11 to all believers.

123. For several primary sources representing such instruction, see Boring et al., eds., *Hellenistic Commentary*, §§ 78–81.

124. Cf. Perkins, "Mark," 596, who rightly points out that Christian mission following this pattern cannot be the agent of colonialism and political expansion.

instructions refer to local households of Christians who provide for traveling missionaries, as reflected in the stories of Acts (9:19b; 10:6, 48b; 18:1–3; 20:6–12; 21:4, 7–8, 16). When missionaries are received into someone's home, they are to remain there during their whole mission in that locale, not to be on the lookout for better lodgings. This instruction seems to presuppose the longer, church-founding missions of the early church, not the mission of the disciples in the time of Jesus. If a locality rejects them, they are not to leave without making a public symbolic act. When Jewish travelers returned from Gentile territory, they shook off the dust from their clothes and sandals as a ritualistic way of reentering the Holy Land without even a touch of Gentile taint upon them. Here the practice is adapted to the Christian mission, as a solemn warning of the severity of rejecting Jesus' emissaries (cf. Acts 13:51; 18:6; see note above).

[12–13] Although Mark's theology of the messianic secret means that the Twelve do not and cannot yet understand the identity and significance of Jesus (see *Excursus: The Messianic Secret* at 9:13), they are portrayed as preaching repentance and casting out demons, precisely as Jesus himself had done (1:14–15). We thus have a double picture of the disciples corresponding to the dual way Jesus himself is presented; ecclesiology corresponds to Christology. Even though the disciples misunderstand and can do no other because their hearts are hardened (6:52; see on 3:5), they carry on a mission of preaching, teaching, exorcising, and healing that corresponds to Jesus' own mission. In Mark's time, the content of the Christian message is "the gospel" (8:35; 10:29; 13:10; 14:9), which the pre-Easter disciples cannot and do not preach. The later Christian mission is nonetheless seen as the extension of Jesus' ministry of word and deed (see on 1:1), and is portrayed in advance in the pre-Easter mission of the Twelve. That they anoint sick people with oil, which Jesus is never reported as doing, is another instance of the practice of the post-Easter church (cf. Jas 5:14) projected onto the time of Jesus. Oil, like wine, was used medicinally (cf. Luke 10:34), but here the act is more symbolic, like the shaking of dust from one's sandals.

[14–16] While the disciples are offstage, not returning until verse 30, the narrative camera shifts from Jesus and his disciples to Herod for the longest story in the Gospel not directly concerned with Jesus.[125] Since verses 14–29 are a Markan intercalation, the new scene is not a fresh beginning, but connected with the previous scene. This means that it is the mission of the *Twelve* that brings *Jesus* to the attention of Herod, and indeed it is Jesus' identity that is the subject of the paragraph—another indication of Mark's theology that binds together Jesus-and-his-disciples as a functional unity, and that ecclesiology and

125. The only other [brief] scenes in which Jesus is not present are 1:4–8; 3:21; 14:1–2 // 10–11, and 14:16, but these are all directly concerned with Jesus. Only here is there an extended story in which Jesus does not appear and not directly concerned with him.

Christology are inseparably related (see on 2:26–27). "Herod" is Herod Antipas, a son of Herod the Great. When his father died in 4 B.C., Antipas had wanted to be king but had to settle for the title of Tetrarch (ruler of a fourth part) granted him by Augustus. In 39 C.E. it was his continuing ambition to be a king like his father that caused Tiberius to depose him and banish him to Gaul. Thus Mark's repeated designation of Herod as "king"—a mistake corrected by both Matthew[126] and Luke—is technically incorrect. Herod comported himself as a petty monarch and may have been called "king" by the populace, but all knew he ruled only at the pleasure of Rome. Whether intentional or not, Mark's inaccuracy allows him to portray the contrast of Herod's "kingship" with that of Jesus, representing the kingdom of God.

All the popular identifications of Jesus come within the category "prophet," which had just been denied to Jesus in his hometown. All the designations are highly positive, though ultimately inadequate, and set the stage for Mark's own view when the same language is repeated in 8:27–29. The most intriguing identification is that Jesus is "John the Baptizer . . . raised from the dead," which identifies Jesus as the risen John because of the "powers at work in him."[127] Here it seems that Mark does not depict this as the opinion of Herod alone, but as the view abroad among the populace. However, such an identification is difficult to understand historically, since it was generally known that John and Jesus had parallel careers, but Jesus-as-resurrected-John seems to require that Jesus did not appear until after the death of John. This understanding of Jesus as *John redivivus* is better understood at the narrative level in terms of Markan theology, in which John is a prototype of Jesus, than in the context of the 30 C.E. history behind the narrative. Mark here switches to a different literary method to address the issue of Jesus' identity. Previously, the issue had been "Who is this?" People, including Jesus' disciples do *not* know, do *not* understand (1:27; 2:7; 4:41; 6:3). In 6:14–8:29, people say "This is . . ."; they "*know*," but *mis*understand (cf. Kingsbury, *Christology of Mark's Gospel*, 85).

[17–29] This approach is strengthened by the fact that the narrative has several other difficulties at the historical level. This story is one of the few points in the Gospel narratives where there are parallel accounts from contemporary historians. This in itself is a remarkable phenomenon. The Christian stories about Jesus have no documentation in contemporary historical literature. This points to the distinctiveness of the Gospel form: it is not a Christian perspective on material also available in the non-Christian world; stories and sayings of Jesus were handed on exclusively within the Christian community. John the

---

126. Matt 14:1 replaces Mark's "king" with the correct "Tetrarch" (though Matt 14:9 reverts to Mark's usage of "king"). Luke uses the correct designation throughout.

127. See *Excursus: Miracle Stories in Mark* at 6:56 on the correlation of resurrection and miracles.

Baptist, however, did come to the attention of Josephus, who around 90 C.E. provided an account of John's execution by Herod (*Ant.* 18.116–119). In Mark, John's arrest was due to his protesting Herod's marriage, which violated biblical law. For Josephus, Herod responded to John's popularity among the populace as a matter of political expediency, deciding "it would be better to strike first and be rid of him before his work led to an uprising, than to wait for an upheaval, get involved in a difficult situation, and see his mistake" (*Ant.* 18.118). There are several other significant differences between Mark's and Josephus's accounts, with Josephus's in each case being the more historically plausible. Thus, while the story has a historical core—Herod and John were real persons, not merely characters in a story—the meaning of the text of Mark is illuminated not by its historical background but by its retelling and reformulation under the influence of biblical models[128] and as an anticipation of the fate of Jesus.

In Mark's view, John is Elijah, and his destiny was already revealed in the Scripture (1:6; 9:11–13). In the biblical story, Elijah is opposed by King Ahab and the wicked Queen Jezebel, who attempts to kill him (1 Kgs 18:13; 19:1–2). Both Ahab and Herod are weak rulers who have a reverential fear of the prophet and want to listen to him, but in each case the petty ruler is led into sin by his wife, whom he should not have married in the first place (1 Kgs 16:31; 21:5–29). The motif of the dancing princess who "pleases" the guests at a royal stag party—the word has erotic overtones—reflects the Esther story (cf. Esth 1:3, 19; 2:12–18; 9:25), and the midrash on Esther even has the head-on-a-platter motif (*Midr. Esther* 1:19–21). In general, the Markan version of the story belongs to the tradition of the rejection and persecution of true prophets who speak against the king.

Not only is the tale influenced by the biblical stories from the past, even more importantly it anticipates the story of Jesus. From the very beginning of the book, John and Jesus are positively linked (1:2–3, 7–11, 14–15; 9:11–13; 11:27–33). Though Jesus is not mentioned, the indirect focus of the story is christological. The story of John's death is introduced in relation to the question of Jesus' identity (vv. 14–16), a question posed in 4:41 and not yet satisfactorily answered. Herod is implicitly contrasted with Jesus. Herod, who is called king, sends (*apostellō*) his men to arrest John. Jesus, who will be called king, sends (*apostellō*, v. 7; cf. *apostoloi*, v. 30) his men to preach, heal, and exorcise. But John is also paralleled to Jesus. John's death anticipates the fate of Jesus and his disciples. The key word *paradidōmi* (hand over, betray, deliver up) connects the destiny of John (1:14), Jesus (3:19; 9:31; 10:33; 14:10–11, 18, 21, 41–44; 15:1, 10, 15), and the disciples (13:9, 11–12). Formally, the story is

---

128. LaVerdiere, *Beginning*, 1:163–68, details the historical problems and especially the influence of the Esther story in biblical and Jewish tradition on the way Mark or pre-Markan tradition has retold the story of John (see on 9:12).

unrelated to the martyr tradition. As in the case of Jesus yet to be told, John is entirely passive, says nothing, decides nothing. There are no scenes in which his brave endurance under torture is praised, no portrayal of his holding fast to his faith despite his suffering and offers of release if he will recant. John is unceremoniously executed offstage. The reader's last picture of John is his being placed in the tomb by his disciples (cf. 15:42–47), with no suggestion of divine vindication.[129] This binds him all the more closely to Jesus. John is intercalated into the Jesus story, not vice versa. The absurdity of his death, in which he is given no voice of his own, finds no resolution apart from God's act in *Jesus*. Jesus is not the resurrected John (vv. 14–16), but the resurrection and Parousia of Jesus will be God's vindication of both John and Jesus.

[30–31] The Twelve return with a successful report. At the pedestrian narrative level, this would mean they were more successful than Jesus himself in the immediately preceding scene (6:1–6a). The actual contrast at the readers' level is the rejection experienced by the earthly Jesus and the success of the post-Easter Christian mission. While the Twelve are a special group (see 3:13–19), it is not clear whether Mark uses "apostle" in the titular sense or only in its generic sense of "one who is sent." This is the only sure occurrence of *apostolos* in Mark (see note *c* on 3:14). The cognate verb *apostellō* occurs twice in reference to Jesus and the Twelve (3:14; 6:7), but eighteen times elsewhere, mostly in its everyday use of "sending," with no "apostolic" overtones (e.g., 3:31; 4:29; 6:27; 11:3; 12:2, 3, 4, 5, 6, 13). Nothing is reported of Jesus' own activities during their absence, for the Twelve function as witnesses to the later Christian community. The Twelve report all they had done and taught, but the reader is not informed as to the content of their teaching, described only as "repentance" in verse 12. *That* the Twelve are authorized to preach and teach is important to Mark, but the messianic secret prohibits his filling in the content of their message. This brief section contains important points of contact with the wider context: the "rest" (*anapauō*) motif connects with the allusions to Ps 23 in the next scene; the "eating" (*esthiō*) motif binds this scene to the whole section 6:14–8:26 in which eating is prominent.

6:31–44 Five Thousand Are Fed

Even the casual reader of Mark notes that the feeding of the five thousand is followed by a story very similar in form and content in which four thousand are fed (8:1–9), and that Mark himself emphasizes their parallels (8:14–21). On closer inspection, it appears that not only the two feedings are parallel, but that Mark has included or composed a double chain of events:

129. Even the account in Josephus contains the element of divine vindication, for the defeat of Herod's armies by Aretas, king of Petra, is regarded as God's punishment for Herod's murder of John (*Ant.* 18.116).

It also seems that Mark has arranged the materials so that Jesus' actions on the west bank represent his ministry to Jews, and those on the east bank the extension of his ministry to Gentiles (cf. also 5:1–43, esp. commentary on 5:1, 21–24).[130] The discussion of purity rules in which Jesus declares all foods to be clean, followed by an exorcism in Gentile territory (7:1–30), stands in the center of this double chain and thus facilitates the transition from Jewish to Gentile mission. The prehistory of these materials and their arrangement in the pre-Markan tradition is disputed (see discussion at 4:35, p. 142), but it seems clear that their arrangement at the Markan level is designed to represent the author's theology.

6:31 And he says to them, "Come apart by yourselves to a deserted place in the wilderness[a] and rest a little." For many were coming to them and then leaving,[b] and they had no opportunity even to eat. **32** And they went away in the boat to a deserted place in the wilderness, to be alone. **33** And many people saw them leaving and recognized them, and they ran together on foot from all the towns and got there ahead of them. **34** And when he had come ashore, he saw a large crowd, and had compassion on them, because they were "like sheep without a shepherd," and he began to teach them many things.

35 And when it had already gotten late, his disciples came to him and were saying, "This is an isolated place, and the hour is already late. **36** Send them away, so that they may go into the surrounding farms and villages and may buy themselves something to eat." **37** But he answered them, "You give them something to eat." And they are saying to him, "Are we to go and buy two hundred denarii[c] worth of bread and give it to them to eat?" **38** But he says to them, "How many loaves do you have? Go and see." And when they had found out, they say, "Five, and two fish." **39** And he ordered them to seat[d] all the people in festive dining groups[e] on the

130. The analyses of, e.g., Kelber and Malbon provide solid evidence that the first feeding is on Jewish soil, the second in Gentile territory (Werner H. Kelber, *Mark's Story of Jesus* [Philadelphia: Fortress, 1979], 33–42; Elizabeth Struthers Malbon, "The Jesus of Mark and the Sea of Galilee," *JBL* 103, no. 3 [1984]: 365–69). Kertelge, *Wunder*, 101–10, 143–44, argues the more precise point that while the first feeding is Jewish, the second is not "Gentile" but universal, embracing Jews and Gentiles.

green grass. 40 And they reclined^f in groups of hundreds and fifties.^{g} 41 And he took the five loaves and the two fish, looked up to heaven, gave thanks to God,^{h} and broke the loaves and kept giving them to his disciples to distribute, and he divided the two fish among them all. 42 And all ate their fill. 43 And they took up enough broken pieces, including fragments of fish, to fill twelve baskets. 44 And those who had eaten numbered five thousand.^{i}

a. See note *e* on translation of *erēmos* as "wilderness" at 1:2–4, p. 34; "wilderness" also at 1:35. "Quiet place" (NIV) misses the point entirely.

b. Literally, "coming and going," but the image of Jesus and his disciples engaged with many people is not of people passing by on some thoroughfare.

c. Due to immense variations in standard of living, buying power, and the fluctuation of currency in both the ancient and modern worlds, it is hazardous to attempt to translate ancient monetary units into modern ones, which in any case quickly go out of date. A general impression of the large amount of money here intended is provided by Matt 20:2, where a day's wage for a laborer is one denarius. Two hundred denarii would thus amount to seven or eight months' wages. Calculating the price of about two thousand loaves of bread at contemporary prices will also suggest the amount of money involved.

d. *Anaklinō* is transitive, "seat, cause to sit," as in the NRSV and others, not intransitive "sit." Jesus does not command all to sit, but commands the disciples to seat all.

e. *Symposia symposia*, lit. "in banquet groups as at a festive drinking party." The symposion was a festive banquet characterized by wine and good conversation. It was a standard institution in the Hellenistic world (cf. the setting of Plato's dialogues in symposia).

f. *Anapiptō* refers to reclining as at a Roman festive meal, not the normal posture of Jews at table, but adopted by them on festive occasions such as Passover.

g. *Prasiai prasiai*, lit., "garden plot by garden plot." The imagery could refer to orderly rows, as in a garden (e.g., one hundred rows of fifty), or orderly groups, some of one hundred and some of fifty.

h. Jesus does not "bless" the bread and then break it, but gives thanks to God and then breaks the bread. The primary meaning of *eulogeō* is to praise, extol. It can then be used in the sense of invoking God's gracious power, i.e., to bless, as often in the LXX. Thus occasionally things can be "blessed," i.e., consecrated to God. The several instances of "saying the blessing" at meals should almost always be understood, however, not in the sense of imparting a blessing on the food, but of giving thanks to God.[131] The accusative is not the direct object of "blessed," but the accusative of reference: "He blessed / thanked God with regard to the food." Cf. the typical Jewish table blessing, ancient and modern: "Blessed art thou, O Lord, King of the universe, who brings forth

131. The sole biblical instance of human beings "blessing" things provided by Bauer and Danker, eds., *BDAG*, 408, is to be understood in this sense. Cf. LaVerdiere, *Beginning*, 175–76: "in biblical times blessing an object was completely foreign to Israelite and Jewish practice. The Hebrew word *barach*, meaning to thank as well as to bless, excluded it. Gratitude was given to persons not to things, . . . Jesus could not have blessed the bread. Raising his eyes to heaven, he blessed God."

bread from the earth." Thus *eulogeō* and *eucharisteō* (give thanks) are used inter-changeably in the Synoptic accounts of the two feedings, the Last Supper, and related passages (cf. *eulogeō* in Mark 6:41 // Matt 14:19 // Luke 9:16; Mark 8:7; 14:22 // Matt 26:26; 1 Cor 10:16; Luke 24:30). *Eucharisteō* is used in Mark 8:6 // Matt 15:36; Luke 22:19 // 1 Cor 11:24; Mark 14:23 // Matt 26:27 // Luke 22:17; John 6:11, 23. In all these contexts, both words mean "give thanks and praise to God"; neither means "bless" in the sense of "consecrate" or "infuse with divine power." Bread and fish are not "blessed" in this scene—God is praised.

i. The Greek text says five thousand *andres*, the plural of *anēr*, which is normally used for "man" in the sense of "male," so that most modern translations render "five thousand men." But, like *homme* in French and *i'sh* in both classical and modern Hebrew, *anēr* can also be used generically for "person," "individual" (as e.g., Jas 1:12). While historically it is more reasonable to suppose that five thousand men followed Jesus to the deserted place, there is nothing in Mark to suggest that the crowd is all male.

This story is found six times in the Gospels, more often than any other, being found in all four Gospels, plus the doublets included in Mark and Matthew (Mark 6:32–44; Matt 14:13–21; Luke 9:10–17; John 6:1–15; Mark 8:1–10; Matt 15:32–39). While it has particular nuances of meaning in each of its bib-lical contexts, the image as such represents a paradigmatic, archetypical scene. Food is a primal human need. Eating is a matter of life and death. To be deprived of food is to be deprived of life; hunger not only kills, it dehumanizes. To receive food is not only to survive, but to have one's humanity maintained or restored. Eating together is a sharing of humanity at the most fundamental level. In this scene, Jesus represents God who grants authentic life, and the story rep-resents not only what happened on a particular day in the life of Jesus, but the act of God in the Christ-event as such.

[31–34] The scene opens with Jesus and the Twelve, who have just returned from the mission on which they shared Jesus' authority and extended his own ministry. Like Jesus alone in 3:20, here the whole group is so intensely engaged in ministry that they have no opportunity to eat—already a contrast to the deca-dent banquet of "king" Herod with its obscene final course that has just been recounted. At Jesus' command, they depart for a deserted "wilderness" place (see note *a* above) in order to eat and rest. At the narrative level, the boat is sim-ply a means of transportation, but it has overtones of the church, the Christian community (see on 4:1, p. 114, and 4:36, p. 145). When Jesus and the Twelve arrive, the huge crowd is already there to greet them.

The omniscient narrator lets the reader know that Jesus, who, so it seems, had attempted to get away from the crowd, actually views them with eyes of divine compassion. "Like sheep without a shepherd" is not an *ad hoc* casual comment of the Markan Jesus as narrator, but echoes the phrase found explic-itly in Num 27:17 (in the context of God appointing a new leader for Israel as Moses' successor) and later in Israel's history when human kingship had failed to represent God's own rule over Israel (1 Kgs 22:17 // 2 Chron 18:16; Jdt 11:19). "Sheep" is often a metaphor for the people of God (e.g., the familiar Ps 100:3; Isa 53:6), and "shepherd" is not a soft, warm-fuzzy image but a royal one (e.g., 2 Sam 5:2; 7:7; 1 Chron 17:6; Ps 78:71). Mark's language of shepherding is resonant with overtones of the kingdom of God (see *Excursus: Kingdom of God* at 1:15). Israelite and Judean kings were charged to represent God's rule among the people, but human kingship failed; God is the true king / shepherd of Israel (Gen 48:15; 49:24; Pss 23:1; 28:9; 80:1; Isa 40:11) and will replace defective and perverse human shepherds (Jer 23:1–4; Ezek 34) by establishing his own kingship in power, either by coming himself or by sending an eschatological king / shepherd (Isa 40:11; 49:9–10; Jer 31:10; Ezek 34:5, 8, 15, 23–24; Mic 5:1–4; Matt 2:6).

This crowd thus represents the harried people of God, as indicated by several traits in the following story that both support this identification and make the story itself understandable. They represent "all the towns" (cf. 1:5 and commentary there). The twelve baskets of broken pieces relate to the twelve tribes of Israel. The wilderness setting connects to the Moses story, and the miraculous supply of bread to the manna (Exod 16). In the wilderness, at the end of Moses' life, God appoints Joshua (*Iēsous* = Jesus in the LXX), to guide God's people, so that they will not be "sheep without a shepherd" (Num 27:17). The plight of the crowd that meets Jesus is not primarily that they are hungry for physical food, but that they are disoriented and scattered. The eschatological shepherd would be a teacher who would instruct the people in the right way. "Torah" was often symbolized by "bread" (Prov 9:5; Deut 8:3; Philo, *Names* 259–60; *Gen. Rab.* 43:6; 54:1; 70:5; cf. the development of this theme in John 6).[132] Thus the shepherd of Ps 23, as understood in some streams of first-century Judaism, is the eschatological shepherd who will give ultimate "rest" (cf. the sought rest of v. 35 above and Heb 4:1–11), will lead in paths of righteousness by his teaching of Torah, will make the people recline on the green grass, and will prepare a table, that is, celebrate the eschatological banquet in the wilderness. All these motifs are found in Mark's story and illustrate that the feeding story is incorporated within this image of Jesus as eschatological teacher. The giving of the loaves is a matter of understanding (6:52; 8:17–21). All this is not to minimize the image of Jesus who provides for the physical needs of hungry people and commands his disciples to do so (6:37; 8:3), but to show that Jesus' initial response of "teaching" is not incidental to his "feeding" but is integral to it, and that teaching takes priority over working miracles. As is the case throughout his narrative, Mark focuses on the affirmation *that* Jesus is the eschatological shepherd who teaches with authority, not the content of the

132. Cf. Peder Borgen, *Bread from Heaven: An Exegetical Study of the Concept of Manna in the Gospel of John and the Writings of Philo* (NovTSup 10; Leiden: Brill, 1965).

teaching itself. The narrator reminds readers in the Markan church that it is not the miracles and charismatic phenomena that continue to happen in their midst that communicates the saving act of God in Christ, but the "teaching," which in Mark's day includes the death and resurrection of Jesus and the call to follow him in the way of the cross.

[35–36] The crowds do not express any need or sense of emergency. It is the disciples who first raise the concern about food.[133] Mark gives no indication of their own hunger. The problem of verse 31 seems to be forgotten, so that to ask when they and Jesus were finally able to eat, and to find the answer, for example, in 7:2, is to understand the story at a historicizing level off-target from its own thrust. Mark spends as much time on the dialogue between Jesus and the obtuse disciples as on the miracle itself. The problem is not so much the hunger of the crowds as the incomprehension of the disciples (6:52). The whole incident belongs more to the story line of Jesus instructing the disciples than that of Jesus helping the sick and demon possessed.

That the story does not move at the level of realistic report is indicated by several features prior to the actual miracle. A crowd of thousands is difficult to imagine in a setting in which the population of Capernaum, for example, was only two or three thousand. That such a mass of people would spontaneously follow Jesus into the wilderness without thought of what they would eat or where they would sleep is difficult to imagine. Likewise, the effort to picture the event historically has problems with their coming from "all the cities," and that they nonetheless reach Jesus' destination before he does—did word first have to be carried to the cities, from which people then formed the crowds, or had they already come to Capernaum from everywhere, yet had no provisions with them? Imagining how such an ungainly multitude outpaced the boat requires some ingenuity, and some explanation for how they knew where Jesus was going. The disciples' suggestion that local farm villages could handle an influx of five thousand hungry people would seem to be a burden for even the lines of fast-food establishments that ring modern cities, and is difficult to see as a realistic suggestion in an actual historical context. That all attention is focused on food, and nothing is said of what people are to drink seems unrealistic in a hot and dry environment. It thus seems that biblical models, not historical recollection of an actual event, provided the basic content of the story. In addition to the shepherd imagery from the biblical texts discussed above, the story has many

---

133. Contrast the parallel situation in 8:1–3, where the focus is on the hunger of the people and Jesus' compassion for their need. Here, the focus is on the people's lack of leadership, and Jesus' extended period of teaching creates the necessity for their feeding, which the disciples first notice and bring to Jesus' attention. There, the "wilderness" setting precludes providing food, and their only hope is a miracle from Jesus; here, neighboring villages are a possibility. Thus the focus here is not on Jesus' miracle, which is not really necessary, but on Jesus' challenge to the disciples: "you give them something to eat." So Schenke, *Wundererzählungen*, 220–23.

points of contact, in both form and content, with the Elisha story of 2 Kgs 4:42–44: there, too, the miracle follows the death of Elijah, the Markan John the Baptist. There, too, the prophet commands his servant to feed a large group with an impossibly small number of loaves. There, too, the objection that such a small amount is not enough for so many is overcome by the prophet's authoritative command. There, too, the miracle not only provides enough, but more than enough. The numbers in 2 Kgs are smaller: twenty loaves for a hundred hungry men, a proportion of one to five. In Mark, there are five loaves for five thousand, a proportion of one to a thousand: here, too, Jesus is not only "more than a prophet" (Matt 11:9); as the eschatological prophet he is *much* more.

[37–38] *You* give them something to eat is emphatic in Greek. The addition of the pronoun gives the command the force of "I mean *you*." The focus remains on the disciples. As they have preached, taught, healed, and cast out demons with Jesus' power and authority, they are now commanded to participate in this dimension of his ministry. When their reply illustrates their lack of understanding, they are told to find out how many loaves they in fact have. (In Mark, the crowds are fed with the disciples' food, not, as in John 6:9, by Jesus' multiplying a little boy's lunch.)[134] The disciples respond that they have only five loaves and introduce the fish into the story. The numbers "five" and "two" in an isolated story would only signify the small amount of food available. In this context replete with symbolism where "bread" already suggests the teaching of the Torah (see above), the image of five scrolls of the Torah may not be far away. The two fish are another matter. Modern Western readers tend to think of fish as the main course and bread as a supplementary side dish, often avoided by calorie-conscious moderns. In first-century Palestine, circular loaves of bread about eight inches in diameter and an inch thick constituted the main course of every meal, so that food as such could be called "bread" (e.g., Mark 3:20; Matt 4:4; 6:11) and eating could be described as "breaking bread" (e.g., Exod 2:20; Jer 16:7; Luke 24:35; Acts 2:42; 20:7; 1 Cor 10:16). Dried fish served only as a condiment. Since Jesus had not asked about fish and they are first introduced by the disciples (and also seem to be an afterthought in 6:43 and 8:7), the fish

---

134. Such details are ignored in the old rationalist interpretation that what we have here is a lesson in sharing: when the disciples were willing to share their food, the others in the multitude who had kept their lunches hidden brought them out, and there was enough for all. Strangely enough, the moderately conservative Vincent Taylor utilizes this explanation in order to hold on to his understanding that Mark is basically the eyewitness report of Peter (*Mark*, 321), and liberation hermeneutic has rejuvenated this old-Liberal moralizing object lesson: "there is nothing 'supernatural' reported to have transpired . . . the only 'miracle' here is the triumph of the economics of sharing . . . ; 'market' economics are repudiated in favor of a practice of sharing available resources so that everyone has enough" (Myers, *Binding the Strong Man*, 206, 229). The political ideal is right and just; finding it in Mark is eisegesis, not exegesis. Transcending all hermeneutical methods, however, the command of Jesus penetrates to the modern disciple: "*You* give them something to eat."

may be only an incidental addition that adds color or a symbolic meaning no longer clear.

[39–40] Jesus does not address the people himself, but commands the Twelve to have the people sit down (see note *d* above). As in the mission the disciples had just completed in verse 30, Jesus' authority is mediated to the crowds through the Twelve.[135] The language of "reclining" and "symposia" gives a festive, celebratory tone to the narrative, with connotations of Christian eucharistic celebrations in the Markan house churches. The "garden plot" metaphor is used in later rabbinic writings of students studying the Torah,[136] and it also connects with the imagery of sowing the word in 4:1–20. The green grass is not, or not merely, a historical reflection of the time of the year, but connects both to the green pastures of the Ps 23 imagery already extensively used and to the blossoming of the desert / wilderness in which the "way of the Lord" is prepared (Isa 35:1; 40:3; 51:3). The "hundreds" and "fifties" suggest the arrangement of the hosts of Israel in the wilderness (Exod 7:4; 13:18; 18:21, 25).

[41] Though the disciples distribute the food, Jesus is the host. The food people receive from their hands comes from him. The series of verbs took / gave thanks / broke / gave is precisely the same as in 14:22 at the Last Supper. Since there is no wine in Mark 6 and no fish in Mark 14, some scholars have argued there are no eucharistic overtones in Mark's portrayal of feeding the multitudes. It is indeed the case that neither is modeled on the other, but that both are modeled on the normal family meal. The Eucharist, however, was a continuation of the table fellowship of Jesus' ministry in which he ate with all sorts of people he was constituting as the new family of God (cf. 2:13–22; 3:31–35). Mark is written for initiated readers, who could hardly hear these words without thinking both of their own eucharistic fellowship and of the account of the Last Supper.[137] Thus many interpreters have rightly seen the account here and in 8:1–9 as an anticipation of the Eucharist, which is itself a foretaste of the eschatological messianic banquet.[138] The Gospel of John, despite the presence of fish and absence of wine, explicitly interprets the story eucharistically (John 6:25–58 interpreting 6:1–14). At the narrative level, the story thus looks backward to Israel in the wilderness, and to Isaiah's prophecy of the new exodus, and for-

135. "Twelve" occurs in this pericope only with reference to the number of baskets in v. 42. It is clear, however, that the Twelve sent in v. 7 are those who return in v. 30, and leave with Jesus in v. 32.

136. See documentation in Strack and Billerbeck, *Kommentar*, 2.13.

137. It is thus wide of the mark (no pun intended) to argue as does Fowler that there is no eucharistic meaning here since the first-time reader does not yet know the story of 14:22–25.

138. For an extensive, perhaps *too* specific, argument for the eucharistic meaning of the feeding stories in Mark, see Quentin Quesnell, *The Mind of Mark: Interpretation and Method through the Exegesis of Mark 6, 52* (AnBib 38; Rome: Pontifical Biblical Institute, 1969). Mark's perspective on the eucharistic is conditioned by his dialectical understanding of the presence and absence of Jesus in the church (see on 6:51; 16:6).

ward to the Last Supper, the church's eucharistic celebrations, and the ultimate future of the messianic banquet. From the reader's point of view, this perspective is expanded to include the memory of Jesus' own table fellowship with the impure, the compromised, and other sinners, and the experience of the threatened and impoverished Markan church that continued this celebratory family fellowship of plenty (cf. 10:29–30).

[42–44] The miracle story concludes without a proper ending; the expected acclamation is missing. The historicizing question of whether the crowds knew what was going on is not even raised; the focus throughout has been on instructing the disciples (and the readers). The story is not really complete until the narrator's comment on the disciples' lack of understanding at verse 52, elaborated in 8:14–20. The magnitude of Jesus' deed of power (cf. 6:5) is emphasized by three concluding statements: (1) All ate and were filled. That people eat their fill is not taken for granted in the biblical world (cf. Ruth 2:14!), but is a mark of eschatological plenty, the return of the abundance of creation (cf. Gen 2:16[139]). (2) Twelve baskets of broken pieces were taken up. The fragments refer to uneaten pieces of the broken bread the disciples had distributed, not to crumbs or half-eaten fragments. That so much food was not only left over, but *left behind* is another indication of eschatological extravagance. The disciples gathering the fragments is a counter-picture of the Mosaic manna, which could not be preserved (Exod 16:4–5; 13–21; see *Excursus: Mark and the Scripture*, at 14:52), and portrays the messianic times, when hunger will be replaced not merely by adequacy but by extravagance (cf., e.g., *2 Bar.* 29.5). The leftover bread is also sometimes interpreted as pointing to the continuing eucharistic presence beyond the time of Jesus' earthly life (e.g., LaVierdiere, *Beginning*, 1:171–72). "Twelve" is another reminder of the Israel / people-of-God theme that permeates the story. (3) For the first time, the reader learns the amazing size of the crowd, five thousand people (see note *i*), which Matthew will expand even further (Matt 14:21).

6:45–52 The Walking on the Sea

6:45 And immediately he compelled his disciples to get into the boat and to go on ahead to the other side, toward Bethsaida, while he dismisses the crowd. 46 And after taking leave of them, he went up on the mountain to pray. 47 And when it had become late and the boat had been in the midst of the sea for some time,[a] and he was alone on the land, 48 and when he

---

139. The grammatical construction of Gen 2:16 with infinitive absolute modifying the modal "you may eat" might be rendered "you may eat to your heart's content" (cf. Allen P. Ross, *Introducing Biblical Hebrew* [Grand Rapids: Baker, 2001], 381). This lavish abundance of creation, not the competition and scarcity of the post-Genesis-3 world, is the will of the Creator, who will restore it at the eschaton.

saw them painfully struggling[b] to make headway, for the wind was against them, about the fourth watch of the night he comes toward them, walking on the sea, and he was intending to[c] pass them by. 49 But when they saw him walking on the sea, they thought that he was a ghost, and cried out, 50 for they all saw him and were terrified. But he immediately spoke with them, and says to them, "Take courage, it is I; do not be afraid." And he got into the boat with them, and the wind ceased. And they were utterly dumbfounded, 52 for they did not understand about the loaves—on the contrary, their hearts had been hardened.

a. *Palai*, which usually refers to a relatively long time in the past as seen from the present perspective, is read by $\mathfrak{P}^{45}$ D f^1 28 2542 and a few other MSS. The context seems to make it inappropriate here, but most MSS of Matt 14:24 have *ēdē* ("already"), apparently deemed by him a more appropriate rendering of Mark's *palai*. Cf. on 15:44, which seems to use *ēdē* and *palai* as synonyms.

b. The basic meaning of *basanizō* is "torture," as 2 Macc 7:13, and can have overtones of the apocalyptic tribulations (Rev 9:5; 11:10; 12:2). Elsewhere in Mark it is found only at 5:7, though it is used by Matthew of the boat being tortured by the waves, Matt 14:24.

c. The use of *ēthelen* is ambiguous ("was about to" or "was intending to"), but the latter is more likely (see commentary below on vv. 47–51).

[6:45] The geographical details are problematic. Jesus commands the disciples to go to Bethsaida, a mainly Gentile city on the east side of the lake. They in fact land at Gennesaret, an area (not a town) on the west bank from which they started (6:53). Only after a long, roundabout way through Tyre, Sidon, the Decapolis (7:31), and an intermediate stop at Dalmanutha (8:10) do they finally make it to Bethsaida (8:22), and this only after having been upbraided for their hardened hearts (8:17–21), already adumbrated at the conclusion of the present story (6:52). These data constitute a problem primarily for modern analyzers of the story, not for the author and original audience, who seem to have been unaware of the actual geography involved—just as modern readers who do not check their biblical maps read the story without reflecting on the location of the sites mentioned. Nonetheless, there are some indications that the geography is intended to convey symbolic overtones.[140] Jesus *compels* the disciples to enter the boat and cross to the other side, a trip they are apparently reluctant to make. The preceding story has been replete with Jewish symbolism (see commentary), but the transition to "other side" and the Gentile city Bethsaida can be understood as reflecting the later experience of the later church. "Boat" connotes "church," which experiences a transition from its original Jewish context to the

140. Here and elsewhere, "Mark has an extraordinary sense of place" (LaVerdiere, *Beginning*, 1:52). "Mark uses geography as theological symbolism" (Senior, "Struggle to Be Universal," 76).

Gentile mission, and not without difficulty (cf. on 4:36). The present crossing-the-sea story is connected to the preceding one and has some of the same motifs, now interwoven into an epiphany story. The searching question as to Jesus' identity raised there (4:41) is definitively answered here (6:50), but the "insider" disciples to whom the mystery of the kingdom has been given (4:10–12) show themselves to belong to the "outsiders" who do not understand because their hearts are hardened (6:52).

[46] Jesus goes up on the mountain to pray. The content of his prayer is not given; the Markan point is that he prays, not the reason for his prayer or its content. Human beings pray; divine beings do not. The initiated reader will think of Jesus' human weakness manifest in the Gethsemane prayer, the only prayer in Mark for which content is given (14:32–42). As Mark prepares to present an epiphany of Jesus on the sea in which Jesus is portrayed with the features of deity, he first presents the human Jesus who prays to God.[141]

[47–51] Like the geographical data, the temporal details are also problematic, pointing to the Markan combination of differing traditions. It was already late in 6:35, and the feeding and dismissal of the enormous crowd must have taken considerable time. Now the disciples are already in the midst of the sea, and the narrator reports again that "it had become late," which stands incongruously alongside the "fourth watch of the night" (3:00 to 6:00 A.M.) of verse 48b. The difficulty in imagining the temporal relations historically was noticed by various scribes, who attempted to adjust it (see note *a*). The miracle story itself, though sharing some elements of the deliverance story in 4:35–41, is primarily an epiphany story modeled on the epiphanies of Yahweh in the Old Testament. (1) The narrator emphasizes the *distance separating* the disciples and Jesus, a separation that cannot be bridged from the human side; the distress of the disciples; and the absence of Jesus (cf., 2:20; 14:25; 16:6). It is humanly impossible that he be with them. (2) Despite the darkness and the distance, Jesus *sees* them in their distress. This is not a matter of a full moon or the dawning light of early morning, but of the God who sees his people in distress (cf. e.g., Exod 3:7; cf. also Mark 2:5, 8; 5:32 where Jesus sees with divine insight). (3) Jesus does what only God can do, coming to them walking on the sea (Ps 77:19; Isa 43:16; Job 9:8b).[142] On interpreting the miracle itself, see *Excursus: Miracle Stories in Mark* at 6:56. (4) Help comes in the early morning hour (e.g.,

---

141. Some patristic authors were concerned in their own pre-critical way that the theology of the cross needed somehow to be included in the miracle stories. Thus, e.g., in Augustine's interpretation of this story, the wood of the boat prefigured the wood of the cross, and the way through the sea on which Jesus walked was the way of the cross. There is "no way to cross over to the homeland unless you are carried by the wood [of the cross]" (Augustine, *Tractate on John* 2.4.3, cited in Oden and Hall, *Mark*, 95).

142. For similar pagan stories of divine beings who walk on the water or give human beings power to do so, see Boring et al., eds., *Hellenistic Commentary*, §§ 110–12.

Ps 46:5). (5) The difficult expression that Jesus intends to *pass by* the disciples is also to be understood in this theophanic framework. In Old Testament epiphany stories, God "passes by" and reveals his glory (Exod 33:19–23; 34:6; 1 Kgs 19:11; Job 9:11). Jesus wanted to pass by them as a divine epiphany and go before them, like Yahweh leading his people in the New Exodus, as Jesus walks ahead of his disciples on the way that leads to the cross and beyond it to the Gentile mission (10:32; cf. 16:7). But this intent is frustrated by the disciples' fear and lack of perception. Thus at one level this narrative represents the retrospective view of the Markan community, mostly Gentile and outside Palestine, of the frustrated and troublesome progress of the gospel from its Jewish beginnings to its present Gentile setting, despite the lack of perception and courage of the disciples (as in Acts 1–15). (6) Jesus speaks to them in the words God uses as his own formula of self-identification, "I am" (Exod 3:13–15 and repeatedly in Deutero-Isaiah, e.g., Isa 41:10; 43:10–13, 25; 45:6, 18, 22; 48:12), thus definitively answering the disciples' question in the previous story of trouble on the sea, "Who then is this?" The Greek *egō eimi* at the pedestrian level merely indicates identity, like the colloquial "it's me," as in John 9:9. At this level of the narrative, when the disciples think they see a ghost, Jesus responds with the reassuring *egō eimi* meaning "Not a ghost, it's me, Jesus." But in the context of all the other marks of divine epiphany, the phrase here must have the connotation of the divine self-revelation, the disclosure of the divine name as Yahweh, the one who says absolutely, "I am." God speaks with this formula especially in Deutero-Isaiah, Mark's key Old Testament text (twenty-two times in the LXX of Isa 40–55, and not elsewhere in Isaiah; the "Do not be afraid" also reflects the divine address in Isa 41:10, 13, 14; 43:1, 5; 44:2, 8; 54:4, 14). The false prophets of 13:6 wrongly appropriate this revelatory formula, which only God and Jesus may use, here and in 14:62—where it will lead to Jesus' death. The Markan church, storm-tossed by the persecution it experiences, may have felt that Jesus had been left behind, back there on the shore of 30 C.E. history. Jesus would reappear as the Son of Man from heaven at the eschaton shortly to come (9:1; 13:24–30). But where is Jesus now? It is impossible for him to be with them, and yet he *is* present. The Markan theme of Jesus' absence between resurrection and Parousia (see on 16:6) is understood dialectically, and the "I am" is the declaration of the divine presence.[143]

The epiphany as a whole has several features of a resurrection story, especially as illustrated in Luke 24:36–41: the sudden epiphanic reappearance of Jesus to his disciples, who are afraid, have hardened hearts, mistake him for a

___

143. See M. Eugene Boring, *Sayings of the Risen Jesus: Christian Prophecy in the Synoptic Tradition* (SNTSMS 46; Cambridge: Cambridge University Press, 1982), 202; Marcus, *Mystery*, 181. Quesnell, *Mind of Mark*, argues that 6:52 is also a reference to the presence of Christ in the eucharistic celebration.

ghost, but are reassured by Jesus' "I am." While we should not think of this as a "misplaced resurrection story" in overtly chronological, linear terms, the story is permeated with resurrection imagery and language. Like other miracle stories, it was told in the pre-Markan church tradition as a pointer to the Christ-event as a whole focused in the death and resurrection of Jesus, and like them, it manifests the language and imagery of the resurrection (cf. on 1:4, 16–20, 29–34, 35–39, 40–45; 2:11–12, 14; 3:3–4; 4:40–41; 5:1–5, 21–24, 28–34, 38–43).

[6:52] The omniscient narrator, who also revealed Jesus' intent to the reader, here discloses the state of the disciples' hearts. They have seen the miracle and do not doubt that it happened. What they lack is understanding. Surprisingly, their being dumbfounded—rather than comforted or assured—by the sea epiphany is linked to their lack of understanding about "the loaves." There, too, they experienced and participated in the miracle, yet it has not enabled them to perceive Jesus' identity. Who Jesus truly is cannot finally be learned from the miracle stories. Their hearts are not merely hard, but harden*ed*, with God as the implied subject (see on 3:5). Their problem is not mere unwillingness, but inability—though they are not without responsibility. Perception and understanding is more than believing the miracle happened; to understand is to receive a divine gift, and others are hardened (see on 3:5; 4:12, and cf. the use of "hardening" terminology in 8:17; John 12:40; Rom 11:7; 2 Cor 3:14). The latter two texts are concerned with the general Jewish rejection of the Christian gospel and its extension to the Gentiles, a frame also important for understanding this story. The disciples are slipping into the category of outsiders (4:11) and even enemies (3:5).

6:53–56 Healings at Gennesaret

6:53 And when they had crossed over, they landed and anchored at Gennesaret. 54 And when they had gotten out of the boat, people at once recognized him 55 and ran around that whole area and began to bring the sick on mats, to carry them around wherever they heard he was. 56 And wherever he would enter into villages or cities or hamlets, they placed the sick in the marketplaces, and pleaded with him that they might touch even the edge[a] of his cloak. And as many as touched it were healed.

a. *Kraspedon,* only here in Mark, is the normal word for edge or hem of a garment, but it is also used for the tassels male Jews were supposed to wear on the four corners of their outer garments (Num 15:38–39; Deut 22:12; cf. Matt 23:5).

[6:53] On the confusing geography, see on 6:45. They "cross over," but do not land on the opposite (Gentile) shore to which they had been directed, but are back on the same side of the lake from which they departed in 6:45, and both the retreat for the disciples and the mission to the Gentiles seem to be frustrated. Gennesaret is not a town, but a section of the western shore of the Sea of Galilee south of Capernaum.

[54–56] The description apparently intends to summarize the popular response to Jesus and to portray the healing power that comes from him almost involuntarily—a generalization of the scene in 5:25–34. It is not intended as a full description of Jesus' ministry, for no exorcisms, teaching, or preaching are mentioned. In contrast to the imperceptive disciples, the crowds immediately recognize Jesus, who both goes to the people and welcomes and heals the vast crowds that come to him. The reader can rejoice that in Jesus the healing power of God erupts into a needy world and that people respond in great numbers.

Excursus: Miracle Stories in Mark[144]

Terminology

Mark uses three words that have been translated "miracle":[145]

1. *dynamis* (NRSV "deed of power"), ten times: 5:30; 6:2, 5, 14; 9:1, 39; 12:24; 13:25, 26; 14:62.
2. *sēmeion* (NRSV "sign"), five times: 8:11, 12 (two times), 13:4, 22.
3. *teras* (NRSV "omen"): 13:22.

The characteristic Markan word for Jesus' "miracles" is *dynamis*, the only term used for his deeds of power. The word is used only in a positive sense, for the acts of God, John the Baptist, and Jesus' followers. *Sēmeion* and *teras*, on the other hand, are used only negatively, either as a perverse demand for Jesus to prove his claims by performing a sign (8:11–12) or to describe what false messiahs and prophets do (13:4, 22). This distinction is a matter of Markan usage, not of inherent meanings of the words themselves.[146] Other New Testament authors use *sēmeion* in a positive sense for Jesus' own mighty works (e.g., John 20:30–31; Acts 2:22). Stories of Jesus' or God's power can be told, however, without using any particular "miracle" terminology, for example, finding the colt (11:1–6), cursing the fig tree (11:12–20), or tearing the temple veil (15:38). The predictions of the resurrection (8:31; 9:3; 10:33–34) and the event itself 16:1–8) are also narrated without using the "miracle" vocabulary.

---

144. See especially Tagawa, *Miracles et Évangile*; Schenke, *Wundererzählungen*; Kertelge, *Wunder*; and the collection of key essays in Alfred Suhl, ed., *Der Wunderbegriff im Neuen Testament* (WdF 295; Darmstadt: Wissenschaftliche Buchgesellschaft, 1980).

145. I am here using the language of "miracle stories" because it has become conventional, though it is not entirely appropriate to Mark. Several English translations, including RSV, NRSV, NAB, ESV, do not include the word "miracle" in Mark, translating *dynamis* more appropriately as "deed of power" or "mighty work," *sēmeion* as "sign," *teras* as "wonder" or "omen." Among those that continue in the KJV tradition of translating Jesus' *dynameis* as "miracles" are NIV, TNIV, REB, NJB, CEV.

146. Cf. Ralph P. Martin, *Mark: Evangelist and Theologian* (Grand Rapids: Eerdmans, 1973), 164–77.

Amount and Distribution

Miracle stories are not a separable or incidental element of the Markan narrative. Stories of Jesus filled with the power of God and doing mighty deeds are fundamental to the narrative, which contains at least sixteen miracle stories, not counting Mark's summary statements. Depending on whether or not one includes the Markan summaries and such stories as finding the colt and cursing the fig tree, miracle stories comprise between 20 and 30 percent of 1:1–16:8 and 40 percent of chapters 1–10.

The stories are not evenly distributed. Almost all occur in part 1 of the Gospel, with the passion narrative being entirely devoid of them. All are in fact prior to the great turning point of Peter's confession and the first passion prediction (8:27–31) except 9:14–29 and 10:46–52, each of which is located in its present context for a particular Markan reason. Jesus heals no sick people and exorcises no demons once he reaches Jerusalem, where his miracles are not even referred to—with the significant negative exception of 15:30–31. The first half of the Gospel thus represents a kind of "theology of glory," with Jesus' power to perform miracles dramatically in the spotlight. The second half of the Gospel represents a kind of "theology of the cross," in which God's power is revealed in weakness. This distribution is a Markan arrangement, integral to his theology and his creation of the Gospel genre.[147] Neither Matthew nor Luke preserve it, inserting miracle stories into the Jerusalem ministry and passion narrative (Matt 21:14; Luke 22:50–51).

Event and Interpretation

The miracle stories are rooted in the life of Jesus and the experiences of the eyewitnesses of his ministry. They were then developed, elaborated, and multiplied in the mission preaching of earliest Christianity, where they adopted the forms and were amplified by the ways in which miracles and miracle workers were understood in both Jewish and pagan traditions.[148] The issue for both Christian preachers and those to whom they proclaimed the Christian message was not whether miracles could or did happen. Nearly everyone believed they happened. During Jesus' ministry, no one disputes the possibility and reality of miracles, and even at the crucifixion scene the issue is not miracles as such, but whether Jesus could miraculously prove his identity (see on 8:11–12; 15:27–32). The key issues were what the stories meant and what they implied about the miracle worker (cf., e.g., commentary on Mark 3:22–30).[149]

147. Tagawa, *Miracles et Évangile*, 49–54, surveys the efforts to explain this as an aspect of the life of the historical Jesus, and finds them wanting.

148. On miracles and miracle stories in the historical context of the New Testament, see especially Kee, *Miracle in the Early Christian World*, and Gerd Theissen, *The Miracle Stories of the Early Christian Tradition* (trans. Francis McDonagh; Philadelphia: Fortress, 1983). For parallels and analogies to individual New Testament miracle stories, noting both similarities and differences, see Boring et al., eds., *Hellenistic Commentary*, ad loc.

149. E.g., Celsus, second-century philosophical opponent of Christianity, does not doubt that Jesus worked miracles, but considered him a magician in league with evil powers. See Origen, *Against Celsum* 5.41. The priestly leadership of the Eleusinian mysteries did not question that Apollonius performed miracles, but refused to initiate him into the mystery cult because they regarded him as a wizard (*goēs*; Philostratus, *Life of Apollonius* 4.18).

In Jewish apocalypticism, a new dimension was added to the interpretation of miracles, which are seen as signs of God's intervention to vindicate his people and establish his rule or kingdom; miracles were correlated with the eschatological kingdom of God. A helpful generalization, with numerous exceptions and nuances, is that pagan miracle stories focused attention on the miracle itself or on the miracle worker as a *theios anēr* ("divine man"), while in Judaism, especially in eschatological and apocalyptic streams, miracles were understood as manifestations or anticipations of the kingdom of God.

Pre-Markan Tradition and Interpretation

Stories of Jesus' miracles were interpreted in a variety of ways in the pre-Markan tradition. Even so, the christological dimension was central, giving the Christian miracle stories a perspective that distinguished them from similar stories in both Judaism and the Hellenistic world at large. The common denominator in the spectrum of interpretations was that they were miracles of Jesus—focus was on the person, mission, and message from and about Jesus, not on the miracle as such. Thus the theme of "faith" rarely occurs in pagan or Jewish miracle stories, and when it does appear, it means "belief that the miracle can happen." In Christian miracle stories, "faith" is a frequent theme, and is directed to God and Christ, not to the phenomenon of miracle itself.

Mission preaching was central among the ways miracle stories functioned in the pre-Markan tradition. The miracle story was proclaimed as the vehicle for preaching the good news of God's act in Christ. The miracle story pointed to the Christ-event as a whole. It is this dimension of the stories that is appropriated and explicitly elaborated in the Fourth Gospel. Thus, for example, John has no exorcisms, though John knows the phenomena of demons and demon possession (John 7:20, 48–52; 10:20–21; 13:2). John interprets the Christ-event itself as a grand cosmic exorcism, using the same word in John 12:31 that the Synoptic stories use for Jesus' exorcisms. Thus also the feeding stories are symbolic of what happens in the Christ-event as a whole (including cross and resurrection), so that the healing of the blind, feeding of the hungry, and raising of the dead point to the Christ-event as such. Feeding the five thousand points to Jesus himself as the bread of life; raising Lazarus points to Jesus himself as the resurrection and the life (John 6:1–59; 11:1–44). John is not here making a radically new, profound interpretation, discontinuous from all that has gone before, but making explicit the motifs that were already present in the individual stories, raising them to the level of conscious theological reflection. This does not mean that we can use Johannine theology to demonstrate the meaning of individual pre-Markan miracle stories. But the explicit interpretation of the stories in the Fourth Gospel does illustrate one of the ways such stories were understood, a way profoundly and reflectively developed by the Johannine school, and shows that this understanding was already implicit in the stories themselves.

Markan Interpretation

Mark affirms, retains, and develops the pre-Markan tradition of miracle stories. Each is not merely a report of an amazing deed of the past, but a picture of God's saving power manifest in Jesus, available to the Markan reader.[150] Mark is not an opponent, but an advocate of epiphany Christology and its pictures of Jesus filled with divine power. He does not introduce the many miracle stories only as negative examples of a false Christology,[151] but affirms them as authentic vehicles of the Christian message. Had he been opposed to them, he could have minimized or eliminated them, or portrayed Jesus as condemning the mob's lust for the miraculous. Instead, he not only includes sixteen stories from the tradition, but composes his own summaries highlighting Jesus' deeds of power (1:32–34, 39; 3:7–12; 6:54–56). The Markan Jesus never offers a critique of the crowds streaming to him for healing; instead he responds to them with compassion as sheep without a shepherd (6:34). He commissions his disciples and empowers them to heal and cast out demons (6:7, 13).

The pre-Markan stories were a valid vehicle for the proclamation of the gospel, but taken by themselves they were also open to profound misunderstanding. Could a Jesus who raised the dead really die? Could a Jesus who walked on the water not come down from the cross? The tradition of Jesus as "divine man" miracle worker was fraught with theological danger: "The seeds of heresy were latent in it from the start."[152]

Mark recognized the dangers inherent in the miracle tradition, and in the process of including and affirming the miracle stories reinterpreted them by setting them in a larger narrative framework that included the cross and resurrection as its climax and hermeneutical touchstone. Previously, each account of a miracle was an individual story. Now, each is an episode in a larger story, and is interpreted only in reference to the narrative as a whole. Within its Markan context, each story is now communicated only with this "eschatological reservation"; its meaning can be rightly appropriated only in the light of the eschatological event of Jesus' crucifixion and resurrection. The resurrection is the inbreaking of the eschaton; the miracles anticipate this. The kingdom of God is the future eschatological reality; the miracles are proleptic of this. Thus the miracle stories, which contain no "teaching" as such, are related by Mark at the redactional level to the teaching of Jesus, which is given priority over the miracles.[153] The content of this "teaching" is rarely explicitly given, but clearly it includes the "mystery of the kingdom of God" in 4:1–34, the coming of the Son of Man in 13:3–37, and the predictions of the suffering, dying, and rising of the son of Man and the call to take up Jesus' cross in 8:31–38; 9:31

---

150. Peter Bolt, *Jesus' Defeat of Death: Persuading Mark's Early Readers* (SNTSMS 125; Cambridge: Cambridge University Press, 2003), argues that Mark's narrative poetics throughout aligns the implied readers with the suppliants in the scenes, which facilitates the actual readers' recognition of their own needs. The healing and exorcism stories portray the shadow of death that already falls on the suppliants, and their deliverance by Jesus already points ahead to God's final defeat of death in the resurrection of Jesus.

151. Contra, most famously, Theodore J. Weeden, *Mark—Traditions in Conflict* (Philadelphia: Fortress, 1971). See *Excursus: Markan Christology* at 9:1.

152. Günther Bornkamm, *The New Testament: A Guide to Its Writings* (trans. Reginald Fuller and Ilse Fuller; Philadelphia: Fortress, 1973), 47.

153. Shiner rightly speaks of Markan "parabolic miracles." "As with the parables, the miracles do not present a clear meaning on their surface. Their meaning must be teased out." Shiner, *Follow Me*, 216.

(specifically designated Jesus' "teaching"). The miracle stories are thus "relativized," not in the sense that their importance is minimized, but that the epiphany Christology they represent must be related to the kenosis Christology of the cross / resurrection kerygma and its call to suffering discipleship. It is only faith in Jesus as the crucified and Risen One that allows one to see the miracle stories as pointing to the saving act of God. Mark thus makes the secrecy motif, already an aspect of some of the miracle stories, into a major hermeneutical key to their interpretation (see *Excursus: The Messianic Secret* at 9:13). The miracle stories are gospel, "good news," only as a constituent element of the Markan literary genre "Gospel."

7:1–23 Defilement—Traditional and Real

This sizeable pericope stands between a section in which Jesus has received widespread acclaim on the Jewish west bank and an extensive trip through Gentile regions. In the next scenes he will exorcize the daughter of a Gentile woman (7:24–30), heal a Gentile man (7:24–30), make a roundabout way through Gentile areas (7:31), and feed four thousand people in Gentile territory (8:1–10). Beginnings in Gentile territory have already been made (4:35–41; 5:1–20; cf. on 6:45), but now as Jesus prepares for an extensive "Gentile mission," the purity issue must first be resolved. The Markan church, predominantly Gentile, struggles with not only the issues that separate them from the Jewish community but the problem of table fellowship among Jewish and Gentile Christians in its own midst. The author here takes up traditional materials from and about Jesus and retells them with this situation in view. "Some" of Jesus' disciples were eating without observing the rules of ritual purity—which means that some were observant (v. 2). The conflict addressed is not between "Christians" and "Jews," but an internal tension among Jesus' own disciples. This section is thus not a digression, but fits into the 6:6b–8:21 section oriented to discipleship and mission.

> 7:1 And the Pharisees and some of the scribes who had come from Jerusalem[a] are gathering around him. 2 And when they saw some of his disciples eating the loaves with ritually unclean hands,[b] that is, without washing them— 3 for the Pharisees and all the Jews do not eat without washing the hands "with the fist,"[c] adhering to the tradition of the elders, 4 and when they come from the marketplace[d] they do not eat without first immersing themselves,[e] and they adhere to many other things they have received from their tradition, the immersion of cups, pots and pans, even beds—[f] 5 And the Pharisees and scribes were asking him, "Why do your disciples not walk[g] according to the tradition of the elders, but eat with ritually unclean hands?"
> 6 He said to them, "How well did Isaiah prophesy about you, you hypocrites, as it is written, 'This people honors me with their lips, but their

hearts are far from me; 7 they worship me in vain, teaching human commandments as doctrines.' 8 You have abandoned the commandment of God and adhere to the tradition of human beings." 9 And he was saying to them, "How good you are[h] at rejecting the commandment of God in order to establish[i] your own tradition! 10 For Moses said, 'Honor your father and your mother,' and 'The one who curses[j] father or mother must surely die.' 11 But you say, 'If a person says to father or mother, "Whatever support you might have received from me is 'corban'[k] (that is, a gift already dedicated to God), 12 you no longer permit that person to do anything for a father or mother, 13 thereby making the word of God null and void by your tradition that you hand on. And you do many such things."

14 And he again called the crowd, and was saying to them, "Listen to me, all of you, and understand. 15 There is nothing that can enter a person from outside and defile that person. But the things that come out of a person are the things that defile a person." [16][l]

17 And when he had gone into a house away from the crowd, his disciples were asking him about the parable. 18 And he says to them, "So you don't understand either? You surely know, don't you, that everything entering a person from outside is unable to make that person ritually unclean, 19 because it does not enter the heart but the stomach, and goes out into the latrine?" (By saying this he declared[m] all foods clean.) 20 And he was saying, "It is what comes out of a person that defiles. 21 For it is from within, from people's hearts, that evil intentions come: sexual sins, thefts, murders, 22 adulteries, acts of greedy selfishness, malicious acts in general, deceit, indecency, an evil eye, slanderous talk, pride, arrogant rejection of God.[n] 23 All these evil things come from within, and they defile a person."

a. The Greek syntax does not make clear whether only the scribes or also the Pharisees come from Jerusalem. In any case, in Mark the scribes from Jerusalem provide the continuity between opposition to Jesus in Galilee and his crucifixion in Jerusalem, in which Pharisees are not directly involved.

b. The adjective *koinos* means "common," which in general Hellenistic Greek would be understood as "shared," "public" (cf. *Koinē* Greek as the common language). In Jewish usage, as here, it is contrasted with "holy, sanctified, ritually pure." Mark explains to his Gentile readers that it means "unwashed."

c. *Pygmē* is lit. "with the fist," but the meaning is unclear (hence ‭א‬ W and some ancient translations read *pykna*, "often," an obvious scribal "correction" of a difficult text). Though the original *text* is virtually certain, the *meaning* is far from clear (see commentary).

d. The words "when they come" are not in the best Greek MSS (only D W and a few others representing the "Western" text, and most of the Latin tradition). The phrase *ap' agoras*, "from the marketplace," alone can imply either "what has been purchased in the marketplace" or "when one comes from the marketplace."

e. Most MSS, including some of the earliest and most reliable, have a form of *baptizō* here, adopted by N-A²⁶⁻²⁷ and GNT⁴, though N-A²⁵ and GNT³ had followed the reading of ℵ B and a few other MSS, *rantizō,* "sprinkle, wash." The basic meaning of *baptizō* is "immerse." A derived meaning "wash ceremonially for the purpose of purification" is given in the standard lexicon (Bauer and Danker, BDAG, 164), but documented only by Mark 7:4 and Luke 11:38. The many mikvehs (ritual baths for immersion) revealed by archaeology confirm the prevalence of ritual immersion in Judaism. Since the practice was not understood by later scribes, who also may have wished to avoid any confusion of Jewish ritual ablutions with Christian baptism, *rantizō* is more likely a later substitution for *baptizō* than vice versa.

f. *Kai klinōn* ("even beds") is missing from 𝔓⁴⁵ (apparently) ℵ B L, but is also well attested. It is likely original, and omitted by some scribes unacquainted with Jewish practice who had difficulty imagining the purification of beds by dipping them in water. Of course, four-posters are not in view, but sleeping mats that had become ritually unclean by bodily emissions including semen and menstrual blood. The *kai* is best translated "even," and expresses a note of Markan sarcasm. After the long parenthesis, the incomplete sentence of vv. 2–4 breaks off and Mark begins afresh in v. 5.

g. *Peripateō* means "walk," and reflects the Jewish terminology of Halakah, the rules for living ("walking"), related to the verb for walk / live, *hālak.*

h. Translating *kalōs,* the same word translated "well" in v. 6, but here used ironically.

i. The reading of some form of *krateō,* "adhere to, hold fast," as in v. 8, is well attested in the MSS, including ℵ A B and most later MSS, but the reading *stēsēte,* "establish," also has good MSS support. Since it is more likely that scribes would have made v. 9 conform to v. 8 than vice versa, *stēsēte* is preferable here. While the difference in meaning is not great, establishing human tradition over against God's command is the more serious charge.

j. While *kakologeō* can mean merely "revile, speak evil of," the Old Testament context indicates "pronounce a curse against" is the intended meaning (Exod 21:17).

k. "Corban" is a Hebrew and Aramaic word (*qorban*) derived from the root *qrb,* "bring near," i.e., "offer" (to God). It became a technical term of Jewish practice, which Mark found necessary to explain to his Greek-speaking readership.

l. "If anyone has ears to hear with, that person had better listen" (cf. 4:9) is found in A D W Θ *f* ¹, ¹³ and most later MSS, but is missing from ℵ B L Δ* and others. It is apparently a scribal addition by a copyist who rightly recognized the similarity between the parable discourse of 4:1–34 and 7:1–23.

m. The Textus Receptus on which the KJV was based followed a few late MSS in reading the neuter participle *katharizon,* which would refer to the preceding infinitive clause, and thus mean that it is the process of digestion and elimination that purifies food. The masculine participle *katharizōn* is certainly original, referring to Jesus as the one who purifies food. The participle is adverbial of manner or means. Since there is no nominative singular masculine word in Jesus' speech to which the participle can refer, it must be a parenthetical statement from the narrator, as punctuated above.

n. *Aphrosynē* is lit. "foolishness," but the context indicates the biblical sense is intended, in which the "fool" is not necessarily lacking in native intelligence but is guilty of arrogant rejection of God (see 1 Sam 13:13; Pss 10:3–4; 14:1 and often in Proverbs and Ecclesiastes; for New Testament usage, see Matt 5:22; 23:17; Luke 11:40; 12:20; Rom 1:22; 1 Cor 15:36).

[7:1–2] The story now takes a sinister turn, again taking up the thread of 2:1–3:30 in which some Jewish leaders had decisively rejected Jesus. He has already been opposed by scribes (2:6, 16; 3:22) who had objected to his eating practices, accused him of blasphemy, and charged him with operating by the power of Satan (2:6, 16; 3:22). Though there were scribes sympathetic to Jesus (12:28–34), these scribes from Jerusalem foreshadow those who will be involved in his condemnation to the cross (11:18; 14:1, 43; 15:1, 31). The scribes' objection is thus no trivial matter. From their point of view, faulty practice on this point could introduce ritual contamination into the whole community. The Mishnah later reports that a rabbi who challenged a ruling of the sages on cleanness of hands, Eliezer b. Hanokh, was excommunicated (*m. ʿEd.* 5:6), and the revered rabbi Akiba ate nothing while imprisoned rather than renounce the ritual washing prescribed by tradition (*b. ʿErub.* 21b, cited Strack and Billerbeck, *Kommentar*, 1:702).

[3–5] In the long parenthesis of verses 3–4, the narrator further explains Jewish customs to the Gentile majority of his audience. "The Pharisees and all the Jews" is a generalizing exaggeration. The statement is not technically correct, since many segments of the Jewish population (e.g., Sadducees and the common people, the *ʿam haʾareṣ*) did not adhere to the strict practice of the Pharisees, and it is disputed how widespread the practice was in the first century even among the observant population. Nonetheless, it is the kind of expression also found among Jews when explaining their practices to outsiders (e.g., *Let. Aris.* 305). Here, in the only occurrence of "the Jews" except for the repeated "king of the Jews" in the Passion Narrative, the phrase has a distancing effect.

The precise meaning of washing the hands "with the fist" (lit. translation; see note *c* above) is not known. It is a technical expression of how properly to hold the hands during the ritual washing, and it may (1) mean that water must be poured on the hands covering the whole fist, up to the wrist, or (2) prescribe how much water—a precious commodity—must be used; that is, a cupped handful, or (3) prescribe the proper position in which the hands must be held as water is poured over them. The issue was later elaborated and regulated in the Mishnah (*Yad.* 2:1–4). While the precise regulations of the Mishnah were not in force in Jesus' or Mark's time, the issue was already a live one, and some such rules had already been developed by some groups. The rules do not come directly from the written Torah, which prescribed handwashing rituals only for the priests. The Pharisaic movement understood all Israel to be a priestly community (cf. Exod 19:6) and was encouraging all Israel to live by the holiness code prescribed for priests. The narrator explains that Pharisees and scribes understood this as adherence to the "tradition of the elders," made explicit in their own words in verse 5. The narrator further explains that it is not merely a matter of handwashing: when observant Jews return from the marketplace, they will not eat without taking a ritual bath (cf. Luke 11:38), and they have water purification rituals for household furnishings. Even before Jesus responds, what began as a criticism of one item of ritual practice has been generalized to become a matter of the validity of the "tradition of the elders" as such.

[6–13] As in 2:18–22, the disciples are criticized, but Jesus responds; both scenes represent the practice of the post-Easter Gentile church, criticized by Jewish and Jewish-Christian objectors, with appeal to the authority of Jesus to settle the issue.

[6–8] Jesus' defense is to go on the attack. Once again Isaiah is quoted as the key biblical prophet. In 1:2–3 the narrator cites a combination of texts including Isa 40:3 as "Isaiah," identifying Jesus with the Lord who speaks in Scripture; in 4:12 the Markan Jesus incorporates key words of Isa 6:9–10 as his own words. Here, Jesus explicitly quotes Isa 29:13 as prophesying his own situation. From the point of view of those who asked the question, the citation is not altogether appropriate, since the issue they have raised is not worship with the lips versus worship from the heart, but ritual purification of the hands before eating. But since this practice is a matter of human tradition rather than divine command, from Mark's perspective the Isaiah text addresses the real issue. In the Hebrew text, at least in the form preserved in the MT (including the Qumran MSS), the problem is that Israel's worship is not from the heart but is a human commandment learned by rote. While it is possible to interpret the Hebrew text of Isaiah as supporting Mark's point, it is only the LXX that specifies the problem as teaching human commandments and doctrines. It is thus likely that verses 6–8, at least in their present form, reflect the Gentile church and its use of the LXX.

[9–13] The new introductory formula *kai elegen autois* (and he was saying to them; see on 2:27) suggests the combination of originally independent elements of tradition (cf. 2:27; 4:1–2, 11, 21; 6:10; 9:1). The modern reader should not reduce the whole matter to a common-sense choice between moral and ritual law, or devotion from the heart versus external religiosity, or Scripture versus tradition in the sense of the older Protestant polemic against Roman Catholicism. "Word of God" does not here mean "Bible," but God's command at Sinai mediated through Moses (Exod 20:12; 21:17; Deut 5:16; Lev 20:9). What began as a challenge regarding handwashing ritual has escalated, from the side of the Markan Jesus, to a countercharge that the scribes and Pharisees reject God's command in order to establish their own tradition. Jesus illustrates his charge by citing the practice of declaring something "corban," that is, solemnly dedicated to God by means of an oath, and thus withdrawn from ordinary human use. The practice here presupposed indicates that it was possible for one who had dependent parents to declare property that could be used to support them as "corban"—unavailable for support of the parents because devoted to God, but still available for the person's own use. The details of this presumed arrangement are vague. No such practice in Jesus' day is known from Jewish sources, and it is likely that the purported arrangement is a matter of

Christian polemics. The Mishnah later discusses the issue of whether vows, which according to Scripture are supposed to be irrevocable (Num 30:2–4), could be changed in order to provide support for one's parents, and decides the issue in favor of changing the vow. The matter was possibly debated in Jesus' day, with the stricter Pharisees and scribes arguing that a vow could not be revoked even to help one's parents. This argument by some Jews could have provided ammunition for later Christian polemics. If so, the later rabbinic tradition came down on the same side of the issue as Jesus, or, said otherwise, the Markan Jesus represents the side of the debate among Jewish scholars that later prevailed (see *m. Ned.* 9.1–2; 5.6). The concluding charge that this is only an illustration of the "many such things" done by Jesus' challengers suggests that the debate has modulated from Jesus addressing Pharisees and scribes to a Christian charge against Jewish traditional practice in general. Thus, although at the narrative level Jesus is still addressing only the Pharisees and scribes, "this people" of verse 6 (= Isa 29:13) already applies to the people as a whole, as in its original context.

[14–23] While 6–13 charges the Jewish leaders / people with undermining the Scripture by their tradition, in 14–23 Jesus himself abrogates one of its key teachings. From Mark's Christian perspective, the contrast was not Scripture versus tradition, but word of God versus human tradition. From the Pharisees' perspective, the oral tradition was not "human tradition" that could be contrasted with "God's command," but was itself God's command revealed at Sinai and faithfully transmitted alongside Scripture (*Abot* 1.1). In the early Christian view represented by Mark, Jesus' teaching was not human tradition opposed to God's command, but itself represented God's command. Both Pharisaic Judaism and early Christianity agreed that Scripture alone was inadequate, but needed authoritative interpretation that itself functioned as word of God. The issue was whether this authoritative word was provided by the oral tradition that became the Mishnah or the person and teaching of Jesus as God's definitive word.

[14] The Pharisees and scribes disappear without a response, and the narrator introduces the crowd as a new audience, reminiscent of the procedure in 4:1–34, and reminding the reader especially of 4:11–12 and the theology of Isa 6:9 associated with it. Jesus' call to "listen" and "understand" suggests that the meaning does not lie on the surface, connects to the parable discourse, and prepares for the explicit reference to the present instruction as *parabolē* in verse 17. The addition of "me" (cf. 4:9) already intimates that it is Jesus' authority that is the decisive issue, not common-sense wisdom—not merely careful, perceptive listening, but listening to Jesus who speaks with the authority of God, not merely as interpreter of the Torah, but as "Lord of the Sabbath" (2:28), one who can overrule it. Whatever else the statement might mean, it seems to present Jesus as abolishing not only the cultic rules of Jewish tradition, but the distinction between clean and unclean foods declared by the Scripture itself. At the narrative level, "all" is a call

to the crowds to hear and understand, but since Jesus' teaching is here called a "parable," the reader might think of 4:10–12, which declares the crowds to be incapable of the true understanding that can come only as a further gift from Jesus himself (4:10–12; cf. also v. 18, which presupposes that the crowds do not understand). The readers, who look and listen over the shoulders of the crowd, know that they are the true addressees of Jesus' word (cf. 13:37).[154]

[15] This statement, in antithetic parallelism, is a comprehensive declaration occasioned by the original challenge, but not a direct response to it. The issue posed by the Pharisees and scribes had to do with unclean hands; this manifesto speaks of unclean foods, but not in a way to distinguish clean from unclean, even in a radically new way. Instead, the distinction itself is abolished, and a complete change of orientation is called for, as in Jesus' parables and his call for repentance. In the Markan form, *nothing* (*ouden*) entering *can* (*dynatai*) defile, but *the things coming forth from the person* (*ta ek tou anthrōpou ekporeuomena*) do in fact defile—presumably all things and all people. So understood, the Markan Jesus declares that in fact all people are defiled—not by what they eat and drink, but by what they will and say and do.

[17–23] As in 3:20–4:13, Jesus' audience changes from Jerusalem challengers, to the crowds, then to his disciples for private instruction, and here as there Jesus expresses surprise that his disciples do not understand. The topic of the debate has likewise shifted from *how* to eat (washed vs. unwashed hands) to *authority* for making such decisions (word of God vs. tradition of the elders) to *what defiles* (what goes in vs. what comes out; the stomach vs. the heart; food vs. intentions and acts). This results in a comprehensive declaration from the narrator that all food is clean and a sample list of "what comes out" of the heart that defiles.

[17–19] The crowds, who have not been given the secret of Jesus' teaching, cannot understand, but when Jesus asks "So you don't understand either?" the disciples are slipping into the same category as the "outsiders" (see on 4:10–12). Their situation will become progressively worse (cf. 6:52; 8:17–21). Jesus' explanation that it is not what "goes in" but what "comes out" that defiles sounds at first as though the subject is still food and what happens to it in the digestive process. The Hebrew Scriptures sometimes considered human excrement as ritually unclean (cf. Deut 23:12–14; Ezek 4:12–14), and rabbis later decided the disputed issue by declaring that excrement does not ritually defile. Thus the reader's initial impression is that Jesus is making use of this Jewish

154. In the present context, the reader might well suppose that the crowd can indeed understand. Cf. Heikki Räisänen, *The 'Messianic Secret' in Mark* (Edinburgh: T. & T. Clark, 1990), 126: "7:14 is thus diametrically opposed to the viewpoint of 4:12." However, Mark's "parable theory" as an element of the messianic secret is not intended to present a consistent historical view of the "life of Jesus," and does not do so (see *Excursus: The Messianic Secret* at 9:13).

principle by declaring that whatever one eats is cleansed when voided into the latrine, and thus one need not worry about eating "unclean" foods. Jesus' explanation, however, turns out to be on another level. No food can defile because it enters only the stomach and has no effect on the "heart"—the center of thinking and willing that determines the real character of a person. The narrator then draws the comprehensive and revolutionary conclusion that Jesus had thereby declared all foods to be clean. This is no longer only a challenge to "human tradition," as in 7:1–13, but an abrogation of the teaching of the Scripture itself (cf. the food laws of Lev 7:26–27; 11:1–47; 19:26; Deut 12:21–25). Neither "explanation" should be understood as rationalistic common sense, as though Jesus is presenting the enlightened teaching that the idea of ritual uncleanness caused by eating the "wrong" food had always been a mistake. The Scripture and Jewish tradition had never taught that some foods were inherently unclean; it was the command of God that made them unclean "for you" (cf. Lev 11; Deut 14:1–21). Thus the real point of the paragraph is not the presentation of an enlightening explanation, but the authority of Jesus.

God had originally declared some foods to be unclean in order to mark Israel out as a holy people distinct from "the nations." Like circumcision and Sabbath observance, the food laws were not a merely a matter of personal, individualistic piety, but were divinely given identity markers of Israel as the people of God. Men and women had died, and had seen their children killed, in order to preserve Israel's witness to the nations (Dan 1–6; 1 Macc 1; 2 Macc 6–8; 4 Macc 5–12). To surrender these identity markers would be unfaithfulness to the command of God and to surrender Israel's God-given mission to the whole world. In Mark's view, as God had originally declared some foods to be unclean for Israel, so Jesus is now acting with the authority of God to declare that all foods are clean, thereby breaking down one of the barriers that separated Jewish from Gentile Christians and facilitating the church's Gentile mission. The language is not descriptive but performative; not explaining what has always been the case, but changing the situation by Jesus' authoritative declaration. In all this, Jesus does not set aside the Law as such; he has already cited the Torah as God's word in this same context, identifying the Law of Moses as the word of God (vv. 9–13). Nor does Mark deal thematically with the place of the law in God's plan and its role in salvation, as Paul does. The point is not to set aside the law but to do the will of God. His focus is on one point at issue in his church, where Christians were charged by their Jewish neighbors with setting aside the word of God (in the Torah) in order to keep their own tradition.[155] Mark responds that

155. This was probably not only a response to criticism from outside. Jewish Christians charged their Gentile Christian brethren with relaxing the command of God in Scripture; conscientious Gentile Christians may too have asked, "Why is it that we do not keep the food laws pronounced by the word of God in our Bible?"

because of Jesus' authoritative word, no Christian, Jewish or Gentile, needs to be concerned that eating certain foods will defile them and make them unacceptable to God. This does not mean that Jesus is presented as the advocate of the modern secularized view that "there is nothing to this defilement business anyway." People can still be defiled, yet defilement is not a matter of eating the wrong food, but a matter of the heart, the intentions and actions that proceed from it.

[20–23] Just as human beings are not victimized and made unclean by what enters them from outside, so they are not made morally unclean by external forces. Despite Mark's awareness and concentration on the role of demons in this rebellious world, he does not here attribute human sinfulness to victimization by demonic powers. Human beings are responsible; it is from their own hearts that sin pours forth (cf. Gen 6:5; 8:21; Pss 55:21; 66:18; 78:18). Mark explicates this by presenting a "vice catalogue," a common means of moral instruction in Stoicism and other Hellenistic philosophies, adapted by Hellenistic Judaism, and then further adapted by early Christianity. There are no other examples in the Gospels (except the parallel in Matt 15:19), but the New Testament epistolary literature has several vice catalogues (Rom 1:29–31; 1 Cor 6:9–10; 2 Cor 12:20; Gal 5:19–21; 1 Tim 1:9–10; 2 Tim 3:2–4; 1 Pet 4:3). Thus "following Jesus" is not a rejection of the law and an invitation to antinomianism. The Markan ethic here presented is not an attack on the law or the purity system as such, but an assertion of what it is that truly defiles.[156] *That* this is true is not a matter of secularized common sense but is christologically grounded in the declaration of the Holy One of God (see on 1:24), who is himself God's agent of purity and cleanness.

The list is not random; it has some structure. Twelve specific evils are framed by the general designations "evil intentions" (v. 21) and "evil things" (v. 23).

---

156. Neyrey, "Purity," 116, offers a helpful summary of the Markan Jesus' alternative to the purity system of the Pharisees.

Pharisees et al.	**Jesus and His Followers**
1. Purity rules are extended to 613 laws, the tradition of the "fence" around the Law.	1. Purity rules are concentrated in the core law, the Ten Commandments.
2. Purity concerns focus on the washing of hands, cups, pots, vessels—external and surface areas.	2. Purity concerns are focused on the heart—interior and core areas.
3. Purity rules prevent uncleanness from entering.	3. Purity rules guard against uncleanness that is within from coming out.
4. Purity resides in specific external actions relating to hands and mouths.	4. Purity resides in a person's interior, in faith and right confession of Jesus.
5. Purity rules are particularistic, separating Israel from its unclean neighbor.	5. Purity rules are inclusive, allowing Gentiles and the unclean to enter God's kingdom.

The initial six items are in the plural, denoting repeatable actions, with the final six entries in the singular, pointing more to traits of character. Although the catalogue is directed to sins against other people, actions that damage relationships and community, the list begins with *porneia* "sexual sins" associated in biblical and Jewish tradition with idolatry, the primal sin against God. Likewise, the list concludes with *aphrosynē,* often translated "foolishness," but in biblical and Jewish tradition understood as the arrogant rejection of God. None of this should be understood as an attempt to contrast "Jewish external ritualism" with Christianity's making religion a matter of attitude and the heart. Doing the will of God is the issue, and both sincere Jews and sincere Christians were concerned to do God's will from the heart. The issue in Mark's church was whether the will of God was revealed in the Torah as interpreted in the oral tradition, also understood to be from God, or whether the will of God was revealed in the Torah as interpreted by Jesus, the ultimate revelation of God's will. Jesus' pronouncement did not absolve his followers from guilt, but universalized it: all are defiled. Though some can avoid ritual impurity by strict adherence to the rules, no one can avoid these evils that arise from the human heart. Yet the paragraph does not function strictly in the Pauline sense to show that all people are guilty and in need of God's grace (Rom 1:18–3:21), but as parenesis urging the reader to avoid those things that truly defile.

Excursus: Jesus the Teacher versus the Scribes

Only Jesus is called "teacher," only he and those he authorizes are represented as teaching,[157] and "teacher" is his own self-designation (14:14; see "Teacher" in *Excursus: Markan Christology* at 9:1). In his first public appearance as teacher, he is set over against the scribes (1:22). Jesus teaches and is called rabbi, but he is not a scribe. "Scribe" does not refer merely to the literate class of professional secretaries who composed and copied documents. The Jewish scribes are the authoritative interpreters of the Scripture and authorized teachers of Jewish tradition (cf. 2:6; 9:11; 12:35),[158] who also functioned in judicial situations.

Scribes are more prominent in Mark than in any of the other gospels or in Jewish literature generally; they are not mentioned at all in Josephus, Philo, Q, or the Fourth Gospel. Historically, scribes could be Pharisees, Sadducees, or neither, but most were Pharisees or sympathized with the Pharisaic interpretation of the law. In Mark's narrative the scribes are distinguished from the Pharisees and associated with Jerusalem and

---

157. Significantly, sixteen of the seventeen usages of the verb *didaskō* have Jesus as subject, and all are in the present or imperfect tense representing continuing activity. The only exception is 6:30, where the Twelve report that they "taught" as part of their mission (aorist rather than imperfect), and they teach only by Jesus' authority. *Didachē* occurs four times, only of Jesus' teaching.

158. Anthony J. Saldarini, *Pharisees, Scribes and Sadducees in Palestinian Society: A Sociological Approach* (BRS; Grand Rapids: Eerdmans, 2001), 152: scribes were "the ordinary teachers with whom the people were familiar."

the Jewish leadership involved in Jesus' death (3:22; 7:1; 8:31; 10:33; 11:18, 27; 12:28, 35, 38; 14:1, 43, 53; 15:1, 31). Scribes form the narrative continuity in the opposition to Jesus. Pharisees are prominent in chapters 1–10, but they have no role in the passion story. "Chief priests and elders" are absent from Galilee but the leading opponents in Jerusalem. Of Jesus' opponents, only scribes are present throughout the Gospel. In Mark's situation, the question "Who are the authorized teachers of the people of God?" was clearly a live issue. This was the situation in the synagogues of Galilee and Syria during and in the aftermath of the 66–70 revolt. Mark presents Jesus as the authority; his opponents are the scribal teachers suspicious of the new Christian movement, attempting in the name of developing mainstream Judaism to discredit Christian teachers (such as Mark himself) and to encourage Christians to conform to emerging "normative Judaism."

7:24–30 The Syrophoenician Woman[159]

That Mark is a two-level drama is nowhere more apparent, or more important in understanding the text, than in his narrative of the Syrophoenician woman's encounter with Jesus. At one level, it is the story of a woman seeking help for her troubled daughter, and who, despite Jesus' initial refusal, attains it by her wit and tenacity. This level of the story is not to be minimized at the expense of the theological meaning of the story at the Markan level. Yet this latter dimension is the focus of Mark's attention: the afflicted daughter and her cure are not directly narrated, and the exorcism itself occurs offstage (contrast, e.g., 5:1–20). Contemporary interpreters are often interested in the story because the central figure (apart from Jesus) is a plucky woman; Mark includes the story because the central figure is a Greek and to illustrate an important aspect of the church's Gentile mission. The issue in this story is not primarily an incident in the biography of Jesus; it has to do with God's plan for history. The Markan narrative as a whole moves in the realm of the problems faced by the church as it moved from a Jewish sectarian renewal movement to a Christian church composed primarily of Gentiles (see Introduction.). This is particularly true of Mark 7. The historical Jesus conducted no Gentile mission.[160] As documented by the

---

159. See p. 5, note 4. David Rhoads, *Reading Mark, Engaging the Gospel* (Minneapolis: Fortress, 2004), 92–93, illustrates the hermeneutical function of giving titles by his sample list of pericope headings for 7:24–30: "Another Healing of the Kingdom"; "Exorcism from a Distance!"; "A Gentile with Faith"; "A Clever Foreigner"; "Finally, A Riddle Understood"; "A Foil for the Disciples"; "Jesus Changes His Mind"; "The Kingdom Shared with Gentiles"; "An Outsider Becomes an Insider"; "Crossing the Final Boundary"; "The Beginning of a Mission to Gentiles"; "Foreshadowing the Mission to the World"; "The Least Are the Greatest"; "The Family of God's Children is Extended"; "The Syrophoenician Woman." His list could be extended almost indefinitely, e.g., "Jesus Admits He Is Outwitted by a Gentile Woman"; "Don't Call Me a Dog!" etc. No title is merely a neutral label.

160. Cf., e.g., Matt 10:5–6; 15:24; Joachim Jeremias, *Jesus' Promise to the Nations* (SBT 24; Naperville, Ill.: Alec R. Allenson, 1958); T. W. Manson, *Only to the House of Israel? Jesus and the Non-Jews* (FBBS 9; Philadelphia: Fortress, 1964).

letters of Paul and Acts 2–15, it was a slow and painful process for the emerging church to become an integrated Christian community of Jews and Gentiles. By Mark's time, Gentile Christianity presupposed a worldwide Gentile mission (13:10; 14:9).

It is not incidental that the key figure in this story is female. In a patriarchal society that influenced the ways in which church life and leadership was conceived, the Spirit overcame the stereotypical male / female roles, and theology found itself attempting to catch up with the reality already created by the Spirit. The Spirit-led insights of Christian women had played a remarkable role in this transition, for, as the modern Pentecostal movement has illustrated, the Spirit transcends and breaks through traditions and institutional conventions. This dynamism of early Christianity forms part of the background of this pericope, and of Mark as a whole. Mark's story is told in the framework of the traditional understanding of salvation history, but in such a way that the explosive newness of God's act in Christ cannot wait. The gospel does not always wait for theology to catch up with it.

7:24 And from there he rose up[a] and went away into the region of Tyre.[b] And he entered a house and did not want anyone to know it, and he was not able to escape notice. 25 But immediately a woman whose daughter[c] had an unclean spirit heard about him, came and fell at his feet 26 (the woman was a Greek, Syrophoenician[d] by nationality), and she was asking him to cast the demon out of her daughter. 27 And he was saying to her, "Let first the children be fed,[e] for it is not right to take the children's bread[f] and throw it to the dogs." 28 But she responded to him, "Lord,[g] even the dogs under the table eat from the children's crumbs." 29 And he said to her, "Because of this saying,[h] go; the demon has come out of your daughter." 30 And she went away to her house and found the child lying on the bed, and the demon gone.

a. Most translations adopt here a rare meaning of *anistēmi*, "set out," "begin a new venture," but the reader should be aware that *anistēmi* is the normal word for "rising up," used repeatedly of Jesus' resurrection. At the narrative level, the word means simply that Jesus "set out" on a trip, but, as elsewhere, it is also a subtle reminder that the narrative, though ostensibly portraying events in the pre-Easter life of Jesus, also deals with post-Easter realities of church life.

b. Although "and Sidon" is found in most MSS, including both ℵ and B and several other of the oldest witnesses, this is best explained by assimilation to Matt 15:21 and the familiar phrase "Tyre and Sidon." The reading of D L W Δ Θ 28 565 it sy[s] and Or is thus adopted here.

c. The original text, probably represented by A B L and most later MSS, had an additional possessive pronoun corresponding to Semitic syntax, and read lit. "whose daughter of her." This and similar phenomena throughout Mark may indicate old tradition originating in Aramaic, or that tradition and / or redaction took place in an environment such as Syria where Greek was influenced by its Semitic linguistic context.[161]

d. As Greeks divided all people into Greeks and barbarians, i.e., non-Greeks, so Jews divided all people into Jews and non-Jews, for which "Greek" was a synonym in such contexts (cf., e.g., Acts 14:1; 19:10; Rom 1:16; 2:9–10; 1 Cor 1:22–24; 12:13; Gal 3:28; Col 3:11), connoting not only "Gentile" but "polytheist," "idolater," "unclean." She is called "Syrophoenician," belonging to Syrian Phoenicia, to distinguish her from Libyphoenicians of north Africa (Libyan Phoenicia).

e. The Greek word order is retained, though awkward in English, to retain the stress on "first."[162]

f. *Artos* is lit. "loaf" (of bread), but is often used generically of "food." It is here translated "bread" to preserve the allusion to the feeding stories and the imagery of "crumbs" that follows.

g. *Kyrios* can be translated as "Lord," "master," or "sir," and, like Spanish *señor*, French *seigneur*, German *Herr*, and Old English "Lord," is used of God (e.g., 12:36), human superiors (e.g., 12:9 NRSV, "owner"), and as a polite address (e.g., Matt 27:63, to Pilate). Mark's usage here seems to be intentionally ambiguous: the woman may mean either "Sir" or "Lord," but the post-Easter Christian reader knows that Jesus is indeed the Lord. Most MSS, including א B and several other ancient and reliable witnesses, include *nai* ("yes") before *kyrios*, but this is likely an assimilation to Matt 15:27 and, as in Matthew, a moderation of the woman's sharp reply.

h. "Saying" translates *logos*, a substantial term used by Mark for the comprehensive message of Jesus himself (2:2; 4:33) and the message about him (1:45; 9:10) as well as for his own incisive one-liners (10:22; 11:29) and for the word of God (7:13). Here the *logos* of the woman stands over against that of Jesus, and he finally acknowledges that it is valid.

Although the pericope has some of the features of an exorcism or miracle story, formally its closest affinity is with dialogue or conflict stories. In particular, it is formally very close to the story of healing the Gentile centurion's son / slave in Matt 8:5–13. The general pattern is the same: a Gentile takes the initiative to approach Jesus and addresses him with *kyrie,* requests healing for a member of the family, receives a critical rebuff from Jesus (Matt 8:7 is to be punctuated as a question) but will not be put off, persisting with an insightful repartee on the basis of which Jesus' initial reluctance is overcome, and Jesus finally heals the afflicted person from a distance. Both stories deal with the relation of Jews and Gentiles in the context of confessing Jesus as Lord; the miracle is in each case almost incidental.

---

161. Cf. Elliott C. Maloney, *Semitic Interference in Marcan Syntax* (SBLDS 51; Chico, Calif.: Scholars Press, 1981).

162. See Rhoads, *Reading Mark*, 197, who uses this an example of the difference between translating for a silent readership (most translations) and translation for an oral presentation to a listening audience.

The larger literary context of this pericope is particularly important. Not only does it immediately follow the crucial episode in which Jesus authoritatively declares that the traditional and biblical restrictions forbidding fellowship between Jews and Gentiles are no longer valid, it is situated between the "Jewish" feeding story of 6:35–44 and the "Gentile" feeding story of 8:1–9, which the narrator has specifically indicated point to a deeper meaning regarding the ministry of Jesus as a whole—a meaning the disciples do not yet grasp (6:52; 8:14–21). But the Gentile woman in this story grasps it, presses her insight with persistent determination, and prevails.

[24] Mark locates the story on Gentile soil. The woman is Gentile, but Mark could have set the story in Galilee, for example, in connection with 3:7–12. By moving the story into the "region of Tyre" the narrator is giving more than a geographical reference. Tyre was a Gentile city, represented in the Bible as the traditional enemy of Jews and stereotypical oppressor of God's people destined for divine retribution. But Tyre also aided in the construction of the temple and was sometimes promised participation in eschatological salvation (1 Kgs 5:1, 7:13; 9:11; Pss 83:5–10; 87:3–6; Isa 23; Ezek 26–28; Joel 3:4–8; Amos 1:9–10; Tyre is also included in the oracle of Zech 9, which plays a role in Mark; cf. 11:2; 14:24). In Mark's day, the Jewish population of Galilee had suffered and continued to suffer at the hands of the powerful urban center that dominated northern Galilee economically (cf. Theissen, *Gospels in Context,* 71). The poor farmers of Galilee saw the products of their labor become bread on the tables of wealthy Tyrians. "Bread" was thus a potent economic symbol as well as having deep theological overtones. Tyrian coinage was used in Galilee. During the 66–70 revolt, Tyrian troops served Rome in the devastation of Galilee, and many Jewish civilians were murdered in pogroms in the city of Tyre, described by Josephus as "our most bitter enemies" (*Ag. Ap.* 1.70). The woman who approaches Jesus thus does not represent the "poor and the outcast . . . one of the poorest of the poor,"[163] but a dominant, oppressive group.

When Jesus enters a house in Gentile territory, Mark may understand this to be a Jewish home, for there were many such in the regions of Tyre. However, since this story immediately follows the discussion of purity rules in 7:1–23, the narrator more likely intends it as a Gentile home (cf. Acts 10:23b–29).

---

163. As previously interpreted by Sharon H. Ringe, "A Gentile Woman's Story," in *Feminist Interpretation of the Bible* (ed. Letty M. Russell; Philadelphia: Westminster, 1985), 64, now retracted in her rereading of the story that acknowledges the woman to represent the "elite economic class" ("A Gentile Woman's Story, Revisited: Rereading Mark 7:24–31a," in *A Feminist Companion to Mark* [ed. Amy-Jill Levine and Marianne Blickenstaff; Cleveland: Pilgrim Press, 2004], 89; cf. 81, 84, 86). Cf. Miller, *Women in Mark's Gospel,* 92: "She is portrayed as a member of the Hellenistic world, cultured and wealthy," while Jesus is one of the Galileans who "went hungry in times of food shortage in order to supply the people of Tyre." This gives bite to Jesus' question of whether it is right to take food from Jewish children in order to feed the "dogs" of Tyre.

Jesus' entering a house also evokes the image of the house churches of Mark's time (cf. on 1:29–34; 2:1–2, 15; 3:20–21; 4:10–11). Jesus' desire to avoid publicity should not be interpreted in biographical or psychological terms as though Jesus were tired or seeking a quiet place to instruct his disciples, but as an aspect of the messianic secret. The similar note in 9:30–31 relates Jesus' ministry to the cross and resurrection as the framework within which his miracles must be understood. In Mark's view, Jesus performed the mighty acts of God's salvation during his earthly ministry, but his intention was that these remain "hidden" until after the resurrection. Yet Mark knows that despite Jesus' intent, such stories circulated as testimony to the power of God at work in him. Thus the narrator's note that Jesus was "not able to escape notice" both acknowledges that his mighty power could not be concealed and that this was against Jesus' intent. Mark regards such stories as proleptic. As this story illustrates, the diachronic scheme of pre-Easter hiddenness / post-Easter revelation is analogous to the scheme pre-Easter mission to Israel / post-Easter mission to Gentiles. Yet the chronological scheme is not absolute. Like the messianic secret, the priority of Israel in God's plan has a temporal limit to be overcome after the fundamental turning point of the cross and resurrection. Both diachronic schemes are "broken" by the synchronic reality that corresponds to the already / not yet character of the kingdom of God and the Christ-event itself.

[25–26] The woman is unnamed, which is typical for the recipients of God's mercy in the Markan miracle stories; later tradition named her Justa and her daughter Bernice (*Ps.-Clem Hom* 2:19; 3:73). That she belongs to the wealthy Tyrian urban class is indicated not only by the results of social-historical studies, but by characterizing her house as having a *klinē* ("bed," 7:30 [contrast the *krabatton* of poor people, as in 2:11]) and a *trapeza* (a table under which household pets can play, cf. Luke 16:19–31). She is specifically identified as a Gentile (cf. note above), the only person for whom Jesus performs a miracle clearly so identified.[164] Like Jairus in 5:23, who also pleads for his daughter, the woman bowed down at Jesus' feet, asking him to expel the demon from her daughter.

[27] Jesus' initial rejoinder is shocking and offensive to the modern reader, just as it was also unexpected to the ancient reader, in view of Jesus' positive response to women, Gentiles, and wealthy people in authority throughout the Gospel (cf. 1:29–31; 5:1–43; 10:17–22; 11:17; 14:3–9). The harshness should not be mitigated by attempted explanations that "dogs" is a diminutive in Greek ("puppies") and not intended seriously, so that Jesus was attempting to dismiss the woman's request with a joke (Iersel, *Mark*, 250), that he spoke with a knowing smile, twinkle in his eye, or a stage wink, intending all along to grant the

---

164. The demoniac healed by Jesus in 5:1–20 is in Gentile territory, but may have been a Jew. There, Jesus only went to the eastern lakeshore before returning to clearly Jewish territory.

request,[165] that he was testing the woman's faith[166] or that his comment was a provocative, parabolic means of evoking a further, deeper response from the woman.[167] The following comments are not intended to excuse or defend, but to facilitate understanding of Mark's theological point.

(1) The opening word, *aphes,* translated "let" in verse 27 above, strikes an authoritative note since it comes from the Markan Jesus, but also has the tone of a respectful request. It is not found elsewhere in Mark, but compare use of the identical word in Matt 3:15, 7:4; Luke 13:8; John 12:7.

(2) *Prōton* used adverbially as "first," "in the first place," is not an absolute rejection, but a relative prioritizing. It points to the election of Israel as God's people, a biblical perspective that Mark does not abandon. It reflects Christian declarations of the priority of Israel in salvation history, including specific statements that the gospel is to be proclaimed first to the Jews, then to the Greeks / Gentiles (Acts 3:26; 13:46; Rom 1:16; 2:9–10; chs. 9–11; 15:8–9; Eph 1:1–13; 2:11–22). It points to the history of the church already experienced by Mark's community, namely that Jesus limited his ministry to Jews, that the church began within Judaism and became a predominantly Gentile religious community only after the death and resurrection of Jesus. Far from suggesting a supersessionism, Jesus' statement maintains the priority of Israel without excluding Gentiles. Mark's readers can affirm this priority without denying it had a temporal limit. They live in the postresurrection time predicted by the Markan

---

165. William Barclay, *The Gospel of Mark* (2d ed.; Daily Study Bible; Philadelphia: Westminster, 1956), 2:122: "We can be quite sure that the smile on Jesus' face and the compassion in his eyes robbed the words of all insult and bitterness." A. E. J. Rawlinson, *St. Mark* (WC; London: Methuen, 1960), 99: "the words are probably spoken half whimsically, and with a smile; there was that in his manner which encouraged the woman to persist; he wanted to see what she would say if he affected to adopt the conventional Jewish point of view." I. Hassler, "The Incident of the Syrophoenician Woman (Matt XV, 21–28; Mark VII, 24–30)," *ExpTim* 45 (1934): 460: Jesus winked as he spoke. Floyd V. Filson, *A Commentary on The Gospel According to St. Matthew* (HNTC; New York: Harper & Brothers, 1960), 180: "His blunt answer is . . . a proverbial statement, used to make clear that his work was with his own people. Its effect would depend much on the speaker's tone and facial expression. The woman senses that his word is not final. . . ."

166. Manson, *Only to the House of Israel,* 22–23; Marcus, *Mark 1–8,* 468, following Petr Pokorný, "From a Puppy to a Child: Some Problems of Contemporary Biblical Exegesis Demonstrated from Mark 7.24–30 / Matt 15.21–28," *NTS* 41 (1995): 328; both tend toward Luther's dictum that such passages seeming to indicate divine refusal teach us to look for the "yes" hidden in God's "no" (WA 17/2.200–204; cf. discussion in Haenchen, *Der Weg Jesu,* 272).

167. France, *Gospel of Mark,* 296: "He functions as what in a different context would be called 'devil's advocate' and is not disappointed to be 'defeated' in argument." While acknowledging that Jesus' response is "negative to the point of offensiveness" and that his explanation "does not remove the harshness of picturing Gentiles en masse as 'dogs'," he also puts quotes around Jesus being "persuaded" by the woman, whose repartee led to "victory."

Jesus, in which the elect people of God includes Jews and Gentiles (13:10, 20, 22, 27), but in the narrative world of 7:27 this is yet to come.

(3) *Tekna*, "children," is not invented ad hoc by Jesus as a metaphor for the Jewish people, but was biblical and traditional terminology (cf., e.g., Isa 63:8, which equates "children" [LXX *tekna*] and God's people—remembering the key role Isaiah plays in Markan theology).

(4) *Chortasthēnai*, translated "be fed," is different from the ordinary word for eating (*esthiō*, used twenty-seven times by Mark), and implies "be satisfied, filled up, eat to the full," something extraordinary in much of human history. Mark uses the term only in the two feeding stories (6:42; 8:4, 8), where he underlines their theological significance (6:52; 8:21!). In combination with *artos* ("loaf, bread, food"), which also has a fullness of symbolic meaning (cf. the profound elaboration in John 6!), the metaphor evokes the image of eschatological salvation. Israel is now being fed with eschatological salvation in the ministry of Jesus. After Easter, under the guidance of the Spirit, this salvation will come to the Gentiles as well.

(5) *Kynarion*, "dog," is the troublesome word, difficult for interpreters to imagine as said by the historical Jesus. The word is harsh, even for Mark. While the inserted vowel "i" makes it diminutive in form (somewhat like "doggie" in English), in Hellenistic Greek the diminutive was often used as simply the equivalent to "dog." The term is here, of course, used metaphorically. The Markan Jesus does not directly call the Gentile woman "dog," just as he does not directly call Jewish people "sheep" (Mark 6:34; 14:27; cf. the typical biblical use of this metaphor: Pss 44:11, 22; 74:1; 95:7; 100:3; Isa 53:6). While it is perhaps possible to use canine metaphors in a nonderogatory way (cf. English "underdog," "top dog," "every dog has its day"), Markan Jesus here taps into a long tradition found in some streams of biblical and Jewish tradition designating Gentiles as "dogs."[168] In the Bible and ancient Jewish tradition, dogs are not pets, beloved insiders to the household and participants in family life, but outsiders—scavengers, disdained as animals that eat unclean food.[169] Jews might throw leftover food out to be consumed by wild dogs, but would never have dogs "under the table" during the meal.[170] Hostility between Jewish

---

168. Cf., e.g., Matt 7:6, and the survey in Reinhard Feldmeier, "Die Syrophönizierin (Mk 7, 24–30)—Jesus 'verlorenes' Streitgespräch?" in *Die Heiden: Juden, Christen und das Problem des Fremden* (ed. Reinhard Feldmeier and Ulrich Heckel; WUNT 70; Tübingen: Mohr, 1994), 218–19.

169. Tob 6:2; 11:4 is a rare exception, suggesting to many interpreters a Hellenistic context for the story in general or even a reflection of Homer in particular (Odysseus's dog).

170. E.g., the Jewish document *Joseph and Aseneth* distinguishes scavenger dogs roaming the streets and countryside from Gentile house dogs (10.14), which also appear in Greek vase paintings. Cf. Sharyn Dowd, *Reading Mark: A Literary and Theological Commentary on the Second Gospel* (Macon: Smyth & Helwys, 2000), 77.

Galilee and Gentile Tyre would have made proverbial statements referring to Gentiles in canine terms particularly relevant in Mark's context. It is also important to see the proverbial nature of the saying, which portrays something about a situation as a whole and does not necessarily apply the metaphors within the proverb to the persons addressed.[171]

(6) The *chronology* of admission of the Gentiles to the blessings of God promised to Israel is the disputed point in the background of this pericope. Broad streams of biblical and Jewish tradition believed that the one God, creator of all, the God who had chosen Israel as his covenant people, would at the eschaton act to bring all people within the scope of divine blessing (cf., e.g., Isa 2:2–3; Mic 4:1–2; Isa 19:25; 25:6–8; LXX Isa 54:15; Dan 7:14; Amos 9:12; Zech 9:10; *Sib. Or.* 3.716–27, 772–75; *T. Benj.* 9.2; *1 En.* 10.21; 48.5; 90.33; *2 Bar.* 68.5; for rabbinic examples cf. Billerbeck 3:150–52). The Christ was expected to come at the eschaton, but for Christian faith Jesus was and is the Messiah who has already come into history rather than at its end; thus the issue in early Christian thought was how this eschatological inclusion of the Gentiles was to be understood in relation to the Christ event. Both Matthew and Luke can allow Jesus to have a ministry limited to Jews during his earthly life, with the risen Jesus commissioning his disciples to carry on a mission to all nations (Matt 28:18–20; Luke 24:45–47). Mark, for his own reasons (see on 16:1–8) recounts no appearances of the risen Jesus, and must compress the message of the risen Christ within the narrative of the earthly Jesus. He thus has Jesus declare that for the present the Jewish "children" are being "fed," but that later the Gentile "dogs" will also be "fed"—will be included in the messianic salvation.[172] While neither Jesus nor Mark created the derogatory metaphor, the originator of the story chose it because it was (unfortunately) particularly suited to illustrate the temporal theological point involved: from the Jewish point of view, wild dogs ate unclean food that was thrown to them *after* the family meal; they did not eat with and at the *same* time as the family itself. The Markan Jesus thus rejects both Jewish-Christian exclusivism ("the Gentiles get no 'bread' unless they become Jews first," requiring the ritually unclean "dogs" to become ritually clean "children" before they can have the children's bread) and Gentile supersessionism ("The Jewish 'bread' has been taken away from them and now given to us Gentiles"). But the metaphor is already intentionally crafted by the narrator to allow the woman to adapt it for her own (Markan) purpose, and she does

---

171. So LaVerdiere, *Beginning,* 1:202, who points out "You can lead a horse to water but you can't make it drink" and "A bird in the hand is worth two in the bush" as examples. Cf. also "Don't count your chickens before they hatch."

172. It may be that "dogs at the eschatological banquet" was already "a fixed image for the participation of righteous Gentiles in the eschatological blessings of Israel." See Marcus, *Mark 1–8,* 464, who cites *Midr. Ps* 4.11.

so. Clearly "bread" here represents the saving work of God in Christ as such, used sixteen times in the section 6:32–8:21, and only once thereafter (14:22!).

[28] The woman does not respond directly to the insulting term ("Don't call *me* a dog!"). She addresses him as *kyrios* (see note *g* above)—the only person in Mark to address Jesus with this title. This is not mere flattery or strategy, but indicates her acceptance of his authority, as had her initiative in coming to him in the first place. At the narrative level, the woman would be saying merely "Sir," but at the level of the Markan reader, it is an affirmation of the Christian confession of Jesus as Lord. The woman accepts Jesus' metaphor, including its affirmation that the "children" are "first," but in the process of accepting it and acknowledging Jesus' authority and power to heal, adapts it to her own need. A shift of imagery takes place in the course of the story. "Dog" in its Jewish context is an outsider, scavenger, unclean eater of unclean food. "Dog" in its Gentile context is an insider, a "member of the family" who, though not "at the table," still plays under it and benefits from the excess of the children's food, and without waiting until the meal is over. Despite acknowledging Jesus' lordship, she does not merely acquiesce ("whatever you say," "the will of the Lord be done"), but like Abraham, Moses, Job, and the biblical psalmists, argues with the Lord. She does not dispute the priority of Israel, but relativizes the diachronic scheme of "first to the Jews, then to the Greeks" by positing a synchronic alternative or supplement to it: the "dogs" do not *only* have to wait to be fed later ("not yet"), but *also* receive the overflow ("crumbs"; cf. commentary on 6:42; 8:8, 19–21) of the messianic extravagance even now ("already"). Jesus' original response had affirmed the traditional salvation history scheme; the woman's response is an affirmation of the already / not yet dialectic of the Christian faith as such. God does indeed have a plan for history, in which Gentiles will be eschatologically included, but God is not bound by this plan (see on 13:20 and diagram in *Excursus: Markan Christology*, p. 247).

[29–30] Jesus reverses his original response and acts on the basis of what the woman has said. Although Matthew correctly interprets the woman's persistence as "faith" (Matt 15:28), in Mark the healing is not a reward for the woman's persistence, and "faith" is not mentioned. The focus is on her statement (*logos*, see note *h* above). As in 13:19–20, the divine plan is changed, the messianic secret is broken but not shattered or abandoned, and the mercy of God triumphs over any theological expression of it. Here as elsewhere, Jesus functions in the role of divine Lord, and the woman represents suffering and imploring humanity. He is not forced against his will to deliver a girl from enslaving demonic power; he remains sovereign throughout. He is not "bested" in an argument, does not "capitulate," but, like God, does reverse a previous decision. The encounter is ultimately not male / female or Jew / Gentile, but divine / human, in which deity ultimately—though not immediately—responds to human need.

7:31–37 Jesus Heals a Man Who Was Deaf
and Impaired in Speech

7:31 And he returned from the region of Tyre and went through Sidon[a] to the Sea of Galilee through the region of Decapolis.[b] 32 And people are bringing to him a deaf man who could hardly speak,[c] and they are pleading with him to lay his hand on him. 33 And he took him away from the crowd by himself, put his fingers in his ears, and he spit and touched the man's tongue. 34 And he looked up into heaven, sighed deeply, and says to him, "Ephphatha" (which means "be opened"). 35 And immediately his ears were opened, and his tongue was freed from its bonds, and he was speaking clearly. 36 And Jesus commanded them to tell no one; but the more he commanded them, the more they proclaimed it. 37 And they were astounded beyond all measure, saying, "He has done everything well; he even makes the deaf to hear and the speechless to speak."

a. Reflecting the familiar expression for the "twin cities" (cf. Minneapolis / St. Paul, Buda / Pest, as in v. 24 some MSS connect Sidon with Tyre, reading "he returned from the region of Tyre and Sidon." But the above text is here preferred on the basis of its strong documentation (including א B D L Δ Θ *f*[13] 33 and many Old Latin MSS) and as representing the more difficult reading.

b. The Greek phrase can be translated so as to locate the Sea of Galilee "in the midst of the Decapolis" or as here, indicating the course of the journey.

c. The rare word *mogilalos* is found only here in Mark, and only in Isa 35:6 in the LXX, where it translates ʾ*illēm*, "mute." The Greek word does not mean inability to speak at all, but having a speech impediment, speaking incoherently.

In terms of both form and content, this story is very similar to the account of healing the blind man in 8:22–26, with which it forms something of a frame:[173] (1) the location of each is specified, in Gentile territory; (2) an anonymous group brings an afflicted person to Jesus, (3) pleading that (4) Jesus will lay his hands on the person. (5) Jesus takes the afflicted person away from the crowd and (6) heals him, (7) by touching him and (8) using saliva, then (9) commands the incident to be kept quiet or sends the afflicted person away from the crowd. (10) Both reflect the eschatological saving work of God as portrayed in Isa 35:5–6. The story of 8:22–26 is understood by the majority of interpreters as symbolic of Jesus' curing spiritual blindness; the similarity of the two stories suggests the validity of a similar approach to this story. The several features that

173. See Robert C. Tannehill, "The Disciples in Mark: The Function of a Narrative Role (1977)," in *The Interpretation of Mark* (ed. William R. Telford; 2d ed.; SNTI; Edinburgh: T. & T. Clark, 1995), 184, who points out that the story of the disciples' inability to see and hear (8:18) is framed by the stories of healing a deaf man and a blind man. Thus the 8:22–10:52 structure is overlapped by this one.

each story shares with standard healing stories in the Hellenistic world, making Jesus resemble the typical "divine man" of the Greco-Roman world,[174] may help to explain why neither Matthew nor Luke includes them in his Gospel. Mark has his own theological reasons, however, for retaining them, despite their openness to misunderstanding.

[31] In 7:24 Jesus had departed for the Gentile "region of Tyre." Here, using the same phrase, Mark narrates his return. It is a very indirect route. Though returning to Galilee in the south, Jesus first proceeds northward at least a day's journey to Sidon. Nothing is narrated as having occurred there, or during the extended roundabout trip to the east and then southward through the Decapolis region, ending up on the eastern shore of the Sea of Galilee. Even a superficial glance at a map will confirm that this is a difficult trip to imagine historically.[175] Mark's main point is not biographical or geographical, but theological, giving the reader the impression that Jesus himself had traveled through the territory in which Gentile churches existed in Mark's own time, giving them a kind of proleptic validation (see on 7:24–30 above).

[32] A person who is deaf and speech-impaired is brought to Jesus. In an oral-aural culture where most people could not read, the inability to hear was a more serious and isolating affliction than in visually oriented modern cultures. The Markan Jesus has repeatedly called for authentic hearing (4:3, 9, 20, 23, 24; 6:11; 7:14). Now, for the first time in the Gospel, Jesus heals a deaf person, showing that as the lack of hearing is divine judgment (cf. 4:10–12), so the ability to hear is divine gift; neither deafness nor perceptive hearing is simply a matter of human choice; each lies in the hand of the sovereign God (cf. Exod 4:11). So also the inability to speak coherently is a serious malady (cf. 9:5–6; 14:40) that only God can heal. There is no reference to the man's faith. This story as a whole reflects the promise of salvation in Isa 35:4–6, when "He [God] himself will come" and heal those who are deaf, blind, and lack understanding, and give them hearing, sight, and the power to speak clearly.

[33–34] Performing the healing miracle apart from the crowd, so that the healer's incantations and techniques could not be known, is a characteristic found in many Hellenistic miracle stories. However this feature may have been understood in the pre-Markan tradition, for Mark this characteristic is integral to his comprehensive messianic secret (see *Excursus: The Messianic Secret* at 9:13). Likewise, the use of touching with the fingers, application of saliva, sigh-

174. Pesch, *Markusevangelium*, 1:395, gives examples of similar healing techniques portrayed in both Jewish and pagan healing stories.
175. Mark seems not to know Palestinian geography very well, but this need not mean that he (or his initial readers) was far removed geographically. In a day prior to maps, few people had a mental picture of geographical relationships. The dissertation of H. R. Preuss, "Galiläa im Markus-Evangelium" (Göttingen, 1966) gives good evidence that most of Mark's geographical detail belongs to the tradition, and confusion or lack of geographical knowledge is expressed in the redaction.

ing (either as groaning during the struggle with the demon causing the affliction or drawing in the breath / spirit as a means of charging the healer with
charismatic power), and pronouncing strings of magic words are for Mark no
longer merely the techniques of Hellenistic magic; there are overtones of Christian meaning as well. For a community steeped in biblical imagery, the healing
touch of the finger is reminiscent of the "finger of God" that performed the exodus miracles, and is related to the power of the Holy Spirit in Christian tradition (Exod 8:19; cf. Q = Luke 11:20 / Matt 12:28). Touching with saliva reminds
the reader that ritual impurity is not communicated by bodily fluids (7:1–23).
Christian readers would note that Jesus looks to heaven as a sign that the power
at work in him comes from God, and that sighing is connected to the presence
of the Spirit in prayer (cf. Rom 8:26); the modern reader must be reminded that
"breath" and "spirit" are the same word in Greek, but the ancient reader knew
this already. "Ephphatha" could have sounded like a magic word to the audience of the pre-Markan story (abracadabra, hocus pocus, open sesame), but
Mark's translation shows it is an ordinary word of Jesus' native language. It is
not magic, but authoritative command.

[35] Unlike other miracle stories that provide a framework for sayings, this
story has detailed description that calls attention to the miracle itself as central.
The healed man instantly hears and speaks clearly. Like seeing and hearing, the
ability to speak clearly, in the sense of confessing and proclaiming the Christian
faith, is likewise a gift of God (cf., 8:38; 13:11). That the man's tongue was
"loosed," set free from its bondage, is the language of exorcism. This reflects not
only the general connection between sickness and demons in ancient understanding (cf. e.g., Luke 13:16), but Mark's conception of Jesus' ministry as a
whole as a divine liberating onslaught against the demonic powers that bind
human life, the victory of God over demonic power in the Christ-event as a whole.

[36] Although the miracle is obvious to all, Jesus commands "them" (including the healed man) not to tell anyone about it. As in 5:43, the command is incongruous historically, and psychological or biographical explanations should not
be attempted, as though Jesus wanted to avoid publicity so as not to be mobbed
by requests for healing, or was using "reverse psychology" to achieve what he
really wanted. Rather, again as in 5:43, the command is to be seen in the context
of the messianic secret (see *Excursus: The Messianic Secret* at 9:13). Likewise,
the zealous proclamation of Jesus' mighty deed of salvation is not to be seen
merely as their disobedience or Jesus' inability to ride herd on unwanted publicity, but as Markan testimony to the "secret epiphany" character of the Christ-
event. Such stories had circulated in early Christianity, glorifying Jesus as
miracle worker but without relating them to the central saving event of the cross
and resurrection, but this was not Jesus' intent. Nonetheless, the word had been
spread because the gospel could not be repressed, and stories like this one constituted a proleptic proclamation of the gospel to the Gentiles.

[37] The exclamation "He has done all things well" has three specific echoes of the concluding words of the creation story in Gen 1:31: *pepoiēken,* here translated "done," is there translated "made" or "created"; *panta,* "all things," is identical to "everything" of Genesis; *kalōs,* "well," is the adverbial form of *kalos,* "good," in the Genesis story. Here Jesus acts in the place of God, renewing the fallen creation, as promised in Isaiah. For Mark, the story narrates not merely an interesting Hellenistic wonder tale but a portrayal of eschatological salvation, the new creation (see on 1:6, 13).

8:1–9 Four Thousand Are Fed

8:1 In those days, once again there was a large crowd that had nothing to eat, and he called his disciples and says to them, 2 "I have compassion on the crowd, because they have already been with me now for three days and have nothing to eat, 3 and if I send them away hungry / fasting[a] to their homes, they will give out on the way—and some of them have come from far off.[b] 4 And his disciples answered, "From where is anyone able to get bread here in the desert / wilderness[c] to satisfy these people?" 5 And he was asking them, "How many loaves do you have?" And they said, "Seven." 6 And he orders the crowd to sit down on the ground; and he took the seven loaves, gave thanks, broke them and was giving them to his disciples to distribute; and they distributed them to the crowd. 7 And they had also a few small fish; and he blessed them,[d] and ordered these to be distributed also. 8 And they ate their fill, and they took up seven large baskets[e] of leftover broken pieces. 9 Now there were about four thousand people. And he sent them away.

a. *Nēsteis* is an adjective that can mean hunger in general or fasting in particular. It is found only here and in the Matt 15:32 parallel in the New Testament, but the related verb is found six times in Mark 2:18–20, where it concerns fasting. At the narrative level, it refers to hungry people for whom Jesus has compassion, but in Mark's own time it would evoke the prediction of Jesus that his followers would later fast (2:20).

b. Once again the two-level character of Mark's composition is illustrated. At the narrative level, *makrothen* simply means some of the crowd had come a long distance. But since the Old Testament repeatedly describes Gentiles as those who are "far off" (e.g., Deut 28:49; 29:22; 1 Kgs 8:41; Isa 39:3; 60:4; cf. Eph 2:13, 17; Acts 2:39), *makrothen* is here translated with the antiquated, biblical-sounding *"from far off"*—like "in those days" of v. 1.

c. At the narrative level, *erēmias* simply means "deserted place," but it is translated "wilderness" here to preserve its biblical connotations. See note *e* on 1:3.

d. "Blessed them" represents *eulogēsas auta,* by far the best attested reading (including ℵ B C L Δ Θ 892). Some MSS substitute *eucharistēsas,* "gave thanks," apparently a scribal assimilation to v. 6, while other MSS omit *auta,* "them," allowing the translation "blessed" [God]. The latter reading would correspond to Jewish usage, in which God, not things, are "blessed" (see note *h* at 6:41). Mark may be intending to portray Gentile usage, or may understand *auta* adverbially, "blessed [God]" with reference to them [the fish], i.e., thanked God for them.

e. *Spyridas*, a different word for "baskets" from the *kophinōn* of 6:43, is here translated "large baskets" to indicate the distinction, maintained by Mark in 8:19–20.

The second feeding story is clearly part of a larger pattern (see at 6:30–44). Mark seems to include dual versions of the same story for two reasons: (1) Mark is developing the theme of the disciples' lack of insight and uses the sequence of feeding stories to drive home this point (cf. 6:52; 8:14–21). (2) In this section Mark is also developing the theme of the transition of the gospel from its Jewish origins to the Gentile context of his own time and place, with "bread" and "feeding" / "eating" as key symbols of this transition (cf. 6:31, 36, 41, 44, 52; 7:2–5, 28; 8:1, 4–6, 14–21). Both the macrostructure and Mark's general interest predispose the reader to think of one feeding as representing God's provision for Jews, the biblical and traditional people of God, and the other feeding as the extension of God's miraculous blessing to Gentiles, that is, a "feeding" of a group that is primarily Gentile but includes Jews, representing the integrated inclusive Christian community of Mark's own time.

[1–3] The location is still in the Decapolis region, mainly but not exclusively Gentile, apparently near the Sea of Galilee, but also in the "wilderness" (see note *c* above). The narrative setting is more theological than geographical. So also "in those days" gives little chronological information, but is a biblical formula with eschatological overtones (cf. 1:9; 13:17, 24). "Once again" (*palin*) reminds the reader to connect the story to the previous feeding in 6:30–44. In contrast to that story, in which the disciples point out the problem of the hungry multitude in the wilderness, here Jesus himself takes the initiative. In the earlier story, Jesus is moved with compassion because the crowds were like sheep (symbol for Israel) without a shepherd, but here in Gentile territory his compassion is aroused because of their hunger—which may be more than physical—and there is no possibility of getting food from nearby villages (contrast 6:36–38). Jesus is their only hope. As elsewhere, the story is told at two levels. At the narrative level it presents Jesus as the compassionate one who by divine power provides food for hungry people. But several elements in this concise description point to a deeper meaning for Mark's postresurrection readers. The story should not be allegorized, yet elements within it point beyond the narrative level: (1) The miracle occurred on the third day. "Three days" could hardly be heard in the Markan church without overtones of the resurrection. Those who left before the three days missed the divine act in which God fed the people through Jesus. (2) "On the way" is resonant with the "way" of Jesus, the path of discipleship his followers are called to walk after Easter (cf. *Excursus: The Way* at 1:3). (3) "Hungry" can be read as the more precise "fasting" (see note *a*), characteristic of the post-Easter Markan church during the time of the absence of Jesus. In 2:20 Jesus had predicted that his followers would fast "in that day," which correlates with the setting of this story "in those days." (4) "Some" have come from "far off" suggests Gentiles (see note *b* above). To be sure, the phrase makes sense at the narrative level, but it also points to the inclusive church of Mark's own day in which some—not all—are Gentiles.

[4–5] One reason Mark includes the doublet is to highlight the disciples' continuing lack of understanding. They pose their question in a way that dramatizes their obtuseness and makes it no longer innocent, as in the prior story, but perverse. "From where" (*pothen*) is oblivious to the divine source of what Jesus provides. "Anyone" (*tis*) places Jesus / God in the same category as everyone else. The verb translated "is able" (*dynēsetai*) and its cognate noun *dynamis* ("power," "mighty act") are key terms throughout Mark for representing the power of God at work in Jesus (forty-three times in Mark; cf., e.g., 2:7; 3:27; 5:30; 6:2, 14; 9:23; 12:24; 14:62). Their response is thus not merely their previous natural human concern for the crowd and lack of awareness of how they could be fed (6:35–36). Here, Jesus shows compassion and they show that they have learned nothing from the previous miracle. The problem is not that they do not believe it happened (Mark is interested in showing that believing in the factuality of miracles is not the same as Christian faith) or that they have forgotten about it (8:19–21 shows that they remember well enough), but they do not understand its *meaning* (6:52).

[5–9] On the feeding miracle as such, see the commentary on 6:30–44. In addition to the suggestions made above, the following points of difference have often been taken as contrasting this "Gentile" story with the previous "Jewish" story. Some may be stretching a valid point, and no single item is compelling. Taken in the aggregate, however, and in the general context suggested above, it does seem that Mark is portraying this story as distinctively Gentile. (1) The feeding of the five thousand is located on the west, Jewish bank; feeding the four thousand takes place on the eastern bank, in Gentile territory (see note 130 at 6:31–44). (2) The note that some had "come from afar" uses phraseology associated with Gentiles. Jews thought of themselves as near to God and Gentiles as far from God (see, e.g., Eph. 2:11–13). (3) The five thousand men suggest the elect of the conquering Israelite army (Josh 8:12). Four, on the other hand, is a universal number representing the world as a whole (four winds, points of the compass, cf. 13:27; Rev 7:1). (4) The "military" connotations of the "hundreds" and "fifties," suggesting Israel in the wilderness, are absent here (see on 6:40). (5) The "green grass" of Ps 23 and the reference to "sheep without a shepherd" are missing here. (6) The five "Jewish" loaves may connote the Pentateuch, the divine teaching with which the Jewish people are fed, while the seven "Gentile" loaves may suggest the Noachic commands binding on all human beings, enumerated as seven in some biblical and Jewish traditions (cf. Gen 9:3–4; *Jubilees* 7.20; *t. Abod. Zar.* 8.4; Acts 15:19–29). In addition or alternatively, seven and its multiples represent the seven Gentile nations of Canaan (Deut 7:1; Acts 13:19). Luke has twelve apostles sent to Israel (Luke 9:1–10) and a later mission carried out by seventy messengers, apparently symbolizing the Gentile mission (Luke 10:1–22). The translation of the Bible into Greek was called the "Seventy," suggesting it was for all nations, since it was often believed that the world as a whole comprised seventy nations (Gen 10; *1 En.* 89.59; 90.22–25; *Tg. Ps.-J.* on Deut 32:8). Luke also has twelve Jewish apostles and seven "deacons" for the Hellenistic part of the church (Acts 6:1–6). Even if "seven" has no specifically Gentile connotation, its widespread use in biblical and Jewish tradition as a symbol for wholeness, for the whole creation, contrasts with the particularity of the covenant people of God represented by "twelve." (7) In the same line of thought, the twelve baskets of leftovers suggests a Jewish group, and the seven baskets a Gentile group. (8) The word for "basket" (*kophinos*) in 6:43 was sometimes specifically associated with Jews, that is, as the small baskets in which they carried their kosher provisions (cf. Juvenal 3, 14; 6, 542). A different word for basket, without the Jewish connotation, is used in 8:8 (*spyris*), with the distinction preserved in 8:20. (9) Blessing God for the food provided reflects Jewish practice (*eulogēsen,* see on 6:41). Giving thanks (*eucharistēsas* 8:6) represents a more universal perspective, while the separate blessing of (not for, as in Judaism) the fish is more Gentile (*eulogēsas auta,* "having blessed *them*," i.e., the fish). The disciples are later challenged to remember these differences and are rebuked for not understanding them (8:19–21).

8:10–13 No Sign Whatsoever

8:10 And he immediately got into the boat with his disciples and went to the district of Dalmanutha.[a] **11** And the Pharisees came out and began to dispute with him, testing him by asking him for a sign from heaven. **12** And he sighed deeply in his spirit and says, "Why does this generation seek a sign? Amen[b] I say to you, absolutely no sign[c] will be given to this generation." **13** And he left them, got back[d] into the boat, and went across to the other side.

a. *Dalmanoutha* and the words associated with it (*oria*, "regions"; *merē*, "district," lit. "parts") occur in various spellings and combinations in the MSS. The best MSS, including ℵ A (B) C L, as well as the great majority of later MSS read as translated above. The uncertainty shows the location given by Mark was unrecognizable even by ancient authors—the word is found nowhere else and cannot be identified with any known location. Already Matthew was unclear, and substituted Magedan or Magdala (variations also exist in Matthean MSS).

b. On "amen," see note *g* at 3:28.

c. A lit. translation of *ei dothēsetai* would be "If a sign will be given . . . ," a fragment of an Old Testament oath formula that represents "May God do so to me and more also, if . . ." (cf., e.g., 2 Kgs 6:31; Ps 95:11; LXX Jer 45:16; LXX 3 Kgdms 17:1, 4 Kgdms 4:30). Coupled with the prophetic "amen" formula, this represents an absolute rejection of the demand for a sign.

d. *Palin*, a characteristically Markan word (twenty-three times) is usually translated "again." Here translating "back" (cf. 5:21; 11:3) highlights the way in which Mark has framed the pericope by Jesus' getting into the boat and departing (*embas eis to ploion . . . ēlthen*) and after a brief exchange with the Pharisees, getting back in (*palin embas*) and departing (*apēlthen*) to the other side. This presents the brief foray to the western "Jewish" bank as an interruption in the extension of Jesus' ministry to the eastern "Gentile" bank.

[10] Jesus sovereignly dismisses the crowd and boards the boat with his disciples. The reader should not ask about the immediate availability of *the* boat (the Greek text has the article) after the long overland journey of many days. Like the crowd of 8:34 that implausibly appears when needed, the boat is available when the story calls for it—another reminder that we are not reading biography or investigative reporting. So also, the brief trip to the west bank (see note *a* on Dalmanutha and note *d* on *palin*, above), where Jesus exchanges three sentences with Pharisees (who likewise appear as needed for the story) before returning to the eastern shore, is not a matter of historical accuracy but theological patterning. This little episode seems to be transferred to the western shore in order to locate there Jesus' final rejection by Jewish leadership in Galilee, to which Jesus responds by his own leaving of them (cf. v. 13). The transition from Jewish beginnings to the predominantly Gentile church of Mark's time is still the overarching theme. An additional reason for Mark's locating the pericope here may be that he or his tradition saw and preserved the connection between the Exod 16 feeding miracle followed immediately by the unbelieving demand for a sign of Exod 17.[176] Previously the Pharisees had challenged Jesus on matters of ritual and tradition; here, the agenda escalates to Christology, the real issue from Mark's perspective.

[11] As Jesus' ministry in Galilee and its northern environs comes to an end, both the reader and the characters in the narrative, including the Pharisees, are aware that Jesus has demonstrated his authority by doing numerous powerful deeds, which Mark has consistently called *dynameis*. No one has doubted that these actually happened, though their meaning has been disputed (see on 3:22–30). Mark's terminology now shifts, and Jesus is asked for a *sign from heaven* (see *Excursus: Miracle Stories in Mark* at 6:56).

[12] The Markan Jesus absolutely refuses to respond to this demand, and declares that no sign whatsoever will be given. The absoluteness of this declaration is only apparently moderated by the Q version adopted and adapted by Matt 12:39–40 / Luke 11:29, each of which portrays the life of Jesus as devoid

---

176. So Marcus, *Mark 1–8*, 504, who also appeals to Ps 95.

of divine miracles, the only sign being Jesus' message (Luke) or the death and resurrection (Matthew). This text, in both the Markan and Q forms, represents old tradition,[177] and belongs to that stream of early Christian tradition that understood the life of Jesus in kenotic, nonmiraculous terms and saw the power of God in the Christ-event as a whole, concentrated in the cross and resurrection (see *Excursus: Markan Christology* at 9:1).

Moreover, the Markan Jesus considers the demand itself to be wrong (cf. 15:29–32 vs. 15:39). Elsewhere in the biblical tradition, asking for signs is not always bad (e.g., Judg 6:36–40; 2 Kgs 20:8–11), and people can even be challenged by a true prophet to ask for a sign (Isa 7:11–17). Other biblical authors evaluate the desire for signs as such to be a mark of unbelief (1 Cor 1:22). Here, the rejection is radical: not only Pharisees are reproached, but "this generation" as such; not only signs "from heaven" are refused, but signs as such. Why does the Markan Jesus here respond with an absolute negative? Is it that, while he could produce such signs if he wanted, he does not work miracles on demand nor to demonstrate his authority? Yet Jesus often does respond positively when asked to work a miracle (e.g., 5:21–24; 9:14–29), and even initiates miracles in order to prove his authority (e.g., 2:1–12, esp. v. 10). The key to understanding the present text probably lies in Mark's understanding of faith. No one can become a believer by putting God to the test, by posing criteria to which God must measure up (cf. Martin, *Mark*, 164–77). For Mark, it is inherent in the nature of faith that it cannot be produced by deduction, as the logical conclusion to evidence that appears valid in the eyes of the inquirer. The problem is not inadequate evidence, but the hardness of human hearts. God does not legitimate divine reality and revelation by meeting human criteria. Even believers do not come to faith on the basis of miracles. Faith is always gift, and the cross / resurrection that upsets all human standards of how God works is the only sign.

Jesus has been challenged by the Pharisees, but his response is in terms of "this generation" (cf. Gen 7:1; Ps 95:10–11; Jer 8:3)—the Pharisees are taken as representative of a comprehensive category (cf. 8:38; 9:19). To ask for a clear sign from God as the prerequisite to faith is not a problem limited to a few Pharisees, but a perversity built into humanity as such. God will not compel faith, and Jesus is weak over against the human demand to prove himself (cf. 2 Cor 13:4), for if God responded on these terms, the result would not be faith. Unbelief leaves God with nothing to do but sigh in deep grief; the scene already points to Gethsemane and the cross.

---

177. The earliest form of the saying may well go back to Jesus. Indications of early tradition are (1) the semitizing oath formula, strange to Greek ears and comprehensible to Mark's audience only because they are familiar with the LXX, (2) the divine passive, (3) the "this generation" formula, and (4) the *amēn legō hymin* formula.

[13] When Jesus leaves the Pharisees, it is his final encounter with the Jewish leadership in Galilee. The brief trip to the west bank and his rejection by (and of) the Jewish leaders there has only reinforced the Gentile mission, to which he returns. Here again, the dual-level Markan story points beyond itself to the church struggles of Mark's own time, and "boat" and "crossing to the other side," here mentioned for the last time, have dimensions of meaning beyond the surface level (see *Excursus: The Way* at 1:3; and comments on 4:1, 10–11, 35–36; 5:31–34; 6:45–52). The reader is challenged to understand this deeper level. Do the disciples get it? The stage is set for the next scene.

8:14–21 The Leaven of the Pharisees and
the Unleavened Bread of Jesus

8:14 And the disciples had forgotten to bring bread,[a] and—except for one loaf—they had none with them in the boat. **15** And Jesus was giving them strict instructions, saying, "Keep alert, watch out for the leaven of the Pharisees and the leaven of Herod."[b] **16** And they said among themselves, "It is because we[c] have no bread." **17** And Jesus knew this, and says to them, "Why are you talking about having no bread? Do you not yet perceive or understand? Do you have hardened hearts? **18** "You have eyes and you do see, don't you? and you have ears and you do hear, don't you? And you do remember, don't you, **19** when I broke the five loaves for the five thousand, how many baskets full of broken pieces you took up?" They say to him, "Twelve." **20** "When I broke the seven for the four thousand, how many large baskets full of broken pieces did you take up?" And they say to him, "Seven." **21** And he was saying to them, "Do you not yet understand?"[d]

a. The Greek is plural *artous*, "loaves." Since the generic singular is often used for food in general (e.g., 3:20; 6:8; 7:5, 27), the plural here is already a reminder of the two feeding stories.

b. Our oldest MS of Mark ($\mathfrak{P}^{45}$), followed by several others including W Θ f^1, f^{13}, reads "Herodians," in accord with 3:6; 12:13. The more difficult reading, also well attested (א B and most MSS) is translated here and in virtually all modern translations. Several translations render *zymē* as the more contemporary "yeast"; the archaic and biblical-sounding "leaven" is here preserved in order to maintain the connection with "unleavened bread" (14:1, 12).

c. Here, I read the first-person *echomen* with א A C L Θ f^{13} 33 and most later MSS, and take the *hoti* as causal rather than recitative, although the alternate possibilities, resulting in the translation "that they had no bread," are also well attested.

d. While the sentence could be a concluding exclamation, "You don't yet understand!" it is here taken as a question, as in most editions of the Greek New Testament and English translations, and is probably intended to leave the door open to future insight for the disciples (and Markan readers).

Jesus' warning about leaven (v. 15) seems to be old tradition independent of its present context, perhaps included in Q.[178] The remainder of the pericope is primarily Markan composition, drawing on the two feeding narratives, having included the doublet partly in order to facilitate making the point of this pericope. As a Markan unit had concluded at 3:6 with the hard[ened] hearts of the religious leaders, and a later unit ended with the unbelief of the folk of his hometown (6:5–6), this major unit now comes to its conclusion with the disciples' manifesting the same hardened hearts and lack of insight. Their downward spiral has been documented in three sea-crossing scenes: in their first boat trip, the disciples are rebuked for their lack of faith and their befuddled question "Who then is this?" though Jesus was with them in the boat (4:35–41). The second sea crossing is at first without Jesus, who joins them in midcrossing, but they "were utterly dumbfounded, for they did not understand about the loaves—on the contrary, their hearts had been hardened" (6:51–52). The boat will disappear from the story after this third and final sea-crossing scene, and Jesus' mighty acts in the meantime have functioned only to further harden the disciples' hearts. Here and elsewhere, the hardened hearts of the disciples is to be distinguished from the popular understanding of "hard-hearted" in the sense of subjective feelings, lack of sensitivity to others, and the like (see on 4:1–34 and *Excursus: The Messianic Secret* at 9:13). In this scene the reader is challenged to realize that human perception and achievement have failed across the board; the only deliverance from theological blindness and deafness is if Jesus himself can open blind eyes and unstop deaf ears. This story of the deafness and blindness threatening the disciples (v. 18) is framed by stories in which Jesus heals a deaf man and a blind man (7:31–37; 8:22–26; cf. commentary to those texts).

[14–15] The scene begins with forgetting and concludes with a call to remember. The subject is ostensibly bread and leaven, but the disciples' problem is that they hear these words at only a superficial level. They think they have no bread, and their concern with literal bread causes them to miss the point of Jesus' instruction about the "leaven of the Pharisees and the leaven of Herod." Jesus does not explain his cryptic speech (contra the procedure announced in 4:34). Will the reader understand? The narrator does not say what the point is that the disciples should have gotten; instead Jesus' words are intended to work provocatively and parabolically. Both Matthew and Luke "explain" the meaning of the leaven—giving differing explanations, Matt 16:12, "teaching," and Luke 12:1,

---

178. So, e.g., Wilhelm Bussmann, I. Howard Marshall, Athanasius Polag, Heinrich Schürmann, and a minority of Q scholars (data in Kloppenborg, *Q Parallels*, 118), but not included in the reconstruction of Robinson et al., *Critical Edition of Q*.

"hypocrisy"—but Mark teasingly gives no explanation.[179] Mark's parabolic meaning may have been rightly divined by Matthew for his situation, and by Luke for his, but Mark indicates to the reader that the disciples did *not* get it without specifying to the reader what they *should* have understood. Readers must ask if they too are without understanding, and "remember" (v. 18).[180]

The "one loaf" has likewise been variously explained. Some have seen the reference as pointing to the continuing failure of the disciples to trust Jesus' power, as though the mathematics of verses 19–20 is the key: if Jesus could feed five thousand people with five loaves (one loaf per 1,000 people) and four thousand with seven loaves (one loaf per 571 people), then surely one loaf will suffice for thirteen![181] It is probably correct that the disciples are faulted for not trusting in Jesus' power, that is, for not recognizing his true identity. However, there is no indication that the disciples know that even "one loaf" was in the boat with them—the communication has been from narrator to readers, and this seems to be another instance in which the readers are let in on something of which the characters in the narrative are ignorant. From at least 6:52 onward, the narrator has given the reader the clue that "bread" points to a deeper meaning. "Bread" has been a continuing motif through this section (sixteen references, 6:8–8:19) but does not occur again until 14:22, where it is specifically identified with Jesus himself—and in a context where *un*leavened bread is important, 14:1, 12. "Bread" thus probably points to Jesus himself, who is in the boat with them. Mark has a dialectical rather than straightforward understanding of the "presence" of Christ in the Eucharist (see on 14:22–25). He writes parabolically rather than allegorically, which prohibits any one-to-one equation of "bread" = "Jesus." Yet it does seem that Mark here points toward not only a christological but a specifically eucharistic understanding. "One" is important in this regard. As Mark is specifically interested in affirming the *one* God (see on 12:28–34) and the *one* people of God of Jews and Gentiles (the thrust of the whole section 6:30–8:21), so he may be affirming the "one loaf"

179. Leaven generally has an unwholesome connotation in biblical thought (e.g., Lev 2:11; 1 Cor 5:6–7), often representing an infectious, corrupting influence. Exodus imagery and the "new exodus" of Isaiah are important to Mark, and Jesus' call to avoid leaven seems to invoke the Passover typology, but we are not told in what way. The Pharisees and Herod form an unlikely combination, leading to the scribal substitution of "Herodians" in numerous MSS (see note *b*). The Pharisees have been implacable enemies throughout, already having plotted Jesus' death (3:6). Herod has appeared only in 6:14–29 as the erstwhile admirer of John the Baptist, but ended up putting him to death. Mark leaves the reader to ponder what the "leaven" of these opponents might be, which Jesus' disciples must take care to avoid.

180. Schenke, *Wundererzählungen*, 302, argues the "leaven" is the demand for an authenticating sign, clearly so for the Pharisees in 8:11–12, and also the case with the Herodians, based on Herod's response to Jesus' "signs" in 6:14–16 (though there *dynameis*, not *sēmeion*, as here).

181. So, e.g., Räisänen, *Messianic Secret*, 202ff.

of the common eucharistic table that unites Jews and Gentiles (cf. 1 Cor 10:17), even though he does not use this specific terminology.[182] As in 4:38 they were panicky even though Jesus was with them in the boat, here they worry about food even though *the* one bread is with them in the boat.

[17–21] The disciples are quizzed on the details of the two feedings, and remember the details exactly, but miss the significance entirely (for the proba-ble Markan meaning of these details, see on 8:1–9). They believe the miracles happened, but are still clueless as to their meaning. The focus of these questions and their correct answers is not on the feedings themselves, but on how much was left over, that is, the sign of messianic abundance, a final pointer to the christological significance of the whole section. If Jesus were ever going to express consternation at the unbelief and lack of perceptive response of those he has tried to teach, one would expect it to be here (cf. 6:6): the disciples have been given the mystery of the kingdom and had Jesus' parables explained to them (4:10–20; 34); they have participated in his mission and experienced his miracles, and have themselves preached, healed, and performed exorcisms (6:12–13). Yet four features of Jesus' reproachful response to his disciples' fail-ure to understand keep his words from being the absolute condemnation read-ers might expect: (1) Jesus almost, but not quite, places them in the same category with his opponents. Like them, they seem to have hardened hearts (see on 6:52), but the Markan Jesus here comes just short of applying the words of Isa 6:9–10 that had been applied to the outsiders of 4:11–12 (though reminis-cent of the Isaiah text, the words here do not come from Isaiah but from Jer 5:21 and Ezek 12:2). (2) Jesus addresses them with questions, not pronouncements. The Greek form of the questions, beginning with the particle *ou*, signals an expected positive response (see translation above). Though the disciples do not understand, the expectation is that they can, and will. (3) The repeated *oupō*, "not *yet?*" points to a future when they will in fact understand (see on 4:21–22; 9:9; 13:9–13; 16:7). (4) The disciples are encouraged to "remember," and it is expected that they will do so, which is something the "outsiders" cannot do.

Major turning points of part 1 end in rejection (see Introduction 2.): as in 3:6 Jesus is rejected by the religious leaders, so in 6:6 he is rejected by his family and hometown (each time in a Jewish synagogue), and in 8:21 even his disci-ples do not understand (in the boat, representing the church). As the readers come to the end of this major section of the narrative, they may become more aware that they always hear themselves addressed over the heads of the disciples,

---

182. So, e.g., Werner H. Kelber, *The Kingdom in Mark: A New Place and a New Time* (Philadel-phia: Fortress, 1974), 61–62; Augustine Stock, *Call to Discipleship: A Literary Study of Mark's Gospel* (GNS 1; Wilmington, Del.: Glazier, 1982), 127, and the thorough argument given by Ques-nell, *Mind of Mark*.

and may realize that, like the disciples, they too potentially stand in the same place as the "outsiders." Just as disciples in the narrative cannot feel superior to the "outsiders," readers cannot feel superior to the "dumb" disciples. Neither disciples in the narrative nor readers who hear it may claim any insight or faith based on their own achievement or virtue. The section concludes with both disciples and readers standing under the sign of hope. There is one who can open the eyes of the blind.

The "Way":
Galilee to Jerusalem
Mark 8:22–10:52

From Blindness to Sight

The section 8:22–10:52 is a transitional section that binds together part one and part two of the Gospel. Such transitions should not be thought of as "divisions" that separate but as "bridges" or "hinges" that overlap and connect (see Introduction 2.). The unit is bracketed with two stories in which Jesus heals a blind person. Other Gospels recount such healings as a common feature of Jesus' ministry (Matt 11:5; 12:22; 15:30–31; 21:14; Luke 4:18; John 7:21–22; 9:1–41; 10:21; 11:37). Mark reserves Jesus' healing of the blind for these two stories, which have an obvious symbolic meaning. In the opening scene the man is healed only gradually and does not see clearly at first, while the concluding scene portrays a blind man truly healed who follows Jesus "on the way" (10:46–52). The internal structure of the section is provided by the three passion predictions (8:31; 9:31; 10:33–34). The recurring pattern is (1) Jesus predicts his suffering, death, and resurrection in Jerusalem; (2) the disciples fail to understand; (3) Jesus renews his call and continues to teach them. Since here as elsewhere Mark is not composing freely but working with traditional materials, the pattern is not crisply neat, but the following general structure does seem to be intended by Mark:

Gradual, secret healing of blind man 8:22–26

Affirmation about Jesus	8:27–30	9:2–29	[9:37; 10:18, 27]
Passion prediction	8:31	9:31	10:33–34
Disciples fail to understand	8:32	9:32	10:35–40
Renewed call and instruction	8:33–9:1	9:33–50	10:41–45

Full, public healing of blind man 10:46–52

This section also includes five other transitional elements that change the character of the narrative that precedes it from that which follows:

(1) The fundamental geographical shift from Galilee to Jerusalem occurs within this section (10:1–52).

(2) Prior to this section, the narrative is dominated by Jesus' mighty deeds, a kind of "theology of glory." After Jesus' arrival in Jerusalem he will perform no salvific deeds of power and no overt miracles at all except the cursing of the fig tree. Within the brackets provided by the two blind man stories, Jesus hardly works a miracle—only the exorcism of 9:25–27 is found in this section, and it is part of a controversy dialogue in which the focus is not on the exorcism itself.

(3) Related to this is the transition from teaching the crowds, who virtually disappear in this section, to private instruction to the disciples.

(4) The major thematic transition that occurs in this section is the transition from veiled, parabolic speech and actions to clear and explicit revelation from God / Jesus regarding the identity of Jesus and his function in the divine plan of salvation. God speaks from heaven, and on the Mount of Transfiguration the disciples hear the same words said about Jesus that had been said to Jesus at his baptism (*Son of God*; 9:7; 1:11). Jesus himself no longer uses parables, but "speaks plainly" (8:32) that he is the *Son of Man* who will suffer, die, and rise (8:31; 9:31; 10:33–34). Peter will correctly confess Jesus as *the Christ* (8:29), though he will not understand the meaning of this confession even when it is explained to him directly by Jesus. These three christological titles are central to Mark's understanding of the answer to the question hovering in the air since 4:41; they are affirmed together and mutually illuminate each other.

(5) As the christological meaning of Jesus' identity comes more clearly into focus, the inseparable bond between Christology and discipleship also becomes more clear, and christological statements are interwoven with teaching on the meaning of discipleship. Thus the "road" motif is particularly important in this section (occurrences of *hodos*, "road," "path," "way," are more frequent in this section than in any other part of the Gospel; see *Excursus: The Way*, at 1:3). From Peter's "confession" in 8:29 onward, Jesus and his disciples will always be together—until their final abandonment of him in 14:50.

8:22–26 A Blind Man Is Healed at Bethsaida

8:22 And they come to Bethsaida. And people are bringing a blind man to him and are pleading with him to touch him. **23** And he took him by the hand and led him out of the village and spit in his eyes, placed his hands on him and kept asking him "Do you see anything?" **24** And he began to recover his sight,[a] and was saying, "I see people—they look like trees, but they are walking around." **25** Then Jesus placed his hands on his eyes again, and he looked intently, his sight was restored,[b] and he saw everything clearly. **26** And Jesus sent him forth to his home, saying, "Do not even go into the village."

a. The aorist participle *anablepsas* can mean either "look up" or "see again," i.e., recover one's sight. It is here taken in the latter sense, and as an inceptive aorist, which in view of the context can be translated "began . . ."

b. *Emblepō*, a strengthened form of the normal word for looking, *blepō*, is found elsewhere in Mark only at 10:21, 27; 14:67.

See commentary on 7:31–37 for similarities in form, content, and even wording between the two pericopes ("people are bringing to him . . ."; "he spit"). In these two cases Jesus resembles the typical Hellenistic miracle worker more closely than in any other stories, which is probably the reason both

Matthew and Luke omit them. The disciples are absent from both stories, which facilitates the readers' seeing the stories as symbolically depicting the disciples as blind, deaf, and not able to speak properly. Both the initial and concluding story show that blindness is not hopeless.

[22] The trip begun at 8:14 reaches its goal, which has been in view since 6:45. The scene is back on the east bank, in what is predominantly Gentile territory. Bethsaida had been rebuilt by Herod Phillip in 2 B.C.E., adding "Julias" to its name in honor of the daughter of the Roman emperor.

[23] Just as, in the prophet's interpretation of the first exodus, God took Israel by the hand and led them out of Egypt (Jer 31:32, which also refers to the promised eschatological renewal of the covenant), so in the eschatological exodus to come, God will grasp Israel's hand, lead them out of captivity, and open their blind eyes (Isa 42:6–7; cf. 18–20). Again, Mark uses Isaiah's new exodus imagery in portraying the Christ-event as God's eschatological redemptive act.[1] When Jesus leads the blind man outside the village, away from the crowd, the reader gets to go along, and here as elsewhere is privileged to overhear what remains concealed from the characters in the narrative. Jesus spits directly into the man's eyes, one of several procedures reminiscent of the techniques practiced by the healers at Epidaurus;[2] saliva was thought to embody the healing potency of the miracle worker, related to his breath / spirit, even his "condensed breath." The Roman emperor Vespasian, a contemporary of Mark, was also reported to have healed a blind man by his saliva (Tacitus, *Histories* 4.81; Suetonius, *Vespasian* 7:2–3).

[24] The healing of blindness, even by Jesus, does not take place instantaneously, but by stages—Mark's ubiquitous *euthys* ("immediately") is conspicuously absent. This is reminiscent of the fact that early Christianity's understanding of the identity of Jesus and the extension of the gospel to the Gentiles dawned only gradually, not all at once (cf. Acts 1–15; Gal 2). Despite the christological difficulties involved, Mark seems to be willing to portray Jesus as having to try more than once to heal the man in order to anticipate the experience of Peter and the disciples he is about to portray. The disciples will begin to have their blindness removed in the next scene, when they perceive him to be the Christ, but will also continue blindly to misunderstand Jesus' plain teaching that the Christ is the suffering and dying Son of Man. Like the man in the story, their blindness and sight is not a quantitative matter, not a partial seeing that can be incrementally completed. The man sees, but does not yet truly see (see Marcus, *Mark 8–16*, ad. loc.). Yet the story is full of promise. As Jesus finally gives the man clarity of vision, so Jesus can be counted on to finish the job he has already begun on the

---

1. For Isaiah imagery as a key to Markan hermeneutic, see *Excursus: Mark and the Scriptures* at 14:52, and commentary at 1:2–3.

2. Cf. Pesch, *Markusevangelium*, 1:416. Seeing "trees" in the process of recovery also has a distant parallel in the healing stories from Epidaurus. Cf. Rudolf Herzog, *Die Wunderheilungen von Epidauros: Ein Beitrag zur Geschichte der Medizin und der Religion* (Leipzig: Dieterich, 1931), #18.

disciples (cf. 1:17—Jesus is the active subject in the transformation of the disciples). When will the blindness be completely healed? Will it be as a result of the revelations in 8:27–10:45, so that Bartimaeus who begins blindly calling Jesus "Son of David" will finally be fully healed and will follow Jesus on his way (10:46–52)? Will it be at the resurrection (16:8)? Or does Mark regard Jesus' disciples of his own time as people who were once blind but still, even after Easter and the reception of the Holy Spirit, only partially healed, so that full sight will come only at the Parousia, when all will *see* Jesus as Son of Man (13:26; cf. 1 Cor 13:12)? Or is asking the question in such diachronic terms already a misunderstanding of Mark's parabolic communication? Is seeing-yet-not-seeing analogous to believing-yet-not-believing (see on 9:24), synchronic and dialectic rather than diachronic and quantitative? In any case, just as the blind man could not initiate his own healing, so he could not complete the process.

[26] Jesus' command to go directly home and not enter the village seems parallel to 7:36 (see notes there) and thus integral to the messianic secret at the Markan level, though the pre-Markan story may have already concluded this way, for other reasons.

8:27–9:1 Christology, Discipleship, and First Passion Prediction

Peter's "confession" and Jesus' response clearly represent a major turning point in the Markan narrative. Interpreters are generally agreed that there are three subunits here: 8:27–30, Peter's "confession" and the command to silence; 8:31–33, Jesus' first "passion prediction" and the mutual "rebuking" of Peter and Jesus; 8:34–9:1, Jesus' instruction to his disciples and the crowds on the meaning of discipleship. These are not discrete units. While synopses and Gospel "harmonies" often subdivide this section, in Mark's narrative these three subunits are integral elements of one scene and will here be treated as a whole. The passage has a complex structure, and is difficult to classify form-critically: two question-and-answer exchanges, followed by three *epitimaō* (strictly, command / rebuke; see note *c* below) exchanges, including the first of three passion predictions, with a scene change from disciples to crowds at verse 34. The focus is on the sayings and dialogue, not the narrative, which only serves as their framework. The passage contains traditional elements, but Mark is the composer of the whole, which bears a Markan stamp and expresses Markan theology.[3]

---

3. Estimates range from the view that the scene is basically an account of a key incident from the life of Jesus based on the reminiscences of Peter (so, e.g., Oscar Cullmann, *Peter: Disciple, Apostle, Martyr* [rev. ed.; Cleveland: World, 1958], 171), through those who regard Mark as primarily dependent on an extensive pre-Markan tradition (e.g., Pesch, *Markusevangelium*, 2:1–27, who sees the pre-Markan passion narrative beginning here), to those who consider the scene to be purely Markan composition (e.g., William Wrede, *The Messianic Secret* [trans. James C. G. Greig; London: James Clarke, 1971], 115–49).

8:27 And Jesus and his disciples came out[a] to the villages of Caesarea Philippi, and on the way he was questioning his disciples, saying to them, "Who do people[b] say that I am?" **28** And they answered him, "'John the Baptist'; and others, 'Elijah'; and still others 'One of the prophets.'" **29** And he was asking them, "And you—who do you say that I am?" Peter replied, "You are the Christ." **30** And he gave them strict orders[c] not to tell anyone about him. **31** And he began to teach them that the Son of Man must endure great suffering, and be rejected by the elders, the chief priests, and the scribes, and be killed, and after three days rise again. **32** And he was speaking the word[d] plainly, openly, and boldly.[e] And Peter took him and began to rebuke him. **33** But he turned, looked at his disciples, and rebuked Peter and says, "Get behind me,[f] Satan! For you are not thinking in terms of the things of God, but in terms of human things."

34 And he called the crowd with his disciples, and said to them, "If anyone wants to follow me, that person must renounce himself, take up his cross, and follow me."[g] **35** For whoever wants to save his life will lose it, but whoever loses his life for my sake and the gospel's[h] will save it. **36** For what does it profit a person to gain the whole world and to lose his own life? **37** For what can a human being give in exchange for his life? **38** For whoever is ashamed of me and my words[i] in this adulterous[j] and sinful generation, the Son of Man will also be ashamed of that person when he comes in the glory of his father with the holy angels. **9:1** And he was saying to them, "Amen[k] I say to you, there are some of those standing here who will not taste death until they see the kingdom of God, which will have come with power."[l]

a. *Exēlthen* does not require that the reader take a stance with regard to the action, and so may be translated "went out" or "came out" (as, e.g., in Matt 8:34; Mark 1:26; 9:26 NRSV). If the author and intended readership were in Syria, northeast of Galilee (see Introduction 6.), the translation preferred here allows them to see Jesus coming from Galilee in their direction.

b. "People" here translates *anthrōpoi*, often used of human beings in contrast to God, not merely to other people. Cf. the bracket with v. 33 concluding this paragraph.

c. Forms of the same word *epitimaō* are used in 8:32 and 8:33, translated "rebuke," but there is no English word that means both "give strict orders" (a warning looking ahead to an action) and "rebuke" (a warning looking back on an action).

d. While the Greek phrase *ton logon elalei* can be accurately translated as "he was saying this" or some such, the more literal translation above is intended to preserve the overtones of proclaiming the Christian message, as in 2:2; 4:33.

e. *Parrēsia* (only here in Mark) refers to a lack of concealment in all three of these senses that can be expressed by no one English word.

f. While *hypage opisō mou* can mean "get away from me" (cf., e.g., CEV) or "get out of my sight" (cf., e.g., REB), the identical words *opisō mou* mean "behind me" in the sense of following, both literally and metaphorically, in 1:17; 8:34.

g. In this brief discipleship section the Greek text uses the masculine singular pronoun in the generic sense ten times (preserved as an English masculine pronoun in the NIV and some other modern English translations). The NRSV achieves gender inclusiveness by rendering them all as English plurals, which are non-gender-specific, but at the cost of losing the reference to individual responsibility and decision. "His or her" language is too awkward in such contexts where the pronoun occurs so frequently, and "one" ("one's cross" and the like) is too impersonal to convey the meaning. I have thus in this passage adopted the practice of the REB, retaining a minimum of generic third-person pronouns (masculine; the feminine has never been used generically in English).[4]

h. Our oldest extant MS of Mark ($\mathfrak{P}^{45}$) and a few others omit *emou kai* ("my and") but the original almost certainly contained the full phrase, which corresponds to Mark's style and theology. *Kai* is here to be understood as epexegetical, identifying "my" and "gospel's" so that the phrase could be translated "for my sake—that is, the gospel's." On "gospel" for *euangelion* (lit. "good news"), see on 1:1, 15.

i. *Logous* ("words") is omitted in $\mathfrak{P}^{45}$ and a few other MSS, resulting in the reading "me and mine (= my followers)." While these omissions may in each case be simply scribal errors, the parallel meaning of the omitted words may indicate a failure to understand a point of Markan theology (see commentary below). Here, too, *kai* is probably to be understood epexegetically.

j. "Adulterous" does not necessarily represent sexual immorality, but is biblical language for unfaithfulness to God (e.g., Isa 1:4; Hos 2:4), where adultery is a symbol for idolatry and abandoning Israel's covenant relationship with God.

k. On initial *amēn,* see note g at 3:28.

l. The combination of aorist subjunctive main verb *idōsin,* "see," and the perfect participle *elēlythuian* (only here in Mark), "having come," means that as Jesus speaks the kingdom is not present, that it will come at some future date in power, and that some of those to whom Jesus is speaking will see that it has arrived.

[27] In any understanding of Markan structure, this scene opens with a literary hinge signaled by a threefold contextualization: (1) The disciples, absent from the previous scene, and last addressed with the question "Do you not yet understand?" (8:21), are reintroduced. This pericope, and the larger context in which it is embedded, is not about Christology in the abstract; in Markan theology, Christology and discipleship imply each other, such that the story of Jesus and the story of the disciples are inextricably interwoven. (2) Caesarea Philippi is at the northernmost tip of traditional Israel, outside Galilee, bordering Syria. While this scene possibly preserves a historical memory of an incident in Jesus' life,[5] the location more likely reflects Mark's theological interests.

4. Cf. on 2:27, and "Preface to the Revised English Bible"; Donahue and Harrington, *Gospel of Mark,* 263; Hooker, *Mark,* 207.

5. The story is located at various places in the Gospels' chronologies: Matt follows Mark in placing the scene here, but Luke 9:10, 18 places it at Bethsaida in direct conjunction with the feeding of the five thousand, and the similar story in John 6:67–71 in the synagogue at Capernaum.

The ancient town had been a center for Baal worship, and later was called Paneas after the Greek god Pan whose shrine was there (still reflected in its modern Arab name, Banias). Herod the Great had built a splendid marble temple in which the emperor was honored as a god. The emperor was the power behind Herod's own throne, having granted him the territory, and Herod's son, Herod Philip, had enlarged the town into a proper Hellenistic city and renamed it Caesarea in honor of the emperor. "Philippi" distinguished it from other cities of the same name, especially Caesarea Maritima on the Mediterranean coast. Mark thus brings the narrative dealing with the identity of Jesus into a setting replete with the ambiguities of Jewish history and its relation to Rome, with overtones of ancient cultic associations and the contemporary deification and worship of the Roman emperor.[6] During the 66–70 war, the area had been used as a staging area for Roman troops invading Palestine and as a rest-and-recreation station for Roman soldiers, where the local Jewish population had been massacred and atrocities committed against Jewish prisoners of war. If the Gospel was written in southern Syria, this dialogue also takes place in an area personally important to writer and readers (see note *a* on *exēlthen* above). (3) Mark sets the conversation not in a house, but *en tē hodō* ("on the way"). The "way" is not merely geography, but connotes the way of discipleship, Jesus' way that now leads from the most distant point in Israel to its capital and temple in Jerusalem, the road to the cross (cf. *Excursus: The Way* at 1:3). Throughout 8:22–10:52 the narrative is bound together by the *hodos* (way) motif as previously by the *ploion* (boat) motif.

Jesus' question is not informational, as though reflecting a 30 C.E. biographical realism in which Jesus had been secluded but his disciples are more in touch with the "word on the street." The Markan Jesus has supernatural knowledge and does not need to be informed. The question is for the readers' benefit, to set up the contrast between what people in general are saying and the disciples' (and readers') own confession of faith. The use of *anthrōpoi* also signals the fundamental contrast between human evaluation and God's (1:11; 9:7).

[28] The question of Jesus' identity has been posed throughout chapters 1–8, specifically, for example, in 1:27 and as the disciples' own question in 4:41. It now finds a definitive answer. The popular evaluations (John the Baptist, Elijah, one of the prophets) have been known to the reader since 6:14–15 (see commentary there). Jesus is popularly known as a prophet, whether this be thought of as one of the dead prophets now restored to life, or as *the* eschatological prophet who stands in the prophetic line. Either way, these are high evaluations, representing a "high" Christology—but in Mark's view they do not do justice to Jesus' true identity.

---

6. Evans, *Mark 8:27–16:20*, lxxxii–xciii, provides a cogent summary of Markan Christology as opposition to the emperor cult.

[29] The "you" is doubly emphatic in the Greek text; the presence of the pronoun, not necessary in Greek syntax, lends emphasis, as does its initial position in the sentence (see translation above). Peter's response, "You are the Christ," is the first use of the word "Christ" by a character in the narrative itself. The titular usage in 1:1 is from narrator to the reader, not from a character in the story. There has been no preparation for it. In Mark's view, it is not an inference from having observed and participated in the miracles of the previous chapters.[7] Yet it is the authentic Christian confession made by the members of the Markan church, the confession Jesus himself will make at the climax of the story (14:61–62), the name by which his followers will be known after the resurrection (9:41), the key designation for Jesus by which Mark wants his narrative as a whole to be known (1:1). Thus, although Jesus here neither accepts nor rejects the title, Mark intends the reader to hear Peter's statement as true, representing the fundamental Christian confession of faith—even though Peter himself does not yet understand what he is saying. "Christ" is clearly a key title to be ascribed to Jesus, yet it does not communicate its full significance when standing alone, but only in conjunction with the other titles, especially "Son of God" and "Son of Man"; all three occur in the section 8:22–10:52, all three are clothed in narrative secrecy for the present, and all three occur in 14:61–62 as Jesus' own "summary" of his identity and role in God's plan.[8] On the meaning of "Christ" and its relation to Mark's other christological terminology, see *Excursus: Markan Christology* at 9:1. While there may well have been speculations about Jesus' identity during his ministry, including some preliminary and inadequate designations of him as the expected Messiah, the present narrative does not reflect the biography of Jesus but the theology of Mark, who is not concerned to report what was once thought about Jesus but to provoke and communicate authentic reflection on Jesus' identity and the meaning of discipleship to his own readers.

[30] Like the "confession" itself, Jesus' command to silence is to be understood primarily at the Markan level as an element in the messianic secret, not

___

7. Matthew rightly understands Mark on this point, and makes explicit that authentic insight into Jesus' identity is not a human attainment, a deduction based on "evidence," but a gift of God (Matt 16:17; so also Paul, 1 Cor 12:3). While Mark values the representation of Jesus in the miracle stories, he does not consider them the basis for confession of Jesus as the Christ (see on 8:11–12; 15:32).

8. Malbon designates this as "refracted Christology"—the Markan Jesus *refracts* or bends the Christologies of other characters and even that of the narrator, principally by juxtaposing their statements with his own statement about the suffering, dying, and rising Son of Man who will reappear at the Parousia. No one "confesses" Jesus as Son of Man, no other character (and not even the narrator) speaks of the Son of Man, but Jesus refracts their confession by placing it alongside his own declaration about himself as Son of Man (Elizabeth Struthers Malbon, "The Christology of Mark's Gospel: Narrative Christology and the Markan Jesus," in *Who Do You Say That I Am? Essays on Christology* [ed. Mark Allen Powell and David R. Bauer; Louisville, Ky.: Westminster John Knox, 1999], 44).

at the biographical level as a strategy of the earthly Jesus, as though he did not want the word of his messianic identity to spread because it would be misunderstood in a political sense[9] or because it would cause people to throng about him and interfere with the private teaching he now wished to devote to his disciples. The biographical explanation must contend with at least four major objections: (1) It is not in the text, which provides no explanation at all; whatever explanation one gives must be based on the interpreter's understanding of the nature of the Markan narrative as a whole. (2) Jesus' proclamation of the kingdom of God would be at least as subject to misunderstanding and as politically explosive as talk of messiahship, yet the Markan Jesus proclaims the kingdom openly. (3) The stringency of the messianic secret is maintained only in Mark. Not only do the other Synoptics relax the secret, in the Gospel of John its Markan form disappears entirely, and Jesus publicly announces himself as the Messiah from the first page on, and encourages others to do so (John 1:41; 4:25–29; 7:26, 31, 41; 9:22; 10:24–25; 11:27). (4) It would have been simple enough to provide a disclaimer along with the announcement of messiahship, along the lines of "Jesus is the Messiah, but do not think of him in the traditional way. He is a different kind of Messiah, who redefines the office by his own life and teaching." This is what the Gospel of John does; this is what the Markan reader does; the historical Jesus and his pre-Easter followers could also have done this. The command to silence simply does not work at the biographical level, but is fundamental to the narrative Christology delineated by Mark, "the hermeneutical presupposition of the genre, 'gospel'"[10] (see *Excursus: The Messianic Secret* at 9:13).

Jesus does not merely command silence. His command is represented by the harsh word *epitimaō*, which will recur twice more in the immediate context, there translated "rebuke" (see note *c* above). It is the same word used to describe Jesus' silencing the demons (1:25) and the demon-storm (4:39). As in 1:34 and 3:12, the demons are silenced because they *know* him. Their identification, like Peter's, is correct, but cannot yet be made known. The narrative here proceeds directly to Peter's own demonic misunderstanding of his correct confession.

[31] Jesus immediately responds to Peter's statement with his own declaration. "Son of Man" has previously occurred only at 2:10 and 2:28, identifying Jesus as the one who acts on earth with transcendent authority (see commentary there), but this is the first indication that the Son of Man must suffer and die. (On the meaning and usage of "Son of Man," see *Excursus: Markan Christology* at 9:1.) While the historical Jesus likely reckoned with the prospect of

9. In any case, readers should be wary of reducing "the" "typically Jewish" understanding of messiahship to the political and military sense. See Klaus Berger, "Die königlichen Messiastraditionen des Neuen Testaments," *NTS* 20, no. 1 (1973): 1–44, esp. 43.

10. Hans Conzelmann, "Present and Future in the Synoptic Tradition," *JTC* 5 (1968): 43.

his own violent death and willingly accepted it, and there are probably traditional antecedents to the Markan passion predictions, in their present form and context they are from Mark himself and should be interpreted as part of the Markan narrative. Mark specifically identifies Jesus' response as *didaskein,* "teaching." Previously, Jesus' teaching has been public, and about the kingdom of God. Now, for the first time, the verb *didaskein* is used for Jesus' private instruction, and for the first time it concerns his own role and destiny. This is the first of three predictions of Jesus' suffering, death, and resurrection (8:31; 9:31; 10:33–34; cf. also 9:12b). Their traditional label "passion predictions" should not be misunderstood as referring only to the suffering and death, since resurrection is integral to each. If "passion" is properly understood as related to "passive," the designation "passion predictions" is appropriate, since Jesus is not the active subject, but is acted upon in both his death (tortured and killed by other humans) and resurrection (raised by God). It is important to Mark that these be seen as an inseparable unity—Jesus' death does not become significant apart from the resurrection, and the resurrection does not supersede the crucifixion, but the Risen One's identity continues as the Crucified One (see on 16:6). The "must" (*dei*) of the Son of Man's suffering applies equally to his resurrection. This means, among other things, that the "must" is unrelated to a theory of the atonement. The necessity of Jesus' death and resurrection is not to allow God to be gracious, but is part of the apocalyptic scheme of things that as a whole represents God's will as revealed in Scripture (see 13:20 and diagram in *Excursus: Markan Christology,* p. 247; 9:12; 14:31, 49). This apocalyptic will of God does not rule out God's own sovereignty that transcends any scheme (cf. on 13:18–20) or human will and responsibility, including Jesus' own decision (see on 14:32–42).

That the passion predictions impute no soteriological meaning to Jesus' death, that they affirm no direct connection between Jesus' death and Scripture (contrast, e.g., 1 Cor 15:3–5), and that neither the cross or crucifixion is specifically mentioned indicates they are not intended as creedal summaries of early Christian faith, but summary accounts of the narrative to follow, which "must" now occur since Jesus has predicted it. The use of *apodokimasthēnai* ("be rejected") is an allusion to Ps 118:22, which will be explicitly cited in 12:11. Those who will reject the Son of Man are identified as the elders, chief priests, and scribes (cf. 11:27; 14:43, 53; 15:1). Together, these make up the official Jewish religious leadership in Jerusalem (cf. 15:1 *holon to synedrion,* "the whole Sanhedrin"). Striking by their absence are the Pharisees, who have been his challengers in Galilee, but who play no role in the passion story. Here it is not said who will kill Jesus; in 10:33 it is the "Gentiles," in 9:31 "human beings."

In each of the passion predictions, Jesus will rise "after three days" (*meta treis hēmeras;* cf. 14:58 *dia triōn hēmerōn* and 15:29 *en trisin hēmerais*), which both Matthew and Luke replace with "on the third day" (Matt 16:21; 17:23; 20:19; Luke 9:22; 18:33; 24:7; cf. also 1 Cor 15:4). There is abundant evidence in the LXX, Josephus, and rabbinic writings that these phrases have exactly the same meaning, representing the Jewish practice of counting part of a day as the whole (cf., e.g., Gen 42:17–18; Exod 19:11–16; Josephus, *Life* 268–69; *Ant.* 2.72–73; *Esth. Rab.* 9:2). In all the Gospels Jesus is killed on Friday and raised on Sunday, and this is consistently represented in their respective passion predictions.

The verb used for "rise" (*anistēmi*) is active, and can be either transitive (as, e.g., Acts 9:41) or intransitive (as, e.g., Mark 1:35; 2:14; 12:23, 25). Since Jesus (i.e., the Son of Man) is here the subject and the verb is active, *anistēmi* must here have the intransitive meaning "rise." Elsewhere, Mark, like other New Testament authors, uses the passive of *egeirō* "be raised" (e.g., Mark 6:14, 16; 14:28; 16:6; 1 Cor 15:4), with God as the actor. However, in 9:27 Mark clearly uses *anistēmi* as synonym of *egeirō,* and active *anistēmi* is used as the equivalent of passive *egeirō* in Matt 12:41–46; Mark 12:23–26; Luke 9:7–8; Luke 9:19–22; 11:8, 31–32; John 11:29–31; Acts 9:6–8. Since both Mark and the LXX (Isa 26:19) use the active of *anistēmi* as the equivalent of the passive of *egeirō,* the meaning here may be: (1) that God will raise the Son of Man from the dead,[11] (2) that the Son of Man is here portrayed as having divine power and functioning as God,[12] as Mark does in fact sometimes portray Jesus; or (3) as meaning simply "rise," without thought as to who does the raising, as is undoubtedly the case in numerous texts where both Jesus and Christians "rise" (active of *anistēmi*) with no thought that they do it by their own power (e.g., Acts 2:41; 17:3; 1 Thess 4:14, 16).

[32–33] Peter's "rebuke" of Jesus uses the same word *epitimaō* associated with exorcism, almost as though Peter considered Jesus possessed (as did his enemies, 3:23). Jesus' response addresses Peter as "Satan"—it is Peter, not Jesus, who needs to be exorcised.

"Speaking the word" is almost a technical term for preaching the early Christian message. Mark regards this message as centered on God's act in the death and resurrection of Jesus. As in 2:2 and 4:33, Jesus is portrayed as himself the proclaimer of the Christian gospel. He does so boldly, as Christians are called to do, plainly (i.e., no longer in parables) and publicly. Even though this nuance of *parrēsia* (see note *e* above) clashes with the private scene of Jesus with his disciples, this aspect is nonetheless present, since Mark wants to portray Jesus as a model of those who forthrightly testify to the Christian faith in public rather than "being ashamed" (see on v. 38) and to contrast him with Peter at 14:66–72.

---

11. So, e.g., Jeremias, *New Testament Theology,* 281–82; cf. also Jeremias's discussion of the "divine passive" on p. 13.

12. Gnilka, *Markus,* 2:16, sees the expression as intentionally chosen by Mark to express his view that it is by his own divine power that the Son of Man overcomes death.

Peter here responds to Jesus' clear and forthright "public" speech with a stern rebuke (see above). Just as nothing in the narrative has prepared the readers for Peter's "confession," so nothing has prepared them for this. *Proslabomenos* (translated "took" above), can mean "take aside" (so, e.g., NRSV), and can be understood in a somewhat patronizing way (cf. Acts 18:26, where Aquila and Priscilla correct Apollos's inadequate understanding). If that is the meaning here, Peter assumes the role of Jesus' teacher, correcting Jesus' "false" Christology. But the word can also mean "take," in a physical sense, "take hold of" (so, e.g., REB). Coupled with the verb *epitimaō* ("rebuke"), this is probably its meaning here, with the prefix *pros-* indicating that Peter now takes a stand *in front of* Jesus, "in his face," almost "by the lapels" (note Matthew's moderating addition in Matt 16:22 and Luke's complete omission at 9:22). As Peter has been the representative spokesperson for the disciples all along,[13] so now Jesus turns and speaks to Peter while looking directly at the disciples. Jesus' counter-counter rebuke (the third occurrence of *epitimaō*) sternly warns Peter to return "behind him" (*opisō mou*, as 1:7, 17; 8:34) to his true place as a disciple—rather than his presumptuous stance in front of him, where Peter is literally in his *way,* an obstacle to the way of the cross Jesus will walk and to which he calls his disciples (cf. 1:7, 17, 20; 8:33–34). Jesus' addressing Peter as "Satan" should not be weakened to its generic meaning "accuser, slanderer." The Markan Jesus addresses Peter as Satan's representative, representing the opposition in the clash of kingdoms (3:22–27), on the side of God's opponent who takes away the word Jesus sows (4:15), putting Jesus to the test as had Satan in 1:13.

The issue in Jesus' charge to Peter has to do with how he thinks: whether he is thinking within the framework of conventional human wisdom or in terms of the things of God. "In terms of" represents the Greek "accusative of general reference." It is not only a matter of what one thinks, but how, in what frame of reference.[14] Since Isaiah plays a formative role in Mark's theology, Isa 55:8–9 may be in the background here; God's "thoughts," God's "way of thinking," is different from human thinking. Peter is called to repent, to think in a radically different way (see on 1:4, 15, and cf. Rom 8:5–6). While "human thinking" is based on the common-sense "values" of trust in oneself rather than faith in God, saving one's life rather than losing it in the service of others, being great and lording it over others, God's "way of thinking" is the opposite of these, embodied in Jesus' own life, a matter of revelation that violates "common sense." Each of the three passion predictions is followed by a statement of the core values of the

13. Interpretations that speak psychologically and novelistically of Peter's "impulsiveness" and the like should be avoided; what we have is Markan theology, not psycho-biography.

14. Josephus, *War,* 1:326 refers to "those of Herod's party" (*tous ta Hērōdou phronounta,* lit. "those who think the things of Herod," "those who think along Herodian lines"; Polyaenus 8.14.3 refers to those who belong to the Roman party as *ta Rōmaiōn phronein,* "those who think along Roman lines."

Markan Jesus, the meaning of discipleship (8:31 is followed by 8:35; 9:31 by 9:35; 10:33–34 by 10:43–45). Christology is not speculation about the nature of Jesus, but inseparably related to discipleship; the proclamation of the kingdom of God is not eschatological speculation but brings a new way of life—giving one's life for others replaces self-centeredness, and the "discipleship of equals"[15] replaces lording it over others or manipulating them for one's own advantage.

[8:34–9:1] These six sayings may originally have been separate sayings or smaller pre-Markan clusters. They are found separately, in different contexts and slightly different forms, in Matt 10:33, 38–39; Luke 14:27; John 12:24–26; *Gos. Thom.* 55. In terms of form and vocabulary, the group of sayings shows considerable variety, representing the diverse origins and previous settings and roles in the pre-Markan tradition: verse 34 is an imperative in the form "if anyone . . . let that person . . . ," a conditional sentence for which the conditions are given in the following sayings. Verse 35 is a double declaration in the form of antithetical parallelism, "whoever does *x* shall *y*." Verses 36–37 are parallel rhetorical questions in the wisdom tradition, beginning with "What . . . ?" Verse 38 is a prophetic declaration in the form of a "sentence of holy law."[16] Each of these five sayings is joined to the preceding saying by *gar* ("for"), together constituting a chain of reasons giving the basis for the imperative of verse 34. The final saying of 9:1 is a prophetic saying with initial *amen*, similar in content and function to 8:38, and providing the concluding eschatological argument and promise. It is joined to the structure with the Markan *kai elegen autois* (as 2:27; 4:2, 21, 24; 6:4, 10; 7:9; 8:21; 9:31; 11:17 [never in Matt; in Luke only 6:5]). Mark is responsible for the present arrangement and location of the sayings cluster, where the unit as a whole functions as the explication of "thinking in terms of the things of God" as opposed to "thinking in terms of human things" (v. 33 vs. v. 27) with the *opisō mou* ("after me") of verse 34 corresponding to the *opisō mou* ("behind me") of verse 33.

[34] Here the typical Markan structure is reversed. Instead of the address beginning with the crowd and being narrowed to the disciples, Jesus begins to speak to Peter, then to the disciples, then imperiously calls "the crowd" to whom the cluster of sayings is addressed. The crowd is an element of Mark's literary technique, appearing when needed, and evaporating after the address. It is a means of making Jesus' demand universal; what is now said is directed to *tis* ("anyone"), disciple or not (cf. the triple *hos an* "whoever" of vv. 35, 38 and the double generic *anthrōpos* "human being," "person" of vv. 36, 37). All, "insiders" or "outsiders," are now called to understand the meaning of

---

15. Elisabeth Schüssler Fiorenza, *In Memory of Her: A Feminist Theological Reconstruction of Christian Origins* (New York: Crossroad, 1983), 140–54.

16. Ernst Käsemann, "Sentences of Holy Law in the New Testament," in *New Testament Questions of Today* (London: SCM Press, 1969).

discipleship. Whereas in 1:16–20 and 2:14 discipleship was the result of Jesus' sovereign call and authority, in these sayings, being a follower of Jesus is a matter of one's decision and responsibility; in verses 34, 35 the verb is *thelō* ("want," "will"; not "wish").

The call to deny oneself does not mean to relinquish the enjoyment of certain *things*, as though doing without or enduring suffering as such made one holy or a disciple of Jesus.[17] The word translated "deny" (*aparnēsasthō*) is found elsewhere in Mark only in reference to Peter's denial of Jesus (14:30, 31, 72). "Deny" is thus the opposite of "confess," "acknowledge"; the hearers are called to deny themselves rather than deny Jesus, that is, no longer to make oneself the top priority and the center of one's own universe, to reverse the Adamic decision made by the *anthrōpos* ("human being") of Gen 3 who wanted to be like God (i.e., to be his own God), and let God be God. It is hardly accidental that *anthrōpos* occurs twice in this passage representing "anyone."

Likewise, taking up one's cross does not refer to the inconveniences, or even the sufferings, that are a part of human life as such, as often interpreted when one's troubles are described as "just the cross I have to bear." The Markan Jesus is not commending endurance of the inevitable pains of life, but the voluntary *taking up* of the cross as sharing the suffering involved in discipleship and Christian mission. While there can be no doubt that Jesus called his followers to radical decision, the specific reference to taking up the cross probably reflects the post-Easter vocabulary of the church.[18] Although this is the first reference to "cross" or "crucifixion" in Mark—and the word will not recur again until 15:13, then ten times in 15:14–16:6—the Greek definite article is anaphoric, referring to a known item from previous reference. Neither the disciples nor the crowd in the narrative has such a point of reference, but the post-Easter readers have two: they are fully aware of Jesus' own crucifixion, and they know that Roman Christians have recently been crucified by Nero (Tacitus, *Annals* 15.44.4), and that Christians were likely among the hundreds crucified by Titus and Vespasian during the war in Palestine. Discipleship to Jesus as willingness to take up the cross was not metaphorical to many of Mark's original readers. Nor was it a matter of internal, private devotion—crucifixion was not only slow

---

17. Cf. Joanna Dewey, "'Let Them Renounce Themselves and Take Up Their Cross': A Feminist Reading of Mark 8:34 in Mark's Social and Narrative World," in *A Feminist Companion to Mark* (ed. Amy-Jill Levine and Marianne Blickenstaff; Cleveland: Pilgrim Press, 2004).

18. In a classic article, Erich Dinkler argued that the saying goes back to Jesus, but did not originally refer to following himself or his own cross. Rather, the challenge is to radical loyalty to God as expressed in Ezek 9:4, where willingness to wear the "sign" of God, the cross-shaped Tau, was not christological but theocentric, the mark of faithfulness to the one God. Erich Dinkler, "Comments on the History of the Symbol of the Cross," *JTC* 1 (1965): 141–43; cf. Pesch, *Markusevangelium*, 2:60, who rightly argues that in any case the present form of the saying is Markan, christological, and refers to the disciples' cross in relation to the cross of Jesus.

and agonizing death, it was public and shameful (cf. v. 38, "ashamed"). Throughout this cluster of sayings, commitment to Jesus is a matter of participation in the mission of the church, the kind of active public testimony and identification with Jesus that draws the fire of the authorities, not merely showing individual kindness to others in private.

[35] As in verse 34, losing or saving one's life / self is here a matter of the will, of one's personal decision, not of divine sovereignty and choice as in, for example, 4:10–12. The word *psychē*, found four times in verses 35–37 (cf. also 3:4; 10:45; 12:30; 14:34), is here used as a synonym for the reflexive pronoun *heauton* in verse 34 ("-self"). Unlike Greek thought, which typically understood the *psychē* as an immortal part of the self, contained in a perishable body, Old Testament / Jewish thought typically understood the human self as a unity, so that *psychē* and other anthropological terms each represented the person as a whole (cf. 12:30). Thus the Lukan parallel replaces *psychē* with the reflexive pronoun *heauton* "-self" (Luke 9:25). All the sayings in Mark 8:34–9:1 represent the reality faced by Markan Christians, that their Christian profession might cost them their life, their whole self. Those who want to save their physical life by denying the faith will end up forfeiting their true life; those who are willing to give themselves for the cause of Christ will in fact preserve their lives in the coming judgment when they stand before the Son of Man (v. 38). "For my sake" (i.e., for the sake of Christ) and "for the sake of the gospel" (i.e., for the sake of the Christian mission in Mark's time) are here inseparably related, though not simply identified (see note *h* above). For Mark, Jesus is present in the Christian message about him, and to be persecuted for it is to suffer for his sake (cf. 8:38; 10:29; 13:9–10).

[36–37] The rhetorical questions of these two verses could have been at home in the world of cynical secular wisdom as well as Jewish religious wisdom (cf. Ps 49:8–16): at the time of death, there is no one who would choose to "keep" all the wealth in the world at the expense of his or her own life, and there is nothing, no matter how valuable, that one can offer in exchange for one's own life. As an expression of Markan theology, the sayings take on new meaning: the Markan Jesus asks for the whole being of the disciple, the life and self, and no one can "save" one's life by offering a substitute.

[38] The Markan Jesus is not rehashing common-sense wisdom; what he says is true not at the level of either superficial observation or sage reflection, but only in the eschatological [ultimate] sense. As Jesus himself is rejected by those who think only "in terms of human things" (cf. v. 33), so his followers will be tempted to be ashamed of their association with him. But just as Jesus was vindicated, so disciples who hold on to their faith despite the shame will be vindicated at the eschatological judgment when the Son of Man returns. The inseparable connection between Jesus and his "words" is analogous to the connection between Jesus and the gospel (v. 35), referring not only to words Jesus has spoken, but to the church's message about him in which he continues to

speak. If the original form of the saying goes back to Jesus, he may have distinguished himself from the Son of Man whose coming in glory will vindicate Jesus' own ministry and those who have acknowledged him,[19] but Mark and his community certainly identify the speaker ("me") as the Son of Man who returns at the Parousia. The Christology of the saying, which combines Son of Man and Son of God, reflects early Christian theological reflection. So also, the terminology of "being ashamed" (cf. Rom 1:16; 2 Tim 1:8, 12, 16; Heb 2:11; 11:16) reflects the vocabulary of the early Christian mission, as does the charge against "this adulterous and sinful generation" referring to the mostly unresponsive and hostile response the Christian preachers had received from Judaism.

[9:1] The chapter division here is unfortunate, for this saying is the conclusion of the preceding sayings cluster, not the beginning of a new unit. The cluster of sayings concludes with a positive eschatological promise balancing the eschatological threat of the preceding saying. The Son of Man is not only integrated into the Son of God image, but directly connected to the coming eschatological kingdom: the coming of the Son of Man will also be the coming of the kingdom "in power." For "kingdom of God," see *Excursus* at 1:15.

The interrelated exegetical issues involve (a) *when* the kingdom is promised to come, (b) what is signified by "in power," (c) the meaning of "seeing" the kingdom, and (d) how to translate the perfect participle *elēlythuian* (see note *l* above). The combination of differing judgments on each of these variables has resulted in many interpretations, often driven by the effort to identify the coming of the kingdom "in power" with some event in the first century that could have been experienced by some of those to whom Jesus is speaking, and thus save Jesus or Mark from an erroneous prediction.[20] The saying has thus been seen as an authentic saying of Jesus referring to the transfiguration, which transpires in the next scene, or as a saying of Jesus or a church teacher or prophet referring to the Parousia, which Mark understands as at least partially fulfilled at the transfiguration.[21] However, the transfiguration story does not speak of the

19. So, e.g., Bultmann, *Theology of the New Testament*, 1:30; H. E. Tödt, *The Son of Man in the Synoptic Tradition* (NTL; trans. Dorothea M. Barton; Philadelphia: Westminster, 1965), 40–46. Though this view has fallen out of favor among more recent exegetes, it is still considered likely by, e.g., Lührmann, *Markusevangelium*, 153 (in the Q-form represented by Luke 12:8–9), and "possible" by, e.g., Donahue and Harrington, *Gospel of Mark*, 264.

20. For a detailed history of interpretation to ca. 1975, see Martin Künzi, *Das Naherwartungslogion Markus 9, 1 par [und Parallelstellen]: Geschichte seiner Auslegung: Mit einem Nachwort zur Auslegungsgeschichte von Markus 13, 30 par* (BGBE 21; Tübingen: Mohr, 1977).

21. E.g., Best, *Gospel as Story*, 87; Pesch, *Markusevangelium*, 2:67; Gnilka, *Markus*, 2:27; C. Clifton Black, "The Face Is Familiar—I Just Can't Place It," in *The End of Mark and the Ends of God: Essays in Memory of Donald Harrisville Juel* (ed. Beverly R. Gaventa and Patrick D. Miller; Louisville, Ky.: Westminster John Knox, 2005), 39. Marcus, *Mystery*, 52, and Marcus, *Mark 8–16*, ad loc. offers a good recent defense of the view that combines transfiguration, resurrection, and Parousia: "The kingdom's coming in power is thus linked both with the transfiguration, which points forward to the resurrection, and with the parousia."

THE MARKAN NARRATIVE WORLD AS APOCALYPTIC HISTORY

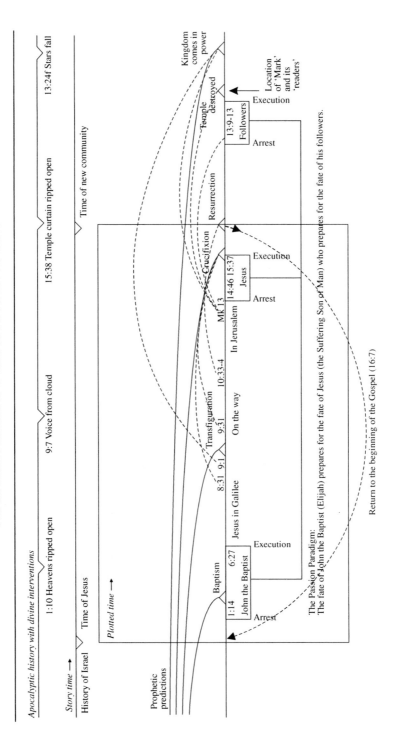

Apocalyptic history with divine interventions

1:10 Heavens ripped open   9:7 Voice from cloud   15:38 Temple curtain ripped open   13:24f Stars fall

Story time →

History of Israel   Time of Jesus   Time of new community

Plotted time →

Prophetic predictions

Kingdom comes in power

Location of 'Mark' and its 'readers'

Temple destroyed

Execution

13:9-13 Followers

Arrest

Resurrection

Crucifixion

Execution

14:46 15:37 Jesus

MK 13

In Jerusalem

Arrest

Transfiguration

10:33-4

8:31 9:1

9:1

On the way

Jesus in Galilee

Execution

6:27 John the Baptist

Baptism

1:14 John the Baptist

Arrest

The Passion Paradigm:
The fate of John the Baptist (Elijah) prepares for the fate of Jesus (the Suffering Son of Man) who prepares for the fate of his followers.

Return to the beginning of the Gospel (16:7)

kingdom or power; it is oriented to Christology rather than the kingdom of God, and is only six days later—hardly justifying the heavy words "before you die." Alternatively, some interpreters have combined "see" with "has come" to mean that the kingdom did in fact come in power in Jesus' own ministry ("realized eschatology") and that Jesus' disciples will come to realize that the reality of the kingdom is in fact already present. C. H. Dodd's early work represents this understanding, which also took a gnosticizing turn in early Christianity: the kingdom is already present, but people don't realize it.[22] So understood, the saying can be seen as from the historical Jesus, who encourages the disciples to see what he sees, and promises that some of them will do so. Closely related to this view is the understanding that the kingdom's coming in power refers to the resurrection of Jesus, the gift of the Spirit at Pentecost, the dynamic mission of early Christianity, and / or the destruction of Jerusalem. Such interpretations must not only regard Jesus as having a nonapocalyptic view of the kingdom, but disregard Mark's apocalypticism, which associates the arrival of the kingdom and the coming of the Son of Man in this very passage. The restriction to "some" and the reference to "tasting death" also pose difficulties for this view.

The saying is probably best understood as an independent logion pronounced as a saying of the risen Jesus by an early Christian prophet.[23] The oracle was a prophetic word of consolation in view of the delay of the Parousia, which promises that at least some of the first generation will live to see it (cf. 13:1–37; 1 Cor 15:51; 1 Thess 4:13–17). The Markan Jesus here points to the Parousia as the coming of the Son of Man and the advent of the kingdom in power as the vindication of those who have given their lives for the sake of Jesus and the gospel.

Excursus: Markan Christology

Christology is the generative and driving force of the Markan narrative. While it has other concerns (e.g., discipleship, eschatology, ecclesiology), it is christological issues that brought the Markan narrative into being and determined its comprehensive structure. Jesus is the central and primary character, and he appears in almost every scene. For example, discipleship is not to be separated from Christology or played off against Christology as though it were a separate theme, just as eschatology is not a discrete "topic" that may be pursued separately, but is wholly determined by the apocalyptic framework in which Jesus returns as Son of Man.

The terms "Christology" and "christological" are here used as umbrella terms for the conceptualization of Jesus' salvific role in God's plan for history. This corresponds to Mark's own use of "Christ" as a comprehensive term. Mark uses a broad spectrum of

22. Dodd, *Parables*, 53. Cf., e.g., *Gos. Thom.* 113, "His disciples said to Him, "When will the Kingdom come?" Jesus said, "It will not come by waiting for it. It will not be a matter of saying 'Here it is' or 'There it is.' Rather, the Kingdom of the Father is spread out upon the earth, and people do not see it."

23. For evidence, argument, and bibliography, see Boring, *Sayings of the Risen Jesus*, 186.

titles, designations, and imagery to communicate the significance of Jesus. All are derived from tradition and influenced by their previous biblical, religious, and cultural contexts; none are created by Mark himself. Titles are important, but their meaning can be explicated only in terms of the Markan narrative. Mark's Christology functions as narrative Christology,[24] and cannot be grasped by cataloging and explicating the traditional meaning(s) of various titles, as though each title were a univocal theological package. Thus each title and image must be examined with regard both to its traditional connotations and function in the Markan narrative. The following is only a summary sketch; see the commentary on key christological texts, and the extensive literature on messianic titles and imagery.[25]

Titles, Designations, and Images

1. Christ (Christos)

The English "Christ" is the transliteration (not translation) of the Greek *Christos*, which is the Greek translation of the Hebrew *Mešiah* (transliterated "Messiah"). Both "Christ" and "Messiah," if translated into English, would be "anointed." While sacral anointing was known in the Greco-Roman world, the background and connotations of this term in the New Testament are drawn entirely from the Bible and Jewish tradition. Anointing was part of the inauguration ceremony for priests (e.g., Exod 28:41; Lev 21:10; Sir 45:15), prophets (e.g., 1 Kgs 19:16; Isa 61:1; Ps 105:15), and kings (e.g., 1 Sam 15:1; 2 Sam 2:4; Ps 18:50), but the understanding of "Christ" in terms of the three-fold office of prophet, priest, and king was a later systematic construction of Christian theology (e.g., John Calvin, *Institutes* II.15). In first-century Judaism, "Messiah" meant primarily "king"—God's anointed king who would defeat Israel's enemies and establish God's kingdom, often understood in eschatological terms. The term itself designates a human being through whom God will act, but in some streams of first-century Jewish tradition the Messiah was already related to or identified with transcendent figures (Son of Man, Son of God).

---

24. Cf. Petr Pokorný, *Der Gottessohn: Literarische Übersicht und Fragestellung* (ThSt 109; Zürich: Theologischer Verlag, 1971), 2–17; Kertelge, *Wunder*, 190. Kingsbury, *Christology of Mark's Gospel*, passim; Robert C. Tannehill, "The Gospel of Mark as Narrative Christology," *Semeia* 16 (1980): 57–96; M. Eugene Boring, "The Christology of Mark: Hermeneutical Issues for Systematic Theology," *Semeia* 30 (1985): 125–54; Edwin K. Broadhead, *Naming Jesus: Titular Christology in the Gospel of Mark* (JSNTSup 175; Sheffield: Sheffield Academic, 1999), 27, 90, 123 and passim; Malbon, "Christology of Mark's Gospel," 33–48.

25. E.g., Reginald H. Fuller, *The Foundations of New Testament Christology* (New York: Scribner, 1965); Ferdinand Hahn, *The Titles of Jesus in Christology: Their History in Early Christianity* (trans. Harold Knight and George Ogg; New York: World, 1969); James D. G. Dunn, *Christology in the Making: A New Testament Inquiry into the Origins of the Doctrine of the Incarnation* (Philadelphia: Westminster, 1980); James H. Charlesworth, ed., *The Messiah: Developments in Earliest Judaism and Christianity* (Minneapolis: Fortress, 1992). Again available is the classic work of Sigmund Mowinckel, *He That Cometh: The Messiah Concept in the Old Testament and Later Judaism* (trans. G. W. Anderson; BRS; Grand Rapids: Eerdmans, 2005).

"Christ" is a *theo*centric term. The ending *-tos* identifies *Christos* as a verbal adjective, the equivalent of a past participle in English, anoint*ed*. The one who anoints is God; the designation "Christ" points to God as the actor. To confess that Jesus is the Christ does not answer the question "Who is Jesus?" but "Who is God?" The point of Christology is not the distinctiveness of Jesus, but that God is the one acting definitively in Jesus.[26] For Mark, to confess that the Christ is Jesus of Nazareth is to affirm an apocalyptic view of history in which the ultimate victory of God will be revealed at the Parousia of Jesus as the Son of Man, through whom God's eschatological kingdom will be realized. The focus of this title is not on the "person" of Jesus, but on the definitive act of God the Creator for the salvation of the world. The Markan Christology is thus not merely a statement about Jesus, but about God and the meaning of history.[27]

Mark uses *Christos* seven times (1:1; 8:29; 9:41; 12:35; 13:21; 14:61; 15:32), all but 12:35 and 13:21 referring directly to Jesus. "Christ" is the encompassing image of Markan Christology. In 1:1 the narrator affirms "Christ" as the comprehensive title that embraces the story as a whole, and Jesus himself affirms it in the climactic trial scene (14:61–62). At a major turning point in the narrative, Peter's "confession" at 8:29 identifies Jesus by this one title. During his ministry, Jesus will proleptically identify his followers as "those who belong to Christ" (9:41).

2. *Son of God* (ho huios tou theou)

Unlike "Christ," "son of God" has a wide range of meanings in Mark's world that cuts across Jewish and Gentile contexts. In the biblical and Jewish worlds of thought, "son" (Heb. *ben,* Aram. *bar*) not only had its usual biological meaning, but often designated the category to which someone or something belonged (see note *c* at 2:19). Thus "son of God" language could be used for a being who belongs to the heavenly world, that is, an angel, a transcendent divine being (Gen 6:2; Job 1:6 [cf. NRSV fn.]). Israel could be called God's son (Exod 4:22). The Judean king was adopted as God's son at his coronation (Ps 2:7), and particularly wise or righteous individuals could be called "sons of God" (Wis 2:16–20), just as Christians could later be so designated (Matt 5:9; Rom 8:14 [sometimes obscured by the gender-inclusive language of modern translations]). In biblical and Jewish tradition there were thus several senses in which a human being could

---

26. Schubert M. Ogden, *The Point of Christology* (San Francisco: Harper & Row, 1982), 19–40.

27. Cf. Lohmeyer, *Markus,* 3; Oscar Cullmann, *The Christology of the New Testament* (Rev. ed.; NTL; trans. Shirley C. Guthrie and Charles A. M. Hall; Philadelphia: Westminster, 1963), 326: "All Christology is salvation history, and all salvation history is Christology"; Via, *Ethics of Mark's Gospel,* 4, 27–39 and passim; Adela Yarbro Collins, *The Beginning of the Gospel: Probings of Mark in Context* (Minneapolis: Fortress, 1992), 1–3, 66, 72. While the dynamism of Mark's understanding cannot be captured in a diachronic two-dimensional chart, the diagram of Keith Dyer (adapted from Burton Mack) is helpful in visualizing Mark's understanding of the setting of his narrative segment within universal history. My adaptation on p. 247 in this volume is a modification of Dyer's chart. See Keith D. Dyer, *The Prophecy on the Mount: Mark 13 and the Gathering of the New Community* (ITS 2; Bern: Lang, 1998), 259; Mack, *Myth of Innocence,* 329. Thus while Mark is rightly regarded as "apocalyptic," this does not mean he is interested either in explicating the signs and chronology of the end of the present age or in depicting what the end of the age and the future world will be like. See further on 13:5–37.

be called "son of God." In Gentile thought, on the other hand, "son of God" would often denote a nonhuman being capable of superhuman feats. Mark is heir to both these cultural and religious streams, but his understanding of "Son of God" as a designation for Jesus cannot be simply identified with or reduced to either. In particular, for Mark "son of God" cannot be reduced to the Israelite idea that the king was adopted as God's son; instead it has an eschatological dimension related to the Son of Man (cf. Strecker, *Theology*, 357).

Mark uses "Son of God" language and imagery nine times (1:1 [disputed; see note *c* there]; 1:11; 3:11; 5:7; 8:38; 9:7; 13:32; 14:61; 15:39). That Jesus is Son of God is declared by the narrator, God, demons, Jesus himself, and the centurion at the cross—the only human being in the narrative to make this confession. What Mark means by the title cannot be determined from the background of the phrase in the history of religions, but only from the Markan narrative itself.

3. *Son of Man* (ho huios tou anthrōpou)

Like "Christ," "son of man" is an expression from the Bible and Jewish tradition that would sound strange in Gentile ears, just as its English translation sounds strange to modern English readers. "Son" in the phrase does not denote a biological relation, but a category (see above on "son of God"). The primary meaning of "son of man" is "member of the category 'human,'" that is, a human being (cf., e.g., the parallelism in Ps 8:4, where "son of man" clearly is the same as "man" [obscured by gender-inclusive translations]). The phrase is used especially of human beings in contrast to God (ninety-three times in Ezekiel, cf. RSV; rendered "mortal" in NRSV). New Testament usage is influenced by the apocalyptic picture in Dan 7, where the succession of pagan empires is symbolized by a series of ferocious animals, concluded when God gives the kingdom to Israel, symbolized by a human being, that is, one like "son of man." While the figure in Daniel was metaphorical and part of a vision, this picture was later objectified, and it was thought that God is reserving in heaven an actual transcendent being, the Son of Man, who will come at the end of history to inaugurate God's kingdom.

The Gospels include Son of Man only in sayings of Jesus; the narrator never refers to Jesus by this title, nor does anyone in the narrative confess or dispute the identity of Jesus using these words. The early Christian tradition of Jesus' sayings included numerous Son of Man sayings, which fall fairly neatly into three categories: sayings that picture the apocalyptic coming of the Son of Man at the end of history, sayings that portray Jesus as the Son of Man acting with authority during his earthly life, and sayings that depict the suffering, dying, and rising of Jesus as the Son of Man. These groups do not overlap; there are no sayings, for instance, that picture the death, resurrection, and Parousia of the Son of Man. Mark has all three types of sayings: "eschatological coming" (8:38; 13:26; 14:62); "present authority" (2:10, 28; 10:45); "suffering, dying, rising" (8:31; 9:9, 12, 31; 10:33–34; 14:21 [two times]; 14:41). The traditional Son of Man of biblical and Jewish apocalyptic sees the plight of the persecuted people of God, identifies with them, and comes to save them (as also in Mark 13:26). In Mark, however, the Son of Man enters into their situation as himself a human being (the original, generic meaning of the term) and suffers with them. While Mark has no explicit doctrine of preexistence or incarnation, his Son of Man Christology is something of a functional equivalent. Though the sayings originated in different streams of tradition, with Mark himself supplying or elaborating the passion predictions, Mark uses Son of Man to portray and bind together the various phases of Jesus' life and work (Collins, *Beginning of the Gospel*, 64). He acts with God's authority on earth, he suffers, dies, and is raised by God, he will come again on the clouds of heaven in the glory of his Father. The image of the future coming of the Son of Man is sometimes parallel to or identical with the coming of the kingdom of God (8:38–9:1). The christological language of the Son of Man sayings is thoroughly theocentric.

4. *Lord* (kyrios)

The Greek term *kyrios* refers fundamentally to one who owns and has authority over, for example, the master of a slave or owner of property. While it can be used as a polite term of respect (like *Herr* in German; *señor* in Spanish; *seigneur* and *monsieur* in French; sir in English; cf. Matt 27:63 to Pilate), usage in Mark's context is fundamentally affected by two factors: (1) the LXX uses *kyrios* hundreds of times as the translation of the divine name YHWH; (2) *Kyrios* was used as a title for deity in pagan cults, including the emperor cult. When early Christianity used this term for Jesus, it raised the question of monotheism for Jews and patriotism for Romans.

Mark exploits the ambiguity of this term, never clearly using it in its diminished secular sense of "sir," but only in ways that can be understood directly or indirectly as referring to God or Jesus. Of the sixteen occurrences (1:3; 2:28; 5:19; 7:28; 11:3, 9; 12:9, 11, 29, 30, 36, 37; 13:20, 35), Jesus is addressed as *kyrios* only in 7:28. At the narrative level, the woman may mean only "sir" (cf. NRSV); the reader hears the truth of her address at a different level. In 12:9 and 13:35, Jesus uses *kyrios* of characters in his parables who point beyond themselves to God or Jesus. So also the narrator has constructed the sentence at 11:3 so that the Greek can be understood either as "The Lord has need of it" or "Its master needs it." From the first occurrence of *kyrios* in 1:3, referring to God in the Old Testament text but to Jesus in the Markan narrative, the ambiguity between the figures of God as Lord and Jesus as Lord seems intentional, and to ask "which" is meant is a misplaced question. The figures of God and Jesus modulate into each other without dissolving the distinction; to identify them compromises monotheism, a compromise Mark adamantly opposes (12:29–30; cf. on 5:19). To separate them too crisply misunderstands Jesus' relation to the one God (cf. 9:37). The post-Easter readers in the Markan church confess Jesus as Lord, but (contrary to all the other Gospels) Mark never allows either the narrator or characters in the story to address Jesus as "Lord" in the christological sense, using this term with an ambiguity which is almost cunning.

5. *Suffering Servant*

"Servant" (Heb. ʿebed; LXX *pais* or *doulos*) is found in the Old Testament and Jewish tradition as a term for the eschatological savior-figure sent by God, sometimes explicitly identified with the Messiah (Ezek 34:23–24; 37:24–25; Zech 3:8; 2 Esd 7:28; 13:32, 37, 52; 14:9; *2 Bar.* 7.9). However, in Jewish tradition the suffering servant of Isa 53 is never portrayed in messianic terms, nor is the expected Messiah ever identified with Isaiah's suffering servant.[28] Explicit christological appeal to Isa 53 is minimal and late in the development of New Testament theology (Matt 8:17; Acts 8:32–33; 1 Pet 2:22–25).

Pais is not found in Mark; the other terms for "servant," *doulos* and *diakonos*, are found seven times, but never applied to Jesus. The parable of 12:1–11 indirectly contrasts the prophets as *douloi* (servants) and Jesus as *huios* (Son). Yet, in the key text 10:45, Mark uses the cognate verb *diakoneō* as central to Jesus' ministry and identity; the one who serves and gives his life a ransom for many seems to allude to the Isa 53 imagery without making an explicit identification. The centrality of Isaiah for Mark (see *Excursus: Mark and the Scriptures* at 14:52), the role of the Isaian servant hymns (Isa 42:1–4; 49:1–7; 50:4–11; 52:13–53:12) in Mark, and the manner in which the narrative as a whole is permeated with Isaian imagery and allusions all make it likely that the image of Isaiah's suffering servant hovers in the background of Mark's Christology.

6. *Teacher* (didaskalos, rabbi, rabbouni)

"Rabbi" is used three times (9:5; 11:21; 14:45), "rabbouni" only in 10:51, and *didaskalos* ("teacher") twelve times (4:38; 5:35; 9:17, 38; 10:17, 20, 35; 12:14, 19, 32; 13:1; 14:14), with the verb *didaskō* used an additional seventeen times, always of Jesus except 6:30 (the disciples teach by Jesus' authority) and 7:7 (Old Testament citation predicting false teaching). *Didache* "teaching" is used an additional five times, always of Jesus' teaching. "Teacher" and "teaching" are used in an unqualified positive sense, but "rabbi" and "rabbouni" have the overtones of failed discipleship or inadequate understanding. Although it was sometimes expected that the eschatological bringer of salvation would settle disputed questions and provide the definitive understanding of God's revealed will, "teacher" per se was not a messianic title or designation. Yet *didaskalos* is a favorite Markan designation of Jesus, used by inquiring crowds, interested individuals, Jesus' own disciples, and Jesus himself (14:14).

Despite its frequency, the term "teacher" is not for Mark Jesus' fundamental identity. He is not basically a teacher in the Hellenistic sense; his mission is not to teach his disciples his system of thought or way of life as a body of teaching independent of his own person. Thus little content of Jesus' teaching is given; *that* Jesus teaches by God's authority, not *what* he teaches, is central for Mark. "Teaching" thus seems to represent Jesus' person, authority, and activity as a whole, including his "mighty works." In the opening scene of 1:21–28, for example, "teaching with authority" brackets the pericope (21, 27), but the content of the pericope is an exorcism, not the subject matter of Jesus' teaching. "All" (in the synagogue) respond to Jesus' authority in casting out the demon by declaring that a "new teaching with authority" has appeared among them. Jesus' exorcisms are

---

28. Contra J. Jeremias, "*Pais Theou* in Later Judaism in the Period after the LXX," Walter Zimmerli and Joachim Jeremias, "*pais theou*," in *TDNT*, 677–700. Most scholars remain unpersuaded by Jeremias's evidence and argument; cf., e.g., Morna D. Hooker, *Jesus and the Servant: The Influence of the Servant Concept of Deutero-Isaiah in the New Testament* (London: SPCK, 1959), and Eduard Lohse, *Märtyer und Gottesknecht: Untersuchungen zur urchristlichen Verkündigung vom Sühntod Jesu Christi* (FRLANT 46; Göttingen: Vandenhoeck & Ruprecht, 1955).

not a parallel phenomenon alongside his teaching, but are subsumed under it. The focus of Jesus' teaching was on the dawning of the kingdom of God; his exorcisms are an aspect of this, as God reestablishes his rule over a rebellious world. So also, as one who can calm the storm on the Sea of Galilee, Jesus is addressed somewhat incongruously as "Teacher" (4:38). Jesus' last salvific miracle is 10:46–52, but his teaching activity continues (12:35; 14:49). Jesus' teaching is the comprehensive category into which his mighty acts of salvation are integrated; Jesus as teacher (of the kingdom of God) is the comprehensive designation within which Jesus as exorcist and miracle worker are included and interpreted.[29] Jesus is not simply a miracle worker; Mark is concerned to show that Jesus' healings and exorcisms represent the divine conquest of the demonic kingdom, bringing the rebellious world back under God's sovereignty. All this is represented as an aspect of Jesus' authoritative teaching (see commentary on 1:27). The contents of the Markan narrative as a whole can thus be considered "teaching," and probably represent the composition of an early Christian teacher.

Like "scribe" for Jesus' opponents, the distribution of "teacher" terminology across the narrative provides continuity between part one (Jesus-the-miracle-worker) and part two (Jesus-the-crucified-man-of-Nazareth). In part one, the authority of Jesus' teaching is manifest in his miracles. In part two, the teaching and authority continue, but miracles cease. "Teacher" is a narrative thread that holds these two portrayals together. Furthermore, "teacher"—like Christ, Son of God, and Son of Man—is a title at home in the Jewish and early Christian tradition inherited by Mark. But—unlike specifically Jewish titles—"teacher" is also at home in his own Hellenistic context as a title for an authoritative, transforming leader who gathers disciples. Furthermore, Mark's own church has teachers who authoritatively represent the message from and about Jesus within the congregations. The multi-layered image of Jesus as authoritative teacher thus serves as a hermeneutical bridge from the Jesus of the text to Mark's own situation.[30]

7. *Prophet* (prophētēs)

Jesus indirectly applies the title "prophet" to himself (6:4), and the narrator with obvious irony has Jesus mocked as a prophet (14:65), indirectly affirming Jesus as truly a prophet. The populace places Jesus in the category of biblical prophets (6:15; 8:28). Though "prophet" is inherently related to "Christ" (see 1. above) Mark does not directly associate the two (as he associates "Christ," "Son of God," and "Son of Man"). John the Baptist is "really a prophet" (11:32), but John himself had declared the one coming after him to be the "mightier one." The passage 12:1–12 indirectly contrasts the biblical prophets with Jesus as the Son. For Mark, "prophet" is a valid designation of Jesus, but inadequate as a christological identification.

---

29. Paul J. Achtemeier, "'He Taught Them Many Things': Reflections on Marcan Christology," *CBQ* 42 (1980): 478–80. Kertelge, *Wunder*, 37–38, 56: Jesus' words and deeds do not in Mark lie alongside each other, but "ineinander," integrated into each other.

30. Cf. elaboration in Boring, "Christology of Mark," 133–34; Robbins, *Jesus the Teacher*, 12–14 and passim; and Edwin Keith Broadhead, *Teaching with Authority: Miracles and Christology in the Gospel of Mark* (JSNTSup 74; Sheffield: JSOT Press, 1992), 187 and passim.

8. *Shepherd* (poimēn)

In biblical and Jewish tradition, "shepherd" is a royal title and image, used both for God and for the king of Israel (e.g., Pss 23:1; 100:3; Ezek 34:15; 2 Sam 5:2). It is sometimes a tender, compassionate image, but for the most part it has the connotation of authoritative rule—the shepherd has absolute power over the sheep. Thus "shepherd" became a title and image for the hoped-for eschatological ruler (Ezek 34:23–24; 2 Esd 2:33–36). The Fourth Gospel explicitly adopts this title and image as a key christological term (John 10:2–16), and Matt 2:6 modifies Mic 5:2 to make the shepherd imagery more explicit. Mark, too, uses the shepherd image of Jesus, but does not make it explicit (14:27; cf. 6:34).

9. *Holy One of God* (ho hagios tou theou)

Though holiness is a central biblical concept, this specific phrase has no background in the Old Testament or Judaism. It is found only in Mark 1:24, where the demons with transcendent knowledge so identify Jesus. The designation is important in the Markan narrative in that Jesus confronts the issue of purity, not as one who opposes the purity concept as such, but as himself the bearer of God's holiness, who authoritatively declares what is holy and what is unclean (see on 2:1–3:6; 7:1–23).

10. *Bridegroom* (nymphios)

"Bridegroom" is not a traditional messianic image; so far as we know, there were no Jewish expectations that represented the coming Messiah as a bridegroom. Nuptial imagery had been used in the Old Testament and Jewish tradition to characterize the relation of God and Israel (Isa 54:4–8; 61:10; 62:5; Ezek 16; Hos 2). From Paul onward, early Christianity tradition used nuptial imagery of the Messiah (2 Cor 11:2; Eph 5:22–32; Rev 19:7; 21:2, 9; Matt 22:1–4; 25:1–13). Mark uses the term "bridegroom" three times in 2:19–20, clearly referring to Jesus. In Mark's understanding of salvation history, the time of Jesus is a special time of celebration in which "the rules were suspended" and to which the Markan church looks back, a period pointing forward to the special time of the Parousia, but not characterizing its own time of trouble and persecution.

11. *King of the Jews/Israel* (basileus tōn Ioudaiōn/Israēl)

The question of whether Jesus is "king of the Jews" (as Romans would have expressed it) emerges five times (15:2, 9, 12, 18, 26), with the more Jewish expression "king of Israel" used in 15:32. The phrase is never found in the mouth of Jesus, the disciples, or the narrator, but at its first occurrence in 15:2 Jesus affirms that he is indeed king of the Jews, though not with the straightforward "I am" of 14:62 with which he claims the title "Christ." The characters in the narrative misunderstand the title and claim in the political sense, yet the narrator has made it clear that Jesus represents the kingship of God in the future kingdom of God that already dawns in Jesus' ministry (see *Excursus: Kingdom of God* at 1:15).

12. *Son of David* (huios Dauid)

The Old Testament portrays David as God's chosen king who established God's rule over Israel and other peoples, "the king par excellence, . . . the standard for all later kings, and . . . a messianic symbol."[31] God promised that David's kingdom would endure forever, that God would be father to the Davidic king, who would be God's son (2 Sam 7:12–16). When historical realities prevented this promise from being understood as the uninterrupted continuation of the Davidic line, the promise was reinterpreted as the hope of a restored Davidic kingdom. The expectation of a messianic "Son of David" was alive in first-century Judaism, as portrayed in *Pss. Sol.* 17: a wise and righteous king empowered by God's Spirit will reunite scattered Israel, subdue the Gentile nations, and rule in God's kingdom on earth.

Some New Testament authors reinterpret this imagery and incorporate it in their own Christology (cf. the pre-Pauline creed cited in Rom 1:3–4; Matt 1:1; 9:27; 12:23; 15:22; 21:9, 15; Luke 1:32, 69; 3:31; 2 Tim 2:8; Rev 5:5; 22:16). Exegetes have variously understood Mark's own use of Davidic imagery.[32] The present commentary understands Mark to be suspicious of "Son of David" Christology, opposing the Davidic messianic imagery current in some Jewish and Christian streams at the time of the 66–70 war. He does not reinterpret the Davidic imagery positively, but dissociates Jesus from the Davidic hope. The Markan Jesus has no Davidic genealogy, and does not come from Bethlehem, the city of David (not mentioned in Mark). His hometown acquaintances reject him as only "son of Mary," with no hint here or elsewhere in Mark that Jesus' genealogy qualifies him as something special. He is misunderstood by the crowds in Davidic terms (11:9–10), challenges the scribal identification of Messiah and Son of David (12:35–37), and heals the blindness of the one person who addresses him with this title (10:47–48).

13. *The Coming One* (ho erchomenos)

The specific expression "the coming one," or "the one who is to come," as a designation for the Messiah is not found in Jewish tradition. Its earliest occurrence seems to be in the Q expression Luke 7:19–20 / Matt 11:3. Mark makes no use of the term, its closest approximation being the crowd's acclamation of Jesus as "the one who comes in the name of the Lord." Their acclamation is misplaced, and is associated with the kingdom of David, also described as "coming" (see on 11:9). Over against the "coming" kingdom of David, Mark places the coming of the Son of Man (13:26; 14:62), who must go through suffering and death to bring the kingdom.

---

31. David M. Howard Jr., "David," in *ABD*, 2:41.

32. In addition to the surveys in note 25 above, cf. the monograph of Christoph Burger, *Jesus als Davidssohn: Eine traditionsgeschichtliche Untersuchung* (FRLANT 98; Göttingen: Vandenhoeck & Ruprecht, 1970), 1–71. Burger summarizes the spectrum of approaches and argues for the view that Mark positively appropriates Son of David in terms of a two-stage Christology analogous to Rom 1:3–4: during his earthly life Jesus *was* Son of David, but is *now* enthroned as Son of God (cf. p. 70).

14. The Mightier One (ho ischyroteros)

From earliest times, the "Mighty One" had been a title for Israel's God (e.g., Gen 49:24; Pss 50:1; 132:2, 5; Isa 49:26; 60:16). Though the Messiah was expected to operate with the power of God, "Mighty One" had not become a messianic title. The hoped-for kingdom of God would be a manifestation of power, God himself coming in strength.[33]

"Power" thus became not merely a characteristic of God, but a circumlocution for the name of God himself, used by the Markan Jesus in the key scene of self-identification (Mark 14:62). Before Jesus appears on the scene, John the Baptist unknowingly points to him as the "Mightier One." Jesus' miracles are consistently called *dynameis*, manifestations of power (of God). His power over demons does not represent internal strife within the demonic realm, but the Mightier One who invades the demonic world from outside (3:22–27). When these manifestations of divine power disappear in part two of the narrative and Jesus suffers and dies in human weakness, the reader is compelled to reflect on how the ultimate power of God is finally manifested in the "Mightier One."

Titular Christology: Summary

The titles have different nuances, but all have the same referent, and fundamentally the same meaning: the human being Jesus of Nazareth as the agent of God's salvation. In the narrative, the titles overlap, not only in that they all are applied to the same figure, the crucified and risen Lord, where they are used interchangeably, but in their actual usage: the Son of Man has God for his Father, that is, is also "Son of God" (8:38); the Messiah is also Son of God, explicated by reference to the Son of Man (14:62). The titles interpret each other, and the reality of the figure Jesus of Nazareth interprets them all. Arguments about which is the "key" or "primary" title for Mark are thus misplaced, based on the misconception that the titles function basically by applying their traditional contents to Jesus. Although there is a sense in which "Christ" is the encompassing image and title,[34] Mark does not use one title to "correct" another. He is not opposing a false Christology represented by one title by replacing it or modifying it with another. The tensions among the contents and nuances of the various titles are not adjudicated by discursive explanations, but by their arrangement in the narrative. While the titles do to some extent interpret Jesus, it is primarily Jesus who interprets the titles, giving them content and meaning determined by the narrative itself. "The Christology of Mark's

---

33. Chilton, *God in Strength.* Cf. Moloney's translation of *hē basileia tou theou* as "the reigning presence of God" (*Mark: Commentary*, 49 and passim).

34. Thus, if one must designate one title that is central or key to all the others, it should be "Christ" (with Donald Juel, "The Origin of Mark's Christology," in *The Messiah: Developments in Earliest Judaism and Christianity* [ed. James H. Charlesworth; Minneapolis: Fortress, 1992], 450), against, e.g., Kingsbury, who argues for "Son of God" (*Christology of Mark's Gospel*, 47–156), and, e.g., Perrin and Achtemeier, who argue for "Son of Man": Norman Perrin, "The Christology of Mark: A Study in Methodology (1971, 1974)," in *The Interpretation of Mark* (ed. William R. Telford; 2d ed.; SNTI; Edinburgh: T. & T. Clark, 1995), 131; Paul J. Achtemeier, *Mark* (2d ed.; Proclamation Commentaries; Philadelphia: Fortress, 1986), 58–60.

Gospel is in the story it tells. . . . Christology is in the story, and through the story we learn to interpret the titles."[35]

Narrative Christology: Summary

Mark's narrative mode of expressing his Christology allows him to juxtapose images of Jesus that, if expressed in discursive language, would be radical contraries. Some Markan images and languages for Jesus portray him as the truly divine agent of God's salvation, acting in the place of God and doing what only God can do. *Epiphany Christology* portrayed Jesus as the powerful, truly divine Son of God, called for triumphalistic Spirit-filled disciples, and could not incorporate a truly human Jesus who truly suffers and dies. Other images portray Jesus as truly human, fully identified with human weakness and victimization. *Kenosis Christology* portrayed the power of God at work in the weakness of the truly human, crucified man of Nazareth, in accord with the Pauline kerygma, and could not incorporate stories of Jesus the miracle worker filled with divine power.[36] In Mark's situation, advocates of each view of Jesus supposed the other view must be rejected. "Miracle stories and passion narrative, the divine man (*theios anēr*) and the Crucified, need relating in a new way. Mark's Gospel grew out of this situation."[37] Conceptually, the two types of christological imagery cannot be combined without compromising one or the other or both. A Jesus who can walk on the water can come down from the cross, and his crucifixion is a sham. A Jesus who cannot come down from the cross cannot walk on the water, and the miracle stories are not really miracles. A truly human Jesus cannot also be truly divine; a truly divine Christ cannot also be truly human. No single theological perspective is ever adequate to do justice to its subject matter. More than one concept is necessary, even if they cannot be conceptually reconciled. Mark affirms both Christologies, and devised a narrative mode of claiming and explicating them both. The narrative juxtaposes the conflicting imagery without synthesizing it (see *Excursus: The Messianic Secret* at 9:13). Mark should not be considered a "synthesis" or "integration" of opposing views; his narrative includes each perspective on Jesus without adjusting it to the other.[38]

35. Frank J. Matera, *New Testament Christology* (Louisville, Ky.: Westminster John Knox, 1999), 26–27.

36. Cf. 1 Cor 1:25–27; 15:43; 2 Cor 12:9; 13:4. Dorothy A. Lee-Pollard, "Powerlessness as Power: A Key Emphasis in the Gospel of Mark," *SJT* 40 (1987): 173–88.

37. Ulrich Luz, "The Secrecy Motif and the Marcan Christology (1965)," in *The Messianic Secret* (ed. C. M. Tuckett; IRT 1; London: SPCK, 1983), 75.

38. Thus Wrede's old view is still to be affirmed, with one important qualification. He argued that "The evangelist has two contrasting motifs but in his consciousness they do not clash. He expresses one, and close beside it the other." While much in Wrede's view has been rightfully modified by subsequent study, on this essential point he was correct. He was wrong, however, when he followed up this insight with the comment that "This juxtaposition is possible only if the narrator simply was not aware of what conclusions for the historical picture must be drawn from each of the two ideas by those reflecting on it" (*Messianic Secret*, 38). Mark did not stumble blindly, like the disciples he describes, into this profound insight. It does not represent naiveté, but careful reflection. Mark was not unaware that reflecting on these two views would produce problems for

9:2–13 The Transfiguration and Discussion about Elijah

9:2 And after six days Jesus takes along Peter, James, and John and brings them up to a high mountain apart, by themselves. And he was transfigured before them, 3 and his clothes became dazzling white, such as no cloth worker in the world could whiten them. 4 And Elijah with Moses appeared to them, and they were talking with Jesus. 5 And Peter says to Jesus, "Rabbi, it is good for us to be here, and let us make three booths—one for you, one for Moses, and one for Elijah." 6 For he did not know what to say, for they were terrified. 7 And a cloud appeared, overshadowing them, and a voice came out of the cloud, "This is my beloved Son, listen to him!" 8 And suddenly, when they looked around, they no longer saw anyone, but only Jesus with them.

9 And as they were coming down from the mountain, he commanded them to tell no one what they had seen until the Son of Man had risen from among the dead.[a] 10 And they observed the warning faithfully,[b] questioning among themselves what this "rising from among the dead"[a] might mean. 11 And they were asking him, "Why do the scribes say that Elijah must come first?" 12 He said to them, "Does Elijah in fact come first and restore everything? Then[c] how is it written about the Son of Man, that he is to endure much suffering and be treated with contempt? 13 But I say to you, Elijah has come, and they did whatever they wanted to him, just as it is written about him."

a. "Dead" in the stock phrase "resurrection of the dead" is plural. In v. 9 *ek nekrōn anastē* can mean "raising of the dead ones" (objective genitive) or someone's "rising from among the dead ones" (genitive of source or origin) But the inclusion of the preposition *ek* ("out of," "from") in v. 10 makes it clear that in both cases the idea is the resurrection of one person from among the dead ones, not the general resurrection. Jewish tradition was familiar with the latter concept, not the former, which is distinctively Christian. The neuter article *to* before the phrase is anaphoric, thus the translation with "this" and the enclosure of the phrase in quotation marks.

b. The phrase *ton logon ekratēsan pros heautous* can also be translated "they kept the matter to themselves" (cf. NIV, NRSV), translating *krateō* as "keep" in the sense of "hold on to" rather than "observe" (a commandment; cf. 2 Thess 2:15), and construing *pros heautous* with *ekratēsan* rather than *syzētountes* ("discussing"). In either case, Mark's point is that the disciples did not divulge the pre-Easter glory of Jesus until after the resurrection.

---

conventional logic. It was precisely his reflection on this problem that generated the narrative form for holding the two traditional christological perspectives together. ". . . resolving these tensions involves unacceptable revisions in other theological loci" (Michael Root, "Dying He Lives: Biblical Image, Biblical Narrative, and the Redemptive Jesus," *Semeia* 30 [1985]: 170). For a good summary of the issues and argument for the approach advocated here, see Phillip G. Davis, "Mark's Christological Paradox," *JSNT* 35 (1989): 3–18.

c. Verse 12a can be punctuated either as a statement or a question (see commentary). If 12a is understood as a question, Mark's ubiquitous *kai*, usually simply "and," here takes on one of its other meanings (see Bauer and Danker, BDAG, 494).

On the way to its incorporation in Mark, several influences may have played a role in the formation and transmission of this story in which the human Jesus not only converses with heavenly beings but is himself clothed with an other-worldly glory. The most popular work of the most popular Roman poet was Ovid's *Metamorphoses,* a collection that integrates some 250 separate myths into a grand story containing tales in which gods are transformed into human form and human beings are transformed into gods. The Jewish Scriptures knew of heroes who were taken to the heavenly world without dying—Enoch, Elijah, and in later Jewish tradition, Moses (whose death is recounted in Deut 34:5–6, but cf. Philo, *QG* 1.86; Josephus, *Ant.* 4.8.48). Jewish apocalyptic knew of human beings who are transformed into the glorious forms of the transcendent world (in *1 En.* 70–71 the man Enoch morphs into the heavenly Son of Man) or who already glow with divine radiance while in this world (*1 En.* 106.2–6 of the newborn Noah). Moses' face glowed with divine radiance after meeting with God on Mount Sinai (Exod 34:29–35),[39] an image that influenced Paul's understanding of the Christian life as a continuing process of transfiguration (2 Cor 3:18; cf. Rom 12:2). In ways that cannot be precisely traced, the imagery associated with Moses and Elijah as prophets who had been persecuted but had been vindicated and exalted to heaven continued to influence Christian imagery (Rev 11:1–13).

It is thus difficult to regard the account as simply a straightforward report-ing of an event in the life of Jesus. Those who have attempted to explain "what really happened" have ventured both subjective interpretations (a "group visionary experience" or the like; Matt 17:9 already calls it a "vision") or ratio-nalistic explanations of some "natural" event (lightning, thunderstorm, fog, sunset or sunrise glow). The literary-theological explanation of a "misplaced resurrection account" has also failed to meet the test of scholarly scrutiny, and has rightly been virtually abandoned.[40] There is an important truth in this gen-

39. For additional parallels and points of contact in pagan and Jewish literature from Homer on, see Boring et al., *Hellenistic Commentary,* §§ 125–29, 1; Gnilka, *Markus,* 2:33; Lührmann, *Markusevangelium,* 156; and esp. Dieter Zeller, "Bedeutung und religionsgeschichtlicher Hinter-grund der Verwandlung Jesu," in *Authenticating the Activities of Jesus* (ed. Bruce Chilton and Craig A. Evans; Leiden: Brill, 1999), 303–21.

40. Wellhausen had already proposed this, followed more recently by, e.g., James M. Robin-son, "Jesus: From Easter to Valentinus (or to the Apostles Creed)," *JBL* 101 (1982): 5–37, and Wee-den, *Conflict,* 118–24. Cf. the discussions and bibliography in Eduard Schweizer, *The Good News According to Mark* (trans. Donald H. Madvig; Richmond: John Knox, 1970), 180; Gnilka, *Markus,* 2:30–31; and Best, *Following Jesus,* 58–60, all of whom reject the theory.

eral approach, however. While the transfiguration is not a story of a specific resurrection appearance retrojected into the pre-Easter life of Jesus, the Markan narrative as a whole is indeed seen from the perspective of the risen Lord of the church's faith, so that there is a sense in which much of his narrative is a retrojection of post-Easter faith onto a pre-Easter screen. In early Christian theology in general and in the Gospels' narrative theology in particular, the line between historical Jesus and risen Lord was not firm or crisp.

[9:2] Prior to the passion story (cf. 14:1), the chronological precision represented by "after six days" is unique in Mark. It may have originally reflected the influence of Exod 24:9–16 and 34:1–35, where Moses takes three companions, ascends the mountain, and after six days God speaks to him from the cloud and Moses' appearance is transformed. The "high mountain" is not to be sought for on a map and identified with a particular mountain, but like Sinai, which is associated with both Moses and Elijah, it is the mountain of revelation. Peter, James, and John are the inner circle of the Twelve (see 5:37; 14:33; *Excursus: Crowds, Followers, Disciples, and the Twelve* at 6:6). The passive verb is a "divine passive," pointing to the *theo*centricity of the whole scene: it is God who transforms, who speaks, corresponding to the "glory of *his Father*" that will characterize the Parousia of the Son of Man (8:38). The transcendent whiteness of Jesus' garments characterizes him as belonging to the divine world (cf. Dan 7:9; *1 En.* 14.20; *2 En.* 22.8–9; *3 En.* 12.1; *T. Job* 46.7–9) and in Rev 6:11; 7:14 are also associated with martyrdom. But, as Matt 17:2 and Luke 9:29 rightly interpret, Mark does not mean merely that Jesus' clothing is transfigured—the subject of *metemorphōthē* is Jesus himself. For Mark, clothing often signifies the person (see commentary on 10:50). Jesus is transformed into a heavenly being, revealing his future resurrection glory to the disciples.

[4] The importance of Elijah and Moses for Mark is their role in salvation history in the past and the expectation that they would each play a role in the eschatological denouement. Moses and Elijah are mentioned together in Mal 4:4–5, which promises that Elijah will return before the final day of the Lord. Deuteronomy 18:15–18 was understood to point to a Moses-like eschatological prophet. That Jesus speaks with them shows he not only belongs in some sense to the heavenly world himself, but that he is to be understood in relation to salvation history—as its climax and fulfiller. In first-century Jewish thought, neither Moses nor Elijah had died, but had been taken directly to heaven. Both were prophetic figures, rejected in their own time, who suffered because of their faithfulness to their mission—but God had vindicated them by taking them into the heavenly world without death. Jesus, rejected in his own time, glows with heavenly glory and ultimately belongs to that world, but remains in this world to suffer and die. The glorious form of Jesus' appearance is a revelation of his form as the Son of Man at the Parousia (8:38), but first he must go the way of suffering and death. Only resurrection will place him in

the transcendent world (thus v. 12 must be considered a part of this context, not a separate pericope).

[5–6] Peter, here as elsewhere, responds on behalf of the disciples (cf. the alternation of singular and plural forms). Here as elsewhere, Peter misunderstands. This, too, is to be understood theologically as a matter of messianic secret and Gospel form, not psychologically as a quirk of Peter's personality. The narrator explicitly notes that Peter and the others were overcome with fear and did not know what to say (see also 6:35–37; 10:38; 14:40). Having just confessed Jesus to be the Messiah, and having just seen Jesus clothed in heavenly glory and conversing with glorified figures of Israel's salvation history, Peter addresses Jesus with "rabbi." This is an obviously inadequate title for the one he has just seen bathed in heavenly glory, immediately corrected by the heavenly voice ("rabbi" and "rabbouni" elsewhere express failed or inadequate discipleship; cf. 10:51; 11:21; 14:45). Peter's offer to build three booths likewise exhibits his lack of understanding, however his intention in making the proposal is understood. Eschatological overtones of the Festival of Booths ("Tabernacles") are often pointed out, but the connection is not evident. Interpreters have generally vacillated between charging Peter with wanting to linger in the aura of the "mountaintop experience" by constructing booths for an extended stay of Jesus and the heavenly participants on the mountain, or erroneously placing Jesus in the same category as the great prophets of Israel's history.

As in Exod 24–25, God speaks from the cloud, as God had spoken from heaven at Jesus' baptism (1:11), in each case declaring Jesus to be Son of God (see *Excursus: Markan Christology* at 9:1). Here, however, the address is to the disciples in the third person, followed by "Listen to him," an echo of Deut 18:18 commanding them to believe and accept the word of Jesus about his way, the way that must also become the disciples' own way (8:31–38).

[9] This is the last of the commands to silence; it sums up them all and is the only one that designates a terminus. The command to silence relates the transfiguration to the resurrection, and can only be understood and proclaimed with it. Here the resurrection (of Jesus) is spoken of matter-of-factly as something presupposed, a matter of common experience that can be looked back on, and from some distance. This is the readers' perspective, but not that of the disciples, who do not (and can not) "get it" until after the resurrection. Thus when they ask what this "rising from the dead" might mean, they are not inquiring about the meaning of resurrection as such—first-century Jews in general readily understood this (12:18–27)—but what Jesus' talk of his own "resurrection from among the dead" could mean (cf. John 11:23–27, which plays on the same distinction).

[11–13] The conversation between Jesus and his disciples reflects a dispute between early Christians and Jewish scribes on the validity of Christian faith. The disciples cite a stock objection: Jesus could not be the eschatological redeemer figure, the Messiah, because Scripture teaches that Elijah will return before the eschaton (Mal 3:1; 4:5–6). Since Elijah has not yet appeared, the Messiah is yet to come (cf. Justin, *Trypho*, 49.1). The details of Jesus' response are not clear. Since 12a can be punctuated either as a question or a statement, the Markan Jesus may be either affirming or challenging this scribal teaching. If understood as a statement, "restores everything" must be reinterpreted, for John-as-Elijah did not perform the expected eschatological work of restoring Israel, society, and the world to its intended state. More likely, Mark presents Jesus as here posing a question that challenges "Elijah's" traditional role. He does not question that John is Elijah, but questions that his eschatological ministry should be understood in the traditional way.

In all this, the Markan Jesus is not concerned with Elijah as such, but switches the focus to the primary issue, the eschatological destiny of the Son of Man. The initial announcement of the suffering Son of Man (8:31) had made no reference to Scripture. Now, Jesus points out that the Son of Man must suffer and be treated with contempt "as it is written of him." There are, of course, no biblical predictions that either the eschatological Elijah or the Son of Man will suffer and die. It is possible to understand Son of Man here as referring not to Dan 7:13, but to the "saints of the most high" represented by the Son of Man (and they did suffer and die before being vindicated by God).[41] However, here the affirmation is made from the Christian perspective, in retrospect, in the faith that the suffering and death of John and Jesus was central to the plan of God; since it represented the will of God, it must be "according to Scripture." This general conviction preceded early Christians' discovery in their Bible of particular texts that Christian faith could understand as predicting the suffering and death of the Messiah (cf. 1 Cor 15:3–5, and *Excursus: Mark and the Scriptures* at 14:52). In the passion story, Mark himself will find this understanding especially in the Psalms, but here the point is simply that the Son of Man suffers and dies according to the will of God as revealed in Scripture. The Markan Jesus then makes the fundamental Christian point that Elijah is not a heavenly figure still expected to arrive in the future, but the earthly figure who has already lived on this earth and suffered a violent death at the hands of its authorities. As the disciples must rethink "Elijah," so they must rethink "Christ," "Son of God," "Son of Man," and God's saving eschatological act as such, which also means rethinking the meaning of being a disciple to such a Christ. A traditional piece of Christian apologetic has thus become a means of instruction on Christology and discipleship. As John the Baptist has shown by his suffering and death to be the authentic Elijah, the forerunner of the Messiah, so the disciples must show themselves to be authentic followers of the Messiah by following Jesus

---

41. So, e.g., Moloney, *Mark: Commentary*, 181. This procedure does not work with the Elijah reference, however.

in the way of suffering and death. In all this it is particularly clear that the narrator is utilizing the address of Jesus to the disciples to speak over their heads to the real addressees, the readers.

In chapters 1–8, Jesus has acted with divine power, doing what only God can do: overcoming Satan, healing the sick, cleansing lepers, calming the storm, walking on the sea, raising the dead. Then for the first time comes the startling revelation that according to God's plan (*dei,* cf. 8:31) the Son of Man will suffer and die; no reason is given, soteriological or otherwise, that might make the suffering of the Messiah and his disciples easier to grasp. The disciples disbelieve and misunderstand, but Jesus takes them to a mountaintop where he consorts with heavenly beings and is himself clothed with divine glory—the glory of the Son of Man reserved for the Parousia in 8:38. Except for the disruptive statements in 8:31, which met with rejection and called for explanation, it seems the next step in the story line developed in the previous chapters would be for Jesus to assume his rightful place among the heavenly beings. The issue in this text is whether Jesus will continue his ascent toward glory or fulfill the mission he has declared for himself in 8:31. When the cloud evaporates, the heavenly voice is gone and so are Moses and Elijah. The disciples see Jesus alone and have been told to listen to him, the one who has been speaking of suffering, death, and resurrection, and they turn to go back down the mountain together.

Excursus: The Messianic Secret

Since William Wrede's epoch-making 1901 publication *Das Messiasgeheimnis in den Evangelien* became known in the English-speaking world as "The Messianic Secret in the Gospels,"[42] the phrase "messianic secret" has become a quasi-technical term to designate a cluster of phenomena in the Gospels, particularly in Mark. Neither "messianic" nor "secret" conveys precisely what Wrede intended; he used "messianic" not only to connote messiahship strictly defined but as a general term to designate Jesus' religious status as a divine being or person endowed by God with transcendent power, and *Geheimnis* had the connotation of "mystery" as well as "secret." Thus scholars have attempted to propose more accurate designations or to separate the "secrecy" data into unrelated categories, distinguishing "messianic secret" from "Son of God secret," "mir-

---

42. Wrede, *Messianic Secret.* Wrede's view is often caricatured and then rejected, as though he simply claimed that Mark devised the messianic secret as a means of superimposing churchly messianic faith on an unmessianic Jesus. Wrede's view, actually quite complex, can be summarized in five steps: (1) Jesus thought of himself as the future Messiah, but made no messianic claims. (2) Christian faith arose that he became Messiah at his resurrection. (3) This was then read back into his earthly life. (4) Prior to Mark, limited circles within the church originated the idea of the secret messiahship in order to combine #2 and #3. Thus already in Wrede's view the messianic secret is related to the tension between the two concepts of pre- and post-Easter messiahship, two Christologies that were already in circulation. (5) Mark did not invent this view (p. 145), but it was Mark who developed it and made it central in composing his Gospel.

acle secret," or "kingdom of God secret."[43] While it is true that the data often related to the "messianic secret" is of disparate origins and kinds,[44] it is better to retain the term as a convenient scholarly designation for a comprehensive Markan narrative pattern representing the author's rhetorical strategy. The cluster of materials consists of the following overlapping categories (see commentary on individual passages):

Commands to silence. Jesus commands those who have recognized him to keep silent (1:34; 3:12; 8:30) and forbids those whom he has helped by his divine power to tell anyone (1:44; 5:43; 7:36; 8:26). In this material, Jesus takes the initiative to keep his identity concealed. The Markan Jesus does not want to be known in terms of the "historical Jesus," the observable historical figure who may be evaluated by customary human norms apart from his true identity as crucified and risen Son of God, which may be known only after the resurrection.[45]

The Markan "parable theory." In Mark 4:10–12, 34, the crowd does not understand the parables, and Jesus does not intend for them to understand. Jesus privately explains the parables to his disciples, but parables are a means to conceal the truth from the crowds. (But see also on 7:14–23; 12:1–12.)

Lack of recognition, misunderstanding, and blindness with regard to Jesus' identity and teaching. John the Baptist, true prophet of God, baptizes Jesus without recognizing that he is the "mighty one" who is to come (1:8–9). Not only opponents and crowds, but Jesus' own disciples and family fail to perceive his true identity or positively misunderstand it—and this despite his clear metaphors, explicit statements, and acts of divine power (1:27; 2:10, 12, 20; 3:7–12, 21, 31–35; 4:13, 41; 5:19, 25–34, 43; 6:2–3, 14–15, 48–52; 7:31–37; 8:17–21, 27–30, 32; 9:34; 10:35–40, 48; 11:1–10). Jesus speaks repeatedly of himself as Son of Man, but this declaration evinces no response from anyone in the narrative (8:31, 38; 9:9, 12, 31; 10:32–34, 45; 13:26–27; 14:21, 41, 62—until the final pronouncement). The disciples continue to fail to understand or to misunderstand even after receiving explanations. Failure to understand is often not directly stated but implicit in the narrative (e.g., 9:34 after 9:31; 10:35–38 after 10:33–34). What they fail to understand is the cross / resurrection (9:10). All this is an aspect of the author's Christology. As summarized by Whitney Taylor Shiner, "The rhetorical purpose for the disciples' lack of understanding appears to be Jesus as hard to understand rather than the portrayal of the disciples as slow of understanding."[46]

43. Cf., e.g., Nils Alstrup Dahl, *Jesus in the Memory of the Early Church* (Minneapolis: Augsburg, 1976), 55; Luz, "Secrecy Motif," 86–87; Kingsbury, *Christology of Mark's Gospel,* 15.

44. The commands to silence, for instance, are often a constituent element of conventional Hellenistic miracle stories, where they have their own function, e.g., in preserving the secrecy of magic words or techniques (see, e.g., Theissen, *Miracle Stories,* 140–51). It is Mark who molds these disparate elements into a comprehensive narrative strategy.

45. So Eduard Schweizer, "Anmerkungen zur Theologie des Markus," in *Neotestamentica: Deutsche und Englische Aufsätze 1951–1963* (Zürich: Zwingli Verlag, 1963), 103.

46. Shiner, *Follow Me,* 30. Accordingly, this is not a matter of the disciples' "stupidity" (contra Sherman E. Johnson, *A Commentary on the Gospel According to St. Mark* [BNTC; London: Adam & Charles Black, 1960], 86, 142, 150, and repeatedly). There are numerous scenes in which the disciples function as those who do understand and participate responsibly in Jesus' mission, e.g., the successful mission portrayed in 6:6–13. Such scenes make the "theoretical" character of

Incognito Christ. The Markan Jesus seeks privacy; he wills to remain unknown and unrecognized. After the "day of the Lord" of 1:21–34, when everyone was seeking him, Jesus avoids publicity and goes elsewhere (1:35–38). This pattern is repeated (6:31–32; 7:24; 9:28–32).

Public instruction, private explanation. Jesus teaches the crowds in public, but gives the key to understanding only to his disciples in private (4:1–20, 33–34; 7:1–16, 17–23; 10:1–9, 10–12; 10:17–22, 23–27; 11:27–12:40; 13:1–37). This motif is similar to the "Incognito Christ," but has the dimension of continuity from the time of Jesus to the time of the reader. In these scenes, the disciples function as the companions of the historical Jesus, "the receivers and transmitters of his teaching who guarantee the continuity between him and the church" (Räisänen, *Messianic Secret*, 118). Despite his focus on the cross and resurrection, continuity with the "life and teaching of Jesus" is important for Mark. The community can rely on the revelation that has been mediated to it by the apostles. This, too, is an aspect of the messianic secret.

Transcendental knowledge. While the human characters in the narrative do not perceive Jesus' identity, he is recognized by beings whose knowledge transcends the narrative: angels (1:13); demons (1:24, 34; 3:11; 5:7); Elijah and Moses returned from heaven (9:2–10), and above all, God himself (1:2–3, 11; 9:7). The reader also belongs to this category, standing outside the narrative, but sharing the transcendent knowledge of God. Though not a transcendent (otherworldly) being, the reader belongs to a different world than the story-world that unfolds on the narrative stage of the Gospel, and is privileged to behold the action on the narrative stage from a God's-eye view. The reader hears the divine voice of 1:11, which the figures on the narrative stage do not hear, and thus knows the divinely disclosed identity of Jesus, which even John does not know. The reader even knows the divinely revealed identity and role of John, which John himself does not know; the reader, not John, hears the offstage divine voice with which the narrative opens. Furthermore, the reader throughout is privileged to be included in the circle of "insiders" who hear and understand (4:10–12), when even the disciples in the narrative fail to comprehend (8:14–21). The reader hears and understands Jesus' passion predictions (8:31; 9:31; 10:33–34); the disciples and others in the narrative only hear, but with hardened hearts—not that they are personally hard-hearted. Their hearts have been hardened by the sovereign God, lest they understand prematurely and superficially (cf. on 3:5; 4:10–12; 6:52; 8:17). The readers see and hear, but such hearing, seeing, and understanding is a gift, not attained but conferred on the reader by the Gospel itself, a matter of grace and election, and not possible prior to cross and resurrection.

---

the messianic secret clear, i.e., that it is a literary strategy, not a historical report. Obtuseness and understanding are not merely sequential periods, but operate dialectically alongside each other (cf. Kertelge, *Wunder*, 138; Shiner, *Follow Me*, 290). The rhetorical role of the disciples varies; the constant is the christological purpose. Similarly, the disciples' lack of understanding does not merely reflect the misunderstandings of post-Easter disciples in Mark's church, which "Mark the teacher" wants to correct, as argued by Karl-Georg Reploh, *Markus, Lehrer der Gemeinde: Eine redaktionsgeschichtliche Studie zu den Jüngerperikopen des Markus-Evangeliums* (SBM 9; Stuttgart: Verlag Katholisches Bibelwerk, 1969), 81–86 and passim. While the disciples in the narrative do often become transparent to the readers' own time, their lack of perception in the narrative facilitates the presentation of Mark's Christology rather than scolding dull Christians of Mark's own community.

"Violations" of the secret. Despite Jesus' will to privacy and commands to silence, from time to time his intention is frustrated, the secret is "leaked," Jesus' command is disobeyed, and his identity or the report of his mighty works is broadcast (1:32–39, 44–45; 5:20; 7:36) and he cannot escape detection (7:24). The importance of this aspect of the messianic secret is threefold: (1) Such scenes are proleptic, already pointing ahead to the post-Easter time of revelation, the Christian readers' own time. Despite such premature disclosures, the characters in the narrative do not come to authentic insight about Jesus—but the reader can do this. (2) The "violations" of the secret show that such revelations are against Jesus' will. The Markan Jesus does not want people to (think that they) recognize him and announce his identity on the basis of his miracles, apart from the cross and resurrection, but they do so anyway, and he is not able to remain hidden (e.g., 6:32–44; 7:24–30). This corresponds to the situation in some circles of Mark's context where Christ was proclaimed as the powerful Son of God but not as the crucified and Risen One. People do not always preach as Christ wants them to. When the powerful, "divine man" Jesus is proclaimed without the cross kerygma, it is against the will of Jesus himself, who forbade it. (3) In any case, such "violations" should not be regarded as merely sporadic and occasional, but as instances of Mark's repeated dialectic of revelation and concealment. Whoever has been healed by Jesus cannot keep quiet about it; the victory of God in the Christ event must be shared.[47] The "violations" are thus not occasional ruptures of an otherwise consistent secrecy theory. There is no consistent secret to be "broken"; secrecy and revelation represent two narrative tracks that are interwoven throughout. In one narrative track the crowds are not blind, not hardened, and not bad, while the disciples are imperceptive and hardened. In the other track these roles are reversed.[48]

Temporal limit. There are several indications that the time portrayed in the narrative is different from the reader's own time (e.g., 2:18–20). There are specific signals that the messianic secret is only temporary (4:22, 40). In 9:9, the resurrection is designated as the time of revelation. At 16:7, the followers of Jesus are commanded to "go and tell." Yet here, too, the Markan dialectic is at work. It is not simply the case that secrecy and misunderstanding prevail before Easter, while the post-Easter readers live in the time of revelation and understanding. The women at the tomb are commanded to tell, but remain

---

47. Keck, "Mark 3:7–12," 354. Cf. Luz's comment on 1:45: "Mark does not use some neutral word for the healed man's speaking, but the positive *kēryssein* ('to proclaim'). *Ho logos* ('the word') is also a very positive expression, meaning the sum total of Christian proclamation: Mark takes the term over from the Church's tradition. So according to Mark the miracle cannot remain secret, even when Jesus does not want it to be made known. By its very nature it breaks through the silence and leads into proclamation. This is to be seen primarily as Mark's positive message" ("Secrecy Motif," 79). Even though Mark affirms that the authentic message about Jesus cannot be proclaimed apart from cross and resurrection, as interpreter of the miracle stories Mark shares the view that the gospel-embodied-in-miracle-stories *generates* authentic Christian proclamation, i.e., he is pro-miracle-story, not an advocate of "corrective Christology."

48. This point is elaborated in Räisänen, *Messianic Secret*, 92–101, who regards this as a confusion caused by Mark's projecting two different concerns on the same narrative screen, a confusion he did not notice or could not prevent, rather than (as here) Mark's intentional strategy inherent in his narrative Christology, in which messianic secret plays a facilitating and positive role.

silent—the pre-Easter situation is ironically reversed. Markan readers live in the time of disclosure and understanding, but not ultimately so. That is still to come. They see, but not perfectly. The ultimate revelation is yet to come when the Son of Man comes with great power and glory, and then "they will see" (13:26), but it will only confirm the revelation already given—the Son of Man to come is none other than the crucified and risen Son of Man of the Markan Gospel.[49] Like that of the Kingdom of God, the disclosure and ultimate resolution of the Messianic mystery is eschatological. The kingdom is proclaimed, but hidden from all during Jesus' ministry, though anticipatory glimmers break through. Then, with the resurrection, Jesus' identity and the present / coming kingdom are revealed to believers. Yet both Jesus and the kingdom await their ultimate revelation at the coming of the Son of Man, which will make known the reality of God's kingdom and the identity of Jesus as God's Son to all.[50] Christians live between the times, in the already / not-yet period when they know—but even they know imperfectly—the Messianic mystery and the mystery of the present and coming kingdom. The messianic secret corresponds to Christology as such: the Christ who is to come has already come, was not recognized during his life, is now (imperfectly) recognized by believers, and will be universally recognized at the eschaton.

Distribution. References to the messianic secret are not evenly distributed throughout the Gospel. The secret is prominent in part 1, the same section of the Gospel which has the miracle stories expressing the epiphany Christology, and only there. Miracles virtually cease after 9:28–32, which comes as a kind of final statement of the secret. This suggests that the secret is closely related to the miracle stories, is the Markan means by which the kerygma of the miracle stories may be communicated to the reader without violating the cross / resurrection kerygma.

Origin and meaning. How should we understand this mass of material in Mark which expresses the messianic secret? The variety of answers that have been given to this question fit into two basic categories:

1. The messianic secret represents a strategy of the historical Jesus, who believed that he was the Messiah but understood messiahship in a radically different sense than his contemporaries. He thus forbade his disciples to announce his messiahship until his

---

49. So Via, *Ethics of Mark's Gospel*, 53–57. See also Tannehill, "Disciples in Mark," 176, who warns against a too-simple view that the problem with the pre-Easter disciples was merely that the passion and resurrection, necessary for authentic faith, had not yet taken place. The Christian reader, who looks back on these events to which the disciples in the narrative can only look forward, is also faced with the challenge of accepting the crucified one as Lord, and following in the way of the cross. "These are not demands that disappear after Easter, . . . nor do they suddenly become easy to fulfill." Strecker rightly insists that for Mark hiddenness and revelation are not mere successive chronological periods, but are dialectically related to each other, "an essential expression of the faith that eschatological salvation has entered into history through Jesus Christ . . . The paradox is to be conceived not only 'horizontally' but 'vertically'" (Strecker, *Theology of the New Testament*, 351).

50. This will be the real conclusion to the Markan story. See on 13:24–27, and Cilliers Breytenbach, "Das Markusevangelium als episodische Erzählung: Mit Überlegungen zum 'Aufbau' des zweiten Evangeliums," in *Der Erzähler des Evangeliums: Methodische Neuansätze in der Markusforschung* (ed. Ferdinand Hahn; SBS 118 / 119; Stuttgart: Verlag Katholisches Bibelwerk, 1985), 154–55.

death and resurrection made it clear that he was not an earthly, political messiah. There are numerous problems with this view, only two of which may be mentioned here:

a. This approach salvages Mark as somewhat historical on this point at the expense of the other canonical Gospels. In Matthew and Luke, Jesus' identity is revealed from the first page on by magi and angels. John the Baptist recognizes Jesus at the baptism (Matt 3:14–15) or already in the womb (Luke 1:44). Matthew omits or modifies every one of the passages in which the Markan disciples fail to understand (cf., e.g., Mark 6:51–52 / Matt 14:47). The Fourth Gospel publicly introduces all the christological titles in the first chapter (1:29–51), Jesus engages in explicit public debate on his identity as Son of God, which he openly declares (e.g. 5:1–39), and Jesus asserts that he has "spoken openly to the world . . . I have said nothing in secret" (18:20). The messianic secret is thus a specifically Markan phenomenon, present in the other Gospels only because they have utilized Mark as a source, and modified by them because it does not fit their own understanding of Jesus' ministry.

b. Numerous scenes in which the messianic secret plays a role are difficult to imagine historically. The demons' announcement of Jesus as Son of God has no effect on the people in the scene; Jesus' commands to silence come too late, for the secret is out, yet the story continues as though the announcement had not been made at all (e.g., 1:24–27; 3:11–12; 5:7). Taken as historical reports, Jesus' commands to those he has healed to keep quiet about it seem to be not only cruel and unnecessary (see, e.g., on 7:31–37) but also impossible to carry out in practice (see on 5:41–43).

2. The messianic secret is an aspect of the author's narrative Christology representing the rhetorical and theological strategy of the evangelist Mark. Mark did not create the secrecy theory from whole cloth. There were traditional elements, some of which may in fact go back to the ministry of Jesus.[51] It is Mark himself, however, who first molds these disparate elements into a comprehensive narrative-rhetorical strategy that facilitates the communication of a story that presents Jesus as the paradoxical unity of divine power and human weakness.[52] It is not the case that Mark formulated the

51. While it is unlikely that Jesus thought of his ministry in terms of the later specific titles and imagery used by the church, he may well have been convinced that in and through his life God was confronting his generation in a decisive way, but discouraged his followers from expressing this in terms of traditional messianic titles. Likewise, the traditional forms of exorcism and miracle stories sometimes had elements of secrecy in them that Mark inherited with his tradition. It was a typical feature of the Hellenistic "divine man" miracle worker, for example, to withdraw from the public in the actual performance of the miraculous deed.

52. This is a different view from that of Malbon, who understands the messianic secret in terms of the Markan Jesus' "deflected Christology" that turns attention falsely focused on Jesus toward God, the true source of salvation ("Christology of Mark's Gospel," 37–44). This view would be more defensible if the Markan Jesus said more clearly something like "I'm not the one doing these amazing deeds—don't admire me, but worship God." Modern faith healers and TV evangelists

messianic secret in order to make the historical Jesus appear more messianic than he actually was. His problem was precisely the opposite, how to interpret a tradition that already understood Jesus as Messiah and powerful Son of God prior to the cross and resurrection. This does not mean, however, that Mark writes a "corrective Christology" in the sense that he simply rejects the image of Jesus as the deity who overcomes all human problems by his divine power. Each miracle story is a paradigm of the Christ event as such, in which God has acted for human salvation. Mark sees the value of this Christology, but also its danger, for it presents a superhuman Jesus untouched by true humanity, and encourages a triumphalistic view of discipleship that has no place for the way of the cross—either Jesus' or the disciples'.

Two opposing Christologies were current in Mark's community (see *Excursus: Markan Christology* at 9:1). Advocates of each Christology opposed the other, unable to reconcile conceptually their own view of Jesus with the other. How could the divine Son of God actually die? How could the one who died on the cross have multiplied the loaves and walked on the water? In discursive, propositional language, the Christologies are contraries and a choice must be made between them. Mark does not choose one Christology over the other, "correcting" one by the other. He saw the values of each Christology and, developing and combining tendencies already in the tradition, devised a narrative-rhetorical means of holding them together: the messianic secret. In Mark, as in the kenosis Christology, Jesus' true identity does not become manifest until the cross-resurrection, when Jesus truly dies as weak-like-us. But also, in Mark, the messianic power is already at work within Jesus' life, as in the epiphany Christology, where he is the powerful Son of God not-like-us. The framework within which both these views are affirmed and held in tension is that of the messianic secret.[53] Within this framework, the true identity of Jesus had to be unrecognized or misunderstood—otherwise, people would have believed in the "Christ" or "Son of God" without the cross and resurrection, which is utterly impossible in Mark's theology. In the narrative framework that the messianic secret makes possible, Jesus' messianic miracles can be portrayed, but they were not known or understood as such until after the resurrection, by Jesus' specific command. This does not matter to Mark, however historically incongruous this may seem, for Mark did not claim to be writing "history." The Gospel is a new 70 C.E. reality, not an abortive effort to reproduce a 30 C.E. reality, and not merely a Christian modification of the *bios* genre already present in the Hellenistic world. This distinctive literary genre was cre-

---

typically make this self-effacing claim, but the Markan messianic secret functions at another level that has to do with chronology and two different types of Christology, not merely misplaced admiration (see on 5:20). Malbon is certainly correct that "God is the one the Markan Jesus wants to speak about" (41), but this is not an alternative to speaking of Jesus as the Christ. To confess Jesus as the Christ *is* to speak about *God* (see on "Christ" as itself pointing to the act of God in *Excursus: Markan Christology* at 9:1).

53. Thus it is off-target to regard the messianic secret as the "theme around which the second evangelist has organized his Gospel," or the "pretentious construct Wrede had made of it," since it is "only one motif among others" (Wrede's view as understood by Kingsbury, *Christology of Mark's Gospel*, 8, 11). The messianic secret is not a "motif" or "theme" at all, but the *framework within which* Mark includes stories expressing both types of early Christian Christology, and without which he is not able to relate the narrative at all.

ated by Mark, a narrative framework in which the two opposing Christologies may be held together and affirmed in such a way that each would dialectically balance the other. This is what a Gospel is. "The secrecy theory is the hermeneutical presupposition of the genre 'gospel.'"[54]

9:14–29 Jesus Heals a Boy Possessed by a Spirit

9:14 And when they came to the disciples they saw a large crowd around them and scribes arguing with them. **15** And when the whole crowd saw him they were awestruck, and they immediately ran to him and were greeting him. **16** And he asked them, "What are you arguing about with them?"[a] **17** And one of the crowd responded, "Teacher, I brought my son to you, for he is possessed by a spirit that makes him unable to speak; **18** and wherever it seizes him it throws him down, and he foams at the mouth and grinds his teeth and becomes rigid; and I asked your disciples to cast it out, and they were not able to do it. **19** But Jesus answers them, "O unbelieving generation, how much longer will I be among you? How much longer will I be putting up with you? Bring him to me." **20** And they brought him to him. And when the spirit saw him, immediately it convulsed him,[b] and he fell on the ground and was rolling around, foaming at the mouth. **21** And he asked his father, "How long has this been happening to him?" And he said, "From childhood. **22** And it has often thrown him into the fire and into the water, to destroy him; but if you are able to do anything, have mercy on us and help us." **23** Jesus said to him, "'If you are able!'[c]—all things are possible for the one who believes."[d] **24** Immediately the child's father cried out, "I believe; help my unbelief." **25** When Jesus saw that a crowd was rapidly gathering, he rebuked the unclean spirit, saying to it, "You spirit that keeps this boy from speaking and hearing, I command you, come out of him, and never enter him again." **26** And it screamed and convulsed him terribly, and came out, and he became like a dead person, so that many said "He has died." **27** But Jesus grasped his hand, raised him up, and he arose.[e] **28** And when his disciples had entered the house, his disciples were asking him privately, "Why were we not able to cast it out?" **29** And he said to them, "No one or nothing[f] is able to cast out this kind except through prayer."[g]

a. Antecedents to the pronouns are ambiguous, since "you" could theoretically refer either to the crowd or the disciples, and "them" either to "scribes," "crowd," or "disciples,"

54. Conzelmann, "Present and Future," 43. For elaboration of all these points, especially the messianic secret as integral to Mark's combining epiphany and kenosis Christologies as a principal factor in creating the gospel genre, see M. Eugene Boring, *Truly Human / Truly Divine: Christological Language and the Gospel Form* (St. Louis: CBP Press, 1984).

depending on the antecedent of "you." Since "one of the crowd" responds, it at first seems that "you" addresses the crowd, but as the story progresses it seems that the dispute is between scribes and disciples, observed by the crowd.

b. The pronoun *auton* is used four times in this verse. The meaning is clear: the crowd brought the boy to Jesus, the spirit saw Jesus and convulsed the boy. Likewise, the "he" that is the subject of "fell" clearly refers to the boy, while the next "he" of v. 21 obviously refers to Jesus, "his" and "him" to the boy, but the translation above has retained the pronouns to correspond to the Greek oral style.

c. The syntax is clear but unusual. The definite article *to* indicates a quotation (as Matt 19:18; Rom 13:9; Gal 5:14); Jesus quotes part of the man's saying back to him, in which "you" had referred to Jesus. Some scribes had "corrected" the apparent meaning, adding *pisteusai* ("to believe"), making the "you" in Jesus' statement refer to the man and making the exorcism a matter of whether or not he had faith.

d. The clause *panta dynata tō pisteuonti* has no verb, which must be supplied. It could thus be understood as in the NRSV, "All things will be done [by God] for the one who believes [either Jesus or the father of the boy]," or as above, preserving the ambiguity (see commentary below).

e. On overtones of the language of resurrection in this vocabulary, see on 5:41.

f. *Oudeni* can be either masculine "no one" or neuter "nothing."

g. While *kai nēsteia* ("and fasting") is in the vast majority of MSS, that it is not original is clear from (1) its absence in ℵ* B 0274 2427 k, (2) the difficulty of the text that generated explanations for the disciples' failure, (3) the later church's practice of fasting, both generally (cf. 2:19–20!), and (4) as an element in the ritual of exorcism.

Except for the healing of blind Bartimaeus, which serves a special Markan purpose (see on 10:46–52), this is the last of Jesus' public miracles in Mark, forming a bracket with his first public miracle, also an exorcism (1:23–27). Like all Mark's exorcism stories, this pericope points beyond the incident of healing an individual afflicted child in Galilee to God's overcoming of cosmic evil in the Christ event (cf. on 1:21–28). The focus of this story, however, is not on the exorcism itself, despite the vivid description, but on discipleship, faith, and prayer. Elements within the story support this interpretation, as does its location in this section of the narrative. Mark has completed part 1 of his narrative, which is filled with miracles, including especially exorcisms. This story is the only healing or exorcism within the brackets provided by the two stories of healing blind men. There will be no exorcisms or other healing miracles in part 2. Were there no sick people or demoniacs in Perea and Jerusalem? To ask the question is to realize that the location of this story, placed within the discipleship section, is a matter not of biographical reporting but of Markan strategy of communication.

[14] Jesus, with Peter, James and John, returns to the other disciples; the "mountaintop experience" becomes a "mountain-bottom experience." The dramatis personae is extensive: Jesus, two groups of disciples, scribes, crowds, demonized boy, his father, the demon. The pronouns throughout do not always have clear antecedents, though as the story progresses the reader has no diffi-

culty in piecing it together. The scribes disputing with the disciples are not mentioned again, nor is the subject of the dispute given. The reader knows the scribes represent Jesus' opponents (see *Excursus: Jesus the Teacher versus the Scribes* at 7:23). They are apparently arguing with Jesus' disciples, and the issue turns out to be the disciples' efforts to exorcise a demon, which in this case have failed. Readers in Mark's church will recognize contemporary disputes about the church's claim to represent Jesus' continuing authority and power, including his victory over demons.

[15] Mark gives no explanation for the crowd's awestruck amazement. Interpreters have sometimes suggested that Jesus' appearance still manifested lingering elements of the transfiguration (Exod 34:33–35; 2 Cor 3:12–13), but Mark does not typically expect this kind of narrative logic to carry over from one scene to the next.[55] If this is not a remnant of the story's composite character, (so e.g., Bultmann, *History of the Synoptic Tradition*, 211–12), then Mark apparently wants to include the crowd's astonished response to Jesus, and locates it here rather than at the conclusion, where he will focus on the "point" of the story as different from the typical ending of a miracle story (see on vv. 27–28). On "greeting," see commentary on 12:38.

[17] Although he has brought his son to the disciples in the absence of Jesus, the father declares he has brought the afflicted child "to you" (sing., i.e., to Jesus). Mark has no explicit hierarchical doctrine of the church, yet he portrays the disciples as operating by power and authority conferred on them by Jesus, so that to deal with them is to deal with him, and to deal with him is to deal with God (3:14–15; 6:7, 13, 30; 9:37). This is one of the ways Mark portrays the church in the absence of Jesus.

[18] The symptoms vividly describe epilepsy—Matt 17:15 so interprets it— but Mark consistently pictures the boy's problem as demon possession. It is the disciples' problem, however, that is the center of the narrator's attention: they have attempted to cast out the demon, but despite their earlier success (6:13) are not able to do it, as both the father and they report (v. 28).

[19–21] In a heightened mode ("O . . . generation" in Greek vocative case), Jesus' response seems to go beyond normal human frustration and address the present situation as typifying the whole unbelieving generation with which his ministry deals. Like Moses in Deut 32:3, Jesus speaks from a God-ward perspective (cf. 8:12, 38, and the contrast between the Son of Man and "humanity" in the next scene [9:31]). So also, with the question "How long am I to be

---

55. Hooker, *Mark*, 223, argues the "only possible explanation" is that, like Moses in Exod 34:29–30, Jesus' appearance was still visibly affected by the transfiguration. Gundry, *Mark*, 488, suggests that Mark might even mean that the transfiguration glory "continues right to the crucifixion." But then Judas would not have needed to identify Jesus in 14:44, but could have simply told the officers, "He'll be the one who glows in the dark!"

with you?" he differentiates himself not only from unbelieving scribes, crowds, and disciples, but from unbelieving humanity as such. The one who here speaks is not merely an exasperated human being, but the Son of God, who does not ultimately belong to this world (cf. Num 14:11; Deut 32:20, where similar phraseology expresses *God's* exasperation).[56] Thus the inquiry "How long has this been happening to him" is not an informational question for Jesus' benefit. As in 8:27 and 9:33, Jesus asks because he knows, and in any case it is a strange bit of conversation while the boy is rolling on the ground in convulsions. The question is for the readers' benefit: such cases were considered incurable.

[22–23] The focus shifts from the afflicted son to the father, then to Jesus as representing God's power. In contrast to the earlier story of the person afflicted with leprosy, who was convinced of Jesus' power but asked about his willingness (see on 1:40), here the issue, posed hopefully but tentatively by the father, is whether Jesus is able to do anything. With divine indignation, Jesus rejects the inquiry as a nonquestion—the one who represents the power of *God* cannot be questioned about his *ability*. The point is christological, not a general statement about the power of faith. Yet, like Mark's Christology as a whole, the point here is expressed dialectically, parabolically, ambiguously. God is not one power among others, but the one God (2:7; 10:18; 12:29, 32), the Creator (10:6; emphatically 13:19) for whom nothing is impossible (10:27; 14:36). It is not "faith" that can accomplish anything, but God. Yet this power is realized (made real, experienced as reality) to and for the one who trusts in God's power (*tō pisteuonti*, "for the one who believes," is singular). Who is this "one who believes"? In 11:23–24 the singular is generic, "anyone who believes," and immediately modulates into the plural. However, even there the occasion for the saying is the power of faith that has been demonstrated in Jesus' cursing the fig tree, that is, the Jesus of 11:14 is the indirect referent and occasion for the statement about faith in 11:23. In 9:23 the statement is certainly not a slogan or proverb about the power of faith in general. While the reference here need not be limited to Jesus, the issue throughout has been whether *Jesus* is able when others, including his disciples, are not. Jesus is able. God's unlimited power is available to and through him. As truly divine, God's power is at his disposal. But also, as *truly* human, he is the one who manifests that ultimate trust in God that corresponds to human beings as their true selves, but which they have perverted as belonging to "this *un*believing generation." In different senses, then, the faithful one may be Jesus, the truly human one who does indeed trust in God's power, or Jesus as the divine one who represents and makes real God's power, or the father who struggles with faith, or the disciples for whom the les-

56. Cf. also the overtones of divine Wisdom, as noted by Pesch, *Markusevangelium*, 2:91, citing Felix Christ, *Jesus Sophia: Die Sophia-Christologie bei den Synoptikern* (ATANT 57; Zürich: Zwingli-Verlag, 1970), 154.

son is intended, in whom the readers may see their own reflections. The next
sentence does not encourage a neat univocal solution to this problem.

[24] The father's anguished affirmation / plea is the climax of the story,
which is not so much about an exorcism as about faith. The belief / unbelief elements in the father's outcry should not be parceled out quantitatively, despite
Matt 17:19–20 and many interpreters since. Mark's point is more dialectic. The
man both believes, and does not believe. He believes but does not have faith as
a possession to which he can appeal, and he knows he must pray (an expression
of faith) for faith (which he does not claim to have).[57]

[25–27] The exorcism leaves the boy in a deathlike state, and Jesus raises
him up as from the dead. The same three verbs are used as in 5:41–42 (*kratē-
sas, ēgeiren, anestē,* "grasped, raised, arose"), again reflecting that Mark's miracle stories point to the Christ event as a whole and communicate resurrection
faith. The meaning of this event is not understood until seen in the light of
Christ's resurrection. So also, Jesus' abrupt ending of the conversation and
authoritative expulsion of the demon when a crowd begins to form is not to be
harmonized with verse 14 in which the crowd has been there all along; instead,
it is a reflection of the messianic secret motif. Indeed, there is no response from
the crowd to confirm the miracle (cf. v. 15 above), just as there is no further reference to the boy or his father.

[28–29] Instead of a public acclamation by the crowd, the conclusion is provided by a private discussion with the disciples. Entering the house is again
reminiscent of the house churches of Mark's own community (cf. on 1:29–34;
2:1–2, 15; 3:20–21; 4:10–11; 7:24), where perplexed discussions about their
own failure to manifest the power and authority they had received continued to
take place. The disciples had lacked faith, but Jesus instructs them that their
failure was due to lack of prayer. This is not a change of topics, for faith and
prayer are two sides of the same coin (11:23–25). At one point in the history of
the story, "this kind" may have referred to a particular kind of demon especially
difficult to exorcise, that is, one that causes loss of speech and hearing and

---

57. Schweizer, *Mark,* 189–90, for eloquent expression of this point. Apparently without plan-
ning it so, Karl Barth literally made this text the brackets for his whole theological career, citing it
in both the first and last pages of his life's work (Karl Barth, *Church Dogmatics, Volume I: The Doctrine of the Word of God* [trans. G. T. Thomson; Edinburgh: T. & T. Clark, 1936], 23; Karl Barth,
*Church Dogmatics, Volume IV: The Doctrine of Reconciliation, Part Four [Fragment], The Chris-
tian Life [Fragment], Baptism as the Foundation of the Christian Life* [trans. Geoffrey Bromiley;
Edinburgh: T. & T. Clark, 1969], 42).

Sharyn Dowd helpfully sums up the thrust of this pericope: (1) Jesus does have the faith for
which nothing is impossible. (2) Inadequate faith on the part of either victim or advocate does not
prevent miracles. (3) The answer to the father's prayer that Jesus help his unbelief is the miracle
itself. "Faith is needed for miracles in Mark, but sometimes miracles are needed to awaken the confidence in Jesus' power that the evangelist labels 'faith'." The relation between faith and miracle is
not linear, but dialectic and circular. Dowd, *Reading Mark,* 95.

epilepticlike symptoms as in the present case. At the Markan level, however, the meaning cannot be that while some demons can be cast out without prayer, this particular type can only be done with prayer. Neither is the contrast between Jesus, who casts out even this demon without prayer, and the disciples, who would have had a successful exorcism if they had only remembered to pray. The instruction is not at the level of exorcistic technique, as in a recipe; as part of the discipleship section 8:22–10:52, it is instruction for the Markan church. Even after the victory of God over demonic powers at the resurrection, the church still finds itself confronted with such powers and is not always able to overcome them. Likewise, the objections of scribes who disputed Jesus' authority and power continue to challenge the church. In this situation the disciples are reminded that despite their past successes (6:12–13), they cannot regard the power and authority given them (3:14–15) as a kind of possession; instead they must continue to depend on the power of God available through faith and prayer. They recognize the father's cry as their own: "I believe / help my unbelief."

9:30–32 Jesus Foretells His Passion Again

9:30 They went out from there and were passing through Galilee, and he did not want anyone to know it; **31** for he was teaching his disciples, and saying to them, "The Son of Man is to be delivered over into human[a] hands, and they will kill him, and three days after he has been killed he will rise again." **32** But they did not understand what he was saying, and were afraid to ask him.

a. The serious word play in Greek ([*ho huios tou*] **anthrōpou**—[*eis cheiras*] **anthrōpōn**), retained by the older translations as "Son of Man—hands of men" is difficult to retain in gender-inclusive English. See on 2:27; 8:34.

In the Markan story line, Jesus is back in Galilee for the first time since 8:27. His ministry there is completed. Though he will again appear in Capernaum in the next scene, he is en route, "on the road" to Jerusalem (see *Excursus: The Way* at 1:3, and notes on the structure of this section at 8:22). The narrator's remark that Jesus did not want anyone to know is explained as providing opportunity to teach his disciples.

Jesus is here pictured as intentionally spending much time in private with the disciples, repeatedly instructing them about his forthcoming death and resurrection. It is not a matter of Jesus simply stating this one sentence, which the disciples hear, fail to understand, and are afraid to ask about. This teaching is summarized in one statement, the second of Jesus' three "passion predictions" (see on 8:31). This is the briefest of these predictions, and, concise as it is, has stylistic traits that have sometimes been regarded as representing an early Aramaic form, even characteristic of the historical Jesus: the *mashal* form, parono-masia wordplay (Son of Man / humans), divine passive, "into the hands of."[58]

Like the other passion predictions, this one has no reference to Scripture, and Mark here omits the *dei* of 8:31 signaling divine necessity. Instead, Mark here uses as the main verb *paradidōmi*, a word he uses more frequently than any other New Testament author.[59] The basic meaning of *paradidōmi* is "hand over," and Mark can use it in the common sense of handing on tradition (7:13) or the derived meaning of "make possible," "permit" (4:29, translated "is ripe," i.e., the grain is ready to be harvested). However, eighteen of his twenty occurrences are used in the sense of someone being "handed over" to judgment or death, a frequent sense in both the Old Testament and Josephus. The combination of God as subject of *paradidōmi* and "into the hands of" is found dozens of times in the LXX (e.g., Gen 14:20; Exod 21:13; Num 21:3; Deut 1:27; 3:2; Josh 24:11; Judges 2:14; Isa 19:4 [which also has "human hands," as here]; Dan 4:14). The Suffering Servant is "handed over" or "delivered up" [by God] in Isa 53:6, 12. In the New Testament, *paradidōmi* can be used of God's judgment of sinners, as three times in Rom 1:24–28, and of God's delivering up his Son for the sins of humanity (Rom 8:32; cf. 4:25). In Mark, Jesus is the object of the action fourteen times; the disciples will be handed over / delivered up, even by their closest friends and relatives (13:9, 11, 12); once John the Baptist is "delivered up" (1:14). Being "delivered up" is the common denominator for Jesus, John, and the disciples. John preaches and is delivered up; Jesus preaches and is delivered up; the disciples will preach and will be delivered up.

The paradigm for all these is Jesus' condemnation by human courts, and his suffering and death. Who is the active agent who "delivers up"? Six times, Judas is named as the one who "delivers," "turns over," or "betrays" Jesus (3:19; 14:10, 11, 18, 21, 44). It is surely significant that *prodidōmi*, the expected word for "betray," is not used, apparently because it lacks this ambiguity. Three times, the chief priests, scribes, and elders are the active subjects (10:33b; 15:1, 10). In 15:15, Pilate "hands him over" to be crucified. In six of the eighteen instances, however, no specific subject is named. Five of these are in the passive voice, presumably a "divine passive" often used in Judaism and the New Testament as a way of expressing the hidden action of God (e.g., 4:11). Mark does not excuse the human actors in the drama in which Jesus is delivered up. But neither does he reduce it to the decisions of human actors. Behind the scenes, in and through

---

58. Cf., e.g., Jeremias, *New Testament Theology*, 281–82; Pesch, *Markusevangelium*, 2:100, vs., e.g., Lührmann, *Markusevangelium*, 163, who points to the Markan vocabulary and theology as evidence of Markan creation.

59. Cf. Norman Perrin, "The Use of (*Para-)didonai* in Connection with the Passion of Jesus in the New Testament," in *A Modern Pilgrimage in New Testament Christology* (ed. Norman Perrin; Philadelphia: Fortress, 1974), 94–103.

the arrest and execution of John the Baptist, the turning of relatives over to the judgment of human courts, the betrayal of Jesus by Judas, the delivery of Jesus to Pilate by the religious authorities, and Pilate's delivery of Jesus to the soldiers for execution, Mark traces the hand of God. Does Mark see all this within in the perspective of the Suffering Servant of Isa 53? There the servant willingly goes to his death, and the innocent one is judged and condemned by others, but his own act of self-sacrifice represents God's act in delivering him up for the salvation of "the many," and God vindicates him after death.

9.33–50 The Meaning of Discipleship, Second Version

9:33 And they came to Capernaum. And after entering the house he was asking them, "What were you arguing about on the way?" **34** But they were silent, for on the way[a] they had been arguing with each other "Who is the greatest?" **35** And he sat down and called the Twelve, and says to them, "If anyone wants to be first, that person must be[b] last of all, and servant of all." **36** And he took a child and placed it in their midst, and took it in his arms and said to them, **37** "Whoever receives one such little child in my name receives me, and whoever receives me is not receiving me but the one who sent me."

38 John said to him, "Teacher, we saw someone casting out demons in your name, and we tried to[c] stop him, because he was not following us." **39** But Jesus said, "Do not stop him; for there is no one who will do a deed of power in my name and will be able soon afterward to pronounce a curse[d] against me; **40** For whoever is not against us is for us. **41** For whoever gives you a cup of water to drink because you are a Christian,[e] amen[f] I say to you, that person will not lose their reward.

42 "And whoever causes one of these little ones who believe in me[g] to fall away,[h] it would be better for that person if a great millstone were placed around his[i] neck, and he were thrown into the sea. **43** And if your hand causes you to fall away, cut it off. It is better for you to enter into life maimed than with both hands to depart into Gehenna, into the unquenchable fire. **45**[j] And if your foot causes you to fall away, cut it off. It is better for you to enter into life lame than with both feet to be cast into Gehenna. **47** And if your eye causes you to fall away, tear it out. It is better for you to enter the kingdom of God one-eyed than with both eyes to be cast into Gehenna, **48** 'where their worm does not die and the fire is not quenched.' **49** For everyone will be salted with fire. **50** Salt is good; but if salt has lost its saltiness, with what will you season it? Have salt in yourselves, and be at peace with one another."

a. The second occurrence of "on the way" is omitted by A D Δ and a few other Greek MSS, as well as most MSS of the Old Latin and Sinaitic Syriac translations, apparently by scribes who did not recognize the deliberate Markan emphasis and considered the phrase too repetitious.

b. The future indicative *estai* is used for the strong imperative.

c. The imperfect *ekōlyomen* is conative.

d. See note *i* on *kakologeō* at 7:10. The persecution context and apocalyptic tenor of this passage suggests that the issue is more than merely badmouthing Jesus, but the either / or of confession of Jesus or cursing him. Cf. 1 Cor 12:3.

e. *En onomati hoti Christou este*, lit. "in the name, because you are Christ's." *En onomati* here means "the classification under which one belongs, noted by a name or category" (so Bauer and Danker, BDAG, 714), the *hoti* is causal, and the genitive *Christou* is possessive, so the clause as a whole means "because you belong to the category 'Christian'" (cf. 1 Pet 4:14).

f. On amen-sayings in Mark, see note *g* on 3:28.

g. *Eis eme* ("in me") is sometimes judged to be secondary (NJB, REB), since it is missing from some good MSS (ℵ D Δ), and scribes familiar with Matt 18:6 could have added it here. However, it is very strongly attested (A B L W Θ Ψ f^1 f^{13} syrˢ copˢ. and others), and a context which so often suggests a post-Easter Christian context points to *eis eme* as original. In this context, even without the two words, "believe" is not generic faith-in-general, but implies Christian faith.

h. On *skandalizō*, see note *d* on 6:3.

i. The Greek masculine pronoun is generic. On the difficulty of translating such passages into gender-inclusive English, see on 2:27; 8:34. Since vv. 42–48 are formulated in the second person, one can reformulate v. 41 as a second-person address (as does the NRSV), but this dissolves the difference in form, preventing the English reader from seeing the variety of types of sayings Mark has bundled together in this speech complex. The TNIV, here and elsewhere, preserves the third singular by using the ungrammatical "anyone . . . them" combination. I have occasionally seen this as the least objectionable solution (see v. 41).

j. Vv. 44 and 46, which reproduce the citation of Isa 66:24 from v. 48, are missing in ℵ B C L W Δ Ψ 0274 f^1 and others. Though present in most later MSS, it is virtually certain they represent a scribal addition made to conform to v. 48.

Verses 33–50 make up a loosely structured unit composed of mostly independent sayings, held together (from Mark's perspective) by the theme of discipleship and by interlocking catchwords ("if," 35, 42, 43, 45, 47, 49; "who[ever]," 37, 39, 40, 41, 42; "one of . . . children / little ones," 37, 42; "name," 37, 38, 39, 41; "cause to stumble," 42, 43, 45, 47; "[it is] good," 42, 43, 45, 47, 50; "be thrown into," 42, 45, 47; "fire," 44, 48, 49; "salt," 49, 50). As was the case with the previous section, an affirmation about Jesus (8:27–30) is followed by a passion prediction (8:31), which the disciples fail to understand (cf. 8:32–33), then by further instruction from Jesus (cf. 8:34–9:1)—who does not give up on them. Thus 9:33–50 corresponds to 8:33–9:1 (see on the structure of this section at 8:22). There are also formal similarities: an initial saying beginning with "if anyone wants" (8:34 / 9:35) followed by a series of sayings beginning with "whoever" (8:35–38 / 9:37–42). While 8:34–9:1 was composed of a collection of sayings dealing with discipleship, here the instruction is a brief narrative in which two sayings are embedded (9:35b, 37), then a dialogue occasioned by the disciples' response to an exorcist who does not belong to their group (9:38–40), to which a series of sayings is appended (9:41–50). Some elements of this unit may be traced back to the historical Jesus, and the unit as a whole reflects his impact, but the vocabulary (e.g., vv. 37, 38, 41, "in my / your / Christ's name") and presupposed situation (e.g., v. 42, believing in *Jesus* and the v. 38 reference to more than one group of Jesus' followers) reflects the post-Easter situation of the church.

[33–34] Jesus does nothing in Capernaum except have this conversation; it is only a way station en route to Jerusalem. The discussion takes place in "the house" with his disciples, again evoking the setting of the house churches of Mark's time (see on 1:29–34). The conversation that ensues is not merely a report of an exchange between Jesus and his pre-Easter followers but reflects the situation in the Markan churches for which he writes, in which arguments about leadership were current. The discussion of relative rank within the group of disciples is not merely a matter of their personal egos, but reflects the conventions of Hellenistic society in which status and honor were very important. It was taken for granted that people would be concerned about their rank on the social ladder. Likewise, rabbinic discussion and documents from the Qumran community indicate that discussion of relative rank in the kingdom of God was a matter of authentic piety.[60] Even so, in the Markan narrative context, the disciples' argument seems absurd: as Peter had responded to the first passion prediction by rebuking Jesus, the disciples now respond to Jesus' announcement that he would suffer and die by arguing about their relative rank in the coming kingdom. Jesus asks what they were arguing about not because he does not know, but because he knows (2:8; 3:1–4; 5:30, 39; 8:27; 9:21); they had not wanted to question Jesus (v. 32), so he questions them. The supreme irony is that their argument about hierarchical order within the group of Jesus' followers had taken place "on the way"—Mark repeats for emphasis (see note *a*)—the self-denying way of the cross which Jesus has chosen and to which he calls his disciples (8:34).

[35] Jesus sits down (the posture of a teacher, cf. 4:1–2) and doesn't get up until 10:1, binding this section into one instructional unit. He calls the Twelve—they are already present; the "calling" has the overtones of the renewed call to discipleship. The saying about "first" and "last" is a logion that circulated independently, appearing in several contexts (Mark 9:35; 10:43–44 [= Matt 20:26–27]; Luke 22:26 / Matt 23:11 = Q; Luke 9:48c). The logion does not provide a strategy for being first after all. Discipleship corresponds to Christology;

---

60. Cf., e.g., the rabbinic references in Strack and Billerbeck, eds., *Kommentar*, 4:1131–32. For Qumran, cf. 1QSa 2.11–22; 1QS 2.20–23.

as the Messiah is the servant who gives himself for others (10:45), so disciples make themselves last in order to serve others, not as a means of getting to be first.

[36] Jesus acts out a parable. In the first-century Mediterranean world, the characteristic feature of children was not thought to be their innocence, but their lack of status and legal rights. Jesus is not teaching a lesson about being child-like, but speaking to the issue of status. Embracing children, contrary to their cultural evaluation as nonpersons with no "rights," was characteristic of the historical Jesus and early Christianity, who accepted the least and the lowly without asking what benefit they could receive from such people. Placing a child in their midst (*mesos*, same word as 3:3, a "congregational" setting), the Markan Jesus speaks directly to the disciples. The child is not a prop or visual aid for a lesson Jesus wants to teach, but belongs within the "congregation"; those who receive it receive Jesus, and those who receive Jesus receive the one who sent him. "Send" is from *apostellō*, with overtones of apostolicity. The apostle represents the one who sent him or her (see on 3:14).

The preceding section had made the scandalous claim that Christ—the *crucified* Christ—represents God. But who represents Christ, and how is Christ's authority mediated to and within the church? Mark has previously affirmed that Christ's chosen apostles, the Twelve, are his authorized delegates (3:13–19; 6:6b–13). He does not take back that claim, and he has no polemic against the Twelve. Yet Mark is greatly concerned that the character of church leadership correspond to the cross-centered character of Christian faith. In this section he shows both that official apostolic leadership cannot be a matter of human greatness and prestige (just as messiahship is not), and that Christ's presence[61] and authority come to the church in irregular, surprising, even scandalous ways. The post-Easter Christian community had readily seen the children as transparent to the "little people" of the church. Here, Christ is represented not only by the "official" apostles, but by the most vulnerable and insignificant members of the community of faith. There is a hierarchy here—God is represented by Christ, and Christ is represented by his own authorized delegates—but the Markan Jesus' teaching subverts the cultural expectations as to who these authorized representatives are, and the nature of their authority. Alongside the "official" apostles stand the weak and vulnerable, who also mediate the presence of Christ.

[37] The loving act of receiving the child is somehow to receive Christ and God; it is the risen Christ who is met in the child (Matthew elaborates in the extensive parable of Matt 25:31–46). The language of doing things "in Jesus' name" or "in Christ's name" was not used during Jesus' lifetime, but in the later

---

61. This passage incidentally indicates that Christ is still present to the church between resurrection and Parousia—in unpredictable and indemonstrable ways. The "absence of Christ" is to be understood dialectically (see on 16:7).

Christian community Jesus' or Christ's name was invoked in prayer, and people were baptized, spoke, or worked miracles in Jesus' or Christ's name, or were persecuted because they bore "the name." As often in biblical theology, "name" is not merely a label but represents the person. Here the expression *epi tō onomati* (vv. 37, 39; cf. 13:6) seems to be equivalent to *en tō onomati* (vv. 38; cf. 41), so that both mean "with mention of the name, while naming or calling on the name," that is, invoking the name as authority, acting on the authority of Jesus (so Bauer and Danker, BDAG, 713). This general meaning can then take on different nuances in different contexts. Here, it means something like "for my sake"—the child is received not only because of its inherent value or because of the open and accepting attitude of the community, but for the sake of Jesus himself who had received the lowly, whose name the community invokes and whose presence and representative is recognized in the child.

[38] Whatever the prehistory of the pericope may have been, in its present Markan context the story continues the theme of discipleship, illustrated by the disciples' wrong attitude. They had themselves just failed to perform an exorcism (9:14–29). Now they report, through their spokesperson *John* (one of the later "pillars" of the Jerusalem church, Gal 2:9), that someone not of their group had been invoking Jesus' name to cast out demons, and they had tried to make him stop, "because he was not following us." The reader expects "following *you*," but the phrase apparently does not mean "not a follower of Jesus": it means "not of our group." In the Markan context, the issue continues to be how the authority of Jesus is mediated in the community. The Twelve have been commissioned to exercise this authority (3:14), and have done so successfully, despite their most recent fiasco (6:12–13, 30). Now they, the Twelve (cf. explicitly v. 35) claim a monopoly on such authority.

[39] The Markan Jesus, without withdrawing the authoritative commission given the Twelve, commands that the work of other Christians who work in his name not be resisted. The imperative is supported with three reasons, each introduced with the typical Markan *gar* clause.

[39b] The first reason identifies exorcism as a "deed of power," that is, uses exorcism as the representative of all Jesus' mighty deeds that manifest God's saving power (cf. 3:22–30), declaring that whoever does this cannot also invoke a curse on Jesus. The context presupposes a context in which radical decisions are made; one either confesses Jesus or curses him. Mark's community is acquainted with this either / or of Christian confession.

[40] The second reason likewise presupposes just two groups, in dualistic apocalyptic fashion. In the critical situation to which Mark speaks, there can be no low-profile neutrality; people are either for or against. As with the preceding reason, however, the Markan Jesus gives an inclusive perspective on such dualism—those not against Jesus are for him (contrast the exclusive Q version reflected in Matt 12:30 / Luke 11:23).

[41] Although the content does not neatly fit, the *gar* introduction to verse 41 shows it is related to the context as the third reason for openness to other Christians who work outside the purview of the authority claimed by the Twelve. The saying about giving you a cup of water because you are a Christian, like the other sayings in this complex, had a variety of meanings in its previous contexts prior to Mark's including it here. Its present meaning is not to underscore the moralism that even the smallest hospitality to others will pay off in the end, but to assure Jesus' disciples, here inclined to magnify their exclusive prerogatives, that those other Christians they are inclined to reject will receive their reward, and that the Twelve should not be exclusive but receptive to their hospitality. "Because you are Christian" (lit. "Christ's") uses the term "Christ" matter-of-factly in identifying Jesus' followers, presupposing they are generally known by this designation despite the messianic secret that encompasses Mark's narrative. This speech complex functions in its post-Easter Christian context, not as a precise report of an incident in the life of Jesus. This is not a matter of Mark's having forgotten the comprehensive messianic secret framework for his story; rather, it expresses another aspect of his theology—as in the Fourth Gospel, the there-and-then account of Jesus' life sometimes modulates seamlessly into the here-and-now address of Jesus to the post-Easter reader (cf., e.g., John 3:1–21; 17:1–26).

[42] The image now shifts from receiving something from others to the seriousness of making others fall away from the faith. *Skandalisē*, literally "put a stumbling block before" (see on 6:3), in this context refers to causing someone to abandon the faith. The initial image of "little ones" referred to literal children, but its use here as a counterpart to those who "belong to Christ" of the preceding verse shows that "little child" has come to represent Christian believers. As in 8:38 future reward is based on one's stance concerning the Son of Man, here one's eschatological status depends on how one treats vulnerable Christian believers. Again, Christology and ecclesiology, Jesus and his disciples, are inseparable. The grotesque image portrays having one's head thrust through the hole in the large upper millstone turned by a donkey, so that it becomes an enormous and deadly collar, and then thrown into the sea from which it is impossible to rise and have a decent burial. This fate, says the Markan Jesus, is better than causing one of the "little ones" to fall away from the faith.

[43–47] These three sayings, all in the same form and all with the same eschatological warning, then turn the threat of verse 42 to the individual who allows himself or herself to fall away. The three sayings equate "entering into life" with "enter into the kingdom of God" (cf. 10:26, 30, which add "be saved" and "eternal life" to the equation). Even though such brutal mutilations were sometimes practiced, the command is not meant literally. Nor is it limited to or focused on controlling the sex drive, a perspective that can be read into Mark from Matt 5:27–30. Nor is it a call to a kind of spirituality that disdains the body

as such. Nor is it doctrine about the nature of future punishment or an explanation of eschatological damnation. Both parts of the threefold "x is better than
y" formulation are metaphorical, but this does not minimize their seriousness.
The most extreme measures are called for—amputation of a hand, foot, or
eye—in order to avoid the unimaginably worse fate of those who are finally
condemned. "Gehenna" is a hellenized form of *gê-hinnōm* ("valley of Hin-
nom"), a valley running south and southwest of Jerusalem (Josh 15:8; 18:16).
Idolatrous worship, including child sacrifice, had been practiced there (2 Kgs
16:3; 21:6; 2 Chron 28:3; 33:6; Jer 7:31; 19:4–5; 32:35). As part of his reform,
Josiah defiled this site (2 Kgs 23:10–14), and it became the rubbish heap of
Jerusalem, pervaded by maggots and the stench of decay, where fire smoldered
day and night. Already by the time of Isa 66:24, cited in verse 48, the valley is
pictured as the destination of the dead bodies of those who had rebelled against
God. In later Jewish apocalyptic this image became the picture of eschatological judgment, and so appears in the New Testament (*1 En.* 27.1; 54.1; 90.26–27;
2 Esd 7:36; Matt 5:22, 29–30; 10:28; 18:9; 23:15, 33; Mark 9:43, 45, 47; Luke
12:5; James 3:6).

[49–50] The final two sayings are apparently linked to this speech complex
by the catchwords "fire" and "salt." Their meaning was already obscure to
Matthew and Luke, who simply omitted them, and to the later copyists, who
made a number of modifications and additions in an effort to make the sayings
comprehensible. The favorite of these was to add some version of Lev 2:13,
"for every sacrifice will be salted with fire," thus making it possible to understand the sayings in terms of Christian self-sacrifice as expressed, for example,
in Rom 12:1. Since both "salt" and "fire" are biblical images with many connotations (purification, preservation, judgment, covenant, etc.), it is possible to
construct a great many edifying explanations of the sayings, but the fact is, here
we have one of the New Testament passages that defy interpretation.

10:1–31 Discipleship, Family, Society

As elsewhere in this section, it is important to keep the Markan structure and
context in mind (see Introduction 2.). The narrative that began briefly in Judea
has transpired almost entirely in Galilee and its environs. In Mark, Jesus makes
only one trip to Jerusalem; chapter 10 is the brief transition from Galilee to
Jerusalem. On the immediate context of this section, see at 8:22. Thus the author
does not decide simply to report here some teaching of Jesus on the subject of
divorce, as though it were a topic of general importance he wishes to discuss,
or an illustration of his conflict with the religious authorities. If this were the
case, the reader might well ask why this pericope was not included in the
debates of 2:1–3:6 or 11:27–12:34. Rather, the meaning of discipleship continues to be the topic. Already in 3:31–35, the Markan Jesus had announced the

formation of a new family that transcended the most sacred obligations and relationships of the conventional family. What did this mean concretely? Was the new Christian movement a sect intent on demolishing family life? Did Jesus' own words about leaving home and family to become a disciple mean that marriage and children had no place in the life of a devoted disciple? The religious and political tensions of Mark's situation had indeed led to the breakup of families—is this an essential cost of discipleship? Can an authentic disciple have a spouse and children? And what is their status within the community? Mark's literary and historical context, including the persecution of (Jewish-) Christians at the time of the 66–70 revolt, is primary for understanding the section. Families were divided against each other (13:12). Marriages came apart under the stress. Disciples were having to make decisions about financial and social matters. Within the framework of the "way to Jerusalem" announced at 8:31, the Markan Jesus spells out some implications of discipleship for marriage and divorce (1–12), relation to children (13–16), property (17–27), family relationships and church leaders (28–31, 35–45).

10:1–12 Discipleship, Marriage, and Divorce

10:1 And he got up and left, and comes into the region of Judea and Transjordan, and again crowds are gathering around him, and, as was his custom, he was teaching them. 2 And some Pharisees[a] came, and were asking, "Is it lawful for a man[b] to divorce[c] his wife?"—testing him. 3 But he answered them, "What did Moses command you?" 4 And they said, "Moses allowed a man to write a divorce certificate and to divorce her." 5 But Jesus said to them, "Because of your hardness of heart he wrote this command for you, 6 but from the beginning of creation 'he made them male and female.' 7 'For this reason a man[b] shall leave his father and mother and be joined to his wife, 8 and the two shall become one flesh'; so they are no longer two but one flesh. 9 Therefore what God has joined together let no human being[b] separate." 10 And in the house again, the disciples were asking him about this. 11 And he says to them, "Whoever divorces his wife and marries another commits adultery against her; 12 and if she divorces her husband and marries another, she commits adultery."

a. The MSS contain at least four versions of the opening words of this sentence. In one version documented by D and the entire Old Latin tradition, i.e., from the "Western" text tradition, as well as from sy[s] and some MSS of the Coptic tradition, the word "Pharisees" is missing and the crowds of v. 1 are the subject. In that case, the "you" of v. 5 would apply to more than the Pharisees. If the crowds were the original subject, this scene already anticipates a shift in their stance toward that of Jesus' opponents (cf. 15:8, 11).

b. *Anthrōpos* ("man," "human being," "humanity") in vv. 2 and 7 is the husband distinguished from the wife. The same word in v. 9 is generic, distinguishing humanity and God.

c. The traditional translation "divorce," retained here for convenience, is actually too modern, and too moderate, a translation for the verb *apolyō* and its cognate noun *apolysis*. Since in the Old Testament and ancient Judaism it was the husband's prerogative, requiring no judicial decision, "dismissal" is more accurate.

The overall form of this pericope is typically Markan: after the travel note (v. 1), there is a two-part scene consisting of public instruction (vv. 2–9) followed by private explanation to the disciples (vv. 10–12; cf. the similar structures in 4:1–20 and especially 7:1–23). The first part has the typical form of a "scholastic dialogue," the traditional form-critical category for a formal unit in which a question is posed to the teacher (v. 2), who responds with a counter question (v. 3) to which the inquirers reply in turn (v. 4), which then receives the definitive answer (vv. 5–9).

[1] "Judea and across the Jordan" is an unusual geographical designation, as in 7:31 reflecting the author's inexact knowledge of geography. Jesus has been teaching in private, but now the crowds reappear, and Jesus will be presented as a public teacher during the Jerusalem days. Mark says nothing about crowds of Passover pilgrims en route to Jerusalem, and the reader need not imagine them here; the Markan crowds can appear wherever the needs of the narrative call for them (see on 8:34). Jesus resumes his customary practice of teaching the crowd, but the content is not given. Jesus' authority, not the content of his teaching, is the point (cf. 1:21–22; 4:1–2, 34).

[2] The Pharisees likewise reappear, again with insincere motives, wanting to put him to the test (cf. 2:16, 24; 3:6; 7:1, 8:11, 15). The omniscient narrator describes their question as "testing him" because they are not seeking his opinion on a disputed point, but already know how he will respond, and wish to use it against him to discredit him. Divorce is assumed in the Torah and was hardly contested in first-century Judaism, where the legitimate *grounds* for divorce was a disputed point (thus Matt 19:3 makes the appropriate change).[62] Given the situation in which the husband could dismiss his wife at will, the divorce certificate was a hedge against the husband's arbitrariness, specifying that she was now free to remarry.

---

62. The only Torah text dealing with divorce, Deut 24:1–4, contains the disputed clause, "because he finds something objectionable about her." The two dominant schools of interpretation were the conservative followers of Shammai, who contended that "something objectionable" could mean only sexual misconduct, while the more liberal followers of Hillel argued that anything that displeased the husband was sufficient ground for divorce, with the famous Aqiba even arguing that finding a more attractive woman was reason enough. The latter view is illustrated by, e.g., Sirach 25:26, "If she does not go as you direct, separate her from yourself," and Josephus's terse comment, "about this time I divorced my wife also, as not pleased with her behavior" (*Life* 426).

[3–9] Jesus responds with a counter question, to which the Pharisees give the biblical answer: the Torah permits divorce, that is, it is simply assumed. There is no contrast between "God" and "Moses." As in 7:9–10, Moses' commandment is identified with God's. Jesus' counterresponse is a citation from Scripture declaring the original will of God set forth in creation, to which the later law of Moses was only a concession to hard-heartedness (Gen 1:27; 2:24). The argument here is not merely pitting one Scripture against another, but is somewhat like that of Paul's train of thought in Gal 3:15–20—the later law, though itself from God, is only a concession, and does not correspond to the original will of God given in creation. Yet for Mark, the authority of Jesus, not the cogency of the argument or the authority of Scripture, is the point of the whole discussion (see on 7:14–23, where Scripture is also cited, but the authority of Jesus is the ultimate court of appeal). Jesus declares that the primal will of God is revealed in the way God originally created humanity as male and female, two persons intended to become "one flesh." This biblical idiom not only refers to the sexual union of husband and wife (cf. 1 Cor 6:16), but also means that the couple are now an actual unity, not two individuals going their own way while united by a contractual arrangement. God the creator is the actor in joining together husband and wife into this new unity. Thus no human being should separate what God has joined together. Though *anthrōpos* here makes the divine / human contrast, the reference is not to a human judge, court, third party, or Pharisaic doctrine, but to a specific human being, namely the husband, for in the Jewish situation presupposed by the Pharisees, only the husband could effect a divorce.

[11–12] There is no further response from the Pharisees; the instruction has been for the church of Mark's time, not for the characters in the narrative. "The house" to which Jesus and his disciples retire for this instruction is the stereotypical house which, like the crowds, appears when needed (*palin*, "again"; cf. on 1:29–34). Verse 11 is an independent logion (cf. Luke 16:18) inserted here by Mark. Unlike the modified and moderated versions in Matt 5:31–32; 19:9; 1 Cor 7:10–13, this saying represents Jesus' absolute prohibition of divorce. Like the Old Testament prophets, Jesus does not temper his command with situational conditions, but announces the absolute will of God. While the Torah permits divorce, as the Pharisees testing Jesus of course knew, the Torah prohibits adultery; by defining divorce as facilitating adultery, Jesus shows that divorce is in fact a violation of God's will revealed in the Torah. Jesus' declaration is also radical in affirming that the man can commit adultery against his wife—in Old Testament and ancient Jewish understanding, only the rights of the husband, not the wife, could be violated by adultery. Verse 12 is probably added by Mark or his Gentile Christian tradition, since it presupposes that a woman could initiate a divorce—possible for Gentile women, but not for Jews. The only instances of Jewish women divorcing their husbands are among the nobility, who live by Gentile standards and were considered scandalous exceptions (cf. Josephus, *Ant.* 15.259; 18.136 [cf. Mark 6:18]; 20.141–43).[63]

Mark's presentation of Jesus' pronouncements on divorce presents him as standing in the prophetic tradition (cf. Mal 2:13–17), declaring the absolute will of God, though it is still directed to the particular situation of Mark's church. As illustrated later by Matt 5:31–32; 19:3–9, this radical ethical demand must be interpreted pastorally in each situation, without losing sight of the ultimate will of God it represents.[64] In some situations, divorce can be the occasion for repentance, acknowledgment that one has failed to live by the will of God, and a means of grace, just as staying married in an impossible situation can express self-righteousness in "living according to the Bible," while distancing one from one's own failure and sense of God's grace. In the light of this text, however, divorce can only be a last resort, and can never be "innocent."

10:13–16 Discipleship and Children

Just as the preceding pericope had dealt with the question of whether the radical demands of discipleship meant leaving behind one's spouse, so this pericope responds to the issue of the disciple's relation to children—including one's own.

10:13 And people were trying to bring[a] little children to him in order that he might touch them, but the disciples rebuked them. 14 But when Jesus saw it he was indignant, and said to them, "Let the little children come to me; do not prevent them, for the kingdom of God belongs to[b] such as these. 15 Amen[c] I say to you, whoever does not receive the kingdom of God as a little child[d] will never enter it." 16 And he took them up in his arms, laid his hands on them, and blessed them.

a. The imperfect *prosepheron* is conative, as in 9:38.

b. The genitive *tōn toioutōn* can be either possessive (as here translated; cf. Matt 5:3, 10) or genitive of content (the kingdom of God "consists of" such as these). The meaning is hardly affected.

c. On "amen," see note g at 3:28.

d. *Paidion* ("child") can theoretically be either nominative, "receive the kingdom as a little child receives it" or accusative, "receive the kingdom as one receives a child" (cf. 9:37). While the syntax is ambiguous, context favors the first interpretation.

63. For other possible examples, cf. Lührmann, *Markusevangelium*, 170.

64. Perkins regards Jesus' saying in Mark as already conditioned by the historical situation of the divorce and remarriage of Herod Antipas. It was this "selfish individualism of the Herodian court" that Jesus opposes. "He was not telling a battered woman that she and her children must risk physical and psychological torment every day just to avoid a divorce" ("Mark," 646).

The passage is not a mini-essay on "the Christian view of children" or the like, but is primarily about discipleship and the kingdom of God. It is similar to 9:36–37, but there the child was an image of the "little people" whom the church should receive. Here, the concern is for children as such, who then become a model for receiving the kingdom.

[13] People presuppose that Jesus' touch communicates God's power (cf. 5:28). Here, however, it is not healing that is sought, but blessing. Despite the recent command of 9:36–37, the disciples not only do not receive the little children but rebuke those who bring them.

[14] Jesus is indignant (*aganakteō*, as 10:41, 14:4, but only here is this term used in Mark to refer to Jesus; cf. Jesus' anger in 1:41 [*orgizō*]; 3:5 [*orgē*]). Mark does not hesitate to portray the human emotion of Jesus, suppressed by both Matthew and Luke—or is it divine indignation? "Do not prevent them" has been seen by some interpreters as reflecting the baptismal practice of early Christianity, since the term used here for "prevent" (*kōlyō*) is related to baptism in Matt 3:14; Acts 8:36; 10:47; 11:17. While this text did become prominent in later debates about infant baptism that persist to our own time,[65] it is not likely that the statement reflects a debate in the Markan church regarding paedobaptism. Since it is disciples, and not the Pharisees or scribes who raise the objection, it is likely that the pericope reflects an internal issue in church life, namely exclusiveness and striving after status.

In the Hellenistic world, children had no status (see on 9:36–37). Religiously they were nonentities, disqualified from participation—as were women. In ancient Judaism, participation in the life of the synagogue began (for males) at age thirteen, when a boy became a "bar mitzvah," a "son of the commandment," responsible for obeying the Torah. Jesus' pronouncement that children as such belong to God's kingdom meant that inclusion in God's kingdom is not a matter of status or attainment of any kind; it is a matter of unconditional acceptance. The statement is not an item in a doctrinal discussion on the innocence of children and the "age of accountability," but a proclamation on the nature of God's kingdom—being included is a matter of God's sovereign grace. Since they already belong to God's kingdom, they should not be prevented from being brought to Jesus for blessing.

[15] This statement, introduced with the solemn *amen*, was originally an independent saying, a slightly modified form of which Matthew adds in a different

---

65. Cf., e.g., Karl Barth, *The Teaching of the Church Regarding Baptism* (trans. Ernest A. Payne; London: SCM Press, 1948), 38–56; Barth, *Dogmatics* IV/4/2, 187, 193–94; Oscar Cullmann, *Baptism in the New Testament* (SBT 1; trans. J. K. S. Reid; Naperville, Ill.: Alec R. Allenson, 1958; Joachim Jeremias, *Infant Baptism in the First Four Centuries* (trans. David Cairns; Philadelphia: Westminsters, 1960); Andreas Lindemann, "Die Kinder und die Gottesherschaft," *WD* 17 (1983): 99.

context (cf. Matt 18:3). By placing it in this context, Mark or his tradition has shifted the meaning from that of the previous statement. Now, it is not a matter of the kingdom belonging to children, but that those who are like children will enter the kingdom at its future advent expressed in the form of a conditional entrance requirement (as 9:47; see *Excursus: Kingdom of God* at 1:15). Only those will enter the kingdom who receive it as does a little child, who make no claims, unself-consciously assume their own utter dependence, and are not concerned about rank, status, and self-image.

10:17–31 Discipleship, Property, and Family

10:17 As he was proceeding along the way, a man ran up, knelt down before him, and was asking him, "Good teacher, what must[a] I do to inherit eternal life?" 18 Jesus said to him, "Why do you call me good? No one is good except the one God." 19 You know the commandments, Do not murder;[b] do not commit adultery; do not steal; do not bear false witness; do not deprive others of their rights;[c] honor your father and mother." 20 He said to him, "Teacher, I have kept[d] all these since I was a boy." 21 Jesus, looking intently[e] at him, loved him, and said to him, "One thing you lack; go, sell everything you have and give to the poor, and you will have treasure in heaven, and come, follow me." 22 But he was appalled at these words, and went away grieving, for he was a man of great wealth.

23 Then Jesus looked around and says to his disciples, "How hard it will be for those who have wealth to enter the kingdom of God!" 24 And the disciples were amazed at his words. But Jesus again responds to them, "Children, how hard it is[f] to enter into the kingdom of God. 25 It is easier for a camel[g] to go through the eye of a needle than for someone who is rich to enter the kingdom of God." 26 But they were greatly astounded, saying to one another, "Then who can be saved?" 27 But Jesus looked intently[e] at them and says, "For human beings it is impossible, but not for God; all things are possible for God."

28 Peter began to say to him, "Look, we have left everything and followed you." 29 Jesus said, "Amen[h] I say to you, there is no one who has left house or brothers or sisters or mother or father[i] or children or fields, for my sake and the gospel's[j] 30 who will not receive a hundredfold now in this present age—houses and brothers and sisters and mothers and children and fields, with persecutions—and in the age to come, eternal life. 31 But many who are first will be last, and the last first."

a. The form *poiēsō* can be either future indicative or aorist subjunctive. In this context it is future indicative, with the force of "what shall I do," in the sense of the same form in the Decalogue, i.e., "must."

b. The LXX Decalogue of Exod 20:1–17 consistently uses the negative of the future indicative, corresponding to the MT's *lō* + imperfect, and appropriately rendered in English by the future, "You shall not . . ." Mark consistently has the negative *mē* + the aorist subjunctive, best rendered in English by the imperative "Do not . . ."

c. *Mē aposterēsēs* is not found in the Decalogue (and is thus omitted by Matthew and Luke in this context, as well as by B* K W Δ Ψ *f*[1, 13] and other MSS), and may be Mark's or his tradition's paraphrasing replacement for the final commandment against coveting, not found in Mark.

d. The middle form *ephylaxamēn* properly means "keep oneself from," "abstain from," which would be inappropriate with regard to commandments. Although the LXX often used the middle form in the sense of keeping commandments (e.g., Exod 12:17, 24, 25; Lev 18:4), both Matt 19:20 and Luke 18:21 correct Mark's incorrect grammar to the active form e*phylaxa*.

e. *Emblepō*, a strengthened form of the normal word for looking, *blepō*, is found elsewhere in Mark only in 8:25, 10:27, and 14:67.

f. Several MSS, including A C D Θ *f*[1, 13] and most later witnesses, add some form of *tous pepoithotas epi chrēmasin* ("for those trusting in riches"). Not only is the phrase absent from ℵ B Δ Ψ and other ancient witnesses, it seems clearly to have been added to alleviate the felt difficulty of the pericope by transferring the problem from possessing wealth as such to trusting in it—one could be a good disciple and retain one's wealth so long as one did not trust in money but in God. In this case, Jesus' statement would no longer declare an impossibility but only pose a challenge to faith.

g. A few MSS (including *f*[13] 28 579 and the Georgian translation) have *kamilon* ("rope," "hawser," "ship's cable") for *kamēlon* ("camel"), again in an effort to make the saying easier to accept. While a rope is smaller than a camel, the proposed solution only seems to help, for it is also impossible for a rope to go through a needle's eye.

h. On *amēn*, see note *g* at 3:28.

i. Most later MSS, and a few ancient ones (including A C Ψ *f*[13]) add *ē gynaika* ("or wife"), but the phrase is missing in ℵ B D W Δ Θ *f*[1], the old Latin, Sinaitic Syriac, and Coptic translations.

j. On this phrase, see note *g* at 8:35. On "gospel" for *euangelion* (lit. "good news"), see on 1:1, 15.

Though elements of verses 17–31 may have had their own history in the pre-Markan tradition, in their Markan context they constitute a unity composed of three scenes: 17–22, a dialogue between Jesus and an anonymous man who turns out to be wealthy; 23–27, instructions to the disciples; 28–31, Peter's question and Jesus' response on the rewards of discipleship, concluded by an aphorism on the eschatological reversal of conventional human evaluations. The first scene, 17–22, originally had the form of a "scholastic dialogue" (see on 10:1–12, p. 286), but at verse 21 it takes a radical turn so that its present Markan form is that of a (failed) call story (contrast 1:16–20; 2:14).

The uninitiated reader does not learn until the end of the story that the man was rich. Most contemporary readers know this in advance, however, and so the problem of wealthy people who want to be followers of Jesus is there from the beginning. The story declares flatly that it is not only difficult but impossible for a rich person to enter the kingdom of God (vv. 23–27; equated with "have treasures in heaven," v. 21; "inherit eternal life," v. 17; "be saved," v. 26). Apart from ancient scribal efforts to alleviate the problem by changing the text itself (see notes *f* and *g* above), the history of interpretation evinces a number of hermeneutical moves that have attempted to enable the church to live by and with this difficult text:

(1) *"Needle's eye" refers to a Jerusalem gate.* Perhaps the most ingenious and well-known attempt is the interpretation that posits a narrow gate in the city wall of Jerusalem known as the "needle's eye." It was difficult, but possible, for a camel to squeeze through it, but only by removing all its baggage, having the camel get down on its knees, and trying *really* hard. The homiletical usefulness of this approach is somewhat obviated by the fact that there was no such actual gate, which first appears in a ninth-century commentary on this passage.

(2) *Jesus' statement was restricted to a particular historical situation, not a general requirement for discipleship.* Numerous interpreters, ancient and modern, point out that during the ministry of Jesus he called a few people to join him in an itinerant ministry, and that the special mission of such people required them to leave everything to follow him. But even the historical Jesus did not ask this of all disciples, for most followers retained their possessions (e.g., Levi of 2:14–17 retained his house in which he continued to have dinner parties, and even the four fishermen who left their boats and homes were not asked to sell them; cf. 1:16–20, 29–31; 4:1, 36; 5:2, 18; 6:32; 8:10).

(3) *Jesus' statement was a prescription for a particular individual, not a general requirement for discipleship.* In this view, it is not rich people in general for whom it is impossible to enter the kingdom, but this particular man, whose moral or theological deficiencies made it impossible for *him.* He was prideful and arrogant, and assumed he could be justified by works.[66] Or he was insincere and was only testing Jesus. Or he is a flatterer ("Good teacher") who expected to be complimented in return. Or he regarded Jesus as merely a good

---

66. So already *Gospel of the Nazarenes*, fragment 16: "And the Lord said to him, 'How canst thou say, "I have fulfilled the law and the prophets?" For it stands written in the law: 'Love thy neighbor as thyself'; and behold, many of thy brethren, sons of Abraham, are begrimed with dirt and die of hunger—and thy house is full of many good things and nothing at all comes forth from it to them!'" So also Hilary of Potiers, *On the Trinity* 9.16; Jerome, *Letters to Julian* 118; Augustine, *Letters to Hilarius* 157, and many after them. For these and other patristic interpretations noted here, see Oden and Hall, *Mark*, 138–46. So also Calvin, and many later Protestant interpreters, pose the issue in Pauline terms, seeing the man's problem as relying on his own confidence in fulfilling the works of the law rather than God's grace (John T. McNeill, ed., *Calvin: Institutes of the Christian Religion* [LCC 20–21; trans. Ford Lewis Battles; 2 vols.; Philadelphia: Westminster, 1960], 1:831 = 3.18.9).

man and thus had a defective Christology. Or he was inordinately attached to his money, Jesus sensed that this was a barrier to discipleship, and prescribed this remedy for his particular spiritual sickness.[67]

(4) *Rejection of "literalism."* The command was not meant literally, but spiritually, for it is not having money, but loving it, that is the problem.[68]

(5) *Law versus grace; the "second use of the law."* The man sincerely supposed he had kept all the law's commands and thus felt no need of God's grace, through which alone salvation is possible. Jesus thus intensified the demand, attempting to bring the man to an awareness that he could not be saved by his own accomplishments, and this is the role the passage is intended to play for the Markan reader. Thus Jesus' response preserved in this story was given as a *praeparatio evangelica* intended to reveal to us our own impotence and drive us to despair, to compel us to stop exerting ourselves in establishing our own righteousness.[69]

(6) *Two levels of discipleship.* Matthew's addition of "If you want to be perfect . . ." before the command to sell all provided the opening for later church interpretation that distinguished two degrees of discipleship, the "ordinary" Christians who keep the basic commandments and the "perfect" who belong to religious orders and live according to the extra "evangelical counsels" of poverty, chastity, and obedience. This interpretation serves to get "ordinary" Christians off the hook of the radical demand to dispose of one's property for the sake of the poor.

In advance of the commentary below on particular verses, we note that the text requires some interpretation to be appropriated at all, and that neither Matthew nor Luke simply repeat it, but incorporate it within their respective hermeneutical schemata. The variety of such hermeneutical approaches, and their common desire to respect the Scripture and live by its injunctions, is a warning to be wary of comforting, "reasonable" explanations. Like the Gospel as a whole, this story works like a parable, retaining its disorienting shock, resisting reduction to something else. In particular, the dialogue itself transforms the man's original request. Asking "How much does God / Jesus want; when is it enough?" turns out to be a wrong question. The answer cannot be quantified; God / Jesus wants *you.*

67. "Insincere": Jerome, *Homily 53*; Gregory Nazianzen, *Theological Orations: On the Son* 30.13. "Flatterer": Kenneth E. Bailey, *Poet and Peasant and Through Peasant Eyes: A Literary-Cultural Approach to the Parable in Luke* (Grand Rapids: Eerdmans, 1980), 162. "Defective Christology": Augustine, *Confessions* 13.19. "Particular spiritual sickness": So Luther, *WA* 47, 348.26–40; 350.13–40.

68. So Clement of Alexandria, *Salvation of the Rich Man* 22.

69. This very Reformation (esp. Lutheran) and Pauline interpretation is represented by, e.g., Schweizer, *Mark*, 215: "The point of all this is found in 25–27, which say essentially the same thing as Rom 3:23–24."

[17–18] The incident takes place "on the way" (cf. *Excursus: The Way* at 1:3). The man in Mark is anonymous, without name or party. He is neither "young" (cf. v. 20, omitted by Matthew, 19:20) nor "ruler" (Luke 18:18). The reader does not learn that he is rich until the scene is over (v. 22). That the man runs and kneels before Jesus indicates both urgency and sincerity. "Good teacher" is likewise sincere, not flattery. The grounds for Jesus' objection are unclear, but we may rule out that the Markan Jesus is straightforwardly making a claim to deity, as though the man too casually uses a predicate for Jesus that should be exclusively reserved for God, just as we may rule out that Mark is here claiming that Jesus is not "good" but a sinner. While Mark is not nervous about placing Jesus in solidarity with sinful human beings (see on 1:4, 9), he is not here making a doctrinal statement analogous to the later dogma of the sinlessness of Christ. This point of Christology has not yet become an issue. Jesus' objection, "No one is good except the one God," echoes the language of both the Shema and the scribes of 2:7. Mark is concerned to make his christological confession in a way that preserves Israel's confession of the One God (see on 12:28–37, which is also concerned with keeping the commandments). As the granting of eternal life is a divine prerogative, so setting the conditions for receiving it belongs to God alone. Jesus qua teacher, however "good" from the human point of view, cannot state the terms of admission to the kingdom of God, which remains God's prerogative. The issue here is not the christological identity of Jesus—how "high on the scale" between humanity and deity—but the sovereignty of God.[70]

"What must I do?" is personal, not abstract. "Eternal life" means eschatological salvation (v. 26) in the kingdom of God (v. 24), the treasures in heaven (v. 21) of the age to come (v. 30). "Inherit" is a fixed biblical form for obtaining the future blessings of God, often used in the LXX for possessing the Promised Land and later adapted in Judaism to express the receiving of eschatological blessings (cf. Exod 32:13; Lev 20:24; Num 34:13; Ps 37:9; Dan 12:2; *Pss. Sol.* 3.16; 9.5; 13.11; 14.4–7, 10; *1 En.* 37.4; 40.9; 58.3; 2 Esd 7:129) and is thus not strictly related to the idea of inheritance, that is, being an heir in the Pauline sense of receiving free grace as a child of God (Rom 4:13; 8:17; Gal 4:7). It would thus be overinterpreting to complain that the man asks what he can "do" to "inherit," as though his question contained a confused built-in contradiction.

[19–20] The question of what to do is answered by what not to do—but see the positive answer at verse 21: "follow me." Jesus' initial response paraphrases the "second table" of the Decalogue, the commandments dealing with relationships with other people, but seems almost studiously to avoid a direct quotation: the form "do not . . ." is different from the biblical form (see note *b* above); the order is different, with the command to respect parents placed last, and the command against

---

70. Cf. M. Eugene Boring, "Markan Christology: God-Language for Jesus?" *NTS* 45 (1999): 451–59.

covetousness is missing, replaced by "do not deprive others." The verb *apostereō* is found elsewhere in the New Testament only in 1 Cor 6:7–8 (NRSV "defraud"); 7:5 (NRSV "deprive"); 1 Tim 6:5 (NRSV "bereft"); and Jas 5:4 (NRSV, the wages of laborers have been "kept back by fraud"; cf. the echo of Mal 3:5; Sir 4:1). This last instance is particularly telling, though the word need not imply deceit, but only injustice. While Mark does not have the modern concept of "systemic evil," he may be signaling that the rich man, though personally moral, understands ethics in personal, individualistic terms and is oblivious to his involvement in corporate guilt,[71] and so he had become rich at the expense of others.

[21–22] Jesus does not challenge or correct the man's claim; the narrator states that Jesus looked at him—the penetrating look of 3:5, 34; 5:32; 8:25, 33; 10:23, 27—and for the first and only time in Mark, states that Jesus loved (*ēgapēsen*) someone. This pericope has several points of contact with 12:28–34; "love" evokes the command of "love your neighbor," which goes beyond avoiding bad behavior and calls for positive action in behalf of the neighbor. Jesus is the embodiment of this love, which he here extends to the man. Jesus then, not as a matter of biblical commands but on his own authority (cf. 1:16–3:6), indicates that the man still lacks one thing. Keeping the negative commands had not affected how he used his wealth; he had not loved his neighbor as himself, and had not thought of entering the kingdom of God and receiving eternal life in those terms. Nor is the man's wealth thought of as merely an impediment to his own spirituality, as though entering the kingdom of God were only a two-party issue between the man and God. Selling his property also involves the poor, who desperately need his money; they do not have reserves, a privilege of the wealthy. The man is asked to transfer his reserves to the heavenly realm, and to join Jesus and his disciples among the poor of the earth who have no this-worldly reserves, to become dependent, like the children of verses 13–16. After divestment, the man can no longer fulfill the role of patron or benefactor, but joins the ranks of those dependent on others. "Follow me" is not an additional command. This selling and giving is not moralizing "doing good," but is the content of the decisive final word, "follow me," which identifies placing one's property at the disposal of others as the meaning of discipleship. Jesus calls, but here his powerful word does not generate followers (cf. 1:16–20). The man, whom the reader only now learns was rich, was appalled and went away grieving. Yet this is not the last word.

[23–27] When the rich man departs, Jesus takes the initiative to address the disciples, shifting the spotlight from the one individual to the comprehensive issue of the relation of possessions to discipleship, eternal life, and entering the kingdom of God. In verse 23, the perspective is broadened beyond this

71. Myers, *Binding the Strong Man*, 272: "The reference in this addition is clearly to economic exploitation."

individual instance to include "those who have wealth" in general, then made universal in verse 24, which is then in verse 25 once again focused on the difficulty—rather, the impossibility—of a wealthy person being saved, now as a focal example of salvation as such. The disciples are astonished at Jesus' initial statement (v. 24). Their amazement indicates they share the general (but not universal[72]) view of Old Testament and Jewish tradition that regards wealth as a blessing from God, a sign of divine favor (e.g., Deut 28:1–14; Job 1:10; 42:10; Prov 10:22). The disciples, along with the reader, must be impressed with the fact that the man is an outstanding example of keeping the divine law as expressed in the Ten Commandments, that he is not self-righteous but implicitly acknowledges he still needs something else, and that he is not too proud to kneel before an itinerant Galilean preacher and ask for help. Jesus does not mollify their consternation with a "reasonable" explanation, but compounds it with the picture of a camel standing helpless before the needle's eye. It is not only hard for the rich man to be saved, it is impossible. He addresses the disciples with "children" (*tekna*, different from the *paidia* of 9:36–37; 10:13–16) for the first and only time in the Gospel (elsewhere as address, only 2:5). This may be only an informal sign of affection, but it also has overtones of the "children of Israel," the people of God (cf. 7:27). The disciples, untypical in their Markan representation, get the point. "Who then can be saved" is not a speculative, theoretical topic of discussion, but the same existential question with which the rich man began (v. 17). Now instructed by what had just happened, the disciples realize that the question concerns everyone; it is not limited to the particular case of the rich man, or even the wealthy as a class. If this man, with every advantage and indication of being near the kingdom, cannot be saved, then who can? Their question is rhetorical: in the light of what has just happened and what Jesus has just said, no one can be saved. Jesus acknowledges and strengthens the validity of their point. Salvation is humanly impossible. But for God all things are possible. God does not merely do the difficult, making up human lack once we have done our best, but does the impossible. Jesus drives the dialogue toward the point where people say "Salvation—of anyone—is humanly impossible." Only then does the good news come: salvation—of anyone, even the rich man—is possible for God (cf. Rom 4:13–20, esp. v. 17).[73]

72. The Old Testament and Judaism also contained a strong tradition opposing those rich people who had no compassion on the poor, so that "poor" could sometimes become practically a synonym for "pious" and "acceptable to God." Cf. Exod 22:21–27; Amos 2:6–8; the Psalms in which the poor are God's chosen; *1 En.* 38.5–6; 63.7, 10; 94.6–9; 96.4–8; 98.2–6, numerous rabbinic statements, and Aloysius M. Ambrozic, *The Hidden Kingdom: A Redaction-Critical Study of the References to the Kingdom of God in Mark's Gospel* (CBQMS 2; Washington: Catholic Biblical Association of America, 1972), 163–69.

73. Karl Barth, *Church Dogmatics, Volume II: The Doctrine of God, Second Half-Volume* (trans. Geoffrey Bromiley et al.; Edinburgh: T. & T. Clark, 1957), 613–30.

[28–31] Peter now takes the initiative, responding on behalf of the disciples to Jesus' instruction. The point has been made. Some have indeed responded to Jesus' radical call and have begun to follow—and this, too, is to be seen as the divine possibility in the face of human impossibility, belonging to the elect (called, chosen) people of God addressed as *tekna* (see above). Some of the Markan community have not only been abandoned by family and friends (13:12), but have actively separated themselves from home and family for the sake of the gospel. What then? Jesus' response rejects both an individualistic and an exclusively future view of salvation. Using the two-ages terminology of Jewish apocalyptic for the only time in this Gospel, Jesus promises that such followers will receive eternal life in the age to come, and that even now they belong to a salvific community of faith; for Mark there is "an inherent relationship between salvation and communal life" (Via, *Ethics of Mark's Gospel*, 143). Even though persecution is involved (v. 30; cf. 13:9–10), eschatological reward is not a matter of suffer-now-reap-later deferred gratification. Modern readers get a sense of Markan ecclesiology, in which Christians are all members of the same extended family (cf. also 3:30–35) where brothers and sisters share with each other.[74] The house church is a household, a true family. In contrast to the rich man who went gloomily away, retaining his wealth but giving up his happiness, Mark provides a warm-hearted picture of the Christian community. Discipleship does not mean abandoning the world, ascetic renunciation of marriage, or abandoning of one's family.[75] Following Jesus does not lead to deprivation but to wholeness and fulfillment, not only in the world to come but in the here and now. The voluntary deprivation of the Markan community was not a matter of ascetic renunciation of the world's pleasures for the sake of one's individual soul, but a testimony to the reality of the coming kingdom already made manifest in Jesus, done for Jesus' and the gospel's sake, which may be the same thing (see on 8:35). Yet the sobering note "with persecutions" (v. 30) shows that while disciples do not abandon the world or withdraw from it, they also cannot settle down comfortably within it. The whole issue is seen in an apocalyptic framework.

10:32–45 The Third Prediction of the Passion and the Argument about Precedence among the Disciples

This subsection beginning with the third passion prediction fits into and forms the climax of the pattern beginning at 8:22 (see commentary there). The initial

---

74. The equation is not 1:1. Mark pointedly omits "wives" from the list of those abandoned (10:1–12!), as he omits "fathers" from the list of those gained—in the extended Christian family only God is father (cf. 3:35).

75. Mark may well be writing in the wake of the wandering charismatics of the Q community, some of whom exalted the life of true discipleship as calling for abandoning home and hearth (see, e.g., Matt 8:18–22 / Luke 9:57–62; Matt 10:37–39 / Luke 14:25–27).

scene "on the road" is not the continuation of the preceding incident, but sets the stage for the following dialogue.

10:32 And they were on the road, going up to Jerusalem, and Jesus was going ahead of them, and they were amazed, and those who were following were afraid. And he again took the Twelve aside and began to tell them what was to happen to him. 33 "Look, we are going up to Jerusalem, and the Son of Man will be delivered over to the chief priests and the scribes, and they will condemn him to death, and will deliver him over to the Gentiles 34 and they will mock him and spit on him and beat him with the scourge and kill him; and after three days he will rise again."

35 And James and John, the sons of Zebedee, are coming to him and saying to him, "Teacher, we want you to do for us whatever we ask of you." 36 And he said to them, "What do you want me to do for you?" 37 And they said to him, "Grant to us that that we may sit, one at your right hand and one at your left, in your glory." 38 But Jesus said to them, "You do not know what you are asking. Are you able to drink the cup that I drink, or to be baptized with the baptism with which I am baptized?" 39 And they said to him, "We are able." But Jesus said to them, "The cup that I drink you will drink and with the baptism with which I am baptized you will be baptized, 40 but to sit at my right hand or my left is not mine to give, but it is for those for whom it has been prepared."[a]

41 And when the ten heard this, they started getting angry with James and John. 42 And Jesus called them and says to them, "You know that those who are recognized[b] as rulers of the Gentiles lord it over them, and their great ones enforce their authority over them. 43 But it shall not be so[c] among you; but whoever wants to become great among you must[c] be your servant,[d] 44 and whoever wants to be first among you must[c] be slave of all. 45 For even the Son of Man has not come to be served, but to serve, and to give his life a ransom for many."

a. The earliest New Testament MS were written in uncials (capital letters) in *scriptio continua* (no spaces between words), so the letters *ALLOIS* can be read as one Greek word, translated "to others," or two words *ALL OIS*, translated, as here, as "but for those." On the first option, the meaning would be "it has been prepared not for you but for others"; on the second, "not for you but for those for whom it has been prepared." In later MSS, after word division had been introduced, most scribes divided the letters into two words, as here, but a few MSS, including the minuscule 225, as well as some Old Latin (pre-Vulgate) MSS and a single Coptic MS and the Sinaitic Syriac read *ALLOIS*.

b. The normal expression would be *hoi archontes*, "those who rule," but Mark has *hoi dokountes archein*, which can be translated "those who seem to rule," "those who appear to rule," suggesting that their "rule" is only apparent and God is the true ruler. However, *dokeō* also often means "have the reputation of," "be considered to be," "be acknowledged as," as in Gal 2:2.

c. The *estin* of v. 43a is present active indicative, but with a futuristic imperative meaning; the future *estai* of 43b and 44 is likewise imperatival, declaring what must be.

[32–34] The location is again significantly "on the road" (see *Excursus: The Way* at 1:3). The scene is dramatic: Jesus strides resolutely ahead, and others follow in amazement and fear. While set in the pre-Easter narrative framework, the imagery again modulates into the time when the readers are themselves called to continue their commitment to follow the risen Jesus, already "out there" in the world ahead of them (cf. 14:28; 16:7). The general image is clear, but how to apportion the groups that follow is not. While the syntax may allow a sorting out of "those who were amazed," "those who followed and were afraid," and "the Twelve" into distinct categories, here it is better not to attempt too much precision in describing the scene (see *Excursus: Crowds, Followers, Disciples*, and *the Twelve* at 6:6). The basic picture comes through clearly: Jesus goes ahead resolutely to his destiny, which he has twice announced (8:31; 9:31), while his followers / disciples / the Twelve continue to follow, though they are astounded and fearful. Amazement and fear should not be explained in terms of the psychology of the 30 C.E. disciples, but as reflecting the numinous, revelatory context of the Christ event. The Markan church recognizes itself in this scene.

Jesus' next words begin with the exclamatory *idou*, "Look!" echoing Peter's exclamation in verse 28. The disciples had claimed that they had left everything, and now follow in fear. Jesus' response to both claim and fear is the final, most detailed of the three "passion predictions." As in verses 29–31, the present suffering of the disciples is not the last word, so here the resurrection is the ultimate reality that overrules Jesus' suffering and death, without superseding or canceling it. Though it has been implicit in previous references to the "chief priests," for the first time, Jerusalem is mentioned as the destination of "the way." Jesus as the Son of Man will be "delivered over" to the chief priests and scribes; though the betrayal of Judas may be included, the passive is probably a "divine passive" (see on 9:31). The chief priests and scribes will condemn him to death and deliver him (now clearly a human act) to the Gentiles, who will mock him, spit on him, and kill him. Despite the expanded detail, there is still no reference to cross and crucifixion. There is no specific allusion to the fulfillment of Scripture, though the selection of some details such as spitting may reflect the church's christological reading of the Old Testament (cf. Isa 50:6).

[35–37] Status among the disciples continues to be the issue. As it turns out, James and John represent all the disciples, as Peter has done previously (vv. 41–42). Their request begins with "Teacher, we want . . . ,"[76] calling to mind

---

76. Wanting ecclesiastical leadership is itself not necessarily a bad thing (1 Tim 3:1); the problem is their understanding of status.

Jesus' instruction they have already received, "If anyone wants to be first . . ."
(9:35)—from which they have learned nothing. Their blindness persists (8:18)
and can only be healed by Jesus himself. Jesus' response anticipates his words
to the blind man in the next pericope: "What do you want me to do for you"
(v. 51). There, the blind man will make the right response, and ask that his blindness be healed. Here, the leading disciples ask for the choice spots in Jesus'
"glory." This has sometimes been misunderstood as though the disciples were
anticipating their own view of an "earthly kingdom," while Jesus is proclaiming a "spiritual kingdom." This misunderstanding does not reflect either the
Markan narrative or the context of early Christianity. A saying had circulated
in early Christianity in which Jesus had promised the disciples they would sit
on twelve thrones judging the twelve tribes of Israel, that is, that they would
share the Messiah's role as judge in the coming eschatological kingdom (Matt
19:28 / Luke 22:30 = Q). In the Lukan form, the disciples sit at table with the
Messiah in the kingdom, while the Matthean form portrays them as sharing the
role of the Son of Man as judge. Mark does not cite this saying, and here seems
to present a polemical rejection of it. The Markan Jesus himself has already spoken of "glory" (*doxa*), the future "glory of his father" when he shall return as
Son of Man (8:38; cf. 13:26; 9:2–8). While the Markan readers may well have
been aware of the Q saying and its view of the disciples' future role, in the
Markan narrative the disciples could only have heard of "glory" in relation to
the coming of the Son of Man, where it is always related to his suffering, death,
and resurrection (8:31; 9:31; 10:33–34). Here the disciples manifest a partial
understanding of Jesus' promise that grasps at the promised transcendent glory
without hearing its inseparable relation to the cross.[77] "Theology of glory" confronts "theology of the cross," and not only as Christology but, as always in
Mark, inseparably linked to discipleship.

[38] Jesus' statement that the disciples do not know what they are asking is
not a reproach but a statement of fact. They do not know and cannot know what
they are involved in until the story is over. Mark's readers look back on the
whole story, and they can know; Jesus' instruction is not aimed at pre-Easter
disciples but post-Easter misunderstandings of leadership in the Markan church
(see *Excursus: The Messianic Secret* at 9:13).

Following Jesus is identified as drinking the same cup that Jesus drinks and
being baptized with the same baptism with which he is baptized. In the Old Testament and Jewish tradition, "cup" is a frequent metaphor for suffering in gen-

---

77. It would thus be a mistake to regard the disciples as here accepting the two-stage schema
of suffering-then-glory presented by Jesus in 8:38, as though they accept suffering and death for
Jesus and themselves, and their only problem is in their mental leap to the time of glory at the Parousia. The passage functions rhetorically, not in terms of narrative logic (contra Shiner, *Follow Me*,
263, who himself usually appeals to rhetoric rather than linear narrativity).

eral, in particular the suffering of God's judgment by the disobedient (Ps 75:8–9; Isa 51:17–22; Jer 25:15; Lam 4:21; 1QpHab 11.14–15; 4QpNah 4.6; *Pss. Sol.* 8.14; *2 Bar.* 13.8; *Mart. Isa.* 5.13; cf. Mark 14:36). God offers the cup. Though Mark has no explicit doctrine of the atonement, here Jesus' voluntarily accepting the cup means accepting God's judgment against human sin on behalf of others. "Baptism," that is, immersion, is well-attested in the papyri for overwhelming trouble. The word *baptisma* itself is not so frequent in this sense in biblical and Jewish tradition, but the image of being overwhelmed by submerging, deep waters is common enough (2 Sam 22:5; Ps 42:7; 69:1–2; Isa 43:2; Isa 21:4 LXX; 1QH 3.13–18; the relation of this Markan text to the saying in Luke 12:50 is disputed). These metaphors could hardly be used in the Markan community without evoking Christian baptism and the Eucharist, in which every Christian participates. Thus for the general reader the text points to the participation of every disciple in Jesus' own obedience to God that led to suffering and death. Yet this sacramental understanding is not Mark's primary point, which has to do with the nature of Christian leadership and the desire for status.

[39–40] The disciples' robust response, "We are able," must, like all similar statements and dialogues, be heard at two levels. At the narrative level, it presents the disciples as overconfident, smug, oriented to the wrong understanding of what discipleship means (cf., e.g., Peter in 14:31, echoed by all the disciples). In the retrospective view of the Markan church, which knows not only of Jesus' crucifixion and resurrection but also that the disciples did become faithful witnesses and that some had already suffered martyrdom, the disciples were indeed "able." The Christians of Mark's time know that the suffering and death of Jesus *did* finally open the eyes of the disciples. The Markan Jesus likewise reflects this post-Easter perspective when he promises that they will indeed drink his cup and be baptized with his baptism, here referring not to the general participation of Christians in the sacraments but to their having learned the lesson of how to give their lives as Christian leaders. Yet Jesus cannot promise them key positions at his right and left hand, for this is not his to give (the infinitive *dounai*, "give," of v. 40 echoes the imperative *dos*, "give," of v. 37). The divine passive "it has been prepared" points to God as the one who makes seat assignments in the eschatological kingdom. It is useless to speculate about who is to receive these seats; that is God's prerogative, a matter of divine sovereignty and election, not something that can be attained either by getting in an early application or even by being faithful to the point of martyrdom. Jesus calls to suffering and death, but this does not become a bargaining chip for special treatment in the world to come.

[41–42] In the honor / shame society of the first-century Mediterranean world, status was a legitimate goal that all were assumed to pursue. The other disciples are resentful of those who had attempted to maneuver themselves into the favored places they all wanted. The "you know" of verse 42 contrasts with the "you do not know" of verse 38: they do not understand Christian leadership, but they understand well enough how rulership works in this world. They understand that all earthly rule—not just that of "bad" rulers—is a matter of status and status-seeking, and that it functions by violence or the threat of violence. They continue to "think in terms of human things," not "in terms of the things of God" (8:33), and they have not perceived the overturning of all conventional values that occurs with the dawning of the kingdom of God. Nor do they perceive that those who rule are "recognized" as rulers but are not the ultimate rulers. Mark's unusual expression (see note *b* above on *dokeō*) reflects his apocalyptic view that behind the apparent rulers of the world stand the real powers, Satan and God, and that of these two only God's rule will ultimately prevail (see *Excursus: Kingdom of God* at 1:15).[78]

[43–44] With "it shall not be so among you" Jesus pointedly summarizes the emphasis throughout this section: as cultural standards do not determine attitudes to marriage, divorce, children, and wealth for Jesus' followers, so they do not determine leadership style. Conventional models of status and self-esteem are reversed, with the Son of Man himself as the supreme role model.

[45] The climactic statement of the whole section that began at 8:22 grounds discipleship in the ministry of the Son of Man, the essence of whose leadership is self-giving, service to the point of dying for others. Even in Dan 7:13–14, which has played a formative role in Mark's Son of Man imagery, the Son of Man in his glory is served. By saying that he as Son of Man "has come" not to be served but to serve, Jesus is not referring to the individual incidents in his ministry, but is looking back on the Christ-event as a whole in a profoundly theological sense (cf. on 1:38 and 2:17). Within the Markan narrative, Jesus is never pictured as "serving," the verb "serve" being found elsewhere only in 1:13 and 1:31, and in each case Jesus is in fact served by others; the footwashing scene of John 13 should not be read into Mark. Instead, Mark has in mind something like the servant ministry of the Christ-event as a whole, as portrayed in Phil 2:5–11 (as does, in fact, John 13).

Though Jesus has referred to his suffering and death in the preceding narrative as the will of God, a necessary part of the divine plan (8:31; 9:31; 10:33–34), in this culminating declaration he for the first time gives it an explicitly soteriological meaning. As in English usage, a ransom (*lytron*) is the payment made to obtain the release of slaves, hostages, or prisoners of war. The *lytron* word group was often used in the LXX in the sense of buying persons out of slavery or redeeming animals or property, that is, paying the necessary sum in exchange for them (e.g., Exod 13:13, 15; 21:8; Lev 25:25–26). By Mac-

---

78. Joel Marcus, "Mark 4.10–12 and Markan Epistemology," *JBL* 103 (1984): 558–62. Mark's apocalyptic perspective is pervasive; it is not restricted to passages dealing explicitly with the eschatological future.

cabean times, "ransom" terminology had been used in Hellenistic Judaism for the death of martyrs, whose death was "as it were, a ransom for the sin of our nation" (4 Macc 17:21, which has *antipsychon* rather than *lytron*; so also 2 Macc 7:37–38, which has the idea without the *lytron* terminology). The Old Testament also frequently uses the *lytron* word group simply as God's saving act, without any thought of a price being paid (e.g., Exod 6:6; Deut 7:8; 9:26; 15:15; 2 Sam 7:23; 1 Chr 17:21; Neh 1:10; Pss 34:22; 44:26; 69:18; Isa 35:9; 41:14; 43:1, 14; 44:22–24; 51:11; 52:3; 62:12; 63:4, 9). In Mark, conceiving Jesus' death as a ransom fits into this latter usage. Mark here pictures Jesus' death as salvific, but does not explain how it saves. Even if the imagery is taken more literally, as a ransom that God or Jesus paid for the salvation of others, this only pushes the question one step further without answering it: If God wills to save, why should God have to pay a ransom in order to do so? This is so quite apart from the later question of to whom the ransom was paid. Mark does not leave the mystery of Jesus' death a meaningless tragedy, but neither does he "explain" why Jesus "had" to die so that God's saving purpose could be fulfilled. *That* Jesus' death was not a meaningless surd, but was a necessary part of God's will and plan is important to Mark's theology (repeated *dei*; cf. 8:31), but he is not concerned to offer a comprehensive schema within which Jesus' death can be incorporated. Declaring Jesus' death to be a "ransom for many" is referential but not objectifying language (see note 104 at 5:11–13).

"Many" does not address the issue of "how many." The contrast is not between many and some other number, whether "few" or "all," but between Jesus' solitary death and the many who are ransomed by it. Nonetheless, "many" in the Semitic sense often is not contrasted with "all" but with "few," and is the functional equivalent of "all"—as in Qumran usage, where "the many" means "everyone" (e.g., 1QS 6.1, 7–25) and as recognized by the paraphrase in 1 Tim 2:6. The word "many" *(polloi)* seems to be an important point of contact with Isa 53, where it occurs three times in 53:11–12 in the context of the Servant's giving his life for the sins of others. Thus the more important issue is whether Jesus' death is here understood in terms of the Suffering Servant of Isa 53, a view that has vigorous defenders and equally vigorous opponents.[79] Except for the word "many," there is little direct contact between Mark 10:45 and Isa 53, and the issue will be resolved on the basis of how the interpreter

---

79. Among the defenders: Gnilka, *Markus*, 2:104; Lührmann, *Markusevangelium*, 181; Witherington, *Mark*, 288–89; Marcus, *Mark 8–16*, ad loc. 10:45. Among the opponents, C. K. Barrett, "The Background of Mark 10:45," in *New Testament Essays: Studies in the Memory of T. W. Manson, 1893–1958* (ed. A. J. B. Higgins; Manchester: Manchester University Press, 1959); Hooker, *Jesus and the Servant*, 74–79; Morna D. Hooker, *The Son of Man in Mark: a study of the background of the term "Son of Man" and its use in St. Mark's Gospel* (Montreal: McGill University Press, 1967), 140–47.

regards the relation of Mark's theology to Isaiah as a whole (see *Excursus: Mark and the Scriptures* at 14:52).

10:46–52 Blind Bartimaeus Healed at Jericho

This story concludes the Markan transitional section between part 1 and part 2, forming a bracket with the only other story of healing a blind person, at 8:22–26 (on the structure of this section, see commentary at 8:22). It is itself a transitional story, not only summarizing and concluding the preceding section, but pointing ahead to the Jerusalem ministry and passion story immediately following.

> 10:46 And they are coming to Jericho. And as he and his disciples and a large crowd were leaving Jericho, the son of Timaeus, Bartimaeus, a blind beggar, was sitting beside the way.[a] 47 And when he heard that it was Jesus of Nazareth, he began to shout, "Son of David, Jesus, have mercy on me." 48 And many were giving him stern orders[b] to be quiet. But he was crying out all the more, "Son of David, have mercy on me." 49 And Jesus stopped, and said, "Call him." And they call the blind man, saying to him, "Take courage; rise up, he is calling you." 50 And he threw aside his cloak, sprang to his feet, and came to Jesus. 51 And Jesus said to him, "What do you want me to do for you?" And the blind man said to him, "Rabbouni, I want to see." 52 And Jesus said to him, "Go, your faith has saved[c] you." And immediately he received his sight, and was following him on the way.

a. *Hodos* could be translated "road" here and in v. 52, but "way" is used to accord with a central Markan theme (see *Excursus: The Way* at 1:3).
b. *Epitimaō*, translated "rebuke" in 1:25; 4:39; 8:32, 33; 9:25; 10:13, carries a reproachful tone.
c. See note *d* at 5:34.

[46] Few miracle stories designate the setting, but here, as in the first story of healing a blind man, the location is given. Bethsaida at the beginning and Jericho at the end bracket this unit. Mentioned twice as Jesus enters and leaves with no intervening action, Jericho, only a day's journey from Jerusalem and the last town before arrival at the Holy City, serves only as a way station en route to the ultimate goal of Jesus' "way" (10:33). While it is likely that there were crowds of Passover pilgrims along the road as Jesus approaches Jerusalem, Mark expresses no interest in such historical details, and the crowd will serve only a narrative role. Bartimaeus is the only person healed by Jesus who is named—a combination of "bar" (Aramaic for "son") and the common Greek name Timaeus (as in Plato's dialogues).

[47] The blind beggar takes the initiative in calling out to Jesus (the blind man of 8:22 was passive, brought to Jesus). He makes no claims, but only asks

for mercy, using the familiar form usually addressed to God (cf. Pss 6:2; 9:13; 122:3 LXX). Bartimaeus is for Mark only the second human being to address Jesus with a christological title. Earlier, Peter had confessed Jesus to be the Christ, correctly, but without understanding what he was saying. Does Bartimaeus get it right? Some interpreters so argue, but it is more likely that for Mark, "Son of David" is a misunderstanding of Jesus' true identity: (1) The "Son of David" was expected to come from Bethlehem, the city of David. Yet Bethlehem is never mentioned in Mark, and Jesus is here named "of Nazareth."[80] (2) Bartimaeus designates Jesus as "son of David" while he is still blind, and he begins to follow only after his blindness is cured. (3) He makes this acclamation while seated *beside* the way, a phrase found elsewhere in Mark only in 4:4, 15 (see commentary there). After his blindness is removed, he follows Jesus *on* the way as a true disciple. (4) Mark elsewhere is suspicious of "Son of David" as a proper title for Jesus (see on 11:10; 12:35–37; on "Son of David" as a christological title, see *Excursus: Markan Christology* at 9:1).

[48] The crowd's attempt to silence Bartimaeus is unrelated to the messianic secret. His addressing Jesus with the christological title is unproblematic for them (cf. 11:10), but that their messianic hero would welcome an appeal from an impoverished beggar was beyond their grasp. The crowd's rebuke and effort to silence him is thus analogous to the disciples' rebuke of those who were bringing children to Jesus in 10:13 (same word, *epitimaō*). In both cases Jesus overrules their well-intended rebuke.

[49] Jesus stops (cf. 5:25–34). The thrice-repeated use of the verb "call," along with "follow" and "way" (v. 52) stamps the story as a call story analogous to 1:16–20 and 2:13–17 (cf. the failed "call story" of 10:17–22). A different verb is used here, *phōneō* instead of *kaleō*, but they are synonyms (cf. 9:35; the words are used interchangeably in Luke 14:12–13 and 19:13–15). Though Jesus is the authoritative "caller," his call is mediated by others, who obey without understanding ("they" called, but "he" is calling; cf. Robbins, *Jesus the Teacher*, 42). In Mark's understanding, the call of Jesus can come through his preachers and missionaries, even if their understanding is inadequate. Bartimaeus is told to "rise," with overtones of the resurrection and the new life that comes in conversion (see comments on 1:29–34; 2:9, 11; 3:3; 9:27). He is called to discipleship, not to apostleship, and is thus transparent to the readers themselves. Like the distressed men in the boat of 6:50 (the only other Markan

---

80. *Nazarēnos* is important to Mark. Transcendent beings who know Jesus' true identity when others in the story do not refer to him as "the Nazarene" (1:24, the demons, who acknowledge him as Son of God; 16:6, the young man in the tomb, as a designation for the crucified and risen one; 10:47, the narrator's own term, in contrast to "Son of David" in the narrative; 14:67, identifying those who belong to Jesus). See Kim Dewey, "Peter's Curse and Cursed Peter," in *The Passion in Mark: Studies on Mark 14–16* (ed. Werner H. Kelber; Philadelphia: Fortress, 1976), 99.

instance of *tharseō*, "take courage"), the blind beggar is addressed with encouraging words, "Take courage, *he* is calling *you*."

[50] The description of Bartimaeus casting aside his beggar's cloak is a strange detail; why is it included here? Two overlapping explanations are suggested by the imagery: (1) It is not merely historical reminiscence or detail added for color, but a further indication that this is a call / discipleship story. The mantle in which he slept and which he spread before him beside the road to collect alms seems to be his sole possession and means of his livelihood; his casting it away corresponds to the other disciples leaving their boats, tax desk, and "everything" (1:18–20; 2:14; 10:21, 28) and provides a dramatic contrast to the one most recently called to follow and who made the great refusal (10:21–22). (2) Throughout Mark, clothing is often symbolic of the significance of the person, and, like the name, partakes of the reality of the person himself or herself (cf. 1:6; 5:27; 6:9; 9:3; 11:7; 14:51).[81] Already in Paul's time, becoming a Christian meant receiving a new identity, symbolized by putting on new garments (Gal 3:27–28; Rom 13:12; 1 Thess 5:8; cf. later elaboration in Col 3:12–14; Eph 4:22–24). By the second century, the practice of taking off the old garments to be baptized and putting on new garments to symbolize the new life had become part of the baptismal ritual. Baptismal imagery is already woven into the context (10:14, 38–39). By throwing his cloak aside, Bartimaeus threw off the garment of his old self and the life he had been living in blindness, beside the way rather than on it.

[51] Jesus' question is exactly the same as previously put to the disciples (10:36), who gave exactly the wrong answer. Bartimaeus, like them, is blind, but his response is the right one. Only Jesus can heal his blindness and let him see things as they really are. He no longer addresses Jesus as "Son of David," but with "rabbouni," a heightened form of "rabbi" meaning "(my) teacher." In this context, the word is double-edged. On the one hand, it is related to "rabbi" (John 1:38; 20:16 regards them as synonyms), always used by Mark to express inadequate or failed discipleship (see on 9:5). Bartimaeus is still blind, not understanding Jesus' true identity. On the other hand, "rabbouni" is a very exalted expression, used by the rabbis themselves only in addressing God,[82] and the reader knows the truth behind this unseeing declaration.

[52] The miracle happens. Bartimaeus does receive his sight. Nothing is made of the miracle itself; there is no elaboration or acclamation from the

---

81. See the incisive development of this Markan theme in LaVerdiere, *Beginning*, 1:30–31, 86–87, 137–38; 2:126–29; 147–48; 254–55; 291–92.

82. So Gundry, *Mark*, 602, who gives bibliography. Cf. the only other use of "rabbouni" in the New Testament, John 20:16, Mary Magdalene to the risen Lord. There, too, it is spoken by one who does not grasp the reality of discipleship (cf. 20:17), but it is also comparable to Thomas's "My Lord and my God" of John 20:28.

crowd. Jesus does not correct his Christology or explain that Bartimaeus must take up his cross and follow. He sees. The spotlight continues to be focused on the healed blind man as convert and new disciple. Jesus does not now call him to be a disciple; this has happened already. "Go" (*hypage*) does not here mean "go away," so that Bartimaeus disobeys by following him; instead it means "no longer sit beside the road begging." "Your faith has saved you" is identical to Jesus' pronouncement to the woman of 5:34, who also had persistently resisted both crowd and disciples in order to receive God's saving / healing power mediated by Jesus. Bartimaeus is addressed as a person of faith, though his theology had been defective; Jesus can heal the theological blindness of those who believe and respond to him. In the narrative, Bartimaeus follows trustingly, not knowing where the way will lead—but the reader, for whose benefit the story is told, knows.

Part 2

Jerusalem
Mark 11:1–15:47

Temple, Confrontation, and Death

For the first time in Mark, Jesus comes to Jerusalem, previously mentioned only as the place from which some of the curious have been attracted (3:8) and hostile scribes have come (3:22; 7:1) and to which Jesus resolutely goes to face the suffering and death he knows await him there (10:32–33). Previously, Jesus has been reactive in regard to those who oppose him. Now he takes the initiative; he goes sovereignly to them. The structure is analogous to part 1: narrative (11:1–12:44) / discourse (13:1–37) / narrative (14:1–16:8), with the long central discourse functioning as the hermeneutical key to the action in the narrative (see Introduction 2.). The discourse sets the narrative within the apocalyptic framework of God's rule of history and the final coming of the Son of Man, presenting all of chapters 14–16 as the elaboration of the passion predictions of 8:31; 9:31; 10:33–34, climaxed by the resurrection of the Son of Man.

Part 2 takes place entirely in and around the temple city Jerusalem. The temple was not only the sacred center of Israel's religious life, where God was enthroned and atonement was made, but the symbol of its national identity and heart of its economic life—serving, as was the case with temples in the Hellenistic world generally, as the national bank and providing employment for many of the city's inhabitants. Jesus' stance toward the temple plays a pivotal role: the first scene concludes with Jesus alone, briefly reconnoitering the temple area (11:11), to which he and his disciples will return the next day to stage a public demonstration (11:15–17). Jesus' longest day of teaching and disputation occurs in the temple (11:27–13:1). In the center of part 2, both textually and hermeneutically, is the long apocalyptic discourse that Jesus delivers "sitting . . . opposite the temple" (13:3), which he has just predicted will be destroyed (13:1–2). Jesus' alleged threat against the temple will play a role in his trial (14:58) and crucifixion (15:29), and, as its destruction had been symbolically predicted in 11:14, 21, so it begins to occur in 15:38 as the temple curtain is torn in two.

Miracles virtually disappear from part 2. While Jesus does manifest supernatural foreknowledge (11:2–3; 13:3–37; 14:13–15), there are no public miracles, none of the salvific miracles of chapters 1–8; there is only one negative miracle (cursing and withering the fig tree, 11:12–14, 20–26). This is not to be explained as due to the lack of faith of the Jerusalem population, as though all those baptized by John had mysteriously disappeared (cf. 1:5). Neither is it a matter of the strategy of the historical Jesus,[1] but as due to the structure of

---

1. See Tagawa, *Miracles et Évangile*, 49–543.

Mark's christological narrative that consigns Jesus' mighty saving acts to part 1 (see *Excursus: Miracle Stories in Mark* at 6:56).

The narrative becomes more explicitly chronological in part 2. The narrative clock slows down, so that the last week of Jesus' life occupies one-third of the narrative, using one-sixth of the whole narrative to recount the last twenty-four hours. Previously, it has been difficult to chart the temporal progress of the narrative: "after six days" (9:2) is the only clear chronological marker prior to 11:11, and even there the reference point is unclear. The reader has no basis for judging how long the preceding ministry has lasted, but presumably less than a year, since this is Jesus' first visit to a Jerusalem festival. Now, however, more sequential data is given, with a firm chronology beginning at 14:1, "two days before the Passover," fixed as Wednesday by 15:42, which locates the crucifixion on Friday. Mark gives sufficient data to allow one to count backward from this date to Jesus' approach to the city at 11:1. Since 11:11–12 clearly separates the first day in Jerusalem from the second, which concludes at 11:19, and the third day beginning at 11:20 apparently extends through 13:37,[2] it is possible to construct the following Markan chronology:

> *Day 1, Nisan 10 (Sunday)*—Approaches Jerusalem (11:1–10); enters temple and looks around (11:11a); leaves city (11:11b).
>
> *Day 2, Nisan 11 (Monday)*—Curses fig tree (11:12–14); "cleanses" temple (11:15–17); conspiracy against Jesus (11:18); leaves city (11:19).
>
> *Day 3, Nisan 12 (Tuesday)*—Discovers fig tree withered (11:20–26); question about authority (11:27–33); parable (12:1–12); on paying taxes to the emperor (12:13–17); question about the resurrection (12:18–27); the great commandment (12:28–34); the question about David's son (12:35–37a); woes to the scribes (12:37b–40); the widow's offering (12:41–44); apocalyptic discourse (13:1–37).
>
> *Day 4, Nisan 13, "two days before the Passover" (Wednesday)*—Jesus' death plotted (14:1–2); anointing in Bethany (14:3–9); betrayal by Judas (14:10–11).

---

2. The chronology is Mark's literary construct, not precise historical reporting. There are several indications Jesus was in Jerusalem considerably longer than the few days before he was killed. The waving of branches and the use of Ps 118 is associated with the festivals of Booths (= Tabernacles, Lev 23:39–43) and Hanukkah (= Dedication, 2 Macc 10:7), not Passover. So also, Mark 14:49 indicates that Jesus' teaching in the temple was not confined to one day. Lane, *Mark*, 405, citing Jewish sources, argues the money changers' tables were authorized to be in the temple court only between Adar 25 and Nisan 1, so that the temple incident must have occurred at least two weeks before Passover itself.

Day 5, Nisan 14 (Thursday)—Preparation, Last Supper, arrest, trial before Sanhedrin (14:12–72).

Day 6, Nisan 15 (Friday)—Trial before Pilate, crucifixion, burial (15:1–47).

Day 7, Nisan 16 (Saturday).

Day 8, Nisan 17 (Sunday)—Discovery of empty tomb (16:1–8a).

11:1–13:4 The Lord Comes to His Temple

Mal 3:1, cited as Mark's opening words (1:2), portrays "the Lord whom you seek [who] will suddenly come to his temple," identified with "the messenger of the covenant," whose appearance will be both promise and threat. In this section, Jesus is constantly in the temple; he speaks and acts with authority as though it is his possession, and in 14:24 will speak of his own blood as the "blood of the covenant." As Zech 9:9 is in the background without being explicitly cited, so Mal 3:1 seems to play a role in the formation of this section.[3] Here, too, the beginning of the Gospel and the way of the Lord to Jerusalem is recalled (see *Excursus: The Way* at 1:3).

11:1–11 The Veiled Messianic Procession

11:1 And when they are approaching Jerusalem, at Bethphage and Bethany, near the Mount of Olives, he sends two of his disciples **2** and says to them, "Go into the village ahead of you, and as soon as you enter it you will find a colt tied on which no human being has ever sat.[a] Untie it and bring it. **3** And if anyone says to you, 'What is this you are doing?' say, 'The Lord / its master needs it,'[b] and he will send it here immediately.'"[c] **4** And they went away and found a colt[d] tied near the door, outside in the street, and they are untying it. **5** And some of those who had been standing there were saying to them, "What are you doing, untying the colt?" **6** And they told them just what Jesus had said, and they permitted them. **7** And they bring the colt to Jesus and throw their cloaks on it, and he sat on it. **8** And many people were spreading out their cloaks on the road, and others were spreading out straw[e] they had cut from the

---

3. Cf. Rau, "Markusevangelium," 2155–56, 2181; John R. Donahue, *Are You the Christ? The Trial Narrative in the Gospel of Mark* (SBLDS 10; Missoula, Mont.: Society of Biblical Literature, 1973), 121.

fields. 9 And those going ahead and those following were shouting, "Hosanna! Blessed is the one who comes in the name of the Lord! 10 Blessed is the coming kingdom of our father David! Hosanna in the highest!" 11 And he entered Jerusalem and went into the temple court[f] and looked around at everything, and since it was already late, he went out to Bethany with the Twelve.

a. Several translations translate *ekathisen* as "has ever ridden," to correspond to the context, but the normal verb for riding a donkey is *epibainō* (e.g., Num 22:30; 1 Sam 25:20), not *kathēmai,* "sit." Mark's or his tradition's peculiar choice of *kathizō* thus appears to be another indication of the royal imagery he intends to suggest.

b. There is an (apparently intentional) ambiguity in both vocabulary and word order. *Kyrios* can mean "Lord" or "master," i.e., owner of the colt. *Autou* can be either "of it" (associated with "need" = "need of it") or "its" (the colt's). The possible translations are thus "The Lord has need of it (= needs it)" or "Its owner needs (it)."

c. Since there were no quotation marks in ancient Greek, how much of the sentence is direct quotation, and thus its meaning, is dependent on the presence or absence of *palin* ("again," "back") after "send it." With *palin*, the whole clause is what the two disciples are to say to the objectors, promising that *Jesus* will send the colt *back* to the owner. Without *palin,* the second clause is Jesus' word to the disciples, promising them that the *objectors* will send the colt to *him*. *Palin* is found, in various combinations, in numerous good MSS, including ℵ B D[Gr] L Θ Δ and in several patristic citations and ancient translations, but is missing from A C[2] G W f^1 f^{13}, the Old Latin and Syriac translations, and most later Greek MSS. The fact that *palin*, when present, is not always in the same place in the sentence, suggests that it is a scribal addition, as does the fact that Matthew apparently did not find the word in his copy of Mark (cf. 21:3).

d. In the Hebrew text of Zech 9:9 here in the background (alluded to but not explicitly cited; cf. also Gen 49:10–11), the animal is a young donkey. Mark's word *pōlos*, taken from the LXX, can refer to the foal of a donkey, horse, or other animals that can be ridden.

e. *Stibas,* only here in the New Testament, in the papyri normally refers to a kind of bed or mattress made of straw, rushes, reeds, leaves. The translation "leafy *branches*" reflects the influence of Matt 21:8 and the palm branches of John 12:13.

f. This is the first reference to the *hieron*, the whole temple complex, used ten times in the following narrative, and to be distinguished from *naos*, the sanctuary proper, used only in 14:58, 15:29, and 15:38.

[11:1] The procession is formed by those already with Jesus, not by people who come out from Jerusalem (cf. 10:46; contrast John 12:13, where Jerusalem crowds go out to meet him). The pilgrim route goes through or by Bethany, about two miles from Jerusalem on the eastern slope of the Mount of Olives. Bethphage is apparently nearer the city, but its exact location is unknown. The Mount of Olives is associated with eschatological expectations, both in the Old Testament (Zech 14:4) and in first-century Judaism; Josephus relates how in the troubled days preceding the war with Rome a self-proclaimed prophet gathered crowds about him to join him on the Mount of Olives, promising to demonstrate that God was now beginning to deliver the people by having the walls of Jerusalem fall down at the prophet's command, just as the walls of Jericho had fallen when Israel first entered the Promised Land (*Ant.* 20.169–72).

[2–6] Mark intends Jesus' detailed description of the disciples' procuring the colt—the details of which are then exactly fulfilled and obeyed—as a demonstration that Jesus is a reliable prophet with foreknowledge and authority, just as is the similar scene in 14:13–15, setting up the later scenes of 14:28, 65; 16:7. In neither case is it a matter of Jesus having made prior arrangements, which are then triggered by his disciples giving the correct "password." Just as the passion predictions had made it clear to the reader that Jesus' suffering and death in Jerusalem would not be that of an involuntary victim, so in the passion narrative itself Mark portrays Jesus as in charge, accurately predicting events in advance rather than being their victim. The texts in the background of verse 2 (cf. note *a* above) were already interpreted messianically in early Judaism. Jesus acts with royal authority in requisitioning the colt. He refers to himself as the *kyrios* ("Lord"); though veiled to the characters in the narrative, the reader perceives this as a reference to Jesus as Lord. Pilgrims were expected to walk into the Holy City at Passover. Riding, whether donkey or horse (see note *d*), was not a mark of humility but of royal authority.[4] Jesus, who elsewhere always goes on foot, here makes a symbolic claim. So also, that the animal had never been ridden designates it as having a sacral quality appropriate for a king (cf. 1 Sam 6:7; Ovid, *Metamorphoses*, 3.11), and that Jesus rides the unbroken animal demonstrates his authority. Mark, unlike Matt 21:4–5 and John 12:14–15, does not cite Zech 9:9 or Gen 49:11 specifically, though both are in the background, and both had already been interpreted messianically in first-century Judaism.

[7–10] The two disciples place their cloaks on the colt, draping it as a kind of makeshift throne (cf. note above on the connotation of the unusual *kathizō*), and the jubilant crowd prepares a makeshift "red carpet" of their own garments and of straw cut from the field. Whether or not the narrator intends the reader to imagine the whole two miles as paved with clothes and straw, the scene is an extravagant one, uninhibited by the constraints of business-as-usual (cf. on 14:4–8). By placing their clothes on the donkey and on the roadway, the disciples and crowds were symbolically offering themselves (see on 10:50). The shouts of the crowd also manifest eschatological joy. "Hosanna" is taken

---

4. If Mark was written shortly after 70 C.E., Mark's description may evoke the imagery of the triumphal procession of the Roman victors, mounted on horses, either in Rome or Jerusalem itself. There is no contrast here between a presumed "Jewish" understanding of messiahship as a this-worldly ruler and Jesus' humility as representative of a "spiritual" kingdom. Already in Zech 9:9 the imagery combines royal triumph and humility.

from Ps 118:25, the last of the Hallel Psalms sung or chanted at all major festivals and familiar to every Jew who visited Jerusalem. "Hosanna" means literally "save now," but it had long since become a liturgical, cultic cry no longer related to its etymological meaning—like "amen," "hallelujah," "kyrie eleison," and "hosanna" in modern English liturgies. The case is different, however, with the cry "blessed is the one who comes in the name of the Lord" (Ps 118:26). Originally a priestly blessing pronounced on worshipers who came to the temple, "Blessed in the name of the Lord is the one who comes (to the temple to worship)," the pronouncement is here no longer generic but directed to Jesus, who is hailed by the crowd as coming in the name of the Lord. They parallel this traditional cultic acclamation with a new one coined for the occasion, "Blessed is the coming kingdom of our father David." This is in continuity with Bartimaeus's repeated identification of Jesus as "Son of David" (10:47–48; see comment there). Though the kingdom of God proclaimed and lived out by Jesus is not the Davidic kingdom of popular expectation,[5] Jesus does not correct the crowd, just as he had not corrected Bartimaeus. Subsequent events, which will manifest an intensification of kingship terminology, will reveal the truth and powerful irony of this scene.

[11] The verb shifts to the singular. Without receiving any response from Jerusalem or the authorities (and leaving readers wondering what all of this means), the procession and celebration halts at the city walls, and Jesus enters Jerusalem alone. Although the Markan Jesus has never been to the temple before, his "looking around at everything" is not the curiosity of a Galilean tourist, but, as in 12:41–44, 13:1–2, his authoritative sizing up of the goings-on in the temple, marking it out for destruction. "His looking around is imperial, stern."[6] Mark postpones the "cleansing" of the temple until the next day, allowing him to intercalate it into the story of the cursing of the fig tree (contrast the chronology in Matt 21:1–10; Luke 19:28–38). What happens the next day will not be the impulsive response of a first-timer, but the calculated demonstration of the temple's impending end.

11:12–25 Barren Temple, Withered Fig Tree, and a House of Prayer for All People

11:12 And the next day, after they had left Bethany,[a] he became hungry. 13 And when, from some distance away, he saw a fig tree in leaf, he went to

---

5. It is likely, as argued by, e.g., Marcus, *Mark 8–16*, ad loc, that the messianic claimants active in the 66–70 revolt had exploited Davidic imagery and associated texts (Gen 49:10–11; 2 Sam 7; Ps 118; Zech 9:9).

6. Gundry, *Mark*, 689, who elaborates.

it to see if he could find anything on it, and when he came to it he found nothing except leaves—for it was not the season for figs. 14 And he said to it, "May no one ever eat fruit from you again!" And his disciples heard it.

15 And they are coming into Jerusalem. And he entered the temple and began to drive out those who were selling and those who were buying in the temple, and he overturned the tables of the money changers and the seats of those who were selling doves, 16 and he would not permit anyone to carry anything[b] through the temple. 17 And he was teaching and saying to them, "Is it not written, 'My house shall be called a house of prayer for all the nations?'[c] But you have made it a 'bandits' hideout.'" 18 And the chief priests and the scribes heard it, and kept looking for a way to kill him; for they considered him a danger,[d] since the whole crowd was astounded by his teaching. 19 And when evening came, they went out of the city.

20 And in the morning as they were passing by, they saw the fig tree withered from the roots up. 21 And Peter remembered, and says to him, "Rabbi, look! The fig tree that you cursed has withered." 22 And Jesus answers them, "Have faith[e] in God. 23 Amen[f] I say to you, whoever says to this mountain, 'Be taken up and be cast into the sea,' and has no doubts in the heart but believes that what he or she says will happen, it will happen for that person. 24 Therefore, I say to you, whatever you pray and ask for, believe that you receive[g] it, and it will happen for you. 25 And whenever you stand praying, forgive, if you have anything against anyone, so that your Father in heaven may also forgive you your trespasses." 26[h]

a. The genitive absolute construction with the aorist participle *exelthontōn* ("having left") indicates the action of the main verb *epeinasen* ("he was / got hungry") occurs later, i.e., the fig tree is not necessarily in the environs of Bethany, and the phrase should not be translated "as they left Bethany." This may be important for the meaning that the incident occurred near the temple, i.e., on the western slope of the Mount of Olives.

b. *Skeuos* may refer generically to any object (as 3:27), or specifically to a vessel such as a jar, bowl, or money bag.

c. Here as elsewhere, *ethnē* may be translated as "nations" or "Gentiles."

d. Lit., "they feared him," but the context (the crowd's amazement) indicates that their problem was Jesus' popularity, not fear of Jesus personally.

e. *Echete* can be either imperative, as here translated, or indicative, "You have faith. . . ." The addition of *ei* ("if") before *echete,* found in ℵ D Θ f^{13} and a few other MSS, makes it necessary to translate as indicative, but this appears to be a scribal assimilation to the more familiar Matt 21:21 / Luke 17:6, and distorts the Markan meaning.

f. On *amēn,* see note g at 3:28.

g. The aorist *elabete* may be translated "you have received," "you will receive," or gnomic "you receive." Both present-tense *lambanete* found in A f^{13} and most later MSS and the future-tense *lē(m)psesthe* of D Θ f^1 and a few other MSS appear to be scribal efforts to soften or clarify Mark's provocative declaration.

h. Verse 26 is missing from ℵ B L W Δ Ψ and several other MSS, as well as from some Old Latin, Syriac, and Coptic translations, and appears to be a late scribal supplement reflecting Matt 6:15 (v. 25 is parallel to Matt 6:14). Some scholars[7] consider v. 25 to be a similar gloss, since it reflects Matthew's language and seems irrelevant to the context, but there is no MSS evidence for omitting it from the text.

On the next day after the triumphal procession, Jesus makes his move—not against the Romans, but against the temple itself. This pericope contains at least three units of tradition that seem at first to fit uneasily together: "cursing the fig tree," the "cleansing of the temple," and "Jesus' teaching on prayer and forgiveness." Several units of tradition that originally circulated independently are combined into what is now a united Markan composition. Mark, in characteristic "sandwich" style (see on 5:21), has split the story of cursing the fig tree and used it as a frame for the account of the temple incident, thereby giving each a symbolic interpretation.[8] Mark's addition of the cluster of sayings on prayer and faith seems to be best explained as possibly his conception that the Jerusalem temple was being replaced by the Christian community as the place of faith, prayer, and the presence of God.[9]

[12] While Christology per se is not the focus of this scene, the reader may well note how unproblematic it is for Mark to portray Jesus as humanly hungry and less than omniscient, not knowing that there was no edible fruit on the tree and that there could not be at that time of the year. Thus the author is not concerned to speculate on why Jesus was hungry (had he not breakfasted with his hosts in Bethany?) and why only he is hungry.

[13–14] From earliest times, the incident of cursing the fig tree has been troublesome for interpreters. It is Jesus' only overt miracle in Jerusalem. It is his only destructive miracle in the Gospels, in contrast both to the apocryphal Gospels (e.g., the *Infancy Gospel of Thomas*) and the punitive miracles of the disciples in Acts (5:1–11; 8:9–24; 13:8–12). It is the only miracle performed on an impersonal object rather than to or for human beings. It seems out of character for Jesus, who appears to respond out of personal pique, and to overreact. And if the hungry Jesus is going to respond with miraculous power, why not

7. Georg Strecker, *The Sermon on the Mount: An Exegetical Commentary* (trans. O. C. Dean; Nashville: Abingdon, 1988), 212; William R. Telford, *The Barren Temple and the Withered Tree: A Redaction-critical Analysis of the Cursing of the Fig-tree Pericope in Mark's Gospel and Its Relation to the Cleansing of the Temple Tradition* (JSNTSup 1; Sheffield: JSOT Press, 1980), 239, who also questions whether v. 24 was originally Markan.

8. This widely accepted view has been elaborated especially by Telford, *Barren Temple*.

9. This interpretation, to be supported below, has been persuasively argued by, among others, Sharyn Dowd, *Prayer, Power, and the Problem of Suffering* (SBLDS 105; Atlanta: Scholars Press, 1988), and Donald Juel, *Messiah and Temple: The Trial of Jesus in the Gospel of Mark* (SBLDS 13; Missoula, Mont.: Scholars Press, 1977). See also Best's ch. 27, "The Church as Temple," in Best, *Following Jesus*, 213–25.

use it to multiply bread for himself and others rather than destroying an innocent tree? Thus interpreters have attempted to find an ethical[10] or symbolic theological meaning.

Mark portrays the Mount of Olives as "opposite the temple," and considers this datum hermeneutically important (13:3). The reader should think of the fig tree incident happening in full view of the temple, with Jesus referring to the temple mount as "this mountain" in verse 23. That Mark inserts the "cleansing" of the temple into the framework of the fig tree episode also suggests that the fig tree symbolically represents the temple. Mark seems intentionally to exclude a literal interpretation by having the narrator comment that it was not the season for figs, which appear at the end of May at the earliest (the Markan event is set at Passover, in late March or early April).[11] The fig tree seems to represent the temple: its leaves, notable from a distance, give it an impressive appearance (cf. 13:1–3). Jesus approaches to inspect it, looking for fruit, as he had inspected the temple (v. 11). Like Yahweh seeking fruit from Israel, Jesus is disappointed (cf. Jer 8:13; Joel 1:7; Ezek 17:24; Mic 7:1, Hos 9:10, 16–17). The use of "fruit" in verse 14, where "figs" is expected, links to this tradition and strengthens the interpretation here presented. Like the prophets of Israel, Jesus pronounces God's judgment on the unfruitful tree. That no one is to eat fruit from it *forever* shows that the pronouncement represents the ultimate, eschatological judgment of God, not a relative, temporary punishment. So also the withering *from the roots up* (v. 20) shows the utter devastation of the tree, which, representing the temple, is destroyed and will not recover.

10. Thus, e.g., Ephrem the Syrian saw Jesus' action as against the unjust owner of the fig tree, who did not obey the law that some fruit should be left on the trees for the poor (cf. Lev 19:9; 23:22; Deut 24:19, which Ephrem finds applicable here). "He cursed it, lest its owner eat from it again, since he had left [nothing] for the orphans and widows." Ephrem also explained that the act had a christological point, showing that Jesus destroyed the tree to exhibit his miraculous power just before the passion, as a sign that he was not a victim of those who arrested and killed him, but was going willingly to his death—for "he would have been able to destroy his crucifiers with a word." *Commentary on Tatian's Diatessaron* (JSSS 2.43–46, cited from Oden and Hull, eds., *Mark*, 159–60).

11. In addition to the ancient symbolical and allegorical interpretations, especially two modern types of interpretation have attempted to provide a rational explanation. (1) The story originally occurred during the fall festival of Booths (Tabernacles), when Jesus would have had every reason to expect figs on the tree. The problem was supposedly created when the pre-Markan or Markan narrator relocated the story at Passover. The preceding story of the procession of people waving branches and shouting "Hosanna" is also supposed to fit better into the setting of the fall festival, which would then explain the impression Mark gives elsewhere that Jesus had spent considerable time in the city (14:49). This view was argued by, e.g., T. W. Manson, "The Cleansing of the Temple," *BJRL* 33 (1951): 271–82. (2) Figs are not actually mentioned, except in the narrator's explanatory comment that it was not the season for figs, taken to mean that Jesus was not looking for them anyway, but for the early buds supposed to be edible, and which he could reasonably expect by Passover time (so Witherington, *Mark*, 352).

The destruction of the temple was a deeply traumatic event for both Judaism and the new Christian movement, especially its Jewish Christian segment. What could it mean that God had allowed the unthinkable to happen? Zealot defenders of the temple had to the very last proclaimed that God was testing the believers, that divine deliverance would come at the last moment, that they needed only to have faith (see Josephus, *War* 6.286–89). But the temple in flames meant that both temple and faith had to be rethought. Both Jews and Christians were refashioning their faith and theology in the light of the temple's destruction. The ultimate curse on the fig tree, from which there could be no recovery, meant that whatever the future path for God's people might be, to hope for a restoration of the temple was a vain hope. That "his disciples heard it" suggests that the scene is unfinished, that it calls for completion, that they and the reader must look beyond this episode for its meaning—which continues into the next scene, and to 20–25.

[15–16] The temple of Jesus' day was an enormous and impressive structure. The modest building constructed by the returning exiles that began the Second Temple period (Ezra 3–6, esp. 3:12; Hag 1–2; Zech 6:9–15) had been desecrated by Antiochus IV Epiphanes and cleansed and rededicated by Judas Maccabeus and his brothers (1 Macc 1–4; Dan 7, 11), and in the first century was in the process of being remodeled on a grand scale by Herod the Great and his successors (see Josephus, *Ant.* 15:11.5–6; John 2:20). The whole temple complex was about 300 by 450 meters (ca. thirty-five acres), comprising, in addition to the sanctuary proper, the large outer "Court of the Gentiles" to which all people were admitted, and then, with increasing degrees of holiness, the successive inner courts for Jewish women, Jewish men, and the priests. The outer Court of the Gentiles was a great public square, where money could be exchanged into the Tyrian coins with no images, the only money acceptable for temple offerings and paying the annual half-shekel "temple tax." In this court unblemished animals acceptable for sacrifice were offered for sale. In some ways it resembled a large stockyard. Both the exchange of money and the sale of animals were services offered to those who came to worship, and were typical of temples throughout the Hellenistic world.

While much ink has been spilled on the topic of what Jesus (and his disciples?) actually did in the temple incident, and what its purpose and significance were for him,[12] that is not our task in interpreting the text of Mark. It is of fundamental importance to distinguish the perspective of Jesus in his time from

12. Among the proposals: (1) Jesus objected to the sacrificial system as such, advocating a purely spiritual religion. (2) Jesus did not oppose the temple cultus as such, but the commercialization of the holy place. (3) Jesus and his followers were a group of nationalist zealots who attempted to take over the temple area with armed force; the size of the temple operation means this must have been a military operation, like that of the later Zealots, but later Christian interpretation attempted to cover this up (so, e.g., S. G. F. Brandon, *Jesus and the Zealots: A Study of the*

that of Mark and his readers. Jesus' action involved an actual temple in which he and his disciples were present (there can be little doubt that some historical event lies at the nucleus of the Markan account); his action and pronouncement envisioned the temple's future. Mark is responding to a situation in which the temple no longer existed (or in which its imminent destruction is virtually certain). Thus Mark is not interpreting the present and ongoing function of the temple in God's plan, but is coming to terms with its destruction. The historical Jesus and his hearers looked at the reality of the temple prospectively, and asked how the temple should function; Mark and his readers looked at the absence of the temple retrospectively, and asked how the people of God could continue after the temple's demise.[13] The presence of the temple is a given for Jesus; its absence was a given for Mark and his readers. These two temporal and situational realities should not be confused or minimized. It is thus fruitless, for instance, to discuss whether *Jesus* could have actually disrupted or closed down the enormous Court of the Gentiles, even temporarily, and if so whether this is a sign of his divine power or an indication that he commanded a paramilitary group, why the Romans did not immediately intervene, and why the charge did not come up at Jesus' trial. Such discussions try to make historical sense of a 30 C.E. incident, on the basis of our knowledge of the size of the temple complex and the Roman responsibility for its security. Not only does the author not have an accurate idea of the size of the temple, his concern is not to portray a historically credible event but to communicate the meaning of the temple's destruction, and to link it to Jesus' own action in the temple. Thus, whether historically credible or not, he does picture Jesus symbolically closing down the temple operation. He drives out both sellers *and buyers* (not just "unjust" sellers), and disrupted the business of those who changed money and sold doves. At the narrative level, this means that the temple operation is brought to a halt. Likewise, Jesus' not permitting anyone to carry anything through the temple means he brings its operation to a standstill, that it no longer

---

Political Factor in Primitive Christianity [New York: Scribner, 1967]). (4) Jesus objected to the injustice of the elite temple leadership who were oppressing the poor people who came to worship by extorting money for sacrifices and rituals (so, e.g., Horsley, *Whole Story*, 19, 41, 100–101, 258 n. 7). (5) As the eschatological prophet, Jesus announced and symbolically acted out the impending doom of the present temple, which would be replaced by the new temple of the end time (e.g., E. P. Sanders, *Jesus and Judaism* [Philadelphia: Fortress, 1985], 61–76).

13. The temple's destruction was also a profoundly troubling question for Judaism. Respect for the Torah did not permit the abrogation of the laws regarding the sacrificial system, but the destruction of the temple did not permit them to be carried out. Thus devotion to God through temple sacrifice was reinterpreted, as in *Aboth of R. Nathan* 4.11a: "It happened that R. Johanan b. Zakkai went out from Jerusalem, and R. Joshua followed him, and he saw the burnt ruins of the Temple, and he said, 'Woe is it that the place, where the sins of Israel find atonement, is laid waste.' Then said R. Johanan, 'Grieve not, we have an atonement equal to the Temple, the doing of loving deeds,' as it is said, 'I desire love, and not sacrifice.'" Cf. similarly Matt 9:13; 12:7.

functions. For Mark, this is not merely an indignant protest against using the temple court as a shortcut, whether this be thought historically possible or not, and whether *skeuos* be thought to denote cultic vessels or everyday objects (see note *b* above). At the level of the Markan narrative, Jesus' dramatic action was not intended to improve the functioning of the temple, but to cancel it altogether. As he had brought an end to the failed leadership of the people of God in the preceding scenes, here he brings an end to the cult center itself. At the close of the day he will announce that the city and temple will come to a literal end, and that finally the world itself will be brought to a worthy conclusion by the Parousia of the Son of Man.

[17–19] Jesus' "teaching" now gives meaning to the whole scene. In verse 17 the Markan Jesus gives his own interpretation of the event, drawn from two texts of Scripture. The first quotation from Isa 56:7 speaks of the temple as a *house of prayer* and *for all people.*

That the temple is to be a "house of prayer" is not a critique of animal sacrifice as such, just as it is not merely a judgment on the commercialization of sacred space in the name of spirituality.[14] Rather, this pronouncement addresses the question implicit in the destruction of the temple for both Jews and Christians, a question that hung heavily in the air of Mark's time: how can the proper worship of God continue, the worship God had commanded in the Torah, now that the one place of sacrifice and atonement has been destroyed, the place of God's presence where God is enthroned over the ark of the covenant, and what did it mean that the temple has been or is being destroyed? The Markan Jesus' answer: as the Scripture says (Isaiah, key for Mark's understanding!), the temple has always been essentially a place of *prayer.* This was also a Jewish answer to the question implicit in the temple's destruction. The local synagogue had never been a cultic center for sacrifice, but a "house of prayer." Thus the rabbinic leaders who reconstituted Judaism after the debacle of 66–70 could explain that the essential function continues in the synagogue.[15] So also for Christians the essential reality of the temple continues in the Christian community as the place of prayer.

14. Commercial activity was a normal and expected activity in any temple in the Hellenistic world, and neither Jesus, Mark, nor the readers would or could have expected it to be otherwise. Modern conceptions of "secular" and "sacred" are unhelpful here. The Jerusalem temple was an economic institution, dominating the city's commercial life, providing employment and security for much of the city's population.

15. See on 12:33. The rabbinic teachers understood that even though the temple had been destroyed, its essential function had always been prayer, and this continued in the synagogue. Though the temple that housed the divine presence was gone, the Shekinah continued to be present in the synagogues and houses of study, where prayers were said in the direction of the temple site (*Deut Rab.* 2:12; *m. Ber.* 4.5; *y. Ber.* 4.5; *b. Ber* 5.8d, 30a). This understanding existed alongside the longing for a new eschatological temple, which was occasionally part of the messianic hope (cf. Tob 13:17; 14:4; Bar 5:1–9; *1 En.* 61.8; 90.28; 91.13; *Jerusalem Targum Isa* 53:5 (cf. Gnilka, *Markus,* 2:280).

Judaism understood the historical temple to be exclusively for Jews, yet many Jews nurtured the biblical hope that this was not ultimately the case—that at the eschaton all peoples would flow to Mount Zion, and the Gentiles would become insiders as the people of God (Isa 2:2–4; 19:23–25). The Dead Sea Scrolls indicate that the Qumran community regarded the Jerusalem temple and priesthood as illegitimate, and that they themselves were the authentic eschatological temple, and they developed this view while the Jerusalem temple was still standing. There were thus Jewish seeds already present in Christian tradition that could well have generated the understanding among some early Christians that the emerging Christian community was the eschatological temple of God, the spiritual house of prayer in which all nations were accepted. In retrospect (or immediate prospect), Mark's community here sees the destruction of the Jerusalem temple as having failed to be a house of prayer for all peoples, a destruction that made way for the true temple of the end time in which "all peoples"—the church of Jews and Gentiles of Mark's own time—will offer up authentic prayers to God. Thus the Markan Jesus appropriately gives instruction on prayer in connection with the destruction of the temple (11:20–25).

When the second quotation (Jer 7:11) refers to the temple as a "bandits' hideout," the reference is not to profiteering and extortion carried out by "thieves" doing business in the temple. Rather, as in the original context of Jer 7, the fatal error was in regarding the temple as a secure place of refuge where bandits could hide out after having perpetrated their crimes elsewhere. In Jeremiah, this was directed to the misunderstanding of sinful Israelites generally, who supposed that they could violate God's law at will, and then retreat to the inviolable temple. This estimate of the temple turned out to be dreadfully wrong, and the temple was destroyed. History is now repeating itself, as both Jews and Christians were inclined to regard the security of the holy temple in Jerusalem as guaranteed by God. During the 66–70 revolt, groups of revolutionaries—called "bandits" by the Romans and by some Jews favorable to the Romans such as Josephus—took over the temple, delivering prophetic oracles that God would not let the temple be destroyed. This situation is in the background of the Markan Jesus' declaration; the temple had turned out not to be the safe refuge, but had gone up in flames.

[18] The incident provoked no Roman response (contrast the scene in Acts 21:27–36, pictured with more historical realism). It served rather as the trigger to revive the plot to kill Jesus; the official resistance begun in Galilee is now transferred to Jerusalem, with a different cast—Pharisees and Herodians are replaced by chief priests and scribes, who, along with the elders, will carry through on the threat that has been hanging over Jesus since 3:6 (cf. 3:6; 10:33–34). Their "fear" is not reverential awe; they have sized up Jesus and consider him dangerous. The plot cannot be carried out immediately, however, since the crowds are still astounded by his teaching (cf. 11:32; 12:12, 37; then

14:43; 15:8, 11, 15). The ensuing confrontations between Jesus and the San-hedrin's representatives (12:13–37) represent, among other things, their attempt to discredit Jesus before the crowds, and thus facilitate his arrest. The attempt is unsuccessful (12:37). Mark's specific indication that Jesus "was teaching" (v. 17a imperfect tense *edidasken*) and the crowd's entranced response to Jesus' "teaching" (v. 18b *didachē*) suggests it was more than the brief Scripture citation of verse 17b. That the narrator does not give the content indicates it is the authority of the teaching itself, not its content, that is the Markan point (see on 1:22, 27).

[20–21] "Rabbi, look! The fig tree . . ." will be paralleled by "Teacher, look! What stones and what buildings . . ." of 13:1, further confirming the view that the fig tree is a transparent symbol for the temple. On "withered from the roots up," see on verse 14. On addressing Jesus as "rabbi," see on 9:5.

[22–25] Mark here inserts a cluster of sayings on faith, prayer, and forgive-ness that was already current in his church. They had been assembled on the catchword principle operative in oral tradition (cf. 9:42–50): cursing / faith; faith / prayer; prayer / forgiveness. Why does Mark insert them here? It is cer-tainly not the case that the author simply decides that this would be a conve-nient spot for the Markan Jesus to pause and offer a few comments on faith, prayer, and forgiveness. The immediate point of contact is the cursing of the fig tree. In response to Peter's wondering statement that the fig tree had been with-ered, Jesus calls for faith in God, backed up with the proverbial statement on the power of faith to move mountains (cf. 1 Cor 13:2), and the saying seems to illustrate the power of Jesus' own faith that caused it to happen (cf. on 9:23). On this basis, the disciples are commanded to have a similar faith in God.

Closer examination of the Markan literary and historical context suggests that the cluster as a whole is particularly relevant to this setting. The sayings are not general edifying teaching on faith and prayer, but speak directly to Mark's situation. The (impending?) destruction was a severe test of *faith* for Mark's church. "Faith that moves mountains" is not a general hyperbolic proverb about the power of faith, but is related to "this mountain," which prob-ably refers to the temple mountain—the subject of the whole section. The tem-ple mountain is no longer the focus of the eschatological events, as pictured in Isa 2:2–4, when all people will come to it to worship at God's house. It had not been "thrown into the sea," but razed by the Romans, a powerful reversal of the Zealots' goal of "throwing the Romans into the sea." Yet the mountain's "removal" is not a meaningless tragedy or frustration of God's plan, but in Mark's interpretation makes way for the ultimate "house of prayer for all peo-ple," the Christian community. This should not be thought of as the church "replacing" the temple in the sense of "Christianity superseding Judaism," for Mark is not dealing with two religions called "Christianity" and "Judaism"; instead it shows the role of the temple in God's continuing plan. Analogous to those Jews who saw the *synagogue* as the "house of prayer" in which the essential function of the temple was continued, Mark sees this function continuing in the church of Jews and Gentiles. It may have seemed utterly impossible to the Christians of Mark's day that the promises of God could still be realized after the temple's destruction, but "nothing is impossible for God." The passive verbs of verse 23, "be taken up" and "be cast into the sea," are divine passives, pointing not to the "power of faith" or "power of prayer," but the power of God for whom nothing is impossible (9:23; 10:27).

The concluding verse 25 is apparently related to the traditional teaching of Jesus' on prayer, preserved more fully in Matt 6:9–15,[16] and for Mark's readers may have called to mind this prayer that had already become traditional in Mark's community. Even so, it is included here not only because it was part of the pre-Markan cluster of sayings, but because forgiveness is an indispensable aspect of community. If the Christian community is to be a "house of prayer for all nations," it must be a forgiving community, for only forgiveness makes it possible for people to live together. In Mark's situation in which family and friends had betrayed each other under the pressure of persecution (cf. on 13:9–13), the praying community must be a forgiving community.

11:27–33 The Question about Authority

11:27 And they are coming into Jerusalem again. And as he is walking in the temple court, the chief priests, the scribes, and the elders are coming to him 28 and were saying to him, "By what authority are you doing these things? Or who gave you this authority to do them? 29 But Jesus said to them, "I will ask you one question; answer me, and I will tell you by what authority I am doing these things. 30 The baptism of John, was it from heaven, or of human origin? Answer me!" 31 And they were discussing among themselves, "If we say, 'From heaven,' he will say, 'Then why did you not believe him?' 32 But if we say, 'Of human origin,'"—they were afraid of the crowd. For all were considering John as really a prophet. 33 And they are answering Jesus, "We do not know." And Jesus says to them, "Neither am I saying to you by what authority I am doing these things."

Here begins Jesus' last day in the temple, which he will leave definitively at 13:1. This pericope is thus related to not only the preceding action in the temple but the similar conflict stories that follow. Yet it is a discrete unit, with its own general challenge to Jesus' ministry, which Mark has placed here as an introduction and anticipation of the passion story to follow. The present shape

---

16. *Ho patēr hymōn ho en tois ouranois* ("your father in heaven") is found only here in Mark, but is an almost exact echo of the tradition of the Lord's Prayer as preserved in Matt 6:9.

of the story, like the analogous stories of encounters with Jewish leaders in 12:13–37, has been influenced by church debates with Judaism in the pre-Markan tradition.

[27–28] "Authority" has been a Markan theme from the opening scenes of the Gospel (1:22, 27; 2:7, 10). In the immediately preceding narrative, Jesus' authority has been manifest from the moment of his arrival in Jerusalem, by his triumphal procession to the city gates, by his withering the fig tree, and by his "cleansing" the temple and teaching in the temple court. It is now explicitly challenged by the chief priests, scribes, and elders, representing the Sanhedrin, who have already decided on Jesus' death (11:18). Their actions, therefore, are not a spontaneous response by curious individuals; instead they anticipate the trial to come (14:43, 53; 15:1), just as the account reminds the reader that Jesus' first passion prediction had said that precisely this group would be responsible for his suffering and death (8:31).

The Jewish officials do not charge Jesus with a specific violation of the sanctity of the temple, but question the authority by which he acts. Their question is general; "these things" refers not only to the dramatic events of the preceding day (11:15–18), but to Jesus' ministry as a whole. They hope to find in Jesus' response a pretext on which to arrest him (cf. 12:13, 15).

[29–30] The answer to the question of Jesus' authority has long since been clear to the reader. Jesus does not operate on the basis of any human authority, but speaks and acts on the basis of his own authority, which Mark does not distinguish from that of God. Jesus thus escalates the issue of authority to a different level, posing the question in terms of divine or human authority, with John the Baptist as the test case. "Heaven" is a common Jewish circumlocution for God, and Jesus challenges them to answer whether John's authority comes from God ("heaven") or human beings—for, like Jesus, John had no human religious credentials. This is not merely an evasive tactic, a strategy to avoid answering the question and place the onus on the questioners. The whole point of the pericope is that Jesus operates with God's authority, and does not need to "outwit" or "embarrass" his questioners. Jesus' own authority is represented in his commanding "answer me" (v. 30b), to which they attempt a futile response.

[31–33] This story has the general form of a "scholastic dialogue" or "school discussion," which normally proceeds on the pattern of initial question from the inquirers, incisive counter-question from the teacher, which then causes the inquirers to get the point (see on 10:1–12). In Mark's adaptation of the form, at the crucial point where the inquirers are expected to respond with their new insight, they refuse to take the obvious next step, but reply, "We do not know." The omniscient narrator had let the reader listen in on their dialogue among themselves, in which they had already acknowledged that they did not in fact believe John. This is in contrast to 1:5, where all the inhabitants of Jerusalem had been baptized by John. This means neither that Mark's previous statement was merely hyperbole (see on 1:5), nor that the Jewish leaders had been baptized along with everyone else, but had done so insincerely. Rather, this is another indication that this scene is to be understood as paradigmatic, not fitting into the narrative story line, but allowing the reader to see that the Jewish leadership knowingly rejected God's messenger John and God's Son Jesus (see the next pericope), that Jesus was aware of all this in advance and is not an unwilling victim to their machinations, but the one who is authoritatively in charge of the whole scenario.

12:1–12 Those Responsible for the Lord's Vineyard Reject the Son, Who Is Vindicated by God

12:1 And he began to speak to them in parables. "A man planted a vineyard and put a fence around it and dug a pit for the winepress and built a tower and leased it to tenants and went away. 2 And he sent a servant[a] to the tenants when the time came, to collect from the tenants his share of the fruit of the vineyard. 3 And they seized him, beat him, and sent him away empty. 4 And again he sent another servant to them, and that one they knocked in the head and treated shamefully. 5 And he sent another, and they killed that one. And he sent many others; they beat some, and killed some. 6 He had still one other—his beloved son.[b] Last of all, he sent him to them, saying, 'They will respect my son.' 7 But those tenants said to one another, 'This is the heir; come on, let's kill him, and the inheritance will be ours.' 8 And they seized him, killed him, and threw him out of the vineyard. 9 What then will the lord[c] of the vineyard do? He will come and destroy the tenants and give the vineyard to others. 10 Surely you have read at least this passage of Scripture, haven't you?

" 'The stone that the builders rejected has become the main cornerstone.[d]
11 This has been done by the Lord, and is amazing in our eyes."

12 And they wanted to arrest him, but they were afraid of the crowd, for they knew that he had told this parable against them. And they left him and went away.

a. *Doulos* properly means "slave," but is here translated "servant" in order to make the association with the traditional biblical phrase that identifies the "servants" as "prophets" (cf., e.g., 1 Kgs 14:18; 2 Kgs 9:7; 17:23; Ezra 9:11; Jer 7:25; 26:5; Dan 9:6; Amos 3:7; Rev 10:7; 11:18; 22:6, 9).

b. There is no "his" in the Greek text, but *huion agapēton* connotes not only "beloved" but "only" (*agapētos* means "only" in the LXX of Gen 22:2, 12, 16; Judg 11:34; Jer 6:26; Amos 8:10; Zech 12:10). "His" is added to bring out this connotation and to correspond to the obvious allegorical meaning that points to Jesus as God's unique son.

The two other uses of *agapētos* in Mark refer specifically to Jesus as the unique Son of God (1:11; 9:7). The reader will inevitably make this connection, but the characters in the story do not.

c. See note *g* on *kyrios* at 7:28. At one level, *kyrios* can mean the owner of the vineyard, and this is the meaning at the narrative level (so NRSV and most modern translations). Since 1:2, however, readers have known that this same word used for God is also applied to Jesus (KJV, ASV preserve this aspect of the word). The Markan ambiguity cannot be preserved in English.

d. While "capstone" or "keystone" (of an arch) is lexically possible, the imagery in Eph 2:20–22 and 1 Cor 3:11 indicates that the term *kephalē gōnias* refers to a cornerstone, as does the citation of Ps 118:22–23 elsewhere in the New Testament.

Mark has placed the parable in this context and adapted it to express his own meaning, but the parable itself is pre-Markan. Whether its earliest form goes back to Jesus and, if so, its meaning in Jesus' context, are disputed points. The interpretation here is restricted to exploring its Markan meaning.

The preceding pericope 11:27–33 is a discrete unit, but it is important to remember that the chapter break here is artificial, that this parable is directly connected with the preceding. Throughout the Gospel, parables appear in situations of conflict and controversy; the conflict is occasioned by Jesus' direct and indirect claims to authority.[17] The Markan Jesus refuses to say (directly) the authority by which he acts and speaks, but he does immediately respond with a parable that calls on his challengers to make their own decision. Mark's interpretation of the parable sets the issue of Jesus' authority in the comprehensive, universal context of God's acts in history as testified to in Scripture as a whole. Jesus' authority is not that of a charismatic individual, a "great man," but is a matter of Jesus' place in God's redemptive plan for history (see on 13:20 and diagram in *Excursus: Markan Christology*, at 9:1, p. 247).

[1] The parable is addressed not to the crowds, but to the chief priests, scribes, and elders of the preceding pericope (11:27). "In parables" is used adverbially, and does not here denote more than the one parable Mark provides. The point is not how many parables Jesus spoke on this occasion, but that his communication was parabolic, indirect (on parables, see commentary at 3:23; 4:1–2). The action is quickly introduced in a series of rapid-fire verbs: a man plants, fences, digs, builds, leases, and departs. The action and vocabulary unmistakably echo Isa 5:1–2, and any biblically literate hearer, either at the narrative level or among Mark's own hearers, immediately makes the connection: God planted a vineyard, Israel. The vineyard = Israel identification is explicitly made in Isa 5:7, with the meaning of the metaphorical narrative as a whole also made plain: God expects the good fruit of justice and righteousness from his

---

17. This point is amplified in the dissertation of Cuvillier, "ΠΑΡΑΒΟΛΗ dans le second évangile"; see esp. 184–85.

vineyard. In the Judaism of Mark's time, the original parabolic "song" had already been allegorized and details had received particular meanings.[18] The tower was understood to represent the temple, and the winevat the altar. Thus the allegorizing aspect of the Markan parable, and Mark's associating it with Jesus' "cleansing" the temple (11:12–17) and prediction of its destruction (13:1–2) represent a Christian extension of a development already under way in the interpretation of Isa 5.

[2] The focus of the Isaian "song of the vineyard" had been on the vineyard itself and its failure to bear good fruit. In the Markan parable, the focus quickly shifts to the tenants and their behavior. The realism of the original story continues. The biblical and ancestral heritage had presupposed Israelites to be small property owners in which the good life was represented as each with his own vine and fig tree (cf. 2 Kgs 18:31; Isa 34:4; 36:16; Zech 3:10), but in first-century Galilee this had given way to an oppressive system in which absentee landowners of large estates leased out their land to tenants who were at their mercy—a severe social and religious problem. As expected, the owner sends his slave ("servant"; see note *a*) to collect his owner's due, the "fruit" owed him (cf. 4:7–8, 29; 11:14).

[3–5] The story takes a violent turn, and the slave is beaten and sent home empty. In the social context of first-century Palestine, this is still within the bounds of "realism," and the hearers might even have some sympathy with the tenants. The violence escalates. A second slave is knocked in the head and treated shamefully; the third is killed. The hearer has already had plenty of reason to suspect that the story is really about something more profound than agriculture and an oppressive socioeconomic situation. When the owner sends *many others*, some of whom are beaten, some of whom are killed, it is now clear that the story is not about a literal vineyard and its bad tenants. The use of "servant" for "prophet" was common biblical language for those who are "sent" (cf. Jer 7:25–26; 25:4; Amos 3:7; Zech 1:6; *apostellō*, used five times for "sent" in this passage, is found thirty times in the LXX in combination with *prophētēs* "prophet"). So also *apokteinō* "kill" and *atimazō* were part of the traditional vocabulary describing the violent destiny of the prophets of Israel. That Deuteronomistic theology according to which the faithful prophets of Israel had been persecuted and killed was widely accepted in early Judaism and by all readers of the LXX, so this description could be readily seen by Mark's hearers as a summary of Israel's history.[19] The parable is here "unrealistic" at the

---

18. Bruce D. Chilton, *A Galilean Rabbi and His Bible: Jesus' Use of the Interpreted Scripture of His Time* (Wilmington, Del.: Glazier, 1984), 112–14. Later Jewish interpreters saw the destruction of the temple prefigured in Isa 5 (cf. Juel, *Messiah and Temple*, 136–37).

19. Odil Hannes Steck, *Israel und das gewaltsame Geschick der Propheten: Untersuchungen zur Überlieferung des deuteronomistischen Geschichtsbildes im Alten Testament, Spätjudentum und Urchristentum* (WMANT 23; Neukirchen-Vluyn: Neukirchener Verlag, 1967).

narrative level, but at the meaning level it dramatically points not only to the injustice and unfaithfulness of those to whom God had entrusted responsibility for the "vineyard," but to a God who is patient and long-suffering, and who endures evil from his subjects rather than retaliate.

[6] The absolute boundary of the unexpected is reached when the owner of the vineyard decides to send his son. Even the initiated reader, who already knows "what the story is really about," is taken aback by a reflective reading, which is even more dramatic in Mark's Greek. The sentence begins with "one," and the reader thinks, "What, he is going to send another 'servant,' his last one?" only to be jolted by the word "son." At any level of meaning, parabolic or otherwise, how could this be? What landowner, what God would do this? Then comes the word *eschaton*, "last," used adverbially.

[7] Here the Markan Jesus, the storyteller within the Markan narrative, assumes the role of the omniscient narrator, and the reader overhears the discussion among the tenants. "Come on, let's kill him," is verbatim from Gen 37:20 LXX, as Joseph's jealous brothers plot his destruction. The *very* perceptive and reflective reader might remember how that story turned out, when after the rejected one had been made the head of all Egypt, Joseph reassures his fearful brothers that what they intended as evil God had transformed into good, to save many people (Gen 45:5; 50:19–20; cf. Mark 10:45). The tenants recognize the son as the heir, and decide to kill him in order to gain the inheritance for themselves. It has been argued that the social context illuminates this strategy and makes it reasonable. The argument is as follows: when the tenants see the son, they assume the father has died and the son has come himself to claim the inheritance. They know he is the only son. They know of a provision within the law that allows the property of one who dies without an heir to be claimed by those already in possession of it, by a kind of "squatter's rights."[20] Whatever the background in social history, the Markan reader knows the christological language of "heir" and "inheritance" as a way of interpreting God's saving act in Christ.[21] Here, as elsewhere in Mark, the reader hears the dialogue in the

20. Among those who provide documentation for this as the legal situation and base their interpretation on it are Jeremias, *Parables*, 75–76, and J. Duncan M. Derrett, *Law in the New Testament* (London: Darton, Longman & Todd, 1970), 86–88. Even if the law would have permitted tenants to assume ownership of unclaimed property (and the point is disputed; cf. Klyne R. Snodgrass, "The Parable of the Wicked Husbandmen: Is the Gospel of Thomas Version Original?" *NTS* 21 [1974]: 142–44), it did not allow murder in order to obtain ownership.

21. Jesus as "heir": Rom 8:17; Heb 1:1–4; Christians as "heirs" mediated by Christ the "heir": Rom 8:17; Gal 3:29; Eph 3:6; Heb 6:17; Jas 2:5; salvation as "inheritance" obtained through Christ: Gal 3:18; 4:30; Eph 1:11, 14, 18; 5:5; Col 3:24; Heb 9:15; 1 Pet 1:4; "inherit" as the verb for receiving salvation: Matt 5:5; 19:29; Mark 10:17; Rom 4:13; 1 Cor 6:9; 15:50; Gal 5:21; Heb 1:14; 6:12; 1 Pet 3:9; Rev 21:7. The whole semantic field related to "inherit" reflects Israel's experience of receiving the promised land as gift, transposed into a transcendent mode, and Jewish-Christian disputes as to who were the legitimate heirs of God's covenant promises.

story at a level the characters cannot be aware of. The tenants are not thinking theology, but property. They not only kill the son / heir, but cast his unburied corpse out of the vineyard, the ultimate humiliation. The Sanhedrin, whose conduct is bringing about the death of Jesus and the destruction of the temple, will likewise make no arrangements for Jesus' burial (cf. 15:38–47, with both temple and burial motifs).

[9] The narrator's voice emerges from the parable, and the Markan Jesus asks the Sanhedrin representatives directly what the owner of the vineyard will do. Without waiting for an answer (contrast 11:33) he responds to his own question, and in the realistic future tense—future to the Jesus and his hearers in the story, but already present or past to Mark's hearers: "He will come and destroy the tenants and give the vineyard to others." The "man" is now the "Lord" (see note *c*), and the action in the story against the tenants has modulated into God's action against the unfaithful temple leadership. This parabolic conclusion can be heard in at least three levels. At the level of the parable, the scoundrels get what they so richly deserve, and the story attains closure. At the level of Markan meaning, the coming of the Lord to destroy the temple establishment points to something in political history that had just happened or was in the process of happening in the 66–70 revolt, when the temple and its leadership were destroyed. But Mark's primary meaning is theological. As the whole parable has been an allegory of salvation history, so the coming of the lord of the vineyard points to the eschatological climax of that history. The tenants are the Jewish leaders responsible for the temple, the chief priests, scribes, and elders—as they themselves recognize (v. 12). It is they who are destroyed, not the vineyard.[22] The parable is not about God's judgment on Israel, but on the Jewish leaders, as in the tradition of the Hebrew prophets.

Who is the "lord?" In a rigidly neat allegory, the son would have been raised and returned to bring judgment on the tenants. In the Markan parable, it is not the "Son" but the "Lord" who comes in judgment. To ask whether this is "God" or "the Lord Jesus" is to misapprehend Mark's Christology. At the story level, the lord is the owner. At the Markan level, the owner who comes himself is the Lord Jesus returning as Son of Man in the glory of his *Father* (8:38). Who are the "others" to whom the vineyard is given? At the level of political history, the "others" are the Romans.[23] At the level of comprehensive church history, the "others" are the predominantly Gentile church (France, *Gospel of Mark*, 462). While each of these may preserve overtones of Mark's parabolic discourse, the primary meaning would seem to be that the old, unfaithful leadership of the

---

22. Contra, e.g., Strecker, *Theology of the New Testament*, 359, who sees the parable as portraying "the history of the Jewish covenant people . . . as an unholy past devoid of salvation, a history of murder of the prophets."

23. Lührmann, *Markusevangelium*, 199; cf. John 11:48.

"vineyard" is to be replaced by new leadership representing Jesus' own authority, that is, the temple hierarchy as leadership of the people of God is to be
replaced by the apostles and disciples of Jesus to whom he has given his own
authority (3:14; 6:7–13). In all this, it is important to be clear that it is not
"Judaism" that is replaced with "Christianity," but leadership of the continuing
people of God that is taken away from unfaithful leaders and given to faithful
ones. All this takes place within the image of the destruction of the old temple
(not the vineyard or the people) and its replacement with the new community
of faith as the "house of prayer for all nations."

[10–11] As the parable began with a clear paraphrase of Isa 5:1–2, so the
Markan Jesus concludes it by appending a Scripture citation from Ps 118:22–23,
one of the Hallel psalms recited at Passover, which had already played a role in
the triumphal procession (11:9–10 = Ps 118:25–26). This text, read christologically, was widespread in early Christianity (Acts 4:11; 1 Pet 2:4, 7; Rom 9:22–33;
cf. Eph 2:20; 1 Pet 2:6). By this addition, the point of the story is shifted from
punishment of the tenants / temple officials to vindication of the Son. The postresurrection perspective is now explicit; in the resurrection the act of God has
reversed the human judgment, and the rejected one has been vindicated. The
imagery also shifts from horticulture to architecture; the tenant farmers have
become the builders. "The builders" was probably a current description of the
temple leadership.[24] They had set aside (or "killed and thrown out of the vineyard") the one who would constitute the new temple that would replace the
destroyed one. The Christian community is the new "building" that replaces the
destroyed temple. A person is the "cornerstone," as the building itself is composed of persons, the new eschatological temple of the Christian community.

The citation could have ended at verse 10 = Ps 118:22, but it was important
to the author to continue the quotation in order to point out that the Christ-event
as a whole, which reverses the human evaluation and rejection of Jesus, was
not a matter of better insight in retrospect, but was God's own doing. "*Our* eyes"
can only be astounded that *God* has reversed the human judgment of who Jesus
was and what he signified. The eyes here spoken of are no longer blind, but have
been opened by the one who gives sight to the blind. It is inappropriate to ask
here whether "the Lord" is God or Christ.

[12] Here, Jesus' parabolic teaching is not mysterious; it is not intended to be
misunderstood and to harden. This shows that Mark has no one consistent "parable theory" (see on 4:10–12; 7:14–23). The parable is intended to be understood,
and is understood, even by "outsiders." The representatives of the Sanhedrin

---

24. Rabbinic interpretation documented only later, but probably already present in Mark's time,
refers to scribes as "builders." Cf., e.g., *Mid Cant.* 1:5; J. Duncan M. Derrett, "The Stone That the
Builders Rejected," in *Studies in the New Testament* (ed. J. Duncan M. Derrett; 6 vols.; Leiden:
Brill, 1977), 2:64–65.

recognize that the parable had been spoken against *them*—not against the people as a whole, not even the crowd that is still entranced by Jesus' teaching. They depart, but do not give up, and will find a way to carry out their will.

12:13–17 The Question about Taxes Paid to a Pagan Government

12:13 And they are sending some of the Pharisees and Herodians to him, to set a verbal trap for him.ª 14 And they come and say to him, "Teacher, we know that you are truthful and answer without regard to what people may think, for you show no partiality, but teach the way of God in accordance with truth. Is it right to pay the poll tax to the emperor, or not? Should we pay it, or should we not?" 15 But knowing their hypocrisy, he said to them, "Why are you putting me to the test? Bring me a denarius and show it to me."ᵇ 16 And they brought one. And he says to them, "Whose imageᶜ is this, and whose title?" They answered, "The emperor's." 17 Jesus said to them, "Give backᵈ to the emperor the things that belong to the emperor, and to God the things that belong to God." And they were utterly astounded at him.

a. The dative / instrumental *logō,* without preposition or pronoun, can refer either to what the inquirers say, "with a question," or what they try to get Jesus to say, "in what he said."

b. *Hina idō* is literally "that I may see [it]," but the subjunctive is imperatival, corresponding to the previous command. On *denarius,* see note *c* at 6:37.

c. *Eikōn,* literally "icon," is used in the LXX for both the image of God in which humanity was created (e.g. Gen 1:26; 5:1; 9:6) and images Israel was forbidden to make, i.e., idols (e.g. Deut 4:16; 2 Kgs 11:18; Isa 40:19).

d. In 14b, "pay" is from the simple verb *didōmi,* the basic meaning of which is "give," though it is the standard verb for the payment of taxes; the verb in v. 17 is a compound from the same verb, *apodidōmi,* which can mean either "give," "give back," "pay," or "pay back."

This traditional material inserted by Mark in this context is in the general form of a "scholastic dialogue" (see on 10:1–12), but climaxes in the memorable pronouncement of Jesus and so is more like the traditional pronouncement story (see on 2:1–3:6). The pronouncement of verse 17, however, may not be abstracted from this context and treated as a general aphorism.

[13] The subject of the sentence is still the chief priests, scribes, and elders of 11:27, continued by the "them" of 12:1, the "you" of 12:10, and the repeated "they" of 12:12. The Pharisees and Herodians do not coincidentally decide to question Jesus, but are sent by the Sanhedrin. In Galilee, early in the narrative, the Pharisees and Herodians plotted Jesus' death (see on 3:6). Here, the narrator incorporates that plot into the machinations of the Sanhedrin, which will carry it out, and Pharisees and Herodians disappear from the narrative.

[14] Those who are attempting to trap Jesus and who will themselves not give a straightforward answer approach Jesus with effusive flattery, which the reader recognizes as ironically true. Jesus is the authentic teacher and does not make what people think of him the measure of his teaching. Their phrase "the way of God" is particularly ironic, in that at one level it poses the issue as a matter of religious law ("way" connotes "Halakah"—cf. note *g* on 7:5). At a deeper level, the reader has known since 1:2–3 that Jesus teaches and embodies the ultimate "way of the Lord" that leads to the cross (see *Excursus: The Way* at 1:3).

The question itself poses a serious issue. Even at this narrative level, the question of paying the Roman tax is not asked in order to obtain legal or political advice, not a matter of one's "civic duty." It is a religious question of conscience, asked by serious religious people. It is not a general question about "religion and politics" or "church and state," but deals with a specific issue, already present in Jesus' time, but particularly sharp in Mark's. The *kēnsos* (lit. "census") was the Roman head tax imposed on Judea, Samaria, and Idumaea when in 6 C.E. the Romans removed these troublesome areas from the rule of local puppet kings, made them a Roman province, and placed them under the direct rule of Roman governors. At that time a census was taken of the new provinces to facilitate the new Roman poll tax. This precipitated a revolt led by Judas the Galilean, who saw this census as an encroachment on God's right to number the holy people and on God's ownership of the Holy Land. Judas proclaimed that only God could be called "Lord" and that to submit to the Roman census was to deny the sole lordship of God, who would deliver the people only when they rose up in armed rebellion against this outrage (see Acts 5:37; Josephus, *Ant.* 18.1.1–6; *War* 2.8.1). Though the Romans quickly put down this rebellion, the movement founded by Judas lived on, led by his sons and grandson, smoldering underground through the time of Jesus and breaking out afresh in Mark's time. When the revolt became the war of 66–70 C.E., this time involving all Palestine and leading to the destruction of Jerusalem and the temple, the members of the revolutionary faction in the tradition of Judas were called "Zealots."[25] The Zealots and their sympathizers saw the *kēnsos* as the litmus test of loyalty to God. The Sanhedrin (including many Pharisees), while resenting Roman rule, saw paying the tax as the necessary price for peaceful coexistence with the Romans, and did not regard it as rejecting the law or rule of God. In this scene the issue is posed cleanly, more from the Zealot point of view from than that of the Sanhedrin, in yes-or-no terms. To say yes places Jesus with the accommodating priestly party and loses popular support; to say no places him

25. The whole movement from 6 C.E. until its final defeat at Masada in 73 has been traditionally referred to as the "Zealots," but the name itself was probably not used until 66 C.E. See Richard A. Horsley and John S. Hanson, *Jesus and the Spiral of Violence: Popular Jewish Resistance in Roman Palestine* (San Francisco: Harper & Row, 1987), xii–xiii, 56–58, 77–78, 121–23, 149–50.

with the Zealots and is ground for his arrest (Luke 20:20 makes this implicit Markan point explicit; cf. 23:2). From the point of view of the Zealot ideology popular with the masses, Jesus must either declare himself to be a political rebel or a religious traitor. While in the Markan story line the whole scene is part of the effort to find grounds on which Jesus may be arrested, the question itself, and Jesus' response to it, is also inherently important for Mark. It was a live issue in his own time, in which the relation of Christians to the demands of the Roman government was not an abstract problem.

[15–16] Jesus knows and unmasks their hypocrisy. "Why are you putting me to the test?" identifies their plot with the machinations of Satan (1:13; 8:11, 33; 10:2). Jesus calls for a denarius, and they produce one. The denarius was a Roman coin, bearing the image of the emperor and an inscription declaring him to be divine and pontifex maximus (high priest). Not only the image, but the inscription, would be offensive to Jewish sensibilities. Whether observant Jews would actually have had a Roman coin in the temple precincts is a disputed point at the level of 30 C.E. history, but Mark's point does not lie at that level. His readers would have known what a denarius was, but not what was permitted or customary in the temple court. Jesus calls attention to the image and to the inscription, and forces them to say whose it is. This then sets the stage for his pronouncement.

[17] Like much else in Mark, the pronouncement functions at two levels. At the narrative level, Jesus' response confounds those who have attempted to trap him, for they must depart without having achieved their purpose of wresting some subversive statement from him that could be the grounds of his arrest. Even at this level, Jesus' response is not merely a clever trick to avoid entrapment, but poses the issue anew, and at a different level (cf. on 11:27–33). Jesus has been in charge throughout. He commands that they produce a denarius, and they obey. The imperatives of verse 15 are important (as in 11:30). Once again, the authority of Jesus is demonstrated, and it becomes ever more clear that when Jesus is arrested, it will be on his own volition in commitment to the will of God, not because he is guilty of any violation of the law—either divine or Roman. Though he will be delivered to them as a political rebel, Jesus here reveals no disloyalty to the Roman government.

The pithy, provocative pronouncement also speaks beyond its narrative context to the setting of the readers. There, too, it does not give a clear yes or no to the question as posed. Like the parables, it calls on the hearers to decide its meaning in their own situation. However, the parable is not so open-ended that it may mean anything; some things are clear:

(1) Jesus does not forbid paying taxes to Caesar. This is in step with other early Christian statements calling disciples to be responsible citizens of the pagan empire, including payment of legitimate taxes (Rom 13:1–7; 1 Pet 2:13–17), without making a blanket statement that this must always be done.

(2) It is also clear that there are things that "belong to Caesar." It may be that this is reflected in the specific vocabulary of verses 14 and 17. It is not clear whether the switch in terminology is deliberate or whether *didōmi* and *apodidōmi* are simply synonyms (see note *d*). If deliberate, the questioners ask about "giving," that is, paying taxes, and Jesus responds in terms of "giving *back*" what belongs to Caesar and God respectively. Is the general principle "If you have what belongs to another, you are obligated to give it back" operative? Then the logic would be, "Since you have a denarius with Caesar's name on it, you have already settled the issue: paying the tax is the return of someone else's property." This would make the line of argument more *ad hominem* than substantial (but cf., e.g., 12:26–27). One can readily think that the Markan Jesus believes that all things already belong to God the Creator, so "giving" to God is giving *back* what God already owns; it is more difficult to think of the tax money as already belonging to Caesar. Likewise, it is not clear whether the use of *eikōn* for the image on the coin is intended to evoke the idea that human beings bear the *eikōn* of God, so that as the coin with Caesar's image belongs to the emperor, the person who bears God's image belongs to God. The statement functions parabolically, and rightfully evokes such reflections rather than postulating clear answers. However these possibilities may be resolved, it is clear that Jesus' disciples are not forbidden to participate in the secular economic and political system as such. They are not called, for example, to emulate the lifestyle of John the Baptist.

(3) There is no paralleling of Caesar and God. God is God and Caesar is not God, in direct opposition to the image and title on the coin. The world is not divided into two parallel kingdoms. There is no encouragement in this text for dividing the world into "secular" and "sacred," with Caesar ruling the one and God the other, nor is there any "balancing" of civic obligation to the state and religious obligation to God. Obligation to God overbalances all else (cf. 12:44, which concludes this section). Caesar is relative and God is absolute, so the two statements are not on the same plane; the second relativizes the first. Even the conjunction *kai* that joins them is not coordinating but adversative (as, e.g., Rom 1:13). Caesar does have a kingdom, and Jesus' followers live in it, but God is the creator of all, and God's kingdom embraces all, including that of Caesar. Thus while the saying itself calls on Jesus' hearers to give both Caesar and God their due, it is not directed to those situations in which one must choose between God and Caesar as Lord. When those situations arise, devotion to God must clearly take precedence over Caesar; God demands all (12:29–30; cf. Acts 5:29). But the saying does not tell the hearer in advance how to discern what those situations are.

(4) Robert C. Tannehill has pointed out that Jesus' response is neither a facile either / or, nor a superficial both / and. By placing Caesar and God together, the saying prevents the reader from thinking of either realm in isolation. "We cannot settle questions of political life without considering the claims of God, nor

seek to live a religious life oblivious to the problems of society. These words should awaken concerned awareness of the (possibly conflicting) claims of Caesar and God. This awareness is the beginning of obedience."[26]

(5) Markan eschatology also plays a role in the appropriation of this word of Jesus. Certainly there is no eschatology in the pericope or the saying as such, but before the narrative day is over, that is, within a few minutes of the hearer's reading time, Jesus will announce not only the coming destruction of the temple, but the imminent coming of the Son of Man, who will bring all earthly dominion to a halt (13:1–37). The nearness of the kingdom of God relativizes the Roman world power and its claims. Thus, though Jesus' followers can in good conscience give Caesar his due, including the payment of taxes, no ultimate commitment can be made to the imperial government, and what is due to it must always be decided from case to case.

12:18–27 The Question about the Resurrection

12:18 And Sadducees, who say there is no resurrection, are coming to him, and they were asking him a question, 19 "Teacher, Moses wrote for us that 'If a man's brother dies, leaving a wife but no child, the brother shall marry the woman and raise up children for his brother.' 20 There were seven brothers, and the first married and, when he died, left no children; 21 and the second married her and died without leaving any children; and the third likewise; 22 and the seven left no children. Last of all, the woman also died. 23 In the resurrection, when they rise, whose wife shall she be? For seven had married her." 24 Jesus said to them, "Is not this the reason that you are wrong, that you know neither the Scriptures nor the power of God? 25 For when they rise from the dead,[a] they neither marry nor are given in marriage, but are like the angels in heaven. 26 But as for the dead being raised, have you not read in the book of Moses, in the passage about the bush, how God said to him, 'I am[b] the God of Abraham, the God of Isaac, and the God of Jacob?' 27 He is not the God of the dead, but of the living. You are totally wrong."

a. "They" here has its generalizing meaning, "people."
b. The Greek sentence, like the Hebrew text of Exod 3:6, is verbless, with "am" understood as required by the context. The LXX supplies the verb *eimi* ("am"). Even though this rendering would support Mark's point, he does not cite it. And even though it is found in the parallel in Matt 22:32, it is remarkable that no MSS of Mark include it.

The pericope, which combines formal features of the "scholastic dialogue" (see on 10:1–12) and controversy story, is divided into two subunits by a double

---

26. Robert C. Tannehill, *The Sword of His Mouth* (Philadelphia: Fortress, 1975), 174.

inclusio. The first part is the Sadducee's question, bracketed by the key word *anastasis*, "resurrection" (vv. 18, 23); the second is Jesus' answer, framed by *planaō*, "lead astray" (vv. 24, 27). While the pericope may well reflect an incident in the life of Jesus,[27] the key exegetical question is the function of the story in this context. It fits into the general collection of controversy stories 11:27–12:34 in which Jesus encounters and defeats a series of opponents who attempt to discredit him (see on 11:27). The story is thus not a general section of "Jesus' teaching on life after death" or the like.

The topic is the resurrection, but not as an abstract theological topic. The Markan church proclaims Jesus as the Risen One, that is, God's act in raising Jesus from the dead, and it found itself having to vindicate the validity of the Christian message (see 1 Cor 15; Acts 17:16–34). The Markan Jesus is vindicated not by the charm of his life or the cogency of his teaching, but by the act of God in raising him from the dead, the keystone of the apocalyptic framework of Mark's theology as a whole. Here as elsewhere, rather than composing an essaylike explanation, the author incorporates an appropriate story from his tradition, a story not originally composed to make this point, but which is already known to his audience and now appears in a new light that illuminates the narrative as a whole. In Mark's theology, Jesus' life, death, and resurrection is in accord with the will of God as revealed in Scripture (14:49), it stands under the necessity of the apocalyptic "must" (*dei*, cf. 8:31; 9:11; 13:7, 10, 14). It is not an illustration of common-sense religious expectations but a surprising manifestation of the apocalyptic power of God (9:1; 13:26; 14:62) who does the impossible (10:27; 14:36).

[18] The Sadducees, mentioned only here in Mark, represented the aristocratic priestly leadership. In characterizing them to his mainly Gentile readership (see 7:3–4), Mark focuses on only one point that is relevant to the present discussion: they do not believe in the resurrection. This does not mean that they were skeptics who had abandoned the traditional faith of Israel, but that they were theological conservatives who did not accept the "modern" theological innovations involved in Israel's late incorporation of apocalyptic concepts such as resurrection, angels, and demons (see Acts 23:6–8; Josephus, *Ant.* 18.16; *War* 2.165). They apparently accepted only the five books of the Torah as Scripture, rejecting the Prophets and Writings as "later additions" to the canon, just as they rejected the oral tradition affirmed by the Pharisees, who accepted all these as authoritative. Israel's theological tradition remained very "this-worldly" until Maccabean times, when under the pressures of persecution the older Deuteronomic and prophetic covenant theology no longer provided an adequate framework within which the justice and faithfulness of God could be affirmed. Thus,

27. John P. Meier, "The Debate on the Resurrection of the Dead: An Incident from the Ministry of the Historical Jesus?" *JSNT* 77 (2000): 3–24.

although there had been previous steps in this direction, it was not until the second century B.C.E. that Daniel presented the first clear affirmation of resurrection (12:2). The Sadducees would have none of this, but maintained the older Israelite theology based on the Torah alone. In debates with Sadducees, Pharisaic advocates of the newer apocalyptic theology, including the resurrection, were thus forced to find biblical justification for the doctrine of the resurrection in the Torah, and the creative exegetical methods accepted on all sides at that time allowed them to do so.[28]

[19] The Sadducees cite the divine law of levirate (Latin "husband's brother") marriage given through Moses, intended in that culture to provide security for the woman, continuation of the male family line, and protection of property and inheritance rights (Deut 25:5–6; cf. Gen 38:6–26; Ruth 3–4). The Sadducees were correct about the original meaning of the text, which was oriented to life in this world, with no presupposition of a future resurrection. It was important for family life within the conditions of that culture.

[20–23] The argument presents an unrealistic case, presumably a stock argument concocted to reduce the doctrine of the resurrection to absurdity and show it could not have been presupposed by the Mosaic legislation: if all eight of the people who have obeyed God's law in the Torah are raised from the dead, how could their marriage relationship be sorted out? The doctrine of the resurrection thus not only presents insuperable difficulties for life in a supposed future age, but is shown to be unbiblical.

[24–25] The Markan Jesus' response is not intended to provide answers for those curious about the nature of heavenly life, but to demonstrate the authority of Jesus and to affirm the apocalyptic view of the world that is the framework for Mark's theology. As with the question about paying the poll tax (vv. 15–17), Jesus does not directly answer the question as posed—he does not declare "whose" wife she shall be—but responds to its presuppositions, which concern the *Scripture* and the *power of God*. Using a chiastic arrangement, he first responds to the latter.

---

28. According to the Mishnah, *Sanh.* 10.1, the Torah teaches the resurrection. The Talmud then gives later illustrations of rabbinic exegesis supporting this argument. The Sadducees punctuated Deut 31:16 to read "And Yahweh said to Moses, 'Soon you will lie down with your ancestors. Then this people will arise and begin to prostitute themselves. . . .'" By punctuating the sentence so that the initial verb of the following sentence is included in the initial sentence, making "Moses" rather than "this people" the subject, the Pharisees read "And Yahweh said to Moses, 'Soon you will lie down with your ancestors and arise. Then this people . . .'" "R. Simai [ca. 210 C.E.] said, 'Whence do we learn resurrection from the Torah? From the verse 'And I also have established my covenant with them [Abraham, Isaac, Jacob] to give them the land of Canaan': it does not say 'to give you', but 'to give them'; thus resurrection is proved from the Torah." Cf. additional illustrations and documentation in G. Baumbach, "Das Sadduzäerverständnis bei Josephus Flavius und im NT," *Kairos* 23 (1971): 17–37.

First, the resurrection is not a matter of the extension of this-worldly realities into the heavenly world, but of a new reality brought into being by God the Creator, not a matter of innate human potential but of transcendent divine power, not a matter of human nature but of God's covenant and the ability to be faithful to it even beyond death. The Sadducees are misled by thinking in terms of human projection rather than divine creativity, "not thinking in terms of the things of God, but in terms of human things" (8:33). In saying that the resurrected ones will be "like the angels," Jesus does not here intend to give a description of the life of the "age to come," but to point out what resurrection life is *not*: the institution of marriage, important for this age, does not continue into the future world, where issues of the propagation of the race and of property and inheritance rights are no longer present. Jewish theology had already interpreted the future life of the transcendent world as like that of the angels (cf. Tob 12:19; *1 En.* 15.7; 51.4; 104.4; *2 Bar.* 51.9–10).

[26–27] Jesus then turns to show that the resurrection, and the apocalyptic plan of God to which it is central, is in accord with the will of God as revealed in Scripture. Although Mark's own canon includes Daniel and the other prophetic books (see 4:32; 9:3; 13:7, 14, 19, 19, 26; 14:62), the Markan Jesus does not critique the Sadducees' limited canon by appealing to the specific affirmation of resurrection there (Dan 12:2). Like the Pharisees, he shows that the doctrine of the resurrection is included in the Torah. They had cited Moses (v. 19) and Jesus responds with Moses, referring to "the passage about the bush" (Exod 3:2–6; chapter and verse numbers were added much later). The Markan Jesus' exegesis does not satisfy modern criteria, but fully accords with ancient practice (see note 28). Even so, its force in the Markan context is not based on the tense of the verb, as though that is the key point: "God did not say 'I *was* the God of Abraham . . .' but 'I *am* the God of Abraham. . . .'" In any case, there is no verb in the Hebrew text of Exodus or the Markan citation (see note *b*). The Markan point is not grammar but the faithfulness and power of God, who had made a covenant with Abraham, Isaac, and Jacob, and who would not allow even death to annul it. Likewise, the probative force of Jesus' "proof from Scripture" is not the cogency of his exegesis in either ancient or modern terms, but the authority of Jesus himself. For Mark, who does believe that his Scripture teaches the future resurrection, the doctrine is true not because Scripture teaches it, but because Christ teaches it. The truth of both Scripture and Jesus' exegesis had been validated in Mark's time not by the logic of Jesus' interpretation, but by God's act in raising Jesus from the dead. Thus the figures in the story cannot be convinced, and are not, but here again Mark is speaking over their heads to his own post-Easter Christian audience whose faith is founded on the resurrection.

The issue of precisely how resurrection should be conceptualized in verse 26 is thus worthy of reflection, but is of secondary importance. God is portrayed as speaking of the patriarchs as somehow living, but obviously not yet resurrected, since their resurrection is future to both Exod 3 and Mark 12, as well as to Mark's readers then and now. On the one hand, this could mean that "resurrection" is here used somewhat vaguely to refer to "life after death." In this view, Jewish authors sometimes used a broad spectrum of language and imagery, including that of immortality, to express their faith in God's gift of life after death.[29] In a Jewish context, this would still not mean belief in the immortality of the soul in individualistic Greek terms, but that hope for life beyond the grave is a matter of God's act and the fulfillment of God's purpose, not a matter of human nature. On the other hand, some authors understand first-century Judaism to have had a consistent doctrine of resurrection, which involved two stages: after death the redeemed are taken into God's presence and are thus not really dead but alive. This, however, is only an intermediate stage before the final resurrection, when they will be restored to transformed bodily existence in the new age of God's justice and righteousness. To claim that the patriarchs are alive with God in the heavenly world would mean that they are destined for the resurrection, and the proof of its reality, though it is yet to come. In this view, "resurrection" is not just a cipher for some form of individual "life after death" or "going to heaven when we die"; it is the key symbol of God's eschatological redemption of history. It is thus a political symbol of the ultimate triumph of God's justice. Like apocalypticism in general, it is not directed to the question, Do we somehow live on after death? It addresses, Will God's justice finally prevail; will the kingdom of God finally come?[30] However the intent of the resurrection of the patriarchs is visualized in this particular text, it is important for Mark's theology as a whole to see its apocalyptic framework, which is concerned not merely with the survival of individual souls but with the redemptive act of God for history and the world, and the political implications for life in this world. The Sadducees are thus not merely mistaken on a point of speculative theology about what happens to people when they die. They suppose that all talk of God's promises and God's justice must be affirmed within a this-worldly framework. For Mark, not only God's covenant with Israel through the patriarchs, but God's ultimate act in Jesus Christ cannot be contained within the confines of life in this world. The resurrection is central to God's salvific plan for history as a whole (see on 13:20 and diagram in *Excursus: Markan Christology* at 9:1, p. 247). To be wrong about *this* is to be "totally wrong."

29. Cf., e.g., George W. E. Nickelsburg, *Resurrection, Immortality, and Eternal Life in Intertestamental Judaism* (HTS 26; Cambridge, Mass.: Harvard University Press, 1972). See the variety and progression in 1 Macc, 2 Macc, 4 Macc. Thus, e.g., Perkins, "Mark," 676, argues that "This argument is directed toward the possibility of immortality in general, not to resurrection as God's eschatological promise."

30. This view is cogently argued by N. T. Wright, *The Resurrection of the Son of God* (Christian Origins and the Question of God 3; Minneapolis: Fortress, 2003) throughout; on this text see pp. 415–29.

12:28–34 The Question about the Great Commandment

12:28 And one of the scribes had heard them disputing, and when he saw that he answered them well, came up and asked him, "Which commandment is above everything else[a]?" 29 Jesus answered, "The primal commandment[b] is, 'Hear, O Israel: the Lord our God, the Lord is one;[c] 30 and you shall love the Lord your God with all your heart, and with all your soul, and with all your mind, and with all your strength.' 31 The second is this, 'You shall love your neighbor as yourself.' There is no other commandment greater than these." 32 And the scribe said to him, "Well said, teacher, for you have spoken the truth when you said that 'he is one, and beside him there is no other'; 33 and 'to love him with all one's heart, and with all one's understanding and with all one's strength' and 'to love one's neighbor as oneself,' is much more important than all whole burnt offerings and sacrifices." 34 And when Jesus saw that he answered with insight, he said to him, "You are not far from the kingdom of God." And from then on, no one dared to ask him any more questions.

a. *Prōtē pantōn* is lit. "first of all [things]." The word for commandment, *entolē*, is feminine; *prōtē* is also feminine, but "everything" is masculine or neuter, so the meaning is not "first of all the commandments," but "first of everything," i.e., "above all things," "above everything else." This is missed by translations that construe "first" to mean "first of the commandments" (e.g., TEV, CEV, NAB, NJB, NIV, REB).

b. Lit. "The first is . . . ," here translated to agree with v. 28. A C *f*[13] and most later MSS have some version of "the first [commandment] of all the commands is . . . ," with the neuter "all" retained and ungrammatically combined with "commandments." This reading represents a scribal attempt to combine "first" and "commandments," i.e., to make the first commandment the first of a series.

c. The Hebrew text of Deut 6:4, its LXX translation, and Markan citation can all be translated in a variety of ways, including: (1) "The Lord our God, the Lord is one" (JPS fn; NRSV Mark; NIV Deut and Mark); (2) "The LORD is our God, the LORD alone" (JPS, NRSV, NAB Deut); (3) "The Lord is our God, the Lord our one God" (REB Deut); (4) "The Lord our God is the one Lord" (REB Mark); (4) "The Lord is our God, the Lord alone"; (5) "The Lord our God is the only Lord"; (6) "Yahweh our God is the one, the only Yahweh" (NJB); (7) "Yahweh our God is the one, the only Yahweh" (NJB Deut); (8) "The Lord our God is the one, only Lord (NJB Mark); (9) "The Lord our God is Lord alone!" (NAB Mark). The Hebrew text is four words, two of which are "Yahweh," with the verb or verbs understood. The variety results from a combination of factors: construing the words as one sentence or two, translating "Yahweh" as a proper name or as the generic "Lord," and understanding the predicate adjective "one" as defining God's nature, God's uniqueness, or Israel's exclusive worship of Yahweh.

Like the preceding pericope, this is a unit of pre-Markan tradition not bound to a particular time or place (note its different context in Luke 10:25–28). Even more distinctly than the preceding pericope, this story bears the formal characteristics of a "scholastic dialogue" (see on 10:1–12), and it likewise easily divides into two parts, the first (vv. 28–31) comprising the scribe's question and Jesus' response, the second the scribe's counterresponse and Jesus' commendation (vv. 32–34). The dialogue alternates in the ABA^{1}B^1 pattern, but since the scribe's counterresponse is a virtual repetition of Jesus' initial response, the unit as a whole has a chiastic structure:

A	Question	*(Scribe)*	A
	B Love God and neighbor	*(Jesus)*	B
	B^1 Love God and neighbor	*(Scribe)*	A^1
A^1	Commendation	*(Jesus)*	B^1

[28] The scribe belongs to the group consistently hostile to Jesus throughout Mark; they will collaborate with the chief priests and elders in his arrest, trial, and death (see on 11:27–28 and *Excursus: Jesus the Teacher vs. the Scribes* at 7:23). Yet, in this scene he is not sent by the Sanhedrin; he manifests no hostility, and he is not trying to test Jesus or trip him up (contrast the Matthean and Lukan versions, Matt 22:34–35; Luke 10:25). He regards Jesus as having given good answers to his critics, and asks a sincere question. He treats Jesus as neighbor, transcends the party strife and us / them mentality of the narrative, and shows that Mark does not present a blanket condemnation of Jews or Jewish leaders. His question, however, is not a spontaneous, individual inquiry about the most important commandment, but reflects the ongoing scribal discussion.[31] Unlike his fellow scribes, he addresses Jesus as a colleague and accepts him as a participant in serious theological discussion.[32] Asking Jesus to

31. For numerous examples of rabbinic discussion of the relative importance of commandments, and which was "first," see Strack and Billerbeck, *Kommentar*, 1:900–908. Something analogous to summarizing the law as the double command of love for God and love for neighbor was present in contemporary Judaism. Cf., e.g., Philo, *Special Laws* 2.63; *T. Dan* 5.3; *T. Iss.* 5.2; 7.6 (though *T. 12 Patr.* material is of questionable date and possible Christian origin). In none of these "parallels" is the point made by citing Scripture texts.

32. This may be illustrated by the well-known story contrasting the responses of Shammai and Hillel, two rabbis of opposing "schools" who flourished shortly before the time of Jesus. A Gentile inquirer, considering becoming a Jewish proselyte, approached Shammai with the request, "Teach me the whole Torah while I stand on one foot." Shammai, representing the more conservative Palestinian Judaism, chased him away for his impertinence. Hillel was also a Palestinian rabbi but he had traveled, had a broader perspective, and was more open to the Hellenistic world. When the same Gentile approached him, Hillel responded with a version of the "Golden Rule" (sometimes therefore called the "Silver Rule"): "What is hateful to you, do not do to your neighbor; that is the whole Torah, while the rest is commentary; go and learn it" (*b. Shabbat* 31a). This story is not, of course, an exact parallel to the Markan story, but does illustrate rabbinic discussion of how and whether the Torah can be summarized and/or its numerous laws prioritized.

identify the first commandment does not refer to the first of a series, relatively the most important, but the command that is above all the other commandments, of a different order (cf. note *a*). This corresponds to the Decalogue, which is not simply the first 10 of the 613 commandments reckoned by the rabbis to be in the Torah, but is considered the primal commands that represent all the others.[33]

[29–30] Jesus' answer joins a long stream of biblical and Jewish affirmations of the love of God and neighbor as the central response to God's saving act at the Exodus and covenant at Sinai. The two tables of the Decalogue, "duty to God" and "duty to the neighbor," functioned as such a summary, as did the Shema itself, here quoted by Jesus (Deut 6:4), so called because its initial word in Hebrew is "Hear" (Sh\u1d49ma). At least twice every day, every pious Jew recited this core statement of Israel's faith and ethics, which is still an integral part of the synagogue liturgy. In Deuteronomy, Moses calls for Israel to love God with all their heart, soul, and strength. While each of these terms expresses a distinctive aspect of human being,[34] the threefold expression is not a dividing up or parceling out of the human self; it means "with all that you are." As God is one, so, too, is authentic love of God. One who loves God is to hold nothing back, not to love God with only part—the "religious" or "spiritual" part—of one's being, but with one's whole self. There is a connection between monotheism and undivided love for God. If there are competing gods, the devotee cannot afford to give total devotion to any one of them. This is also true, of course, in modern secular society, unaware of its own polytheism. The Markan Jesus cites the text in roughly its LXX form, but with two modifications: (1) for the LXX's *dynamis* ("strength," "power") Mark has the synonym *ischyos*, "strength." *Dynamis* is an important theological term for Mark, even used as a name for God (see 5:30; 6:2, 5, 14; 9:1, 39; 12:24; 13:26; 14:62), but never used for human power. (2) To the biblical "heart, soul, and strength" Mark adds a fourth: "mind" (*dianoia*). Such

---

33. So R. Simlai [ca. 250] in *b. Mak.* 23b. Then in *b. Mak.* 24a follows: "R. Simlai said: 'Six hundred and thirteen commandments were given to Moses, 365 negative commandments, answering to the number of days of the year, and 248 positive commandments, answering to the number of man's members. Then David came and reduced them to eleven [Ps 15]. Then came Isaiah and reduced them to six [Isa 33:15]. Then came Micah and reduced them to three [Mic 6:8]. Then Isaiah came again, and reduced them to two, as it is said, 'Keep ye judgment and do righteousness' [Isa 56:1]. Then came Amos, and reduced them to one, as it is said, 'Seek me and live' [Amos 5:4]. Or one may then say, then came Habakkuk [2:4] and reduced them to one, as it is said, 'The righteous shall live by his faith.'" *Makkot* 23b–24a, cited in C. G. Montefiore and H. Loewe, eds., *A Rabbinic Anthology* (New York: World, 1963), 199.

34. Roughly speaking, "heart" (*levāv*) refers not so much to the emotions, but to the internal center of thinking and the will—one thinks with the heart and "feels" with the liver or kidneys; "soul" (*nefeš*) to the internal vital force, the "self"; "strength" (*me'ōd*) refers to physical weight and power and to one's material substance. In Jewish thought, each of these three refers to the person as a whole. The "heart," for instance, is not a "part," but integrates all dimensions of human existence.

language reflects Hellenistic Judaism, where the reasonableness of Jewish faith had been emphasized as part of its missionary outreach to thoughtful Gentiles, many of whom were attracted to the high ethics and monotheism of the Jewish community—both of which are also emphasized in this scene.

[31] The scribe had asked the traditional question of the one most important, all-embracing command. Jesus responds by giving not one but two, citing the command to love the neighbor found in Lev 19:18. While in its biblical context "neighbor" had originally referred to one's fellow Israelite, by the first century it was widely understood to refer to human beings as such; Jesus does not oppose a presumed "narrow" Judaism with his more "inclusive" understanding of neighbor. Although the substance of Jesus' "summary of the law" would not have seemed radical or surprising, his particular way of joining the command to love the neighbor found in Lev 19:18 with the Shema of Deut 6:4–5, and regarding the two in tandem as an inseparable unity as the primal commandment "above all else" is distinctive of Jesus. Though they remain two commands, they are inseparable: love of God cannot exist without love for all fellow human beings as its content. Love of humanity cannot exist without love of God as its basis. The two commands are not numbers "one" and "two" of the longer list, relatively more important than the others. They belong to the same order, so that the "first" commandment is not relatively more important than the "second," which is then more important than the third, and so on. The double commandment of love transcends all the others as their essence and meaning. Yet it is also true that "love" is not an extra-Torah "principle" that stands outside the Torah itself. The two commands are within the Torah, but together they are "above everything else" and reveal the meaning and orientation of the Torah as a whole.

[32–33] Only here in Mark does one of the religious authorities agree with Jesus. The scribe not only repeats Jesus' answer but amplifies it with allusions to Exod 20:3, Deut 4:35, and Isa 45:21. He then adds his own comment, significant both in its literary context in Mark and its narrative context in the courts of the temple, that the double command of love is "much more important than all whole burnt offerings and sacrifices." The statement, affirmed by the Markan Jesus (v. 34) but placed by the narrator in the mouth of a Jewish scribe rather than presented as a saying of Jesus himself, also addresses the burning issue of Mark's day about the continuation of authentic faith and worship after the destruction of the temple (see on 11:11–25). This statement, too, joins a significant stream of Jewish theology that, without denying the validity of sacrifice and the temple cultus, makes love of God and others far more important (cf. 1 Sam 15:22; Pss 50:14, 23; 51:17–19; Isa 1:12–17; Mic 6:6–8; and especially Hos 6:6, which has identical vocabulary to the scribe's response).

[34] The Shema and the kingdom of God had already been related in Jewish thought, where to recite the Shema and the related "first commandment" was to take upon oneself the yoke of the kingdom. Jesus' declaration that the

scribe is "not far" from the kingdom is a positive affirmation, made of no one else in the narrative. Yet the scribe is not [yet] "in" the kingdom, which for Mark is an eschatological reality, still future. The language of being "in" the kingdom is found only once in Mark, of its future consummation (14:25; cf. *Excursus: Kingdom of God* at 1:15). The scribe is in the same situation as Joseph of Arimathea, another Jewish leader who responds sympathetically to Jesus: he is prepared for the kingdom and can enter it when it comes (15:43). Yet neither the scribe nor Joseph are called "disciples," which depends not only on a positive evaluation of Jesus' teaching, but a response to Jesus himself.

Mark's insertion of the story at this point in the narrative makes five particularly Markan points:

(1) A *missionary / apologetic* point. Jesus' teaching is in continuity with the best of biblical and Jewish thought. If a Jewish scribe can commend Jesus' teaching, there is in principle no reason that Jews must reject him on the basis of his teaching.

(2) A *narrative and historical* point in the context of the temple's (imminent) destruction. The temple is not necessary for the continuing life of the people of God, since the community of faith can continue as a "house of prayer" where the command to love God and neighbor is central, and can thus do without the sacrificial apparatus of the temple. Mark's critique of the temple is in step with the best of biblical and Jewish thought. This is a crucial issue in the time of the composition of Mark, when the temple had just been destroyed or was about to be. Mark locates this story in the narrative context between Jesus' "cleansing" of the temple (11:12–17) and his prediction of the temple's destruction (13:1–2), in the courtyard of the temple itself, and in conversation with a scribe whose professional concern was often focused on the rules of the temple cultus.

(3) A *theological* point regarding the uniqueness of the one God. The repeated emphasis on the "one God" is peculiar to Mark, not picked up by either Matthew or Luke in their versions of this story. They rightly recognize that the response to the question about the "first commandment" need not cite the Shema, which is not really a "commandment." It is important to Mark, however, to emphasize that the Christian community's christological use of God-language for Jesus is not an infringement on monotheism, important not only in its dialogue with Judaism, but with the polytheistic pagan world.[35]

(4) A *christological* point about the authority of Jesus. This has been the underlying theme since 11:27: Jesus has succeeded in silencing all of his challengers, and he now shows that he is a master interpreter of the Scripture who is commended by a scribe.

---

35. Cf. *Excursus: Markan Christology* at 9:2; Boring, "God-Language," and Joel Marcus, *The Way of the Lord: Christological Exegesis of the Old Testament in the Gospel of Mark* (Louisville, Ky.: Westminster John Knox, 1992), 145–46.

(5) An *ethical* point. In good Jewish fashion it simply assumes that what is right is defined by the will of God made known by revelation, and that ethics is obedience to this command, not adherence to an ideal or principle. Like the Old Testament and Judaism, the Markan Jesus teaches no ethics as such, but response in faith and love to the act of God. The Markan Jesus does not teach ethical principles, but reaffirms and radicalizes the biblical call of God to obedience—ethics is discipleship, and the Markan ethic makes sense only to those who respond to the Markan Jesus' call to discipleship. Yet Mark's is not a sectarian ethic focused only on insiders, but makes sense to those who affirm the ethics of Judaism, and "the scope of the Markan neighborhood extends beyond the Christian community."[36]

12:35–37 Is David's Lord the "Son of David"?

12:35 And as Jesus was teaching in the temple, he was saying, "How is it that the scribes say that the Christ is the Son of David? 36 David himself said, speaking in the Holy Spirit, 'The Lord[a] said to my Lord, "Sit at my right hand, until I put your enemies under your feet." ' 37 David himself calls him 'Lord.' And how then is he his son?" And the large crowd was listening to him eagerly.

a. In the Hebrew text, the first "Lord" is the proper name of Israel's God, YHWH, and the second "lord" is *adōnāy*, the generic term for "lord," including kings and masters of slaves. The LXX translates both words as *kyrios,* "lord."

[35] The scene is not a separate thematic section, "Jesus' Teaching about Messiahship" or the like, but is an integral part of the present context. The change of topic may seem abrupt, but it has been prepared for in the narrative. Blind Bartimaeus had hailed Jesus *of Nazareth* as "Son of David" (see on 10:47), and the crowds had greeted the arrival of Jesus in Jerusalem with shouts about the "coming kingdom of our father David" (11:10). This scene is also appropriate to the historical context of Mark's readers, who confess that Jesus is the Messiah who has already come, yet the national and religious hopes embodied in Jerusalem and the temple have gone up in flames, or are about to be destroyed. The Romans seem to have triumphed, and those who believed in Jesus as the Messiah must have had to deal with the contradiction between the destiny of Jesus and the messianic hopes expressed by the "son of David" imagery. Was not the Messiah supposed to be the mighty Son of David who would establish the justice of God that triumphs over Roman power? How can Jesus be the fulfiller of these hopes if the Davidic image remains unfulfilled?

36. Via, *Ethics of Mark's Gospel,* 87; see his helpful book as a whole.

This question troubled Christian believers, and was confronted directly in the teaching of the Jewish scribes as a challenge to Christian faith. As the scribes had objected that Jesus could not be the Messiah because Elijah had not yet come (see on 9:11), so the scribes teach that Jesus could not be the Messiah because the Davidic hope remains unfilled. The issue is whether the Messiah as God's agent will establish God's justice in Davidic terms, as the righteous king empowered by God to bring in God's kingdom (in the tradition of Isa 9:2–7; 11:1–9; *Pss. Sol.* 17.31–51), or whether Christology is conceived in Markan apocalyptic terms as the suffering, dying, and rising one who will return in glory to establish God's eschatological kingdom.

At the narrative level, the issue is not Jesus' own identity as the Christ, which has not yet been publicly disclosed. Nor does Jesus introduce the subject to respond to a challenge about his own Davidic descent, which is not an issue in Mark. There is no indication in Mark that the author or his community contends that Jesus is descended from David, and that this was disputed by Mark's opponents. The issue is the general image and mission associated with messianic faith: Son of David empowered by God to bring in the kingdom "from below," or suffering Son of Man who will return from heaven to establish God's kingdom "from above." The events of 66–70 had not discredited Davidic messianism as such, but had made it impossible to believe in *Jesus* as Messiah in traditional Davidic terms. The Markan Jesus challenges this image of the Messiah as such; it is the scribes, Jesus' opponents, who falsely designate the Messiah as Son of David. The Markan Jesus does not acknowledge that the Messiah is in fact the "Son of David," as though the only issue were "how" in the sense of "in what way," or "to what extent" this is so. "How" (*pōs*) is here a challenge to the idea as such, as in 3:23 (cf. Job 25:4; 33:12 LXX).

[36] The Markan Jesus cites Ps 110:1 (slightly conflated with Ps 8:6; "as a footstool" becomes "under"). This is the most-quoted christological text in the New Testament (Mark 12:36; 14:62; Matt 22:44; 26:64; Luke 20:42–43; 22:69; Acts 2:34–35; Rom 8:34; 1 Cor 15:25; Eph 1:20; Col 3:1; Heb 1:3, 13; 8:1; 10:12). In its Old Testament context, a court prophet delivers an oracle declaring that Yahweh invites the Judean king to sit at his right hand while he (Yahweh) defeats the king's enemies. The "right hand" is the place of honor and power (Exod 15:6; 1 Kgs 2:19; Pss 45:9; 80:17; Matt 25:33–34). Since in the ancient Near East orientation was toward the east, "right hand" also meant "south," and so the imagery also pictures the Judean king enthroned in his palace, to the south of the temple where God himself is enthroned. In the Judaism of Jesus' and Mark's day, Ps 110 was not generally understood as a messianic text.[37] Early Christian teachers interpreting their Scripture in chris-

---

37. See a more nuanced discussion of this in France, *Gospel of Mark*, 486, and the literature he cites.

tological terms saw Ps 110:1 as portraying the Christ-event in which God had exalted Jesus to heaven and declared him to be Lord (cf., e.g., Phil 2:5–11; see *Excursus: Mark and the Scripture* at 14:52). In accord with first-century conceptions, David himself, speaking as a prophet, is thought to be the author of the psalm. This is the meaning of *en tō pneumati tō hagiō*, "in the Holy Spirit." Not only is he "inspired," but like the prophets he has a vision of the heavenly world and / or the future (cf. Acts 2:30–31; Josephus, *Ant.* 6.166), where he sees one he calls "my Lord," identified by Christian interpreters as "the Christ." It is not clear whether the Markan text pictures David as looking into heaven where he beholds the ("preexistent"; cf. on 1:2–3) Lord, or whether he looks into the future and sees the post-Easter Lord enthroned at God's right hand. Probably Mark does not have or want conceptual precision on such matters. The point here is that this one, who has been exalted to heaven as Lord of all, is addressed by David as "Lord" and thus cannot be his "Son." Biological descent is not at issue; the point is how the Christ is understood—as a David-like one who will fulfill Israel's national hopes, or as the transcendent Lord who will come again as Son of Man.

12:38–40 Woe to the Scribes

12:38 And in his teaching he was saying, "Watch out for the scribes [,] who[a] like to walk around in long robes and greetings in the marketplaces 39 and the prominent seats in the synagogues and places of honor at the banquets, 40 [the ones] who devour widows' houses, which they encourage[b] by saying long prayers. In the judgment they will receive the more severe sentence.

a. The Greek participial construction can indicate a particular group of scribes, not the whole class of scribes as such, which is indicated in English by the presence or absence of a comma after scribes and by omitting the bracketed words. The preceding pericope has shown that not all scribes are bad. Judaism, too, had criticism of insincere and ostentatious religious teachers. Yet the tendency of originally restrictive judgments to be generalized, and the generally negative picture of "the scribes" (not just some of them) as the chief opponents of Jesus throughout the Markan narrative suggests that here too the condemnation is intended to be global—with an occasional exception such as found in the preceding pericope.

b. There are three possibilities, each grammatically correct, for understanding the meaning of *prophasei*:[38] (1) related to the preceding clause, "as a covering for," i.e., "to *cover it* [taking the widows' houses] *up* with long prayers" or "*to facilitate it* [taking the widows' houses] with long prayers; (2) related to the subject, "the scribes," to mean "for appearance' sake," "for show," "insincerely"; (3) related to the prayers, "offer long,

38. Cf. Robert G. Bratcher and Eugene A. Nida, *A Translator's Handbook on the Gospel of Mark* (Leiden: Brill, 1961), 392.

unreal prayers," "make long but insincere prayers." The context suggests a connection between taking the widows' houses and the long prayers, i.e., they pray in a way that attracts vulnerable widows to them as apparently pious and trustworthy people, then take advantage of them.

The speech against the scribes appears to be a Markan excerpt from a more extensive tradition represented in Q and elsewhere (cf. Matt 23:1–36; Luke 11:37–52). In its context, this brief portrayal of the scribes' constant courting of public approval is not merely an incidental bit of Christian "anticlerical" propaganda or condemnation of external showy religion, but fits into the context in which the authority claimed by the scribes is contrasted with the authentic authority of Jesus. This last public teaching contrasts the authority of Jesus and that of the scribes, as did his first public appearance (1:21–27). The charges against the scribes are traditional, in the realm of general ethics, not their particular plot against Jesus, which is known to both Jesus and the disciples, including the readers (8:31; 10:33).

[38–39] The warning to "watch out for" the scribes is verbally identical to that against the Pharisees and Herodians of 8:15 and the warning against false prophets of 13:5 (*blepete;* see also 13:9, 23, 33). While in the narrative setting the warning is given to the crowds, the Markan readers hear it as the directive of Jesus to beware of the Jewish scribes of their own time, the synagogue teachers who cultivate and receive popular respect, while Christian teachers such as the author himself are considered sectarian or apostate. The Jewish teachers have special seats in the Sabbath worship in the synagogue and the Sabbath festive meals (cf. Luke 14:7–11; Jas 2:2–4), while the Markan churches meet in private homes on a different day not recognized as holy. The "long robes" (*stolais*) are not liturgical garments (analogous to a pulpit or choir robe) or the Greek philosopher's robe, that is, not a distinctive scribal costume, but the festive religious garments worn on special occasions. The scribes wear them every day, in order to impress people with their piety. The "long robes" may also have developed a quasi-official function, signaling prayer, making a legal pronouncement, or absolving one from a vow.[39] Greetings in the market places were taken seriously in social protocol (like salutes in the military), so that inferiors in the social scale were expected to greet first. Like the Gentile rulers of 10:42–45, they love the image of authority and position. Jesus' disciples and those who teach in the Christian community are to avoid such ostentation.

[40] Widows represent the vulnerable members of society; they had no inheritance rights in first-century Jewish culture, and most had to rely on family or community welfare programs. To ensure their well-being was the respon-

---

39. "Rabbi Gamaliel dismounted from his donkey, wrapped himself in his robe, seated himself, and absolved the man from his vow" (b. Ned 77b Bar).

sibility of the community as a whole, specified in the Torah. Neglecting this responsibility was severely condemned by the prophets, since God was their ultimate advocate (e.g., Exod 22:22; Deut 10:18; 14:29; 27:19; Pss 68:5; 146:9; Isa 1:17; Jer 7:6; 22:3; 49:11; Ezek 22:7; Zech 7:10; Mal 3:5). The Mal 3:5 reference may be especially important here, since it pictures the Lord who will suddenly come to his temple and judge those who oppress the vulnerable, including the widows. It is not clear just how the scribes "devoured" the widows' houses, that is, cheated them of their property. They may have become trustees or managers of their estates, then misused their position of trust. Scribes apparently could not directly charge fees for their services, but their positions facilitated the financial exploitation of those without legal defense. However it was carried out, the charge that *scribes* exploited *widows* was an extremely serious charge in a Jewish context, which had great respect for the Torah and those charged with teaching it, and great responsibility for caring for the defenseless, symbolized by the widow. The evil of the scribes will be immediately contrasted with the authentic devotion to God by the poor widow.

12:41–44 True Piety in Contrast to False

12:41 And he sat down opposite the treasury and was observing how the crowd was putting money into the treasury. And many rich people were putting in large amounts. 42 And one[a] poor widow came and put in two lepta, which make a quadrans.[b] 43 And he called his disciples and said to them, "Amen[c] I say to you, this poor widow has put in more than all those putting money into the treasury; 44 for all put in from their surplus, but she from her deprivation has put in everything she had, her whole life."[d]

a. Greek has no indefinite article, so *tis* ("someone," "a certain one") or the numeral *heis* ("one") can be used as its simple equivalent (as 9:17; 10:17). Here it is better to preserve the translation "one," in contrast both to the "many" rich people and as parallel to the "one" exceptional scribe of 12:28.

b. It is difficult to translate ancient coinage into modern equivalencies (see note *c* on *denarii* at 6:37). The *leptos* was the smallest Greek copper coin, the *quadrans* the smallest Roman coin. Two *lepta* were very roughly equivalent to 1/64 of a denarius, which would be somewhat like two half-dollar coins in contemporary U.S. currency (again, calculated very roughly). While a very small amount, it is more than the traditional translation "penny." The traditional "widow's mite" derives from the fourteenth-century Wycliffe translation of this passage, where it represented a Flemish copper coin of very small value, and from there into the KJV, though there was never an English coin called a "mite." The influence of the KJV led to the "mite" as representing a small amount of anything.

c. On *amēn*, see note *g* at 3:28.

d. *Bios*, "life," can also mean "living" in the sense of the resources one has to live on, as in "making a living," and by extension all one's "property," as in Luke 15:12, 30. "Life" is chosen here to correlate with Jesus' teaching in 8:35–37 (where "life" is *psychē*).

[41–42] Having concluded his teaching in the temple, Jesus sits in an area of the temple court known as "the treasury" and observes the crowd placing their gifts in the offering receptacles. The narrator is not interested, however, in how Jesus knew how much each person had given, but in the contrast itself: rich and poor, many and one, much money and two lepta.

[43–44] Attention is focused on Jesus' statement. Except to explain that the woman gave out of her poverty and the others from their wealth, Jesus' declaration that the woman has given more than all the others is not elaborated. The narrator makes nothing explicit, but the reader's imagination is provoked in several directions. The Greek may mean that the woman not only gave "more" than any one of the rich people, but more than all of them together. That she is a poor widow evokes the image in the preceding pericope of scribes who devour widows' houses (see comments on v. 40). Is she poor precisely because the religious leaders have taken advantage of her vulnerable economic position? Does the Markan Jesus lament the foolishness of her deed, duped by the scribes to give her whole living to their false program?[40] They have given from their surplus and will not miss the gift. She has given her whole life. Though Mark spells none of this out, the reader thinks of the rich man who made the great refusal (10:17–22), of the disciples (including the readers) who are called to give their lives for Jesus and the gospel (8:34–9:1), and of Jesus himself, who does give his life for others (10:45). Although Jesus does not explicitly commend the woman, he obviously holds her up as an example, recognizing and affirming the "small" acts of the "little" people from God's own perspective. In this regard, it is not distinctively Christian; there are Jewish and pagan parallels, and Jesus here takes up wholesome Jewish teaching the scribes have perverted.[41] The woman illustrates the unity of love for God and others (vv. 28–34); her gift is at once to God, and for all Israel in supporting the temple where offerings are made in behalf of the people as a whole.

In and of itself, the story speaks of wholehearted, single-minded devotion to God, especially in the realm of giving one's money for God's work. By placing it in this context, Mark has given it a particular set of meanings. It shows that Jesus and the Christian teachers represented by Mark do not consider the temple inherently wrong. This story affirms the temple offerings; Mark has no "temple polemic" as such. Rather, the author is responding to the known event of the temple's (impending?) destruction. This story is not brought into con-

---

40. Some exegetes oriented to liberation theology or postcolonial hermeneutic, uncomfortable with Mark's seeming approval of supporting the temple establishment, so argue. See, e.g., Addison G. Wright, "The Widow's Mites: Praise or Lament?—A Matter of Context," *CBQ* 44 (1982): 256–65; Myers, *Binding the Strong Man*, 320–22; R. S. Sugirtharajah, "The Widow's Mites Revalued," *ExpTim* 103 (1991–1992): 42–43; Horsley, *Whole Story*, 258 n. 7.

41. Cf. the often-cited rabbinic parallels, Pesch, *Markusevangelium*, 2:263; Gnilka, *Markus*, 2:177.

junction with 11:17 and the temple as a refuge for "robbers." Mark's point here
is that the *robbed* widows, in contrast to the *robber* scribes, are those who truly
serve God.

13:1–4 Leaving the Temple; Its Coming Destruction

The chapter division is here especially unfortunate. Verses 1–2 are the conclusion of Tuesday's "great day in the temple," which began at 11:27, and should
not be separated from the preceding section, while verses 3–4 respond to Jesus'
announcement about the coming destruction of the temple, thus setting up
Jesus' discourse in 5–37.

> 13:1 And as he is leaving the temple, one of his disciples says to him,
> "Teacher, look! What stones and what buildings!" 2 And Jesus said to him,
> "Do you see these great buildings? Absolutely not one stone will be left
> here upon another. Every last one will be thrown down."[a] 3 And as he was
> seated[b] on the Mount of Olives opposite the temple, Peter, James, John,
> and Andrew were asking him privately, 4 "Tell us, when will this[c] hap-
> pen, and what will be the sign when all these things[c] are going to be[d]
> brought to an end?"

a. The double negative *ou mē,* which intensifies the negation, is found twice in this
declaration, before the verbs "left" and "thrown down." This is represented by
"absolutely" and "every last one," which are not in the Greek text.
    b. See note *a* on *kathēmai* at 4:1, in each case signaling a major teaching discourse
of Jesus that forms the center of a major unit of the Gospel.
    c. The singular "this" and plural "these things" are both expressed by the same Greek
word, *tauta.* While *tauta* is often used for the singular, translation and interpretation
require a decision as to whether the author distinguishes the first instance from the second, i.e., whether there are two questions or two versions of a single question. In the latter case, both instances of *tauta* should be translated the same.
    d. *Mellē* can (1) mean "about to be" in the sense of "to be at the point of," (2) mean
"must be" in the sense of "is destined to be," or (3) be a periphrasis for the simple future,
"will be," "going to be" (see Bauer and Danker, BDAG, 627–28).

[13:1] Jesus leaves the temple for the first time since his arrival in 11:27. It
is a definitive exit; Jesus will not return. Mark explicitly states "leaving the *temple,*" for the perceptive reader evoking the image of the "glory of Yahweh" (the
presence of God) leaving the temple and pausing on the Mount of Olives before
the final departure (Ezek 10:18–19; 11:22–23). In the next scene Jesus, too, will
pause on the Mount of Olives. Josephus reports that several divine signs
appeared during the war, including a voice from within the temple announcing
"We are departing hence" (Josephus, *War* 6.300).

The unnamed disciple's exclamation about the magnificence of the temple is not merely the response of a country yokel in the presence of the big city's buildings. Nor is it inappropriate at this juncture in the story, as though he has been in Jerusalem some days, including three visits to the temple (11:11, 15, 27) and only now notices its splendor. The temple was indeed an impressive architectural wonder (see on 11:15–16); such comments could be made at any time, even by residents of the city. The narrative function for including the statement, and precisely here, however, is to set up Jesus' response.

[2] Jesus' public ministry ends with a double reference to the temple. In the preceding scene, he had commended the poor widow who had given her all to it. On leaving, he now predicts its total destruction. That the temple was burned by Titus's armies, not torn down, is sometimes offered as evidence that Jesus' statement was a real prediction given in advance that does not reflect the actual event, or that Mark must be dated prior to 70 C.E. But Caesar's command to level the city was carried out; after the fire, the temple was razed. However, since the language is stereotypical, it cannot be used as evidence for either a pre- or post-70 date for Mark or the composition of the discourse. Although these particular words cannot with certainty be attributed to Jesus, it is likely that he spoke against (the leadership and abuses of) the temple, since he stood in the prophetic tradition of such critique (cf. Mic 3:12; Jer 7:14; 26:6), and the New Testament contains various indirect indications of such statements (11:15–17; 14:58; 15:29; Acts 6:14). When the charge of destroying the temple comes up at his trial (14:58) and crucifixion (15:29), readers will know what the Markan Jesus "really" said.

[3] Every visitor to Jerusalem knows the fabulous view of the Temple Mount from the Mount of Olives. The author or his tradition may also have known this, or may have located the apocalyptic discourse here on the basis of his interpretation of the Bible, where the Mount of Olives had apocalyptic overtones (cf. Ezek 11:22–23; Zech 14:4–5). For Mark, too, the "mountain" is the place of secret revelation (cf. 3:13; 9:2). The typical pattern of Jesus' instruction has been public, enigmatic statements followed by explanations to his disciples in private (4:1–9 // 10–20; 7:1–15 // 16–17; 10:1–9 // 10). Here, it is not the Twelve, but the inner circle of Peter, James, and John, which here includes Andrew (see *Excursus: Crowds, Followers, Disciples, and the Twelve* at 6:6). The last word of the discourse opens up what is said to this inner circle to "all"—including especially the readers.

[4] Jesus' prediction had been clear and specific, but the disciples' response to it is somewhat ambiguous (see note *c* above). It seems best to understand the disciples as asking two questions. The first asks about a single event, when the destruction of the temple will occur. In their second question, the plural form of *tauta*, along with the addition of "all," refers to an all-embracing complex of events; the *tauta panta* of verse 4 corresponds to the same phrase in verse 30

that looks back on both the terrors of history and the Parousia of the Son of Man. This is also signaled by the different verbs in the two questions, the first having the future form of the most common verb "to be" (*estai*) while the second has a verb related to "end" (*synteleisthai* from *syntellō*; cf. *telos* "end," 13:7, 13). Mark here uses precisely the same vocabulary as Dan 12:6–7, which combines the question "when?" with "all these things" and the verb "be brought to an end." Matthew rightly understood the second question to deal with eschatology and made this explicit (Matt 24:3). In Mark the disciples' question does not yet have a specific eschatological program in mind, as though the first *tauta* referred only to the historical event of the destruction of the temple and the second *tauta panta* referred specifically to the coming of the Son of Man.[42] Yet the first *tauta* and the second *tauta panta* are not to be identified; the disciples' dual question does involve both history and eschatology, and already raises the issue of what sort of connection there might be between the temple's destruction and the eschatological end, although it does not do this explicitly.[43] Their question is not for information, but already presupposes some sort of connection between the tragic events of the 66–70 war and the end of the age, and serves as the foil for Jesus' answer given in verses 5–37. This connection did not have to be made for Mark's readers; the frightful events of their own experience had already raised this question. For them, the destruction of the Holy City and its temple was a given or imminent reality. For them, the two questions pointed to a single nexus of reality, "the destruction of the temple and all that goes with it," and they wondered how the destruction of the temple is related to the end of the age. Is the destruction of the temple itself the sign of the immediate end? The Markan Jesus addresses this double question, with verses 5–23 addressing the first and verses 24–27 the second, concluding with instructions and warnings on the all-embracing question "When?" While the Markan Jesus does end up giving indications of the readers location on God's timetable, and insights on how to relate the past or anticipated demise of the temple and the future appearance of the Son of Man, he does not immediately or directly address the disciples' request for a "sign." *Sēmeion* is a negative word in Mark's theological vocabulary, found only in 8:11–12, in the Pharisees' request (refused; no sign

---

42. It is important to distinguish two questions, without making their content too specific in advance. Cf. Moloney, *Mark: Commentary*, 253. The somewhat vague questions serve to set up the specific response of Jesus addressed over the heads of the disciples to the situation of the Markan readers (v. 37).

43. A minority of interpreters regard the question as entirely about the destruction of the temple, with no eschatological dimensions. N. T. Wright, *Jesus and the Victory of God* (Christian Origins and the Question of God 2; Minneapolis: Fortress, 1996), 339–68, understands both the question and all Jesus' answer to deal only with the destruction of the temple and Jesus' vindication, not with the Parousia. France, *Gospel of Mark*, 500–507, argues the question is a single inquiry about the destruction of the temple, to which Jesus responds in 5b–31, then adding 32–37 addressing the time of the Parousia, which was not involved in the disciples' question.

will be given this generation), and 13:22, where *false* Messiahs and prophets deliver signs.

13:5–37 Central Discourse of Part 2: Historical Troubles and the Coming of the Son of Man

Interpreting the Apocalyptic Discourse[44]

The following preliminary statements are important for understanding the discourse, which must be read and understood as a whole. Comments on individual texts will be given below explaining and supporting these general perspectives.

- *The setting of this discourse in the narrative, including its relation to the parable discourse of 4:1–34, is important for interpreting not only the apocalyptic discourse itself, but the narrative as a whole.*[45] Mark places an extensive discourse in the center of each of his two narrative sections, interpreting the meaning of the whole (see Introduction 2.). This discourse is even more fundamental to the whole narrative than its counterpart in chapter 4, in that it comes in the climactic final position, is an unbroken monologue with no dialogue or change of location, and has no transitional formulae such as *kai elegen autois* ("and he was saying to them"). Except for the narrator's parenthetical "let the reader understand" of verse 14, it is absolutely uninterrupted, the longest speech in Mark. It is thus not the case that the Markan Jesus decides to pause

---

44. Use of the traditional term "apocalyptic discourse" is here continued for convenience, without claiming that the discourse, which has some apocalyptic elements and perspectives, is generically an apocalypse. That it is a narrated speech, rather than a vision report, is only one of the significant differences from traditional apocalyptic. Cf. Robbins, *Jesus the Teacher*, 173–78, who points out the similarities to the Old Testament "farewell discourse" and the Hellenistic "temple dialogue." There is a sense in which Mark 13 is in fact *anti*-apocalyptic, opposing the apocalyptic speculations of the "false prophets" of Mark's time (cf. Frans Neirynck, "Le discours anti-apocalyptique de Mc. XIII," *ETL* 45 [1969]: 154–64). Yet the apocalyptic perspective should not be minimized.

45. See especially Willem S. Vorster, "Literary Reflections on Mark 13:5–37: A Narrated Speech of Jesus," *Neot* (1987): 203–22.

here for a bit of apocalyptic teaching. While it goes too far to claim that Mark as such is a "narrative apocalypse,"[46] the narrative as a whole is conceived in an apocalyptic framework, with the ministry, death, and resurrection of Jesus as the defining segment of a history that extends from creation to eschaton. Mark places the discourse not after the resurrection, its "natural" place,[47] but at a key point *within* the narrative, where it serves both to complement the other extended discourse revolving around the seed parables and to reject claims to post-Easter revelations.

• The seed parables have often been interpreted as illustrating the gradual growth of the kingdom in history (continuity) rather than portraying the kingdom of God as an intervention that ends history (discontinuity). Posing the alternatives in this manner is not helpful, and not in accord with Mark's theology. Mark expects history to end with the sudden coming of the Son of Man to bring the kingdom (13:26; 9:1). At the Markan level, the parables, including the Seed Growing Secretly (4:26–29) and the Mustard Seed (4:30–32), must be interpreted in that framework. But even the seed parables, interpreted by the hermeneutic current in the older liberal theology in relation to the parable of the Leaven (Matt 13:33; Luke 13:20–21), are not parables of slow, gradual growth. The Mustard Seed pictures only the small beginning and the amazing end, not a long and gradual period of growth. Nonetheless, the insights of old liberalism are important in emphasizing that the future apocalyptic kingdom of Mark is not an utterly new discontinuity with the life of Jesus and the life of the church. For Mark, too, the word of the kingdom was planted by Jesus and continues to be planted by Christian preachers and teachers. And when the apocalyptic kingdom comes, it will not be

46. So Norman Perrin, *The New Testament, an Introduction: Proclamation and Parenesis, Myth and History* (New York: Harcourt Brace Jovanovich, 1974), 144–45. The revision by his student Dennis Duling suggests an "apocalyptic drama" or "apocalyptic myth" (Dennis C. Duling and Norman Perrin, *The New Testament: Proclamation and Parenesis, Myth and History* [3d ed.; Fort Worth: Harcourt, Brace, & World, 1994], 295, 323). See also Kee, *Community of the New Age*, 65–71 and passim. Cf. Adela Yarbro Collins, *Is Mark's Gospel a Life of Jesus? The Question of Genre* (Milwaukee: Marquette University Press, 1990), 63: "history in an eschatological or apocalyptic sense." For a vigorous argument against understanding Mark in apocalyptic categories and an interpretation of the Gospel as a political statement opposing Roman rule, see Horsley, *Whole Story*, especially ch. 6, "The Struggle against Roman Rule," 121–48.

47. In later gnosticizing literature, the risen Jesus gathers a few chosen disciples on a mountain, typically the Mount of Olives, giving instruction about eschatological secrets. Cf. the *Apocryphon of John, Sophia Jesu Christi, Gospel of Eve, Pistis Sophia* (ch. 2), and *Apocalypse of Peter.*

utterly discontinuous with all that has been, but will maintain continuity with what is already mysteriously, paradoxically present in Jesus and his disciples. But it will not simply grow out of their work; the Son of Man will come from the transcendent world to bring it to consummation.

- *The apocalyptic discourse is the only place in the narrative where the Markan Jesus predicts the future lying beyond the narrative itself, the present and future of the readers.* Only here do we have a direct reflection of the events of the author's and readers' own time. The discourse presents Jesus to the reader as a reliable predictor of the future. This is important for the tense and uncertain times in which the Markan community lives. Within the narrative itself, Jesus had said he would be betrayed by one of his own (14:18–21), and so it had happened (14:10–11; 43–46). Jesus predicted the details of his trial and death, and they happened as predicted (8:31; 9:31; 10:32–34; chs. 14–15). The reader knows more than the characters in the narrative, namely that some things Jesus has predicted in the plotted narrative have already happened after Mark 16:8. The unfaithful disciples have met the risen Christ in Galilee (16:7) and have become faithful disciples (13:9–13) empowered by the Holy Spirit (1:8; 13:11) who have been made into "fishers for people" (1:17) in the service of Christ. The bridegroom has been taken away, and they do fast (2:20). James and John have died as martyrs (10:39). The preaching of the gospel in the whole world is indeed under way (13:10; 14:9). That Jesus would build a new temple not made with hands and open to all peoples is now being realized (cf. 14:58; 11:17). Thus the readers are prepared to accept the picture of their own ultimate future in chapter 13 from one who has shown he knows the future.

- *This discourse contains substantial pre-Markan elements, including some that go back to Jesus, but as it stands the discourse is a Markan composition.*[48] The interpreter's primary focus should therefore be on the address to Markan readers in their situation ca. 70 C.E., not on the original meaning of sayings of the historical Jesus and / or the oracle of a Jewish or Christian prophet included and reinterpreted in the discourse. Nonetheless, the pre-Markan

---

48. The most persuasive and detailed case for considerable pre-Markan content with a thoroughly Markan form is made by Jan Lambrecht, *Die Redaktion der Markus-Apokalypse: Literarische Analyse und Strukturuntersuchung* (AnBib 28; Rome: Päpstliches Bibelinstitut, 1967), 293 and passim.

elements in the text, to the extent that they can be identified, provide an important aspect of interpreting the final form of the text.

• *Mark 13:5b–37 resembles the New Testament book of Revelation
more than it resembles anything elsewhere in Mark or the other
Gospels.* This is one indication that Mark here incorporates and
reinterprets a Christian prophetic oracle current in his situation.
This oracle was set forth as a revelation of the risen Jesus interpreting the events of 66–70 C.E. as signs of the imminent end and
the Parousia of the Son of Man. This oracle may itself have been
a reinterpretation of a Jewish prophetic oracle evoked by
Caligula's 40 C.E. attempt to place his image in the Jerusalem temple.[49] Mark's composition of the apocalyptic discourse and insertion of it into the narrative presents it as words of the pre-Easter
Jesus rather than post-Easter revelations from the risen Lord. In
this framework the teaching of the earthly Jesus serves to correct
the misinterpretations of such post-Easter Christian prophets.
Mark presents the earthly Jesus as having already warned his followers that they should not be deceived by such "prophecies"—
the Son of Man will return soon enough, within their own
generation, but not immediately in connection with the destruction
of the temple.[50] Mark's main point is not speculative apocalyptic
("When will the end come?"), but a matter of the worldwide Christian mission, for which God provides time (v. 10). The missionary
task, not the Parousia, lies in the immediate future of the disciples.

---

49. For elaboration of this widespread view and evidence and argument for it, see Boring, *Continuing Voice of Jesus*, 236–46. For a comprehensive history and critique of the many permutations
of this theory, see George R. Beasley-Murray, *Jesus and the Last Days: The Interpretation of the
Olivet Discourse* (Peabody, Mass.: Hendrickson, 1993). Egon Brandenburger also surveys the
attempts to reconstruct the pre-Markan apocalypse, concluding that Mark adopted and adapted a
written document (13:7–8, 14–20, 24–27) that originated in Christian circles in Jerusalem after the
beginning of the war in 66 C.E., though including memories and motifs from the Caligula crisis of
40 C.E. (*Markus 13 und die Apokalyptik* [FRLANT 134; Göttingen: Vandenhoeck & Ruprecht,
1984], 22–50). Among those who argue for the interpretation pursued here, that Mark reinterprets
an oracle of early Christian prophecy, cf. Lloyd Gaston, *No Stone on Another: Studies in the Significance of the Fall of Jerusalem in the Synoptic Gospels* (NovTSup 23; Leiden: Brill, 1970);
Grundmann, *Markus*, 259–66.

50. Thus, e.g., Moloney, *Mark: Commentary*, 256, overstates a valid point when arguing that
Mark "established that a long history will follow the fall of Jerusalem." Mark is concerned to separate the fall of Jerusalem from the expectation of the *immediate* end, not to set his own time within
a generations-long history of salvation.

• *The discourse is structured by the disciples' duplex question and Jesus' duplex response. This structure is important for interpretation.*

The relative length of each part indicates Mark's emphasis:

A   Disciples' question: *When*? (4a)

  B   Disciples' question: *Sign*? (4b)

  B¹   Jesus' answer: *Non-signs and Sign* (5b–27)

A¹   Jesus' answer: *When* (28–37)

Jesus' response dealing with the "sign" is by far the longest, and is divided into two parts, "historical troubles" (5b–23), which are *not* the sign of the end, and "cosmic events" (24–27), which will signal the immediate end, thus giving the following outline:[51]

   I. *The end is not yet*: current events are not signs of the imminent end (5b–23).

  II. *The end will come*: cosmic signs will signal the Parousia of the Son of Man (24–27).

 III. *When*? Two parables communicate the dialectic of knowing and not knowing (28–37).

13:5–23 I. The End Is Not Yet

13:5 Then Jesus began to say to them, "Watch out,[a] that no one leads you astray. **6** Many will come in my name, saying 'I am,'[b] and will lead many astray. **7** When you hear of wars and reports of wars, do not be alarmed; such things must happen, but the end is still to come. **8** For nation will rise against nation, and kingdom against kingdom; there will be earthquakes in various places; there will be famines. This is the[c] beginning of the 'labor pains.'[d]

9 "Watch out for yourselves; for they will hand you over[e] to councils and you will be beaten in synagogues and you will stand before governors and kings because of me, to offer testimony to them. **10** And the gospel must first be proclaimed to all the nations.[f] **11** And when they bring you to trial and hand you over,[e] do not worry beforehand about what to say, but say whatever is given you in that hour, for it is not you who will be speaking, but the Holy Spirit. **12** And brother will hand over[e] brother

---

51. Cf. the careful study of Dyer, *Prophecy*, who likewise argues that the discourse has elements that go back to the pre-Easter Jesus and includes additions and modifications by Christian prophets, and that the turning point from the present of the author and his community to its own future is found at v. 24.

to death, and a father his child, and children will rise up against parents and cause them to be put to death, 13 and you will be hated by all because of my name. But the one who endures to the end will be saved.

14 "But when you see the 'abomination of desolation'^d standing where he^g must not (let the reader understand), those in Judea must flee to the mountains. 15 The one on the housetop must not go down or go inside to take anything out of the house, 16 and the one in the field must not turn back to get a coat. 17 How terrible it will be for pregnant women and nursing mothers in those days! 18 Pray that it will not be in winter. 19 For those days will be 'tribulation'^d of a sort that has not happened from the beginning of creation that God created until now, and will never be in the future. 20 And if the Lord had not cut short the days, no one would survive. But for the sake of the elect whom he has chosen, he has cut short the days. 21 And if anyone says to you then, 'Look! Here is the Christ!' or 'Look! There he is!' do not believe it. 22 For false Messiahs^h and false prophets will appear and perform signs and wonders to lead astray the elect, if that were possible. 23 But you watch out; I have told you everything in advance.

a. *Blepete* occurs four times in the discourse (vv. 5, 9, 23, 33), as thematic and structural markers. It is the second-person plural imperative of the common word "to see" (*blepō*), but in such contexts must be translated with the meaning "watch out [for]," "beware," "be careful." Cf. the same word in 4:24, 8:15.

b. "I am" literally translates *egō eimi*, which can be an identification formula "I am he / it," "It is I," colloquially "It's me," but also has a technical meaning better preserved by the literal translation (see commentary below).

c. Some translations (e.g., RSV, NRSV, ESV, CEV, NET) insert "but" or "only" here. While this is true to the meaning (see commentary), there is no such word in the Greek text. Word order does place emphasis on *archē*, "beginning."

d. "Labor pains," "abomination of desolation," and "tribulation" are placed in quotation marks to indicate they had become traditional, quasi-technical terms of eschatological expectation in Mark's setting and that of the modern English reader as well. *Ōdines*, "labor pains," had become a metaphor for the terrors of the last days just before the birth of the new age. A more precise translation of *to bdelygma tēs erēmōseōs* would be "the sacrilege that makes (the temple) desolate," i.e., causes the temple to be deserted because it has been profaned. Since the phrase was a biblical expression (Dan 9:27; 11:31; 12:11) that had already become traditional, as has "abomination of desolation" in English, it is better to retain the somewhat strange expression in the English translation. Similarly, "tribulation" is retained for *thlipsis*, which could also be rendered simply "trouble" or "distress," but which had attained a quasi-technical sense in eschatological contexts.

e. On *paradidōmi*, see commentary at 9:31.

f. *Eis panta ta ethnē* can also be translated "in (or among) all the Gentiles."

g. "Abomination" is neuter; the pronoun is masculine.

h. The phrase "false Messiahs" is omitted from D and a few other Greek MSS, as well as two MSS of the Old Latin translation, but its overwhelming MSS attestation indicates the phrase is probably original. The interpretation advocated in this commentary would be strengthened if the words could be considered a later addition; though possible, the MSS weighs heavily against it. It may be, however, that the few scribes who omitted the words considered them problematic because they interpreted the text in the same way proposed here. On the other hand, if not original, the phrase may have been added by scribes on the basis of Matt 24:5.

The narrative now becomes directly relevant to the time of the reader, as the Markan Jesus looks beyond the plotted narrative and speaks directly to the Markan readership, predicting the times in which they live. The "tribulation" that precedes the coming of the Son of Man is described in detail, but not the Parousia itself. The emphasis is on the this-worldly time of the reader, not the apocalyptic finale.

[5–8] The first word is not a statement answering the question "When?" but an imperative, *blepete* ("Watch out"), setting the tone of the whole speech, which contains twenty imperatives. The keynote of the speech is not prediction, but warning. "Watch out" recurs at verse 9 and verse 23, where it concludes the section, then in verse 33 with its synonym *agrypneite,* is then continued with a form of *gregoreo* ("stay alert") in verse 35, which then appears as the final word to "all" in verse 37. Here the disciples are urged to "see," corresponding to the call to "hear" in the parable discourse (4:3, 9, 23, 24; cf. 4:12; 8:18, where these are combined). The repeated "lead astray" had become almost a technical term for the activity of false prophets and false teachers who led Israel aside from the path marked out for them by God (see Deut 4:19; 13:5; Hos 4:12; Mic 3:5; Isa 28:7; cf. 2 Thess 2:11; 2 Tim 3:13; Rev 13:14–15) and is thus related to the Markan imagery of the "way of the Lord" (cf. *Excursus: The Way* at 1:3).

The "many" deceivers are often identified with the "false Messiahs" of verse 22 (see below on vv. 21–23). In this interpretation, the followers of Jesus are warned against an external danger, being misled by Jewish messianic claimants. Accordingly, "in my name" would not mean "in *Jesus'* name," but "in the name that properly belongs to Jesus, namely 'Christ,'" that is, "claiming to be Christ." "I am" would then require a predicate nominative, "I am the Christ," as understood by Matt 24:5. Each element of this interpretation is strained, just as it is difficult to see Jesus as warning his own followers not to be taken in by the claims of militant Jewish nationalists asserting their messianic role. This would mean giving up their faith that Jesus is the Christ, and nothing in the speech indicates this is a threat. Thus other interpreters have understood the church of Mark's time to be threatened by those who claimed to be Jesus himself, returned from heaven, or a reincarnation.[52] Here, too, it is difficult to imagine the Markan Jesus warn-

52. E.g., Schweizer, *Mark*, 268; Pesch, *Markusevangelium,* 2:279; Lührmann, *Markusevangelium,* 219.

ing his own followers not to mistake some other figure for (the returned) Jesus himself. What then was the danger? After Easter, within the Christian community, there were those who came "in Jesus' name" and spoke in the first person as the voice of the risen Lord, using the revelation-formula "I am."[53] Just as there were Jewish prophets who saw the threat to the temple in 66–70 as an indication of the last days and the eschatological intervention of God (cf. Josephus, *War* 2.17.18 [§ 433–34]), so there were Christian prophets who spoke in Jesus' name and with his revelatory formula "I am." Mark is suspicious of such prophets; the Markan Jesus warns his followers against them. They are not to be alarmed by such "prophetic" announcements; Mark here uses *throeō*, found elsewhere in the New Testament only in 2 Thess 2:2, addressed to an analogous situation.

In apocalyptic thought, wars, earthquakes, and famines are the standard signs that the end of history is drawing near. These were the standard features of eschatological expectation (cf. Rev 6; 2 Esd 13:30–32; *2 Bar.* 70.8). They are also the persistent ingredients of history's pageant of suffering as such, and the list fits any period of history. But neither the one nor the other is Mark's point. He is concerned to interpret the particular events of 66–70 to his particular readers, and to place these events in a particular perspective, interpreting how they fit into the "must" (*dei*) of God's plan for history (see on 8:31; 13:20 and diagram in *Excursus: Markan Christology*, p. 247). The events of the readers' own time are *not* merely one more instance of the ongoing tragedy of history, but *neither* are they harbingers of the imminent end. Mark and his readers do live in the last generation of human history, the generation of the Christ and the Son of Man (v. 30). But the events of 66–70 are not the end, or even the direct prelude to it, and Jesus' followers of Mark's time should not be deceived by those Christian prophets who identify the destruction of Jerusalem and the temple as the prelude to the immediate end. Thus the first answer to the disciples' double question "When?" and "What is the sign?" is that the end is *not* yet, and the historical troubles through which the Markan Christians are living, terrible as they are, are *not* the sign that the *end* has already begun or is immediately at hand, but only the *beginning* of the "labor pains" that usher in the new age.[54] The troubles of

---

53. For documentation of these formulae as indicating Christian prophecy, see Boring, *Continuing Voice of Jesus*, 158–61.

54. The imagery of labor pains for the troubles the world must go through in bringing forth the Messiah is a Jewish idea developed from biblical roots (cf. Isa 13:8; 26:17–18; 66:7–9; Jer 4:31; 6:24; 13:21; 22:23; 49:22; 50:43; Hos 13:13; Mic 4:9–10; 1QH 3; 1QM; *1 En.* 99.1–100.6; *Sib. Or.* 2.153–73; 3.538, 635–51; *Jub* 23.11–25; 2 Esd 4:40–43; *2 Bar.* 27.1–15; 48.31–41; 70.1–10; *Gk. Apoc. Ezra* 3.11–15; *b. Sanh.* 97a, 98ab; *b. Sabb.* 118a; *b. Ketub.* 111a; *Gen. Rab.* 42.4). Later rabbinic thought made "labor pains" into a specific technical term, the "messianic woes," not documented in Jewish literature of the first century. However, New Testament data reveal that the idea and imagery were already present in Mark's time (1 Thess 5:3; Rom 8:21–23; Rev 12; John 16:20–22). Cf. Dale C. Allison Jr., *The End of the Ages Has Come: An Early Interpretation of the Passion and Resurrection of Jesus* (Philadelphia: Fortress, 1985), 8–10.

the Jewish revolt his church is living through are not merely historical, but are to be interpreted in an eschatological framework. But the war is distanced from the end itself. Readers with Christian faith may live in hope, but not as though they lived in the very last days; there will be no *historical* sign of the appearance of the Son of Man to bring history to a close and to bring the kingdom of God with power. Mark's readers experience "tribulation" and persecution (cf. 4:17), but they are not yet at the end.

[9] As verse 5 had called the disciples to watch out for seductive prophets, here they are called to watch out for themselves, that is, to endure the persecution that will befall them—which the readers were already experiencing. The key term is "hand over," which refers both to the betrayal by friends and family and being delivered over to persecution as part of the eschatological plan of God (see on 9:31). The disciples' suffering is not random evil, but is modeled on that of Jesus, and it is part of a pattern that embraces John the Baptist, Jesus, and the disciples. In the narrative, their suffering is predicted before Jesus' is narrated; in the experience of the readers, they look back from their own time of suffering to that of Jesus who had already walked the way of the cross before them. As Jesus had been tried and condemned in the council (*synedrion* 14:55; 15:1) in Jerusalem, so his disciples will be brought before the local Jewish courts (pl. *synedria*). The charges against them are not specified, but they are to understand that their suffering is "because of" Jesus and "because of" his name, that is, because they are Christians (cf. 9:41). The beatings they receive in the synagogue are not mob violence, but judicial punishment of "heretics" as part of synagogue discipline (cf. Deut 25:1–3; Matt 23:34; Acts 22:19; 2 Cor 11:24–25). That they are subject to such punishment means they are still considered insiders to the Jewish community, and consider themselves to be such; it is not a case of agents of one religion, "Judaism," persecuting adherents of another religion, "Christianity," but of discipline of dissidents within the Jewish community. The Markan Jesus points forward to a time when his followers will not only offer their testimony within synagogues but will be brought before governors and kings, during the time of the Gentile mission of Mark's own day. Here, too, the missioners will be arrested, but their standing before the court is not a time to back down, but a time to bear witness to their faith.

[10] This text contains both eschatological instruction, and, on the basis of this, a command to evangelize the world. It is still a part of Jesus' response to the "When" question but is not offered as part of an eschatological timetable. The word *prōton* ("first") does indeed mean that the end will not come before the gospel is preached to all nations. This is not abstract eschatological doctrine, however, but is directed to the concrete question in the air in Mark's time: "Is the destruction of the temple part of the end-time events?" Answer: it is not;

as part of God's plan (*dei*) all the nations must be evangelized.[55] There is a mission to accomplish, and there is time to do so. The statement is both theological argument and missionary assignment.

[11–13] This disintegration of family life that the Markan community is experiencing should not surprise them; it was already foreseen as a mark of the last times by biblical prophets (e.g., Mic 7:1–7) and Jesus himself, who had been rejected by his own family (3:30–35) and had specifically predicted it. When they stand before Jewish or Gentile courts, Jesus' disciples need not be anxious about what to say and need not prepare a defense beforehand (contrast 1 Pet 3:15, and Jesus' own near-silence before the court, Mark 14:61–62; 15:1–5), for the Holy Spirit will give them words to say. This is the only specific reference to the role the Holy Spirit will play in the life of post-Easter believers. It is not presented as part of "Mark's teaching about the Holy Spirit" (cf. on 9:21–25; 10:1–12; 12:18–27), but by inserting the saying here Mark makes three specific points: (1) Since the activity of Christian prophets is in the background of the whole discourse (see above), the point here is that prophecy (speaking in the power of the Spirit) is democratized, something that belongs to the whole community of faith. Prophecy is not a special gift that belongs to only a few, but is God's gift to every Christian under duress. When inspired prophetic speech occurs, it is not for the purpose of providing speculative answers to eschatological questions, but for strengthening the community in its witness to the world. Nor is the Spirit a general, abiding "gift" in the possession of the prophet; it comes on needed occasions as the gift of God. This somewhat sporadic concept of the work of the Holy Spirit is more like that of the Old Testament than the understanding of, for example, Paul and John, where the Spirit abides in the community and the believer, and may also be related to the Jewish view that the Spirit is a special gift to martyrs. (2) Receiving the power of the Spirit to function as God's witnesses is another parallel to the life of Jesus. As Jesus was rejected by family, and denied and betrayed (handed over) by friends, so this will happen to the disciples. But as Jesus endured as one who had been baptized and received the Spirit, so also will the disciples. (3) The saying about the Spirit is here a promise, not only to the disciples in the narrative, but to the reader. So far in the story, the disciples have been dull, imperceptive, and inarticulate. They will turn out to be cowardly (14:50). What will they be able to do when they stand before the courts of kings and governors? How will they ever become God's instruments in proclaiming the gospel to all nations?

---

55. Thus the "first" of 13:10 makes the same point as "the end is *not* yet" (v. 7), and the terrors of war, earthquake, and famine are only the "*beginning* of the labor pains" (v. 8). Cf. Rev 14:6 and Rom 11:1–36, which concludes with a revealed mystery that the proclamation of the gospel to the Gentiles is part of the eschatological events.

The Markan Jesus answers: they are not alone; they need not worry, the Spirit will make it happen. Like the martyrs, they must endure to the end, and those who do will receive salvation. "Saved" here does not necessarily mean being set free by the court; those who lose their lives for the sake of Jesus and the gospel are ultimately saved even if not delivered from death in this world (8:35–38). "End" (*telos*) here probably has the double connotation of enduring under persecution even to death, for those who become martyrs, but also enduring to the end of the age, which will come in the lifetime of (some of) Mark's readers (v. 30; cf. 9:1).

[14–23] This section especially contains indications of a composition from discrete sayings that have passed through more than one setting. The direct second-person address is maintained (v. 14, "when you see . . ."; v. 18, "pray . . ."; v. 21, "if anyone says to you . . ."; v. 23a, emphatic "*you* watch . . ." forming a bracket with v. 5; v. 23b, "I have told you"). But third-person statements are enclosed within this second-person framework (v. 14, "those in Judea"; v. 15, "the one on the housetop . . ."; v. 16, "the one in the field . . ."; v. 17, "pregnant women and nursing mothers"; vv. 20, 22, "the elect"). The relation between these two strands of tradition is not clear. Mark's readers can readily find themselves addressed in the second-person statements and imperatives, but the third-person statements and imperatives, especially those addressed to "those in Judea," have a distancing, objectifying effect. The temporal location of the prophetic composer of the pre-Markan oracle was between verse 13 and verse 14; he or she looked ahead to the appearance of the "abomination of desolation" (though not to the distant future), while the temporal location of Mark himself is between verse 23 and verse 24.[56] If Mark was written after the destruction of the temple (or in its immediate and inevitable prospect) and elsewhere than in Judea, the third-person element has no direct message to his readers, just as it has none for the modern reader, who must ask what Mark's intention is in including it.

[14] "Let the reader understand" cannot be a directive from the historical Jesus or the Markan Jesus of the narrative to the four disciples hearing his oral discourse. It may belong either to a pre-Markan apocalyptic fly sheet, if there was such, or to Markan redaction. In either case, it is probably not directed to individual readers with their own personal copies of the document—which would be rare in that society—but to the lector who reads the document aloud to the gathered community (cf. Rev 1:3). The interjected command points out

56. Cf. the analysis in Rudolf Pesch, *Naherwartungen: Tradition und Redaktion in Mark 13* (KBANT; Düsseldorf: Patmos-Verlag, 1968), 203–18. The view that Mark himself regards the climax of the tribulation and the revelation of the "abomination of desolation" as the Antichrist as still to come is represented by, e.g., Martin Hengel, "The Gospel of Mark: Time of Origin and Situation," in *Studies in the Gospel of Mark* (ed. Martin Hengel; Philadelphia: Fortress, 1985), 14–30.

that the meaning of the text is not on the surface, but calls for reflection and insight (cf. Rev 13:18; 17:9). Since it corresponds to apocalyptic style, the reader is expected to recognize the meaning, but only after reflection; the revelatory dimension is accentuated by including a bit of planned obscurity.[57] Whatever its origin, the reader is directed to the Markan text (in contrast to Matthew, where the reader is referred to "the prophet Daniel" here cited), and Markan readers are expected to recognize the allusions as referring to something in their own experience.

What is this "abomination of desolation"? The phrase comes from 1 Macc 1:54; Dan 9:27, 11:31; 12:11, where it refers to the pagan altar erected in the temple by Antiochus IV Epiphanes on December 15 in 167 B.C.E., defiling the temple and making it impossible for Jews to worship there, that is, making it deserted.[58] On later occasions when the temple was threatened with defilement or actually was defiled, this biblical language and imagery was available for interpreting it. In the 40 C.E. Caligula crisis (see above), there may have been a Jewish or Jewish Christian prophetic oracle proclaiming that such an event was imminent. Likewise, the actual desecration and destruction of the temple in 70 C.E. by the Romans may have evoked such an oracle from a Jewish or Christian prophet.[59]

The Markan Jesus in the narrative ("30 C.E.") predicts this event as something in the future. Whether Mark, writing around 70 C.E., still regards it as future, and if so, whether he considers it to be the destruction of the temple or some subsequent event ("appearance of the antichrist" or the like) depends both on the dating and the interpretation of Mark. In the interpretation pursued here, the "abomination of desolation" is cryptic apocalyptic language for the desecration and destruction of the temple, which is about to happen or has just happened. The grammatical shift from neuter "abomination" to masculine "standing" points to the desecration of the temple not by an altar, but by a human act. In Mark's perspective, this could have referred to the actions of Titus

---

57. The disciples had asked for a sign, *sēmeion*, v. 4. Apocalyptic signs neither conceal nor directly reveal, but signify, i.e., communicate through revelatory signs that still require some interpretation. Thus Plutarch, *Moralia* 404e, with reference to the Delphic oracle, *oute legei, oute kruptei, alla; sēmainei*, "she neither speaks openly nor conceals, but *sign*ifies," the verb being cognate to *sēmeion*.

58. See note *d* above on translation of the phrase. Related vocabulary and imagery are found in Jer 25:18 and Ezek 33:29, but there the land becomes desolate because of the abominations (idolatry) committed by Israel.

59. Vicky Balabanski, *Eschatology in the Making: Mark, Matthew, and the Didache* (SNTSMS 97; Cambridge: Cambridge University Press, 1997), has recently made a plausible case for the historicity of the Judean Christians' flight to Pella in the early days of the 66–70 war, influenced by a prophetic oracle. Others regard this as a late Christian legend. For a balanced evaluation, including references to primary sources and bibliography on both sides of the issue, see Moloney, *Mark: Commentary*, 260–61.

and his soldiers in 70 C.E. or the actions of the Zealots who occupied the temple from the winter of 68 until its destruction (Josephus, *War* 4.150–57, 196–207; in 4.388 Josephus himself cites an "ancient prophecy" that this would occur). So understood, what can be the meaning of the directive to "those in Judea" to "flee to the mountains"? Mark and his readers are not in Judea, and the time for flight is past. Thus discerning the precise moment to flee with such urgency was not a practical problem for them, as it is not for the modern reader, and its message to them must be indirect. For first-century readers, as for modern ones who look back on the temple's destruction as a historical reality, this might be fourfold: (1) The destruction of the temple was simply a given element in the first readers' experience. What sense could be made of it? It was no cause for despair, for it was no surprise to God or Jesus who had predicted it, and it was part of the divine plan for history (*dei*). The future of God's people is not dependent on the temple, but lies in a different direction (see above on 11:12–25; 13:2). (2) The authority of Jesus as one who can reliably predict the future is confirmed. (3) The interpretations of current events being made by the Christian prophets Mark opposes are wrong. Jesus had predicted the destruction of the temple, and had given instructions for those in Judea at the time: they were to flee away from the temple, not to it as though it were a place of refuge, for the temple was doomed to destruction. If Mark is post-70, he is showing that the disastrous flight of people *to* the doomed city had been forbidden by Jesus, who knew and predicted its fate. In any case, Jesus had thereby separated this historical event from the eschatological event that was still to come. (4) The sufferings of Mark's own community are to be seen in the context of the temple's destruction. These sufferings are not merely the unfortunate tragedies caused by the misunderstanding of Jewish and Roman authorities, but are included in the "tribulation," the horrific sufferings unleashed during the terrible war that devastated Judea, Jerusalem, and the temple. Mark neither looks back on a previous persecution in Judea that does not involve his church, nor forward to some great "tribulation" in which he is not yet involved. By providing this framework, the sufferings of his own church take on a meaning that gives courage to endure.

In all this, Mark does not need to be specific. As in the analogous situation of the book of Revelation, the first readers knew only too well the historical circumstances to which the imagery of the document alludes. It is only later readers not in the situation who need historical study to get within hearing distance of a text that spoke directly to its original audience. This understanding of the text lends support to its ca. 70 date and Galilean or Syrian provenance.

[18–20] Fleeing "to the mountains" takes up traditional, biblical imagery that compares the destruction of the doomed city to God's judgment on Sodom (cf. Gen 19:17). The danger is that the need to flee might come in winter, when the rainy season makes flight impossible because of swollen wadis and especially the Jordan. This instruction, though historicizing for Mark and his church, who already look back on this event, indirectly makes an important theological point. Both the events of the destruction of Jerusalem and the eschatological events still to come are not random, but part of God's plan. Such apocalyptic knowledge functions to reassure the reader that God the creator has not abandoned history, but is in control and will bring it to a worthy conclusion (cf. the repeated *dei*, 8:31; 9:11; 13:7, 10, 14). Yet this is not understood in a rigidly fixed manner as though every detail is determined and history can only follow its prewritten plan, with no human decision or responsibility involved. Believers can still pray that it will happen in one way and not in another, at one time and not at another. Likewise, God's plan for the end includes the "tribulation," the specified period of suffering just before the end. But God the Creator is not subordinate to the plan, and shortens the days for the sake of the elect. While the "tribulation" is a typical apocalyptic motif, rearranging the apocalyptic timetable en route is not. There is a clear contrast to the kind of apocalypticism in, for example, 2 Esd 4:35–37, where the apocalyptic scheme seems firmly in place, and even God is helpless to do anything but follow it. Mark's God is like that of Daniel, the Creator who can change times and seasons (Dan 2:21). There is thus throughout this discourse a dialectic of determinism and indeterminism, divine sovereignty and human responsibility, knowing and not-knowing. "The elect," a Markan term for God's people found only in this context, is on the "divine sovereignty" side of this dialectic: though the false prophets pose a danger, it is not ultimately possible for them to succeed in deceiving God's elect (see note *h* on v. 22).

[21–23] The warning against "false prophets" is readily understood within the interpretative framework presented here; the reference to "false Messiahs" poses problems for any interpretative framework.[60] Such deceivers are mentioned both in Josephus (*Ant.* 20.97–99, 102, 167–72, 188; *War* 2.264; 6.288) and the New Testament (Acts 5:36–37; 21:38). While there were various claimants to be the messianic deliverer sent by God, so far as our sources indicate no one before Bar Kochba in the second Jewish revolt (132–35 C.E.) explicitly claimed to be

60. Two possibilities in addition to the one pursued here: (1) Matthew had extended the "I am" of Mark 13:6, according to his own interpretation, to mean "I am the Christ." Most MSS of Mark were then contaminated by the more familiar Matthean reading, so that only D and a few other MSS preserved Mark's original reading. This would relieve Mark of this troublesome phrase, but is difficult to justify in terms of text criticism (cf. note *h* above). (2) Though the explicit claim to be the Messiah was not made by the Jewish rebel military leaders of 66–70, their claims to be Israel's saviors were understood by Mark to be counterclaims to Jesus' exclusive Messiahship. "Salvation comes only by the one 'Christ'—Jesus the Son of Man or Messiah. Every other claim to mediate God's salvation is from a 'false Christ' who—from the Christian point of view—is actually claiming to be the bringer of salvation and thus to be a false 'Christ'." (So Brandenburger, *Markus 13*, 158. See Richard A. Horsley and Richard S. Hanson, *Bandits, Prophets, and Messiahs* [Minneapolis: Winston, 1985], ch. 3: "Royal Pretenders and Popular Messianic Movements," 88–134.)

the Messiah. Is the Markan Jesus worried that his followers in Mark's time will be tempted to abandon their faith that Jesus is the Christ and accept one of the nationalist military figures of 66–70 as the real Messiah? Are those who say "Look! Here is the Christ!" false prophets who are identifying one of these claimants as the Messiah sent by God to save Jerusalem and its temple, and deliver Israel from the Romans?[61] Such warnings might be appropriate from a Jewish teacher to Jewish believers in 66–70, but hardly to the followers of Jesus—though one could conceive of a warning to Jewish Christians of a nationalistic bent who were marginal Christian believers and were tempted to exchange their Christian faith for belief that the savior sent by God had finally appeared as one of the Jewish nationalist military leaders. Or is the warning directed against recognizing some figure as the Christian Messiah, the returned Jesus? This, too, is difficult to imagine—were there people masquerading as Jesus who had returned from heaven, but in such an unobvious manner that some would regard such a person as the Christ and some not? And could there have been "many" such to be warned about? Or does Mark understand the phenomenon still to be future, not to be identified with anything in his past or present experience? Within the interpretative framework here proposed, the warning against false prophets points to the internal danger to the Christian community of being misled by those who speak in Christ's name and with his authority, announcing that the destruction of the temple is part of the eschatological drama, proclaiming that Christ will appear from heaven in immediate connection with the fall of the temple. Such prophecies could be seen as announcing "false Messiahs," that is, the various expectations of the return of Christ associated with the fall of the temple. Likewise, saying "here is the Christ" or "there he is" could point to those prophecies that identified the return of Christ with current events. Such prophets operated with charismatic power, and their miracles were considered signs and wonders confirming their message. But Mark's readers are warned against such prophets. "False messiahs and false prophets" thus seem to constitute one category, those who promise God's final salvation and claim to represent it.[62] Alternatively, the Markan Jesus could be understood as warning against a double danger: within the Christian community are "false prophets" misinterpreting the times as the end; outside it are "false Messiahs," the Jewish nationalist messianic claimants. However the referent of this passage is understood, its intent is clear: to encourage the followers of Jesus to persevere in their faith that the crucified

---

61. Some scholars point to the Jewish doctrine of the hidden Messiah, already present and waiting to be revealed at the crucial moment, as the context for this expectation. Cf., e.g., Beasley-Murray, *Jesus and the Last Days*, 122.

62. As argued by, e.g., Heinz Giesen, "Christliche Existenz in der Welt und der Menschensohn: Versuch einer Neuinterpretation des Terminwortes Mk 13,30," *SNTU* 8 (1983): 39, who points out the parallel to 5–6.

and risen man of Nazareth is the Christ, and that following him is a call to endure and suffer as he suffered, a faith that will be vindicated in his return as Son of Man. This vindication will be evident to all, and will not depend on trusting in the prophetic interpretation of current events or the evaluation of the miracles of the prophets who interpret them.

[23] The concluding "Watch out . . ." forms a bracket with verse 5 and signals the end of this section, just as the beginning of verse 24 signals the transition to a new unit. The Markan Jesus' claim that he has "told you everything in advance" serves to indicate that Jesus is a reliable predictor. Mark's readers know that the things he predicted have taken place in their own experience. It also once again documents the author's suspicion of those Christian prophets who continued to give post-Easter revelations from the risen Lord. The Jesus of the Markan narrative had already told the readers *all* they needed to know, eliminating the need for any additional speculative "revelations" from contemporary "revealers." Mark's narrative itself is a check on such new revelations.

13:24–27 II. The End Will Come

13:24 But in those days, after that 'tribulation,' the sun will be darkened, and the moon will not give its light 25 and the stars will be falling from heaven, and the powers in the heavens will be shaken. 26 And then they will see the Son of Man coming in clouds with great power and glory. 27 And then he will send out his angels and will gather his elect from the four winds, from the end of the earth to the end of the sky.[a]

a. Here, as elsewhere, *ouranos* may be translated "heaven" or "sky." Since the worldwide scope of the gathering of the elect is in view here, "sky" is preferred to express the "horizon to horizon" range of the angels' activity. The singular *akron* means extremity, usually the highest point, but here the end of earth and sky, i.e., the horizon.

There is a sense in which these verses represent the real conclusion of Mark's story, a conclusion in which the story finds its resolution.[63] The resolution of the human problem is not finally solved by the ministry of Jesus, or his death, or even by his resurrection. The solution to the human problem will be resolved at the coming of the Son of Man and the kingdom of God. Mark does not narrate this; it still lies in the future not only of the characters in the story, but in his own future. The resolution of the tensions of Mark's own narrative is not narrated, but prophesied; it lies not in the narrative itself, but in the narrative world it projects.

63. So Breytenbach, "Markusevangelium als episodische Erzählung," 154–55, in concord with Norman R. Petersen, "When Is the End Not the End? Literary Reflections on the End of Mark's Narrative," *Int* 34 (1980): 151–66.

[24–25] A clear temporal break occurs here, signaled both by the adversative conjunction *alla* and the specification "in those days after the 'tribulation.'" The preceding long section 5b–23, bracketed by admonitions to "watch out" and by references to false prophets, had described the time of the church's mission, a time in which the followers of Jesus would experience great persecution. It would be a time filled with historical terrors, including the destruction of Jerusalem and its temple, but these would *not* be the eschatological signs. This was Mark's own time; with verse 24 he begins to speak of events in his own future, describing the cosmic events that will be unambiguous signs to the Christian community that the end is to come immediately.[64] The answer to the disciples' question of verse 4 now contrasts the ambiguous signs of historical events that could be misinterpreted with the unambiguous cosmic events that cannot be missed. "Mark's message is a warning against looking for false signs."[65] War, persecution, even the destruction of Jerusalem and the profanation of the temple are not signs of the end. When the end comes, its arrival will be clear to all.

The failing of the light of sun and moon, the falling of stars, and the shake-up of the heavenly world was traditional eschatological imagery for the end of the world and the coming of God (cf. 2 Esd 5:4; *Sib. Or.* 3.801–803; *1 En.* 80.4–7; 102:2; *T. Mos.* 105; Heb 12:26–27; Rev 6:12–13; 8:10). Mark limits his depiction of the final events to a brief selection and combination of Scripture texts (Isa 13:10; Joel 2:10, 30–31; Isa 34:4; Dan 7:13–14; Zech 2:6; Deut 30:4). In the Old Testament, such imagery was sometimes applied as dramatic metaphors to the "world-shaking" events of the fall of empires (e.g., Isa 13:9–22). While some interpreters have so understood the present passage, in the context of Markan and New Testament theology as a whole it is more likely intended to portray the Parousia and the coming of the Son of Man at the end of the age, as understood from Matthew onward (cf. Matt 24–25). In the first-century context, heavenly bodies were often thought of in personal terms, identified with or associated with the gods, influencing or controlling events on earth. Their "fall" would indeed indicate a change in the rulership of the universe. But the meaning cannot be reduced to this symbolic aspect; the Markan Jesus predicts that the final act of world history will begin with cosmic signs that cannot be overlooked. Such language is referential but not objectifying; it refers to something real. While it is not literal, it is not "*merely* a metaphor."[66] Readers cannot wait until they see these signs to begin to be obedient servants. The cosmic convulsions are not a sign that the Son of Man is *about* to appear,

---

64. This is the main point of Conzelmann, "Present and Future," 26–44, who argues this thesis quite apart from the history of the pre-Markan tradition and Mark's incorporation of the oracle of a Christian prophet advocated here.

65. Morna D. Hooker, "Trial and Tribulation in Mark XIII," *BJRL* 65, no. 1 (1982): 99.

66. On the Bible's referential but nonobjectifying language, see Boring, *Revelation*, 51–58.

but the response of the creation to the advent of the Creator. When the signs can be seen, it will be too late to get ready (cf. vv. 33–37).

[26–27] Mark's only depiction of the final events is very sparse, limited to the Parousia of the Son of Man[67] and the ingathering of the elect by his angels. Only the saving work of the Son of Man is pictured. Missing are such typical elements in the eschatological scenario as the resurrection and the judgment. The imagery involves only those alive at the time, but there is no speculation about those who have died in the meantime. There is no concern to present the whole apocalyptic drama, or to depict events that may be fitted into some more comprehensive scheme. Attention is focused only on the vindication of the Son of Man and his own, only here in Mark called "the elect." In biblical and Jewish tradition, God's people Israel are called by this name (Wis 3:9; 4:15; Sir 46:1; 2 Esd 15:21; 16:73–74). A feature of God's eschatological salvation is the promised regathering of God's scattered people from throughout the earth (Zech 2:6; Deut 30:4). The Son of Man will gather the elect, *wherever* they are—it is not important to be in or near Jerusalem, which is not the center of God's eschatological saving act. When the Son of Man returns, the gospel will have been preached to all nations (13:10), and the angels will gather the faithful elect from among them. Here, the elect are those who belong to the Son of Man, who functions in the role of God. The angels traditionally play the role of God's agents in the eschatological harvest (cf. Matt 13:39, 41). Here, God's agents are servants of the Son of Man, and once again the imagery of God, Lord (cf. v. 20), and Son of Man modulate into each other.

13:28–37 III. When?

The end will come (vv. 26–27). There will be signs, but the historical events of 66–70 are not the signs that the end is near (vv. 5b–23). The unmistakable sign will be in the sky for all to see (vv. 24–25). But when? Mark's readers now receive a specific reply to the disciples' question of verse 4, albeit a twofold parabolic response instead of a straightforward calendric answer. The apocalyptic discourse of chapter 13 corresponds to the parable discourse of chapter 4 (see Introduction 2.) As the coming of the kingdom of God can only be expressed in parables, so the coming of the Son of Man requires parabolic speech for its communication. Two parabolic images concerned with waiting for the end are here dialectically juxtaposed.[68] In the first (vv. 28–31), there will be signs that

---

67. The imagery borrowed from Dan 7 here means that the Son of Man comes from God's right hand, not to it. In Jesus' own key and climactic christological statement in 14:62, the session at God's right hand precedes the final coming. *This* is the Markan order.

68. C. E. B. Cranfield, "St. Mark 13," *SJT* 6–7 (1953–1954), 189–96, 287–303; 284–303, argues that Mark intentionally holds these together, so that each controls and interprets the other. The tensive combination of knowing that one lives in the last times without claiming to know exact chronology is found in some Jewish apocalyptic. E.g., *Ps. Sol.* 2.25 announces the end time to be at hand, yet 17.21 affirms only God knows the time of Messiah's coming.

unmistakably signal the advent of the Son of Man, and believers are instructed to "know." In the second (vv. 32–37), the Son of Man will arrive suddenly, without warning, and believers "do not know," but must be ready at all times. The discourse ends on this note. Here as elsewhere in the discourse, the large number of imperatives shows that the tenor of the whole is not that of speculative apocalyptic information, but that of prophetic parenesis, communicating challenge and hope (cf. 1 Cor 14:3). The section is structured around the two parables, as follows:

I. (a sign; "you know")

Introductory imperative "learn"	28a
Parable of the Fig Tree	28b
Application: when you see this, know he is near	29
All will happen in this generation	30
Heaven and earth will pass away, not my word	31

II. (no sign; "you do not know")

Only the Father knows the day or the hour	32
Introductory imperative "watch out, keep alert"	33a
Parable of the Returning Householder	34
Application: watch, you do not know	35–36
The instruction is given to all	37

13:28 "But from the fig tree learn the parable:[a] when its branch becomes tender and puts forth leaves, you know that summer is near. **29** So also you, when you see these things happening, know[b] that he is near, at the gates. **30** Amen[c] I say to you, this generation will not pass away until all these things happen. **31** Heaven and earth will pass away, but my words will absolutely not[d] pass away.

32 But as for that day or hour, no one knows it: neither the angels in heaven, nor the Son—no one except the Father. **33** Watch out, stay alert, for you do not know when the appointed time will arrive. **34** It is like a man going on a journey; he leaves his house and gives authority to his servants,[e] to each his work, and commands the doorkeeper to stay alert. **35** Therefore, stay alert—for you do not know when the lord of the house will come, whether in the evening, or at midnight, or at cockcrow, or at dawn—**36** or else he might come suddenly and find you sleeping. **37** What I say to you I say to all: stay alert."

a. Though *parabolē* can be translated here as "lesson," it is better to preserve the word that has been so significant in the narrative (cf. 3:23; 4:2, 10–13, 30–34; 7:17; 12:1, 12), which the Markan Jesus here uses for the last time, and which correlates this discourse with the parabolic discourse on the kingdom of God in 4:1–34.

b. The form *ginōskete* can be either indicative ("you know") or imperative ("know"). Context indicates v. 28 is indicative, v. 29 is imperative.

c. On *amēn*, see note g at 3:28. Five times in Mark (9:1, 41; 10:15; 13:30; 14:25) this prophetic formula is coupled with the emphatic negative *ou mē*, as here (". . . will not pass away" in vv. 30, 31), which could be (over-)translated "absolutely will not . . ."

d. On the strong negative *ou mē*, see note *a* on 13:2.

e. On *doulos* as slave / servant, see note *a* on 12:2.

[28–31] The parable has eschatological overtones. "Near" already evokes eschatological imagery. Israel has basically two seasons, winter (the rainy season) and summer (the time of growth and harvest; cf. Gen 8:22). The nearness of summer is signaled by the budding of the fig tree. The word for "summer" is related to the word for harvest (*theros / therizō*), and "harvest" is loaded with eschatological connotations (cf. Jer 51:33; Hos 6:11; Joel 3:13; 2 Esd 4:28, 35; Matt 9:37; 13:30, 39; Mark 4:29; Rev 14:15). Just as the budding of the fig tree makes obvious to all that summer is near, the cosmic signs of verses 24b–25 make it obvious to all that the Son of Man is near.[69] The fig tree of the parable is unrelated to the "cursed" fig tree representing the temple (11:12–21). Nor is the fig tree here a symbol for Israel. The story simply portrays a phenomenon of nature that provides an analogy for understanding the nearness of the Son of Man. In Mark, the budding of the fig tree is the sign of the nearness of summer, just as the cosmic disturbances of verses 24–25 are the sign of the nearness of the advent of the Son of Man.

[30] Initial *amen* is an indication of the prophetic authority with which the saying was delivered and transmitted. Though the author is suspicious of the prophetic phenomena in his church, he preserves these marks of prophetic authority in his tradition: it is the Markan Jesus of the narrative who delivers the prophetic word, not the contemporary claimants to the authority of the risen Lord who speak in his name. The phrase *tauta panta* ("all these things") includes not only the historical and cosmic signs, but the coming of the Son of Man and the ingathering of the elect by the angels. *Genea* ("generation") refers, as elsewhere in Mark (8:12, 38; 9:19) to those alive at the time of Jesus, that is, the contemporaries of Jesus and Mark.[70] Regarded historically, this means that,

69. *Tauta* ("these things") refers most naturally to the signs just spoken of in vv. 24b–25. It is artificial to attempt to limit "these things" to the historical events of 6–23, and to contrast the *tauta* of v. 29 with *tauta panta* ("all these things") of v. 30 (contra Pesch, *Markusevangelium*, 2:308, followed by, e.g., Collins, *Beginning of the Gospel*, 79).

70. The conclusion that the Markan Jesus mistakenly predicted the Parousia to occur in the first century has been resisted by proposing alternative interpretations. There have been many such, but the two classical approaches, each of which still has its advocates are (1) "This generation" does not refer to the contemporaries of Jesus or Mark, but to the Jewish people, the generation of the church, the human race as a whole, or the last generation. This view was popular among the church

while Mark opposes those who proclaim the immediate Parousia in connection with current events, he holds on to the expectation of early Christianity that Christ would return in their own time (cf., e.g., 9:1; Matt 10:23; 1 Thess 4:13–17, esp. v. 17; 1 Cor 7:26–32; 15:51–52; Rev 1:1, 3; 3:11; 12:12; 22:6, 7, 10, 20; Jas 5:7–9; 1 Pet 4:7). In Mark's situation, this did not serve as doctrinal information about the time of the end, but as encouragement and hope: the immediate troubles are no cause for eschatological panic; there is time for mission before the Lord returns, but those who faithfully endure and confess Jesus before the world will be acknowledged by the Son of Man who will return in power and glory in their own lifetimes (8:38; 9:1).

[31] Jesus here speaks the same language as God in Isa 40:7–8. The words of the Markan Jesus are as valid and lasting as God's own words. Adherence to them (and not the "new revelations" of charismatic prophets who claim to speak Jesus' words) is what will count when the Son of Man appears (8:38). Mark wants his community to be wholly oriented to and dependent on these words, and assures them of their eternal validity, for the Markan Jesus has told them everything, needing no later supplementation from those who claim to deliver messages from the heavenly Lord (v. 23).

[32–37] The concluding words here take a dramatic shift of perspective, from signs to no signs, from knowing to not knowing (see structural outline above). Only the Father knows the time of the end. It is surprising that Jesus professes his own ignorance of the time of the end so emphatically. Theologians of the patristic period were bothered by the christological implications as though the divinity of Christ were compromised, since the Second Person of the Trinity did not know something the First Person was unwilling to share (cf. 10:40; Acts 1:7). Mark does not have these later theological issues in mind. He is rather concerned to cut the ground from under the charismatic prophets who claim to have received revelations from angels[71] and from the exalted Christ about current events as signs of the end. The Markan Jesus declares that this is impossible, since neither angels nor Christ have any information on this subject to reveal! To the extent that Mark is making a christological point, this datum would, like Jesus' identification with sinners, fall on the "truly human"

---

fathers and in the middle ages. (2) "All these things" does not refer to the final events including the Parousia of the Son of Man, but only to the historical events leading up to the destruction of the temple. This view first became widespread in modern times, beginning with its popularization by John Calvin.

71. Mark has angels present at Jesus' temptation (1:13), in the transcendent realm of God (12:25), and at the Parousia under the authority of the Son of Man (8:38; 13:27), but, in contrast to, e.g., Luke and Revelation, has no revelatory angels who provide eschatological revelations to Christians—the angels themselves do not know these things, and Christians should not trust those who claim to receive such angelic communications. Here Mark is more like Paul (Gal 1:8!).

side of the Chalcedonian ledger, just as placing his own words in the same category as God's in the preceding statement places him on the divine side.

This paragraph's emphasis on not knowing means not only that the present historical "signs" (wars, earthquakes, famines) cannot be interpreted as "signs of the end," but that there will be no future *historical* sign signaling the end, that is, that Mark does not anticipate an antichrist figure to emerge just before the Parousia.

[34] A parable that probably goes back to the preaching of the historical Jesus has been allegorized and used for apocalyptic instruction. Mark's allegorical application shines through the parable itself. That the man is *apodēmos* ("on a journey") already suggests that his return will not be immediate. The "house" suggests the house churches of Mark's community (cf. 1:29–34; 2:1–2, 15; 3:20–21; 7:24; 9:28–34; 10:28–31). The *douloi* ("servants" / "slaves") are transparent to Christian ministers, especially apostles and prophets (10:44; Acts 4:29; Rom 1:1; Titus 1:1; Rev 10:7; 11:18) who have received Christ's authority to represent him in the Christian mission (cf. 3:15; 6:7), and whose ministry is called *ergon* ("work"; cf. Acts 13:2; 15:38; Phil 1:22; 2 Tim 4:5). It is a picture of the absent Lord of the church who has assigned it a missionary task involving the whole world. Their responsibility is neither to busy themselves with calculating when the Lord might return nor to neglect the reality that he will do so, but to be about their missionary task, so that whenever the Lord returns he will find them ready. The evangelist holds his community in the tension between fanatical misinterpretation of current events and lackadaisical disinterest in the sure hope of the coming of the Son of Man.

[35] The last word of the parable becomes the first word of direct address, as the command to "watch out" flows from the world of the parable into the narrative world of the four disciples on the mountain, and from there into the world of the reader (v. 37!). The four watches of the night correspond to the widespread Roman system of dividing the twelve-hour period between 6:00 p.m. and 6:00 a.m. (6:00–9:00, *opse*, "evening"; 9:00–12:00, *mesonyktion*, "midnight"; 12:00–3:00, *alektorophōnias*, "cockcrow"; 3:00–6:00, *prōi*, "dawn"). As the suffering predicted for the disciples already anticipates the story of Jesus' passion that is about to begin, these four watches will be reflected in the way the story of Jesus' last night is depicted.[72]

[37] The readers have almost forgotten that they are overhearing a narrated speech of Jesus to four characters in the story. The address throughout has modulated back and forth from the narrative world to that of the reader. But now it

---

72. So numerous scholars, following especially R. H. Lightfoot, "The Connection of Chapter Thirteen with the Passion Narrative," in R. H. Lightfoot, *The Gospel Message of St. Mark* (Oxford: Oxford University Press, 1962), 48–59, who may have claimed too much precision regarding a valid point.

becomes explicit. The character Jesus looks up from the page and directly addresses the reader. Better said, in Mark's oral-aural frame of reference, the listening congregation, who have known they were spoken to by the numerous second-person imperatives throughout, are explicitly told that this is what the Markan Jesus intended all along.

The speech closes on the imperative "watch out." We readers hear nothing of the disciples' reaction. The there-and-then report has modulated into here-and-now address, and without any transition the passion story begins, as Jesus begins to model and live out the suffering predicted for his disciples. The story is bound together christologically: the Son of Man who is to come on the clouds (v. 26) is the one who goes the way of the cross (8:31) and calls his disciples to follow (8:34).

14:1–15:47 Trial and Death

From a narratological point of view, three important plot lines converge in the passion story:[73] (1) Jesus fulfills his commission from God; (2) the disciples fail to fulfill the commission they have received from Jesus; (3) Jesus' opponents (now including Judas and the crowd) seem to succeed in their purpose to destroy him. These aspects of the passion story have often been anticipated in the preceding narrative. Even so, the narrative that begins here is distinctive within Mark as a whole:

- There is little in this section that could have circulated in early Christian tradition as an independent saying or story.[74] For the most part, the unit 14:1–16:8 functions only as a connected whole. Thus most scholars are persuaded that Mark adopted and adapted an extensive pre-Markan passion narrative.[75]

---

73. Following Robert C. Tannehill, "The Gospels and Narrative Literature," in *The New Interpreter's Bible* (ed. Leander Keck; NIB 8; Nashville: Abingdon, 1995), 8:66, and Tannehill, "Narrative Christology," 57–96.

74. Two obvious exceptions are 14:3–9, which does occur independently in other Gospel contexts (Luke 7:36–50; John 12:1–8), and 14:22–25, which was used in the eucharistic liturgy without its larger context (cf. 1 Cor 11:23–26).

75. There are two extreme positions, with a variety of mediating views. One extreme is represented by Pesch, *Markusevangelium*, 2:1–27, who argues that Mark adopted, with minimal editing, a narrative that extends from 8:27 through 16:8, with 14:1–16:8 being incorporated almost verbatim. The other pole is represented by Norman Perrin and his students, who argue that there was no connected pre-Markan passion narrative, but Mark himself creatively composed 14:1–16:8 on the basis of a minimum of traditional material (Werner H. Kelber, ed., *The Passion in Mark: Studies on Mark 14–16* [Philadelphia: Fortress, 1976]).

- Jesus works no miracles. The christological dynamic (truly human / truly divine) of the Markan story as a whole is still present, but there are no surface manifestations of Jesus' divine power.[76] Jesus becomes passive. The subjects of sentences shift; Jesus becomes the direct object of the actions of others rather than the acting subject (cf. on "passion" at 8:31). Jesus is no longer the authoritative actor in the same way as before. His authority continues but is now seen only indirectly by the readers; it is not manifest to characters in the story. He goes willingly to his death. He is not coerced, but voluntarily places himself in the hands of those who will bring about his death.
- The Pharisees, among Jesus' opponents in Galilee, disappear from the narrative and play no role in the passion story (last appearance was 12:13).

14:1–11 Betrayal and Anointing

These verses are now a compositional unit created by Mark's intercalation of the story of Jesus' anointing by an anonymous woman into the account of the Sanhedrin's plot to kill Jesus.[77] Both framework (human plotting) and central core (Jesus' sovereignty) are focused on Jesus' death. In 14:1–2, 10–11, Jesus' enemies plot his death; in 14:3–9 Jesus predicts it himself, and interprets the woman's act as anointing his body for burial. The story of the plot to kill Jesus was a unit in pre-Markan passion tradition, with the story of the anointing an independent unit placed at other locations in the narrative at Luke 7:36–50 and John 12:1–8 (Matthew simply follows Mark). Mark's insertion of it here, at the very beginning of the passion narrative, framed by the plot to destroy him, enables the reader to see that Jesus' death cannot be reduced to the machinations of his enemies against his will, for Jesus foresees and affirms his own death and resurrection (cf. 8:31; 9:31; 10:33–34). While Mark has a more subtle way of doing this than the author of the Fourth Gospel, in Mark, too, Jesus is not simply victim, but *Christus Victor*. Jesus is passive in this section, but beneath the surface of the narrative Jesus still represents the sovereignty of God. Placing the story here makes it the opening scene that forms a bracket with the final scene in which women will come to complete the burial ritual by anointing his body (16:1)—which will not be necessary or possible because of the resurrection.

---

76. Broadhead rightly points out that while there are no formal miracle *stories* in the passion story, miraculous *events* continue (*Teaching with Authority*, 180–81). The epiphany Christology of part one continues not overtly, but as a narrative substratum. Jesus the powerful Son of God and Jesus the victimized human being are not only presented diachronically but synchronically and dialectically.

77. On intercalation as a Markan compositional technique, see on 5:21.

14:1 It was now two days before[a] the Passover[b] and the Festival of Unleavened Bread. And the chief priests and the scribes were looking for a way to arrest Jesus by stealth and kill him. 2 For they were saying, "Not in the presence of the festival crowds,[c] so that there will not be a riot among the people."

3 And while he was in Bethany in the house of Simon the leper, as he was reclining at mealtime, a woman came who had an alabaster bottle of perfume, pure[d] nard, very expensive, broke the alabaster bottle and poured its contents on his head. 4 But there were some who said indignantly to each other, "Why has this waste of perfume happened? 5 For this perfume could have been sold for more than three hundred denarii, and the money given to the poor." And they snorted[e] at her. 6 But Jesus said, "Let her alone; why are you bothering her? She has done a good work for me. 7 For you always have the poor with you, and whenever you are willing, you can do good to them. But as for me—you will not always have me. 8 She has done what she could; she has poured the perfume on my body beforehand, for its burial. 9 Amen[f] I say to you, wherever the gospel[g] is proclaimed in the whole world, what this woman has done will also be told in remembrance of her."

10 And Judas Iscariot, one of the Twelve, went away to the chief priests in order to hand him over[h] to them. 11 And when they heard it, they were very glad, and promised to give him money. And he started looking[i] for a good chance to hand him over.

a. *Meta dyo hēmeras* is lit. "after two days." As 8:31, "after three days," means Friday–Sunday on the Jewish reckoning of time, so "after two days" can be translated "on the next day."

b. *Pascha* is not a native Greek word, but the transliteration of the Aramaic *pashā'*, derived from Hebrew *pasah*, the Hebrew verb "pass over." Mark finds it in his Bible, the LXX, where it is used forty-three times.

c. *En tē heortē* may be translated either temporally, "not during the festival," or spatially, "not in the presence of the festival crowds." In the former case, the chief priests and scribes change their plans in response to Judas's proposal; in the latter case followed here, Judas facilitates their intention by enabling them to arrest Jesus away from the crowds.

d. *Pistikē* may be related to the name of the plant from which the perfume was derived, perhaps the *pistakia*, the pistachio tree. More likely the word is related to *pistis*, "faithful, trustworthy," and thus means "genuine," "unadulterated." The perfumed oil was so rare (nard was imported from India) that it was often diluted with less expensive ingredients. Mark's point is that the large quantity of perfume was entirely pure.

e. On *embrimaomai* as "snorting" (in indignation), see note *d* on 1:43, its only other occurrence in Mark.

f. On *amēn*, see note *g* at 3:28.

g. On "gospel" for *euangelion* (lit. "good news"), see on 1:1, 15.

h. See discussion of *paradidōmi* at 9:31.

i. The ingressive imperfect *ezētei* emphasizes the beginning of an action, with the implication that it continues.

[14:1–2] Despite the ambiguities entailed by the difference between the Roman reckoning of days (sunrise to sunrise) and the Jewish mode (sunset to sunset) and the meaning of "after two days," it is clear that Mark understands the crucifixion to have taken place on Friday, and the Passover meal / Last Supper on Thursday evening, so that the events of "two days before the Passover" took place on Wednesday (see on 11:1). The name is derived from the Exodus account in which the destroying angel "passed over" the homes of the Hebrews during the deliverance from Egypt (Exod 12:1–32). The Festival of Unleavened Bread that followed immediately after Passover was originally a separate festival, but by the first century both were often thought of as one feast (so also Josephus, e.g., *Ant.* 14.2.1; 18.9.3; cf. the merging of "Advent" and "Christmas" in the popular mind). Passover was a pilgrimage festival celebrating the exodus events, with nationalistic overtones. This, combined with the fact that the population of Jerusalem increased by four times during the festival, made the authorities nervous about patriotic crowds filled with religious fervor. The Roman governor moved his residence from Caesarea on the coast to Jerusalem during the festival, with increased numbers of soldiers and higher levels of security. The "chief priests and scribes" represent the official opposition to Jesus that has continued from 3:6 (cf. on 11:18). Their fear of a riot "among the people" (*laos,* not *ochlos,* "crowd") contrasts the leadership with the people as a whole, and shows the leadership, not the people, are responsible for Jesus' death. They have already decided to kill Jesus, but need to find a way to arrest him when the festival crowds are not present. In the pre-Markan tradition, the narrative goes directly to verse 10.

[3–9] While this story may reflect some event in the life of Jesus, the variations as to time, place, people concerned, action (anointing head or feet?), nature of the objection and Jesus' reply illustrate how the story was modified and reinterpreted in various situations of the oral tradition and by the Evangelists (Matt 26:6–13; Luke 7:36–50; John 12:1–8). In Mark the woman remains nameless. She is not, as in John 12:1–8, the hostess for the occasion, nor is she a sinner, as in Luke 7:37. The New Testament never identifies her as a prostitute, which enters the tradition only later. Not until the fourth century is she identified with Mary Magdalene.[78]

78. Ephraem the Syrian, Gregory the Great. The Western church made the identification with Mary Magdalene, who on the basis of Luke 8:2 was sometimes considered a prostitute, combining the name "Mary" from John 12:3 (though this was a different Mary, the sister of Martha and Lazarus) and the "sinful woman" of Luke 7. The Eastern tradition kept the three distinct.

[3] Though Mark does not specify it, Jesus seems to have made Bethany his temporary residence while in Judea (11:1, 11–12), as Capernaum had been his Galilean headquarters (1:21–34; 2:1; 9:33). "Simon the leper" is not otherwise known. Since there are nine different persons named "Simon" in the New Testament (five in Mark), some distinguishing epithet is necessary. He is not called the *"former* leper." While it is difficult to imagine a person with such an affliction hosting a dinner party, it is by no means inconceivable, and Mark may be suggesting that as Jesus enters the house of sinners and eats with them (2:15–17), and enters the house of a dead person (5:35–43), so in sovereign disregard of purity conventions (cf. 7:1–23) he dines with one afflicted with leprosy. If so, it is striking that the issue of Jesus' ability and willingness to heal him does not even come up (cf. 1:40–45)—but this is in keeping with Mark's limiting epiphany-Christology miracle stories to the first part of his Gospel. Jesus reclines among guests at a formal dinner, which would have been held in late afternoon. The Jesus who will shortly affirm the woman's extravagant gift is himself no ascetic (cf. 2:18–20).

During the meal, an unnamed women enters. Without a word, she breaks the flask, showing she intends to empty it (her gift is total; cf. the woman of 12:44) and pours the very expensive contents on Jesus' head. It was customary in the hot, dry climate of the Middle East to anoint the head with oil (cf., e.g., Ps 23:5; Matt 6:17). At fashionable dinner parties, expensive perfume could be used. The woman's act, however, is extravagant beyond all imagining.[79] This becomes the objectionable point.

[4–5] While it violated cultural conventions for a woman to intrude into a men's festive meal, the objection is not to her gender but to her extravagance. It would take almost a year for a laborer to earn this much money, which would have supplied bread for about 7,500 people (see note *c* at 6:37; 200 denarii for 5,000; 300 denarii would satisfy 7,500). Mark does not identify the "some" who object; he does not suggest that they were his disciples, nor does he explain that their protest was insincere. It is a reasonable objection, in line with biblical teaching (e.g., Deut 15:7–11), with the custom at the Passover to be especially generous to the poor (cf. John 13:29), and with Jesus' own demand to help the poor (10:21). Readers who are not shocked by the extravagance of the radical act of a woman who squanders a year's wages on cosmetics in apparent disregard for the needs of poor people, and who do not share something of the indignation of those who objected, will tend to interpret the scene according to their own agenda and to rationalize and domesticate Jesus' radical counterresponse that becomes the focus of the story.

[6] The woman has done a *good work* for *Jesus*, therefore the objectors should leave her alone—colloquially, "stop giving her a hard time." *Kalon*

---

79. Cf. John 19:38–40, where more than seventy-five pounds of spices are used in the burial of Jesus, worth the equivalent of more than half a million dollars.

ergon ("good work") is not a trivial expression ("doing something nice for someone"); it has quasi-technical overtones. (1) In Judaism, "good works" were distinguished from giving to the poor as such ("alms"), which was considered the religious duty of every Jew. The latter could be given only in cash, could be given only to the poor, and must be given to the living. "Good works" could be done for poor or rich, for the living or the dead, and in addition to money required personal engagement and concern. Thus the rabbis considered "good works" superior to "alms."[80] (2) In the Hellenistic world generally, in which "honor" was a supreme value and "shame" a great detriment, *kalos* had the connotation of "honor." To do an "honorable deed" needed no further justification. (3) In the Christian community, a "good work" was an act of Christian ministry that did not have the pietistic and moralistic flavor of being a do-gooder. To do good works was to live in imitation of and in obedience to Christ. The following texts render *kalon ergon* in various ways, but all have the same vocabulary as Mark 14:6: Matt 5:16; John 10:32; 1 Tim 3:1; 5:10, 25; 6:18; Titus 2:7, 2:14; Heb 10:24; Jas 3:13; 1 Pet 2:12. Thus Jesus' defense of the woman's act is to place it in the category of "good works," not to explain that she understood his coming death. The woman's motive is not given, but there is no indication that she had heard Jesus' passion predictions (8:31; 9:31; 10:33–34) or that she knows Jesus is about to be killed.[81] The woman does not interpret her deed symbolically, but makes an extravagant, personal, spontaneous gift to Jesus.

[7] Jesus' declaration, "You always have the poor with you," is not a despairing comment on the problem of poverty or a decree that poverty will never

80. Primary sources cited in Strack and Billerbeck, *Kommentar*, 4.2.536ff, 559ff. Summarized in Joachim Jeremias, *Abba: Studien zur neutestamentlichen Theologie und Zeitgeschichte* (Göttingen: Vandenhoeck & Ruprecht, 1966), 110, and Pesch, *Markusevangelium*, 2:333.

81. In any case, the passion predictions include the prediction of Jesus' resurrection, which, if the woman had understood, she would have recognized there was no need to anoint Jesus' body, for God would vindicate Jesus despite his dishonorable burial without being anointed (see on 15:46–16:1). The suggestion that with prophetic insight she anoints Jesus as the suffering Messiah is to be rejected. (This older view [e.g., Johnson, *Mark*, 224] has again been popularized by, e.g., Schüssler Fiorenza, *In Memory of Her*, xiv, but rightly opposed by, e.g., Pesch, *Markusevangelium*, 2:332, and Gundry, *Mark*, 812–14.) For Mark, Jesus has already been anointed as the Christ by God; he does not just now become Messiah by a human anointing. The verb for messianic anointing is *chriō*, and the material is olive oil; Mark's word is *myrizō*, used in reference to everyday cosmetics and skin-care, and the material is not olive oil but *myron*, used 16x in the LXX, but never of royal anointing. Anointing the head is normal (Ps 23:5; Matt 6:17; cf. Eccl 9:8). The author knows that Jesus will be buried unceremoniously without anointing, and provides for this aspect of an honorable burial in advance (15:42–16:1). Those present object to extravagance, not to a misplaced messianic anointing. Neither the Markan Jesus nor the narrator relates the incident to Jesus' messianic office, directly or ironically (as though as suffering messiah he is "messianically" anointed, but for death). Mark is a master of irony, as shown by his use of royal terminology in the paragraphs to follow ("king of the Jews," etc.), and had he intended the reader to perceive a messianic anointing here, even if hidden from the characters in the story, he could have done so much more adroitly.

cease. The statement echoes Deut 15:11 and God's concern for the poor; it expresses Jesus' own concern, and his call for disciples to be concerned for the poor (10:21–22). The issue is not compassion but time, the contrast between "always" and "not always" (as in 7:24–30, where a woman is also the central figure). The case is analogous to 2:18–20, when Jesus affirms fasting for "normal" time but considers the time of his presence a "special" time (2:18–20) in which otherwise-valid rules are suspended. Here, too, what is always right and valid is affirmed, but overruled by the once-for-all encounter with Jesus. The woman exemplifies that devotion which transcends ordinary responsibility that is "always" right, and makes the extraordinary response that transcends all general rules. As in 2:18–20, the objection (in Mark) is not made by Jesus' disciples, but by those outside his circle, and the contrast is between those rightly concerned to be responsible adherents of law and religious duty and those who celebrate the unique presence of God in Jesus. The readers, who live in the time of the absence of Jesus, are not confronted with the alternative posed by the objectors in the story, "Jesus or the poor," but are called to proclaim the gospel and to care for the poor and needy of this world.

[8] The woman is praised because she "did what she could," that is, she gave what she had to give. As the poor woman of 12:44 gave what she had, so this wealthy woman gives what she can give. Mark's point is that the woman shows her great devotion by making a fabulous, spontaneous gift. *She* does not understand her act as the proleptic anointing of a corpse for burial, but the Markan *Jesus* prophetically interprets it as pointing to his death.[82] Jesus, not the woman, is the prophet in this scene and throughout, as Mark once again emphasizes Jesus' predictive powers.

[9] The scene concludes with a solemn prophetic *amēn* declaration. If the scene and saying go back to the life of Jesus,[83] it may have originally meant that the woman's good work, despite its rejection by human observers, will not be in vain, but will be remembered before God (cf. Acts 10:1–4, where the same word *mnēmosynon* is used, not the *anamnēsis* of 1 Cor 11:24–25). Whatever the prehistory of the saying may have been, for Mark it is a declaration about the church's worldwide proclamation of the gospel in his own time (cf. 13:10). It illustrates and makes real Mark's own understanding that the individual stories representing the pre-Easter life of Jesus are vehicles for the proclamation of the good news of God's saving act in Christ. The single story becomes the medium of the gospel. Wherever this gospel is preached, this woman's extravagant, loving deed will be recounted. The gospel is not an abstraction, nor a

82. Cf. Matt 25:31–46, where those who understood themselves to be acting out of human kindness learn to their surprise that they have been serving Jesus, risen Lord and Son of Man.

83. So Joachim Jeremias, "Die Salbungsgeschichte Mc 14,3–9," *ZNW* 35 (1936): 75–82, and several later interpreters.

summary statement such as "God loves you" or "Christ died for you," nor even the grand narrative of the life, death, and resurrection of Jesus, but is always bound up with the concrete stories of the "little people," the nameless individuals through whose devotion the gospel becomes real.

[10–11] Mark does not indicate that Judas (or the other disciples) was present at the occasion when the woman anointed Jesus, or that his "going away" was a reaction to this event. "Went away" is Mark's redactional means of knitting the two stories together, and corresponds to 3:19, the only previous reference to Judas. There, too, he is "one of the Twelve" and *paradidōmi* ("hand over," "betray") is used of him. There, too, he "went away" (*apēlthen*), but there it was to become a member of the Twelve; here he "went away" to betray Jesus. Judas has been a low-profile member of the Twelve since 3:19; this is the first specific reference to him since. Unlike later interpreters of the Gospel of Mark, beginning already in the New Testament, Mark himself has no speculation on Judas's motives in handing over Jesus to the authorities. They promise to give him money without his asking for it—in fact Judas has no speaking part in the whole narrative (contrast Matt 26:15, where the initiative is with Judas). Mark does not mention any amount; Matthew specifies the "thirty pieces of silver" of Zech 11:12. Mark shows no interest in the later fate of Judas, and mentions him only once more, when he delivers on the promise made here (14:43). Mark is only interested in the unseen hand of God at work in these events (cf. on *dei* at 8:31, *paradidōmi* at 9:31).

14:12–25 Passover and Eucharist

14:12 And on the first day of Unleavened Bread, when they kill the Passover lamb,[a] his disciples are saying to him, "Where do you want us to go and prepare for you to eat the Passover?" 13 And he sends two of his disciples and says to them, "Go into the city, and a man carrying a jar of water will meet you. Follow him, 14 and wherever he enters, say to the owner of the house, 'The Teacher says, "Where is my guest room where I may eat the Passover with my disciples?"' 15 And he will show you a large upstairs room, furnished and ready. And there make preparations for us." 16 And the disciples went out and came into the city, and found everything just as he had told them, and they prepared the Passover meal.

17 And after it had become evening he comes with the Twelve. 18 And as they were reclining for the meal and were eating, Jesus said, "Amen[b] I say to you, one of you will hand me over, one who eats[c] with me." 19 They became terribly upset, and were saying to him one by one, "Surely not I?"[e] 20 But he said to them, "One of the Twelve, one who dips[d] into the bowl with me. 21 For the Son of Man is going away just as it stands written about him, but woe to that man[e] by/through whom the Son of Man

is handed over/delivered up.[f] It would have been better for that man if he had not been born."

22 And while they were eating, he took a loaf of bread, gave thanks and praise[g], broke it and gave it to them and said, "Take; this is my body." 23 And he took a cup, gave thanks, gave it to them, and they all drank from it. 24 And he said to them, "This is my blood of the covenant,[h] which is poured out for many. 25 Amen[i] I say to you, I will no longer drink of the fruit of the vine until that day when I drink it anew[j] in the kingdom of God."

a. The third-person plural imperfect *ethyon* is impersonal and customary, "when they killed the Passover lamb" (= "when the Passover lambs were killed").

b. On *amēn,* see note *g* at 3:28.

c. The substantival present participle *ho esthiōn* may be translated either "the one who is eating" or "the one who eats." In English, the former translation points to a present act in progress, the latter to a characteristic act. The LXX Ps 49:10 alluded to in this phrase clearly understands it in the latter sense. Whether Mark understands it in the former sense depends on whether he specifically thinks of Judas as present at the Last Supper (see commentary below). Likewise, *ho embaptomenos* is used in Greek for actions distinguished in English as "the one who is dipping" or "the one who dips."

d. The interrogative pronoun *mēti* expects a negative answer, and is thus not the soul-searching "could it be me?" but is also not the matter-of-fact, "It's not me, right?" It can be used in contexts in which the questioner is in doubt concerning the answer (cf. Bauer and Danker, BDAG, 650), and thus has the overtone of uncertainty. The starkness of both their question and Jesus' response is expressed in verbless sentences.

e. The Greek relates *ho huios tou anthrōpou,* "the Son of Man," to *tō anthrōpō ekeinō,* "to that man."

f. In contrast to *hypo,* which means "by," Mark expresses Judas's agency with the preposition *dia,* which can be "by," but here means "through," focusing on the originator of the action, as, e.g., Heb 1:2. So also, *paradidotai* can be "is being handed over / betrayed" or "is being delivered up" (see on 9:31). The meaning here is that *Judas's* act of *betrayal* is the instrument of *God's delivering up* Jesus, but all these nuances are impossible to preserve in a single English translation.

g. On *eulogeō* and *eucharisteō* (v. 23) see note *h* at 6:41.

h. *Kainēs* ("new") is found in A *f*[1, 13], some ancient translations, and most later Greek MSS, but its absence from ℵ B C Dc. L Θ Ψ 565 k, and the intrinsic probability that it would be more likely added from the familiar parallels in Luke 22:20; 1 Cor 11:25; 2 Cor 3:6, Heb 8:8; 9:15 than an original *kainēs* would be omitted make it virtually certain that the reading translated above is original.

i. On *amēn,* see note *g* at 3:28. With the double negative *ou mē,* the phrase could be translated "I will absolutely not . . ." (cf. note *c* at 13:30).

j. *Kainon* ("new") is adverbial accusative, not an adjective modifying "wine." It does not refer to "new wine," but to how it will be drunk—in the eschatological newness of the kingdom of God.

[**12–16**] Whether or not the actual Last Supper of Jesus with his disciples was a Passover or was so understood in the pre-Markan tradition (see discussion of Markan chronology at 11:1; 14:1), Mark emphatically describes it as a Passover, repeating the term *pascha* four times in this brief section. This subunit is often called the "preparation for the Passover," but Mark devotes only a brief clause devoid of details to the actual preparation (16c, "they prepared the Passover meal"). A more appropriate title would be "Jesus' foreknowledge and authority exhibited in securing a room in which to celebrate the Passover" (see Introduction 2.). Since Passover was a pilgrim festival that could be celebrated only in Jerusalem, and since the Passover lamb had to be consumed before the morning, requiring groups of at least ten people for the meal, it was necessary to arrange for a suitable location in advance. The Holy City was understood to belong to no one of the tribes but to Israel as a whole (cf. Washington, D.C.). Residents had traditionally considered it a pious duty to open their homes for this celebration, welcoming pilgrims and asking no fee for the service.

[**12**] The reader is presumably to picture Jesus and his disciples as still in Bethany, since there has been no indication of a change of location since 14:3, and the command to "go into the city" presupposes they are outside it, as does the wording of verse 16 ("went out and came into the city").[84] According to Markan chronology, the day is Thursday, Nisan 14. The Torah specified that the Passover lambs were to be killed on Nisan 14 "between the two evenings," that is, in the twilight between dusk and dark. The Passover meal was then to be held after dark on the same day, according to our reckoning, but on the next day, Nisan 15 in Jewish reckoning. By the first century, the large number of pilgrims had made it necessary to move the beginning time to earlier in the afternoon. Contrary to the impression given by Mark, Passover was a one-day festival, followed immediately by the seven-day Festival of Unleavened Bread. Mark's reversal of the order may simply reflect his lack of precise knowledge of Jewish customs (see on 7:3–5), but the necessity of clearing leaven from the house that began at noon on Nisan 14 contributed to the popular understanding that the festival itself began then, and such language is used even by Josephus (*War* 6.3.1; cf. *Ant.* 2.15.1, which speaks of an eight-day Festival of Unleavened Bread).

[**13–16**] Jesus' sending two disciples to secure a room for the Passover meal is similar, in structure and vocabulary, to his previous sending of two disciples

---

84. Mark does not always signal such transitions, however; the narrative is not structured by firmly linking the assumed topography of one scene to that of the preceding or next (cf. 13:37 / 14:1). It is thus possible that Casey is correct that this scene transpires in the temple courts, where Jesus and his disciples are sacrificing the Passover lamb, and that the text should be translated "when they (Jesus and the disciples) were sacrificing the Passover lamb" (see Maurice Casey, *Aramaic Sources of Mark's Gospel* [SNTSMS 102; Cambridge: Cambridge University Press, 1998], 219–52).

to secure a colt for the procession into Jerusalem, as a comparison of verses 13–16 with 11:2–6 will make clear (see commentary there); note especially the identical wording of 11:2 / 14:13. The meeting of a man carrying a jar of water is only moderately unusual. To be sure, carrying water was mostly women's work, and when men carried water they usually used skin bottles rather than jars, but men, especially slaves, could be seen in the streets of Jerusalem carrying water jars without raising eyebrows. What is surprising is that the man will meet them, as though looking for them. It is likewise remarkable that the owner of the house offers the upper room without objection or question. When the readers hear the disciples repeat Jesus' words beginning with "The Teacher says," that refer to "my guest room," they think of 11:3, which they understood as "The Lord needs it" (see commentary there). This is the key to the Markan understanding of this scene. Historicizing interpretations have attempted to discern in all this some prearranged plan secretly made by Jesus and his contacts in Jerusalem on previous visits undocumented by Mark, or have claimed that Jesus is resorting to secret signs to locate a secure room in which he and his group could celebrate the Passover. All such approaches miss the Markan point, which is to emphasize the foreknowledge and authority of Jesus. When Jesus predicts in advance how it will be, and the disciples find it "just as he had told them," Mark is showing the reader once again that the events of the passion do not take him by surprise. He is in control and goes willingly and resolutely to meet his suffering and death in full awareness of what lies ahead.

He will celebrate the Passover "with his disciples," not with his family. So, too, his disciples are not with their families. The group about the table represents the new family to which they belong (3:20–21, 31–35; 10:28–31).

[17–21] Jesus' disciples have prepared the Passover. Jesus comes with the Twelve. The meal that follows has thus been placed in a Passover framework: a lamb has been killed; it is after sunset; the group stays in the city, contrary to their usual practice, for only there can the Passover be celebrated; they recline to eat (the prescribed Passover ritual even for poor people[85]); there is unleavened bread and wine, normal for Passover but not for ordinary meals; the wine is called "fruit of the vine," as in the Passover liturgy; and at the conclusion of the meal they sing a hymn (v. 26). All this points to a Passover celebration, yet in Mark's spare description of the meal itself, distinctive Passover elements are missing: there are no bitter herbs, no recitation of the Exodus story explaining the meaning of the occasion, and no reference to the Passover lamb. Some scholars have seen this as evidence that historically Jesus' last meal was not a

---

85. Mishnah *Pes* 10.1. Reclining was the aristocratic form of dining. *Anakeimenōn* is found elsewhere in Mark only at 6:26 of the banquet in Herod's palace (though cf. 2:15; 14:3, *katakeimai*; and 6:40; 8:6 *anapiptō*). At Passover, however, all Jews reclined in the manner of nobility, illustrating that they had been slaves in Egypt, but now celebrate as free people.

Passover, while others have worked hard at showing the Markan account does after all fit the Passover pattern.[86] For Mark, it is important that the occasion be understood as a Passover meal, but the Markan Jesus refocuses its meaning for his disciples. Interpreters should not import their later awareness of what the Passover ritual was "really" like. If Mark's readers had such knowledge, which is probably not the case, Mark makes no point of it; the author himself may not have known the details of the Passover ritual. The Markan portrayal of the Last Supper contains only two items, the announcement of a traitor among the Twelve (17–21) and Jesus' interpretation of the bread and wine (22–25), each introduced with the participle *esthiontōn* "as they were eating."

[17] "After it had become evening" signaled a new day in the Jewish reckoning, Nisan 15, the Passover, which began at sundown on Thursday. That Jesus arrives "with the Twelve" (v. 17) could mean the two sent ahead did not belong to the Twelve and had remained at the guest room of verses 14–16, in which case the Last Supper would have included more than Jesus and the Twelve. However, Jesus' address to those present in verse 18 as "one of you" suggests that Mark thinks of only the Twelve as present (cf. the pointed identification of Judas in v. 10 as "the one of the Twelve," literally translating *ho heis tōn dōdeka*). It thus seems that Mark assumes throughout that only Jesus and the Twelve, including Judas, were present in the upper room. Mark's focus is on the words of Jesus, spoken to the reader over the heads of the characters in the scene, rather than providing information that allows readers to envision the tableau of the Last Supper in a historicizing manner.

[18] Mark's readers most likely knew from general Christian tradition that one of Jesus' own disciples had betrayed him to the authorities, and they had certainly known since 3:19 that Judas was the culprit. At the narrative level, the Twelve had been told since 8:31 that Jesus would suffer and be rejected by the Jewish leaders. Since 9:31; 10:33–34 they had known that this would involve a "handing over," but only now do they learn that this will involve one of their own number. What Jesus had predicted would happen to *them* in time to come (13:9, 12) was already happening in their midst, but instead of their being handed over to the authorities by family and friends, one of them will actually hand over *Jesus* to his death. Without directly quoting Scripture, Jesus clearly uses the language of the Psalter (Ps 41:9). "Eating with" is serious language in first-century Judaism, indicating a very close relationship, almost comparable to "sleeping with" in modern culture. That the traitor is someone who eats with Jesus strongly emphasizes that the new community Jesus has called into being is undergoing an extremely serious crisis.

---

86. E.g., Joachim Jeremias, *The Eucharistic Words of Jesus* (trans. Norman Perrin; New York: Scribner, 1966), 41–83; Schweizer, *Mark*, 294–97; Pesch, *Markusevangelium*, 347–49, 356–60.

[19–20] The disciples' reaction is grief, distress, anxiety, shock, dismay—
lypeisthai has all these connotations. Their shock is not a response to the
announcement of Jesus' coming death, which they here seem to take in stride,
but to the possibility that one of them will participate in bringing it about (see
notes *e, g* above). "One who dips (bread) into the (common) bowl with me" is
not here, as in John 13, a specific pointer to Judas, but continues the imagery
of Ps 41:9—it is one of Jesus' closest associates, one he has called to be with
him (3:14), one of the Twelve, who will hand him over to death.

[21] Although this saying takes up the "woe" terminology adopted by
Israel's prophets from the language of lamentation and used by them in pronouncing of God's judgment (e.g., Hos 7:13; 9:12; Amos 6:1; Isa 5:8; 31:1; Jer
13:27), here as in 13:27 (the only other instance in Mark) it is not a "woe oracle" pronouncing judgment, but an expression of compassion bewailing the situation of the betrayer. It is not a pronouncement about his eternal destiny, but
expresses sorrow for the wretched present existence of the betrayer. The saying expresses the paradox of divine sovereignty and human responsibility. Jesus
foresees his death and goes willingly to it as integral to the will of God revealed
in Scripture ("as it stands written"; cf. 9:12 and the *dei* of divine necessity in
8:31; 9:11; 13:7, 10), yet this does not absolve the betrayer of responsibility for
his own decision. It is this theological point, not a psychological ploy on Jesus'
part to get Judas to renege, with which Mark is concerned.

[22–25] The discussion here is focused on Mark's meaning, and will necessarily leave out of account the complex questions of the original form and
meaning of these words in the life of Jesus, the relation of the Markan form to
the other New Testament accounts (Matt 26:26–29; Luke 22:15–20; 1 Cor
11:23–26), and the centuries-long discussion within the church, sometimes
acrimonious, regarding eucharistic doctrine and practice. Mark's church must
have regularly celebrated the Eucharist, the meaning of which would be further
illuminated by his terse narrative, but this brief scene is intended neither to be
the founding narrative for "the institution of the Lord's Supper" nor an exposi-
tion of eucharistic doctrine, either for the disciples in the story or for the reader's
situation. Mark focuses on Jesus, not on church practice, on Christology not
ecclesiology. Readers overhear what Jesus *once* said to the disciples; it speaks
to them indirectly, not, as in 1 Cor 11:23–26, directly.[87]

[22] The interpreter should not attempt to correlate this second reference to
"while they were eating . . ." with the order of the Passover ritual (Mark does
not do so). The phrase serves as the transition to a new set of sayings, introducing a fragment of tradition that circulated independently. The meal contin-

---

87. The Markan narrative throughout portrays a network of disciples en route, on "the way" (cf.
Excursus: The Way at 1:3). It does not directly "establish communal rites to be repeated, either Baptism or the Lord's Supper." See Rhoads, *Reading Mark*, 106.

ues as though nothing had happened, somewhat anomalously after the explosive announcement in the preceding verses. Jesus assumes the role of the head of the family, gives thanks to God for the bread, which he breaks and distributes to the disciples. The words of blessing and thanksgiving said with regard to the bread and wine are directed to God, not to the bread and cup, and do not effect a change in their substance (see on 6:41). No appeal to Aramaic or Greek vocabulary or grammar can settle the disputed issue of how the relation of the bread and Jesus' body is to be understood. The Greek *estin* ("is") can mean "is" or "means," but just how either is to be understood requires further clarification. In any case, to translate as "symbolizes" or "represents" is too restrictive. Jesus gives no soteriological comment regarding the bread, and there is no suggestion that "breaking" (the normal act in distributing bread) points to his violent death. By eating the bread, the disciples are to know that they somehow become participants in Jesus' own destiny, but this saying does not specify how this is to be. Receiving and eating bread that Jesus has somehow identified with his very self may be an enactment of what he had said in 8:34–38. It is not said that the disciples at the narrative level now finally grasp what they had failed to understand in the two previous scenes where Jesus broke the bread (6:52; 8:21)—but the reader understands.

[23–24] Jesus passes the cup, and at his command they all drink from it. The words then said over the cup identify it (i.e., its contents) with Jesus' blood. Both "body" and "blood" refer to the person's life or self as a whole, not to parts or aspects of one's being. The "pouring out" or "shedding" of blood is biblical idiom for death. The blood is identified with or related to the blood of the covenant, in words taken from Exod 24:8. After God's deliverance of Israel from Egypt, at Sinai God constituted them as God's own covenant people. Jesus applies such language to himself; his death is the means of God's ultimate covenant-making act for "many," biblical idiom for "all," and here there are echoes of Isa 53:12 (see on 10:45 for the soteriological interpretation of Jesus' death and for its universal scope). This is Mark's only reference to "covenant." While it is not a major theological category for him, the imagery places Jesus' death within the framework of God's eschatological saving event in which God's covenant with Israel is not nullified or superseded, but eschatologically renewed.

[25] The Last Supper dialogue concludes as it began, with an *amēn* saying (v. 18). As the bread and cup words had pointed ahead to Jesus' impending death, this saying points beyond death to Jesus' presence in the coming kingdom of God. A powerful image of the eschatological kingdom is that of the messianic banquet, with God's salvation portrayed as a great feast in which there is food and drink for all (cf. Isa 25:6–9; *1 En.* 62.13–16; *2 Bar.* 29.5–8; 1QSa 2.11–22; Luke 13:28–30; Rev 19:9). Jesus does not explicitly picture himself as presiding as Messiah in the transcendent world, nor does he include the disciples (Matt 26:29 adds "with you"). There is much in later church eucharistic

reflection that is missing here. Mark's interest is directed to portraying Jesus as the one who foresees both his own death and God's vindication of him beyond death, not in teaching eucharistic doctrine.

There is no command to repeat, no "in remembrance of me." It is not clear whether Jesus himself eats and drinks. Since Jesus insists he will not drink wine until the kingdom of God, from this scene alone the reader would not have the image of Jesus' followers celebrating his eucharistic presence with them in the time between resurrection and Parousia. While Mark is not developing a doctrine of the "Real *Absence*," when Jesus' statement in verse 25 is combined with 2:20 (also an eating and drinking scene), 14:7, and 16:7, it does seem clear that Mark has no explicit doctrine of Jesus' eucharistic *presence* with his church.

14:26–31 Predictions of Suffering and Scattering, Resurrection and Regathering

14:26 And when they had sung the hymn,[a] they went out to the Mount of Olives. 27 And Jesus says to them, "You will all fall away,[b] for it is written, 'I will strike the shepherd, and the sheep will be scattered.' 28 But after I am raised up, I will go before you into Galilee." 29 And Peter was saying to him, "Even if all fall away, I will not." 30 And Jesus says to him, "Amen[c] I say to you, this day, this very night, before the second cockcrow,[d] you will deny me three times." 31 But he kept emphatically insisting, "Even if I must die with you, I will not deny you." And so said they all.

a. *Hymnēsantes* is a participle, lit. "having hymned," so whether the article is included in the English translation and whether the singular or plural is understood is a matter of context. If the later Mishna accurately portrays the earlier Passover practice, and if Mark was aware of this, the reference here is to Ps 118 (or 115–18 or parts thereof; see commentary below).

b. On *skandalizō*, see note *d* at 6:3.

c. On *amēn*, see note *g* at 3:28.

d. The omission of *dis* ("a second time") here by ℵ D W and a few other MSS, and the variations of its position in the clause in other MSS, is related to the omission of the first cockcrow in v. 68 in key MSS. The textual transmission is complex, since only Mark has the two cock-crowings, which is difficult to understand in any case. Thus scribes tended to make Jesus' prediction accurate and Mark internally consistent and to harmonize Mark and the other Gospels, which predict only one cock-crow and later report only one. Yet *dis* is both well-attested and the more difficult reading and is thus to be preferred as original.

Mark has framed the Passover meal with references to Jesus' betrayal, abandonment, and denial by his own disciples (cf. 14:10–11, 18–21), and emphasizes that Jesus predicts these in detail. This scene revolves around the three predictions that God will strike the shepherd (Jesus), and the sheep (the disciples) will be scattered; that Jesus will be raised and go before the disciples to Galilee; and that Peter will deny Jesus three times. The narrator emphasizes again that the events about to happen will not take Jesus by surprise; instead he knows them and willingly goes to meet them.

[26] Tradition only documented later (*m. Pes.* 10.5–7) specifies that the Hallel psalms (113–118) were to be sung at the Passover meal. The rabbis debated which were to be sung before and which at its close; the prominent school of Hillel specified 113–114 before the meal and 115–118 after the fourth cup. Since Mark nowhere else refers to Jesus and the disciples singing, either he or his tradition may have been aware of this aspect of the Seder prescriptions. Conversely, Mark or his tradition may have been influenced by the Christian practice of singing at eucharistic meals. Psalm 118 has already played a role in the shaping of the Markan story (cf. Ps 118:22 / Mark 8:31; Ps 118:22–23 / Mark 12:10–11; Ps 118:25–26 / Mark 11:9–10). Likewise, the Mount of Olives plays a role not only in Old Testament predictions of the eschatological events (Zech 13–14; cf. 14:4) but in the previous Markan narrative (11:1; 13:3). Jesus and the disciples do not return to Bethany where they had been staying (11:11–12; 14:3), but remain in the city as specified in the Passover regulations (the festal meal lasted until very late). To facilitate compliance with the requirement that Passover participants remain in Jerusalem the whole night, the rabbis had declared part of the Mount of Olives to belong to the city.

[27] In 2 Sam 15:16–30, David is betrayed by a trusted friend, goes to the Mount of Olives, weeps, and prays to God. The passion narrative as a whole is deeply influenced by biblical imagery (see esp. Brown, *Death of the Messiah*, 1:145–67), but only here is the Scripture formally quoted (see *Excursus: Mark and the Scripture* at 14:52). The text here agrees with neither the MT nor the LXX of Zech 13:7; Mark is not concerned with the ancient meaning in the literary and historical context of Zechariah, but reads the text christologically as an expression of his own theology.[88] "Strike" is an imperative in both the MT and LXX; God commands someone else to strike the shepherd. In Mark's citation, this becomes "I will strike," with God as the obvious speaker. Mark's change may have been influenced by his reading of Isa 53:4, 6, 10 it which it is Yahweh who "bruises" and "puts to grief" the servant. As in Mark 1:2–3 (also "Isaiah"), Scripture modulates into the voice of God. Mark appeals to Scripture to show that the death of Jesus, though carried out by human beings who bear

---

88. The Zechariah text seems to have played a role in the nationalist-military theology of the Zealots during the 66–70 revolt. Mark may cite it here in terms of his alternate understanding: the promises of God's faithfulness are not fulfilled by a militarist messiah, but one who willingly goes to suffering and death. Discipleship to such a messiah is not to take up arms against Rome, but to follow him on the way to the cross. Cf. Marcus, *Way of the Lord*, 161–63.

responsibility for their decisions, is nonetheless the act of God. For Mark, the "shepherd" is Jesus, but here, too, biblical imagery for God is applied to Jesus (see on 6:34). The "sheep" are here Jesus' disciples, who will be scattered by the overwhelming events.[89] The passive voice is important; they will not "scatter" but their being-scattered by the shepherd's being-struck is incorporated into God's act that affects not only Jesus but the disciples.

[28] The *alla* ("but") indicates that this promised meeting in Galilee can restore the relationship between Jesus and his disciples, a relationship they do not even realize is [going to be] broken. The death of Jesus and the scattering of the disciples is not the end. The God who strikes Jesus and scatters the disciples will raise Jesus and regather the community. Neither resurrection nor reunion in Galilee are plotted in Mark's narrative, but both are presupposed in its narrative world (see on 16:7). The shepherd imagery continues. As in 10:32, where the same word, *proagōn*, is used, Jesus will go before his frightened and dismayed disciples, but this is to be visualized as the resurrected Lord preceding his disciples to Galilee and encountering them there, not as though Jesus will rejoin his disciples in Jerusalem and lead them to Galilee. Yet 16:7 leaves the imagery open, for readers to fill in. The Markan point is not how the resurrection is to be conceptualized, but the promise that following Jesus and belonging to the community of faith will still be possible after the disciples have denied and been dispersed. As the scattering is divine judgment, the regathering is divine grace.

[29–31] Peter emphatically distinguishes himself from the other disciples; the *ouk egō* at the end of the sentence places the emphasis on "I" over against the others. The events of the passion that will cause the community to disintegrate and result in each individual's own response has already begun. Jesus' response, introduced with the solemn prophetic *amēn*, corresponds to Peter's own claim, emphasizing the second-person singular pronoun "you." Both Jesus and Peter understand they are now talking about more than being scattered, more than a momentary lapse, but whether one will remain a disciple or repudiate Jesus. The whole interchange reflects the terminology and meaning of 8:31–38. Here Peter seems to understand, at least at one level, that Jesus will die and calls others to follow him even it means their own death. Peter asserts that he will not deny Jesus, even if he must die with him, using a form of the verb *dei* that Jesus had used to express his own death as part of the divine plan (cf. on 8:31; 9:11–12). All the other disciples say the same, but the "all" here is no longer the one community of faith, but a group of individuals who enter the calamitous events on their own resources; the community dissolves. The readers know what the characters in the story cannot know, that all will forsake Jesus

---

89. On "flock" as metaphor for the people of God, an image that binds together Israel and the church, see Best, *Following Jesus*, 210–12.

and that Peter will deny him. They also know that the community has been regathered, and that Peter has died as a martyr only a short time before the Gospel was written, and from this story they take courage for the trials they, too, are facing.

14:32–52 Jesus Prays, Is Arrested; Disciples Sleep, Abandon Him

The narrative of Jesus' agony in Gethsemane is often treated separately from the account of his arrest. Yet the location is the same, and "immediately, while he was still speaking" of verse 43 fuses the two episodes into one scene, which contrasts the constancy of Jesus with the failure of the disciples. As in the preceding scene, the story of Jesus and the disciples is interwoven throughout; to ask whether it deals with Christology or parenesis is a misplaced question.

14:32 And they come to a place[a] called Gethsemane, and he says to his disciples, "Sit here while I pray." 33 And he takes with him Peter and James and John, and he began to be overwhelmed with horror and anguish. 34 And he says to them, "I[b] am overwhelmed with sorrow, to the point of death; stay here and stay alert.[c] 35 And he went a little further, and was falling to the ground and praying that, if possible, the hour might pass him by. 36 And he was saying, "Abba, Father, everything is possible for you. Take this cup from me. Yet not what I want, but what you want." 37 And he comes and finds them sleeping, and says to Peter, "Simon, are you asleep? Could you not stay alert for one hour? 38 Stay alert[,][d] and pray[,][e] that you may not be put to the test. The Spirit[f] is willing, but the flesh is weak." 39 And again he went away and was praying, saying the same words. 40 And again he came and found them sleeping, for their eyes were weighed down, and they did not know what to say to him. 41 And he comes the third time and says to them, "Are you still sleeping and resting?[g] It is settled.[h] The hour has come. See, the Son of Man is being betrayed into the hands of sinners. 42 Get up! Here we go! See, here comes the one who is handing me over!"[i]

43 And suddenly, while he was still speaking, Judas, one of the Twelve, arrives, and with him a crowd with swords and clubs, from the chief priests, the scribes, and the elders. 44 Now the one who is handing him over had given them a sign, saying, "He is the one I will kiss; arrest him and take him away under guard." 45 And when he came he immediately went up to him and says, "Rabbi," and kissed him with a show of affection. 46 And they laid hands on him and arrested him. 47 But one of the bystanders drew his sword, struck the slave of the high priest, and took off his ear. 48 And Jesus said to them, "Have you come out with swords and clubs to arrest me, as though you were going after a bandit? 49 I was

with you daily,[j] teaching in the temple, and you did not arrest me. But this is happening to fulfill the Scriptures.[k] 50 And they all deserted him and fled. 51 And a certain young man was following him[l], wearing nothing but a linen cloth, and they seized him, 52 but he left the linen cloth behind and fled naked.

a. In contrast to a city, *chōrion* ("place") refers to any unpopulated area, e.g., a field or group of fields surrounding a city, or to a particular field or piece of land. Gethsemane probably means "olive press," and refers to a particular field or place. Mark does not call the place a garden (*kēpos*), which comes from John 18:1, which has no reference to "Gethsemane."

b. *Hē psychē mou* is lit. "my soul," but this is the typical LXX rendering of the common Hebrew expression *naphshi,* which refers to the self, the whole person, not an interior "part," and is thus the equivalent of "I." One might translate it as "my whole being."

c. *Grēgoreite,* exactly the same as the final word of 13:37.

d. Here the verbs shift from second-person singular to second-person plural.

e. The Greek syntax may be so construed that the conjunction *hina* refers to the purpose of staying alert and praying, signaled in English by inserting the comma after "pray," or the *hina* may indicate the content of the prayer, indicated by the comma after "alert."

f. The Greek text does not distinguish capital and small letters. The English word is capitalized to indicate the Holy Spirit (see commentary).

g. Since the indicative and imperative forms are here identical, and since the ancient MSS had no punctuation apparatus, there are three translation possibilities, all of which are represented in English translations and commentaries: (1) as an exclamatory statement, "You're still sleeping and resting!" (2) as a command, either seriously or sarcastically, "Go ahead and sleep . . . ," (3) or as a question, not for information, but as an expression of shock, "What, you're still sleeping and taking your rest?"

h. The notorious translation and exegetical problem is posed by the dual facts that *apechei* itself has several meanings and its subject in this sentence is not clear. Matthew, Luke, and a few MSS of Mark simply omit it, while others add *to telos* ("the end"), apparently to facilitate the meaning "Is the end far off?" (as you sleeping disciples seem to think). The Vulgate renders it *sufficit,* "it is enough," followed by many translations. Since the word sometimes refers to completing a financial transaction, some interpreters have understood the word as referring to Judas's deal with the chief priests, now complete as he delivers Jesus to them. No interpreter or translator can operate with confidence here. The above translation understands the word as Jesus' concluding word on the ordeal he has just undergone, a way of expressing resolute acceptance of God's will.[90]

i. Literally, "the one who is handing me over has come near." Mark uses *ēngiken* only here and 1:15, of the kingdom of God. See note *d* there.

90. Eta Linnemann, *Studien zur Passionsgeschichte* (FRLANT 102; Göttingen: Vandenhoeck & Ruprecht, 1970), 24–28, so understands the word, regarding it as referring not just to the Gethsemane experience, but to the passion narrative as a whole. So also Collins, *Beginning of the Gospel,* 96, who differs from Linnemann in regarding the Gethsemane pericope not as a story that could have existed independently, but as an introduction to the following stories.

j. *Kath' hēmeran* is regularly used in the distributive sense, "day by day," "daily," "day after day," but could mean "in the daytime" (in contrast to the covert night arrest you have chosen).

k. The clause is elliptical, *all' hina plērōthōsin hai graphai,* lit. "but that the Scriptures may be fulfilled," requiring something to complete the sense. Other possibilities understand the *hina* as imperatival, resulting in "let the Scriptures be fulfilled" or "the Scriptures must be fulfilled."

l. *Synēkolouthei,* not *akoloutheō,* Mark's typical word for "following" in the sense of discipleship, but the only other occurrence of the word in the Gospel (5:37) shows Mark can use the word of a disciple.

[32–34] The three disciples who constitute Jesus' inner circle have witnessed Jesus' power over death (5:37), his transfiguration (9:2), and (along with Andrew) have heard Jesus' eschatological instructions that concluded with the command to "stay alert" (13:3; cf. 13:37). They have been especially privileged to become witnesses of the divine power at work in him ("truly divine"); now they are challenged to witness his human weakness as he struggles with death ("truly human"). They will falter and fail Jesus in his hour of need. Yet the Markan readers know that all three have in fact suffered martyrdom (see on 10:39–40, which is also connected to this pericope by the "cup" imagery). The words *ekthambeisthai kai adēmonein,* translated as "overwhelmed with horror and anguish," represent Jesus as barely in control, on the verge of panic, reflecting not only the depth of suffering of a human being who shudders on the threshold of torture and death, but also the numinous terror of the eschatological, transcendent nature of what is about to transpire, a sorrow and anguish so intense it already threatens his life. Jesus' words represent the language of God's eschatological act, without explicating a theory of the atonement. Both "cup" (v. 36) and "hour" (vv. 35, 37, 41) are eschatological terms. The "cup" often represents the final judgment of God (Rev 14:10; 18:3; see on 10:38–39), while "hour," like "day," refers to the hour of God's eschatological judgment and salvation (13:32; 14:25, 30, 35; cf. Rev 9:15). As in his only articulate words from the cross (15:34 = Ps 22:1), Jesus' misery is expressed in words reflecting the suffering righteous one of the Psalter (Pss 42:6, 11; 43:5; 55:4–5; 118:17–18, the latter psalm having just been sung as part of the Passover liturgy). Jesus seeks human companionship; he wants his closest friends to be with him, to remain alert and pray.

[35] Falling on the ground is not the normal posture for prayer. It is the attitude of worship, supplication, and awe in the presence of the holy (Matt 17:6; Luke 5:12; 17:16; 24:5; 1 Cor 14:25; Rev 7:11; 11:16); it can also be the expression of desperation and exhaustion. Mark's language throughout this scene is shocking to the reader, presented without restraint and without comment. Jesus has previously announced his suffering and death with sovereign objectivity (8:31; 9:31; 10:33–34); now he quakes before its reality, and prays that the cup

and the hour might pass him by. He prays to the God for whom all things are possible (cf. 9:23), the God who is not bound by any preordained system or constraints, even those of his own making (see on 13:19–20). Three levels are interwoven in all serious grappling with this text, which the modern reader might well attempt to distinguish, though they cannot be separated: (1) The historical man of Nazareth was a human being who, despite his trust in God, trembled at the prospect of death. He is not a Stoic, serene in his transcendent philosophy, who is unperturbed by what people might do to his flesh, nor is he the triumphant martyr who scoffs at his tormentors. In terms of heroism, the Jesus of Gethsemane comes off poorly when compared to Socrates. Jesus was about thirty years old, celebrated life, and did not want to die. (2) Mark views the scene not only as an instance of human suffering, the result of human sin and injustice, but christologically. Mark's Christology incorporates and affirms the reality of the human Jesus, his weakness and his suffering. It is important for Mark to represent Jesus as truly human and truly divine. Yet the Markan Jesus is not a cardboard theological figure who only serves as a cipher for Mark's Christology. The present scene locates Jesus on the human side of the ledger, but as one who finally submits his will to God's. Mark believes Jesus' death is not an isolated tragedy but integral to God's saving plan. Jesus' death is salvific, yet Mark elaborates no theology of the atonement (10:45; 14:24). It is important to Mark not to see Jesus as a scapegoat for the sins of humanity, not a third party in the transaction between God and humanity. Mark respects the ultimate mystery of God's saving act in the weakness and death of the truly human Jesus of Nazareth, and acknowledges the mystery of God's acting through the sinful acts of those who betray, condemn, and execute him. Mark affirms and narrates this mystery, but does not elaborate or explain it, does not incorporate it within some larger theological system. (3) Later Christian theology, which has affected many modern readers' approach to this text, did develop doctrinal statements that attempt to do justice to the christological issues involved, especially by developing Trinitarian theology and theories of the atonement. Mark provides beginnings and raw materials for both christological doctrine and atonement theory; in both cases Markan elements are in line with and the basis for later developments, but Mark does not spell them out.[91]

[36] Jesus addresses God in prayer as *abba,* the respectful but familiar Aramaic word used in the intimacy of the family, not only by children but by mature

---

91. Cf. not only the ecumenical creeds, but, e.g., Karl Barth, *Church Dogmatics, Volume IV: The Doctrine of Reconciliation, Part One* (trans. Geoffrey Bromiley; Edinburgh: T. & T. Clark, 1956), 268–70. Barth reflects on the coincidence of human obedience and divine will, and the coincidence of God's saving act and human evil acts involved in this narrative. He argues that confronting the shocking depth of this mystery was an element in Jesus' own consternation and suffering in Gethsemane, and this has been preserved by Mark.

men addressing their fathers, and sometimes by students addressing a revered rabbinic teacher. It is not the equivalent of English "daddy." Whether Jesus was absolutely unique in this usage remains disputed,[92] but it is clear that this was a distinct, somewhat shockingly unusual address to God, expressing Jesus' own understanding of his relationship to God. The Old Testament and Jewish tradition sometimes referred to God as "Father," but there is no clear instance of *abba* as address to God in prayer. On the basis of Jesus' usage, his followers adopted this language, even in Greek-speaking Hellenistic Christianity (cf. Rom 8:15; Gal 4:6). Jesus will receive the cup from the hand of his Father, not from some dark impersonal fate; he is not the tragic hero of Greek drama. He prays in trusting obedience, but nonetheless asks if there is not some other way. Neither the Markan Jesus nor the narrator provides an explanation for why it was God's will that Jesus die. The interpreter should not provide one either, but should remember that Mark writes retrospectively when the horrible death of Jesus was a given fact of history; *that* it was the will of the God for whom all things are possible seemed clear. Mark and his community have a retrospective view and place the event as somehow within the salvific plan of God. The Markan Jesus still sees the event prospectively, trembles but does not rebel, prays that not his will but God's be done. Later Christian theology's quest for a viable theological explanation is based on Mark's own dialectical perspective that "God" and "Jesus" are not finally separable persons.

The narrative has points of contact with the Lord's Prayer: address as "Father," prayer for God's will to be done (v. 36) and deliverance from testing / temptation (v. 38; cf. also the echo in 11:25). The scene also evokes the transfiguration (9:2–8), where Jesus is accompanied by the same three disciples, there is a divine revelation of Jesus' identity, and they do not know how to respond (v. 40). There, it was the revelation of Jesus' divine glory, here, of his human weakness. The disciples do not yet know how to see either in their full manifestation; seeing them together as God's definitive self-revelation in the humanity of Jesus is still altogether beyond them. At the transfiguration, Jesus and the inner circle of three heard the heavenly voice. Here, Jesus speaks, the disciples sleep, and the heavens are silent. The events themselves will reveal God's response to the prayer.

---

92. The classic arguments for this view are found in Joachim Jeremias, *The Prayers of Jesus* (SBT 2/6; Naperville, Ill.: Alec R. Allenson, 1967), 11–65, considered too extreme by, e.g., Mary Rose D'Angelo, "'Abba' and 'Father': Imperial Theology and the Jesus Traditions," *JBL* 111, no. 4 (1992): 611–30. James Barr, "'Abba' Isn't 'Daddy'," *JTS* 39 (1988): 28–47, is not a refutation of Jeremias, but a correction of the way his point is popularly misunderstood. Joseph A. Fitzmyer, S.J., "*Abba* and Jesus' Relation to God," in *A cause de l'Evangile: Études sur les Synoptiques et les Actes: Offertes au P. Jacques Dupont, O.S.B. à l'occasion de son 70e anniversaire* (ed. Jacques Dupont; LD 123; Paris: Cerf, 1985), 15–38, essentially supports Jeremias. See now the balanced discussion of Marcus, *Mark 8–16*, ad loc.

[37–40] Jesus returns to find the disciples sleeping, rebukes and challenges them, and returns to pray. This happens three times, emphasizing both Jesus' constancy in prayer and the disciples' repeated failure. The three times correspond to Peter's threefold denial, already predicted and shortly to happen, and to the threefold designation of the hour in Jesus' crucifixion. He speaks to Peter as the representative of all (the verbs become plural in mid-sentence at v. 38). As Jesus had addressed God personally and intimately, so he speaks to Peter (the narrator's designation) as "Simon"—the only instance in the Gospel of Jesus addressing a person by name. If this is a question (see note *g* above), it expresses not only surprise and rebuke, but promise, "You are able to stay alert with me one hour, aren't you?" The command to "stay alert and pray" addresses the situation—if they do what Jesus does in his hour of trial, they will be strong and endure as he does. He prays and they sleep; he endures and they run away. The instruction transcends the situation, however, and speaks over the heads of the sleepy disciples to the Markan readers, who are exhorted to stay alert and pray that they will not come into a situation of testing they cannot withstand. Likewise, the basis for this exhortation transcends the situation.

"The spirit is willing, but the flesh is weak" can be understood as a commonplace comment on human nature, as though "spirit" is one's "inner self" and "flesh" is one's material nature. Then the comment would be an expression of general Hellenistic wisdom: "our inner self wants to do what is right, but our weak flesh hinders us from carrying out the will of the inner self," a comment on the general human condition. They should then pray for more inward stamina to overcome the weakness of the flesh, which gets reduced to "try harder." In this view representing commonplace Greek anthropology, "spirit" and "flesh" are understood dualistically as two parts or aspects of human life that struggle against each other, and prayer is to strengthen the "good" part of this internal struggle. It is more likely, however, that "Spirit" and "flesh" are understood in the biblical and Hebrew sense, in which "flesh" represents human being as such and in its totality, with "Spirit" representing God's power. In this view, the disciple as "flesh" is weak through and through, has no "good" internal "part" that struggles against the flesh, and as a human being relying on human resources is destined to fail. This is the situation of the disciples in the story; it includes Jesus' own humanity. This is the situation the Markan readers are warned against. Stay alert and pray for the Spirit, the gift of God, that alone can deliver from the time of testing. This terminology is found only here in Mark, but cf. Gen 6:3; Ps 51, Isa 31:3; Joel 2:28; John 3:6; 6:63; Acts 2:17; Rom 8:4–13; Gal 5:16.

[40] The persistent and repeated sleep of the disciples, in the presence of Jesus' own sufferings and despite his rebukes and challenges, makes even the reader who has become more-or-less accustomed to their failure and obtuseness call for an explanation. The narrator inserts a clarifying *gar* ("for") clause explaining the disciples' persistent sleepiness. It is not at the level of historicizing explanations attempting to excuse the disciples' conduct ("it was late"; "they had had a big meal"; "stress"), but on the same plane as the numerous other *gar* clauses in which the narrator gives his own explanation as an aside to the reader, often with explicit theological overtones (cf., e.g., 1:22; 3:21; 5:8, 42; 6:18, 52; 7:3; 9:31; 10:22; 11:13, 18, 32; 12:12; 14:2, 56; 15:10; 16:8). The passive is important: their eyes were weigh*ed* down, not just heavy. This corresponds to their hearts that are not just hard, but have been harden*ed* (see on 3:5; 6:52). They are not absolved of responsibility, but neither they nor anyone else can be alert to what is happening until seen in the light of the cross and resurrection. Thus their not-knowing-what-to-say is more than nonplussed embarrassment, but corresponds exactly to 9:6.

[41–42] However the words of Jesus are interpreted and translated (see translation notes above), it is clear that Jesus has regained his composure, that his prayer has been answered and will be answered in the ensuing events, and that he is again in charge. Though the ones who betray, arrest, condemn, and execute Jesus are culpable, the "sinners" into whose hands the Son of Man is betrayed are not merely the notorious offenders of the passion story, but are identical with the "human hands" of 9:31. The "one who is handing me over" is at once Judas, who has fulfilled his assignment in delivering Jesus into the hands of the Sanhedrin, and God, who delivers Jesus up as the suffering servant (see on 9:30–31), the One whose kingdom "comes near" in the approach of Judas and the cross. "Here comes the one / One who is handing me over" fuses the approach of Judas and the crowd with the approach of God who is active even in human evil, and correlates with the approach of the kingdom Jesus has proclaimed and lived out. Though a bit too slangy for the context, the resolute "Here we go!" catches the nuances of Jesus' performative language as Jesus himself affirms and initiates the final events, and bids the disciples to get up and join him.

[43–47] Judas is mentioned for the first time since 14:10. Though he was apparently present at the Last Supper, nothing is made of this, and no mention is made of his departure. This is the last reference to Judas. Mark shows no interest in him as a narrative character or in his tragic fate, variously elaborated in the other Gospels and later Christian tradition (e.g., Matt 27:3–10; Acts 1:16–20), but is only interested in his role in delivering up Jesus to be killed. The crowd that emerges with Judas is not a lynch mob, nor even a posse of angry citizens deputized by the temple authorities. Since they are armed; are specifically designated as sent by the chief priests, scribes, and elders (cf. 10:33b; 11:18, 27–28; 15:1, 10); have Judas as their leader; know the sign he will give to designate the one to be apprehended; take Jesus into custody; and bring him to the high priest, they are portrayed as an authorized police force including a slave of the high priest. They are probably not the temple police, but a group of officers under the authority of the Sanhedrin whose duty it was to apprehend and keep in custody those to be tried by the Sanhedrin, and to have charge of them until their case was disposed of (cf. the "guards" of v. 54, and note *b* there). In Mark, they do not include Roman soldiers (contrast John 18:3). Thus by "crowd" Mark does not here mean the multitude of potential disciples that throughout the narrative has been attracted to Jesus' teaching and miracles (see *Excursus: Crowds, Followers, Disciples, and the Twelve* at 6:6). However, by using the word "crowd" here, Mark signals that the group of potential disciples who have not decided for him will ultimately be against him (cf. 9:40; 15:11, 15; note *a* at 10:2). Like Judas, the crowd is switching sides.

The scene is realistic. "Rabbi" was a customary address, but in Mark it has the overtones of failed discipleship (cf. on 9:5; 10:51; 11:21). A kiss was a customary form of greeting (cf. Gen 29:13; Exod 18:7; Luke 7:45), continued in the life of the church (cf. Rom 16:16; 1 Cor 16:20; 2 Cor 13:12; 1 Thess 5:26; 1 Pet 5:14). Biblical examples already existed of the deceitful, traitorous kiss (2 Sam 20:9; Prov 27:6; Sir 29:5). Even so, there is an overtone of Mark's Christology: Jesus looks like an ordinary human being; there is nothing distinctive about his appearance; in the darkness and confusion the deputies need to have Jesus pointed out to them. Jesus alone is taken into custody. The arresting party is not interested in the disciples as members of a "Jesus movement," but only in Jesus.

"One of the bystanders" seems to refer neither to a disciple nor to one of the arresting party, but to one of a group who had followed Judas and his group out of curiosity. Thus his wounding the slave of the high priest seems to have been an abortive attempt to defend Jesus by one of his sympathizers—there must have been many such in Jerusalem at the festival. Neither the narrator nor the Markan Jesus makes anything of the incident, but later Gospels clarify the ambiguities of the scene: the swordsman was one of the disciples; Jesus rebukes him and provides an explanation to the reader (Matt 26:51–54; Luke 22:49–54; specifically Peter, John 18:10, who also gives a name to the slave).

[48–49] The Markan Jesus seems to ignore the dramatic events that have just happened (cf. the relation of 14:22–25 to 14:17–21). He responds neither to Judas nor to the sword episode, but addresses the arresting party. He rebukes them for coming after him as though he were a bandit. The word "bandit" occurs for the second time in Mark (see on 11:17), and will occur again at the cross (see on 15:27). They could have arrested him in broad daylight as he taught in the temple, for neither he nor his followers are armed and they would not resist—incidentally indicating that the swordsman does not belong to his own group. Armed force is not necessary, because Jesus is voluntarily being delivered up according to the will of God revealed in Scripture, not overtaken by the force of arms. The characters in the story act on their own volition, as though they were in charge, with no sense of what is "really" happening.

[50–52] As Jesus had predicted (14:27–31), all the disciples flee. The narrator reports it laconically, without comment. Except for the scene in the courtyard of the high priest in which Peter denies his association with Jesus—a specific dramatic illustration of the failure of all the disciples—this is the disciples' last appearance in the Gospel (but cf. on 16:7). The abandonment of Jesus by all his followers is further illustrated by the strange incident of the young man who fled away naked. It is not comic relief. The modern reader may smile, but running away naked was a matter of deep shame; the young man chose shame over confession of the Son of Man (cf. 8:38). Among the several interpretations attempting to explain this bizarre episode,[93] within the story line of the Markan narrative as a whole it seems best to regard it as the final

93. The general interpretation here followed is now widely accepted; among those who argue for it are Ludger Schenke, *Studien zur Passionsgeschichte des Markus: Tradition und Redaktion in Markus 14, 1–42* (FB 4; Würzburg: Echter Verlag, 1971), 356–59, 427–29; Howard M. Jackson, "Why the Youth Shed His Cloak and Fled Naked: The Meaning and Purpose of Mark 14:51–52," *JBL* 116, no. 2 (1997): 273–89, who provides further bibliography. The following alternatives to the interpretation pursued here are not all mutually exclusive; some may have been factors in Mark's primary meaning suggested above.

(1) Assuming the episode has "no obvious theological significance," it is considered to simply reflect a fragment of historical tradition (Hooker, *Mark*, 352). A popular variation of this view, in the traditional understanding of Mark, is that here the author adroitly inserts himself into the narrative. The naked young man was John Mark, in whose house the Last Supper was held, who was awakened from his sleep by the temple police who came to the house after Jesus had left, then followed the group without taking time to dress, hid in the bushes and overheard Jesus' prayer while the disciples slept, and barely escaped being apprehended himself (cf., e.g., Zahn, *Introduction*, 2:492–95, rejuvenating one of several patristic interpretations [Victor of Antioch, *Catena on Mark* 14:51]).

(2) The scene was composed or shaped by Mark or by someone in pre-Markan tradition on the basis of Amos 2:16, "And those who are stout of heart . . . shall flee away naked in that day" (cf., e.g., C. G. Montefiore and Israel Abrahams, *The Synoptic Gospels* [2d ed.; LBS; New York: Ktav, 1968], 349–50; Frederick C. Grant, "Introduction and Exegesis of Mark," in *The Interpreter's Bible* [ed. George Arthur Buttrick; IB 7; 12 vols.; Nashville: Abingdon], 7:886).

(3) The cryptic story is the result of Mark's inept attempt to cover up an incident reported more accurately in the *Secret Gospel of Mark*, in which Jesus initiated naked young men into the mysteries of the kingdom of God (Morton Smith, *Jesus the Magician* [San Francisco: Harper & Row, 1978], 134; on the *Secret Gospel of Mark*, introduction, 4, note 18).

(4) The reappearance of the linen cloth as a burial shroud (15:46) and the young man clad in a white robe in the tomb on Easter morning (16:5) have generated a variety of symbolic interpretations. The young man represents Jesus who, though arrested and killed, "escapes" death, leaves behind his shroud in the tomb and reappears at Easter. Or: the young man represents the disciples who fled but are renewed by the Easter event, or reflects the baptismal practice of the early church, in which candidates removed their old clothing, were baptized nude, and emerged to put on new garments, all related to the death and resurrection of Jesus (cf., e.g., Albert Vanhoye, "La fuite du jeune homme nu [Mc 14,51–52]," *Bib* 52 [1971]: 401–6; LaVerdiere, *Beginning*, 2:254–55, 320–22). Or: since *sindōn* is used only here and for the shroud in which Jesus is buried, it has been argued that the young man represents those disciples, both in the narrative and in Mark's situation, who too-eagerly declared their willingness to be martyrs but changed their mind in the reality of the situation (10:38–39 vs. 14:52; 14:31 vs. 14:66–72). ". . . this man is so sure of his loyalty that he comes all dressed for death, but suddenly changes his mind when his death is a real prospect" (Tannehill, "Disciples in Mark," 194). Jesus accepts his shroud and dies; the last disciple rejects his shroud and escapes—but reappears on Easter morning, renewed by resurrection faith.

abandonment, the reversal of Jesus' original call to discipleship. Jesus had called people to follow him (not only the Twelve, cf. 8:34–38), and they had left everything to do so (1:16–20; 2:14; 10:28–31). Then they began to abandon him. First his family (3:20–30), then Judas (14:1–2, 10–11), then the "crowd" that had supported him (14:43; 15:8–15), then Peter and all the others (14:27–31, 50, 54, 66–72). The women who had followed Jesus, who have been more faithful than others, will also finally fail (15:40–41; 16:1–8). In this scene one of those who had been called to "leave everything" to become a disciple of Jesus literally "leaves everything" to become a nondisciple. From 1:6 on, clothing is often deeply symbolic in Mark. In abandoning his clothing, the young man had abandoned not only Jesus, but the new identity he had received as a follower of Jesus (see on 10:50). But the ultimate abandonment is yet to come (see on 15:33–34). Who will stay with Jesus? (see on 16:8).

Excursus: Mark and the Scriptures

Mark sees the entire story as in accord with Scripture

Mark's narrative is deeply influenced by his Bible.[94] The opening sentence is a collage of quotations from the Old Testament under the heading of "Isaiah" (1:2–3); the last words in the narrative that Jesus speaks to his people are "Let the Scriptures be fulfilled" (14:49), and his last words from the cross cite Ps 22:1. The Markan story is thus bracketed with references to Scripture.

Exactly how many direct quotations Mark contains depends on how precisely one draws the lines between "quotation," "clear allusion," "echo," "background imagery," and the like. The following list includes those texts most often considered citations or clear allusions:[95]

1:2–3	Mal 3:1; Isa 40:3
1:11	Ps 2:7; Gen 22:2; Isa 42:1
4:12	Isa 6:9–10
4:29	Joel 3:13
6:34	Num 27:17, (1 Kgs 22:17; Ezek 34:5)
7:6–7	Isa 29:13
7:10	Exod 20:12; Exod 21:17
8:18	Jer 5:21 (Ezek 12:2)
9:7	Ps 2:7; Gen 22:2; Deut 18:15

94. For full-length monographs on this theme, see Marcus, *Way of the Lord*, and Watts, *Isaiah's New Exodus in Mark*, and the bibliography they present.

95. Among other such lists, cf. Robert G. Bratcher, *Old Testament Quotations in the New Testament* (London: United Bible Societies, 1961), 11–16, and Henry Shires, *Finding the Old Testament in the New* (Philadelphia: Westminster, 1974), 235–37 and passim. The margin of the Nestle-Aland[27] text adds the following: Mark 4:32 / Ps 104:12; Mark 9:11 / Mal 4:5; Mark 13:24–25 / Isa 13:10; 34:4; Mark 14:34 / Ps 42:5, 11; 43:5.

9:48	Isa 66:24
10:4	Deut 24:1
10:6	Gen 1:27
10:7–8	Gen 2:24
10:19	Exod 20:12–16
11:9–10	Ps 118:25–26
11:17a	Isa 56:7
11:17b	Jer 7:11
12:1	Isa 5:1–2
12:10–11	Ps 118:22–23
12:19	Deut 25:5
12:26	Exod 3:6
12:29–30	Deut 6:4–5
12:31	Lev 19:18
12:32–33	Deut 6:4–6; 4:35, Lev 19:18
12:36	Ps 110:1
13:24–25	Isa 13:10; 34:4; Joel 2:10, 31
13:26	Dan 7:13
14:27	Zech 13:7
14:62	Ps 110:1; Dan 7:13
15:24	Ps 22:18
15:34	Ps 22:1
15:36	Ps 69:21

In addition there are at least scores (Kee says "hundreds"; *Community*, 45) of other instances where Mark echoes the language of the Old Testament, or biblical imagery influences his narrative, such as the description of John's clothing in 1:6, which evokes the image of Elijah in 2 Kgs 1:8. From the earliest days the Christian community believed that the Christ event happened *kata tas graphas* ("according to the Scriptures," 1 Cor 15:3–5), and so the tradition Mark inherited was often already permeated with biblical language. There can be no doubt that Mark both affirmed this and added his own references to Scripture. The better the readers know the Old Testament, the better they will understand Mark. Only occasionally does the evangelist make his allusions to Scripture explicit. Here, too, the reader must have "ears to hear" (4:9).

Mark draws upon a wide range of Scripture, but Isaiah plays a central role

It is clear from the above list that Mark draws on a wide range of Scripture. As in early Christianity generally, the Psalms are understood eschatologically, which also corresponds to a tendency already present in first-century Judaism. Especially Pss 2 and 110 are key christological texts for Mark; Pss 22 and 69 play an important role in the formation of the passion narrative. Apart from the more obvious allusions, the ubiquitous presence of imagery from the Psalter in the background of Mark's thought is illustrated, for example, by the several features of Ps 95 reflected in 1:2–15.

Some have seen Daniel as the primary biblical influence on Mark.[96] While it is true that the apocalyptic perspective and Son of Man language and imagery are indeed constituent elements of Mark's narrative, it seems that the central prophetic book for him is Isaiah.[97] Isaiah is the only prophet named in Mark, and Mark quotes Isaiah more often than all the other Old Testament books together: Mark 1:2–3 = Isa 40:3; Mark 4:12 = Isa 6:9–10; Mark 7:6–7 = Isa 29:13; Mark 9:48 = Isa 66:24; Mark 11:17 = Isa 56:7; Mark 12:32 = Isa 45:21; Mark 13:24 = Isa 13:10; Mark 13:25 = Isa 34:4. Not only specific quotations and allusions, but numerous items of the basic structures, situation, and content of Isaiah correspond to Mark. The word "gospel" itself with which Mark begins has its biblical roots in Deutero-Isaiah. The imagery of the second exodus in which Yahweh (LXX *ho kyrios,* "the Lord") defeats the enemies of the people of God becomes the paradigm for the "way of the Lord" followed by Jesus, to which he calls his people. Mark accepts the Isaian pattern of the holy war in which Yahweh triumphs, but transforms it by the image of the cross, so that the Isaian "way of the Lord" from Babylon to Jerusalem now leads from Galilee to Jerusalem and crucifixion. Thus Mark can be appropriately read as "The Gospel according to Isaiah," with the *kathōs* of 1:2 understood as programmatic for the entire narrative: the story that follows, taken as a whole, corresponds to Scripture, "as written in Isaiah the prophet." Dowd points out that "A comparison of these two texts—Mark and Isaiah—uncovers at least the following common threads: announcements of the good news of God's reign, healing for the lame and those unable to speak, the conversion of the Gentiles, the 'way of the Lord,' suffering on behalf of others, repeated injunctions to 'listen' and 'look,' provision of bread, critique of religious leaders, cosmic conflict, redemption, forgiveness of sins, and the use of blindness and deafness as metaphors for the people's failure to perceive and understand the ways of God."[98] It is thus an exegetical and hermeneutical issue throughout whether the interpreter may appeal to the presumed Isaian background, even if Mark does not make it explicit. This issue becomes particularly important, for example, in deciding whether

---

96. Ibid., 45–46; Howard Clark Kee, "Scriptural Quotations and Allusions in Mark 11–16," in *SBLSP* 2 (Atlanta: Society of Biblical Literature, 1971); A. C. Sundberg, "On Testimonies," *NovT* 3 (1959): 268–81.

97. Already argued in 1979 by Rau, "Markusevangelium," 2040, 2051, 2053 and passim. More recently, cf. Beavis, *Mark's Audience*, 110 and passim; Marcus, *Way of the Lord*, 12, cf. 20, 23, and esp. Watts, *Isaiah's New Exodus in Mark*, 60 and passim.

98. Sharyn Dowd, "Reading Mark Reading Isaiah," *LTQ* 30, no. 3 (1995): 133–44, now comprehensively developed in Dowd, *Reading Mark*. One might add at least three items: (1) Deutero-Isaiah, from whom Mark's initial quote is taken, begins like Mark, with a "Prelude in Heaven" (Isa 40:1–11). (2) The motif of the eschatological king who establishes peace with the animal world is shared by Isa 11:1–9 and Mark 1:13. (3) For Isaiah the "strong[er] one" is a predicate for both God and for God's messenger (49:26, 28:2; 11:2), a motif adopted by Mark (e.g., 1:7; 3:22–27; 9:28). John Kenneth Riches also affirms the importance of Isaiah for Mark, but offers a critique of too easily accepting Isaiah as Mark's pattern, pointing out significant differences. According to Riches, Mark is not so directly dependent on Isaiah for his theological scheme, but "Underlying both Isaiah and the Markan story is a salvation historical view which sees God as enabling his people to overcome sin by teaching and leading them." (*Conflicting Mythologies: Identity Formation in the Gospels of Mark and Matthew* [SNTW; Edinburgh: T. & T. Clark, 2000], 140]).

Isa 53 is part of Mark's understanding of the death of Jesus, and whether "Galilee of the Nations / Gentiles" is sometimes connoted by his orientation toward Galilee (Isa 9:1).

Mark does not have a single specific hermeneutical approach to Scripture, but has a variety of ways in which the Scriptures function in relation to his narrative

Most fundamental is the Markan conviction, not spelled out, that the Christian message is in accord with Scripture as a whole. It is not merely that particular events are "prophesied" or "predicted," but that the Christian story as such unfolds in accord with Scripture, that is, in accord with the will and plan of God—see his use of the *dei* of apocalyptic necessity, that is, divine sovereignty (8:31; 9:11; 13:7, 10). This is clearly illustrated when the Markan Jesus declares that the imprisonment and death of John the Baptist (= "Elijah") happened "just as it was written of him" (9:13). Mark does not elaborate, and no one would affirm that Mark has in mind particular texts "prophesying" the fate of John, which have now been "fulfilled."[99] Yet exactly the same expression is used in the preceding verse with regard to the Son of Man, who will suffer and be treated with contempt (9:12). Cf. also 14:21, where "the Son of Man is going away just as it stands written about him." Mark obviously does not have in mind particular Scripture texts that were fulfilled in the sufferings of either John or Jesus, but sees their destiny as in accordance with the will of God expressed in Scripture as a whole. Mark only uses the *plēroō* ("fulfillment") vocabulary once in reference to Scripture (14:49). Here, too, these last public words of Jesus indicate that his arrest, trial, and death are in accord with the will of God as represented by Scripture as such, not that particular biblical texts are "fulfilled" by particular events in the passion story. It is not only the passion story that is interwoven with echoes of biblical language and imagery; the narrative throughout is resonant with subtle allusions to Scripture that Markan readers familiar with their Bible will recognize without having it made obvious. One example: without ever citing the Bible directly or using the word "manna," the story of feeding the multitudes in the wilderness evokes the exodus story, places Jesus and the church in continuity with it, and contrasts the manna that could not be preserved with the amazing twelve (!) baskets of fragments that remain available (6:43). The later Gospels also continue this allusive hermeneutic, but also make it explicit in a way that Mark does not yet do (cf., e.g., Matt 1–2; Luke 24:13–47; Acts 1:16; 3:18; John 18:9, 32; 19:24, 36).

Mark, like the Christian tradition he inherits and interprets, rereads his Bible christologically. The God of the Scripture is the God definitively revealed in Jesus Christ. The God of Jesus Christ is the God whose will and voice speaks in Scripture—so that the words of Scripture can be taken as first-person address in which God speaks directly (1:2–3; 14:27). The process is circular, but presupposes Christian faith. When biblical texts are applied to Jesus, or biblical imagery and vocabulary are used to narrate the story of Jesus, the idea is not only or primarily that the Old Testament now helps the Christian

---

99. For a helpful, detailed discussion of how the biblical tradition (Esther, esp. as interpreted in Jewish tradition) was formative for the narrative of the death of John the Baptist in Mark 6:14–29, see LaVerdiere, *Beginning*, 1:163–68.

reader to make sense of the present, but that the Christ event now makes sense of the Old Testament, and provides the key to its interpretation. While at the story level it is primarily Jesus who cites the Scriptures, communication is made almost entirely at the discourse level. It is the reader who hears the christological meaning not only of the direct citations, but of the many allusions to Scripture in the discourse from narrator to reader of which the characters in the story are oblivious (cf. Fowler, "Rhetoric," 220 and passim).

14:53–72 Trial before the Sanhedrin:
Jesus' Confession and Peter's Denial

53 And they conducted Jesus in custody[a] to the high priest, and all the chief priests, the elders, and the scribes are assembling. 54 And Peter had followed him at a distance, right into the courtyard of the high priest and he was sitting with the guards[b] and warming himself at the fire.

55 Now the chief priests and the whole Sanhedrin intended to have Jesus put to death, and were looking for testimony against Jesus to support their case, but they were not finding any. 56 For many were giving false testimony against him, but their testimony was not consistent. 57 And some stood up and were giving false testimony against him, saying, "We heard him saying, 'I will destroy this temple made with hands, and within three days I will build another, not made with hands.'" 59 And even so, their testimony was still inconsistent. 60 And the high priest stood up in the midst of the assembly and asked Jesus, "Are you not going to respond to what these have testified against you?" 61 But he was silent, and gave no answer. Again the high priest was interrogating him, and says to him, "Are you the Christ, the Son of the Blessed One?" 62 And Jesus said, "I am, and you [pl.] will see the Son of Man seated on the right hand of Power, and coming with the clouds of heaven." 63 And the high priest tore his clothes and says, "Why do we need witnesses? 64 You heard his blasphemy! What do you decide?" And they all condemned him as deserving the death penalty. 65 And some began to spit on him, and to cover his face[c] and to hit him and to say to him, "Prophesy!" And the guards took charge of him, and beat him.

66 And while Peter was in the courtyard below, one of the high priest's servant-girls comes up, 67 and when she saw Peter warming himself at the fire, she looked him over intently[d] and says, "You too were with the man from Nazareth, Jesus." 68 But he denied it, saying, "I do not know nor understand what you are talking about."[e] And he went out into the forecourt. And a cock crowed.[f] 69 And the servant-girl saw him, and again began to say to the bystanders, "This man is one of them." 70 But he was denying it again. And after a little while, again the bystanders were saying to Peter, "You are certainly one of them, for you are a Galilean." 71 But he began to invoke a curse,[g] and to swear a solemn oath, "I do not

know this man you are talking about." 72 And immediately a cock crowed
the second time.[f] And Peter remembered the saying, how Jesus had said
to him, "Before a cock crows twice, you will deny me three times." And
he broke down[h] and cried.

a. *Apagō*, legal technical term as in v. 44.

b. *Hypēretēs* is a generic term for "helper," "assistant," "attendant," that takes on its
specific meaning from the context. Here it apparently refers to the officers sent by the
Sanhedrin who had been instrumental in Jesus' arrest (cf. commentary on the "crowd"
of v. 43).

c. "Covered his face" is missing from D, one MS of the Old Latin, and some MSS
of the Syriac and Coptic translations.

d. *Emblepō*, a strengthened form of the normal word for looking, *blepō*, is found elsewhere in Mark only in 8:25; 10:21, 27.

e. My translation into flawed English reflects the rough Greek. The syntax, grammar,
and punctuation of this sentence are all unclear, perhaps incorrect Greek. *Oute . . . oute*
("neither . . . nor") cannot be combined with two synonymous verbs. The pronoun *sy*
("you") seems superfluous or out of place. Explanations range from poor translation of
an Aramaic original to the narrator's intentional representation of Peter's stammering,
disconcerted response, to Mark's lack of command of elegant Greek. Thus some later
scribes adjusted the text to the more correct *ouk . . . oude*. The words can be divided into
two sentences, the second a question: "I don't know, neither do I understand. You, what
are you talking about?"

f. The MSS tradition on the number of cock-crowings is very confused, with some
MSS omitting the first reference in v. 68 and "the second time" in v. 72, some retaining
both, and some retaining one or the other. Scribes were clearly concerned to harmonize
the Markan text with itself, i.e., to make the fulfillment in vv. 68 and 72 correspond with
Jesus' prophecy in 14:30 and with the other Gospels. It is here judged that all the Markan
references to two cock-crowings are original, the variations in the MSS representing
scribal attempts to make Mark consistent with himself and the other Gospels. See note
d at 14:30.

g. *Anathematizein* can be either intransitive (Peter invoked a curse on himself, so that
the two actions are synonymous) or transitive (Peter invoked a curse on someone else,
namely Jesus).

h. Like *apechei* in v. 41 above, no one knows the meaning of *epibalōn* in this context. The word itself (aorist participle of *epiballō*) is simple enough, a compound of the
common verb *ballō* ("throw, cast"; cf. "ballistic") and the preposition *epi-*, meaning
basically "on." Like the English preposition, it has a wide variety of contextual meanings. The combination may mean, for example, "lay on," "throw or place on," "beat
against" (of waves), "fall one's lot" (by inheritance), "throw oneself into" (work, a project), and "begin" (as understood by D Θ and the Latin and Syriac translations). *Epiballō*
is found seventy-one times in the LXX and eighteen times in the New Testament, Mark
himself using it in 4:37 of the waves beating against the boat and breaking over it, and
in 11:7 of the disciples placing their garments on the colt. Some have suggested "place
upon" in the sense of "cover" (his head), with the sense that Peter pulled his garment

over his head and sobbed, but normal grammar would require the mention of the garment. The meaning remains unclear, but "Probably Mark intends the reader to understand a wild gesture connected with lamentation."[100]

The narrative certainly has a historical core, and its basic structure of Jewish leaders who apprehend a religiously dangerous prophetic figure and deliver him to the Romans for punishment or death is historically plausible.[101] The factual core has been interpreted and elaborated in Christian tradition between Jesus' death and the composition of the Gospel, and the present structure appears to be Markan. The Jewish trial and the Roman trials are remarkably parallel and stylized, representing the concerns of later Christians.

The unit 14:53–72 is a Markan intercalation in which the two scenes interpret each other (see on 5:21). This is a major clue on how to interpret this unit. At the center stands Jesus, for the first and only time in the Gospel declaring his true identity, proleptically making the full Christian confession of faith, and it costs him his life (vv. 55–65). This scene is framed by the episode in which Peter denies his (and Jesus') true identity, and it saves his life (8:34–38). Both Peter and Jesus are challenged by a threefold accusation, and each makes a definitive response. Jesus makes the "good confession" and is a model for Christians under duress. Peter is a negative example of those who crumble under pressure (cf. 4:17; 14:32–42). This Markan structure combining the trial of Jesus with that of Peter shows that Jesus' trial is narrated as a reflex of the trials of Christians in Mark's own time (cf. 13:9–13). Jesus' declaration is the ultimate christological word about himself. Peter's word about himself is not ultimate; here, too, Jesus will have the last word (see on 16:7).

[53] Although the hearing will take place in the residence of the high priest, Mark emphasizes the formality of the occasion by listing again the groups that constitute the Sanhedrin (cf. on 8:31; 11:27–28) and by stating that all the members were present. We know from other sources, including the other Gospels, that the high priest in office at the time was Caiaphas, but neither here nor elsewhere does Mark give his name. This is not because Mark could assume his readers already knew it—this would be unlikely for Gentile readers who needed

---

100. So Bauer and Danker, BDAG, 368, who provide a thorough discussion of the possibilities.

101. The remarkably similar case of another first-century Jewish prophet, also named Jesus, is reported by Josephus (*War* 6.5.3 [300–309]). Jesus ben Ananias, ca. 62 C.E., appeared at the Festival of Booths, and constantly cried out, day and night, his prophetic oracle, "A voice from the east, a voice from the west, a voice from the four winds, a voice against Jerusalem and the holy house, a voice against the bridegrooms and the brides, and a voice against this whole people!" The religious leaders arrested and beat him, and turned him over to the Romans, but he said nothing in his defense, and when released continued his woeful oracle. When the leaders saw their disciplinary warning had no effect, they arrested him again and delivered him to the Roman governor Albinus. There, too, he did not defend himself, though beaten "until his bones were laid bare." The governor considered him a harmless madman, and released him.

purity rules to be explained to them (see on 7:1–4)—but because most of the characters in the passion story are important for their function, not as individuals. It is important that the leading officials in Jewish religious matters play a primary role in Jesus' death, but nothing about the high priest himself, including his name, is significant for Mark. It is the "chief priests, elders, and scribes" who condemn Jesus. Unlike the Roman governor, the high priest does not function as an individual judge (the Apostles' Creed has no "condemned under Caiaphas" that corresponds to "crucified under Pontius Pilate").

[54] The narrative camera shifts momentarily to note that Peter, who had fled with the other disciples (v. 50) has not yet totally abandoned Jesus. He is still "following," also in the theological sense, albeit "at a distance" (cf. the same phrase of the women at 15:40). This is analogous to his earlier portrayal in 8:22–24, in which the blind man sees-but-doesn't-see. Peter finds a place among the guards warming themselves at the fire, apparently the same group that had arrested Jesus (cf. note *b* above and commentary on 14:43).

[55–56] Mark emphasizes again that the whole Sanhedrin is present, and will have them all accompany Jesus to deliver him to Pilate (15:1), emphasizing that Jesus was rejected and condemned not by a few arbitrary individuals acting on their own, but as an official act of the Jewish leadership. Mark portrays them in a very bad light. They have already resolved to kill Jesus (cf. 14:1, in continuity with 3:6) and wish to do it judicially, but they cannot themselves put anyone to death, since capital cases come under the jurisdiction of the governor.[102] They have already reached a verdict and are only looking for a charge against Jesus that can be supported when they deliver him to Pilate. Nonetheless, Mark does not portray their desire to kill Jesus as personal malice, but their sincere commitment to rid their country of one they consider a threat to authentic religion. There is thus no contradiction between their intent to kill and their attempt to base their decision on valid and documented charges. The witnesses against Jesus are called "false witnesses" by the narrator, but there is no indication they were insincere or had been bribed by the Sanhedrin. When the testimony of the witnesses is inconsistent, the Sanhedrin does not disregard this problem and proceed against Jesus anyway, but considers their purpose frustrated. There are thus two levels interwoven into the narrative. There are the trappings of a proper judicial procedure to which the Sanhedrin is committed (cf. Deut 17:6; Num 35:30), yet the Christian narrator knows in retrospect that Jesus was falsely tried and condemned, that the testimony against him was a violation of the central Jewish commandments (Exod 20:16; Deut 5:20). In all of this, the narration is colored by the conviction that events are unfolding according to Scripture (cf. 9:12–13;

---

102. Mark clearly assumes this, but, unlike John 18:29–32, does not make it explicit. The historical situation in Jesus' day is disputed, but the majority argue that the Gospels are accurate on this point.

14:49); Jesus is the righteous sufferer of the Psalms, who is betrayed and lied against (cf. Pss 27:12; 37:32; 38:12; 54:3; 63:9; 69:4; 86:14).

[57–59] Mark does not give the content of the inconsistent testimony of the "many" false witnesses, but focuses on only one charge: Jesus had purportedly said he would destroy the temple made with hands and build another not made with hands. Mark must intend the reader to understand that they had reported various versions of what they had "heard him say," otherwise their testimony would not have been inconsistent. There were indeed various versions of Jesus' saying(s) about the temple in circulation in early Christianity, for which there must have been a historical core that goes back to Jesus himself (cf. 13:2; 15:29; John 2:19–22). Our purpose here, however, is not to reconstruct what Jesus "really said" in contrast to the testimony of the "false witnesses." The reader knows that the Markan Jesus has spoken about the destruction of the temple (13:2) but has not claimed that he will destroy it or rebuild it. The Markan Jesus opposes the temple as it is currently misused, but he does not claim to be its destroyer. Mark probably regards the Christian community as the eschatological temple (see on 11:12–26). While there is no explicit doctrine of a "spiritual temple" in Mark, it is likely that Mark's readers could not hear "within three days" without thinking of Jesus' resurrection. In addition, the contrast "made with hands" / "not made with hands" would evoke imagery of the old temple made by human beings and the eschatological temple that replaces it, the Christian community called into being by God.

[60–61] The high priest stands up in their midst, that is, not as one of the group but as its president, standing before the assembly pictured as arranged in a semicircle, as though they were in their normal assembly hall. The narrative setting in the high priest's house seems to be forgotten, and the scene is portrayed in terms of an official trial. Jesus' silence in response to both the witnesses and the high priest contrasts with his own instructions to his disciples (13:11) and continues to portray him as the suffering righteous one (Pss 27:12; 35:11; 38:14–16; 39:9–10; 109:2–27), and the Suffering Servant of Isaiah (53:7).

The witnesses having failed to provide a conclusive case against Jesus, the high priest addresses him directly. Those who argue that the trial scene represents a historical report, or a plausible account of what might have happened, strive to show that there is a logical connection between the unproven charge of claiming to destroy the temple and the direct question, "Are you the Christ?" The argument is that the question is not arbitrary, but follows from the temple allegation, since it was expected that God or the Messiah would replace the present sanctuary with a new eschatological temple.[103] Likewise, the identification of "Christ" and "Son of God" was once thought to be a Christian formulation,

---

103. Among the advocates of this view are Pesch, *Markusevangelium*, 2:435–36; France, *Gospel of Mark*, 607.

but now it is often argued, especially on the basis of Qumran evidence, that it is not unhistorical or anachronistic for the high priest to have made this identification.[104] To the extent that such arguments are persuasive, they show that Mark uses his tradition to compose a historically plausible narrative. However, such historical verisimilitude is almost incidental to Mark's purpose, and should not divert attention from the primary meaning at the Markan level of the text. Whether or not a Jewish official could speak of "Christ, the Son of God," this was the Christian confession affirmed in Mark's community.[105] Jesus, for the first time in the narrative, clearly makes the (later) Christian confession that he is the Christ, the Son of God. The revelatory *egō eimi* ("I am"; cf. 6:50; 13:6) is not a claim to be YHWH or an enunciation of the sacred name of God, but is a straightforward affirmation of the Christian credo Jesus' disciples are called to make in their own situation. Jesus now confesses the identity declared from heaven (1:11; 9:7), recognized by demons (3:11; 5:7), declared at the beginning of the Gospel by the narrator (1:1), and once confessed by Peter (8:29)—who now denies it in the courtyard below.

These are the climactic words of Jesus in the whole Gospel. Jesus' *egō eimi* makes the trial into an *epiphany* scene.[106] He will not speak again, except to reaffirm this confession before Pilate (15:2), and in the anguished cry from the cross (15:34). Now, in words that will seal his death, the messianic secret is definitively dissolved—Jesus' true identity as Son of God can be openly declared, but only in inseparable union with his identity as the Crucified One. His *egō eimi* ("I am") corresponds precisely to the high priests *sy ei* ("are you"), yet his response does not merely affirm the question, as though christological meaning is determined by preexisting expectations. As in 8:27–31, the Markan Jesus' affirmation of traditional christological titles reinterprets them in terms of the Son of Man. The imagery is a combination of Ps 110:1 (already developed in 12:35–37 repudiating the traditional Davidic Christology) and Dan 7:13 (already developed in 13:24–27). Such combination of scriptural texts reflects the exegetical work of Christian teachers who, after Easter on the basis of their resurrection faith, continued to interpret the meaning of confessing Jesus as the Christ through their christological rereading of their Bible (see *Excursus: Mark and the Scriptures* at 14:52). Here, the definitive aspect is that confessing faith in Jesus as Christ and Son of God is integrated into the divine drama of the Son of Man, who acts on earth with the authority of God (2:10, 28); who is rejected

104. Cf. Juel, *Messiah and Temple*, 77–116, who nevertheless argues that at the level of the Markan text the Christian understanding of the terms is primary.

105. So, e.g., Norman Perrin, "The High Priest's Question and Jesus' Answer," in *The Passion in Mark: Studies on Mark 14–16* (ed. Werner H. Kelber; Philadelphia: Fortress, 1976), 87, and numerous others.

106. Georg Bertram, *Die Leidensgeschichte Jesu und der Christuskult: Eine formgeschichtliche Untersuchung* (FRLANT N.F. 15; Göttingen: Vandenhoeck & Ruprecht, 1922), 55–61.

by the religious authorities; who suffers and dies in fulfilling the will of God, the hidden actor in Jesus' being delivered up by human hands; who is vindicated by God, who raises him from the dead (8:31; 9:31; 10:33–34; 14:21, 41, 49); who is now, in Mark's time, seated at God's right hand (Ps 110:1); and who will come on the clouds of heaven as God's representative to judge the world and gather his elect (8:38; 13:26). This paradigm is a call for Markan readers to confess their own faith in Jesus the suffering Son of Man who has been vindicated by God as Son of God. Just as Jesus' confession "provokes and indeed causes the death sentence,"[107] so also for the readers. Thus the reason for Jesus' condemnation and death in Mark is not to be explained in political and juridical terms, but is a matter of Markan Christology and discipleship.[108] Six streams of Markan christological imagery converge in this crucial scene: Messiah (Christ), Son of God, Son of Man, Suffering Servant of Isa 53, suffering righteous one of the Psalms and the Wisdom of Solomon, and true prophet of God (see *Excursus: Markan Christology* at 9:1).

All this, of course, is full-blown Christian theology, clear to the reader but not what the high priest had in mind. Nonetheless, he considers it blasphemy, and tears his garments—not a spontaneous outburst of emotion, but a prescribed ritual act in response to blasphemous words (cf. 2 Kgs 18:37; 19:1; *m. Sanh.* 7.5). The later rabbinic definition of blasphemy was very restrictive, limited to pronunciation of the Tetragrammaton YHWH. While some interpreters have related this to Jesus' *egō eimi* or his pronunciation of God's name in the original Hebrew of Ps 110:1 that he quotes, this is unnecessary and unlikely either for the historical actuality of Jesus' trial or for Mark's intended meaning. First-century Judaism had a broad understanding of *blasphēmia*, which could include various types of arrogant speech against God, the Torah, or God's people, or arrogating divine prerogatives to oneself (cf. Mark's own usage in 2:7; 3:28–29).[109] Neither at the historical nor the narrative level was Jesus' presumed "blasphemy" pronouncing the divine name or claiming to be divine, but his claims could be taken as an affront to God, the temple, and the Torah, which qualified as blasphemy in Jewish eyes, and his declaring himself to be the Christ

---

107. Werner H. Kelber, "Conclusion: From Passion Narrative to Gospel," in *The Passion in Mark: Studies on Mark 14–16* (ed. Werner H. Kelber; Philadelphia: Fortress, 1976), 161.

108. "Without doubt the trial is phrased in the light of later Christian experience. In it we are hearing how Christians in the last third of the 1st cent. understood Jewish adversaries who considered Christian claims about Jesus to be blasphemous." Brown, *Death of the Messiah*, 1:544.

109. Cf. among many others, esp. Darrell L. Bock, "The Son of Man Seated at God's Right Hand and the Debate over Jesus' 'Blasphemy,'" in *Jesus of Nazareth: Lord and Christ* (ed. Joel B. Green and Max Turner; Grand Rapids: Eerdmans, 1994), 184–91, developed in detail in Darrell L. Bock, *Blasphemy and Exaltation in Judaism and the Final Examination of Jesus: A Philological-historical Study of the Key Jewish Themes Impacting Mark 14:61–64* (WUNT 2/106; Tübingen: Mohr, 1998).

could be represented to Pilate as claiming to be a king. The awkward Greek translated as "condemned him as deserving the death penalty" is not a formal legal verdict, but expresses the judgment of the court, which now has what it needs in order to hand Jesus over to Pilate.

[65] Mark's portrayal of "some" (vs. "all" of vv. 53, 64) of the Sanhedrin spitting on Jesus and striking him is not merely an expression of personal animosity and disdain. Spitting on the accused and condemned man is shameful for him, and expresses one's own distance from his shameful error (Num 12:14; Deut 25:9; Job 30:10). For Mark, it further identifies Jesus with the suffering righteous man and Servant of the Lord (Isa 50:6; 53:5 LXX). According to the Torah, false prophets who lead Israel astray were to be killed by stoning, with the hands of the judges first upon them (Deut 13:1–11; 18:20). Striking Jesus after covering his face and challenging him to "prophesy"—to identify who struck him by his supernatural knowledge, but also a mocking rejection of his prophetic claims in general—indicates Jesus is considered a false prophet. Witnesses were to participate in the execution. The Sanhedrin were all witnesses (vv. 63–64), but since the court did not have the power to execute him according to the Torah, they ritualize their rejection and participation in the sentence. Their mockery and abuse of Jesus as a false prophet is doubly Markan irony, since Jesus has in fact prophesied both this very scene and the one simultaneously transpiring in the courtyard below.

[66–72] The narrative camera zooms in on Peter, who has been on the periphery of the readers' vision during the trial of Jesus. Jesus affirms he is the Christ; Peter denies he belongs to Jesus' group. Jesus tells the truth that leads to his death; Peter lies, and saves his life (8:35). Peter too undergoes a trial. Though not in a courtroom, the account has several legal overtones, suggesting imagery of Christians in Mark's situation when they are brought before local sanhedrins (13:9). The threefold form itself may reflect courtroom procedure in which the accused are given three opportunities to deny their membership in the suspect group (cf. Pliny, *Letters* 10.96.3; *Mart. Pol.* 9–10). The charges increase in seriousness, as do Peter's responses: from feigned lack of understanding to denial to rejection sealed with a formal oath. The first challenge is from a slave woman, directly to Peter. Her social status and the one-on-one address should pose no particular threat, but Peter denies, using language that may carry juridical connotations.[110] The second denial is occasioned by the slave girl's accusing him to a larger group, and the third a response to this group's identifying him as "one of them." The charge that he is with "the Nazarene" is similar to the later charge of belonging to the "sect of the Nazarenes" (Acts 24:5). Throughout, the accusation is not that he believes

---

110. So William Lane, who cites M. Shebuoth 8.3, 6, "I do not know what you are saying," as a formal, legal denial of a charge. Lane, *Mark*, 542.

something false about Jesus, but that he belongs to a suspect group; the charge is "ecclesiological" rather than "christological," though in Mark's mind the two are inseparable. Peter had wanted to be a low-profile disciple, but ends up solemnly, before witnesses, with a formal oath disavowing his association with Jesus. Peter's "cursing" and "swearing" (v. 71) is not a matter of profanity, but refers to the oaths taken in the courtroom, in which God is invoked to punish the one making the statement if it is not true (cf. 1 Sam 14:44; 1 Kgs 20:10). It may well be that Peter also attempts to establish his dissociation from Jesus by invoking a curse on *Jesus* (see note *g* above),[111] as was later done when Christians were on trial (cf. Pliny, *Letters* 10.96.5; 1 Cor 12:3). The ambiguity here may be intentional—Mark is capable of such subtleties (cf. 11:3; 15:40–41, 47; 16:1).

The story is highly ironical. As one of the Twelve, Peter had been called to "be with" Jesus (see on 3:14). Now he denies that he is "one of them." The last words of Peter, who had vowed to be faithful to death (14:29), are "I do not know this man." Peter's words have turned out to be frail enough. When the cock crows, fulfilling Jesus' powerful word, Peter remembers Jesus' word. This word begins to work its transforming act, as in 1:16–20. Peter weeps. This is the reader's last sight of Peter, apparently a step in the direction of repentance. The word of 16:7 will single him out for restoration, but the narrative ends without recounting this. The readers know Peter died a martyr.

15:1–15 Trial before Pilate

15:1 And as soon as it was morning, the chief priests, with the elders, the scribes, and the whole Sanhedrin, held a consultation,[a] bound Jesus, led him away, and handed him over to Pilate. **2** And Pilate asked him, "Are you the king of the Jews?"[b] But Jesus answers him, "So you say."[c] **3** And the chief priests were solemnly[d] accusing him. **4** And Pilate was asking him again, "Are you not going to give any answer at all? Just look at the seriousness of the charge they are bringing against you." **5** But Jesus no longer answered at all, so that Pilate was amazed. **6** Now at each festival Pilate released[e] one prisoner to them, whomever they wanted. **7** Now there was a man called Barabbas held in prison with the rebels who had committed murder during the uprising. **8** And the crowd came up and began to ask him to do as he regularly did.[e] **9** And Pilate responded to them, "Do you want me to release to you the king of the Jews?" **10** For he knew it was out of jealousy that the chief priests had handed him over. **11** But the chief priests stirred up the crowd, to have him release Barabbas to them instead. **12** And Pilate spoke to them again,[f] "Then what do you want me to do with

111. Cf., e.g., Helmut Merkel, "Peter's Curse," in *The Trial of Jesus: Cambridge Studies in Honour of C. F. D. Moule* (SBT 2/13; Naperville, Ill.: A. R. Allenson, 1970), 66–71; Dewey, "Peter's Curse," 101, 109; Lührmann, *Markusevangelium*, 253.

the man whom you call[g] king of the Jews?" 13 And they shouted back,[f] "Crucify him!" 14 But Pilate kept saying[h] to them, "Why, what crime has he committed?" But they shouted even louder, "Crucify him!" 15 So Pilate, wishing to placate the crowd, released Barabbas to them, and, after having Jesus scourged, he handed him over to be crucified.

a. The translation takes the original text to be *symboulion poiēsantes*, attested in A B W Ψ *f*[1, 13] and most later MSS. The possible originality of *symboulion hetoimasantes* ("having reached a decision") of א C L and a few other MSS is also to be taken seriously. Neither reading is to be understood as the (re-)convening of the Sanhedrin after daylight to finally resolve the issue of Jesus' guilt or to make their decision "official," which is not Mark's concern. See on the analogous phrase *symboulion edidoun* at 3:6. The participle *poiēsantes* may be resumptive, "having (already) held a consultation (during the night)."

b. Vocabulary and word order (*sy legeis ho . . .*, "are you the . . .") provide no basis for translating a presumed sarcastic tone of voice ("*You* are the king of the Jews?"). Precisely the same phraseology is found in, e.g., Matt 11:3, John the Baptist's question to Jesus, "Are you the one who is to come?" and several other times in the New Testament and LXX, with no suggestion of sarcasm. To be sure, the Markan Pilate does not believe Jesus is a king, but both the historical Pilate and the character in Mark's narrative could intend the question quite seriously: does Jesus in fact make this claim, or is he only charged with it by others (cf. v. 12)?

c. *Sy legeis* is lit. "you are saying." Except in Jesus' responses in the trial scenes in the Gospels, there are no instances in the LXX or the New Testament of *sy legeis* as a response to a direct question. The analogous *sy eipas* of Matt 26:25, where only the tense of the verb is different, clearly means "yes." Here, the translation of the phrase depends on one's understanding of the contextual meaning (see commentary below).

d. Adverbial *polla;* see note *f* on 1:45. Correspondingly, the *posa* of v. 4 is here translated adverbially, "how serious the charge is" rather than "how many" (accusations). The chief priests are not bringing many charges against Jesus, but one—and it is ultimately serious.

e. The imperfect *apelyen* here expresses customary, habitual, regular, or general action, what Pilate did at "each festival." Similarly, the imperfect *epoiei* in v. 8 refers to what Pilate regularly did.

f. *Palin* may mean either "again," "in turn," or "back."

g. In this sentence the originality of both *thelete* ("you want") and *hon legete* ("whom you call") are borderline cases, with *thelete* the more doubtful. Each is missing from some important MSS and included in others. Without either or both, the sense is "What shall I do with the king of the Jews," which would be understood sarcastically or ironically.

h. Iterative imperfect *elegen*.

[1] There were, of course, no chapter breaks in the original document. Mark's typical *euthys* (see on 1:10) continues the preceding narrative seamlessly. The

narrative camera, just focused on Peter in the courtyard below, now swings back to the Sanhedrin and resumes the scene left at 14:65.

Roman courts were normally held at sunrise.[112] The modern reader should not think of the Jewish leaders as "getting Pilate out of bed" in order to conduct the trial. They were eager to get Jesus to the governor by the regularly scheduled hour. The seemingly redundant "and the whole Sanhedrin" after naming its three constituent groups expresses Mark's emphasis that it was not a few disgruntled individuals, but the whole Jewish governing body acting officially that condemned Jesus. For the first time the narrator mentions that Jesus is bound (like our "handcuffed"), now treated like a condemned criminal. "Handed him over" is the proper secular legal term, but is also resonant with Mark's theological meaning (cf. on *paradidōmi* at 9:31). Jesus' prediction of 10:33 is fulfilled exactly.

[2–5] While the modern scholar knows quite a bit about Pilate from other sources,[113] and Mark may have presupposed the same of his original readers, he makes nothing of Pilate as a historical figure. The reader assumes that he is the Roman official who has authority to decide Jesus' case, to put him to death, or to release him, but Mark gives him no title (as the high priest is given no name). The narrative is very spare, and parallels the previous portrayal of Jesus before the Sanhedrin.

14:60–62	15:4–5, 2
And the high priest . . . asked	And Pilate was asking him again
"Are you not going to respond to what these have testified against you?"	"Are you not going to give any answer at all?"
But he was silent, and gave no answer.	But Jesus no longer answered at all
Again the high priest was interrogating him, and says to him, "Are you the Christ, the Son of the Blessed One?"	And Pilate asked him, "Are you the king of the Jews?
And Jesus said, "I am, . . .	But Jesus answers him, "So you say."

For the first time, "King of the Jews" appears in the narrative. The title is central to the passion narrative, where it occurs five times in addition to asso-

---

112. Cf. Seneca, *De ira* 2.7.3 *prima luce*, "at first light," and the other evidence given in A. N. Sherwin-White, *Roman Society and Roman Law in the New Testament* (Sarum Lectures; Grand Rapids: Baker, 1978), 45.

113. His official title was *praefectus*, prefect, as we now know from a Latin inscription on a statue found in Caesarea Maritima in 1961. He is anachronistically called "procurator" in Tacitus and Josephus; "governor" is a generic term, not a specific office.

ciated imagery (15:16–20). It is a Gentile term—Jews themselves said "King of Israel" (15:32)—and in Pilate's world of thought it placed Jesus in the category of those nationalist revolutionaries rebelling against Roman rule. There were several revolutionary leaders in the tumultuous years prior to and during the revolt of 66–70. Some Zealot leaders claimed the title "king" (e.g., Simon, Athronges, and Judas; cf. Josephus, *Ant.* 17.271–278; *War* 2.4.3.60–62). The Sanhedrin had accused Jesus of blasphemy on the grounds that he claimed to be the Christ; "king of the Jews" is a translation of this charge into Roman political terms, and this is the accusation they present to Pilate. It is a serious charge.[114] The reader knows that Jesus is the Christ, God's anointed eschatological king in the coming kingdom of God, but that in Pilate's categories Jesus has not claimed to be "king of the Jews." All this is presupposed in this scene, which opens with Pilate's question.

Jesus had responded with a clear affirmative to the high priest's question whether he is the Christ (*egō eimi,* "I am"; see on 14:61–62). His response to Pilate is not so straightforward (*sy legeis,* "you are saying"; see note *c* above). It, too, can be taken as an emphatic affirmative (somewhat like the colloquial "you said it"); as a denial (*you* say I am a king; I do not); as intended ambiguity that puts the ball in Pilate's court; as noncommittal, evasive, suggestive ("you might put it that way"); as corrective ("king is your word, not mine, for what I claim and who I am"); or even as a question ("are you saying so?" i.e., "are you serious?").[115] The Jesus who had commended forthrightness to his followers when they stood before the courts (13:9–13; cf. 8:38) is not being coy himself, yet he cannot give a clear answer to a question wrongly conceived. In the narrative, Pilate does not take the response as a clear "yes," and he seems to regard Jesus as innocent. He is not bothered by Jesus' failure to respond with the courtesy and respect governors can expect from provincials hailed into their courts. He states that others may claim Jesus to be a king (v. 12) but refers to no claim of Jesus' own. All this shows that the narrative does not aim at historical or psychological realism, but presents christological issues to the reader. The chief priests continue to press their charge against him (v. 3), which would not have been necessary if Jesus had acknowledged it (contrast 14:62–64).

These are Jesus' last words until his cry from the cross. Pilate, who—unlike the reader—is unaware of the silence of God's Servant who is unjustly accused and condemned (Isa 53:7), can only be amazed that Jesus does not even attempt

---

114. Though Herod Antipas had wanted to claim the royal title, he was hesitant to do so for fear of Roman reprisals. When his wife Herodias finally persuaded him to petition Rome for the title, he was promptly banished to Gaul (Josephus, *Ant.* 18.8.2).

115. Of the numerous discussions of the Markan meaning of the phrase, perhaps the most cogent is David R. Catchpole, "The Answer of Jesus to Caiaphas," *NTS* 17, no. 2 (1971), who concludes that Jesus' answer is affirmative in content, but circumlocutory in form.

to defend himself (Isa 52:15). This silence is in contrast to the Jewish and Christian martyrs, who take the occasion of their unjust death to make extended speeches (*2–4 Mac*; Acts 7), just as it contrasts with Jesus' own instruction to his disciples (13:11). Theologically, the Markan reader might ask why Jesus does not speak his powerful, transforming word (as, e.g., 1:16–20). Yet here it is not the powerful Son of God who acts, but the truly human Jesus, who has resolved to suffer and die according to the will of God (14:32–42). His silence is an expression of Markan soteriology.

[6–12] The scene is interrupted by the narrator's explanation of a practice that is difficult to accept historically. Except for the parallel accounts in Matt 27:15 and John 18:39 (Luke 23:17 is textually dubious, yet seems to be presupposed by 23:18–19), the custom of releasing a prisoner at the Passover is not otherwise attested. Proposed parallels are not convincing, and the practice seems inherently unlikely[116]—why would the government grant amnesty to some notorious rebel every year? Historically speaking, Pilate's administrative track record in particular makes it unlikely that, even if there had been such a custom, he would have acquiesced to Jewish pressure. Likewise, despite the Hollywood versions of this scene, it is historically difficult to imagine that a crowd could intrude itself into the court of a Roman governor. While the name Barabbas is attested as a fairly common Jewish surname, there is no known Jewish uprising against the Romans connected with his name or near the time presupposed in the narrative.

While the historical realities behind the narrative remain vague and disputed, important aspects of Mark's theological intent in the narrative seem to be clear, and laden with irony:

(1) *The narrative-theological role of Barabbas.* Mark's Jewish-Christian readers would recognize the Jewish name "Bar-abbas" as meaning "son of the father." While Mark does not explain this to his Gentile readers (contrast his practice in 5:41; 7:34; 15:22, 34, and elsewhere; cf. 7:3–4; 14:12; 15:42), he has explained "abba" as "father" (14:36), and since "abba" was a prayer in Gentile churches (Rom 8:15; Gal 4:6), many Gentile Christians could be expected to see "Barabbas" as an ironic counterpart to Jesus, the true Son of the Father. The parallel and contrast may go further: Barabbas has already been convicted of insurrection and sentenced to death, but will escape; Jesus is falsely accused of insurrection and will die in Barabbas's place, although he is innocent and has not been convicted or sentenced. During the whole period from the Roman takeover of Palestine (63 B.C.E.) to the actual revolt in 66 C.E., the only people crucified in Palestine were those convicted of being revolutionaries and their followers. It is important for Mark and his readers to distinguish Jesus from revolutionaries such as Barabbas. The point will again be made at the cross, where

116. The practice is defended as historical by, e.g., Pesch, *Markusevangelium*, 2:462.

those crucified as actual revolutionaries will dissociate themselves from Jesus (15:32).

(2) *The narrative-theological role of Pilate.* Whatever the character and policy of the historical Pilate, in Mark the literary character Pilate appears as a weak character who delivers Jesus over to death against his better judgment, believing him to be innocent. Like Herod in 6:14–29 (where some of the same themes and vocabulary appear), Pilate left himself open to being manipulated by the evil of others, and will not stand firm on his own convictions. Pilate attempts a strategic move in which he believes the crowd will call for the release of Jesus, miscalculates and is outmaneuvered by the chief priests, and delivers Jesus to their will without ever pronouncing a verdict himself.

(3) *The narrative-theological role of the chief priests.* While everyone in the scene except Jesus is guilty, Mark makes the chief priests the chief culprits. The omniscient narrator lets the reader know Pilate's thoughts, which express the reality of the situation: "it was out of jealousy that the chief priests had handed him over." While *zēlos*, a frequent biblical word for "jealousy," can also mean "religious zeal," that is not the word Mark uses here. There is less ambiguity in *phthonos*, which usually means "envy" pure and simple, and is rarely used positively in the religious sense (cf. Phil 1:15; Jas 4:5). However the historical chief priests might have been motivated in their action against Jesus, the Markan characters seem to be driven by envy. Jesus, a nobody from Galilee, attracted the crowds, even in their own religious capital.

(4) *The narrative-theological role of the crowd.* Regarded historically, it is unlikely that the crowd that confronts Pilate and is manipulated by the chief priests has the same constituency as the crowd that has followed Jesus about, welcomed him into Jerusalem, and was feared by the Sanhedrin (see *Excursus: Crowds, Followers, Disciples, and the Twelve* at 6:6). This, however, is beside the Markan point. The crowd plays a narrative role within the Markan structure of the abandonment of Jesus. All those who have been close to him will one by one forsake him (see on 14:50–51). In Mark's apocalyptic dualism in which there is no neutrality (see on 9:40), this means switching sides, and this is what the crowd does. They, too, choose a this-worldly deliverer and reject the suffering Christ sent by God.

[13–15] Though the noun "cross" has appeared once previously (8:34), this is the first reference to crucifixion. Not only the figures in the narrative, but every reader knew what was involved. Claiming to be a king was treason, insurrection, a capital offense. Roman citizens could not be crucified; the horrible, degrading death by crucifixion was reserved for slaves and rebellious provincials. The crowd knew that their choice influenced who would be executed and knew that the standard means of execution in such cases was crucifixion. In such a situation, crying out "crucify him" is not per se sadistic or bloodthirsty, but means they choose Barabbas over Jesus. Pilate caves in to the will of the crowd, and orders that Jesus be beaten as preliminary to crucifixion.[117] This beating, horribly cruel in itself, was carried out by scourging the victim with leather lashes that had bits of bone or metal knotted into them. Then Pilate, too, handed Jesus over (see on *paradidōmi* at 9:31).

15:16–39 Jesus Is Mocked and Crucified

15:16 And the soldiers led him away into the courtyard of the palace, that is, the governor's headquarters,[a] and call together the whole battalion.[b] 17 And they are dressing him up[c] in purple[d] and wove together a crown out of thorns and are putting it around his head; 18 and they began to salute him, "Hail, king of the Jews!" 19 and they were repeatedly striking his head with a reed, and were spitting on him, and they knelt down and were worshiping him.[e] 20 And when they had finished mocking him, they took off the purple and put his own clothes on him.

And they are leading him out to crucify him. 21 And they compel a passerby who is coming in from the countryside,[f] a certain Simon of Cyrene, the father of Alexander and Rufus to take up[g] his cross-beam. 22 And they bring[h] him to the place called Golgotha, which means "Skull Place." 23 And they were trying to give[i] him wine mixed with myrrh to drink, but he did not take it. 24 And they crucify him, and are dividing up his garments, casting lots to decide who takes up[g] what. 25 And it was nine o'clock in the morning[j] and they crucified him. 26 And the inscription giving the legal charge against him was written, "The King of the Jews." 27 And with him they crucify two bandits, one on his right and one on his left.[k] 29 And the passersby blasphemed[l] him, shaking their heads and saying, "Ha! you who are going to destroy the temple and build it in three days, 30 save yourself by coming down from the cross!" 31 Likewise the chief priests were mocking him among themselves, along with the scribes, saying "Others he saved, himself he is unable to save. 32 Let the Christ, the King of Israel, come down from the cross now, in order that we may see and believe." Even those who had been crucified with him kept insulting him. 33 And when it became noon,[j] darkness came over

117. The Roman legal system had a variety of punishments by beating and flogging, with a variety of prescribed instruments. Some were punitive and disciplinary, after which the prisoner was released, while others were preliminary to crucifixion. The latter type could be administered with varying degrees of severity, depending on whether or not the judge and executioners wanted the condemned person to be able to survive a long time on the cross. Mark and his readers were aware of this general picture, but Mark is not concerned to specify the particulars of Jesus' case, if he was aware of them. While Roman legal terminology was sometimes precise, distinguishing *fustigatio* (beating), *flagellatio* (flogging), and *verberatio* (scourging), Mark uses one Greek word (*mastigoō*) in the passion prediction of 10:34 and a different term here for the actual beating (*phragelloō*). That Jesus died so quickly on the cross may well indicate that the beating itself was near-fatal.

the whole earth[m] until three in the afternoon.[j] 34 And at three o'clock Jesus shouted in a loud cry, "Eloi, Eloi,[n] lema sabachthani?" which means "My God, my God, why have you abandoned me?" 35 And some of the bystanders heard it and were saying, "Look! He is calling Elijah!" 36 And someone ran, soaked a sponge in sour wine, placed it on a stick, and was trying to give[o] it to him to drink, saying "Wait, let's see if Elijah comes to take him down." 37 But Jesus let out a loud cry[p] and breathed his last. 38 And the temple curtain was torn in two, from top to bottom. 39 Now when the centurion who had been standing facing him saw how he had[q] drawn his last breath, he said, "Truly this man was the[r] Son of God."

a. The Latin loanword *praitōrion* (praetorium) is not a specific building, but a generic term for the governor's headquarters, even if, as here, only temporary.

b. Greek *speira* corresponds to the Latin cohort, one-tenth of a Legion, six hundred troops.

c. The rare verb *endidyskō* of the ancient Doric dialect, rather than the common *endyō,* is found elsewhere in the New Testament only in Luke 16:19, there, too, related to "purple," and adds a note of burlesque pomposity to the mockery. I have attempted to capture this by translating "dressing *up*" rather than merely "dressing."

d. A few MSS (including Θ *f*[13] 565 700) follow Matthew in reading "scarlet robe," which is historically more realistic (see commentary), but *porphyran* ("purple") is clearly original.

e. *Prosekynoun* can mean "do reverence," "do homage," but the parallel to Caesar and the context designating Jesus as Son of God (14:61; 15:39) makes "worship" the appropriate translation.

f. *Ap'agrou* does not here mean "from a field," as though Simon had already been at work and was returning at this early hour, but contrasts city and countryside. Simon was either a Diaspora Jew now living in the environs of Jerusalem, or a visitor in Jerusalem for the festival whose temporary quarters were outside the city (like Jesus and the Twelve, 11:19; 14:3).

g. *Airō* can mean "carry," but is here translated with its basic meaning "take up," to correspond to 8:34. Exactly the same word is found in v. 24.

h. The word translated "bring" (*ferō*) can mean either "lead" (as 11:7) or "carry" (as 1:32; 2:3; 7:32). Mark could have used the specific word for "lead" (*agō,* as in 20b), but seems to leave the door open to the understanding that Jesus collapsed and was carried to the place of crucifixion. Both Matt 27:33 and Luke 23:33 omit the possibly offensive word, and D ϕ 565 and some old Latin MSS change it to the unproblematic *agō.*[118]

i. *Edidoun* is conative imperfect.

118. Mark uses *ferō* fourteen times (Matt 4 times, Luke 4 times, John 8 times). The other evangelists generally limit the meaning of the word to "carry," and thus replace it whenever Mark uses it in a way they consider inappropriate. See C. H. Turner, *"Ferein* in St Mark," in *The Language and Style of the Gospel of Mark: An Edition of C. H. Turner's "Notes on Marcan Usage" Together with Other Comparable Studies* (ed. J. K. Elliott; NovTSup 71; Leiden: Brill, 1993), 13–15.

j. Lit., "the third hour," reckoning from dawn at 6:00 a.m. So also "the sixth hour" translated "noon," and "the ninth hour" as "three in the afternoon." In v. 25 a few witnesses (Θ syr^hmg eth) read "the sixth hour," an obvious secondary harmonization with John 19:14.

k. Verse 28 is missing from the best ancient MSS, including both א B C D Ψ, and is very probably a scribal insertion from Luke 22:37 = Isa 53:12.

l. *Blasphēmeō* in such contexts usually means "insult, slander, revile" (cf. 7:22) but is here translated "blaspheme" to correspond to 14:64 (and cf. 3:28).

m. *Gē* can mean either "earth" (cf. "geology") or "land" (cf. "geometry"). The other eighteen instances of *gē* in Mark refer either to the ground as such (e.g., 4:1, 5) or the earth as a whole (e.g., 9:3; 13:27), never to a particular country, which would require a supplementary noun in the genitive (e.g., "land of Judea," as interpreted in *Gos. Pet.* 5:15 in accord with its intense anti-Judaism).

n. Mark's text is a Greek transliteration of a mixture of Aramaic and Hebrew. A few MSS read *ēli ēli, elei elei*, or *ēlei ēlei* to correspond more closely with the Hebrew text of Ps 22:1, as in Matt 27:46. The spelling of the other words in the quotation is likewise slightly adjusted in various MSS to agree with the Hebrew spelling.

o. *Epotizen* is conative imperfect.

p. The vocabulary is the same as v. 34, *phōnē megalē / phōnēn megalēn* ([with] a loud cry). The function of the aorist participle *apheis* is not absolutely clear. Instead of referring to a separate and final "loud cry," as translated above, it can be resumptive, "having let out *that* loud cry . . ." (cf. note on *poiēsantes* at 15:1). That Matthew considered the text ambiguous is indicated by his adding *palin* ("again," 27:50) to specify that there was a second cry.

q. A large number and wide range of MSS, some ancient and generally reliable, include some form of *kraxas* ("cried out") here. The text translated above is found in א B L Ψ 892 and a few other Greek MSS, in the Sahidic Coptic and part of the Bohairic Coptic translations. There is good, but not overwhelming, probability that the Markan text has been assimilated to the text of Matt 27:50, where a form of *krazō* is more appropriate.

r. There is no article in the Greek text, so the phrase could theoretically be translated "a son of a god," but the Markan narrative as a whole makes this impossible in this context (see commentary below). It is perfectly in accord with Greek grammar to translate the construction using the English article.[119] Exactly the same Greek construction appears in nine other Gospel texts (Matt 4:3, 6; Luke 4:3, 9; Matt 14:33; 27:40, 43, 54; John 10:36). The RSV translates all nine as "the Son of God;" NRSV translates the first six as "the Son of God," the last three as "God's Son." REB, attempting to represent what a historical centurion might have meant, translates inconsistently "This man must have been a son of God" (consistency would require "a son of a god"). If this historicizing approach is pursued, one must ask whether the centurion spoke Latin (in which there are no articles, definite or indefinite) or Greek—and if the latter, whether he knew the subtleties of the use of the Greek article—all of which only illustrates the error of that approach.

---

119. Ernest Cadman Colwell, "A Definite Rule for the Use of the Article in the Greek New Testament," *JBL* 52 (1933): 12–21; Maximillian Zerwick and Joseph Smith, *Biblical Greek* (Rome: Scripta Pontificii Instituti Biblici, 1963), 56. See, however, the reservations of Philip B. Harner, "Qualitative Anarthrous Predicate Nouns: Mark 15:39 and John 1:1," *JBL* 92 (1973): 75–87, who prefers the translation "God's Son" as emphasizing relationship and leaving the definite / indefinite issue open.

[16] Jesus is now in the hands of Gentile soldiers, no longer in the custody of the Jewish police who had arrested him. Historically, these were probably not the crack Roman Legionnaires under the command of the governor of Syria, but auxiliary troops recruited from the surrounding areas. However, this is irrelevant to the Markan point that now, in accord with Jesus' own prediction, he is to be mocked and abused by Gentiles. For the first time in Mark, Jesus is led inside the governor's headquarters. It is historically unlikely that a whole battalion of six hundred troops assembled in the courtyard to mock Jesus, but this is beside the point dramatized by Mark: as the "whole" Jewish Sanhedrin had gathered together to condemn and mock Jesus, so the "whole" Gentile battalion joins in mocking him.

[17–20a] As the mocking by the Sanhedrin was an ironic parody of true prophecy (see on 14:65), so the mocking by the Roman soldiers is a parody of imperial rule. "Purple" was extremely expensive, a symbol of Roman authority and wealth. Again, it is historically unlikely that soldiers could have come up with a purple robe[120]—somewhat like enlisted men in a modern barracks having an ermine robe or gold crown at their disposal—but this is again beside the point: Mark presents a theatrical scene in which the soldiers dress Jesus up to parody a Roman ruler. Likewise the "crown" woven of thorns should not be thought of as further torture, or as mocking the metal headpiece worn by later kings, but as a parody of the wreath worn by imperial figures (thus it was placed "around" rather than "on" his head). The divine emperor was sometimes represented with a radiant wreath, the rays projecting from his head as Apollo-like manifestations of divinity. "Hail, king of the Jews" is a parody of the familiar "Ave, Caesar." Since there was an aura of divinity associated with the emperor, bowing the knee and "worshiping" the humiliated Jesus has the overtones of his claim to be Son of God. The only other instance of kneeling (*proskyneō*) before Jesus is 5:6–7, where the demoniac acknowledges him to be Son of God. While there are various historical parallels to such mockery that have been cited either to make Mark's narrative plausible or to show that he or his tradition could have created it from such precedents,[121] neither the one nor the other is crucial to understanding the scene at the level of the Gospel narrative, which intends to express the deepest irony: the one whom they mock as "king of the Jews" is in fact the Messiah, the king of Israel, whose lordship is expressed precisely in his suffering and humiliation.

The soldiers remove his "royal" garments (nothing is said about removing the crown, hence the traditional pictures of the Crucified One wearing the crown of

120. Matthew recognizes this and alters the cloak to "scarlet," the color of the Roman soldier's garb that would have been readily available. Mark is more interested in dramatizing a theological point than such historicizing touches.

121. Often cited is Philo's account (*Flacc.* 6.36–39), in which, during the visit of Herod Agrippa I, an Alexandrian crowd set up a mentally challenged Jewish peasant named Carabas as "king," complete with improvised "robe," "crown," and "scepter."

thorns). Jesus is passive throughout. The soldiers are the only actors in the entire scene. Mark writes to a persecuted church (13:9) that sometimes knows its own powerlessness in the face of institutional power "acting in the public good."

[20b–39] Mark's depiction of the death of Jesus is remarkably reticent on three points: (1) In contrast to accounts of martyrdom current in the first century and to later cinematic and novelistic treatments, his account of the crucifixion is extremely brief, comprising the three Greek words *kai staurousin auton* ("and they crucify him"). He does not sensationalize the suffering of Jesus; he gives no gory details. His restraint is not a matter of squeamishness—both Mark and his readers knew what was involved. The effect of the cross is not psychological. Mark does not want to arouse either sympathy for Jesus or hatred for his tormentors; the message lies in another direction. (2) Even though Mark's concern is primarily theological, he does not depict the suffering of Jesus in terms of a theory of the atonement. It is the fact of Jesus' suffering and death that is revelatory and saving, not a theory about it. (3) Mark narrates the crucifixion as the truly human death of the Son of God, without attempting an "explanation" of how the Son of God could die.

[21] It was standard practice for the condemned prisoner to carry the crossbeam for his own execution to the stake already in place outside the city, but the Markan Jesus does not carry his own cross. Occupied and colonized countries are familiar with the law that soldiers can impress local residents into their service (cf. Matt 5:41). Mark may intend to depict Jesus carrying the beam part way before Simon is impressed to carry it for him, as in traditional pictures, movies, and the Stations of the Cross, but has no interest in clarifying such details or explaining why Jesus did not carry his own cross. Without being obtrusively didactic, Mark may allow the reader to see Jesus bearing his own cross, and then, following him, Simon takes up the cross of Jesus. Simon thus seems to be introduced not only because his sons Alexander and Rufus are known to the readers,[122] but as a counterpart to 8:34, which has the same vocabulary (*aratō ton stauron autou* "let him take up his cross" / *arē ton stauron autou*

---

122. It is possible, but not likely, that Rufus is identical with the figure Paul greets in Rom 16:13. Like Simon and Alexander, Rufus was a very common name. Just as Simon should not be identified with any of the numerous other biblical Simons, and Alexander is not the same person as the figures of Acts 19:33; 1 Tim 1:20; 2 Tim 4:14, so the Rufus of Rome, who was probably a Gentile, cannot be assumed to be the same person as the son of Simon the Cyrenian Jew. If they were the same, one wonders why Paul refers to Rufus's mother, but not his famous father, who had actually carried Jesus' cross. So also Pesch, who is committed to a Roman provenance for the Gospel (Pesch, *Markusevangelium*), 2:477, and Peter Lampe, who is not (Peter Lampe, "The Roman Christians of Romans 16," in *The Romans Debate: Revised and Expanded Edition* (ed. Karl P. Donfried [Peabody, Mass.: Hendrickson, 1991], 226). Peter Lampe, *From Paul to Valentinus: Christians at Rome in the First Two Centuries* (trans. Michael Steinhauser; ed. Marshall D. Johnson; Minneapolis: Fortress Press, 2003), has not a single reference to Mark 15:21. There is thus no reason to take the reference to Rufus in Mark as evidence for a Roman provenance.

"to take up his cross"). The 8:34 saying was in response to a Simon who misunderstood and who would later deny and abandon Jesus; the Simon of 15:21 does take up "his" cross, identifying Jesus' cross with his own. Of course, this is all at the level of evocative imagery; the Simon in the narrative evaporates from the story line, with no suggestion that he instantly becomes a disciple. The story would not have been related, however, unless Simon and his sons had later become Christians. As in the case of the centurion, the women, and Joseph of Arimathea, the reality of post-Easter discipleship already breaks through the darkness of the crucifixion story.

[22–23] Both Jewish and Roman law specified that executions were to take place outside the city (cf. Lev 24:14; Num 15:35–36; on theological overtones Mark does not here make specific, cf. Mark 12:8; Heb 13:12–13). If Mark intends or allows the reader to picture Jesus as being carried (see note *h* above), it was not against his will, but a theological expression of Jesus' victimization and passivity (see 8:31 on "passion" and "passive"). Golgotha / Skull Place was apparently the traditional name for the Jerusalem place of executions. We do not know the origin of the name, which gave rise to later topographical speculations that supposed the name is derived from a skull-shaped hill—no New Testament author locates Golgotha on a hill—and theological speculations that Adam's skull was buried there.[123]

As portrayed by Mark, the wine mixed with myrrh seems to be understood as a narcotic given to victims to deaden the pain.[124] Mark does not say who offered it, but later Jewish tradition (*b. Sanh* 43a) refers to a humanitarian gesture by Jerusalem women to condemned prisoners, following the lead of Prov 31:6. This would fit Mark, but not Matthew, who changes the myrrh to gall on the basis of Ps 69:21, and regards it as further hostility on the part of Jesus' tormentors. Mark gives no explanation of the offer or Jesus refusal, leaving the reader to reflect on the significance. Two meanings are likely: the compassionate offer illustrates that the whole Jewish population was not against him, but Jesus' refusal of the stupefying drug seems to indicate that he wants to remain conscious throughout the ordeal; his suffering is passive, but he is not a victim in the sense that his suffering is involuntary.[125]

---

123. In some ancient Eastern traditions, Adam was buried on Golgotha and his son, Seth, planted a tree on his grave which was later used to make Christ's cross. From the late tenth century onward in Western art Adam's skull was sometimes shown at the foot of Christ's cross, where the atoning blood touches it, removing Adam's sin and atoning for all humanity.

124. There is only minimal evidence for the mixture understood as a narcotic. Myrrh was more generally associated with embalming and perfume, with perfumed wine regarded as a delicacy. The wine itself may have been thought of as moderating the suffering.

125. Tertullian later relates that a Christian condemned to die had been given "medicated" wine to numb the pain, but it had made him so drunk that he was incoherent and could not properly confess his faith. In this reading, the Markan Jesus refused the narcotic because he did not wish to die in a drunken stupor.

[24] The citation of Ps 22:18 is the first explicit citation of this psalm, which has profoundly influenced the telling of the passion story;[126] its opening words will be the last words of the Markan Jesus (v. 34). Even so, Mark does not indicate that the words are from Scripture, but here and elsewhere expects his (predominantly Gentile) readers to recognize them as such (see *Excursus: Mark and the Scriptures* at 14:52). Receiving the remnants of the condemned man's property—namely what he was wearing, for victims were crucified naked—was apparently a customary perquisite of the execution squad. While it is not implausible that they gambled to decide who should receive what, this detail is more likely supplied from the Scripture than historical memory.

[25] The narrative clock was very vague in part 1 (1:1–8:21) and the transitional section 8:22–10:52. It began to designate days when Jesus arrived in Jerusalem (part 2, 11:1–16:8; cf. 14:1), and now slows to designate the hours (15:25, 33). As the Synoptics (following Mark) differ from Johannine chronology for the last week of Jesus' life (see on Markan calendar at 11:1 and 14:1), so their chronologies for Jesus' last day differ from that of the Fourth Gospel. In Mark, Jesus is crucified at 9:00 A.M., while in John he is still being tried before Pilate at noon (John 19:14). Efforts to harmonize these are in vain; each author has dramatized the event for his own theological purposes.

[26–27] Crucifixion was a public execution intended as a deterrent, so it was important to placard the crime of the executed criminal. This was usually done by placing a wooden plaque around the condemned person's neck or having it carried before him on the way to execution. Mark gives no indication that the placard was affixed to the cross (as in Matt 27:37; John 19:19). "King of the Jews," though laced with sarcasm, is probably historical, and confirms that Jesus was executed on a political charge as ostensibly a rebel against Rome, and that Mark and his readers so understood it.

Mark calls the two men crucified with Jesus *lēstai*, found elsewhere in Mark only in the citation of Jeremiah in 11:17 and in Jesus' response to those who come to arrest him in 14:48, in each case translated "bandits," as in, for example, Luke 10:30; John 10:8. Josephus used this term disparagingly of the Jewish rebels of 66–70 and their predecessors, and John 18:40 (but not Mark) designates Barabbas a *lēstēs*. They considered themselves to be religious zealots and patriotic freedom fighters; their opponents called them "bandits." Thus Mark does not refer to the two who were crucified with Jesus as thieves or robbers in the usual sense. Robbery was not a capital offense punishable by crucifixion, which was reserved for slaves and political rebels who were not Roman citizens. Whatever the historical reality may have been, Mark's portrayal of Jesus crucified between two *lēstai* would have been understood by his readers, in the polit-

---

126. Mark 15:24 / Ps 22:18; Mark 15:29 / Ps 22:7; Mark 15:34 / Ps 22:1; cf. also the imagery of Ps 22:6, 8.

ically charged atmosphere of or just after the 66–70 revolt, as falsely condemned on the charge of claiming to be a king opposing Roman rule.

[29–32] The charges at Jesus' two trials are mockingly echoed at the cross: claiming to destroy the temple and claiming to be the Messiah / King / Son of God. Both claims are called "blasphemy," a significant word throughout Mark (2:7; 3:28–29; 7:22; 14:64; 15:29). The insults hurled at the suffering Righteous One also draw on biblical imagery (Ps 22:7–8; 109:25; cf. Lam 2:15). The specific term *blasphēmeō* is not a reflection of Old Testament imagery, however, but of the preceding Markan narrative (2:7; 3:28–30), especially the trial before the Sanhedrin in which Jesus was charged with blasphemy (14:64). *Blasphēmeō* can refer either to slander of humans or blasphemy against God. In another Markan ironic double entendre, those who suppose they are insulting a human blasphemer are themselves guilty of blasphemy against God. Their insult echoes the charge of claiming to destroy and rebuild the temple (14:58) as well as Jesus' previous instruction to his disciples (8:35). At the historical level, passersby at the execution site are not likely to have been aware of either, but the reader has heard them both, and recognizes the perversion of Jesus' previous teaching and its ironic truth.

The taunt directed to Jesus by the passersby is taken up as an inside joke by the chief priests and scribes, who mockingly repeat it to each other, focusing it even more specifically. Like the demand for a sign in 8:11, the religious leaders claim that if they can see a sign of his divine power, they will believe, and state the ironic truth that the one who did in fact save others cannot save himself. Seeing signs is falsely made the basis of faith; one can "see" and still not believe (4:12). The perceptive reader knows that the narrative as a whole repudiates this understanding of faith, and that "come down from the cross" is the polar opposite of Jesus' call to take up the cross (8:34), just as "save yourself" is a perversion of the word of Jesus that to try to save one's own life is to lose it (8:34–35; see Excurses on *Miracle Stories in Mark* at 6:56; *Markan Christology* at 9:1, and *Messianic Secret* at 9:13).[127]

Those crucified with Jesus join their insults to the chorus. In Mark, no voice, earthly or heavenly, speaks in Jesus' behalf, and as the darkness descends, Jesus is utterly alone.

[33] The darkness is a cosmic, divine sign, but without a word of interpretation. Attempts to fit it into a rationalistic view of the universe ("sandstorm,"

---

127. Others have argued that the historical and/or Markan Jesus did indeed have the power to come down from the cross, but that to have done so would be to "fail in his mission" of dying for the sins of the world (so, e.g., C. E. B. Cranfield, *The Gospel According to Saint Mark* [Cambridge: Cambridge University Press, 1966], 457; Evans, *Mark 8:27–16:20*, 505). Does not such an understanding, desiring to honor the "divinity of Christ," miss the Markan dialectic, the nature of the Gospel genre, and at least border on Docetism?

"dark, low-lying clouds") began with Luke's "eclipse" (Luke 23:45).[128] Whatever may have happened historically, the Markan darkness probably has connections with the folkloristic motif of darkness that signals the death of a great ruler,[129] the apocalyptic failing of the sun (e.g., Mark 13:24), and biblical imagery (cf. darkness preceding creation, Gen 1:2–3; darkness plague of Passover, Exod 10:21–23; the failure of the sun for those who mock the suffering just one, doubting that he is a "son of God" (Wis 2:12–20); especially Amos 8:9–10, which not only has the "sun going down at noon," but "mourning for an only son"). Mark's depiction is distinctive in that the darkness does not signal Jesus' death, but *ends* at his death.

[34] Jesus' last words, his only words from the cross in Mark, are a citation of Ps 22:1. This does not mean that Jesus is piously quoting Scripture as he dies. The psalm is one of the numerous laments in the Psalter, a complaint to God, expressing the human experience of sickness, suffering, rejection by others, and the sense of abandonment by God. While Mark and (some of) his readers were presumably aware of the psalm as a whole, which concludes on a trusting and triumphal note, to reduce these words to an incipit of a prayer of trust violates the Markan portrayal of Jesus as here experiencing the ultimate abandonment (see on 14:50–51).[130] Jesus does not doubt the existence of God or God's power to help—he still calls out to "*my* God"—but challenges the God who has kept silent and remained distant. The Markan Jesus here expresses the depths of faith in a paradoxical form that must not be reduced to consistent pedestrian logic (cf. 9:24). Likewise, there is nothing in Mark to suggest that God had to "turn away" from Jesus at the cross because he was laden with the sins of all humanity, or that on the cross Jesus is enduring God's wrath for the sake of others.[131] Mark regards the death of Jesus as salvific, but explicates no theory of the atonement.

[35–37] The Jesus who has been misunderstood throughout the narrative experiences the final irony that his last words are misunderstood by

---

128. Not that Luke was a rationalist. Describing the phenomenon in natural terms is part of Luke's interpreting the events of the first Christian generation in historical rather than eschatological terms as a damper on eschatological enthusiasm. In any case, a solar eclipse is an astronomical impossibility at Passover, the time of a full moon.

129. Of numerous examples, cf. the darkening of the sun at Caesar's death (Plutarch *Caesar* 69.4; Josephus, *Ant.* 14.309; Pliny *Natural History* 2.97).

130. Contra Pesch, *Markusevangelium*, 2:494, and numerous others. Matthew, who follows Mark in most of the details of the passion story, includes this prayer of abandonment, but both Luke and John felt constrained to omit it and substitute something more appropriate to their own theological portrayal of Jesus (cf. Luke 23:46 = Ps 31:5; John 19:30's sovereign "It is finished")—thus indicating they did not perceive the Marcan version of Jesus' last words as a prayer of trust.

131. Anselm of Canterbury (ca. 1033–1109) was apparently the first to relate Jesus' cry of abandonment with the theory that on the cross Jesus endured the wrath of God for the sake of others. See P. Rogers, "The Desolation of Jesus in the Gospel of Mark," in *The Language of the Cross* (ed. P. Rogers; Chicago: Franciscan Herald Press, 1977), 57.

bystanders who continue to be curious about the possibility of miracles but are oblivious to the presence of God in the suffering of Jesus. A later tradition documents the folk-religion belief that Elijah might come in answer to the prayers of pious Jews to deliver them from various troubles. To the bystanders, apparently Jewish since they know this tradition, "Eloi" sounds enough like "Elijah"[132] to suggest that they might yet see some marvelous phenomenon— though they no longer claim that if it happens, and Elijah appears to take Jesus down from the cross, they will believe. The involved reader, but not the curious bystanders, knows that the Elijah question has already been dealt with: Elijah has come, and like the Messiah, has already been rejected and killed (9:11–13).[133] The drink of sour wine, standard fare of soldiers and poor folk, is offered not for humanitarian or punitive intent, but to make Jesus last a little longer. They want to prolong his life in hopes of seeing a miracle. Instead, they see his death.

It is not a triumphal death. If Jesus' final cry is separate from the cry of verse 34 (see note *p* above), his "letting out" a loud cry is not a shout of triumph, nor demonstration of spiritual power, but a passive letting-go—a nadir, not an acme. There is no good English translation of the one word Mark uses to express Jesus' dying. *Exepneusen* is literally "breathed out," often used as a synonym for the common word for dying, which in this case would have been *apethanen*. It is analogous to English "expire," which also literally means "breathe out," but to translate "expire" would sound entirely too clinical in this context (like "deceased"). Thus even though "breathed his last" has a more delicate tone than expressed by Mark's *exepneusen*, it is perhaps the best we can do.

Jesus had pointed to his death as cup and baptism (10:38; 14:36; cf. 1:9–11). Mark narrates the story of Jesus as transpiring between his two baptisms, in both of which he is passive and God is the actor.[134]

[38–39] There are two immediate and direct responses to Jesus' death: the temple curtain is torn, and the centurion in charge of the execution squad

132. It is often noted that Matt 27:46 changes Mark's Aramaic "Eloi" to the Hebrew "Eli," which sounds more like "Elijah," or argued that Jesus must have originally cited the psalm in Hebrew. Such speculations are beside the point. Even at the historical level, if Jesus had uttered this prayer, the agonized gasps of a dying man will not necessarily make fine distinctions in pronunciation. The key point is that the characters in Mark's narrative (mis-)understand the word in this way.

133. In Mark's theology the appearance of Elijah as part of the eschatological scenario is intertwined with the appearance of Jesus as Messiah and Son of God. Thus John-as-Elijah is present at the first heavenly announcement of Jesus' Sonship (1:6–11), Elijah is present on the Mount of Transfiguration for the second divine announcement (9:2–13), and Elijah is mentioned at the cross in the context of the centurion's confession (15:33–39).

134. Cf. Corina Combet-Galland, "L' Évangile selon Marc," in *Introduction au Nouveau Testament: Son histoire, son écriture, sa théologie* (ed. Daniel Marguerat; MB 41; Geneva: Labor et Fides, 2004), 55.

confesses Jesus to be the Son of God. Both responses are acts of God to the death of Jesus. Though he had heard no answer to his prayer, Jesus' prayer was heard after all; though he experienced abandonment and the absence of God, Jesus had not been forsaken. The tearing of the temple curtain is God's act: the verb *schizō* forms an inclusio with 1:10, its only other occurrence in Mark, and God is there the actor; God is the hidden subject in the passive "was torn"; "from top to bottom" points to a heavenly rather than this-worldly origin. Just as Mark does not offer an interpretation of the event of tearing the temple curtain, so he does not specify which of the several temple curtains he intends. Later interpreters have focused on two possibilities: the outer curtain separating the temple court from the Holy Place or the inner curtain between the Holy Place and the Holy of Holies. It is unlikely, however, that either he or his readers were familiar with the specifics of Herodian temple architecture. Two symbolic meanings have been proposed, which are not mutually exclusive: (1) the destruction of the temple (that was imminent or had already happened in Mark's time) already begins, understood not only as God's judgment on the temple but God's act in the vindication of Jesus (see on 11:12–25). Jesus' words about the temple destruction had played a role in his trial, and had been mockingly thrown in his face as he hung on the cross. But now God acts to vindicate Jesus. Thus the one who had died in God-forsakenness was not abandoned after all. (2) Jesus' death is the removal of a barrier, the opening of the way into God's presence for both Jews and Gentiles, as the eschatological temple not made by human hands becomes a house of prayer for all nations. Mark may have thought of this as a barrier being removed, so that Gentiles now have access to the presence of God (cf. Eph 2:14–18; Heb 9:1–8; 10:19–22; the specific imagery here must not, however, be imported into Mark). Alternatively, tearing the curtain may signal the departure of God from the earthly temple, which is no longer the place where Gentiles must seek God (cf. Ezek 10, where the symbol of God's presence departs the first temple prior to its destruction by the Babylonians; cf. also *2 Bar.* 6:7; 8:2). In either case, the curtain is torn not so much to let people in as to let God out—the divine presence is not localized, either in an earthly holy place or in the heavens. Both have been split (15:38 corresponds to 1:10; cf. also the rejection of Peter's building proposal in 9:5–6). As the tearing of the curtain is a proleptic realization of the temple's destruction, the immediate response of the centurion is a proleptic realization of the faith of Gentiles who respond to the gospel of the crucified Jesus.

What caused this response in the Gentile centurion? Mark says that it was when he *saw* (*idōn*, from *horaō*) that Jesus *thus* died (*houtōs exepneusen* translated above as "how he had drawn his last breath"). Looking for some reasonable explanation for the centurion's declaration, some interpreters have avoided the problem and flattened the narrative to manageable proportions by reading the centurion's response as nonserious, of a piece with the other mockery about the cross.[135] Others have argued that the centurion saw some supernatural sign on which to base his confession, such as seeing the temple curtain torn or that Jesus was able to muster a last supernatural shout of triumph.[136] In the interpretation pursued here, the centurion's confession is sincere, and "how Jesus died" does not refer to some external sign, but to the manner of Jesus' death as a whole: rejected, misunderstood, unheroically crucified in weakness, exhibiting nothing from which one could *infer* that he is the Son of God. The centurion does not arrive at the conviction that Jesus was truly the Son of God as an inference on the basis of "signs"—this is the very concept of faith Mark is against (8:11–12).[137] Those who mocked Jesus asked to "see" so that they might "believe," but such seeing and believing would be on their own terms and their own attainment (15:32). The centurion "sees," but "seeing" must be understood within the framework of Mark's development of this theme throughout (cf., e.g., on 4:12, where outsiders look and look but do not see; 4:24–25; 8:29, 35, and especially on the two stories of healing the blind 8:22–26 and 10:46–52, where seeing is not an attainment but a gift). Multitudes had "seen" the miracles but did not really see. Now, at the climax of the story, one who has seen no

135. So, e.g., Earl S. Johnson, "Is Mark 15.39 the Key to Mark's Christology?" *JSNT* 31 (1987): 3–22; Brian K. Blount, "Is the Joke on Us? Mark's Irony, Mark's God, and Mark's Ending," in *The End of Mark and the Ends of God: Essays in Memory of Donald Harrisville Juel* (ed. Beverly R. Gaventa and Patrick D. Miller; Louisville, Ky.: Westminster John Knox, 2005), 16. Some cannot consider the centurion's statement to express the Christian confession, since he did not defect from the oppressive Roman army. Like the other enemies who "know who Jesus is," this only leads them to want to destroy him (so Myers, *Binding the Strong Man*, 393). Since the centurion's words *can* be read as an expression of mocking unbelief, correct but ineffective identification, or as authentic confession, C. Clifton Black regards this as another example of intended Markan ambiguity (Black, "Face Is Familiar," 44–45). The reader must decide, especially the one who reads aloud (see Juel, *Gospel of Mark*, 146–47, who considers the traditional interpretation affirmed here as too satisfying, an effort on the reader's part to impose a happy ending on Mark).

136. The fact that the Greek words for breath and breathing (*pneuma, [ek-]pneō*) also mean "spirit" and "wind" has allowed some interpreters (beginning with John 19:30) to interpret Jesus' last act in terms of the power of the Holy Spirit. Cf., e.g., Gundry, *Mark*, whose massive commentary throughout argues that Mark has no theology of the cross in the sense of God's power manifest in weakness and that Mark "makes the passion itself a success story" (p. 3). Jesus' last breath is the final expression of divine power he has manifested throughout, "making a wind strong enough to rend the veil of the temple" (p. 948, following Howard M. Jackson, "The Death of Jesus in Mark and the Miracle from the Cross," *NTS* 33 [1987]: 27–28). This, coupled with Jesus' loud shout which presumably no ordinary victim of crucifixion could make, was the evidence that convinced the centurion that he was indeed the Son of God. Why other sign-seekers at the cross were not convinced remains unexplained. All this is the polar opposite of Mark's own view of the relation of signs and faith.

137. Kee's summary statement: "For Mark *understanding of reality is not achieved by availability of evidence but by revelatory insight*" (emphasis his; Kee, *Community of the New Age*, 58).

miracles, but sees only the crucified Jesus *sees* who he really is (*alēthōs,* "truly"). This seeing is not a human attainment, but the gift of God, and in this respect the centurion is a model for all later believers.

The centurion's confession is the climactic christological statement of the Gospel, carefully composed, with every word important. It is to be understood at the level of the Markan narrative, not at the level of historical reporting. The questions of what a 30 C.E. Roman officer might have said at the crucifixion of Jesus, and what he might have meant by the statement in the Markan narrative, or what tone of voice he might have used, are irrelevant to the Markan meaning—just as irrelevant as what the high priest might have meant in 30 C.E. terms by his question before the Sanhedrin (see on 14:61–62). "This man" (*houtos ho anthrōpos*) refers precisely to the human being Jesus, the particular suffering and dying person before whom he stands, and whose truly human death he will verify to Pilate (v. 44).[138] "The Son of God" is central to the christological claims of the Gospel of Mark and the Markan Christian community, confessing Jesus to be the one in whom God is present and active, the one who belongs on the divine side of the infinite qualitative distinction that separates humanity and deity (see *Excursus: Markan Christology* at 9:1). This man is truly (*alēthōs*) human, truly divine. Of course the historical centurion, if he said something like this, did not have this Christian confession in mind, nor is Mark himself thinking in terms of the metaphysical categories of the later creeds.

The Christian confession is that Jesus *is* the Christ, the Son of God (1:1), responding to and echoing God's own "confession" of Jesus (1:11; 9:7), the confession of a present reality brought about by God's act in Christ. It is not an evaluation of Jesus as a figure of the past. The centurion uses the verb "was" (*ēn*). The past tense of the verb may mean, from the reader's perspective, that now, for the first time, it can be grasped who Jesus really was during the whole of his earthly life (so, e.g., Gnilka, *Markus,* 2:327). Without denying this aspect of the centurion's declaration, more central is the Markan perspective that a full, authentic Christian confession cannot be made apart from the resurrection; while God and the demons know of Jesus' transcendent origin and thus can identify Jesus as God's Son, for human beings it is only in the light of the res-

---

138. "This man *was* . . ." has also been understood as vindicating Jesus' claim to be God's Son made before the Jewish authorities that they had rejected, a claim accepted by a representative Gentile (14:61–64). In this case the *alēthōs* would have the sense of settling a disputed issue, as in 14:70, its only other occurrence in Mark. This interpretation is appropriate to Mark, but secondary to the primary christological point. P. H. Bligh, "A Note on *Huios Theou* in Mark 15:39," *ExpTim* 80 (1968): 51–53, argues that the thrust of the statement is that "*This* man [not Caesar] is the *real* Son of God." Cf. also Evans, *Mark 8:27–16:20,* lxxxii–xciii, 510–12. The cult of the divine Caesar was in the air in Mark's time, and Mark here juxtaposes the Christian confession to the emperor's claim to deity without specifically focusing his Christology on opposition to the emperor cult.

urrection that it can be said that Jesus *is* the Son of God.[139] While Jesus' teaching and mighty deeds are integral to his identity, they are not a sufficient basis for authentic faith in him prior to the cross and resurrection. The centurion's "confession" is correct but inadequate, and is not to be understood apart from the actions of the women, Joseph, and the statement of the young man at the tomb that immediately follow.

15:40–47 Jesus Is Buried

15:40 Now there were also women looking on from a distance, among whom were Mary Magdalene, Mary the mother of James the less[a] and Joses, and Salome, 41 who were following him when he was in Galilee and were serving[b] him, and many others who had come up with him to Jerusalem. 42 And after it had already become late, since it was Preparation Day,[c] that is, the day before the Sabbath, 43 Joseph of Arimathea, a respected council member who was also himself waiting expectantly for the kingdom of God, summoned up his courage and went to Pilate and asked for the body of Jesus. 44 But Pilate was surprised to hear that he had already died, and called the centurion and asked him if he was already dead.[d] 45 And when he had ascertained from the centurion [that this was indeed so], he granted the corpse[e] to Joseph. 46 And he bought a linen cloth, took him down, rolled him up in the linen cloth and placed him in a tomb which had been hewn out of the rock, and he rolled a stone against the entrance of the tomb. 47 Mary Magdalene and Mary the mother of Joses were watching where he was placed.

a. The identity of these three (or four) women involves numerous interrelated problems of textual transmission, interpretation, and translation, as well as the relation of this list to those of 15:47 and 16:1. The translation given above understands the text to refer to three women. This reading presupposes (1) the absence of the second article before Joses. If the reading with the article found in B Ψ 131 is considered original, the mother of Joses could more easily be regarded as a different person from the mother of James, i.e., a fourth woman whose name is not given. However, not only is the article supporting the four-women reading absent from practically all MSS, Matthew—older than all of our extant MSS—clearly understood Mark to be referring to three women, the second of whom he designates simply "the other Mary" (Matt 27:61; 28:1). (2) The genitive *Iakōbou* ("of James") is parallel to *Iōsētos* ("of Joses"), thus identifying Mary as mother of both, though it is possible to take the first as meaning "daughter of" and thus referring to a different person. (3) *Tou mikrou*, translated "the less," retains the ambiguity of the Greek, which could refer to stature or age, i.e., "the smaller" or "the younger."

139. So, e.g., Gerd Theissen, *The Religion of the Earliest Churches: Creating a Symbolic World* (trans. John Bowden; Minneapolis: Fortress, 1999), 172: the centurion's "confession" was correct but inadequate, "corrected" at 16:6. Cf. his earlier comment in *Miracle Stories*, 218: "The imperfect [*ēn*] looks back on a life which is over. . . ."

b. The connection between following Jesus and serving him is also made in John 12:26. There, as here, it is pointed out that to serve him is to be the same kind of servant that he was. On the overtones of the *diakoneō* / *diakonos* word group, see on 1:31.

c. *Paraskeuē* means lit. "preparation," but it had become the standard term for Friday, the day before the Sabbath—as is still the case in modern Greek. This text makes it clear that Jesus died on a Friday; the chronology of Mark's "Holy Week" is reckoned forward and backward from this fixed point.

d. *Palai* normally means "for a long time," but can mean simply "already." The presumably more appropriate *ēdē* ("already") is found in B D W Θ 2427 and a few other MSS (see on 6:47).

e. *Sōma* ("body") is read by A C W Ψ 083 $f^{1, 13}$ 33 and most later MSS, perhaps under the influence of 14:22, but *ptōma* ("corpse"), though less elegant, is likely the more original—another Markan emphasis on the reality of Jesus' death.

[40–41] For the first time, the reader learns that a large number of women had come to Jerusalem with Jesus, some of whom watch the crucifixion scene from a distance. Three are specifically named. The delayed introduction of the women into the narrative, and the somewhat odd ways they are described, suggests analogies to the (male) disciples, who disappeared at the arrest and will not be mentioned again until 16:7. The women are not specifically called disciples, though they are said to "follow him," exactly the same phrase used for the initial disciples in 1:16 and 2:14. The women are said to serve Jesus, which at one level may mean they provided for his itinerant ministry from their own resources (as understood by Luke 8:1–3), but also connotes obedience to him as Lord and ministry in his service (see note *b* above). The pattern of a smaller group of three named persons within a larger group is reminiscent of the large group of male followers, the smaller group of disciples, with three representative leaders (see *Excursus: Crowds, Followers, Disciples, and the Twelve* at 6:6). Yet Mark seems hesitant to clearly designate the women as "disciples," and in 16:7 the women and the disciples seem to be distinguished. Why this hesitancy, and why this delayed portrayal of them as people who have followed Jesus from his ministry in Galilee through the passion, burial, and resurrection? There is no reason to suppose that Mark has suppressed the actual role of women in Jesus' ministry, and that he only now must grudgingly acknowledge their role, against his will, because historical circumstances will not allow him to completely falsify the actual facts.[140] One should rather seek a rhetorical, literary-theological explanation.[141] Judas has betrayed Jesus, Peter has denied him, all the male disciples have forsaken Jesus and fled. No one in Jesus' family was present at the cross,

---

140. Contra, e.g., Winsome Munro, "Women Disciples in Mark?" *CBQ* 44, no. 2 (1982): 225–41, and David Rhoads et al., *Mark as Story: An Introduction to the Narrative of a Gospel* (2d ed.; Minneapolis: Fortress, 1999), 149.

141. As argued by Tolbert, *Sowing the Gospel*, 288–99.

and none will attempt to claim his body. The women are now introduced as the only hope that at least some of Jesus' followers will remain faithful to the end, though the note that they only gaze "from a distance," like Peter's following in 14:54, sounds foreboding (see further on 16:8). The women only look; they are not involved in the burial itself, either by washing and anointing the body, or by the customary lamentation. The women thus represent continuity of service and testimony from Jesus' ministry in Galilee through the death, burial, and resurrection. They also supplement the "confession" of the centurion, who represents faith in the identity of Jesus as Son of God and the kerygma of the cross, but whose confession necessarily lacks any relation to Jesus' life and ministry.[142] The alternative to the mocking unbelief around the cross, demanding authenticating signs, is not only the right confession of the Crucified One as Son of God, but placing one's life in Jesus' service (*diakonia*), yet the narrative constraints prevent the centurion from representing this aspect of discipleship. Thus Mark points out that the women had *followed him* and *served him in Galilee*. In Markan theology, not only Jesus' suffering in Jerusalem, but his salvific ministry in Galilee is essential to the gospel message. The women constitute this link, which neither the male disciples nor the centurion can provide.

Who are these women? *Salome* is mentioned only in Mark and is otherwise unknown, though apparently recognized by the Markan readership (cf. "Alexander and Rufus," 15:21). In Matthew she is understood to be, or is replaced by, "the mother of the sons of Zebedee" (Matt 27:56).

Mary Magdalene appears here for the first time in the Gospel. Although the name was surely already known to most Markan readers from the tradition, modern readers may not import information from the other Gospels and later tradition to interpret her significance in Mark. Hers is the only name that remains constant in the three lists 15:40–41, 47, 16:1; she is (along with the reader) the sole continuing witness to Jesus' life, death, burial, and resurrection.

In terms of narrative function, the most intriguing figure is *Mary the mother of James and Joses*. Unless she is identical with the mother of Jesus, she too is otherwise unknown. Unless two different women are referred to (cf. note *a* above), she is mentioned again, oddly, in verse 47 as the "mother of Joses" and in 16:1 as the "mother of James." Neither source-critical theories nor reference to Mark's clumsy construction resolves this odd series of descriptions; it seems intentionally but subtly designed to provoke reflection. Except for Mary Magdalene, the only other Mary in Mark is Mary the mother of Jesus (6:3; cf. 3:20–35). The only other reference in Mark to brothers named "James" and "Joses" is 6:3, where they are listed as sons of Mary among the brothers of Jesus. But if Mark intends the reader to think of Jesus' mother, why this oblique,

---

142. Though the "was" of his confession embraces the life of Jesus as Son of God, not only his death.

indirect reference? Thus most interpreters have decided that Mark refers to an otherwise unknown Mary.[143] This judgment may do less than justice to Mark's evocative subtlety. Just as he has portrayed one good scribe as a representative exception to the generally unbelieving scribes (12:28–34), just as he has portrayed one good Roman soldier who is "converted" by beholding the crucified Son of God as an exception to the class of unbelieving Romans (15:39), and just as he will portray Joseph of Arimathea as a representative exception to the generally unbelieving Sanhedrin (15:43–46), so with understated literary artistry and lack of compulsion, he presents a figure who could be Jesus' mother, the exception to his generally unbelieving family. It thus may be that the picture of Mary in 3:31–35 is not Mark's final picture. In the light of Jesus' suffering and death, she too may have become a fallible follower, but Mark does not make this explicit, and the reader must decide.[144]

[42] Depending on their physical health and the severity of the preliminary scourging, some victims of crucifixion lingered for days before death. The normal Roman practice was to place a guard at the site of crucifixions to prevent friends or relatives from taking the victims down from the cross. Although there were exceptions in which the Romans released the remains of a person executed by crucifixion to allow for a decent burial,[145] normal procedure was then to leave the corpse on the cross until it decomposed and was eaten by birds or animals. Like burning at the stake and being thrown to wild animals in the arena, the other brutal means of Roman capital punishment, nothing was left of the victim to bury—this was part of the intended shame and presumed deterrent power of the horror of crucifixion.[146]

143. Lührmann, *Markusevangelium*, 264, speaks for many: "obviously not the mother of Jesus." This interpretation at least seems to be strengthened by Mark's comment that the women followed him and served [with] him while he was in Galilee (v. 41), for Jesus' mother had not done this. Also, since they were already followers, it is not the cross that transforms them. Or is Mark committed to this sort of linear logic?

144. For an elaboration of Mark's dialectic, particularly on this point, see Boring, "Christology of Mark," 136–45. If the Mary of 3:31–35 is thus here subtly reintroduced, this would be analogous to what Matthew did more clearly with the "mother of the sons of Zebedee" (Matt 27:56), also an unnecessarily awkward phrasing. In Matthew's case, this woman had been presented in an unfavorable light (Matt 20:20), but now at the cross she is potentially a faithful disciple. Did Mark intend something similar by his oblique characterization of "Mary"?

145. A tomb discovered at Giv'at ha-Mivtar just outside Jerusalem in 1968 contained an ossuary with the heel bones of a young man, twenty-four to twenty-eight years old, who had been crucified in the period before 70 C.E. Since the 7.5-inch nail had hit a knot and bent, it could not be extracted, so the feet had to be amputated for the body to be removed from the cross. Thus the heel bones, nail, and fragments of the plaque and cross were all buried together. The tragic remains provide evidence that the Romans did sometimes release the body of the condemned for burial. Cf. James F. Strange, "Crucifixion, Method of," in *IDBSup*, 199–200, and the bibliography he gives. Josephus, *War* 4.5.2 also tells of Jews who were permitted to bury executed relatives.

146. Cf. John Dominic Crossan, *Jesus: A Revolutionary Biography* (San Francisco: HarperSanFrancisco, 1994), 124–27.

After six hours on the cross, Jesus had died around 3:00 p.m.; the Sabbath would begin at sunset, about 6:00.[147] This is the meaning of Mark's reference to "getting late." If the body is not to remain on the cross for two days, it must be buried immediately.[148]

[43–45] Historically, it was politically and even personally risky to request the body of a condemned criminal. In Mark's narrative, neither Jesus' family nor his disciples (in contrast to the disciples of John, 6:29) make any move to procure his body. The one who summoned up the courage to do so had much to lose. Joseph is not from Galilee, and he is a "respected member of the council," which suggests that he belongs to the Sanhedrin, "all" of whose members had condemned Jesus (14:64). This "all" is not to be treated in a historicizing manner as either Markan exaggeration or as meaning "all who were present," supposing that Joseph, a nonresident of Jerusalem, was absent for the vote. Nor is Joseph necessarily to be assigned to a local council, not involved in the Jerusalem Sanhedrin. Again, Mark seems intentionally to leave the matter somewhat ambiguous, though the reader has the impression that Joseph is a member of the Sanhedrin that had condemned Jesus. Likewise, in describing him as "waiting expectantly for the kingdom of God," the reader could understand Joseph to be a pious Jew who had rejected Jesus' proclamation of the kingdom, but who cared for the Torah regulations about burying the dead, and did not want a dead body defiling the land. Yet the *dawning*—the essential futurity—of the kingdom of God had been the core of Jesus' message. This may be an oblique way of relating Joseph specifically to Jesus and his message; he accepts Jesus' message and looks for its fulfillment despite Jesus' death.[149] Yet—as in the case of the women—Mark does not explicitly make him a disciple. The Markan Joseph remains an ambiguous figure; the reader must decide whether or not to follow Mark's open-ended hints (in contrast to Luke 23:51, which specifically identifies Joseph as a member of the Sanhedrin, and Matt 27:57, which specifically makes Joseph a disciple). Mark does not bring Joseph into sharp focus for the reader, but leaves the door open to understanding him as another instance of those who, in contrast to other members of their own group, are "converted" by the events of the passion. But as is the case with the scribe, the women, and the centurion, the conversion can only be proleptic and must await its fulfillment and validation at the resurrection.

Pilate responds to Joseph's request with surprise that Jesus is already dead, and wants his death certified by the centurion in charge; this certification is duly

147. In Mark's putative chronology, this Friday is also Passover day, but since after 14:25 Mark makes no further reference to Passover in any of the events of the arrest, trial, crucifixion, burial, and resurrection, Passover seems not to play any role in his understanding of these events.

148. Nothing is said of the other victims, who are presumably still alive.

149. Contra, e.g., Dowd, *Reading Mark*, 164, who takes the description of Joseph as still *waiting* to mean "he, like so many in this story, has missed the whole point." This follows only if the kingdom in Mark is seen as unambiguously present in Jesus' ministry (see *Excursus: Kingdom of God* at 1:15).

given. In this scene, the centurion does not "confess" his newfound "faith," but serves to validate that Jesus had truly died, and to squelch possible alternatives to the resurrection faith, as though Jesus' relatively short time on the cross meant that he had been taken down by friends or relatives and had recovered.[150] From the earliest days, the Christian kerygma had included "he was buried" as the validation of a real death (1 Cor 15:4).

[46–47] Jesus' burial is described as without ceremony, completed before the onset of the Sabbath. If there were difficulties regarding purchasing a linen cloth on Passover, Mark is not concerned with them, just as he does not bother to explain how one person could purchase the linen cloth, take the body down from the cross, carry it to the tomb (whose location or ownership is not mentioned in Mark), and roll the stone before the door. The other Gospels note the starkly minimal, barely decent burial in Mark, and enhance its respectability by ennobling Joseph, the burial cloth, the burial procedure, and the tomb.[151] In Mark, all attention is focused on the fact of the burial as the guarantee of Jesus' death and the placing of his body in the tomb as the prelude to his resurrection. The three women are named as witnesses, with Mary the mother of Joses identified in a different way than in the prior or in the following scene, teasing the reader to identify her.

150. Josephus describes finding three of his acquaintances among the hundreds crucified by the Roman army besieging Jerusalem, and requesting and receiving permission from Titus to take them down. One survived (Josephus, *Life* 75).

151. According to Matt 27:57–60, Joseph is a "rich man" and "disciple"; the cloth is "clean," the tomb is "his own new" tomb, the stone is a "great" stone. In Luke 23:50–53, Joseph is a "good and righteous man" explicitly identified as a "member of the council [who] had not agreed to their plan and action"; the tomb had never been used. In John 19:38, Joseph is a "disciple," assisted by Nicodemus a "leader of the Jews" and "teacher of Israel" (3:1, 10), who had defended Jesus before the chief priests and Pharisees (7:50–51) and had brought "a mixture of myrrh and aloes, weighing about a hundred pounds" (and thus worth more than half a million dollars) and buried Jesus in a "new tomb" in a "garden," "according to the burial customs of the Jews."

16:1–8 EPILOGUE: RESURRECTION AND MISSION: BACK TO GALILEE

Just as calling 1:2–15 the "prologue" does not mean "optional introduction," designating these concluding verses "epilogue" does not mean "appendix" or "optional supplement." As the prologue gives the prospective framework within which the narrative as a whole is to be understood, so the epilogue provides the retrospective key to the whole.

16:1 And when the Sabbath was over, Mary Magdalene, and Mary the mother of James, and Salome bought spices, so that they might go and anoint him. 2 And very early on the first day of the week, they go to the tomb after the sun had come up. 3 And they were saying to one another, "Who will roll away the stone for us from the entrance to the tomb?" 4 And when they looked up / recovered their sight[a] they saw that the stone had already been rolled back—for the stone was very large. 5 And they went into the tomb and saw a young man sitting on the right side, dressed in a white robe. And they started to panic. 6 But he says to them, "Don't panic! You are looking for Jesus of Nazareth, the Crucified One.[b] He has been raised; he is not here. Look, here is the space where they placed him. 7 But go, tell his disciples, especially / even Peter,[c] that[d] he is going ahead of you to Galilee; there you will see him, just as he told you." 8 And they went out and fled from the tomb, for terror and consternation[e] took hold of them. And they said nothing to anyone, for they were afraid . . .[f]

a. The prefix *ana-*, when attached to the common word for seeing, *blepō,* may mean either "up" or "again," so that the word may mean either "look up" (as 6:41) or "see again," i.e., recover one's sight (as 10:51–52). The ambiguity here is intentional, as in the similar case in 8:24.

b. The perfect passive participle indicates a past event whose reality continues into the present, differently from an aorist participle, which would simply point to an event of the past. For Mark as for Paul (cf. 1 Cor 1:23; 2:2; Gal 3:1), the crucifixion is not an episode in the past that is left behind at the resurrection. Even after the resurrection, Jesus' identity continues as the Crucified One. The phrase has a formal, almost titular tone, communicated in the translation by initial capital letters.

c. *Kai* can here be understood either as "especially" or "even." Peter has been the leader of the Twelve from the beginning; 1 Cor 15:5 likewise distinguishes Peter from the other disciples in the context of narrating resurrection appearances. But though Peter has disavowed any connection with Jesus, *even* he can be restored.

d. The translation of *hoti* is important but ambiguous. It may be *hoti recitativus,* a marker of direct quotation, in which case the "you" refers to the disciples and Peter (so, e.g., NIV, NJB, NAB, REB, TEV). Or it may indicate indirect discourse, so that it should be translated "that," as in the translation above (with RSV, NRSV, CEV, ESV), in which case the women (and the readers) are also addressed. The Greek MS D and one MS of the Old Latin translation (k) have "clarified" the ambiguity by substituting the first person for the third ("*I* am going ahead of you . . . you will see *me* . . . as *I* told you"), but there can be no doubt that the ambiguous reading is original.

e. *Ekstasis* can mean "astonishment" in the positive sense, as in its only other occurrence in Mark (5:42, also in response to deliverance from death). Here, however, the word does not mean reverent amazement, but fear resulting in disobedience, as the next clause makes clear.

f. The Gospel concludes in six different ways in the various MSS, either ending at 6:8 or having some combination of three additional endings. On the basis of א, B and the testimony of Eusebius and Jerome that most MSS in their time ended at 16:8, critical editions of the Greek New Testament and most scholars regard this as the oldest attainable text.[1]

Mark now brings the reader to the explicit scene of the resurrection, which is integrally related to the preceding narrative as a whole, not a postscript. The scene is a strange climax to the Gospel, for the story is only briefly recounted, and the resurrection event itself is not pictured.[2] There are neither accounts of Jesus' appearances nor sayings of the risen Jesus, just as there is no speculation about where Jesus was between Good Friday and Easter Sunday. Mark shows no awareness of or interest in the idea of Jesus' descent to the world of the dead, trip to Paradise, or foray into the realm of demonic powers, reflected in such early Christian texts as Luke 23:43, Eph 4:8–10; 1 Pet 3:18–22; *Gos. Pet.* 9:35–10:42, and the "descended into hell" of the Apostles Creed. Like the other canonical Gospels, he is concerned to affirm the reality of the resurrection, but not to narrate it in a way that requires fitting it into a conceptual and chronological framework. The other Gospels themselves have differing conceptions of the "chronological stages" of Jesus' exaltation to be with God (including variations

1. For full details and discussion, see Bruce M. Metzger, *A Textual Commentary on the Greek New Testament* (2d ed.; Stuttgart: United Bible Societies, 1994), 122–26, and D. C. Parker, *The Living Text of the Gospels* (Cambridge: Cambridge University Press, 1997), 124–47. For a dissenting view arguing for the originality of 16:9–20, see William R. Farmer, *The Last Twelve Verses of Mark* (SNTSMS 25; London: Cambridge University Press, 1974).

2. In contrast to the *Gospel of Peter,* where the reader gets to see Jesus emerge triumphantly from the tomb, and a late addition to one Old Latin MS (it^k), which provides an actual description of the resurrection.

within the same Gospel). That they uninhibitedly adopt more than one image shows that they too (implicitly) reject the identification of any particular way of imaging the reality with the thing itself. By not narrating resurrection appearances, Mark almost entirely avoids this problem.[3] The resurrection *faith* existed long before Mark; whether and to what extent the Markan *account* of discovering the empty tomb rests on pre-Markan tradition is a disputed point.[4] The interpretation below focuses entirely on the Markan meaning.

[16:1–4] In the Markan narrative, the plot too rests on the Sabbath. Just as there is no picture of Jesus between burial and resurrection, so the narrator is silent about the activities of both enemies and followers. When the Sabbath is over at sunset on Saturday, the three women (cf. 15:40–41, 47) purchase spices. No reference had been made to washing and anointing the body in the hasty burial of 15:42–47, in which the women had not been involved. They presumably intend to complete the procedures of a decent burial and achieve some kind of closure to their relationship with Jesus, described as "following." They approach the tomb to anoint a corpse, not proclaim a resurrection.

The scene calls to mind 1:35–38, including its specific vocabulary, already a subliminal call to return to "Galilee" (Sabbath is over, early morning, seeking Jesus, misunderstanding, mission elsewhere). The reference to the "first day of the week" is not mere chronology—what other day could it be after the Sabbath?—but reflects the Christian practice of meeting on this day (1 Cor 16:2; Acts 20:7) as the Lord's Day. Though this is also the "third day" Jesus had predicted (8:31; 9:31; 10:33–34), and the day of God's help predicted in the prophet (Hos 6:2), Mark makes nothing explicit of this.

The women's question, "who will move the stone?" (which the narrator points out was "very large")—makes little sense historically or psychologically, as though the two Marys who had seen the stone put in place only now ask the practical question of how they can actually enter the tomb. The narrative moves on a level other than logic or psychology. The comment is for the readers' benefit, emphasizing both that the women have no expectation of

3. E.g., Mark has no ascension, and his narrative does not explicitly raise the question of when Jesus was exalted to heaven. However, depicting Jesus as meeting the disciples in Galilee *and* as the Son of Man who will return on the clouds of heaven nonetheless seems to call for some conceptual framework within which these are held together. Mark refuses to take the step into objectifying language that makes such conceptualizing necessary. For a concise discussion of the whole issue, see Brown, *Death of the Messiah*, 2:1127–29.

4. The options vary from totally pre-Markan narrative (Pesch, *Markusevangelium*, 2:519–28) through various degrees of Markan redaction of traditional materials (e.g., Taylor, *Mark*, 602), to total creation by Mark (e.g., "The Empty Tomb and the Resurrection according to Mark" in Collins, *Beginning of the Gospel*, 119–38). The main positions are summarized in Pheme Perkins, *Resurrection: New Testament Witness and Contemporary Reflection* (Garden City, N.Y.: Doubleday, 1984), 115–16. For a detailed argument that the Markan narrative rests on reliable early tradition somewhat edited by Mark, see Wright, *Resurrection*, 587–631, who debates with other positions.

finding the stone rolled away and the tomb empty, and that such a stone, large as it is, will not finally seal Jesus in the tomb. Nor is it merely a reminder that the men disciples, presumably capable of handling the stone, have disappeared. The statement does not contrast absent men and present women,[5] or strong men and weak women, but functions on another level, standing in the same series as 1:10, in which God's hand splits the heavens, and 15:38, in which God's hand splits the temple curtain. The resurrection will be the divine finale of removing barriers that separate God and the world. They see that the stone has been rolled away, expressed in the Greek perfect tense (*apokekylistai*), which is analogous to the perfect participle "the Crucified One" of verse 6 (see note *b*). The stone was not only once-upon-a-time-rolled-away, but once-for-all-time-rolled-away; the past act of God definitively affects the present, and cannot be undone.

The women "look up" and "see"—or perhaps they "have their sight restored" and then "see" (cf. note *a* on *anablepsasai* above). The usual translation seems rather pedestrian, as though Mark wants us to picture the women walking along, looking at their feet or the path, and then they "look up" and see the tomb. Mark has given no indication the tomb is on some sort of rise or hill. But this author, for whom blindness and recovery of sight is a powerful metaphor (see on 4:10–12; 8:14–20) has used precisely this word in 8:24 to signify the divine healing of blindness—which turns out to be preliminary and partial. So in this scene, devoted followers of Jesus who have nonetheless been blind to what God was doing in the life and death of Jesus—they are, after all, coming without hope to anoint a dead body—recover their sight, but only in a preliminary way. In contrast to the man of 8:26 who will be sent forth (*apesteilen*) as one whose sight has been restored so that he sees everything clearly, this semi-recovery of sight is as far as the women get in the plotted narrative. Whether they, and the readers, will get past the semi-blindness to true following in the way (10:46–52) must happen, if at all, beyond the plotted narrative in the readers' own world.

[5–7] When the women enter the tomb they do not find the body of Jesus, but this does not generate faith in the resurrection, which in Mark's view is not an inference from data but is the response to the divine word. As Mark's earliest extant interpreter knew, and rationalistic interpreters have repeatedly reminded us, empty tombs can be explained in other ways than by God's act in raising Jesus from the dead (Matt 28:11–15). Events in themselves are mute, and require an interpreting word. The "interpreting angel" frequently plays this role as a standard feature of apocalyptic literature (Zech 1–6; Dan 7–12; Rev

---

5. It is true enough that the male disciples have fled while the women did not, but this is not Mark's present point—the women, too, will shortly flee, just as the men have done (contrast Fowler, *Let the Reader Understand*, 245).

1:1; 19:9–22:16). Angels can be represented as young men (cf. 2 Macc 3:26, 33; 5:2). The young man the women encounter in the tomb has all the accoutrements of an angel who authoritatively represents this divine, interpreting word: he is seated in the position of an authoritative teacher; he is on the "right side," the propitious side of authority; he wears a white garment as do angels and heavenly beings (e.g., Dan 7:9; Mark 9:3; Acts 1:10; Rev 4:4; 19:14); he has supernatural knowledge and gives authoritative commands; the women respond in fear, as regularly in biblical angelophanies (e.g., Gen 21:17; Matt 1:20; Luke 1:13, 30; 2:10); even the stone that has been inexplicably rolled back may be thought of as the angel's deed. The figure is clearly an angel, and the other Gospels make this explicit (Matt 28:2, 5; Luke 24:23; John 20:12). Why does not Mark simply call him an angel? The most likely explanation accords with Mark's reluctance to narrate appearances of the risen Jesus: he does not wish to open the door to post-Easter revelations from the risen Lord, including those mediated by an angel.[6]

The angelic figure identifies Jesus not in terms of christological titles, but only as from Nazareth, and as the Crucified One (see note *b* above); the Risen One, the Christ and Son of God, the Son of Man who is to come on the clouds, is not to be separated from the career of the crucified man of Nazareth. The resurrection does not mean that the earthly life and shameful death of Jesus are now made passé or obsolete. The story does not go forward, taking the gospel to all nations, apart from the narrative just told. The passive verb is here emphatic; Jesus does not "rise" but has been raised by God. The story is not christocentric in a way that keeps it from being finally theocentric. The story of the one who cried out to God as abandoned turns out to be God's own story.

"He is not here" points primarily to the empty tomb: Jesus is not to be found there, but the stone has been rolled away and Jesus is out, "on the loose,"[7] going

---

6. See on 13:5, 20–21, 32, and Introduction sections 2, 4, 6. Mark's seeming reluctance to use the word "angel"—which may have been in his source or tradition, and he has suppressed—has opened the door to complex and subtle modern theories. Sometimes the young man is thought to represent Jesus himself, and/or the believer who is united with him in baptism, who has taken off the old garments of death and is now clothed in the garments of the new life. Associations are sometimes made with the young man of 14:51–52 who, like Jesus, was "seized" and fled away naked, but who has now returned clothed in the garments of discipleship—a bad disciple restored. On the historicizing level, this same young man has then been identified with the presumed author, John Mark, who witnessed the last supper, Gethsemane, and the arrest, the one who fled naked in terror but who has now returned to be a witness of the resurrection. For a more sympathetic presentation of such interpretations and further bibliography, see Vanhoye, "La fuite du jeune homme," 401–6, and John Dominic Crossan, "Empty Tomb and Absent Lord," in *The Passion in Mark: Studies on Mark 14–16* (ed. Werner H. Kelber; Philadelphia: Fortress, 1976), 147–48.

7. Donald Juel, "A Disquieting Silence: The Matter of the Ending," in *The End of Mark and the Ends of God: Essays in Memory of Donald Harrisville Juel* (ed. Beverly R. Gaventa and Patrick D. Miller; Louisville, Ky.: Westminster John Knox, 2005), 6.

before the disciples into the world. The narrative that began with address from God to the offstage Christ the Lord concludes with a reference to the offstage Jesus "out there" in the world ahead of the disciples. The Lord who from the opening words had "a way" (1:2–3) is the Jesus who has been constantly under way during the narrative. This Jesus does not now rest in peace, but is still under way, going ahead of the fearful disciples (cf. 10:32). In addition to this primary meaning, the messenger's announcement has deeper overtones. As the Markan Jesus experienced the absence of God, so the resurrection faith of the suffering Markan community does not deliver it from experiencing the absence of Christ. The bridegroom has been taken away, and it is the time for fasting, not feasting (2:20). There is no promise at the Last Supper that Jesus will be present in the church's eucharistic meals; they will eat and drink without him until the kingdom comes (14:22–25). Jesus will not make himself present in the miracles and oracles of prophets who speak in his name (13:5, 21–23). And yet "he is not here" does not sharply conceptualize where Jesus is now, in the readers' own time. The absence of Jesus is an aspect of the community's experience that is to be acknowledged over against glib claims of the presence of Christ, but it is not made into a dogma. The Markan Jesus is not "present" and available in the charismatic life of the church in which angels deliver new messages from the risen Christ. As the risen Lord, he is already with God, seated at the right hand of Power, whence he will come as Son of Man in the glory of his Father, and *then* angels will accompany him (8:38). In a way not to be conceptually combined with his heavenly session and future coming, Jesus is presently "out there" in the world ahead of the disciples, and there they will see him.[8] At one narrative level, this encounter of the disciples with Jesus in Galilee, announced but not narrated, posits the appearance of Jesus to his disciples that made the resurrection real to them and reconstituted them as authentic disciples who would continue as his faithful witnesses despite persecution (13:9–13). The promised meeting in Galilee involved restoration and forgiveness even to those who had abandoned and denied—"even Peter." As the community of Jesus' followers disintegrated in the two scenes in which the disciples flee and Peter denies (14:50–52, 66–72), so there is a twofold reconstitution of the community: "tell the disciples, tell Peter." Even at this level, there was a message to the Markan readers, including those who had fled and denied under the pressure of persecution. In accord with the two-level nature of the Markan narrative, this final scene modulates from a scene of reconciliation in Galilee in the readers' past to their own present. The risen Jesus "goes ahead" of them in their

---

8. On the Markan dialectic of the presence and absence of Christ, cf. Marcus, *Mark 1–8*, 267, 288. Even the resurrection does not bring a complete fulfillment and closure, and after Easter the disciples (and reader) still live in the tension between *already* and *not yet*, awaiting the complete *seeing* at the Parousia. See "Temporal limit" in *Excursus: The Messianic Secret* at 9:13.

own mission, and there they too will "see" him. Blindness is finally overcome when the gift of sight is received on the road of discipleship, a road that does not end until they finally "see him" at the Parousia (13:26).

The messenger points the disciples, both those in the narrative and those reading it, back to Galilee. Again, at one level this points to actual Galilean appearances of the risen Jesus to his disciples.[9] But, without suggesting that Mark is an allegory, "Galilee" is resonant with layers of symbolic overtones.[10] The community is directed away from Jerusalem. It has sometimes been argued this represents a Markan polemic against the leadership of the Jerusalem church, the original Twelve, and the relatives of Jesus,[11] or that the Gospel of Mark itself is the oracle reported by Eusebius directing the Jerusalem church to leave the city just before the disastrous war of 66–70 (Marxsen, *Mark the Evangelist*, 151–88). Neither of these interpretations has proved viable. More likely is the view that Mark is opposing the apocalyptic interest that centered on Jerusalem in the final phases of the war and the destruction of the city and its temple. Mark's message throughout has been that the future of the people of God is no longer bound up with Jerusalem and its temple; the church, whatever its geographical location, is to look beyond Jerusalem to its Gentile mission represented by Galilee (11:17; 13:10; 14:9).[12] Galilee represents the openness to Jesus' message of the later Gentile church. Throughout the narrative the troublemakers are Pharisees and scribes from Jerusalem. Mark's own community may be located in the environs of Galilee or have engaged in mission there.

The primary function of Galilee as it appears in the final words of the Gospel, however, is internal to the narrative itself. Galilee, in specific contrast to Jerusalem, has been the locus of Jesus' preaching of the kingdom (1:14–15), of his mighty deeds and exorcisms that bind the demonic "strong man" and the plunder of his house (3:23–27). All these are characteristic of the Galilean part 1 of the narrative; all are missing from the Jerusalem part 2 (cf. Introduction, 2). Mark does not want to replace the picture of Jesus' powerful salvific deeds with the kerygma of the cross; Mark presents both together. Now that the power of God is seen to be manifest in the weakness of the crucified, truly human

9. Mark promises an appearance of the resurrected Jesus to his disciples in Galilee, not the Parousia of the Son of Man. A few scholars have advocated the view that the Markan church is directed by the Gospel to go to Galilee to meet the returning Lord (e.g., Ernst Lohmeyer, *Die Briefe an die Philipper, an die Kolosser und an Philemon* [14th ed.; KEK IX/1; Göttingen: Vandenhoeck & Ruprecht, 1974], 359; and especially Willi Marxsen, *Mark the Evangelist* [trans. Roy A. Harrisville; Nashville: Abingdon, 1969], 90–92).

10. Cf. the analogous use of "Judah" and "Damascus" at Qumran, where the migration of the group away from involvement in Jerusalem and its temple to their community of the new covenant by the Dead Sea is repeatedly called going from "Judah" to "Damascus" (CD 6:5, 19; 8:21 4Q266–269).

11. E.g., by Weeden, *Conflict*; Crossan, "Empty Tomb," 145–49.

12. See C. F. Evans, "'I will go before you into Galilee'," *JTS* 5 (1954): 3–18.

Jesus, the pictures of Jesus as truly divine Son of God can be reappropriated, and the reader is pointed back to "Galilee," that is, to Mark 1–9.[13] The messenger points ahead to "Galilee" of the Christian mission of the readers' own time, but does not narrate this; there is no narrative of reunion in Galilee, receiving the Spirit, and continuation of the church. In terms of narrative, the story folds back on itself, and readers who are willing to have the gospel continued in their own lives are directed back to the *archē* of the gospel itself, in Galilee (1:1), which can now be reread in ever-new perspective. The final words of the messenger, "just as he said to you," point the reader back not only to 14:28, but into the narrative as a whole. The series of predictions made by the Markan Jesus have been fulfilled; the one mocked and condemned as a false prophet has shown himself a faithful spokesman for God, and the reader may be sure that this prediction of the postresurrection reunion of Jesus with his disciples will be fulfilled, though its fulfillment is not plotted in the narrative itself. Moreover: the future will unfold not as new revelations from the risen Jesus, but as the continual reappropriation of what the Markan Jesus has already said in the narrative the readers have just heard. The Gospel seems to end on an incomplete and troubling note, but "this ending is not the end of the gospel, but only the end of 'the beginning of the gospel.'"[14] Back to the *archē* . . .

[8] Within the plotted narrative, however, the story ends on a disturbing note. Jesus has been rejected not only by his family, the religious leaders, and the crowds, but has been abandoned by the disciples he has personally called, who have forsaken him and fled (see on 14:51–52, the memory of which is here evoked by the occurrence of the same word "young man"). The women are the

---

13. Cook, *Narrative Quest*, 95: "Mark invites us to return to Galilee where Jesus is still going before us, to complete the circle ['Galilee' means 'circle'] and read the whole gospel from the beginning in the light of the end." So also Schenke, *Markus-Evangelium*, 75–79. Thus the way of Jesus has a "geographical" structure: from Galilee to Judea, then back to Galilee, I > II > I again, = "III" (ibid., 80). The "fear" and "ecstasy" at the empty tomb is thus related to the response to the miracle stories of chaps. 1–9. The resurrection is the grand miracle, pointing the reader back to the previous miracle stories in Galilee, which now may be reappropriated as pointers to God's act in the Christ-event as a whole.

14. LaVerdiere, *Beginning*, 1:9. The story comes to an end, but without closure. This point is developed especially by Focant, *L'évangile selon Marc*, 594–600: Beginning and end correspond, in both a complementary and antithetical manner. The prologue announces, in prospect, one who prepares the way, which, in retrospect, is seen to be the way of the cross. As John goes before the one to come, so now Jesus goes before the disciples in their continuing mission. The narrative begins with a cry and ends with a silence that can only be broken by the reader. The narrative circles back on itself, but the return is not a vicious circle; it is a spiral, in which the reader can go back to the beginning with eyes to see and ears to hear. Initially, the reader supposes the *archē* of 1:1 refers to the following narrative; by the end, the perceptive reader can see (though the conclusion is not forced) that the narrative as a whole is the *archē* of the larger story that embraces the readers' own time. "The epilogue of the Evangelist constitutes a prologue to the work of the reader" (599).

last hope that someone *within* the narrative will continue as faithful followers. They have now seen the empty tomb and been commissioned by the heavenly messenger. But they flee, filled with terror and consternation, and say nothing to anyone, for they are afraid. . . . The story that began with the trumpet call announcement of the dawning of God's kingdom ends not with a bang but a whimper, trailing off in midsentence.[15] After all, no one in the story who has been with Jesus is willing to carry the message and continue his mission. Is there anyone else who might after all be a faithful disciple?[16] Throughout the story, there has been a nonparticipant observer who has been with Jesus in every scene. The narrator has permitted the reader to be "with Jesus" the whole time, from beginning to end. The reader heard the voice of God declaring Jesus to be his Son, when no one else heard; the reader was present with Jesus in the wilderness, tested by Satan, when no one else was there. When family rejected him, the reader persisted. When religious leaders, crowds, and disciples misunderstood and abandoned Jesus, the reader stood by him. When the inner circle went to sleep in Gethsemane, oblivious to Jesus' plea to watch with him one hour, the reader stayed awake and heard Jesus' anguished prayer. When the disciples fled and were absent at the cross, the reader was present. When Jesus cried out to God in abandonment, the reader was still there. Now, the readers stand at the brink of the incomplete narrative in which all have failed, and, with terrible restraint, the narrator breaks off the story and leaves the readers, who may have thought the story was about somebody else, with a decision to make. . . .

15. The final word of Mark is *gar*, a conjunction, usually translated "for" and requiring additional words to complete the sense. While not absolutely unprecedented, it is extremely unusual to end a sentence, paragraph, and especially a book with this word, something like concluding an English volume with "and" followed by ellipsis dots, "and . . ." Mark brings no closure to his narrative, not even an "Amen" or benediction.

16. At the narrative level of presenting past events, the reader is aware that the disciples did somehow get the message, did encounter the risen Christ, did become faithful disciples. Yet the concluding scene functions more as address to the reader than as report of past events. The Markan *text* does not resolve this issue; the existence of the church, the Markan community of faith, testifies that God has nonetheless resolved it (cf. Moloney, *Mark: Commentary*, 353–54).

ALTERNATIVE ENDINGS

The plethora of interpretations of the ending of Mark, necessarily involving combinations of text-critical judgments, exegesis, and hermeneutics, may be sorted into the following categories:

1. The reading given in this book, which assumes Mark intended to end his narrative at 16:8 with an implicit challenge to the reader, a "positive" reading of the failure of all the characters in the narrative.[1]

2. Mark intended to end his narrative at 16:8 and did so, but the Markan conclusion is to be interpreted differently than the interpretation here advocated:

    a. More "positive" readings understand the fear and silence of the women as reverent awe in the presence of the numinous, and their silence as only temporary, thus making good historical sense—the disciples certainly did receive the message—and reassuring the readers as well. A few interpreters have sometimes tried valiantly

---

1. Reynolds Price, *The Three Gospels* (New York: Scribner, 1996), 59: "Such an apparently reckless last-minute abandonment by an author of his reader's keenest final expectation is thoroughly characteristic of the kind of narrator Mark has been throughout his book. *This is my story, suddenly told—you tell it from here.*"

    The interpretation advocated here is of course not original. In the wake of Frank Kermode, *The Genesis of Secrecy: On the Interpretation of Narrative* (Cambridge, Mass.: Harvard University Press, 1979), 49–73, this has become almost the standard interpretation. Among those who offer more detailed arguments for it are Tolbert, *Sowing the Gospel*, 295–96; Myers, *Binding the Strong Man*, 399–404; Marcus, *Mark 8–16*, 2: ad loc., and Moloney, *Mark: Commentary*, 350: "Mark 16:1–8 is the masterstroke of a storyteller. . . ." For a detailed and technical argument leading to this conclusion, see Paul L. Danove, *The End of Mark's Story: A Methodological Study* (BIS 3; Leiden: Brill, 1993), esp. 220–30. See especially Juel, *Master of Surprise*, 107–22, whose intense insistence that 16:1–8 not be read in isolation but as the proper conclusion of the preceding narrative has been very influential. Juel emphasizes that the concluding challenge to the reader *not* be understood in the sense that, whereas the disciples in the narrative all "failed," it is now up to the reader to "succeed." The kingdom of God announced by Jesus will not finally be realized by disciples, in the narrative or out, unfaithful or faithful, but by God. For elaborations and responses to Juel's contribution, see Beverly R. Gaventa and Patrick D. Miller, eds., *The End of Mark and the Ends of God: Essays in Memory of Donald Harrisville Juel* (Louisville, Ky.: Westminster John Knox, 2005).

to present the women as heroic examples of discipleship to the very end.[2]

b. More "negative" readings oriented to early Christian history understand Mark's intent as polemical, explaining that the leaders of the Jerusalem church, the Twelve, and Jesus' relatives never received the message and were never redeemed, in contrast to Mark's own Gentile church (e.g., Kelber, *Mark's Story*, 88–90). Other "negative" readings oriented to Mark as literature see the author as a Kafkaesque composer who intentionally confounds the readers and leaves them hopeless.[3]

3. Mark in fact ended his narrative at 16:8, but did not intend this to be the conclusion. He intended to complete the story by recounting the fulfillment of the promise of 14:28 and 16:7, thus bringing the narrative to a satisfactory conclusion. The women's failure, like that of the male disciples, was only temporary, and was to be resolved within the narrative itself, but Mark was unable to complete the narrative for reasons unknown to us.

4. Mark did in fact extend the narrative beyond 16:8, but the original ending was early lost and is no longer extant.[4]

5. Mark's original ending, in whole or in part, is preserved in resurrection narratives of one of the other Gospels.[5]

6. Mark's original ending is preserved in one of the endings appended to many manuscripts of Mark (so Farmer, *Last Twelve Verses*).

However, both internal and external evidence make it virtually certain that Mark ended at 16:8, and none of the additional endings can be considered "canonical."[6] They belong to the *Wirkungsgeschichte* and reception history of

2. E.g., Schüssler Fiorenza, *In Memory of Her*, 316–23. Among scholars who reject this straightforward "positive" reading are Tolbert, *Sowing the Gospel*, 295–96; Elizabeth Struthers Malbon, "Fallible Followers: Women in the Gospel of Mark," *Semeia* 28 (1983): 29–48; Perkins, "Mark," 729–33; Dowd, *Reading Mark*, 170–71; Miller, *Women in Mark's Gospel*, 178–92.

3. E.g., Stephen D. Moore, "Deconstructive Criticism: The Gospel of the Mark," in *Mark and Method: New Approaches in Biblical Studies* (ed. Janice Capel Anderson and Stephen D. Moore; Minneapolis: Fortress, 1992), 84–102, esp. 86–87.

4. The most complete treatment of this view is now found in N. Clayton Croy, *The Mutilation of Mark's Gospel* (Nashville: Abingdon, 2003), who also provides a thorough documentation of the text-critical data and its recent evaluation.

5. Edgar J. Goodspeed, *An Introduction to the New Testament* (Chicago: University of Chicago Press, 1937), 144, claims there can be "no reasonable doubt" that Matt 28:8–20 preserves the lost ending of Mark. Bultmann regards the view that the story of John 21 formed the "original conclusion" of Mark as having "a certain probability" (Rudolf Bultmann, *The Gospel of John: A Commentary* [trans. G. R. Beasley-Murray et al.; Philadelphia: Westminster, 1971], 705), and Streeter argued in favor of this "interesting speculation" (Burnett Hillman Streeter, *The Four Gospels: A Study of Origins* [London: Macmillan, 1964], 333–62).

6. Vs. the decision of Trent that 16:9–20 is "the" canonical ending.

Mark, not to Mark itself. Yet they should not be disdainfully dismissed as though they were mindless additions by those who "didn't understand what Mark was doing." Not only the scribes who copied Mark, but Mark's earliest interpreters, Matthew and Luke (and John?), supplemented Mark's abrupt ending. After other Gospels were written, scribes and teachers in the church that treasured Mark came to regard Mark's conclusion as not adequate. As the parables rightly generated endings because they were felt to be "incomplete," so the parabolic Gospel of Mark generated endings. As we benefit from, for example, 4:13–20 as the edifying word of the church, an early reading of the parable, so we benefit from the later endings of Mark, early responses to the parabolic Gospel narrative. The phenomenon illustrates that the line between Jesus, church, and text is dynamic and synchronic, not crisp and diachronic, that the text of the Gospels continued to be living and dynamic.[7] The "spurious" endings, along with the readings of Matthew, Luke, and John, are in fact the earliest commentaries on Mark's generative text. This process of reading, interpretation, and making of commentaries continues until this moment.

---

7. Cf. Painter, *Mark's Gospel*, 212; Parker, *Living Text*.

INDEX OF ANCIENT SOURCES

INDEX OF SUBJECTS

CPSIA information can be obtained
at www.ICGtesting.com
Printed in the USA
FFOW04n1012100915
16772FF